NEW MEXICO PLACE NAMES

A GEOGRAPHICAL DICTIONARY

Edited by T. M. PEARCE

Assisted by INA SIZER CASSIDY

and HELEN S. PEARCE

THE UNIVERSITY OF NEW MEXICO PRESS

Publication of this book was assisted by a grant from the Ford Foundation. Manufactured in the United States of America by the University of New Mexico Printing Plant, Albuquerque. Library of Congress Catalog Card No. 64-17808. ISBN: 0-8263-0082 0.

Sixth paperbound printing 1983.

CONTENTS

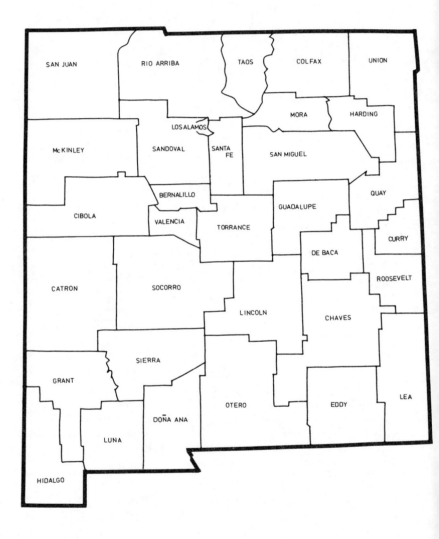

INTRODUCTION

The materials for *New Mexico Place Names* were first collected by workers of the New Mexico Writers' Project, between 1936 and 1940. Except for information used in the volume *New Mexico, A Guide to the Colorful State* (1940), these materials were never published and remained in the files of the project. At the third annual all-state meeting of the New Mexico Folklore Society, held in Las Vegas on June 26, 1948, President Ina Sizer Cassidy proposed that the Society sponsor the *Dictionary.* Her recommendation was approved, and Mrs. Cassidy was named chairman of the place name committee. Working with T. M. Pearce, editor of publications, Mrs. Cassidy distributed mimeographed instructions to collectors, and material began to come in. On May 14, 1949, the *First Collection* of place names was published in mimeographed form. It consisted of 334 items, and was followed by the publication of 251 place names in the *Second Collection,* May 13, 1950, and 138 items in the *Third Collection,* May 12, 1951. These relatively small publications were edited from several thousand cards, based upon material contributed by members of the Folklore Society, by workers in the Spanish Place Name Project, sponsored by the Modern Language Department, the University of New Mexico, and by letters solicited through Ward Fenley of the University of New Mexico News Bureau. The editorial work was done by T. M. Pearce, who was elected editor of *New Mexico Place Names* at the fifth state meeting of the Society in Albuquerque, May 13, 1950. Grants-in-aid from the University of New Mexico Committee on Research defrayed preliminary expenses during these and subsequent years.

PLACE NAMES AND PLACE NAME CLUSTERS

Some curious problems face the editor of place names. One is the matter of recognizing a place name when he sees it. This is not as simple as it sounds. A place name is the word or words identifying a geographical entity, that is, topographical features such as mountains, hills, mesas, rivers, lakes, arroyos, and settlements or areas within settlements, such as districts, streets, railroad stations. Anything that occupies an area in space, horizontal or vertical, in a sense becomes a place name. But not all place names are of sufficient general interest to justify including them in a dictionary for public use. Furthermore, the names of resorts and tourist lodges, even though identifying geographical locations, have not been included, since they are individual commercial establishments and, like famous stores or hotels in cities, identify a place of very limited area and of circumscribed interests. The names of ranches and trading posts, unless they are also post offices or serve to name a community center, fall into this class of restricted names. We have, therefore, not included them unless they have unusual historical or geographical importance.

When an editor finds a number of separate geographical features, such as Pajarito (a settlement), Pajarito (a creek, canyon, plateau, mountain, and park), does he have one place name or six? There are really six place names here, because six places are involved even though but one name is used for all six. They form a name cluster. Clusters are of three types: those made from generic terms, such as bear, wolf, horse, or Spanish *gallinas*; those made from descriptive terms like red, black, dark, pleasant; and those that employ personal names as the basis for the grouping. Illustrations will make the process clearer: *pajarito*, Spanish, "little bird" (a descriptive name which was also used as a surname) forms a generic cluster naming a settlement south of Albuquerque and a number of places northwest of Santa Fe. Bear Creek, Bear Canyon, Bear Springs, Bear Wallow and their parallel forms in Spanish, Oso Creek, Oso Ridge, are also generic clusters. Red Bluff, Red Hill, Red Lake, and Pleasant Hill, Pleasant Valley, and the community name Pleasant illustrate descriptive clusters. Padillas Creek, Padillas Canyon, the village name Los Padillas show how a personal cluster forms. Any of these terms, however, can separate themselves from the cluster pattern. When a generic is modified by or merged with other words, as Little Bear Lake or Redland or Pleasanton, it becomes both a separate name as well as a distinctive designation of a place.

For purposes of economy, the clusters have been printed in block paragraphs, except where the groups were so large that such an arrangement was impractical. In enumerating the total number of names in the *Dictionary*, we counted each individual place listing whether identified with a cluster or not.

A Spanish abbreviation for "saint" is *san* and it appears 152 times in our files, being used for settlements, canyons, creeks, lakes, peaks, mesas, springs, land grants and other locations. The individual saints honored by this generic number 41. The nouns *santo* and *santa* add 15 more holy personages whose names are applied to both communities and topography, and the Virgin Mary as *Nuestra Señora*, "Our Lady," appears under 15 different titles, some of which are only parish names and have not been included in this collection. The term *sierra*, "mountain range," appears 28 times, with qualifying words that name elevations in descriptive, commemorative, and possessive categories. "Ranch" is a generic term, Anglicized from American Spanish *rancho*, "a cattle raising settlement," but unless the ranch names in New Mexico have become names of communities or have post office designations they have not been entered in this dictionary. The names of mines, too, have been omitted unless they have been associated with some historical or geographical fact of importance.

DESIGN OF THE DICTIONARY

How much historical and economic data to include with the place names has been a difficult decision. Sometimes no very satisfactory answer can be given about the naming of a community and the impulses and motives behind the naming, and a place name dictionary is not a gazeteer prepared to describe the resources of a community or to give its Chamber of Commerce assets. Nevertheless, we have tried to present at least an item or two giving data locating and identifying each place name.

There are approximately 5,000 names in the *Dictionary*. Their forms and locations are based primarily upon the United States Geological Survey Map, Provisional Edition, 1955, and the quadrangle maps provided by the Geological Survey. We found the detailed maps in the *New Mexico Sportsmen's Guide* helpful, since they are based upon maps of the U.S. Department of Agriculture, U.S. Forest Service and other state and federal surveys. They also contain an index to many settlement and field names. Our collection of New Mexico place names contains: 1) all the counties and county seats; 2) all the present post offices, and all of those discontinued before 1964; 3) the state and national parks; 4) the state and national monuments; 5) the more important cities, towns, settlements, and land grants; 6) the better-known lakes, creeks, mesas, mountain ranges, and peaks. We abandoned the search for all the canyons and arroyos. They were numberless and the information on them is largely unavailable. Even with the names we have listed, information as to origin is frequently missing, but we decided to include all the names we were able to assign to county locations even though detailed information was lacking. Some of the early post offices have just a county designation plus the nearby town where mail was sent when the office was discontinued. "Mail to" means that the post office shifted elsewhere; "name changed" indicates that the post office or community took a new name.

For reference, in addition to the maps previously mentioned, the following historic maps were checked for places named at strategic time intervals.

Map of Domingo del Castillo, 1541. Reproduced in *Cartography of the Northwest Coast of America to the Year 1800* (Berkeley, 1937), p. 31; also in *New Mexico History and Civics* by Lansing Bloom and T. C. Donnelly (Albuquerque, 1938), p. 18.

Michael Lok's map dedicated to Sir Philip Sidney and inserted between pp. 54 and 55 of *Hakluyt's Voyages* (1582), edited by John Winter Jones for the Hakluyt Society in 1850.

Map of California and New Mexico from L'Atlas Curieux of N. de Fer, 1700. Reproduced in *Mercurio Volante*, by Sigüenza y Góngora, translated by I. A. Leonard (1932), p. 89.

Mapa de la Frontera del Vireinato de Nueva España, by Nicolas de Lafora, Mexico, 1771, in *The Frontiers of New Spain*, ed., Lawrence Kinnard (Berkeley, 1958).

"Nuevo Mejico" as outlined in 1828 by Mapa de los Estados Unidos de Mejico, in Genaro Garcia Collection, The University of Texas Library. Reproduced in *Three New Mexico Chronicles*, translated by H. Bailey Carroll and J. Villasana Haggard (1942); also the "Caravan Map," in this volume used to illustrate Escudero's *Noticias Históricas y Estadísticas*, 1849.

Plano de la Provincia Interna del Nuebo México made under the direction of Lieutenant Colonel and Captain General of the Province Don Juan de Anza by Bernardo Miera y Pacheco of the Royal Garrison of Santa Fe in 1775. Original in the Biblioteca del Palacio in Madrid, Spain. Copy reproduced by A. F. Thomas in *Forgotten Frontiers* (1932).

Maps in such modern gazetteers as Cram's *Atlas of the World* (Chicago, 1884, 1895) and Winston's *Atlas of the World* (Chicago, 1921).

TIME CYCLE IN NEW MEXICO PLACE NAMES

The time cycle for the names in New Mexico extends from the prehistoric period to the present, for names were here when the first Europeans arrived and they are being added as this volume goes to press. The prehistoric period began with the arrival of the Southwest Indian groups, early in the European Christian era, and extended to the arrival of the first European visitors in 1539, at which time Friar Marcos de Niza and a Negro slave (as a forerunner) led a company of Indians across Arizona to Zuñi Pueblo in New Mexico, searching for the fabled Seven Cities of Cibola. The Spanish period may be divided into three distinctive intervals: the period of exploration between 1539 and 1598; the first period of colonizing between 1598 and 1680; and the second period of colonizing after the Pueblo Indian Rebellion in 1680 and the Reconquest by Don Diego de Vargas in 1692. The latter event was important to place naming because it brought new groups of European settlers and new activity in the naming of settlements and landmarks. The Spanish period ended in 1821 when Mexico separated from Spain. This year also brought the opening of the Santa Fe Trail. Anglo-Americans gave English names to the places where they stopped, such as Rabbit Ear Creek and Wagon Mound. Today English and Spanish place names are in the great majority and are about equal in number. The Indian names constitute a small minority.

SIX LANGUAGE GROUPS

In a state where the language sources are more complex than in most geographical areas, many problems have arisen. In New Mexico, there are six general language divisions from which the name words are drawn. There are four Indian stocks: Tanoan, Keresan, Zuñi, and Athapascan. The Tanoan has three groups: Tiwa (Taos, Picuris, Sandia, Isleta pueblos); Tewa (San Juan, Santa Clara, San Ildefonso, Nambe, Tesuque pueblos and Pojoaque—now defunct); Towa (Jemez Pueblo, Pecos—now defunct). The Keresan group includes the active pueblos of Cochiti, Santa Domingo, San Felipe, Santa Ana, Zia, Laguna, and Acoma. The Zuñi language has only the one community, Zuñi Pueblo, to represent it. Speaking the Athapascan languages are the Navajos in the northwest corner of the state and the Apaches at Jicarilla and Mescalero. Spanish becomes the fifth language stock, and the term English, or Anglo, includes all the other American as well as European name sources.

Intermingling of languages has been one of the most engrossing aspects in the study of these place names. South of San Ildefonso Pueblo is a high mesa associated with stories of the giant Tsahveeyo, who dwelt on another mesa nearby and was a central figure in Tewa Indian mythology. This giant was said to prey upon children in the pueblo. He was finally slain by the Twin War Gods, who allowed Tsahveeyo to gulp them down; then they cut open his stomach and destroyed him. The Spanish name for the mesa of Tsahveeyo is *gigantes*, "giants." Certainly before naming the spot, the Spanish settlers learned of this background in Indian lore. Another illustration of language interplay is the name of a creek in Rio Arriba County. The creek is called Coyote Creek in both the Spanish and the Indian languages. The Tewa terms are *nday*, "coyote," *po* "water," creek. Since the Tewa frequently use animals as subjects for geographical naming, one concludes that the name was probably translated into Spanish, rather than vice versa. The same applies to the name Crystal, given to a trading post and settlement located in San Juan County. The Navajos named the place "crystal water flows out." The English name is derived from the Navajo. Other instances of the commingling of Indian, Spanish, and English may be found if the reader will turn to such names as Tesuque, Pecos, Canadian, Navajo, Seneca, Sugarite, and Tucumcari.

PATTERNS OF PLACE NAMING

A check list of the Indian names in New Mexico will show few if any names honoring individuals or places where the tribes may have previously lived. Indian names are almost entirely descriptive, that is, identifying a place in terms of some characteristic registered by the senses. Illustrative of this pattern are the names Abiquiu, Spanish corruption of the original Tewa for "timber end town"; Pecos, Towa for "place or water"; Chuska, Navajo for "white spruce"; Puye, Tewa for "cottontail rabbit place"; Pojoaque, Tewa for "drink water place." However, there are Indian names based on personal incidents such as Callamonge, Tewa "place near where the Spanish live," and Totavi, Navajo for "place where water is dug out." Although the Indian names may not be as romantic and sentimental as some eastern poets and writers of fiction have imagined, they are frequently concrete and vivid. If known in their English equivalents, some of them would be: Arroyo Where Two Maidens Sit, Down at Alkali Point, Stone on Its Head Place, Sliding Stone Mountain, Place of the Twisted Corn Husks (referring to ceremonial objects), Place of the Blue Water Man (referring to a sacred pool), and Wrestling Mountain (referring to sports held on this hill). Absent, however, are names commemorating political or military events, their leaders or their achievements. The Indian names, like the Indian himself, remained a part of, not separate from, the land in which he lived.

Spanish place name patterns, by contrast, include not only descriptive and incident names, but employ many names which commemorate personages or places important to Spanish history. Such are names like Santa Fe, the many place names honoring saints in the Roman Catholic Church, the name Albuquerque (honoring a Viceroy of Mexico), and the name Mexico itself, in Nuevo Mejico. The place name of an Indian pueblo, San Juan de los Caballeros, commemorates the Spanish soldier and knight on horseback. Descriptive Spanish names are Arroyo Hondo, "deep wash"; Escondida, "hidden place"; Polvadera, "dusty spot"; and Rio Vermejo, "red river." The Spanish made use of identifications like Los Lunas, "the Luna folks," and Los Ladrones, a mountain range which was the hideout of cattle rustlers. Incident names, too, are common, such as Jornada del Muerto, "journey of death," named for the perils of heat, thirst, and marauding Indians. Oñate said he named a spring El Ojo del Perillo, "because on this day a dog came into camp with its feet coated with mud and we found waterholes." Of course the Spanish transferred many names such as Madrid, Valladolid (once the name of the settlement at Taos), and Valencia, but this category sometimes coincides with a commemorative like Guadalupe or an identification like Cordova.

The English made use of the same varied patterns as the Spanish adding, perhaps, a category or two, such as those displaying English humorous irony or the modern practice of merging parts of words and also combining initial letters to form acronyms. Samples of these naming patterns are given below:

1. Descriptive names recounting the appearance or the qualities of a place: Alkali Lake, Aspen, Black Butte, Broke Off Mountain, Graveyard in the Sky, High Lonesome, Mocking Bird Gap, Rattlesnake Siding.
2. Possessive names identifying a place with a person, group, or wild life which make the place a habitat: Adams Diggings, American Creek, Cureton, Five Dollar Canyon, Jack's Peak, Nester Draw, Peacock Canyon, Coyote Valley.
3. Incident names which associate a place with an encounter or a particular date, that is, calendar names: Dead Man's Arroyo, Dog Canyon, Fourth of July Canyon, Pie Town, Signal Peak, Six Shooter Siding, Truth or Consequences, Wild Cow Canyon.

4. Commemorative names which honor a person, abstract concept, or another locality: Aden, Beulah, Gladstone, Grant, Hope, McKinley, Roosevelt, Thoreau, Shakespeare.

5. Idealistic or sentimental names which suggest the future in terms that may be more hopeful than real: Beauty, Bible Top Hill, Cloverdale, Columbine Creek, Melrose, Pleasant Hill, Pool of Siloam, Rosebud.

6. Manufactured or coined words, using initial letters (acronyms) or syllables (blends) of other words: Anzac, Gamerco, Hiway, Jal, Maljamar, Maypens, Stanolind, U.S. Hill.

7. Names transferred from one geographical area or feature to another: Carlsbad, Crater, Delphos, Des Moines, Hanover, Hollywood, Tunis. A type of transfer name called shift name applies to the change of a specific name from one generic group to another, as Black Lake, Black Mesa, Black Mountain, Black River.

8. Names exhibiting humor or playful imagination, some of which encourage folk etymology: Belly Ache Mesa, Humbug Creek, Me Own Hills, Pep, Pothook, Tinpan Canyon, Tooth of Time Mountain, Wahoo Peak.

Perhaps one might generalize by pointing out that the Indian patterns stress the descriptive elements in identification plus the use of some incident data; the Spanish employ a considerably greater variety of naming processes in which the descriptive and incident patterns are supplemented by historical memories illustrated in transferred and commemorative names recalling and honoring people, places, and events, especially the religious experience. In like manner, the English name patterns illustrate not only impressions of the landscape and experiences encountered in a new environment, but honor places and individuals, both familiar and famous, coin names with the freedom characteristic of the English language, and illustrate the humor and irony of the Anglo-Saxon temperament.

SOME PROBLEMS IN EDITING

From the welter of language elements came the greatest of editorial trials in the preparation of this volume. The problem of accents upon Spanish names in English was solved by the rule that no accents would be used in the writing of proper names in English, a language free from such stress marks. However, where Spanish is used in a publication or reference exclusively Spanish, every effort was made to use the correct diacritical markings. There is one diacritical mark in Spanish which cannot well be dispensed with. That is the tilde over the *n*. Peña Blanca cannot be pronounced when written as one word, as on the U.S. Geological Survey maps, and without the tilde over the *n*: Penablanca. The same is equally true of Espanola without *ñ*. Consequently, we have kept the

Spanish ñ and suggest that American geographers dealing with the place names of the Southwest insist upon adding this letter to the English alphabet.

English syntax has influenced the form of Spanish place names, as in the loss of *el* and *la*, *los* and *las* before nouns in the formal syntax of the Spanish language. El Rio de las Vacas, "the river of the cows," could appear on maps in this form, or as Rio de las Vacas, Rio las Vacas, or Vacas River. Las Trampas, "the traps," will appear on some maps with Las and on others as just Trampas. Some maps prefer Rio Peñasco and others Peñasco River. The Spanish-English and English-Spanish parallelism continues with cañon and "canyon": Cañon Blanco or White Canyon, Cañon de Manuelito or Manuelito's Canyon. Regional spelling has warped Spanish Cebolleta to Seboyeta, and San Agustin to San Augustine, which is neither English nor Spanish.

The areas of language dominance may be traced, east and west, north and south, where Spanish *arroyo* in place names becomes English "wash" or "draw," and Spanish *ciénaga*, "marsh," is replaced by "swale" or "sink." As before said, *cañon* and "canyon" are one and the same field generic in two different languages. Both persist in New Mexican place naming, and with the help of the Spanish ñ, they can continue to add variety and descriptive color to their respective settings. It is difficult to oppose popular usage. Spanish San Agustin seems to be destined to turn into San Augustine, and Fray Cristobal Range seems to have lost out to Fra Cristobal. This is regrettable. Our place names tell the story of our historical and linguistic inheritance. By preserving their integrity, they tell the story with greater honesty, accuracy and truth.

ACKNOWLEDGMENTS

Since the collecting of place names for New Mexico has been a co-operative venture over a period of years, the acknowledging of helpers cannot possibly indicate everyone who has contributed to the success of the project. From the first literary records, by such soldier-historians as Pedro de Castañeda in 1540-42, to the investigations of the New Mexico Folklore Society, the place name story of New Mexico has been written by many hands over a long period. A line may be drawn, however, between the adventurer in a new land who inquires of natives their names for landmarks and the collector of such materials for a reference work. The latter type of collecting seems not to have begun in New Mexico earlier than the *29th Annual Report* of the Bureau of American Ethnology (1908) which contained a list of place names covering the ethnogeography of the Tewa Indians, prepared by John P. Harrington. The work of Frederick Webb Hodge in his *Handbook of American Indians North of Mexico* (1907), constitutes another landmark in place name materials. Henry Gannett of the U.S. Geological Survey provided some material in his *American Names* (1902, 1947), and the members of the Writers' Project between 1936 and 1940 undertook a survey which was never completed. The microfilmed documents of the Records Survey, Office of Land Management, held by the Library of the University of New Mexico, provided the information on land grants. The increase in publication since the New Mexico Folklore Society became interested in collecting is witnessed by the items in the Bibliography dating after 1948.

The editor expresses his gratitude and appreciation to a number of individuals whose help was indispensable to the building of this book: Fray Angelico Chavez, priest and historian, for Spanish place names and those with Aztec and Nahuatl sources; W. A. Keleher, attorney and historian, for material on certain of the land grants with their legal backgrounds; Dr. Sheldon Dike, for permission to use data from his list of territorial post offices of New Mexico up to January 6, 1912, and Charles G. Finke for bringing this list up to the year 1964; Mr. and Mrs. Gilberto Espinosa, for reading the manuscript and for suggestions relating to the significance and history of many Spanish names in the state; Eldred R. Harrington, for checking the out-of-the-way localities, many of them ghost towns, known to him from long acquaintance and wide travel throughout the state; Frances L. Newcomb, for guidance in locating and interpreting Navajo Indian names, and for assistance in reading copy; Philip Shamberger, for checking the names with his travel notes of places in the state; Ina Sizer Cassidy and Rose P. White, for sustained encouragement in the project from its beginning; Dr. G. Adlai Feather and Howard Bryan, for adding names and supplying the data to go with them; G. Ward Fenley, Director of the University of New Mexico News Bureau, for press releases as well as personal interest in the place name story.

Finally, the editor acknowledges that without the assistance of Helen S. Pearce, his wife, who co-ordinated material in the files and carried on countless other types of investigation, this book would never have appeared. To Roland Dickey, Director of the University of New Mexico Press, hearty thanks are given for his advice and guidance in all the details of publication; and the same to Winifred W. Gregory, also of the Press, for her general surveillance of data and details of the manuscript both before and during printing; for library help, the editor expresses thanks to Frank D. Reeve, for many years editor of *New Mexico Historical Review*; to Fern Young, Albuquerque Public Library; to W. Michael Mathes, Special Collections Librarian, and Genevieve R. Porterfield, University of New Mexico Library; and for the details of deciphering my script and typing it, to Mrs. Florence J. Shoemaker, Mrs. W. E. Kiefer, Mrs. Joseph E. Kaye, Mrs. Eunice Hauskins, Mrs. Robert Lawrence, and Robert Romero.

The Bibliography at the end of this volume will indicate many of the printed sources to which the editor has had access and, we hope, all of the individuals who have contributed to the published collections.

T. M. PEARCE

The University of New Mexico

Locations are indicated in terms of the cardinal points of the compass as these directions relate to the national and state highways, the intra- and interstate railroads, the better-known towns and geographical features. Where two counties are indicated for a settlement, the second county named was created from the first. Early or existing railroad lines have been abbreviated in the following manner:

A&NM RR	Arizona and New Mexico Railroad
AT&SF RR	Atchison, Topeka and Santa Fe
A&P RR	Atlantic and Pacific
CRI&P RR	Chicago, Rock Island and Pacific
C&S RR	Colorado and Southern
D&RGW RR	Denver and Rio Grande Western
EP&NE RR	El Paso and Northeastern
EP&SW RR	El Paso and Southwestern
NMC RR	New Mexico Central
NMM RR	New Mexico Midland
PV&NE RR	Pecos Valley and Northeastern
SFC RR	Santa Fe Central
SFNW RR	Santa Fe Northwestern, also called Santa Fe, San Juan and Northern
SLRM&P RR	St. Louis, Rocky Mountain and Pacific
SP RR	Southern Pacific
TNM RR	Texas, New Mexico

ABAJO (Bernalillo). Span., "down, below." Flag stop on AT&SF RR, 5 mi S of Bernalillo. Formerly BERNALILLO ABAJO. In early times, towns strung along a road named their extremities *Arriba*, Span., "above," and *Abajo*. This was true of Bernalillo, Corrales, and other towns. An English equivalent would be "Upper" and "Lower" in reference to a locality.

ABBOTT (Colfax). Also called NEW ABBOTT. On NM 58, 19 mi E of Springer near Abbott Lake. Named for Horace C. Abbott, who became the first postmaster. Post office, 1881-1963. In 1936 a number of the settlers moved to a location called THE FORKS, at the junction of NM 58 and 39. A post office is also listed at ABBOTT (Mora) in 1905; formerly SAUZ. ABBOTT LAKE (Harding). Artificial lake 10 mi SW of Abbott. ABBOTT STATION (Harding). 2 mi below Colfax County line, 19 mi SE of Springer. Established when SP RR built its line through the area in the later 1870's. Two brothers, Horace and Jerome Abbott, owned a big sheep ranch here.

ABEYTAS. A family name, i.e., "the Abeyta folks"; from the de Veitia family which came to NM some time after the Reconquest of 1692. Name seems to be of Basque origin. Don Diego de Veitia, origin unknown, settled in the vicinity of Santa Cruz. In the eighteenth century one of his grandsons married into a Rio Abajo family, and a cluster of these families came to be known as the PLAZA DE LOS ABEYTAS between Belen and Socorro.

ABEYTAS (Socorro). On US 85 and AT&SF RR, 14 mi S of Belen. Also called LOS ABEYTAS. Post office, 1914-45.

ABIQUIU (Rio Arriba). 18 mi NW of Española on US 84. First settled by the Spanish in 1747 and resettled in 1754. There was a Tewa pueblo ruin (probably abandoned in the 1500's) over which Abiquiu was built. In 1776 Escalante speaks of the settlement SANTA ROSA DE ABIQUI (Twitchell, *Leading Facts NM History*, III, 524). Name may be a Spanish corruption of Tewa *pay shoo boo-oo*, "timber end town," for San Juan Pueblo. The Tewa-speaking peoples took over the new Spanish approximation and gave it a folk etymology, "chokecherry end," *abay*, "chokecherry." ABICUI on Mapa de los EUM (1828). Post office, 1852 to present, with interruptions and one name change, to JOSEPH, in 1884. ABIQUIU CREEK (Rio Arriba). Rises S of Abiquiu, flows into Chama River. ABIQUIU PEAK (Rio Arriba). 12 mi SW of Abiquiu. TOWN OF ABIQUIU GRANT (Rio Arriba). Granted on May 10, 1754, by Governor Cachupin to Indians and others for the grazing of animals and the cultivation of land. Previously this grant had been given to Antonio Montoya, a captain under Gov. Diego de Vargas, who raised sheep and cattle near the Indian ruins. The Montoya family lost the Abiquiu property for failure to settle. They were given land E of the Rio Puerco by Governor Cachupin, to compensate them for the loss. See M. AND S. MONTOYA GRANT.

ABO (Torrance). Town in SW part of county, 6 mi SW of Mountainair on US 60. Post office, 1910-14. ABO STATE MONUMENT (Torrance). Ruins left by a former Tompiros division of the Piro Indians, on Arroyo Empedradillo. First mentioned in 1598 by Juan de Oñate. Became seat of Mission of San Gregorio, founded 1629 by Fray Francisco de Acevedo, who erected a large church and monastery, the walls of which are still standing. Abo is shown on L'Atlas Curieux (1700). Population during early mission days was probably two thousand.

Prior to the Pueblo Rebellion of 1680, the village was abandoned because of Apache raids. The ruins have been excavated by the Museum of New Mexico and were declared a state monument on Aug. 30, 1939. Abo is said to have been dedicated to San Gregorio, patron saint of the old city of Abo, Finland, but the name is a Piro Indian word used for the pueblo in 1598, whereas the mission was not established until thirty years afterward. Settlement takes its name from the state monument. Post office, 1910-11. ABO ARROYO (Socorro). N on US 60 between Veguita and Scholle.

ABREU (Colfax). Former settlement on Rayado River, 20 mi W of Springer. Named for a prominent family of that section, owners of a large ranch in the old Maxwell Land Grant.

ABUELO (Mora). Span., "grandfather." Little town in Cebolla Valley, 1½ mi from Mora. Its provincial pronunciation as "agüelo" is evident among the earliest documents. This is an old New Mexico expression for "bogeyman," an ugly old man to scare children with, used interchangeably with the more classic *coco.*

ACEQUIA MADRE. Span., "mother ditch." This is a peculiar place name, for it really designates an irrigation ditch. In New Mexico, however, it has a symbolic value, since it personifies the role of water streams in the history of various regions of the state. An *acequia* is a man-made canal to carry water to the fields. The chief of these, which feeds other smaller canals, has for centuries been called the *acequia madre.* There are more than sixty of these in the Rio Grande Valley alone, each of them controlled by a *mayordomo,* or ditch boss. The San Juan Indians call their chief irrigation ditch by the Tewa terms, *kwee-o-yee yah,* "mother irrigation ditch," a probable translation from the Spanish name. A small stream flowing through the city of Santa Fe is called the Acequia Madre and the name has passed to a city street.

ACME (Chavez). Former stock-raising community on US 70 and AT&SF RR, 25 mi NE of Roswell. Named for Acme Gypsum Cement Co., which in 1906 constructed a cement mill nearby. Plaster and cement blocks were manufactured until 1936, when high freight rates caused the plant to close down. Post office, 1906-46.

ACOMA (Valencia). Indian pueblo 56 mi W of Albuquerque, 12 mi S of US 66 at Casa Blanca; situated on top of a 357-ft-high mesa, accessible either by a staircase cut into the rock

or by a sand dune filling a large fissure. This village was first reported in the fall of 1540 by Hernando de Alvarado, one of Coronado's soldiers. At that time, several thousand Indians may have lived in the village. Today only a few members of the tribe remain, the others having settled in a community nearer the highway or in the valley below. The name is from the Keres Indian language: *ako* meaning "white rock," and *ma,* "people"; the full name, then, means "people of the white rock." Espejo first used the present spelling in 1583. The mission was established in 1629, and dedicated to St. Stephen. It is the largest of the early NM churches. The capture of Acoma, in a siege lasting from Jan. 21 to 23, 1599, is reported by Gaspar Perez de Villagra in his *History of New Mexico* (1610). A number of celebrated stories dealing with early days at Acoma are to be found in Willa Cather's *Death Comes for the Archbishop* (1926). Acoma and a Lago d'Acoma appear on L'Atlas Curieux (1700). ACOMA CREEK (Valencia). E of pueblo; flows N to join the Rio Jose at New Laguna. ACOMA GRANT (Valencia). Sealed by the Spanish Crown in 1659, according to *New Mexico,* American Guide Series (1940), p. 331; confirmed by the US on Dec. 22, 1858, and approved by President Lincoln with the gift of a silver-headed cane in 1863. In the following year, canes were sent to twelve more of the pueblo governors, in recognition of their peaceful conduct after the US acquired NM and during the Civil War. They are still passed on as the badge of office when the governors are elected in January of each year. See PUEBLO LAND GRANTS.

ACOMITA (Cibola). Village on US 66, settled by the Indians of Acoma, who have irrigated farms here. The name derives from the Spanish diminutive, *ita,* suffixed to the Keres Indian word, *Acoma.* It means, therefore, "little Acoma" or "little place of the people of the white rock." Post office, 1905-06; 1912-58.

ACREY LAKES (Eddy). 27 mi NE of Cienaga near Eddy County line.

ADAIR SPRING (Catron). 2½ mi SE of Luna.

ADAMS DIGGINGS (Catron). 15 mi NE of Quemado. Named for a man reputed to have discovered a fabulous gold mine in the malpais W of Grants during the fall of 1864. Other reports place the location in the Mogollon Mts. Adams and his companions were reported to have mined a considerable amount of gold and then to have sent men for supplies to

Ft. Wingate, which at that time was established a few miles S of Grants, near San
Rafael. These men were waylaid and killed
by Apaches, as were all the other members of
the party except Adams, a companion named
Davidson (who was away from camp with
Adams when the Apaches attacked), and a
man named Brewer, who may have escaped
and found his way to the Spanish settlements
on the Rio Grande. Post office, 1930-46.

ADAMS LAKE (Colfax). Small lake covering
about two acres of land near Cassel Rock and
Ash Mtn. Named for a prominent family of
the vicinity.

ADBERG (Quay). On CRI&P RR, 5 mi NE of
Tucumcari. Family name of first settler.

ADELINO (Valencia). Spanish-American settlement 3 mi S of Tome, on Old River Road E
of the Rio Grande. Named for Adelino Sanchez, the son of Jesus Sanchez, one of the
original settlers. Post office, 1911-16.

ADEN (Doña Ana). Community on SP RR
in SW part of county. A nearby extinct volcano is called Crater of Aden. Since the railroads chose names from many disconnected
sources, this may be named after the seaport
town of Aden in Arabia. Post office, 1894-98;
1905-24.

ADOBE (Socorro). Span., "sun-dried brick."
Former trading point on US 380, 32 mi E of
San Antonio. Named for the nature of the soil.
Post office, 1933-38.

AFTON (Doña Ana). Former post office on SP
RR, 20 mi SW of Las Cruces. Possibly named
for the Afton River in Scotland, as a number
of Scotsmen settled here in the early days.
Post office, 1924-41.

AGRICULTURAL COLLEGE (Doña Ana). Post office,
1905-12. See UNIVERSITY PARK.

AGUA AZUL. Span., "blue water." Many place
names in NM use the Spanish word for water,
agua, plus a descriptive adjective, such as fría,
"cold"; negra, "black." AGUA AZUL (Lincoln).
Named for a pool where Jesus Maes settled in
1878. AGUA AZUL CREEK (Mora).

AGUA CHIQUITA CANYON (Otero). Span., "little
water." Runs through Sacramento and Weed
on E slope of Sacramento Mts. AGUA CHIQUITA
CREEK (Otero). In canyon of the same name.
Summer camps and cabins have been established along its banks by people from Artesia,
Weed, and elsewhere.

AGUA DEL LOBO (Taos). Post office, 1888-1905;
changed to LOBO.

AGUA FRIA (Colfax). Span., "cold water." Small
community between Taos and Eagle Nest.
Post office, 1924-34. AGUA FRIA (Valencia). 1
mi S of Paxton, near the Continental Divide,
on Agua Fria Creek. AGUA FRIA CRATER (Valencia). Near the Continental Divide, 3 mi SW
of town of Agua Fria. AGUA FRIA CREEK
(Catron). N tributary of the Rio La Casa;
drains into a basin in NW part of county.
AGUA FRIA LAKE (Catron). At head of Agua
Fria Creek. AGUA FRIA PEAK (Colfax). Altitude 11,000 ft; near village of Agua Fria.
AGUA FRIA RITO (Colfax). Rises near Agua
Fria Mt. and forms Cieneguilla Creek to
empty into Eagle Nest Lake.

AGUAJE DEL MUERTO (Sierra). See LAGUNA DEL
MUERTO.

AGUAJE DEL PERRILLO (Doña Ana). See OJO DEL
PERRILLO.

AGUA NEGRA. (Mora). Span., "black water."
Once a town on Mora River in Maxwell Land
Grant. Post office, 1884-92. AGUA NEGRA (San
Miguel). Post office, 1868-69. AGUA NEGRA
CHIQUITA CREEK (Guadalupe). Small stream
near Santa Rosa.

AGUA PIEDRA (Taos). Winter sports area, S of
Taos. AGUA PIEDRA CREEK (Mora).

AGUA SALADA GRANT (Sandoval, Valencia). Luis
Jaramillo, a discharged corporal of the Royal
Garrison, on July 20, 1769, presented his petition to Pedro Fermin de Mendinueta, Governor and Captain General, for a grant of un-
cultivated land on the slope of the Navajo
country, bounded on N by land of Antonio
Baca, on S by land of Pedro Padilla, on E by
road crossing the place leading to Laguna
Pueblo, and on W by land of Salvador
Jaramillo. W border of this grant is about 5
mi E of Marquez.

AGUA SARGO (Taos). See AGUA ZARCA.

AGUA VIVA (Taos). Span., "living water." Trading point on US 64, 10 mi E of Taos in Taos
Canyon.

AGUA ZARCA (San Miguel). Span., "light blue
water." Village 4 mi SW of Las Vegas. AGUA
ZARCA (Taos). Flows W to enter the Rio
Pueblo, 1 mi SE of Tres Ritos.

AGUDO (De Baca). Span., "sharp, keen, acute."
Siding on AT&SF RR, 6 mi S of Ft. Sumner. The place boomed during the building
of the railroad in 1906-07. Post office, 1909-14.

AHMEGO (Quay). Post office, 1908-12; changed
to LOCKNEY.

AHOGADERA (Colfax). See SAN FRANCISCO MESA.

AIR FORCE MISSILE DEVELOPMENT CENTER (Otero). Experimental station in Tularosa Basin, near US 70 and US 54, 12 mi W of Alamogordo. To the S is the White Sands Missile Range. Center was formerly known as ALAMOGORDO ARMY AIR FIELD when construction started on Feb. 6, 1942. Renamed HOLLOMAN AIR FORCE BASE in September 1948 in honor of the late Col. George V. Holloman, pioneer in guided missile research. Became HOLLOMAN AIR DEVELOPMENT CENTER on Oct. 10, 1952; changed to AIR FORCE MISSILE DEVELOPMENT CENTER at HOLLOMAN AIR FORCE BASE, Sept. 1, 1957.

AIROLO (Union) Post office, 1905-09; mail to Pasamonte.

AKELA (Luna). Siding on SP RR, 22 mi E of Deming. Today there is a trading post of the same name near here. US 70, 80, and the railroad almost meet at this point. Akela, like Lisbon or Luxor, is a railroad name chosen in the 1880's by some railroad official or the relative of an official, and the reasons for such choices are not known. Akela might be identified, however, as the leader of the wolf pack in Kipling's Mowgli stories. See *The Jungle Book* (1883). Post office, 1922-41.

ALACRAN HILLS, (Eddy). Span., "scorpion." Descriptive name for barren hills 3 mi NE of Carlsbad.

ALAMEDA, Span., "poplar or cottonwood grove, public park." In NM, where public parks were unknown until the nineteenth century, an *alameda* served the same purpose and consisted of tracts of cottonwoods like those along the middle Rio Grande Valley, or groves of mountain poplars along streams like those at Taos and Santa Fe. ALAMEDA (Bernalillo). On US 85, 7 mi N of Albuquerque; site of a Tiwa Indian pueblo in the seventeenth century, but one of the Span. Arch. NM, I, 818, dated Nov. 26, 1696, tells of a group of settlers petitioning to remove from La Villa Nueva de Santa Cruz to Alameda. The Indians removed to Isleta sometime after this date and the Spanish settlers took their place. The name appears on L'Atlas Curieux (1700). Post office, 1866-68; 1890—. ALAMEDA GRANT, or TOWN OF ALAMEDA GRANT (Bernalillo, Sandoval). Large grant N and W of settlement, crossing Bernalillo line into Sandoval. Made on behalf of the King of Spain to Montes Vigil "as a reward for military service." Vigil took possession on Jan. 27, 1710. Title was conveyed to Capt. Juan Gonzales on June 18,

1712, and on Sept. 13, 1713, to Juan Isidro Flores Mogollon, Governor and Captain General of the Province of New Mexico.

ALAMILLO (Socorro). Span., "little cottonwood." Seventeenth-century Piro Indian pueblo, on the Rio Grande, 50 mi S of Isleta. Name appears on L'Atlas Curieux (1700). ALAMILLO ARROYO (Socorro).

ALAMITOS (San Miguel). In NE part of county, W of Canadian River. ALAMITOS CREEK (San Miguel). In W part of county; empties into Pecos River 5 mi SE of Rowe.

ALAMO. Span., "poplar or cottonwood." The cottonwood tree or *álamo*, which grows profusely in NM, has left its name on both settlements and topographical features. "Cottonwood, Little Cottonwood, Big Cottonwood, Cottonwood Grove, The Cottonwood" are English translations of the same Spanish place names drawn from *álamo*. ALAMO (Guadalupe). 17 mi SE of Cuervo. Post office, 1906-30. ALAMO CANYON (Otero). On W side of Sacramento Mts. ALAMO CREEK (Catron). Heads in Datil Mts., and flows E to the Rio Salado. ALAMO CREEK (Harding). See UTE CREEK. ALAMO CREEK (Santa Fe). Flows W 6 mi N of Cerrillos. ALAMO PEAK (Otero). On W side of Sacramento Mts., in Lincoln National Forest. First called HURSCHBURGER PEAK for an early prospector.

ALAMOGORDO (Otero). Span., "large cottonwood." On US 54, 70, and SP RR, at W base of Sacramento Mts. and on E side of plain known as Tularosa Basin. Townsite was purchased, laid out, and named in 1898 by the Eddy brothers, John and Charles B., early promoters of the Pecos Valley and the Tularosa Basin. Post office, 1898—. ALAMOGORDO ARMY AIR FIELD (Otero). See AIR FORCE MISSILE DEVELOPMENT CENTER. ALAMOGORDO CREEK (Quay, Guadalupe). Tributary of Pecos River, called ALAMOQUADO CREEK from its head in W Quay County to the settlement of Alamo; from Alamo to the Pecos, known as ALAMOGORDO CREEK. ALAMOGORDO RESERVOIR (De Baca). Dam on Pecos River in NW corner of county.

ALAMO HUECO MOUNTAINS (Hidalgo). Span., "hollow, full of holes, spongy cottonwood tree." In SE corner of county, 3 mi from Mexico and N of NM 79.

ALAMOQUADO CREEK (Quay, Guadalupe). See ALAMOGORDO CREEK.

ALAMOSA RIVER (Sierra). Span., "place of cottonwoods." See MONTICELLO CREEK. ALAMOSA

CREEK (Quay, Curry, Roosevelt). Rises S of Ima; flows SE to Curry County line, turns and flows SW to enter Taiban Creek just W of De Baca County line.

ALBEMARLE (Sandoval). Old gold mine camp. Post office, 1901-03; mail to Bland, 2 mi E.

ALBERT (Harding). At junction of Tequesquite and Carriso creeks, 13 mi NE of Mosquero. Named for Albert Mitchell, one of the early and prominent ranchers of the state. His son, Albert K. Mitchell, was a candidate for governor in 1938. The Mitchell Ranch is near Albert and uses the town as headquarters. Post office, 1890—.

ALBUQUERQUE (Bernalillo). On the Rio Grande at the crossing of US 66 and US 85, and on AT&SF RR. The industrial and population hub of NM and one of its medical and cultural centers as well; seat of the University of New Mexico, founded in 1889, and of the College of St. Joseph, established in 1940. Originally, the name was spelled "Alburquerque," like that of a city once lying in Portugal, now in the province of Badajoz, Spain, about 10 mi E of the Portuguese border. This area was held by the Moors from the eighth century until Fernando II expelled them in 1166. A derivation for the name has been sought in the Latin *albus quercus*, "white oak." This may be further developed or complemented by such Latin and Spanish forms as *arbor quercus*, "oak tree"; *albor* or *albur quercus*, "oak of whiteness" (the trunk of the cork oak after the outer layer has been exposed); *albura quercus*, "oak with white foliage" (*alburnum*, a white blooming tree). The seal of the Spanish city of Alburquerque bears the design of an oak upon it.

The records of New Mexico's twenty-eighth colonial governor, Don Francisco Cuervo y Valdez, state that in the early part of 1706 the governor founded a villa which he named SAN FRANCISCO DE ALBURQUERQUE, in honor of Don Francisco Fernandez de la Cueva Enriquez, Duque de Alburquerque, the thirty-fourth Viceroy of New Spain, then resident in Mexico City. Don Francisco Fernandez was the second duke titled Alburquerque to serve as Viceroy of New Spain, and was the tenth in succession from the first Duke of Alburquerque, Don Beltran de la Cueva, who received the Portuguese dukedom in 1464 from King Enrique IV.

When Governor Valdez placed the new villa of Alburquerque under the patronage of San Francisco, he selected the name of his own patron saint (Saint Francis Xavier) and that of the viceroy, but the latter, fearing the displeasure of King Philip V of Spain (who had not authorized the villa) decided to rename it SAN FELIPE DE ALBURQUERQUE, honoring the patron saint of the monarch. The spelling *Alburquerque* appears in the report of the Marques de Altamira to the auditor general of war, dated Sept. 16, 1750 (AGN, Provincias Internas, 37, No. 2), but the "r" in the second syllable of the name was dropped by English-speaking people early in the nineteenth century, as the narratives of Zebulon Pike, 1807; George W. Kendall, 1841; and J. F. Meline, 1866, testify. All record *Albuquerque* not *Alburquerque*. Yet the "r" spelling persists in Spanish documents as late as Escudero's *Noticias* (1849). It is possible that some confusion with a titled Portuguese family bearing the surname *Albuquerque* and *Alboquerque* may have contributed to the present spelling ("Two Dukes of Alburquerque," *El Palacio*, 61, June 1954, 171-184). Governor Cuervo's letter to the Viceroy-Duke of Alburquerque dated Apr. 24, 1706, states that he had founded the villa "on the margins and meadows of the Rio del Norte in a goodly place of fields, waters, pasturage and timber" and there were thirty-five families now living there, comprising 252 persons. Furthermore, a church had been built and other public buildings were being constructed. Descendants of these founding families still live in the city.

The modern section was founded in 1879 by the New Mexico Townsite Co., an auxiliary of the AT&SF RR, which entered the new station on Apr. 22, 1880. Post office, 1851-82; New Albuquerque, June 21—July 1, 1882; Albuquerque, 1882—. ALBUQUERQUE GRANT (Bernalillo). Actually there never was a grant of land to the settlement of Albuquerque, either to the community or to the individuals, under the laws of Spain or Mexico. Various efforts were made in the Congress of the United States and before the Court of Private Land Claims to establish the existence of a "Town of Albuquerque Grant." None of these efforts was successful. A decree was handed down by the Court of Private Land Claims on May 21, 1892, finding as a matter of law that the Villa de Albuquerque, "which was founded in the year 1705 and continued in existence up to the year 1846, was entitled, under the laws of Spain and Mexico, to four square Spanish leagues of land in a square body, measuring one Spanish league from the center of the plaza or public square of said villa to each of the four cardinal points of the compass, and this finding and the confirmation in this decree contained are based upon the provisions of titles V, VII, XII and XIII, Book IV of the *Recopilación de Leyes de los Reynos de Las Indias.*" The case was appealed to the Supreme Court of the United States and the case was reversed on Oct. 17, 1898. (See decision in U.S. Supreme Court Reporter 171, p. 685.) Finally, in order to cure the defect in titles in the Albuquerque area, the Congress of the United States on Feb. 18, 1901, enacted a law entitled "An Act to Confirm In Trust To The City of Albuquerque in the Territory of New Mexico, The Town of Albuquerque Grant, and For Other Purposes." This law quitclaimed to the City of Albuquerque as Trustee for the use and benefit of those actually entitled thereto "the land or any part thereof which was in eighteen hundred and eighty-three surveyed under the direction of the Surveyor General for New Mexico, as the TOWN OF ALBUQUERQUE GRANT, the surveying having been approved by the said Surveyor General on the 28th day of November, eighteen hundred and eighty-three, and including four Spanish leagues; all the right, title, claim and interest of the United States in and to the said premises embraced in the said grant is hereby vested in the City of Albuquerque in trust for the benefit of all persons claiming title to their individual holdings of real estate at the time of the acquisition of New Mexico under the Treaty of Guadalupe Hidalgo and their successors in interest of who have been in open adverse possession for the period of ten years prior to the passage of this act." Albuquerque was not alone in the matter of lacking a land grant title. Both Santa Fe and Socorro lacking land grant title, were obliged to ask for an Act of Congress to assist them in perfecting the titles to individual owners, which titles had been clouded by reason of the fact that the United States had a superior claim, at least on paper.

ALCALDE (Rio Arriba). Span., "mayor or judge, magistrate." Agricultural community on US 64, 7 mi N of Española. Name refers to the official appointed to keep the peace and administer affairs during the days of the Span-

ish and Mexican governors, 1598-1846. Post office, 1890, intermittently, to present.

ALCATRAZ (San Juan). Post office, 1892-94; mail to Largo.

ALCOR (Guadalupe). On SP RR, 12 mi NE of Santa Rosa.

ALELLEN (Chaves) Post office, 1904-7. See ORCHARD PARK.

ALEMAN (Sierra). Ranch and AT&SF RR siding S of Engle and 18 mi SE of Truth or Consequences. Post office, 1869-78; 1884-90.

ALEXANDER VALLE GRANT (San Miguel). Small tract on canyon of Pecos River N of Pecos Pueblo. Original petition was made to Governor Maynez in 1808 by Juan de Dios Peña, Francisco Ortiz, Jr., and Juan de Aguilar. Valley Ranch is on the edge of this area.

ALGODONES (Sandoval). Span., "cotton, cotton plants." 7 mi N of Bernalillo, on US 85. Settlers moved here in 1839, and Writers' Project records indicate that the town was named for cotton fields nearby. However, there is no record of cotton growing in Spanish colonial times. On the other hand, there is an abundance of cottonwood trees in the area, and the seasonal lint they shed may have contributed the name. Post office, 1855, intermittently, to present.

ALHAMBRA (Grant). Post office, 1890-1902; mail to Silver City.

ALICIA SIDING (Harding). On SP RR, 5 mi SE of Abbott Station.

ALIRE (Socorro). Name of mining camp near Carthage; a family name. Post office, 1923-25.

ALIVIO (Sierra). On AT&SF RR, 21 mi NE of Hatch.

ALKALI LAKE (De Baca). In SE corner of county.

ALLEGROS MOUNTAINS (Catron). 7 mi E of Mangas.

ALLEN (Quay). Post office, 1906-16.

ALLIE (Roosevelt). 3 mi S of Causey. First postmaster, Allie M. Gilmore. Post office, 1912-23.

ALLERTON (Sandoval). NW of Cochiti on road to Bland, and once a flourishing timber and mining camp; in Bernalillo County before 1903. Post office, 1894-96; mail to Bland.

ALLISON (Grant). Named for postmaster, John H. Allison. Post office, 1893-1901.

ALLISON (McKinley). 3 mi NW of Gallup near US 666. Named for Fletcher Allison, official of Victor American Coal Co. Post office, 1913-37; mail to Gallup.

ALMA (Catron). Established in 1881, 8 mi W of Mogollon. Named for wife of one of original settlers. Post office, 1882-96; 1900-31.

ALPS (Union). Station or passing track on C&S RR, 5 mi NE of Folsom and 6 mi S of Colorado border. Named in 1887, when railroad was built, because of terrain similar to Swiss Alps.

ALTAMONT (Rio Arriba). Post office, 1883-84; mail to Tierra Amarilla.

ALTA VISTA (San Miguel). 2 mi W of Trujillo.

ALTAIR (Luna). On SP RR, 18 mi E of Columbus.

ALTO (Lincoln). Span., "high." 11 mi SW of Capitan. Settled in 1882 by W. W. Brazel, named by postmaster, W. H. Walker, in 1901 for high elevation, 7,300 ft. Post office, 1901—.

ALUMINA (Grant). At base of Alum Mtn. about 3 mi below confluence of E and W forks of Gila River. The residents, however, mined meerschaum, not alum. Post office, 1890-94; mail to Pinos Altos.

ALVARADO (Otero). On SP RR, 5 mi NE of Hueco and 9 mi from Texas line. An officer of the Coronado expedition in 1540 was named Alvarado. There were no settlers in NM by this name from 1598 to the present century. The name is common, however, south of the border, and the town's extreme southern location prompts the belief that it was named for an Alavardo who moved up from Mexico in modern times. Nevertheless, the town may have been named by someone, whether Anglo or Hispano, who wished to honor Coronado's man.

AMADO (Cibola). Post office, 1900-05; mail to San Mateo.

AMALIA (Taos). Span., feminine personal name. Post office 5 mi SE of Costilla on NM 196.

AMARGO (Rio Arriba). Span., "bitter." Post office, 1881-94; 1913-23. See LUMBERTON. AMARGO RIVER (Rio Arriba). Rises 18 mi W of Chama and flows NW into Colorado, following D&RGW RR to border. Name refers to chemical content of the water.

AMBOY (Union). On C&S RR, 3 mi NW of Des Moines.

AMBROSIA LAKE (McKinley). 14 mi NW of San Mateo. Ranch area with a lake now dry; center of uranium mining and milling. Original name was LA LAGUNA DEL DIFUNTO AMBROSIO. The story is that an individual named Ambrosio was found floating in the lake, his body pierced by Indian arrows. The form "ambrosia" is modern.

AMERICAN CREEK (Rio Arriba). Small tributary of Rio de las Vacas in Jemez Mts. AMERICAN CREEK (Colfax). Flows into Cieneguilla Creek in Moreno Valley S of Eagle Nest. AMERICAN VALLEY (Socorro). Post office, May 27—Oct. 11, 1887; mail to Socorro.

AMISTAD (Union). Span., "friendship." Near Texas line, E of NM 18. Founded in 1906 by the Rev. H. S. Wannamaker, a Congregational minister, who named it as a token of his hope for the enterprise. A number of the early settlers were clergymen from the East. Post office, 1907—.

AMIZETTE (Taos). Boom town, 1893-95, in Hondo Canyon, 14 mi NE of Taos. Named for Amizett(e) Helphenstine, wife of Al Helphenstine, a prospector who led the first miners to ore strikes there. Post office, 1893-1902. See TWINING.

ANALCO (Santa Fe). Mexican-Spanish word for a minority district on the other side of a river. Referred to in 1680 as a suburb S of Santa Fe River, and originally the home of Tlascalan or Mexican-Indian servants of the Spaniards in Santa Fe.

AMOLES (Doña Ana). Span., "soapweeds." On Refugio Grant, 2 mi SE of Gadsden; washed away by floods, 1876, 1884, and abandoned after 1886.

AÑAL, also AÑIL, CREEK (Guadalupe). Span., añal, "offering in memory of a person one year after his death"; añil, "indigo plant." N of Ft. Sumner. Probably named for an herb growing here. See ARROYO DE AÑIL. In 1916, a country post office was established at the head of this creek. The new postmaster spelled the name as it sounded to him, Añal. Old-timers still used Añil for the creek, but were obliged to have their mail addressed to Añal. The post office was discontinued in 1924, but the community is still known by that name.

ANALLA (Lincoln). Post office, 1903-09. See TINNIE.

ANAPRA (Doña Ana). Post office, 1907-19. See SUNLAND PARK.

ANASTACIO ROMERO GRANT (Santa Fe). "From the side of a hollow and above a house lot and from same hillside and lot the line runs from east to west to the river below the Pueblo of Pojoaque where the junction of the rivers is, and from a stake which is driven in said hollow." Quoted from grant by Gov. Pedro Rodriguez Cubero on Dec. 9, 1699.

ANCHETA CREEK (Grant). Flows S into Mimbres River 8 mi E of Santa Rita. Named for either Joseph A. Ancheta or his father, Nepomuceno Ancheta. The father came to NM in 1856, a refugee from the Mexican

Revolution. He was mostly Yaqui, and was said to have had a secret mine to which he made trips, returning with plenty of gold. The son became an attorney and was admitted to the bar in Indiana and NM. In 1891, while a member of the Territorial Legislature, he was the innocent victim of an evident attempt to murder Thomas B. Catron.

ANCHO (Lincoln). Span., "wide." On SP RR, 2 mi SW of Luna. Named because of location on the side of a wide valley. Shipping and supply point for ranchmen after it became a railroad station in 1899. Post office, 1902—. ANCHO PEAK (Lincoln). 7 mi SE of Ancho in Jicarilla Mts. ANCHO VALLEY (Lincoln). 1 mi NW of Ancho.

ANCONES (Rio Arriba). On NM 111, on the Rio Vallecitos 9 mi N of Ojo Caliente.

ANDRECITO CREEK (Doña Ana). In San Andres Mts. 25 mi SW of Tularosa.

ANDREWS (Sierra). 4 mi NE of Hillsboro. Named for William Andrews, who managed the Andrews Mine here. Post office, 1898-1907; mail to Hillsboro.

ANGLE (Sierra). Post office, 1881; changed to ENGLE.

ANGOSTURA (Doña Ana). Span., "narrows." 2 mi E of Hatch. ANGOSTURA (Rio Arriba). Reference may be to a narrow pass. ANGOSTURA GRANT (Sandoval). Small grant between Algodones and the Jemez River. Given to Andres Montoya, lieutenant and chief alcalde of the pueblo of San Felipe, Nov. 10, 1745.

ANGUS (Lincoln). On NM 37, 8 mi SW of Capitan. Settled in 1881 by Amos Eakers. Named by P. G. Peters, first postmaster, in 1898. Name honored VV Ranch which was stocked with Polled Angus cattle. It is reported that the SP RR bought up the ranches in this area for their water rights and allowed the orchards and farms to go to ruin. Post office, 1898-1913.

ANIMAS (Hidalgo). Span., "departed souls." Pre-Spanish Indian village on SP RR, 15 mi NE of Rodeo. First settled and named by Spanish people in 1843. Post office, 1909—. There are two words for "soul" in Spanish: *alma*, which is usually applied to the soul of a living person; *ánima*, to the soul of one who has died. Thus *ánimas benditas* (blessed souls in Purgatory); *ánimas perdidas* (lost souls in Hell). ANIMAS CREEK (Hidalgo). NW of Kingston. ANIMAS CREEK (Sierra). 9 mi N of Kingston. ANIMAS PEAK (Hidalgo). ANIMAS RIVER (San Juan). Stream flowing SW from above Durango, Colo., into northwestern NM; parallels US 550 for 40 mi, then empties into San Juan River at Farmington. Name is probably a shortened form of *ánimas perdidas*. So named because of the treacherous quicksands of the river crossings where many Indians and early Spanish explorers lost their lives. Formerly called RIO DE LAS ANIMAS. Not the same as Animas Purgatoire ("Picketwire") River in central Colorado, which empties into Arkansas River.

ANNISTON (Quay). Post office, 1909-13.

ANSONIO (Grant). May be a transfer name from Ansonia, Conn., which is named for Anson G. Phelps, senior partner of Phelps Dodge Corp. This company has extensive copper reserves and a mine at Morenci, Ariz., just across the state line at this point. Post office, 1890-92; mail to Hanover.

ANNVILLE (Bernalillo). Post office, 1881-82; changed to Wallace.

ANTELOPE (Hidalgo). On SP RR, 18 mi NE of Rodeo. ANTELOPE (Lea). Boom settlement of short duration, 6 mi W of Crossroads. Said to have been named for anticipated "swiftness" of growth, by its founder, Charles Burks. ANTELOPE (Torrance). Post office, 1891-95; mail to Chilili. ANTELOPE CANYON (Otero). Named for antelope herds found by early settlers of Sacramento and Guadalupe mts. ANTELOPE LAKE (Lincoln). 19 mi W of White Oaks. ANTELOPE LAKE (Otero). 34 mi SE of Alamogordo. ANTELOPE PEAK (Colfax). E of Cunico at Union County line; extends into Doña Ana County on NE side of Organ Mts. ANTELOPE SPRING (Torrance). Near Estancia. Stocked with cattle by Robert McAtee in 1874. ANTELOPE WELLS (Hidalgo). Trading point on NM 79, 1 mi N of Mexican border. Settled by 1847 and named for the many antelope that found a water hole here.

ANTHONY (Doña Ana). On US 80 and 85, 20 mi N of El Paso; in the heart of the cotton-growing area of the Mesilla Valley along the Texas border. When the AT&SF RR built its line in 1881, the station was placed on the Texas side and named La Tuna. A Spanish-American woman named Sabrina had a chapel on the NM side dedicated to San Antonio, and when a town was started she rejected the name La Tuna and insisted upon Anthony. Previously the location on the NM side was called HALF WAY HOUSE. Another version states that a Catholic priest came through the mountain pass to establish a church here and found that the outline of a face on the mountain was called St. Anthony's Nose. There is a promontory on the Hudson River named Anthony's Nose, but commemorating the nose of Anthony D. Hooges. Post office, 1884—.

ANTOINE LEROUX GRANT (Taos). Large tract E of the Rio Grande and N of Taos Pueblo. See MARTINEZ or GODOI GRANT.

ANTON CHICO. Span., "little Anthony." A common nickname, but no particular individuals can be associated with the communities or land grants so named in NM. Span. Arch. NM, I, 899, refers to the Sangre de Cristo Grant as "Antonchico." ANTON CHICO (Guadalupe). Shopping center for ranch community 6 mi W of US 84 at Guadalupe County line. Post office, 1872—. ANTON CHICO GRANT (Guadalupe, San Miguel). Large grant in NW corner of Guadalupe County crossing into San Miguel. Name may commemorate an early grantee or settler. Petition for the grant was made on Feb. 13, 1822, and approved by the Mexican Congress on Aug. 18, 1824. The Texas-Santa Fe Expedition under McLeod came near or through this area in 1841.

ANTONIO DE ABEYTA GRANT (Rio Arriba). Small tract 5 mi W of Embudo along the Rio Ojo Caliente. An Antonio de Abeytia is listed as an officer of the militia at Santa Cruz in 1735. The grant was made as early as 1736.

ANTONIO DE SALAZAR GRANT (Rio Arriba). Petition of Antonio de Salazar and his brothers to the Governor and Captain General on Aug. 25, 1714, for a grant of land in Rio Arriba County, bounded on N by junction of Chama River with the Del Norte, on S by the land of Santa Clara Pueblo, on E by the Rio del Norte, and on W by the hills.

ANTONIO ORTIZ GRANT (San Miguel). Large area SE of Las Vegas extending nearly to county line. Records in the Court of Private Land Claims for NM show that on Dec. 18, 1818, Antonio Ortiz petitioned Governor Melgares for a grant situated on the Gallinas River. His request was granted, and he took possession on June 28, 1819.

ANTONIO SEDILLO GRANT (Bernalillo, Valencia). Large grant crossing two county lines and the Rio Puerco, 20 mi W of Isleta. In April 1769 Antonio Sedillo petitioned for a tract of land known as Cañada de los Apaches. His request was granted and he took possession on April 25 of that year.

ANZAC (Cibola). Section house and siding on AT&SF RR, 9 mi SE of Grants. Company-conferred name, from initials of the Australian and New Zealand Army Corps in World War I.

APACHE. Since there are reservations in two parts of the state for these Indians, the place name appears frequently. APACHE (Colfax). Post office, 1877-82; mail to Chico Springs. APACHE CANYON (Quay). On NM 88, 6 mi N of its junction with NM 18. Some say that the last Apache Indian killed by cattlemen was slain near the mouth of the canyon on a small hill. Others say the canyon is so named because it was the Apaches' favorite spot for attack on wagon trains, as this was the only trail leading from the caprock to the valley. APACHE CANYON, CREEK (Santa Fe). Runs S 2 mi W of Glorieta. Scene of battle between Union and Confederate forces on Mar. 26, 1862. The Union forces withdrew to Pigeon's Ranch and Glorieta where two days later they won a decisive victory. APACHE CITY (Quay). Former settlement 30 mi S of Tucumcari. Townsite and sale of lots about 1907. APACHE CREEK (Catron). Settlement on NM 12, at junction of Apache Creek and Tularosa River, 10 mi NE of Reserve. Post office, 1928—. APACHE CREEK (Catron). Flows S from Apache Canyon to join Tularosa River. APACHE HILLS (Hidalgo). APACHE NATIONAL FOREST (Catron). Originally created on Mar. 2, 1899, and known also as the DATIL FOREST. Since then, numerous boundary changes have been made in the interest of better administration. Today the Apache National Forest has a gross area of 1,009,553 acres in NM and 707,989 acres in Arizona. APACHE PASS (Taos). APACHE PEAK (Catron). APACHE SPRINGS (San Miguel).

ARABELLA (Lincoln). See LAS TABLAS. In the late 1870's or early 1880's, three Spanish families came from Walsenburg, Colo., and settled on ranches at the SE end of the Capitan Mts. They called the settlement LAS TABLAS, probably with reference to timber used for building. In 1886, Andy Richardson moved to Las Tablas and opened a general store. When he was appointed postmaster in 1901, he changed the name to honor the daughter of one of the settlers. Post office, 1901-28. ARABELLA (Guadalupe). On SP RR, 7 mi SW of Santa Rosa.

ARAGON (Catron). Settlement 23 mi SW of Mangas. Originally the name of an ancient Spanish province. The town's name comes from a family which arrived in NM in 1693. Aragon is old FORT TULAROSA, which served as an Apache Indian agency from 1872 to 1874. The Indians were moved here from the Ojo Caliente reservation, then moved back and the fort abandoned in 1874. Post office, 1906—.

ARCH (Roosevelt). 12 mi SE of Portales. There are two accounts of the naming of this settlement. One reports the name as suggested by Ila Nichols for Arch Williams, a settler when the post office was established here on Sept. 22, 1903. Another version says that the name was for Arch Gragg, or Gregory, an early sheriff of Roosevelt County, but this report is challenged by some present-day residents. A later postmaster says that Ila Nichols did not name the locality for any person, place, or thing. The Post Office Department asked for short names; she wrote "Arch" down, liked it, and sent it in. Vincent H. Ogburn declares that the name commemorates Archie Roosevelt, son of President Theodore Roosevelt, for whom the county was named in 1903. Post office, 1903—.

ARCHULETA. Ascencio de Arechuleta, a native of the Basque province of Guipuzcoa, came to NM as a captain in Oñate's 1598 expedition. His own children dropped the first "e" as early as the beginning of the seventeenth century. Their descendants clung pretty closely to the country N of Santa Fe, pushing over northward into the present Colorado. ARCHULETA (Bernalillo). Post office, 1888-94; changed to PEREA. ARCHULETA (San Juan). On San Juan River, 16 mi NE of Bloomfield. Post office, 1919-30. ARCHULETA CREEK (Union).

ARCO DEL DIABLO (Luna). Span., "arch of the devil." Peak of Florida Mts. S of Deming, containing a natural windowlike opening.

ARD (Quay). Post office, 1907-14.

ARENA (Luna). On SP RR and NM 9, 14 mi E of Columbus.

ARENAL (Bernalillo). Span., "sandy ground." Located outside city limits of SW Albuquerque, W of Armijo. Settlement was once called LOS ARENALES.

ARENAS VALLEY (Grant). On US 260, 7 mi E of Silver City, 3 mi W of Ft. Bayard. The present postmaster reports that there was a debate on the names Whiskey Creek and Arenas Valley, but, through the influence of a state senator, Arenas Valley was chosen. Post office, 1947—.

ARMAS (Grant). 5 mi E of Silver City.

ARMENTA CANYON (San Juan). Runs into San Juan River 3 mi SW of Blanco and 8 mi above Bloomfield. Named for the Jose Armenta family, which settled near the mouth of the canyon about 1878.

ARMIJO (Bernalillo). Settlement 3 mi S of Albuquerque, on NM 85. Jose de Armijo, a native of Zacatecas, came to NM in May 1693 with his wife, Catalina Duran, and four grown sons. One of his grandsons settled in the Rio Abajo area, and there his many descendants intermarried with the prosperous families of Atrisco. A cluster of these Armijo families gave the name to this place S of Atrisco on W bank of the Rio Grande. Post office, 1883-86; changed to Old Albuquerque; Armijo, 1906, intermittently, to 1936. ARMIJO (Valencia). Siding on AT&SF RR, 6 mi W of Suwanee.

ARMS (Colfax). First postmaster, Henry M. Arms. Post office, 1879-80.

ARMINTA CANYON (San Juan). See ARMENTA CANYON.

ARRAGON (San Miguel). Post office, 1884-85; mail to El Pueblo.

ARREY (Sierra). 15 mi SE of Hillsboro. First postmaster, Urbano P. Arrey. Post office, 1901—.

ARRIBA (San Miguel). On AT&SF RR 6 mi N of Las Vegas. See ABAJO.

ARROYO (San Juan). Span., "stream, brook"; Southwestern Spanish, "dry water bed, wash or gulch." ARROYO COLORADO (Torrance). "Red." ARROYO COLORADO (Valencia). Flows into the Rio San Jose, W of Correo. ARROYO DE AÑIL (De Baca). Rises in Guadalupe County and flows S to enter Pecos River, 3 mi NW of Ft. Sumner. Named for wild flowers on its banks. ARROYO DE COMALES (Rio Arriba). "Pottery griddles for cooking corncakes." 7 mi NW of Abiquiu. ARROYO DE LA JARA (Mora, San Miguel). On border of the two counties, W of Watrous. ARROYO DE LA MATANZA (Socorro). Dry watercourse W of Socorro, where cattle and sheep used to be slaughtered. ARROYO DE LA PARIDA (Socorro). ARROYO DE SALADA (De Baca). "Salt." Named because of salt content of land through which it runs. ARROYO DEL CEJITA (Harding). Named for Cejita Creek. Also known as RIDGE CREEK. ARROYO DEL CUERVO (Torrance). "Crow."

ARROYO DEL GUIQUE (Rio Arriba). Flows into the Rio Grande N of Guique. See QUIQUI. ARROYO DEL MUERTO (Harding). "Dead man." Possibly from tragedy to people trapped by the sudden rush of water in a stream bed usually dry. ARROYO DE SAN LORENZO (Socorro). Named for the patron saint, honored in NM by communities in both Taos and Grant counties. See SAN LORENZO. ARROYO DE TAJIQUE (Torrance). See TAJIQUE CREEK. ARROYO DEL TAJO (Socorro). "Mountain gap." ARROYO HONDO (Taos). "Deep." Settlement 12 mi NW of Taos. Named for deep valley in which it is situated. Post office, 1885—. ARROYO HONDO GRANT (Taos). Extends between Arroyo Hondo and San Cristobal. After a proclamation was made on Feb. 28, 1813, inviting settlers to go on vacant land, a petition was signed on Mar. 27, 1815, by Nerio Sisneros and forty-two others requesting from 40 to 300 varas of land at the "Rio Ondo Place." Petition was approved Apr. 10, 1815. ARROYO LA PETACA (Taos). "Trunk or chest." ARROYO SECO (Taos). "Dry." 7 mi N of Taos. Settlement began in 1804 when Cristobal Martinez and Jose Gregorio Martinez from Rio Arriba County planted crops here for three years before building their houses in 1807. Post office, 1881—. ARROYOS NEGROS (Socorro). Named for black lava formation.

ARTESIA (Eddy). On US 285 and AT&SF RR in N part of county. Farming and stockraising were once the principal activities of this community, but since 1923 the oil industry has contributed to its rapid development. Location was originally on the homestead site of J. F. Truitt, a Union soldier, the first to settle here. In 1894, the old stage line ran through what is now the city, where there was a spring (still running) called BLAKE'S SPRING. Location was a part of the Chisum holdings and known as SOUTH CHISUM CAMP. When the railroad built a siding here it was called MILLER. In 1899, a post office was established and called STEGMAN, for an early-day promoter who married Mrs. Sallie Robert, a niece of John Chisum. The post office siding was then known as MILLER-STEGMAN. In 1903, a townsite was laid out on land bought from Mrs. Robert, and named Artesia because of the discovery of artesian water in the vicinity. Post office 1903—.

ARUNAS CREEK (Sierra). 9 mi N of Kingston.

ASH CANYON (Doña Ana). In San Andres Mts. Named for large ash trees growing beside springs. Contains ruins of stone house used often by the Lincoln County desperado, Billy the Kid. ASH CREEK (Hidalgo). Rises in Gillespie Mts., flows NE to Playas Lake. ASH MOUNTAIN (Colfax). 3 mi E of Taos County line on the Rito Leandro, in Maxwell Land Grant.

ASPEN. These trees of the Canadian life zone, above 8,000 ft, are responsible for at least two place names N of Santa Fe. ASPEN HILL (Santa Fe). 3 mi N of Hyde Park. ASPEN MOUNTAIN (Santa Fe). 3 mi E of Aspen Hill.

ATALAYA GRANT (Santa Fe). Span., "watchtower, height." Small grant SE of Santa Fe, surrounding Atalaya Peak. Spanish grant within northeast-central portion of Santa Fe Grant and mentioned in early documents as both Atalaya Grant and Talaya Grant. Petition for grant was made in 1735 by Manuel Trujillo; confirmed by U.S. in 1895. Grant consists of 319.20 acres. ATALAYA PEAK (Santa Fe). A small cone-shaped hill ½ mi E of St. John's College, SE of Santa Fe.

ATARQUE (Quay). Span., "diversion dam." Founded in 1884. First settlers were Juan Garcia and his mother, Señora Cecelia Garcia, who built a dam on the natural lake, developing a water tank for stock. Name may be related to atarquinar, "to fill up with mud." The word was used for an earthen dam, and was extended later to mean any dam across a small stream. ATARQUE (San Miguel). 17 mi SE of Bell Ranch. ATARQUE (Cibola). On NM 36, 5 mi NW of Fence Lake. Post office, 1910-55. ATARQUE CREEK (San Miguel). E of Atarque, 3 mi from Harding County line. ATARQUE LAKE (Cibola). 5 mi NW of Atarque.

ATENCIO (Union). 7 mi from Texas line, 24 mi N of Clayton. Name of Spanish family, the earliest of whom, Jose de Atienza de Alcala y Escobar, arrived in NM in 1693. Post office, 1910-14. See CUBA.

ATKINS (Catron). Settlement 1½ mi from corner where Catron, Sierra, and Socorro counties come together.

ATOKA (Eddy). On AT&SF RR, 5 mi S of Artesia. This is a place name found in Virginia, Tennessee, and Oklahoma, and is said to be a Choctaw word meaning "in, or to, another place."

ATRISCO. Written Atlisco by Fray Atanasio Dominguez in 1776. Atlixco was the name of a valley and city SW of Puebla, Mexico. The river valley location S and W of Albuquerque must have reminded the colonists of their previous home. Today it is a section of Albuquerque called Westgate Heights (formerly Snow Vista). Post office, 1892-93; 1907-08.

ATRISCO GRANT (Bernalillo). On Oct. 28, 1692, a grant was made by King Charles II of Spain, through the Governor and Captain General of New Mexico to Fernando Duran y Chavez, founder of the community. At that time, the grant embraced 41,000 acres on the W side of the Rio Grande across from the present site of Albuquerque. Then, however, the river was farther east. The Atrisco Grant was enlarged to 82,000 acres on May 7, 1768. Today it is controlled by a corporation established on Apr. 11, 1892, and has been reduced to about 46,000 acres.

ATSINNA (Cibola). Ruins of a Zuñi Indian Pueblo, on top of 200-ft-high Inscription Rock in El Morro National Monument. Name means "writing on the rocks."

AUGUSTINE (Socorro). Former settlement 2 mi from W county line on US 60. Post office, 1927-55. Supplied from Magdalena.

AURORA (Mora). Point 6 mi N of Ocate. Post office, 1902-21.

AURUPA RUINS (San Miguel). 3 mi W of US 84, and 2½ mi S of Apache Springs.

AVALON (Eddy). On AT&SF RR. 4 mi N of Carlsbad. Name is commemorative of British King Arthur, whose last resting place was assigned to an island so called by writers from the twelfth to the nineteenth centuries. AVALON RESERVOIR (Eddy). Dam and lake at head of Pecos irrigation system canal. Named by a Mr. Kidder, a retired sea captain, who built a clubhouse on the shore of the lake and had sailboats here.

AVE MARIA (Rio Arriba). Latin, "Hail Mary." Named for opening words of the Angelic Salutation. As the title of this prayer, it was taken over into Spanish untranslated, as was done in pre-Reformation English. Post office, 1923-25.

AVIS (Otero). 7 mi SE of Weed. Town bears as its name the Latin word for bird. Aviz is a Portuguese family name given to a town and a castle in Portugal. It referred originally to the two black birds on the family shield. Post office, 1903-30.

AZOTEA. Span., "flat roof." Descriptive of the flat roofs and platforms characteristic of the stone houses of Mexico and the adobe ones of NM. AZOTEA (Rio Arriba). Post office 1887-93; mail to Monero. AZOTEA FORK (Eddy). Flows SW through Azotea Mesa. AZOTEA MESA (Eddy). 10 mi W of Carlsbad. AZOTEA PEAK (Eddy). W of Azotea Mesa.

AZTEC (San Juan). City at crossroads of NM 550, 173, and 44, just SE of Animas River. Planned in 1890 and named for the ruined pueblo nearby. Post office 1879—. AZTEC RUINS NATIONAL MONUMENT (San Juan). Across Animas River from Aztec. Excavated by Earl Morris who was director here for the American Museum of Natural History until 1924. Named in the belief of many that the old ruins were those of a northern branch of the Aztec Indians.

AZUL (San Miguel). Span., "blue." On AT&SF RR, 6 mi N of Las Vegas. Added to the list of stations July 12, 1883. AZUL CREEK (McKinley). Flows into Bluewater Reservoir from NW.

AZURE (Grant). Post office, 1895; mail to Silver City.

Baca. Span., "cow." The family name originated in the thirteenth century during the Moorish wars in Spain. An individual who had marked a strategic river ford with a cow's skull was rewarded by the King with the name Cabeza de Vaca (Cow's Head). Members of this family came to the New World even before famed Alvar Nuñez Cabeza de Baca made his transcontinental trek (1528-36). In 1600, Capt. Cristobal Baca, a native of Mexico City, came to NM, and several of his great-grandsons returned with the Reconquest of 1692, settling in the Santa Fe region. Around 1800, Luis Maria Baca, one of the many sons of Juan Antonio Baca of La Cienaga began using the full name, Cabeza de Baca. Civil as well as church records show that it is the same family. BACA (Lincoln). 3 mi N of Lincoln. BACA (McKinley). BACA (Mora, Union). First postmaster, Louis A. C. de Baca. Post office, 1884-98; mail to Bueyeros.

BACA GRANT, LOCATIONS. These terms refer to land areas associated with the descendants of Cristobal Baca. On Apr. 6, 1835, under the laws of Mexico, a grant was made to Juan de Dios Maese and twenty-five other citizens of Las Vegas designating a tract of land containing approximately 500,000 acres. On June 11, 1841, another grant was issued to Don

Luis Maria Cabeza de Baca, who was born in Santa Fe on Oct. 26, 1754. Complaints arose because the grants appeared to overlap, and on June 21, 1860, the Congress of the United States confirmed the Town of Las Vegas as Trustee for the grant of Apr. 6, 1835. On the same day the Congress also authorized the heirs of Don Luis Maria C. de Baca to select in lieu of the land claimed by them under the grant of 1841, an equal quantity of vacant land, not mineral, in NM to be located in square bodies not exceeding five in number. The first choice, called BACA LOCATION No. 1, was in present-day Sandoval County, a tract containing approximately 100,000 acres located in the Valle Grande W of present-day Los Alamos and extending to the Cebolla embracing originally the property known today as Sulphur Hot Springs. This Baca Location was acquired later by Frank Bond and Company and Redondo Development Company, finally being transferred to Texas owners. BACA LOCATION No. 2 was selected in the area of Ft. Bascom on the Canadian or Red River which was then San Miguel County. This particular Baca Location eventually became part of the Bell Ranch. See LAS VEGAS GRANT. Third and fourth Baca Locations were selected in parts of New Mexico which later became incorporated into Colorado and Arizona. Both were involved in litigation settled in 1863. A fifth Baca Location in eastern New Mexico was chosen in territory the federal government allocated for a Navajo and Apache Indian reservation. Claimants abandoned their efforts because the three-year limitation prescribed in the Congressional action of 1860 had expired.

BADEÑOS (Torrance). Abandoned town near Punta de Aguas. Named for a Spanish family.

BADGERVILLE (Eddy). See HOPE.

BADO DE JUAN PAIS (Guadalupe). Span., *vado,* "ford." Crossing of Pecos River just below Dilia. Once a prominent place on road from Las Vegas to Santa Rosa. Stage and mail station for the early Star Route mail deliveries. The stage stopped at the Juan Pais ranch for dinner.

BAKER (Grant). 30 mi SE of Lordsburg, and 2 mi W of NM 81. BAKER DOMES (San Juan).

BAILY CREEK (Sierra). 20 mi NW of Hermosa.

BALDWIN (Catron). 5 mi NW of Datil. Named for Levy Baldwin, a rancher there in early 1880's.

BALDY. Peaks in Catron, Colfax, Mora, and Santa Fe counties are so named because of the absence of timber on their rocky summits. BALDY (Colfax). Settlement 5 mi NE of Elizabethtown. Post office, 1888-1926. BALDY (Taos). Gold-mining camp. Named for BALDY MOUNTAIN. BALD KNOLL (Grant).

BALENZUELA (Socorro). 10 mi SW of Socorro. Also called VALENZUELA.

BALLEJOS (Valencia). Span., *vallejos,* "small valley." Post office, 1910-26.

BALTAZAR BACA GRANT (Cibola). Small Spanish grant in 1769 to Baltazar Baca and his two sons. 4 mi W of Cebolleta and 3 mi N of the Laguna pueblo of Encinal.

BANDELIER NATIONAL MONUMENT (Sandoval). 20 mi NW of Santa Fe. Named for Adolph F. Bandelier, Swiss-American archeologist, who explored Indian ruins of Frijoles Canyon and Pajarito Plateau between 1880 and 1886. On Feb. 11, 1916, these prehistoric buildings were established by Presidential proclamation as a national monument to be administered by the National Park Service. See EL RITO.

BANKS (Roosevelt). 15 mi NE of Ft. Sumner. Named for sand banks nearby. Post office, 1909-13.

BARANCOS (Quay). Span., *barranco,* "gorge." Post office, 1906-12.

BARCLAY'S FORT (Mora). See FORT BARCLAY.

BAR LAKE (Catron). 8 mi N of Luna.

BARD (Quay). Farming and ranching community 28 mi E of Tucumcari, near US 66 and CRI&P RR. First named BARD CITY when townsite was laid out in 1906. Walter R. Haynes recalls that this was a transfer name from a small watermelon-loading place in Texas which his father had named Bard because of a group of wandering music makers who held dances here. Post office, 1908—.

BARELA CANYON (Taos). Spanish family name. 7 mi NW of Tres Piedras. Runs E and W.

BARELA MESA (Colfax). On N boundary of county. Named for Senator Barela, a prominent Spanish-American resident of Trinidad, Colo., in the 1890's. See CHICARICA MESA.

BARELAS (Bernalillo). Suburb of Albuquerque, named for early nineteenth-century settlers.

BARILLIS CREEK (San Miguel). 12 mi E of Pecos. BARILLIS PEAK (San Miguel). 13 mi E of Pecos.

BARKER ARROYO (San Juan). Named for A. N. Barker, famous old stockman who happened to be in this vicinity when he was killed by a member of the Stockton and Ethredge gangs of outlaws who plagued this section. He was brought to Farmington for burial but the grave remained unmarked. When the early-day cemetery was moved, about 1925, J. B. Arrington reports that Barker was identified by his fine suit of clothes and cowboy boots which, despite the crumbling coffin, were in an excellent state of preservation. BARKER DOME (San Juan). Named for A. N. Barker.

BARNEY (Hidalgo). Stage stop for the Butter-field Overland Mail, 5 mi NE of Lordsburg. Named for an official of the Butterfield Co. BARNEY (Union). Former settlement on Pina-bete Creek, 24 mi SW of Clayton. Post office, 1896-1930.

BARR (Bernalillo). 10 mi S of Bernalillo on AT&SF RR. Named for Leo J. and A. J. Barr, brothers who were attorneys in Albuquerque in the early 1880's and who filed homestead claims here. Also called BARR STATION.

BARRANCA (Rio Arriba). Span., "gorge, ravine." Farming community 2 mi W of Abiquiu, S of NM 96. BARRANCA (San Miguel). BA-RRANCA (Taos). 4 mi N of Dixon. Post office, 1881-90. BARRANCA CREEK (Quay). BARRANCA GRANT (Rio Arriba). Near Abiquiu, E of the Piedra Lumbre. Made to Geronimo Martin and others, Mar. 2, 1735.

BARTLETT MESA (Colfax). N of Raton at Colo-rado line. Named for Carlos Bartlett, an early settler and founder of the Bartlett Estate in Vermejo Park in 1906.

BARTOLO CANYON (Torrance). Empties into Arroyo de Manzano, N of Manzano. BARTOLO VACA (Bernalillo). Settlement 19 mi E of Albuquerque on US 66.

BARTOLOME FERNANDEZ GRANT (McKinley). Small grant in SE corner of county in Cibola National Forest. Bartolome Fernandez is listed as a family man between 1750 and 1763 and was alcalde mayor of Jemez Pueblo at the end of this period. He received this grant from Governor Mendinueta on Sept. 2, 1767.

BARTON (Bernalillo). 22 mi E of Albuquerque, on US 66. Named for an early homesteader. Post office, 1908-36; mail to Edgewood.

BASCOM (San Miguel). 8 mi N of Tucumcari on SP RR.

BAT CAVES (Eddy). See CARLSBAD CAVERNS NATIONAL PARK.

BATHTUB DRAW (Grant). Runs S below Brushy Mtn.

BATTLESHIP ROCK (Sandoval). 3 mi S of La Cueva.

BAYARD (Grant). 10 mi E of Silver City on US 260. Named for Ft. Bayard, an early fort and Army hospital. Post office, 1902—. See FORT BAYARD.

BEAR. This place appears as English "bear" and as Spanish oso, and is used for canyons, creeks, mountains, and lakes. BEAR CANYON (Bernalillo). On W slope of Sandia Mts. BEAR CANYON (Colfax). Small stream E of Raton. BEAR CANYON (Otero). 9 mi S of Cloudcroft. The Mary White Camp for Girls is located here, on a tract of land donated by Eliza White, an early rancher of the vicinity. BEAR CANYON RESERVOIR (Grant). 25-acre lake, 2 mi N of Mimbres. BEAR CREEK (Grant). Rises in Pinos Altos Mts. and flows W into Gila River. BEAR CREEK (Hidalgo). In SE corner of county, 12 mi S of Big Hatchet Mts. BEAR CREEK (Mora). Tributary of Mora fork of Pecos River. BEAR CREEK (Rio Arriba). See RIO DEL OSO. BEAR LAKE (Colfax). W of Eagle Nest Lake. BEAR MOUNTAIN (Grant). 8 mi W of Buckhorn in NW part of county. BEAR MOUNTAIN (San Miguel). BEAR MOUN-TAIN (Socorro). BEAR SPRINGS (Otero). Near Cloudcroft. In 1858, two battles were fought near here by mounted riflemen against hostile Indians: on Aug. 29 by Detachment I, on Oct. 1 by Companies A, F, and I. BEAR SPRINGS (Socorro). 10 mi S of Riley; flows NE to the Rio Salado. BEAR TRAP CANYON (Socorro). BEAR WALLOW MOUNTAIN (Catron). 16 mi NE of Alma.

BEATTY (Mora). 7 mi N of Cowles. BEATTY'S CREEK (Mora). See RITO DEL PADRE.

BEAUBIEN-MIRANDA GRANT. See MAXWELL GRANT.

BEAUTIFUL MOUNTAIN (San Juan). 24 mi SW of Shiprock, at the Arizona line.

BEAUTY (Lea). Shown on 1921 map 18 mi NE of Tatum. Post office, 1916.

BEAVER. There are place names in at least five NM counties contributed by the amphibious rodent which in the 1820's and 1830's drew French and English trappers to the territory. BEAVER (Socorro). Post office, 1880-82. BEAVER CREEK (Catron). Flows S to Gila River. BEAVER CREEK (Colfax). Flows into the upper Rayado River in SW corner of county. BEAVER CREEK (Rio Arriba). Flows into Los Pinos River. BEAVER CREEK (San Miguel). N fork of El Porvenir Creek. BEAVERHEAD (Catron). Near the head of Beaver Creek, and once the site of Beaverhead Lodge. Named by the Evans brothers, local ranchers, because of the creek. Post office, 1922-38. BEAVER RIVER. See CANADIAN RIVER.

BECKER (Valencia). Named for John Becker, pioneer merchant of Belen. Illustrates names in this part of NM growing from commercial development along the railroads. Mr. Becker was instrumental in securing money for extending the railroad into Belen. Officials of AT&SF RR named the first water tank E of Belen for him, and the first one on the W side for his partner, Paul Dalies. See DALIES.

BEENHAM (Union). Former ranch settlement on a branch of Tramperos Creek, 9 mi SE of Pasamonte. Owned and named about 1880 by Charles John de Haviland (Uncle Charley) Bushnell, a sea captain from Beenham, England. He served as first postmaster. Post office, 1890-1924.

BELCHER (Roosevelt). Near town of Inez. First postmaster, Everett E. Belcher. Post office, 1910-11.

BELEN (Valencia). Span., "Bethlehem." Commercial center on US 85, 31 mi S of Albuquerque. Two small settlements, one Spanish and one of *genízaros* (captive Indians) disputed for this land in 1746. Although authorities in Mexico City ruled in favor of the Spanish settlers, there were a few Indians at Belen as late as 1766. One archive mentions a village here destroyed by Indians in the Pueblo Rebellion of 1680. Another source credits the founding to the year 1740 and the name to the Belen Grant. Post office, 1865-68; 1873—. BELEN GRANT (Valencia). Spans the Rio Grande S of Belen to Bernardo. Grant was made by Gov. Gaspar Dominguez de Mendoza, Nov. 15, 1740. A group of Spanish settlers took possession of NUESTRA SEÑORA DE BELEN (Our Lady of Bethlehem) GRANT on Dec. 9, 1740.

BELL (Colfax). 12 mi NE of Raton. Settled by a group of dissatisfied miners from Blossburg, who went on Johnson Mesa to farm. Named for Marion Bell, leader of the settlers. First postmaster, Alonso S. Bell. Post office, 1891-1933. BELL CANYON (Otero). 8 mi E of Cloudcroft. BELL LAKE (Lea). 19 mi S of Lea. BELL RANCH (San Miguel). In center of Pablo Montoya Grant, in E part of county. Post office at Bell Ranch takes its name from the ranch brand, which is bell-shaped. The brand, in turn, came from BELL MOUNTAIN, named for resemblance to the outline of a bell. In 1871, Wilson Waddington bought virtually the entire interest in Pablo Montoya Grant and

established a number of ranches, one of which was called Bell Ranch, using the brand of a bell on the left ribs. Post office, 1888—.

BELLVIEW (Curry). 7 mi NE of Broadview. Received name through a process of evolution. First post office was named PRESTON and was ¾ mi W of where Bellview now stands. Later the post office was renamed LEGANSVILLE, but other people had different ideas about where the town should be located. First schoolhouse was built 2 mi S of Bellview and named Liberty Bell. In 1918, the name Bellview was decided upon for the settlement. L. V. Ray and Glen Turner were the first settlers in the Bellview community. Both cattlemen, they established ranches there in 1905.

BELLY-ACHE MESA (Grant). N of Silver City, on the road between Alma and Stevens. This grazing area was named Belly-Ache Mesa or GUT-ACHE MESA, because a cowboy cook warmed over some soured frijoles, thus upsetting all the cowhands on a roundup. Another version blames bad son-of-a-gun stew for the upset.

BENNET (Lea). Oil and ranch community 3 mi S of Jal and 2 mi W of TNM RR. Post office, 1940-57.

BENNETT (San Juan). Named for F. T. Bennett, Navajo Indian agent at Ft. Wingate, 1869-71. BENNETT CREEK (Hidalgo). 21 mi NE of Cloverdale.

BENSON (Roosevelt). 10 mi W of Floyd. First postmaster, John O. Benson. Post office, 1911-19.

BENT (Otero). Farming and ranching community 10 mi NE of Tularosa. Named for George B. Bent, miner and promoter, who operated a mine and mill here about 1906. Post office, 1906—.

BERENDA. See BERRENDA. BERENDA CREEK (Doña Ana). Enters the Rio Grande N of Garfield. BERENDA CREEK (Sierra). 2 mi N of Lake Valley.

BERINO (Doña Ana). On US 80, 19 mi SE of Las Cruces; former town of COTTONWOOD, on route of Butterfield Overland Mail. Berino is said to be an Indian word meaning "ford." Post office, 1902—.

BERNABE MONTAÑO GRANT (Sandoval). Long tract spanning the Rio Puerco in both Sandoval and Bernalillo counties. Bernabe Montaño and other settlers were granted this land on Nov. 25, 1753, by Thomas Velez Cachupin, Governor of the Province of New Mexico.

BERNAL (San Miguel). Community on US 84, 16 mi SW of Las Vegas. Bears the Spanish surname Bernal, probably Vernal originally, "pertaining to spring." The ancestor of the Bernal family in NM was Juan Griego, a native of Greece, who came with Oñate in 1598. Juan Griego means "John the Greek." His wife was Pascuala Bernal. Some of his sons passed on the Griego surname, but at least one son and several daughters chose Bernal, the name of the mother. Post office, Feb. 14, 1881-95; changed to CHAPELLE.

BERNALILLO (Sandoval). Trading center and county seat 17 mi N of Albuquerque. Name may be translated "little Bernal." So called soon after the Reconquest by De Vargas in 1692. Before 1680 and also after 1693, members of the Gonzales-Bernal family lived in this district, and Bernalillo may have been named for one of these Bernals, perhaps one of small stature, or else a "Junior" who was thus distinguished from the "Senior" of the same name. Another possibility is that Don Fernando de Chavez, the leading citizen of this area and no friend of the Bernals, named his hacienda after his friend Fray Juan Bernal, who was martyred in 1680. Adolph F. A. Bandelier in his *Final Report of Investigations among the Indians of the Southwestern United States* (Cambridge, John Wilson & Son, 1890-92) says Bernalillo was founded by De Vargas in 1695. In 1704, Governor De Vargas led a campaign in the Sandia Mts. against Apaches and, falling ill, was brought to Bernalillo, where he died on Apr. 4, 1704. He was buried at Santa Fe "in the principal church." Post office, 1855-59; 1865—. BERNALILLO COUNTY. Created by the New Mexico Territorial Legislature on Jan. 9, 1852, at which time it included Sandoval County. Bernalillo was the county seat. Once the largest county in size, Bernalillo became the smallest, until Los Alamos County was created in 1949. County was set up by the Republic of Mexico in 1844, and reinstituted by the US on Jan. 6, 1852. Area today is 1,169 sq mi, with Albuquerque the county seat. BERNALILLO GRANT (Sandoval). N of Bernalillo and E of the Rio Grande. There were several petitions claiming eleven square Spanish leagues of land submitted to the U.S. Land Court and Court of Private Claims in 1893 and 1894 by petitioners claiming to be the heirs of Felipe Gutierrez, to whom a land grant was made by Governor Cubero on Jan. 21, 1704. Because boundaries were ill-defined and documentation inadequate, the courts made adverse rulings.

BERNARDO (Socorro). On US 85, 17 mi S of Belen. Named about 1902 for a friend of John Becker of Belen. Post office, 1902-19.

BERRENDA. Span., "spotted, two-colored." Name is in the category of "incident names" and is applied to localities where antelope have been discovered. The Western pronghorn antelope is light brown with a whitish section or two on each side. BERRENDA CREEK (Sierra). W of Lake Valley. BERRENDA PEAKS (Sierra). Series of three peaks named for the antelope found here. BERRENDO RIVER (Chaves). 5 mi N of Roswell on US 70 and 285.

BESS (Guadalupe). On W side of Pecos River, 12 mi SE of Puerto de Luna. Once a "cancellation" post office for joint communities of Los Ojitos and Bess, but when water from Alamogordo Dam covered the land of Los Ojitos, the Bess community diminished, too, and only a few families remained.

BEST LAKE (Chaves). 16 mi N of Caprock.

BETHEL (Roosevelt). Hebrew, "house of God." 10 mi W of Portales. Community founded by a colony of Christians who started a ministerial school. Post office, 1902-07.

BEULAH (Rio Arriba). Post office, 1894-95; mail to Abiquiu. BEULAH (San Miguel). 25 mi NW of Las Vegas. First post office was in the home of S. Omar Barker's father. Named for the old Methodist hymn "Beulah Land." Post office, 1896-1932.

BIBLE TOP HILL (Union). 3 mi W of Rabbit Ears Mtn. and N of US 87. A deep depression runs E and W across the top of the hill, which thus appears like an open book; hence the name Bible Top. This hill was used as a lookout point by Indians, and numerous flint arrow points have been found here.

BIBO (Cibola). On road to Cebolleta, 12 mi N of Laguna. Named for the Bibo brothers who settled in this area in the early 1880's. Ben Bibo, the youngest of six brothers, operated a trading post and post office, 1905-20.

BIG BEAR SPRING (McKinley). See FORT WINGATE.

BIG BURRO MOUNTAINS (Grant). W of Silver City. Separated from Little Burro Mts. by Mangas Creek.

BIG CREEK (Hidalgo). 10 mi SE of Rodeo.

BIG DRY CREEK (Grant). Tributary of San Francisco Creek, 15 mi from Glenwood, heading in Mogollon Mts.

BIGGS (Rio Arriba). On D&RGW RR 7 mi E of Monero. President of company which built lumber road from Lumberton to Hillcrest was named Biggs. Also called BIGGS SPUR.

BIG HATCHET MOUNTAINS (Hidalgo). See HACHITA (Grant).

BIG HORN (Rio Arriba). On D&RGW RR, 8 mi W of Los Pinos. Named for wild bighorn sheep of the Rocky Mts. Also called BIG HORN SIDING.

BIG MIKE (San Miguel). See SAN MIGUEL MOUNTAIN.

BIG SPRING (Union). See RABBIT EAR CREEK.

BIG TESUQUE (Santa Fe). Winter sports area, 14 mi NE of Santa Fe. BIG TESUQUE CREEK (Santa Fe). Small stream 10 mi N of Santa Fe.

BIG TURKEY CREEK (Grant). Rises in Diablo Range and flows SW to Gila River 11 mi NE of Cliff.

BIKLABITO (San Juan). Navajo trading post, 25 mi W of Shiprock.

BILLING (Socorro). On AT&SF RR between Socorro and Magdalena. Probably named for Gustav Billing, a mining engineer.

BILLY THE KID SPRING (Chaves). On San Juan Mesa, 6 mi NE of the town of Olive. Named for its association with William H. Bonney, the famous desperado of the Lincoln County cattle wars. Bonney, whose real name seems to have been Henry McCarty, came to Santa Fe with his mother in 1873. He lived in Silver City for three years, and subsequently worked for John Chisum and other ranchers, including an Englishman, John Tunstall. The murder of Tunstall in a dispute over a debt catapulted the Kid into a four-year feud ending with his death at Ft. Sumner, on July 14, 1881. Famed for both courage and villainy, the Kid was reputed to have slain twenty-one men, one for every year of his life, and he captured the imagination of writers. He is memorialized in poetry, drama, fiction, song, even ballet, as well as in a single place name.

BIRCHVILLE (Grant). See PINOS ALTOS.

BISHOP CAP (Doña Ana). Peak in Organ Mts., 10 mi N of Berino.

BLACK CAÑON (Grant). In NE corner of county. The stream here is a tributary of the Gila River, entering from the E and flowing from the Black Range 25 mi S of Silver City. BLACK HAWK (Grant). Post office, 1884-87; mail to Fleming. BLACK LAKE (Colfax). In SW corner of county. Named because, when viewed from a distance, dense timber surrounding the water makes it look black instead of blue.

First inhabitants here were Don Jose Maria Mares and his wife, Doña Jenara Trujillo, in 1886. Years earlier, in 1857, Jose Maria Mares had been captured by Indians while he and his brother were with a hunting party. They were taken to Taos, where they were sold to Don Juan Mares, who adopted them and brought them up as his own children. Post office, 1903-27. BLACK LAKE (San Juan). 3 mi W of Crystal. BLACK MESA (Colfax). 8 mi SE of Raton. Distinguished by interesting carvings on W side. BLACK MESA (Rio Arriba). Called by the Tewa Indians *tsee kwah yay*, "basalt height," and crossed by two Indian trails, the old Ute Trail and the "eagle gap trail," between San Juan Pueblo and Ojo Caliente. Also called CANOE MESA. BLACK MESA (Santa Fe). Probably the most famous mesa by this name in the state; just N of San Ildefonso Pueblo. The Tewa name is *toonyopeeng ya*, "very spotted mountains," from the large green spots on the N side of the blackish basalt composition. The place looks like a big, black fort and has served as a fort more than once. In historic times the Indians from San Ildefonso were besieged on top of the mesa by the Spanish at the close of the Pueblo Revolt. De Vargas made three unsuccessful attempts to assault it. Ruins of temporary adobes atop the mesa date from the De Vargas siege. Black Mesa has much to do with the mythology and religion of the Tewas. Other names are SACRED FIRE MOUNTAIN, SAN ILDEFONSO MESA, ROUND MOUNTAIN. BLACK MESA (Socorro). Near Valverde Battlefield. BLACK MESA GRANT (Rio Arriba). Small grant N of Alcalde and E of Chama River; made on Oct. 5, 1743, to Juan Garcia de Mora and Diego de Medina, by the Governor and Captain General under authority of the King of Spain. BLACK MESA OF SANTO TOMAS (Doña Ana). Lava flow 6 mi S of Las Cruces. BLACK MOUNTAIN (Colfax). BLACK MOUNTAIN (Grant). BLACK MOUNTAIN (Otero). BLACK PEAK (Sierra). See CUCHILLO NEGRO PEAK. BLACK RANGE (Sierra). W of Truth or Consequences. BLACK RIVER (Eddy). Rises in SW corner of county and flows NE into the Pecos. BLACK RIVER VILLAGE (Eddy). BLACK ROCK (McKinley). Post office, 1904-26. BLACK SPRINGS (Catron). Settlement 70 mi E of Reserve. Named for springs nearby in a dense and dark section of the forest. Post office, 1935-42. BLACK TOWER (Curry). Post office, 1905-12. See PORTAIR. BLACK WATER (Lincoln).

BLACKWATER DRAW (Curry, Roosevelt). In Oasis State Park, 7 mi NE of Portales. Site of fossil beds discovered by highway crew in 1932.

BLACKSMITH CANYON (Union). 2½ mi N of Dry Cimarron River on N side of Black Mesa. Heads in NM and opens out into North Carriso Canyon in Colorado. In the early 1860's a band of outlaws, led by the notorious outlaw Coe, did their blacksmithing in this canyon, where later settlers found a part of the anvil block. It was made from a piece of fine, hard wood, very rare in this part of the country; hence the name.

BLAKE's SPRING (Eddy). See ARTESIA.

BLANCHARD (San Miguel). Established 15 mi SW of Las Vegas as a switch and loading point for the shipment of timber. Named for Charles Blanchard, pioneer citizen of Las Vegas.

BLANCO (San Juan). Span., "white." Settlement 14 mi SE of Aztec. Named for prominent outcropping of rhyolite in adjacent hills. Post office, 1901—. BLANCO (San Miguel). 5 mi E of Rociada at Mora County line. BLANCO CANYON (Curry). 4 mi N of Ranchvale. BLANCO CANYON (San Juan). Runs N into Carrizo Creek, 8 mi SE of Blanco. BLANCO CREEK (Curry, Quay). Rises in Quay and flows E through Curry; named for the canyon through which it flows.

BLAND (Sandoval). Sixty years ago a thriving gold- and silver-mining community; now a ghost town, 12 mi NW of Cochiti Pueblo. Named for Richard P. (Silver Dick) Bland of Missouri. Post office, 1894-1935. BLAND CANYON (Santa Fe).

BLIND CANYON (Colfax). At head of Vermejo River; extends E from Caliente Canyon. Cowboys called it "blind" because it has but one entrance.

BLOODGOODS (Grant). On Little Creek, SE of Gila Hot Springs. Named for a rancher who had a butcher shop in Kingston and whose sons were Dean and Ellsworth. He sold his cattle in 1887 and moved to Mexico.

BLOOMFIELD (McKinley). 8 mi SE of Crownpoint. BLOOMFIELD (San Juan). On NM 17, 9 mi S of Aztec. Settled in 1878 and named for an early settler. The early history was of cattle rustling, terrorism, and violent death. Notorious Port Stockton, an outlaw from the Lincoln County War, came here after the war was over. He was killed in 1881 while hiding a man named Truitt, who had shot a man at a dance. Formerly called PORTER. Post office, 1879—.

BLOSSBURG (Colfax). 5 mi up Dillon Creek NW of Raton. Settled about 1881 as a coal-mining town, by a Colonel Savage from Blossburg, Pa., and named for his home town. There is now little left at the site. Post office, 1881-1905; mail to Gardner.

BLOSSER CREEK, GAP (Colfax). Flows into Eagle Tail Creek, which empties into Hebron Reservoir. Creek flows through the gap about 15 mi SE of Raton. This opening through the mountain range was named for a man by the name of Blosser, who had been evicted from his ranch by the Maxwell Land Grant Co., and who used the gap to run cattle through to the piñon country south of the mountains where the grazing was good.

BLUEBIRD MESA (Sandoval). 8 mi E of Lagunitas.

BLUE CANYON (Socorro). On the old road from Socorro to Magdalena; mineral deposits in the rocks, at certain times of the day, are as blue as giant peacock feathers. BLUE CREEK (Grant). Flows S into Gila River. BLUE HOLE (Quay). 5 mi N of Tucumcari. Blue pools on pioneer trail to Las Vegas. BLUE HOLE SPRING (Guadalupe). See SANTA ROSA CREEK. BLUE LAKE (Guadalupe). 1 mi E of Santa Rosa; so deep the water shows an intense blue. BLUE LAKE (Taos). At upper end of Hondo Canyon, sacred lake of the Taos Indians. During August, no permits are issued by the U.S. Forest Service to visit here, because this is the period when the Taos Indians hold sacred ceremonies at the lake. Indian sentinels guard all trails at this time. BLUE MESA (Catron). 6 mi E of Madre Mtn. BLUE SPRINGS (Eddy). BLUE SPRINGS (Socorro). BLUE WATER (Lincoln). In SE part of county, 13 mi NE of Lincoln. BLUEWATER (Valencia). On US 66, 11 mi NW of Grants. Post office, 1889-92; 1895—. BLUEWATER CANYON (Valencia). In this canyon, a dam was built across BLUEWATER CREEK, which formed BLUEWATER LAKE. BLUE WATER CREEK (Chaves). BLUEWATER CREEK (McKinley). BLUEWATER CREEK (Otero). 5 mi S of Weed. BLUEWATER LAKE or RESERVOIR (McKinley, Valencia). Crosses border of the two counties, in Zuñi Mts. Lake is L-shaped, 7 mi long, 3 mi wide, and the waters are of a bluish hue. Fed by Azul Creek and by other springs, Triangle Bar Spring, named for Triangle Bar Ranch, among them. In 1850 a Frenchman, Martin Boure, had a small irrigated farm above the present lake;

the ruins still stand. His farm was 14 or 15 mi from the present town, but was the beginning of the settlement of BLUEWATER VALLEY. In 1870 other Frenchmen came and organized a cattle company, irrigating their ranches from a small reservoir. They built the first dam of dirt in 1885. It washed out the next year. In 1891-92 there was a terrible drought, their cattle died, and the project was abandoned. In 1894 Mr. A. Tietgen, from near Ramah, recognized the possibilities of the valley and built a dam across Bluewater Canyon. He induced several Mormon families to join him, and a Mormon settlement was founded. Later he induced the AT&SF RR to help, and a cement dam was built impounding enough water for irrigating the valley. In 1904 the dam was again washed out and a new one built.

BLUFF CREEK (Hidalgo). Empties into Bear Canyon, 18 mi NE of Cloverdale.

BLUITT (Roosevelt). Ranching and farming community on NM 262, 9 mi E of Milnesand. Name suggested by J. T. Hadaway, from the Bluitt Ranch in Texas where he had worked before settling in NM. Post office, 1916-44.

BLUMNER (Rio Arriba). Near Vallecitos, 20 mi E of Cebolla. Post office, 1905-07.

BOAT LAKE (Chaves). 12 mi E of Weed.

BOB CAT CREEK (Taos). 1 mi SE of Red River settlement.

BOAZ (Chaves). 40 mi NE of Roswell on US 70. Site established in 1907 and named by W. W. Weatherby for the Boaz mentioned in the Book of Ruth in the Bible. Post office, 1907-55.

BOGLE (Lincoln). Post office, 1920-25. See COYOTE.

BONANZA (Santa Fe). First of the Cerrillos mining camps reached on traveling south from Santa Fe. Settled in spring of 1880, and once a town of 2,000 inhabitants. Now it is a ghost town. Post office, 1880-83; mail to Turquoise.

BONNER LAKE (De Baca). 12 mi SE of Ft. Sumner.

BONITA CREEK (Colfax). Span., "beautiful." Runs through BONITA CANYON in W part of the county. BONITA DAM (Lincoln). BONITO (Lincoln). Post office, 1882-1911; mail to Parsons. BONITO LAKE (Lincoln). 26 mi SE of Carrizozo and 11 mi NW of Ruidoso. Supplies water to Alamogordo and Holloman Air Force Base. BONITA RIVER (Lincoln). Has its source in White Mts. and joins Ruidoso River to form Hondo River, which empties

into the Pecos 6 mi below Roswell. BONITO VALLEY (Lincoln). 14 mi NW of Ruidoso.

BORICA (Guadalupe). Span., *borrica*, "jenny donkey." 30 mi S of Santa Rosa, on the mesa 10 mi SE of Puerto de Luna. Also called Borica Springs. Post office, 1917-20.

BORKE SPRING (Doña Ana). In San Andres Mts., 21 mi NE of Doña Ana settlement.

BORRACHO CANYON, RANGER STATION (Rio Arriba). Located at Vallecitos. See CAÑON DEL BORRACHO.

BORREGO ARROYO (Sandoval). Span., "sheep, lamb." Spanish surname in neighboring Rio Arriba County.

BOSQUE. Span., "wood, forest, grove." The term in NM was used for a junglelike thicket of large trees with a heavy undergrowth of vegetation, as with cottonwood groves and areas covered with tamarisks, willows, or other kinds of brush. BOSQUE (Valencia). Also called BOSQUE FARMS. 6 mi S of Belen. Original community was founded in eighteenth century as a *genízaro* (captive Indian) group. In the 1930's the federal government established a resettlement project here with farmers from drought-stricken areas. BOSQUECITO (Socorro). BOSQUE DEL APACHE WILDLIFE REFUGE (Socorro). Wildlife reserve 9 mi S of San Antonio. BOSQUE DEL APACHE GRANT (Socorro). Tract spanning the Rio Grande between San Antonio and San Marcial. Granted to Antonio Sandoval on Nov. 28, 1845, by the "active and actual" governor, Manuel Armijo. BOSQUE GRANDE (Chaves). On Pecos River 50 mi below Ft. Sumner. Named by Spanish settlers about 1860. Became headquarters for the first herd of Jingle-Bob cattle brought to the valley by John S. Chisum in 1867. This famous brand became distinctive because it was not a body brand but a deep slit in both ears of a steer so that one part of the ear flapped downward and the other part stood up in its natural way. When cattle had to be identified in a big herd, the Jingle-Bob animals only had to lift their heads to be instantly identified. BOSQUE PEAK (Torrance). In Manzano Mts. W of Manzano between Mosca and Osha peaks. BOSQUE REDONDO (De Baca). On Pecos River near Ft. Sumner. An area said to have been on trail followed by Coronado in 1541 and Espejo in 1583. Campground of the Comanches before the Spaniards came. A licensed trading post was established here in 1851, and a fort named for Gen. E. V. Sumner, commander of the 9th

Military Department in New Mexico, was erected. When many of the military posts in NM were abandoned in 1861, the major portion of the territory was exposed to attacks by Indians. Kit Carson, who served as Indian agent for eight years, carried out the government policy of rounding up hostile groups. In 1863 he brought six hundred Apaches to the Bosque Redondo, and in 1864 he defeated the Navajos at Canyon de Chelly and transferred seven thousand of them to the Bosque. The Bosque Redondo scheme did not work. The Navajos did not succeed as farmers, and the Apaches fled from the reservation and took to the warpath. In 1868 the Navajos were sent back to their own country in northwestern NM and northeastern Arizona. Ft. Sumner was subsequently abandoned by the military.

BOSQUE SECO (Doña Ana).

BOTTOMLESS LAKES (Chaves). In BOTTOMLESS LAKES STATE PARK, 12 mi E of Roswell. State Park on US 380. Named by cowboys in the early days, who measured the depth of the water by tying several lariats together as a plumb line. They found no bottom, and pronounced the pools bottomless. The lakes are sinkholes developed when surface rock drops after being undermined by water. Few are deeper than 80 or 90 ft. Created a state park in 1934.

BOULDER LAKE (Rio Arriba). 12 mi NW of El Vado. Named for parapet of rock which surrounds the natural lake. The Tewa Indian name was *kookaeeway pokwee*, "lake enclosed by stone barrier or wall." Also called STONE LAKE

BOUNDARY BUTTE (Utah). So named for its proximity to the boundaries of NM, Colorado, and Utah.

BOVE (Santa Fe). See SAN ILDEFONSO.

BOX CANYON (Colfax). 30 mi SW of Raton; 3 mi N of Dawson. The name, in general, applies to a canyon closed at the far end, or so narrow as to make traffic through it difficult or impossible, that is, a man is boxed in. Box CANYON (Doña Ana). Runs S and E into the Rio Grande, N of Picacho Mtn. BOX CANYON (Sandoval). BOX LAKE (Catron). SW of Quemado and 6 mi S of US 60. Once called CAJON, which means "big box" in Spanish. Post office, 1919-20.

BRABA (Taos). See TAOS PUEBLO.

BRACKETT (Colfax). Post office, 1910-17.

BRAKES (Quay). Post office, 1907-09; mail to Norton.

BRAMLETT (Grant). First postmaster, Nathan N. Bramlett. Post office, 1911-12.

BRANCH SEVEN RIVERS (Eddy). S of Seven Rivers. Old-timers say that Branch Seven Rivers is now called NORTH SEVEN RIVERS. Named for seven springs which formed the sources of the river. Artesian wells have caused these springs to dry up.

BRAZIL SPRINGS (De Baca). See TAIBAN SPRINGS.

BRAZITO. Span., "little arm, tributary." Gen. Stephen W. Kearny, commanding the Army of the West, occupied Santa Fe on Aug. 18, 1846. On Sept. 25, he set out for California, leaving Col. Alexander W. Doniphan in charge of New Mexico, with orders to march southward to assist in the conquest of Chihuahua as soon as Col. Sterling Price arrived to take command in Santa Fe. Colonel Doniphan and his Missouri Volunteers moved south to Brazito, Doña Ana County, and on Christmas afternoon, 1846, the only battle of the Mexican War to be fought in New Mexico took place. The Mexican forces consisted of 1,200 men led by General Trias. The Americans were victorious and moved on to occupy El Paso without a struggle on Dec. 28. On Feb. 8, 1847, they began their advance on the city of Chihuahua. BRAZITO (Doña Ana). The area below Mesilla Park is in the old BRAZITO GRANT. The schoolhouse and the farm community still bear the name. Referred to as early as 1776 as HUERTO, Span., "orchard," DE LOS BRAZITOS. BRAZITO GRANT (Doña Ana). Extends 8 mi along the Rio Grande, S of Las Cruces. Made to Juan Antonio Garcia in 1822 or 1823, and confirmed by U.S. Congress on July 22, 1854.

BRAZOS (Rio Arriba). Span., "arms of a human being, branches of a stream." Town at junction of NM 95 and 84, 4 mi N of Tierra Amarilla. Post office, 1898-1900. BRAZOS, UPPER, and BRAZOS, LOWER (Rio Arriba). Arms or branches of North Chama River. BRAZOS CANYON (Rio Arriba). 20 mi SE of Chama. BRAZOS FALLS (Rio Arriba). BRAZOS LAKE (Rio Arriba). Near the Brazos meadows. BRAZOS PEAK (Rio Arriba). Imposing granite precipice E of Park View, 12 mi NE of Tierra Amarilla.

BREECE (McKinley). 5 mi SW of Thoreau. Post office, 1921-27.

BRENMAND (Catron). On South Fork of Negrito Creek, 11 mi SE of Reserve.

BRICE (Otero). Post office established in 1899 W of Orogrande in Cornucopia Canyon. Called

JARILLA JUNCTION, and changed to Brice when the railroad ran a spur 2 mi into the canyon. A superintendent of the company which operated here about 1901 was named Brice. Post office, 1904-09; 1919-20.

BRICK (Doña Ana). 1 mi N of point where NM, Texas, and Mexico join. At one time there was a brick plant here. BRICKLAND (Doña Ana). On AT&SF RR 3 mi N of El Paso, 2 mi N of Brick.

BRIGGS CANYON (Union). 12 mi NE of Folsom; heads a few miles N of Des Moines and opens into Cimarron Canyon. Named for a family who located here in 1866. It is a spot abounding in wildlife.

BRILLIANT (Colfax). Former coal-mining community on AT&SF RR, 6 mi NW of Raton. Post office, 1906-35; 1940-54. BRILLIANT CANYON (Colfax). BRILLIANT CREEK (Colfax).

BRIMHALL (McKinley). 15 mi N of Gallup. Named for an Indian trader. BRIMHALL (San Juan). 60 mi NW of Gallup, 13 mi W of US 666. BRIMHALL WASH (San Juan). Runs W into Captain Tom Wash NE of Newcomb.

BROADVIEW (Curry). On NM 18, 30 mi N of Clovis.

BROIS SPRINGS (De Baca). Named for Jim Brois, who settled on land surrounding the springs in 1885. These springs do not create any flow of water for a runoff, but a draw leads from them to La Mora Creek.

BROKE OFF MOUNTAIN (Rio Arriba). 6 mi NE of Hopewell. Name describes a volcanic "stump."

BRONCHO, BRONCO, Span., "rough, sturdy, wild." There are two communities which commemorate the transfer of this Spanish adjective to an unruly or spirited horse. One is the standard Spanish spelling in BRONCO (Lea), and the other, the American cowboy misspelling BRONCHO (Torrance).

BROOM MOUNTAIN (Valencia). 17 mi S and W of Acoma Pueblo. Spanish settlers called it SIERRA LA ESCOBA, because they came here to get the long grasses used in making brooms. The grasses were tied together in small bunches, near the cut end. The long end was used for sweeping, and the short, stiffer end was used for brushing the hair. These native brooms are occasionally seen today.

BROWNHORN (Roosevelt). Post office, 1905-06; changed to MELROSE.

BRUSHY CREEK (Hidalgo). 18 mi E and N of Cloverdale. BRUSHY MOUNTAIN (Catron). Extends N and S, 2 mi E of Pueblo Creek.

BRUSHY MOUNTAIN (Catron). A second by the same name, 6 mi SW of Alma and 3 mi W of Glenwood. BRUSHY MOUNTAIN (Grant). 6 mi S of Gila Cliff Dwellings National Monument.

BRYAN (Grant). Post office, 1913-14. BRYAN LAKE (Lincoln). 7 mi W of Gallinas.

BRYANTINE (Harding). 25 mi SE of Mosquero. First postmaster, Sarah P. Bryant. Post office, 1903-20.

BUCHANAN (De Baca). On AT&SF RR, 10 mi W of Yeso. Founded in 1907 with building of railroad. Named for James Buchanan, fifteenth President of the United States (1857-61). Subsequent to building of the railroad, the population declined. Post office, 1907-40.

BUCKEYE (Lea). Oil-field community on NM 8 17 mi SW of Lovington. Named for Buckeye Ranch owned by A. J. Crawford of Carlsbad.

BUCKHORN (Grant). On US 260, 30 mi NW of Silver City.

BUCKMAN (Santa Fe). Formerly a village and station on D&RGW RR, 5 mi S of San Ildefonso Pueblo. Founded in 1899-1900 by H. F. Buckman, an Oregon lumberman, who built sawmills and cut timber on the Pajarito Plateau. The bridge, road, and mesa here bear the Buckman name. Post office, 1899-1903; 1913-25. BUCKMAN MESA (Santa Fe). Large lava-topped mesa on S side of the Rio Grande between Buckman village and San Ildefonso Pueblo. According to San Ildefonso legends, the hole in the top is one of the four places from which fire and smoke came forth in ancient times. The old bridge here led to Los Alamos Ranch School, now the site of the city of Los Alamos.

BUDVILLE (Cibola). On US 66, 23 mi E of Grants. Site of Laguna-Acoma Baptist Mission. Named for H. N. "Bud" Rice, who started automobile service and touring business here in 1928.

BUENA VISTA (Harding). Span., "beautiful view." 28 mi SE of Mosquero on NM 39. BUENA VISTA (Socorro). S part of town of Socorro; built since 1895. BUENA VISTA (Mora). 20 mi N of Las Vegas. Name emphasizes natural advantages.

BUEY CANYON (Santa Fe). Span., "ox." Water from canyon flows into the Rio Grande from the E, just below Buckman Bridge. The Tewa name is *abay bay hoo-oo*, "arroyo of the little corner of the chokecherry."

BUEYEROS (Harding). Span., "ox-team drivers." On Bueyeros Creek and NM 57, 8 mi S of

Union County line. Settled in 1878. So named because teams of oxen were used for the work done here. Post office, 1898—.

BUFFALO. At least five place names commemorate the "cows covered with frizzled hair which resembles wool," as Castañeda called the buffaloes in 1540. BUFFALO CREEK (De Baca). Flows W and N into Pecos River, S of Ft. Sumner. BUFFALO GRASS CREEK (Rio Arriba). BUFFALO GRASS CREEK (Taos). Flows into the Rio Pueblo de Taos, 4 mi E of Taos Pueblo. BUFFALO HEAD (Colfax). High point of rock N of Folsom; named for its resemblance to the head of a buffalo. BUFFALO VALLEY (Chaves).

BUFORD (Torrance). On US 66, 40 mi E of Albuquerque; once a neighbor to, but now a part of, Moriarty. Mr. H. Crossley owned the townsite E of the railroad at Moriarty, and from 1930 to 1933 that part of the town was named Buford, for his infant son Buford Crossley.

BUG SCUFFLE CANYON (Otero). See ROCKY WATER HOLE CANYON.

BULLARD PEAK (Grant). 15 mi SW of Silver City. Named for John Bullard, prospector and miner, killed while leading a successful campaign against the Apaches in the neighborhood of Silver City during the summer of 1871. He had developed properties here in the gold rush days of the 1870's. BULLARD CANYON (Grant). Also named for him. See CHLORIDE FLATS.

BULL CREEK (Hidalgo). 29 mi E of Cloverdale. BULL CREEK (San Miguel). Small tributary of Pecos River, first flowing into Cow Creek; rises in Santa Fe National Forest. BULL OF THE WOODS MOUNTAIN (Taos). E part of county, W of Elizabethtown. BULL SPRINGS (Socorro). 8 mi S of Riley. In 2-mi stretch below it are Cow Spring, Deer Spring, and Bear Spring.

BULLIS LAKE (Eddy). 18 mi S of Dunken.

BURFORD LAKE (Rio Arriba). See STINKING LAKE.

BURLEY (Socorro). Shown on 1921 map on the Rio Salado, 15 mi W of Puertocito. Post office, 1901-19.

BURNHAM (San Juan). See FRUITLAND. BURNHAM (McKinley). 34 mi NE of Gallup.

BURNING HILL (San Juan). N and W of Fruitland. A fire has smouldered inside this hill since 1891. Much red shale has been hauled from the vicinity to beautify nearby homes. The old lime kiln from which building lime was hauled in pioneer days was near this site. Sightseers still visit Burning Hill, the kiln, and the nearby site called The Meadows.

BURNING MOUNTAIN (Catron). This name given because heat remaining in this volcanic area causes the ground to steam after a slight rainfall.

BURNS CANYON (Rio Arriba). Runs SW into Vaqueros Canyon, 7 mi NW of Pounds. Named for wealthy sheep-owner near Chama.

BURNT RIDGE CREEK (Taos). Canyon, creek, trail about 4 mi E of Taos Pueblo; stream flows into the Rio Pueblo de Taos.

BURRO. Span., "jackass, donkey." A place name map of NM would not portray faithfully the story of the land if the picture of patient, wood-hauling burros did not appear. The services of this faithful beast of burden are recorded in a number of place names. BURRO ARROYO (Harding). Flows down BURRO CANYON 6 mi SE of Roy, crossing into San Miguel County. BURRO MOUNTAINS (Grant). In Gila National Forest W of Silver City. BURRO MOUNTAIN JUNCTION (Grant). BURRO SPRINGS (Grant). 15 mi NW of Silver City. J. C. Brock, whose father settled here in the 1870's, says, "It was the only watering place in the vicinity, and man, beast, and devil on their way to the Mogollons stopped there for water."

BURSUM (Socorro). Post office, 1904-05; mail to Chloride. BURSUM TRAIL (Catron). Runs from Mogollon to O Bar O Ranger Station in SW part of county. Named for Holm Bursum, U.S. Senator from 1921 to 1924. It was broken through by the state with prison labor, then taken over by U.S. Forest Service, and finished by Civilian Conservation Corps workmen at Willow Creek, from 1936 to 1940.

BURTON FLATS (Eddy). Flat country 12 mi NE of Carlsbad. Named for old Burton Ranch in this area. On the edge of Burton Flats, V. H. McNutt first found potash in the Carlsbad area.

BUSH RANCH (Catron). See GLENWOOD.

BUTTE CITY (Sierra). Small settlement 2 mi N of Truth or Consequences.

BUXTON (San Miguel). On Buxton Ranch near Cherryvale, 30 mi NE of Las Vegas. First postmaster, Gerald H. Buxton. Post office, 1909-14. A siding N of Las Vegas on AT&SF RR was also given this name.

BYNAM (Chaves). First postmaster, John F. Bynam, 1907-10; mail to Olive.

BYRIED (De Baca). Post office, 1909-21.

CABALLO. Span., "horse." The first horses were introduced into the Southwest as early as the *entrada* (Span., "entrance, arrival") of Coronado in 1540. Subsequent Spanish expeditions brought more horses, many of which were stolen by the Indians. Soon herds of wild horses were concealed in mountains and canyons, contributing place names to such localities. CABALLO (Sierra). 14 mi S of Truth or Consequences. Named for the mountains. CABALLO LAKE STATE PARK AND RECREATION AREA (Sierra). Storage reservoir built in 1937-38, 11 mi below Elephant Butte Lake. CABALLO HOT SPRINGS. See MANBY HOT SPRINGS. CABALLO MOUNTAINS (Sierra). Extend S of Truth or Consequences on E side of the Rio Grande. Also called SIERRA DE LOS CABALLOS on Mapa de los EUM (1828).

CABEZA (San Miguel). Span., "head." 4 mi S of Mosquero, on SP RR.

CABEZON (Sandoval). Span., "big head." Former town N of Cabezon Peak, W of Ojo del Espiritu Santo Land Grant. Abandoned when U.S. purchased the grant in 1934. First settled when Juan Maestas arrived here in 1826 from Pagosa Springs, Colo. Oliver Perry Hovey settled at this place when the town was called LA POSTA. Mr. Hovey was instrumental in changing the name to Cabezon in 1891. Stage coaches from Santa Fe to old Ft. Wingate used to get fresh horses at E edge of town. Today Cabezon is a ghost town. Post office, 1891-1949. CABEZON PEAK (Sandoval). Great volcanic plug or hill, rising 2,200 ft above the plain 40 mi NW of Albuquerque. Called by the Navajos *tse najin,* "black rock," and identified as the head of a giant killed by the Twin War Gods. Shown on Miera y Pacheco map (1775) as El Cabezon de los Montoyas. CABEZON STATION (Sandoval). Post office, 1879-81; changed to CABEZON.

CABO LUCERO CREEK (San Miguel). Span., "Lucero knoll." Enters Tecolote Creek 1 mi N of San Geronimo.

CABRA SPRINGS (San Miguel). 35 mi SE of Las Vegas. Named for a spring used as a watering place by *cabras,* "goats." Post office, 1878-91. Re-established as CABRA, 1900-04.

CABRESTO CREEK CANYON (Colfax). Regional Span., "rope, halter, lead ox." Runs into Red River NE of Questa. CABRESTO CREEK (Rio Arriba). CABRESTO LAKE (Colfax). 4 mi SW of Baldy Mt. CABRESTO LAKE (Taos). Near Questa.

CACTUS FLAT LAKE (Lincoln). 22 mi SE of Jicarilla.

CAJA DEL RIO GRANT (Santa Fe). Span., "box canyon of the river." Large tract E of Rio Grande, W of Santa Fe, and SE of present Bandelier National Monument. Made to Nicolas Ortiz and Nino Ladron de Guebara, on May 30, 1742.

CAJON (Catron). See Box LAKE.

CALAVERAS CREEK (Sandoval). Span., "skulls." Small stream 2 mi long, entering Cebolla Creek in Jemez Mts.

CALF CREEK (San Miguel). Small tributary entering Gallinas River 24 mi W of Las Vegas.

CALIENTE (Valencia). See OJO CALIENTE. CALIENTE CANYON, CREEK (Colfax). Span., "hot or warm." At head of Vermejo River, 12 mi N of Dawson.

CALLAMONGE (Santa Fe). See CUYAMUNGE.

CALLEY'S LAKE (Mora). 8 mi S of Wagon Mound.

CALVERT (Torrance). Station on AT&SF RR, 45 mi S of Santa Fe. Named in 1959 for F. W. Calvert, officer of the Ideal Cement Co., which established a plant at Tijeras 16 mi E of Albuquerque.

CAMALEON (Torrance). Span., "chameleon." On old NMC RR between Willard and Torrance. Named when the railway was being built in 1903 because of the large number of chameleons or lizards in that section.

CAMBRAY (Luna). Span., "cambric or fine linen cloth." Small railroad village between Las Cruces and Deming. Became a water station on SP RR in 1892 when a well was drilled here. Post office, 1893-1953.

CAMEL MOUNTAIN (Luna). In extreme SE corner of county. Name was suggested by its configuration, as was the case for CAMEL ROCK, familiar landmark on highway between Santa Fe and Pojoaque.

CAMEO (Roosevelt). Trading point 10 mi NE of Portales on AT&SF RR. Name said to have come from pretty black rocks in vicinity which Mexicans on construction crews called "cameos." Post office ordered on May 27, 1907, but never established.

CAMERON (Quay). On NM 39, near Curry County line, 6 mi N of Grady. Arthur H. Cameron, first postmaster. Post office, 1908—. Formerly called WHEATLAND. CAMERON CREEK (Grant). Rises 10 mi E of Silver City; flows S to AT&SF RR, where it enters San Vicente Arroyo, 2 mi NW of Whitewater.

CAMP (Otero). Post office, 1908-10; 1912-16. See VALMONT.

CAMPANA (San Miguel). Span., "bell." SP RR station 14 mi S of Mosquero, on Pablo Montoya Grant; generally known as the Bell Ranch. There was already a settlement called Bell, named for the bell-shaped mountain which gave the name to the ranch; so the station took the Spanish word for bell.

CAMPBELL'S SWITCH (Chaves). Siding NE of Roswell on AT&SF RR, between Acme and Elkins.

CAMP CITY (Otero). See VALMONT.

CAMP CODY (Luna). Former Army encampment 2 mi W of Deming. Area about 2,000 acres. In 1917, during World War I, over 30,000 troops were here. Named for William F. Cody, better known as Buffalo Bill, an American plainsman and circus manager, who was born on an Iowa farm in 1846. He went West when he was fourteen, worked in the Colorado gold mines, served as an Indian scout, and later promoted a famous "Wild West" show. He died in 1917. Camp Cody, after the war, was used as a tuberculosis sanitorium for ex-soldiers. It was transferred in 1922 from the U.S. Public Health Service to the Deming Chamber of Commerce. The sanitorium was then managed by the Sisters of the Holy Cross. See HOLY CROSS.

CAMP HENLEY (Hidalgo). U.S. Army post near Lordsburg; established and active during the Apache uprisings in the 1890's.

CAMP MONARCH (Grant). Post office, 1907-08; mail to Lake Valley.

CAMP SEPARATION (Grants). See SEPAR.

CAÑADA. Span., "ravine, gulch." In the broken terrain of NM, many places use the Spanish word cañada to describe a gulch made by erosion or by volcanic activity. CAÑADA (Sandoval). Originally, CAÑADA DE COCHITI. Settlement active until 1735; later abandoned on account of drought. A small church was standing here in 1920 and several families were living here. Townsite is now owned by James W. Young, whose apple orchard lies ½ mi N along Cañada Bonito Creek. CAÑADA ALAMOSA (Socorro, Sierra). Runs from Ojo Caliente to Monticello. See MONTICELLO. CAÑADA DE ARCHIBEQUE (Taos). CAÑADA DE COCHITI GRANT (Sandoval). Long, narrow strip running to the Rio Grande N of Cochiti Pueblo Grant. Original grantee, Antonio Lucero, petitioned Governor Bustamente on Aug. 2, 1728. His grant was certified at a later date

by Juan Antonio de Cabeza de Baca, chief alcalde of Cochiti. CAÑADA DE LA CUEVA (Rio Arriba). CAÑADA DE LA CRUZ (Valencia). See SEAMA. CAÑADA DEL AGUA GRANT (Santa Fe). Small area in SW corner of county S of Golden. Made to Jose Serafin Ramirez, Feb. 12, 1844. CAÑADA DE LA JARITA (Taos). "Little boar." CAÑADA DE LOS ALAMOS (Santa Fe). "Cottonwoods." Village 15 mi SE of Santa Fe. CAÑADA DE LOS ALAMOS GRANT (Santa Fe). Tract 10 mi S of Santa Fe, W of US 85. Lorenzo Marques petitioned for this land on Sept. 23, 1785, and was put in possession on Oct. 7, 1785, by Antonio Jose Ortiz, senior alcalde and war captain, in obedience to the command of Juan Bautista Anza, colonel of Royal Armies and civil and military governor. CAÑADA DEL OSO (Rio Arriba). "Bear." CAÑADA DEL ROCIO (San Miguel). "Dew, mist." CAÑADA DE LOS TRES HERMANOS (San Miguel). "Three brothers." CAÑADA JAQUES (Rio Arriba). 4 mi E of Lindrith. CAÑADA JOSE (Otero). CAÑADA OJITOS (Rio Arriba). "Little springs ravine." Also known as CAÑADA DEL OJITO. Runs through Sebastian Martin Grant 6 mi N of Chimayo. CAÑADA TANQUES (Rio Arriba). 4 mi E of Gavilan. There was once a Tanque Indian Pueblo in Rio Arriba County.

CANADIAN (San Miguel). On SP RR, 11 mi N of Tucumcari. CANADIAN HILLS (Mora). Extend E from Wagon Mound across E end of county. CANADIAN RIVER. When Frederick Webb Hodge prepared his Handbook of American Indians North of Mexico (1907), he gave the Caddo Indian word kanohatino, "red river," as the name source for the Red River of Louisiana and the Colorado River in south-central Texas, colorado being Spanish for "red." The Red River of Louisiana, of course, forms the S boundary line of Oklahoma and extends W through the Panhandle of Texas to the NM state line. N of it is the Canadian River also called the RED RIVER or the CANADIAN RED RIVER, which starts in northern NM and flows through Colfax County to form the Mora-Harding county separation, then turns E through San Miguel and Quay counties until it goes across Texas into Oklahoma, where it is known for awhile as Beaver River. Finally, as the North Canadian River it joins the Arkansas. Canadian, then, as a place name could be derived from this Caddo word for red. However, in The Masterkey, XXIII (May 1949), p. 91, Dr. Hodge printed a quotation from the journal of Lt. J. W. Abert describing an excursion to the river and the great canyon through which it flows, and he thus seemed to favor the derivation of the name from *cañada*, and the original name as *Cañadian*. But Mapa de los EUM (1828) shows the stream as *Canadiano Rio*, without the *ñ*, which would favor a Spanish adaptation of the Indian *kanohatino*, "red river." The red salt which washes down in time of floods to color the water is responsible for the descriptive name. Spanish land titles call it the RIO ROJO, "red river," as well as the RIO CANADIAN. In the upper reaches it is called today the LITTLE RED RIVER. While trying to find the source of this river, Zebulon Pike got into trouble with the Spanish authorities in 1806, resulting in his nominal arrest and deportation to Mexico. A map drawn by Bvt. 2nd Lt. Jno. G. Parke in 1851 shows the river with the name Goo-Al-Pay, said to be a Kiowa word, *gu'adlpah*, "alongside a red hill or bluff."

CANDELARIAS (Bernalillo). Suburban community in NW Albuquerque. Named for a family of early Spanish settlers.

CANJILON (Rio Arriba). Community 16 mi SE of Tierra Amarilla at junction of NM 115 and 110. Settled in 1774 by descendants of followers of De Vargas. Their names were Juan Ramon Velasquez, Jose Antonio Martinez, Pedro Jose Esconderos, and Jose Alejandro Madrid. The name may be related to Spanish *cangilón*, "earthen jar, pitcher," or *canja*, "ditch on which one builds a house." However, Fray Angelico Chavez writes that for a long, long time, and for reasons unknown, New Mexicans have had only one meaning for *canjilón:* "deer antler." In Spain, the word denotes each knob on a water wheel (*noria*) to which a water trough or scoop is attached; "knobs on deer's heads" might have suggested its NM application. There is a tradition that the original Indian name of the place meant "deer horn." Post office, 1892—.

CANJILON CREEK (Rio Arriba). Tributary of Chama River, heading at E base of Canjilon Mtn. CANJILON MOUNTAIN (Rio Arriba). In Carson National Forest. CANJILON LAKES (Rio Arriba). Five or six small lakes 10 mi N and E of Canjilon.

CANN CREEK (Colfax). Small stream entering the Ponil.

CANNON AIR FORCE BASE (Curry). Established in 1942 as CLOVIS AIR FORCE BASE, and first occupied by the 302nd Bombardment Group.

Redesignated and dedicated to the late Gen. John K. Cannon on June 7, 1957. At present it is a component of the Twelfth Air Force, Tactical Air Command, and the home of the 832nd Air Division.

CANODE (Quay). Former community on CRI&P RR, 5 mi NE of Logan. Post office, 1908-14. Now only a railroad siding.

CANOE MESA (Rio Arriba). N of Chamita. Presumably named for its oblong, boatlike shape. See BLACK MESA.

CAÑON. Span., "canyon, gulch." *Cañon* and "canyon" are synonymous, though English "canyon" has no such convenient diminutive as *cañoncito*. There is confusion in the use of the words, as appears in *canyoncito* in which the English and Spanish forms are combined; also as in *Canyon Bancos*. CAÑON (Sandoval). Trading point on NM 4, 3 mi N of Jemez Pueblo. CAÑON (San Juan). Post office, 1902-03; mail to La Boca. CAÑON (Taos). 1½ mi SE of Taos plaza. Settled about 1700 because of plentiful water and location at foot of Sangre de Cristo Mts. CAÑON BLANCO (San Juan). Span., "white canyon." In E central part of county, S and E of Blanco. Post office, 1917-20. CAÑON CREEK (Rio Arriba). Rises on S border of county and flows N and E to the Chama. CAÑON DE CARNUEL GRANT (Bernalillo). See CARNUEL GRANT. CAÑON DE AGUA GRANT (Santa Fe). Original grantee was Jose Serafin Ramirez, on Feb. 12, 1844; his grant was approved by special act of Congress on June 12, 1866. CAÑON DE LA VIRGEN (Sandoval). CAÑON DEL BORRACHO (Rio Arriba). "Drunk." A dry wash near Vallecitos where a celebrated old yellow steer named Borracho died. CAÑON DEL DIEZMO (Santa Fe, Sandoval). Reference is to the church tithe. CAÑON DE MANUELITOS (San Miguel). "Manuel or his children." CAÑON DE PEDERNALES GRANT (Rio Arriba). 8 mi SW of Abiquiu, and S of Cerro Pedernal. Granted on Dec. 16, 1807, to Juan Bautista Baldez, along with seven other companions. CAÑON DE TIO GORDITO (Rio Arriba, Taos). "Fat little uncle." CAÑON DE TREMENTINA (San Miguel). "Turpentine." CAÑON GALLEGOS (Torrance). See GALLEGOS CANYON. CAÑONES (Rio Arriba). "Canyons." Settlement on NM 96, 7 mi W of Abiquiu; listed as a settlement by Escudero in *Noticias* (1849). Also called CAÑONES PLAZA. CAÑONES CREEK (Rio Arriba). Joins Polvadera Creek at Cañones; flows N to Chama River. CAÑON

LARGO (San Miguel). "Long canyon." In NE part of county, entering Canadian River. CAÑON NUANES (Bernalillo). "Canyon of the Nuanes family." CAÑON PLAZA (Rio Arriba). In E part of county, 4 mi NW of Vallecitos. CAÑONES PLAZA (Rio Arriba). See CAÑONES.

CAÑONCITO (Bernalillo). Span., "little canyon." Settlement on a byroad from NM 10 at foot of Sandia Mts. CAÑONCITO (Bernalillo). Navajo settlement and day school, N of US 66 and NE of Laguna. CAÑONCITO (Santa Fe). Trading point 15 mi SE of Santa Fe; in a defile where the old Santa Fe Trail enters Apache Canyon. Here the Mexican governor, Armijo, failed to hold his troops against General Kearny in August 1846, and here the Confederate supply train was destroyed by the Union general, Canby, in 1862, determining the battle of Glorieta in favor of Union forces. On the rise of a hill is an old adobe house which served as the last station on the Santa Fe Trail before entering Santa Fe. Post office, 1879-80. CAÑONCITO (Guadalupe). CAÑONCITO (Mora). CAÑONCITO (Rio Arriba). On Embudo Creek, 3 mi S of Dixon. CAÑONCITO (San Miguel). On NM 94, 7 mi NW of Sapello. CAÑONES CREEK (Rio Arriba). Enters Chama River a few miles S of Chama. CAÑONES CREEK (Sandoval). Small stream on N side of Jemez Mts., 8 mi SE of Youngsville.

CANOVA (Rio Arriba). On W side of the Rio Grande opposite Velarde.

CANTARA (Curry). Span., "pitcher." 30 mi W of Clovis. Post office, 1908-12.

CANTO RECIO (Socorro). Span., "rough stone, edge." 40 mi S of Socorro. In 1880's, first stop on stage line from San Marcial to Black Range mines in Chloride district.

CANTON (De Baca). 15 mi SE of Ft. Sumner, N of Buffalo Creek. Post office, 1910-25.

CANTRELL LAKE (Otero). In Guadalupe Mts., 27 mi S of Dunken.

CANYON (Sandoval). Post office, 1910-13. See CAÑON. CANYON BANCOS (Rio Arriba). CANYON DE SAN DIEGO GRANT (Sandoval). An area beginning 4 mi above Jemez Pueblo and extending to Fenton Lake; between the Sierra Nacimiento and the Jemez Mts. Testimony in the Surveyor General's office on June 13, 1859, presented claims by virtue of a royal grant made by Gov. Fernando Chacon on Mar. 6, 1798. CANYON PLAZA (Rio Arriba). See CAÑON PLAZA.

CAPILLA PEAK (Torrance). Span., "hood, cap." At top of Manzano Mts., 9 mi W of town of Manzano. Said to have been named by the early Spaniards at Quarai because the peak is shaped like a hood. Also spelled CAPILLO PEAK.

CAPITAN (Lincoln). Span., "captain." Takes its name from CAPITAN PEAK, a commanding eminence in the CAPITAN MOUNTAINS, which extend in an easterly direction from the Sierra Blanca Mts. In 1884, Seaborn T. Gray homesteaded on the Salado Flat and put up a small store. A post office was established in 1894 and he was appointed postmaster, naming it GRAY for himself. In January 1900, the EP&NE RR (later to become the Southern Pacific) built a branch line into Gray and changed the name to Capitan for the surrounding mountains. Post office, 1900—.

CAPITOL PEAK (Sierra). NE corner of county in San Andres Mts.

CAPROCK (Lea). Community 47 mi E of Roswell, on US 380 at Chaves County line. Named in 1913 by Ed Charles E. Crossland, founder and first postmaster, for the presence of caprock in surrounding land. Located on the first rimrock of the Llano Estacado, Span., "staked plains." Crossland planted the first cottonwood trees, now seen from miles away. See LLANO ESTACADO. CAPROCK (Quay). See RAGLAND.

CAPTAIN TOM'S WASH (San Juan). Flows from Chuska Mts. N through Newcomb into Chaco River. Named for the commanding officer under Col. John M. Washington, civil and military governor of NM in 1848. See NEWCOMB.

CAPULIN (Rio Arriba). Mexican-Span., "wild cherry." In Santa Fe National Forest in south-central part of county. CAPULIN (Union). On US 64 and 87, 27 mi SE of Raton and 8 mi W of Des Moines. First named DEDMAN in honor of E. J. Dedman, superintendent of AT&SF RR in 1909. In 1914, when Mr. Dedman died, the name was changed to Capulin because of the proximity to Mt. Capulin. Post office, 1879—. CAPULIN CREEK (Sandoval). In Jemez National Forest; a tributary to Gallinas Creek. CAPULIN MOUNTAIN (Union). 20 mi S of Colorado line and 4 mi NE of Capulin. Named because of the wild cherries (chokeberries) which grew inside the cone. It is one of the most symmetrical volcanic cones in North America. CAPULIN MOUNTAIN NATIONAL MONUMENT (Union). The high elevation affords a view into five states. CAPULIN PEAK (Rio Arriba). W of Abiquiu, and 3 mi NW of Capulin.

CARACAS (Rio Arriba). See CARRACAS.

CARBONATE CREEK (Sierra). 2½ mi N of Kingston. CARBONATEVILLE (Santa Fe). Once a flourishing mining town, 5 mi S of Bonanza City, in the center of Los Cerrillos District. Post office, 1879-80. First called TURQUESA.

CARDENAS (De Baca). Span., "chains." In NW corner of county, 5 mi NW of Buchanan. It is reported that when the AT&SF RR was under construction at this place, one of the local Spanish workmen was honored by having the switch named for him.

CARESSO CREEK (Colfax). Flows SE into Cimarron River E of Springer.

CARISA CANYON (Otero). Also spelled "Carissa." Tributary to Sacramento River. Both Caresso and Carisa may be variants of Carrizo.

CARISBROOK (Colfax). See CARRIS BROOK.

CARLISLE (Grant). Ghost mining camp 50 mi NW of Lordsburg. Named for Claude Carlisle Fuller, the first child born in the town, Apr. 21, 1884. Post office, 1884-96; changed to Steeplerock.

CARLITO SPRINGS (Bernalillo). In Tijeras Canyon, 5 mi from Albuquerque city limits on slope of Sandia Mts. Named for Carl Magee, once editor of the *Albuquerque Tribune*. Formerly called WHITCOMB SPRINGS, for a Union veteran of the Civil War who homesteaded here.

CARLSBAD (Eddy). On Pecos River, in SE corner of state, on US 285 and 180. Organized in 1888 and first named for John A. and Charles B. Eddy, brothers who held large ranch interests and promoted railroad building and townsites in this section. The spot chosen for the ceremony was at the old ford of the Pecos River, an area called LOVING'S BEND, for a Texas cattleman who was wounded here. Lillian Green, daughter of one of the town promoters, broke a bottle of champagne and named the town EDDY. When it was learned that the mineral content of a spring NW of town rivaled that of the Carlsbad springs in Bohemia, agitation arose to change the name of the town from Eddy to Carlsbad. At an election on May 23, 1899, the change was voted. The city was officially proclaimed Carlsbad by Gov. W. E. Lindsey on Mar. 25, 1918. Post office, 1899—. CARLSBAD CAVERNS NATIONAL PARK (Eddy). 25 mi SW of Carlsbad, in Guadalupe Mts. First explored in 1901 by a cowboy named Jim White and called BAT CAVES because of millions of bats which flew nightly from the cavern mouth. Extending 750 ft below the surface, these caverns are the largest yet explored in the world. They were made a national park by act of Congress in 1930. CARLSBAD RESERVOIR (Eddy). 4 mi NW of Carlsbad.

CARMEN (Mora). 12 mi S of Mora near Cebolla River. Possibly a reference to Nuestra Señora del Carmen, "Our Lady of Carmen."

CARNAHAN (Santa Fe). In the area of Golden and San Pedro. Named for a prospector who filed some mining claims here. Post office, 1927-30.

CARNE (Luna). A siding of SP RR, 3 mi N of US 70 and 80, 14 mi E of Deming. Post office, 1909-12.

CARNERO. Span., "sheep, mutton, ram." In NM the word *borrego* or *borrega* took its place as a general term for sheep, and *carnero* came to signify a full-grown ram, especially one kept for breeding purposes. CARNERO (Torrance). On AT&SF RR, 6 mi E of Encino. CARNERO CREEK (Catron). 8 mi NW of Luna.

CARNUEL (Bernalillo). Also CARNUE. Small settlement at mouth of Tijeras Canyon, at edge of Albuquerque city limits. Carnue seems to have been an earlier name for the canyon later called TIJERAS. CARNUEL GRANT, also CAÑON DE CARNUEL GRANT (Bernalillo). Small grant in foothills of Sandia Mts. E of Albuquerque between Carnuel and Tijeras. Three petitions were presented to Governor Melgares, chiefly by some people of Albuquerque: on Nov. 1, 1818; in January 1819; and a third still later, all asking for land at Carnue. On Feb. 3, 1819, the governor instructed the alcalde of Albuquerque to report the names of those people who had no land of their own. On Feb. 24, 25, and 26, the alcalde gave possession to forty-eight persons, and on Mar. 15, he gave possession to twenty-nine more. Boundaries of grant were from San Antonio on N, to foothills of canyon on S, and Cerro Huerfano on W.

CARPENTER (Bernalillo). 15 mi E of Albuquerque, in Sandia Mts. First postmaster, Jose R. Carpenter. Post office, 1903-07; mail to Albuquerque.

CARR (Cibola). Locality near Ramah. Post office, 1893-95; 1915-17.

CARRACAS (Rio Arriba). Post office, 1881-82. CARRACAS CANYON (Rio Arriba). Runs N to

Colorado line 12 mi E of Rosa.
CARRIS BROOK (Colfax). AT&SF RR stop in Sugarite Canyon. Post office, 1907-08; mail to Raton.

CARRIZALILLO HILLS (Luna). In SW part of county at Mexican border.

CARRIZO (Otero). Span., "reed grass." 4 mi S of Ruidoso. CARRIZO CREEK (Catron). Rises in Valencia County, flows W into Arizona. CARRIZO CREEK (Harding). Rises in NW corner and flows SE to form Tesquesquite Creek. CARRIZO CREEK (Rio Arriba). Flows W to San Juan River. CARRIZO CREEK (Union). Empties into Dry Cimarron Creek. CARRIZO SPRING (Lincoln County). Seems to have given names to CARRIZO PEAK and CARRIZO MOUNTAINS. CARRIZO (Otero). 3 mi S of Ruidoso.

CARRIZOZO (Lincoln). In SW Lincoln County, at junction of US 54 and 380. Named for Carrizo Springs. In 1899, the EP&NE RR built their line to this point and a town was started, but it was not platted until 1907. James Allcook, foreman for a cattle ranch, then added a second zo to Carrizo, making the name Carrizozo, the extra syllable indicating "abundance." A. H. Harvey was first postmaster, as well as first depot agent. Post office, 1902—.

CARROS CREEK (Harding). 12 mi W of Pleasant Valley.

CARRSEY (Roosevelt). See CAUSEY.

CARRUMPA CREEK (Union). See CORRUMPA.

CARSON (Taos). Nearly abandoned farming community 15 mi SW of Taos. Named for Kit Carson, who came to NM with Bent and St. Vrain in 1826, and became famous as trader, government scout, and Indian agent. CARSON (San Juan). SE of Farmington. CARSON NATIONAL FOREST (Rio Arriba). On both E and W borders of Rio Arriba County. Created on Oct. 12, 1905, and at that time included as a part of Jemez Forest. Taos Forest was created on Nov. 7, 1906. These areas were combined on Mar. 2, 1909, and were designated as Carson National Forest, which today has a gross area of 1,188,138 acres.

CARTER (Roosevelt). 12 mi N of Causey. Named for O. B. Carter, according to information supplied by his son, Harvey Carter. Post office, 1906-17.

CARTHAGE (Socorro). Near US 380, 27 mi SE of Socorro. The Carthage coal mines were developed in 1880-85 and for economic reasons later abandoned. Named by a U.S. Army officer for the ancient city of Carthage. Post office, 1883-93; 1906-51.

CASA BLANCA (Cibola). Indian village 4 mi W of New Laguna on US 66, 51 mi W of Albuquerque. The houses are coated with white clay, hence the name. Post office, 1905—. CASA COLORADO (Valencia). Span., "red house." Small settlement on a secondary road which parallels the bank of the Rio Grande and is opposite Bosque. An old town was here in 1788 when Governor Concha was returning from the Gilas and found a missing horse herd at this place. At one time the old stage road ran on the E side of the river and Casa Colorado was a stage stop between Albuquerque and Socorro. Now called TURN. It was abandoned for many years prior to 1823. A modern report is that the stage depot was in a large adobe general store which had been colored red. CASA COLORADO GRANT (Socorro and Valencia). Small tract in SE corner of Valencia County between Belen and Tome grants. Don Jose Maria Perea and a number of citizens of Manzano were granted this tract on June 23, 1813, and took possession on July 19, 1823. CASA GRANDE (San Miguel). Post office, 1907-12. CASA MORENO (McKinley). CASA SALAZAR (Sandoval). "House of Salazar." Settlement on NM 279 and W bank of the Rio Puerco, 35 mi NW of Bernalillo. The seventeenth-century Salazar name in NM came from Sebastian Rodriguez de Salazar, who arrived in 1619. However, no member of this family is listed among the Spanish who left NM during the Pueblo Rebellion of 1680. The Salazars named after 1692 are new settlers or those who survived the Rebellion. Post office, 1888-1919.

CASAUS (Guadalupe). First postmaster, Juan Casaus. Post office, 1894-1911; mail to Dilia.

CASITA (Rio Arriba). Span., "little house." 12 mi S of El Rito.

CASS (Lincoln). Post office 1888-90; mail to Lookout.

CASSEL ROCK (Colfax). Near Taos County line.

CASTLEBERRY (Quay). First postmaster, Ritta Castleberry. Post office, 1910-15; changed to LESBIA.

CATALPA (Colfax). Post office, 1882-84; mail to Madison.

CAT MESA (Socorro). 3 mi SE of Monte Prieto and 2 mi E of Chupadero Mesa.

CATRON COUNTY. Created by state legislature on Feb. 25, 1921. Named for Thomas B. Catron, who came to Santa Fe from Missouri in 1866, served in the Constitutional Convention of 1910, and was chosen U.S. Senator at the first session of the State Legislature in 1912. Area is 6,898 sq mi, making it the largest county in the state. CATRON WASH (McKinley). 1½ mi S of Mexican Springs, flowing into Figueredo Wash.

CATSKILL (Colfax). Former community on Little Red River, 30 mi NW of Raton. Originally settled in August 1890 by a group of lumbermen under company management of H. G. Frankenburger. The Union Pacific Railroad built a spur from Trinidad, Colo., and C. F. Meek, the railroad's general manager, is said to have named the town because the scenery resembled the Catskill Mts. near his home town in New York. As the timber resources failed, the railroad pulled up its tracks in 1902. By 1916, Catskill was a ghost town. Now a tourist attraction. Post office, 1890-1905.

CAUSEY (Roosevelt). 25 mi SE of Portales, off NM 92. Said to have been named for one of the vice-presidents of a railroad whom Dr. Joseph M. Manes, founder and first postmaster in 1907, hoped to influence toward building a line through here. Present settlement is 3 mi N of the old Causey, and was begun by Ezra Ball after World War I. The story of the vague vice-president of the nameless railroad has been challenged. An old-time buffalo hunter, George Causey, seems to be the likely first owner of the name in this area. He came from a family who lived on a ranch some 40 or 50 mi E of Portales in 1881. Some member or members of the family evidently later moved to the present site of the town. Post office, 1907—.

CAVARISTA (Taos). Post office, 1895; mail to Labelle.

CAVE CREEK (San Miguel). Extreme S fork of Panchuela Creek about 3 mi above ranger station near Cowles. CAVE CREEK (Sierra). Flows E into Animas Creek 8 mi S of Hillsboro.

CEBOLLA. Span., "onion." This word was applied to a number of NM streams and locations because of wild flowers of the onion family, not the garden product. In some areas, such as parts of Rio Arriba and Sandoval counties, the name described sulphur water, which had an onionlike odor. CEBOLLA (Mora). Valley in W part of county 3 mi SE of Mora. CEBOLLA (Rio Arriba). On US 84, 12 mi S of Tierra Amarilla. Post office, 1907—. CEBOLLA CREEK (Rio Arriba). Flows W to Chama

River. CEBOLLA CREEK (Sandoval). Flows S to the Rio de las Vacas. CEBOLLA GRANT (Taos). Land at Lama between settlements of Rio Colorado and San Cristobal. Made by Governor Armijo, Dec. 31, 1845, to Juan Carlos Santistevan for himself and five others. CEBOLLA RIVER (Mora). In the Mora Grant; crosses NM 3 SE of Mora and enters Mora River. CEBOLLETA (Valencia). See SEBOYETA. CEBOLLETA GRANT (McKinley, Sandoval, Valencia). Large grant covering mountainous terrain at corners of three counties. Given by Gov. Fernando Chacon to thirty settlers on Jan. 15, 1800. CEBOLLETA MOUNTAINS (McKinley, Valencia). SE corner of McKinley County and NE corner of Valencia County; in Cibola National Forest. CEBOLLETA PEAK (Valencia). See MOUNT TAYLOR. CEBOLLETITA. "Very small onion," a further diminutive of cebolla, but it actually means "little Cebolleta," since it was settled by people from Cebolleta (Valencia). 2½ mi S of Cebolleta and 3 mi N of Paguate.

CEDAR. This name is commonly found where there is an abundant growth of juniper trees (Juniperus scopulorum, the common cedar). CEDAR CREEK (De Baca). Joins Pecos River 25 mi S of Ft. Sumner. CEDAR CREEK (Lincoln). Joins the Rio Ruidoso 2 mi W of Hollywood. CEDAR CREEK (Otero). Winter sports area 4 mi NW of Ruidoso. CEDAR CREST (Bernalillo). Health resort 18 mi E of Albuquerque. CEDAR GROVE (Luna). See KLONDIKE HILLS. CEDAR GROVE (Santa Fe). 35 mi NE of Albuquerque. CEDAR HILL (San Juan). On D&RGW RR, 10 mi NE of Aztec. Post office 1892—. CEDAR HILLS (Colfax). At mouth of Cerrososo Canyon. CEDAR LAKE (Eddy). 2 mi S of NM 83, 27 mi E of Artesia. CEDAR LAKE (Lea). CEDAR LAKE (Sierra). 3 mi N of Engle. CEDAR MOUNTAINS (Luna). Run NW and SE in SW corner of county. CEDAR SPRINGS (De Baca). On Pecos River 20 mi N of Ft. Sumner. Settled in 1865 by John Gerhardt, but abandoned after the soldiers were removed from Ft. Sumner. CEDARVALE (Torrance). 24 mi SW of Encino. Named by its founders for Cedarvale, Kans., because it was similarly situated in a valley with cedars (junipers) nearby. Established in 1908 by Ed Smith, William Taylor of Wellington, Kans., and Oliver P. DeWolf, who selected the townsite and had it surveyed by engineers of the U.S. government, with lots being sold through the General Land Office. Post office, 1908—. See SABINA.

CEDRO (Bernalillo). Span., "cedar." Settlement in Cedro Canyon 5 mi S of Tijeras. CEDRO CANYON (Bernalillo). Enters Manzano Mts. S of US 66, 12 mi E of Albuquerque.

CEJITA CREEK (Harding). CEJITA DE LOS COM-ANCHEROS (Harding). Span., "little mountain summit of Comanche hunters or traders." A little W of Union County line in NE corner of county. Name is descriptive of Indian warfare between Spanish settlers and Indians before the American occupation. Comancheros were traders licensed by the U.S. They bartered with the Indians for buffalo hides or stolen horses and cattle, and sometimes fought the Indians with Indian methods and on their own terms. After the American occupation there were Anglo Comancheros, sometimes accused of disguising as Indians and raiding American wagon trains.

CENTER (Curry). E of US 70 and within boundary of Bivens Ranch. Named in relation to ranch headquarters. CENTER FIRE CREEK (Catron). NE of Luna. CENTER FIRE BOG (Catron). 10 mi NE of Luna. Texas and NM cowboys fastened their saddles with a double cinch; California riders used a single "center-fire" cinch. This mudhole must have been named when a cowboy riding a "center-fire" saddle got into trouble here. CENTER VALLEY (Doña Ana). Post office, 1913-19. See VADO.

CENTERVILLE (Union). 8 mi S of Amistad and 13 mi N of Nara Visa. Established by homesteaders in December 1907. Post Office, 1907-44.

CENTRAL (Grant). In central part of county, 1 mi from Ft. Bayard. Name probably came from central location and was given by settlers who followed the troops to the Army post. Superseded Spanish name for the place, which was SANTA CLARA. Post office, 1887—. CENTRAL CITY (Grant). Post office, 1870-71; mail to Ft. Bayard. CENTRAL CITY (Union). See HAYDEN.

CERNADA (Union). Span., "cinder," with probable reference to volcanic ashes. Near Mt. Dora, 18 mi W of Clayton.

CERRILLOS, CERRITO, diminutive forms of CERRO, Span., "hill." In seventeenth and eighteenth centuries, name was applied to haciendas located near Turquoise Mtn., SW of Santa Fe. CERRILLOS (Santa Fe). Also called Los CERRILLOS. Former coal-mining community 18 mi SW of Santa Fe. Built by AT&SF RR in

1879. Took its name from topography in the vicinity. Historic evidence shows that Indians enslaved by the Spaniards mined turquoise N of here with crude hand tools before 1680. Post office, 1880—. CERRITO DEL CHIBATO (Rio Arriba). See CHIVATO MOUNTAINS. CERRITO DEL LOBO (Torrance). "Little hill of the wolf." CERRITO HUERFANO (San Miguel). "Orphan." CERRITO NEGRO (Taos). "Black." 7 mi NE of No Agua. CERRITOS (San Miguel). 3 mi NE of Villanueva in SW part of county, on Pecos River.

CERRO (Taos). Span., "peak, hill." Community 3 mi NW of Questa and 32 mi N of Taos. Settled in 1854 by families from Taos and Questa. Named for Cerro Guadalupe Mts. Post office, 1880—. CERRO ALESANDRO (McKinley). In SW part of county. CERRO ALESNA PEAK (McKinley). "Shoemaker's awl." Volcanic peak N of San Mateo. CERRO AZUL (McKinley). "Blue." CERRO CHAVES (McKinley). In SE part of county. CERRO CHIFLO (Taos). 5 mi W of Cerro. CERRO COLORADO (Socorro). "Red." CERRO CRISTOBAL (Taos). CERRO DEL AIRE (Taos). "Breezy." 3 mi SE of No Agua. CERRO DE LA OLA (Taos). "Wavy." 11 mi W of Questa. CERRO DEL ORO (Valencia). "Gold." CERRO DEL Oso (Taos). "Bear." CERRO DE LOS TAOSES (Taos). 6 mi E of Servilleta. CERRO DEL PEDERNAL (Rio Arriba). Near Abiquiu. Mentioned in a boundary grant of 1813. Span. Arch. N.M., 1006-07, CERRO DE TOME (Valencia). See TOME. CERRO GUADALUPE (Taos). See GUADALUPE MOUNTAIN. CERRO MAGDALENA (Doña Ana). See MAGDALENA PEAK. CERRO MONTOSO (Taos). 7 mi SW of Questa. CERRO NEGRO (Taos). 2 mi S of San Cristobal. CERRO OLLA (Taos). On Taos-Mora border, 15 mi SE of Taos. CERRO PEDERNAL (Rio Arriba). See PEDERNAL MOUNTAINS. CERRO PELON (Rio Arriba). "Bald." CERRO PRIETO (Socorro). "Black." N of Quemado; near headquarters for Hubbell Ranch. CERROSOSO CREEK (Colfax). Crosses US 64, 3 mi E of Cimarron.

CHACO. Regional Span., "desert." Name may be derived from Navajo phrase for the arroyo and valley, tsé ya chahatquel nlini, "which flows along," "darkness under the rock," and reinterpreted into chaco. CHACO (San Juan). 16 mi SE of Burnham. CHACO CANYON (San Juan). Settlement on NM 56, and on Chaco North Fork Creek, at Pueblo Bonito. Post office, 1936-42. CHACO CANYON NATIONAL MONUMENT (McKinley, San Juan). Contains some of the greatest surface ruins in the U.S.

Among the eighteen major ruins and countless smaller ones, archeologists have identified house sites of the Basket Makers dating back more than 1,500 years. Pueblo Bonito, Chetro Ketl, and Pueblo Alto are among the larger ruins.. Here also are the unit-type houses of the first Pueblo Indians, a civilization that flourished between the ninth and twelfth centuries. Chaca, on Mapa de los EUM (1828). CHACO RIVER (San Juan). Heads S of the settlement of Chaco Canyon; flows W and N and joins San Juan River E of Shiprock.

CHACON (Mora). Settlement at upper end of Mora Valley, 7 mi N of Holman. Named for members of the Chacon family. Albino, Damasco, and Pedro Chacon are listed among the first settlers of San Antonio de Mora (now Cleveland). Diego A. Chacon, first postmaster. Post office, 1894—.

CHACRA MESA (McKinley). NE corner of county.

CHAMA. Span. approximation of Tewa *tzama,* name of a pueblo on Chama River below El Rito River, which might still have been occupied at the coming of the Spaniards. Name was taken over and applied first to the general area around the pueblo and then to the river. J. P. Harrington gives the meaning of *tzama* as "here they have wrestled." Dr. Edgar L. Hewett says in *Ancient Life in the American Southwest* (1930), p. 239, that the word means "red" and is a name descriptive of coloring of the "river water." Appears on Mapa de los EUM (1828). CHAMA (Rio Arriba). 6 mi S of Colorado line at junction of US 84 and NM 29. Post office, 1880—. CHAMA RIVER (Rio Arriba). Rises in southern Colorado and flows S into the Rio Ojo Caliente at Española. CHAMITA (Rio Arriba). On NM 285, 6 mi N of Española.

CHAMBERINO (Doña Ana). On NM 28, W of the Rio Grande, 18 mi S of Las Cruces. Reported to be an Indian word meaning "deep ford"; and also as a corruption of the Spanish word for brush that grew in this section. On E side of river is the settlement called BERINO. Post office, 1880-82; 1893—.

CHAMISAL. Span., "place overgrown with chamiso." Several varieties of grayish, narrow-leaved, Southwestern brush called by the Spanish name *chamisa* (*Chrysothamnus nauseosus,* variety *graveolens* and variety *bigelovi*), also known as rabbitbrush. This is commonly seen growing along stretches in the Santa Fe and Taos regions. Another common brush,

the saltbush, is called *chamiso* (*Atriplex canescens*). *Flowers of the Southwest Mesas,* by Pauline M. Patraw (1951), pp. 6, 41. The name is a folk name that may be related to Span., *chamuscar,* "to singe or burn," probably because the people used the brush as firewood. CHAMISAL (Socorro). Name applied to N part of city of Socorro. CHAMISAL (Taos). Established about 1851, 30 mi SW of Taos. Post office, 1904-13; mail to Llano. CHAMIZAL CREEK (Taos). Heads near Rio Arriba border; flows N below town of Chamisal. CHAMISO MESA (Sandoval). 4 mi E of Jemez Pueblo.

CHAMITA (Rio Arriba). Span., "little Chama." 7 mi N of Española on US 285. Named for colony at Chama, possibly at time of Oñate or shortly afterward. Post office, 1881-1944. CHAMITA GRANT (Rio Arriba). Also called TOWN OF CHAMITA GRANT. Conferred by acting governor, Juan Domingo de Bustamente, on June 8, 1724, upon Antonio Trujillo. CHAMITA REGION (Rio Arriba). Describes a triangular area whose apex is at confluence of Chama River and whose sides are formed by Chama River and the Rio Grande. It is generally considered to go N up to the hilly country of Canoe Mesa.

CHANCE CITY (Grant). Named for Last Chance Mine, owned by William Randolph Hearst in the early 1880's. Post office, 1885-86; mail to Gage.

CHAPELLE (San Miguel). Trading point 25 mi S of Las Vegas. Established as a switch on AT&SF RR. Said to have been named for a contractor employed at that time by the railroad. However, from 1895 to 1899, Archbishop Chappelle was head of the Roman Catholic Church in NM. Previously called BERNAL. Post office, 1895-1939.

CHAPERITO (San Miguel). Span., "little hat." 25 mi SE of Las Vegas. This place name preserves a Spanish archaism of *chapero,* related to French *chapeau,* "hat." Chaperito is, of course, a diminutive. Post office, 1875-1957.

CHAPMAN (San Miguel). First postmaster, John L. Chapman. Post office, 1879-80.

CHAPPEL (Doña Ana). Point on SP RR, 25 mi SW of Las Cruces, 7 mi E of county line.

CHARCO (San Miguel). Span., "pool, puddle." Post office, 1893-94; mail to Liberty.

CHARETTE LAKE (Mora). 7 mi W of Nolan.

CHARLOTTE (De Baca). Former small community 10 mi N of Taiban. Post office, 1907-23.

CHASE CANYON (Colfax). 6 mi N of Cimarron. Named for M. M. Chase, a pioneer settler in the canyon.

CHATFIELD PEAK (Otero). On SE slope of Sacramento Mts. just outside boundary of Lincoln National Forest. Named for a rancher who settled in a canyon at base of the peak about 1890.

CHAUNTE CANYON (Socorro, Sierra). Runs SE into upper end of Elephant Butte Lake at Socorro—Sierra county line.

CHAVES, CHAVEZ. In old Galician Spanish and in Portuguese, the word meant "keys," and was conferred upon two brothers who wrested the ancient town of Chaves from the Moors. Fray Angelico Chavez says the general spelling of the name in NM is Chavez, but Chaves is the older form. The ancestor of the NM families bearing this name was Don Pedro Duran de Chavez, a native of Derena in the province of Extremadura, Spain. This Chavez may be the Pedro Gomez Duran in the Oñate lists of 1600. Don Fernando de Chavez returned with the Reconquest of 1692, and his descendants spread from the ancestral lands of Bernalillo and Atrisco all the way down to Belen. Three members of the Chavez line were governors of NM between 1822 and 1834: Francisco Xavier Chavez, 1822-23; Jose Antonio Chaves, 1828-31; Mariano Chavez, 1833-34. Jose Francisco Chaves, son of Don Mariano, was a prominent figure in nineteenth-century political and military life. In 1865, he was elected delegate to Congress, where he served three terms. CHAVES (Chaves). On US 285, 30 mi N of Roswell. Founded in 1929, by Mrs. Mathie Griffith and named for county. Post office, 1932-42. CHAVES (San Miguel). First postmaster, Francisco S. Chaves. Post office, 1901-06; mail to Trementina. CHAVES (Socorro). 10 mi W of Riley. CHAVES (Valencia). Post office, 1886-92; mail to Mitchell. CHAVES CANYON (Chaves). CHAVES CANYON (Socorro). CHAVES COUNTY commemorates the name of Jose Francisco Chaves. Created by Territorial Legislature, Feb. 25, 1889, out of land from the county of Lincoln. Area comprises 6,095 sq mi, fourth largest county in the state. CHAVES CREEK (Rio Arriba). Rises W of Brazos Peak; enters the Chama N of Brazos.

CHEECHILGEETHO (McKinley). Navajo, ch' e ch' il, "oak," bi, "by," tqo, "water." Trading post, mission, and day school, 8 mi from Arizona line and 24 mi SW of Gallup. In the COUSINS community.

CHEROKEE BILL CANYON (Lincoln, Otero). Empties into the Rio Ruidoso just W of Hollywood.

CHERRY CREEK (Grant). Small stream NW of Silver City. CHERRY TREE LAKE (Lincoln). 3 mi W of Lone Tree. CHERRYVALE (San Miguel). 28 mi E of Las Vegas. Post office, 1910-26. Also called CHERRY VALLEY. CHERRY VALLEY LAKE (Mora). 2 mi SE of Shoemaker. CHERRYVILLE (Socorro). Civilian part of Ft. Ojo Caliente. Only walls of the fort remain. Post office, 1881-86; mail to Monticello.

CHETRO KETL (San Juan). See CHACO CANYON.

CHICAL CREEK (San Miguel). Rises 9 mi SE of Bell Ranch. Flows S into Canadian River. CHICAL CREEK (Quay). Named for burnt charcoal from Indian camps along the creek.

CHICARICA, CHICORICO. Also called SUGARITE. This curious name, according to F. Stanley, is a corruption of Span., achicoria, which refers to a wild native endive or chicory. However, Calvin Jones testified in litigation over the Maxwell Land Grant in U.S. District Court in Colorado on Sept. 13, 1883, the creek, canyon, and mesa known by the word chicarica were named by the Comanches for the great quantity of birds which lived in the pine timber here. The Comanche word for bird, he testified, was rico and the word for spotted was choco. (W. A. Keleher, Maxwell Land Grant, p. 89). Elliott Canonge, of Walters, Okla., advises that the Comanche word for bird is huhtsúu, but comments that it would help to know the type of bird Jones was referring to as common in the region. A glossary of Comanche words by D. Manuel Garcia Rejon, Vocabulario del Idioma Comanche (Mexico, 1886), pp. 13, 22, gives the word cocorá as la gallina, "hen." Prof. F. M. Kercheville, of the University of New Mexico, points out that the reference might be to "prairie chicken" or the wild fowl known as "road runner." Cocorá could be from the Spanish verb cacarear, "to cackle." CHICORICO CREEK (Colfax). Named first. Rises near Colorado line and flows down the canyon into Raton Creek, then into a stream called Uña de Gato (Cat's Claw), and finally joins Canadian Red River. The Spanish developed the name by folk etymology into Chico rico, "rich little bit" or "rich little fellow," which did not have much meaning, but made quite as much sense as the Anglo transposition, Sugarite. The creek is now called SUGARITE RIVER. In SUGARITE CANYON the river flows through Lake Maloya and Lake Alice. Lake Maloya is the reservoir from which the city of Raton gets its water supply. CHICARICA MESA is now called BARELA MESA. See BARELA MESA. As Sugarite River flows into Raton, it runs by Sugarite Street. Raton Mesa is separated from Chicarica, *i.e.,* Sugarite, *i.e.,* Barela Mesa, by Manco Burro Pass. SUGARITE CANYON (Colfax). 2 mi S of Lake Maloya.

CHICO. Name means "small" in Spanish, but it also used to be an abbreviation or nickname for "Francisco." In NM, the word *chico* is identified with green corn, soaked in water, and heated in an oven overnight. In the morning, the husks were pulled back and tied in knots, and the corn hung along vigas for future use in *posole* and other dishes. CHICO (Colfax). 12 mi N of Abbott and 22 mi E of Maxwell. Post office, 1895-1956. CHICO CREEK (Colfax). Rises near Chico; flows into Canadian River. CHICO ARROYO CREEK (McKinley, Sandoval). Rises in McKinley and flows into Sandoval County to enter the Rio Puerco, 5 mi NW of Guadalupe. CHICO HILLS (Colfax). Roughly, in the area between Chico and Abbott. CHICO SPRINGS (Colfax). Post office, 1877-95; changed to CHICO.

CHICOMA PEAK (Rio Arriba). See TSCHICOMA PEAK.

CHICOSO (Colfax). Post office, 1876-77.

CHIHUAHUA TRAIL. See EL CAMINO REAL.

CHIHUAHUEÑOS CREEK (Rio Arriba). E of Youngsville, heading on N side of Jemez Mts.

CHIJUILLA ARROYO (Sandoval). Rises near the Continental Divide; flows SE to the Rio Puerco, 8 mi N of La Ventana. Also settlement named CHIJUILLA.

CHILI (Santa Fe). On US 84, at junction of the Rio Chama and the Rio Ojo Caliente. Station on old D&RGW RR, which was called locally "the chili line."

CHILILI (Bernalillo). In Manzano Mts., SE of Albuquerque, on US 10. One of the oldest place names in NM records, since the site was visited by Chamuscado in 1581 and probably is referred to by Oñate in 1598 as *Chiu Alle.* Fray Alonso de Benavides men-

tions it in 1630 as the first pueblo of the Tompira Indian group, and refers to missionary activity begun by the Franciscans about 1613. Pueblo was abandoned between 1669 and 1676 because of Apache raids. Chililí on L'Atlas Curieux (1700). Ruins of Indian pueblo lie on W side of Arroyo de Chilili. Present Spanish village was established in 1841 and lies on E side of the stream. Post office, 1882-1937. CHILILI ARROYO and CANYON (Bernalillo). In SE corner of county; flows through Chilili. CHILILI GRANT (Bernalillo). In SE corner of county at Torrance County line. On Mar. 8, 1841, Santiago Padilla and six others, for themselves and twenty more heads of families, petitioned Gov. Manuel Armijo. Grant was approved on March 20 and the men took possession on March 29.

CHIMAYO. Spanish village 9 mi E of Española, formerly inhabited by a group of Tewa Indians. The name in Tewa was *tsimayo* and meant "good flaking stone," i.e., obsidian of superior quality. Span. Arch. NM, I, 882, mentions the Spanish settlement in 1695 by De Vargas: "and will tell the said governor and captain to go to the said place of Chimayo, where they asked my permission to settle." Span. Arch. NM, I, 1021, for the year 1716, spells the name *Chimaco.* Span. Arch. NM, I, 353, Aug. 18, 1752, refers to the settlement as SAN BUENAVENTURA DE CHIMAYO. Across a small brook from the village is the celebrated El Santuario de Chimayo, a shrine under the patronage of Nuestro Señor de Esquipulas. Post office, 1894—. CHIMAYOSIS PEAK (San Miguel).

CHIMNEY CANYON (Catron). Flows NE to Negrito Creek 8 mi S of Reserve. CHIMNEY CANYON (Colfax). Runs E from Caliente Canyon which branches from Vermejo River Canyon 10 mi N of Dawson. CHIMNEY ROCK CANYON (Catron). Heads on Saddle Mtn. and runs SE to West Fork of Pueblo Creek. CHIMNEY WELLS (Eddy). 15 mi SE of Oil City in Clayton Basin.

CHINA SPRINGS (McKinley). Near US 666, just N of Gamerco, and 8 mi N of Gallup.

CHINCHONTE ARROYO (Torrance). Span., *sinsonte,* "mocking bird." Flows E to NM 41, 5 mi N of Tajique.

CHIQUITA CREEK (Otero). Flows N from Sacramento Mts. through Weed to join the Rio Peñasco.

CHIQUITO CREEK (Taos, Sandoval). See RIO CHIQUITO.

CHISE (Sierra). Trading point 24 mi NW of Truth or Consequences. Farming community once near mining activities. Now ruined by floods with only a few families remaining. Name may refer to the Apache chief Cochise, who camped here in 1871-72. He commonly was referred to as Chise or Cheis.

CHISUM (Lincoln). Named for John Chisum who drove cattle from Brown County, Tex., to Honeywell, Kans., in 1866 and shortly afterward established headquarters in the Bosque Grande 30 mi S of Ft. Sumner. In the 1870's he was credited with the largest holdings of cattle in the world, and his domain extended from Ft. Sumner southward for 200 mi to the Texas line. After Chisum's death in 1884, the ranch was purchased by a Colorado group which sold it in 1904 to Cornell University for an experimental station in range control. Post office, 1884-85; mail to Roswell.

CHIVATO MOUNTAINS (Rio Arriba). Span., "kid, young he-goat"; also applied to the wild mountain goat. Located 8 mi S of Abiquiu. Sometimes called CERRITO DEL CHIVATO.

CHIWILLA ARROYO (Sandoval). See CHIJUILLA.

CHLOE (Valencia). Siding on AT&SF RR, 27 mi S of Albuquerque.

CHLORIDE (Sierra). Former mining community 30 mi NW of Truth or Consequences, just off NM 52. Mining district started in 1879 when Harry Pye hauled freight to military posts in the West. Pye knew something about minerals and while crossing this country with a pack train recognized ore where Chloride now stands. He had the ore assayed and discovered that he had made a silver strike. When his contract with the government was finished, he returned with a party of friends and worked the claim. Name was given to site because of character of the ore. Pye did not live to enjoy his wealth. He was killed by an Apache shortly after he began mining operations here. The area has not continued to be productive of mineral wealth. Post office, 1881-1956. CHLORIDE CREEK (Sierra). CHLORIDE FLATS (Grant). Mining district in W part of Silver City received this designation from the chloride of silver ore mined here. Named by John Bullard and his party in the early part of 1870.

CHORRO DE AGUA (Socorro). Span., "jet, spurt of water." Name given to SW part of Socorro because of a stream of water coming from a pipe as an overflow from the spring.

CHOUKAI WASH (San Juan). Navajo, "white spruce." See CHUSKA. 3 mi N of Pueblo Bonito; flows W and N to Chaco River.

CHUPADERA (Santa Fe). Span., "sink hole," from chupar, "to suck, drink." The word, however, can also refer to a sucking insect, as a cattle tick. Community on NM 22, 3 mi NE of Tesuque and 12 mi NE of Santa Fe. Post office, 1927-28. CHUPADEROS CANYON (Santa Fe). CHUPADERA CREEK (Sandoval). CHUPADERO MESA (Socorro). In E Socorro County extending into Torrance.

CHURCH ROCK (McKinley). Community 8 mi E of Gallup, 1 mi N of US 66. Named for a prominent rock nearby, resembling a church. Post office, 1952—.

CHUSKA or CHUSCA RANGE (San Juan, McKinley). In SW San Juan County extending into McKinley County. Approximation of Navajo, chusgai, "white spruce." According to the Franciscan Fathers, the higher regions of this range are covered with growths of white pine (pinus ponderosa), but no mention is made of white spruce. The Navajos may have used the word interchangeably. Escalante in 1776 called the mountains Chuska. A long, low range, they are really a mesa or plateau. CHUSKA PEAK (McKinley). NW corner of county, 6 mi NW of Tohatchi. CHUSKA VALLEY (McKinley).

CIBOLA. This may be the earliest NM place name to appear on a map, since it is shown on Castillo's map in 1541. It appears as "la Ciudad de Cibola," and is shown with towers and walls, on a somewhat smaller scale than those of "la Ciudad de Mexico," farther S and E. After Friar Marcos de Niza described Cibola as a very beautiful city (the smallest of seven cities like it) with terraced houses all of stone, and bigger than Mexico City, the entire northern region was sometimes spoken of as Cibola, the Seven Cities of Cibola, and men were willing to hazard all for its reputed wealth. Frederick Webb Hodge points out that Fray Marcos learned the name in the language of one of the Piman tribes of northern Sonora or southern Arizona, and he ventures the suggestion that Cibola may be a transliteration of Shiwina, the Zuñi name for their tribal range. Fray Escobar, in his diary of the Oñate expedition to California, 1605, says the Spaniards called the Zuñi pueblo of Hawikuh by the name of Scibola. This place name was transferred in Spanish to the great animal native to the region, the buffalo (*Bison Americanus*). Casteñada describes the Seven Cities as "seven little villages . . . all within a radius of four leagues . . . together they are called the kingdom of Cibola." (*Narrative of the Coronado Expedition*, eds. Hammond and Rey, 1940). Cleve Hallenbeck, annotating his translation, *The Journey of Fray Marcos* (1949), p. 87, says that the Isleta Indians have a word *si-bu-la-da*, meaning "buffalo," that may have been learned from the Aztec term for the animal. CIBOLA COUNTY. Created by the state legislature in 1981. Comprises much of what was formerly western Valencia County. CIBOLA NATIONAL FOREST (Catron, Socorro, Torrance). Composed of areas in the Datil, Zuñi, Mt. Taylor, Magdalena, and Manzano forests. Datil division was created on Mar. 2, 1899; Mt. Taylor division on Oct. 5, 1906; Zuñi division on Mar. 2, 1909; Manzano and Magdalena forests on Mar. 6, 1906. The areas were combined on Dec. 8, 1928, as Cibola National Forest. Gross area is 2,275,282 acres. CIBOLA CONE (Sandoval). CIBOLA DRAW (Rio Arriba).

CIENAGA. Span., "marsh, marshy place." Anglo-Americans pronounced the Spanish word as "sienaga, sinigie, senigie" or other variants. See SENECA. CIENEGUILLA and CIENEGUITA, "Little cienaga," has the diminutive of *illa* or *ita*. CIENAGA (Catron). CIENAGA (McKinley). Also spelled SIENAGA. CIENAGA (Otero). Small community 55 mi SW of Carlsbad. CIENAGA (Santa Fe). Small farming settlement 15 mi SW of Santa Fe. A Queres Indian pueblo here in 1680 participated in the Pueblo Rebellion. The location is shown on L'Atlas Curieux (1700). CIENAGA (Socorro). Post office, 1894-1902; mail to Salt Lake. CIENAGA (Taos). CIENAGA (Torrance). CIENAGA CREEK (Union). See RABBIT EAR CREEK. CIENAGA DEL BURRO (Union). See RABBIT EAR CREEK. CIENAGA DEL MACHO (Chaves). "Mule." 22 mi N of Roswell on US 285. CIENAGA DEL MACHO RIVER (Lincoln). Formed by several creeks 18 mi E of White Oaks and flows E. CIENAGA GRANT. Given to Capt. Diego Arias by Governor Mogollon, July 30, 1715. CIENAGA GREGORIO (Rio Arriba). Small lake and valley, 6 mi E of Cuba. CIENAGA PEAK (Hidalgo). 18 mi N of Rodeo. CIENEGUILLA (Colfax). CIENEGUILLA (Santa Fe). CIENEGUILLA (Taos). Post office, 1903-04; mail to Rinconada. CIENEGUILLA CREEK (Union). Formed by

several tributaries 3 mi N of the settlement of Mt. Dora; flows E into Oklahoma. Formerly called CIENEGUILLA DEL BURRO. CIENEGUILLA CREEK (Santa Fe). Crosses US 85, 9 mi SW of Santa Fe. CIENEGUILLA GRANT (Santa Fe). 10 mi SW of Santa Fe and 4 mi W of NM 85. CIENEGUILLA GRANT (Rio Arriba). Grant made by the King of Spain through the military governor of New Mexico, Don Fernando Chacon, to twenty persons, who took possession on Feb. 12, 1795. CIENEGUITA (Socorro).

CIMARRON. The term *cimarrón* is an Americanism in Spanish, having originated to describe a maroon or fugitive slave in the West Indies. Meaning of the word generalized to describe a wild or unruly person or untamed animal. Applied in NM to the wild bighorn sheep of the Rocky Mountains: *ovejas y carneros cimarrones*, Don Pedro Bautista Pino calls them. Fray Angelico Chavez points out that the wild red-plum which grew abundantly along the NE rivers of NM was called *ciruela cimarrona*. J. Frank Dobie, however, in *The Mustangs* (1952), p. 94, says, "The word specifies mountain sheep, whence the Cimarron River, which heads in mountains once inhabited by aboriginal sheep, took its name." Both wild horses and wild cattle later came to be called *cimarrones*. CIMARRON (Colfax). On US 64, 38 mi SW of Raton. Settled in 1841 with filing of the Beaubien and Miranda Grant. In the 1860's and 1870's Cimarron was the principal stopping place for travelers on the Santa Fe Trail via Taos. Cowboys in northern NM, both lawless and law-abiding, made it their hangout, and Buffalo Bill organized his Wild West show here. The first postmaster was Lucien B. Maxwell. Post office, 1861—. CIMARRON CANYON (Colfax). W of town. May have been named earlier. CIMARRON CREEK, RIVER (Colfax). Flows through canyon E and then S to form Canadian Red River with its famed Palisades of the Cimarron; shown as SEMERONE on Mapa de los EUM (1828). See DRY CIMARRON. CIMARRON RANGE (Colfax). CIMARRONCITA CREEK (Colfax). Flows into the Cimarron River. CIMARRON PASS (Union). See EMORY GAP.

CIMILORIO (Colfax). See VERMEJO PARK.

CINIZA (McKinley). Span. *ceniza*, "ashes." On AT&SF RR, 7 mi E of Wingate.

CIRCLE SEVEN CREEK (Sierra). 3 mi N of Hermosa. CIRCLE S MESA (Quay). 15 mi S of Tucumcari and about 12 mi W of NM 18.

Once headquarters of the Circle S Ranch, one of the famed brands of pioneer ranches of the region. The Circle S Ranch has long since passed into oblivion, but the mesa is still a monument to its name.

CIRUELA CREEK (Mora). Name means wild red-plum (Span., *ciruela cimarrona*), which is common in northern counties.

CITY OF ROCKS (Grant). Strange rock formation about 33 mi N of Deming on W side of Shepherds' Canyon. Name came from resemblance of large boulders to buildings, standing in rows as if in a street. Area became a state monument in 1952.

CLAIRMONT (Catron). See CLERMONT.

CLANCY (Guadalupe). Probably named for Capt. John G. Clancy, a native of Vermont and a retired sea captain, who came to NM in 1879 to develop large ranch holdings on Alamogordo Creek near Ft. Sumner. He died in 1916. Post office, 1908-09; mail to Salado.

CLAPHAM (Union). 22 mi SW of Clayton on NM 57. Named for Tom Clapham who, in 1888, filed with Jim Davis on adjoining claims. They built a long, two-room house on the section line, so that one room was on Clapham's claim and the other on Davis's claim. Post office, 1888-1954.

CLARK (Santa Fe). Shown on 1920 map as 15 mi S of Galisteo, SE of Placer Mtn.

CLARK'S LAKE (Eddy). 6 mi W of Artesia. Originally a mere sinkhole, but because of seepage from leaky and abandoned artesian wells, a lake has been formed. Owes its name to the fact that it is on former Clark Ranch.

CLARKVILLE (McKinley). Shown on 1920 map as 5 mi NW of Gallup. Post office, 1898-1908.

CLAUD (Curry). 11 mi N of Clovis on NM 18. Named for Claud V. Kelly, who in 1906 owned a mercantile store here and was the town's postmaster, 1909-20.

CLAUDELL (Roosevelt). 14 mi NW of Elida. Name is a blend of the two names of the first postmaster, Claude D. Wells. Post office, 1908-25.

CLAUNCH (Socorro). Settlement at junction of NM 41 and NM 10, near Lincoln County line. Name taken from Claunch Cattle Co. which had headquarters nearby. Post office founded in 1930, although local men carried mail on their own in 1929 from Gran Quivira.

CLAVERIE (Rio Arriba). 16 mi S and W of Nutrias, 3 mi W of Arroyo Seco.

CLAYTON (Union). Railroad shipping center and county seat 10 mi W of Texas line. Founded in 1887 by John C. Hill, range manager of the Stephen Dorsey Ranch and named for Clayton C. Dorsey, son of Sen. Stephen W. Dorsey of Arkansas. The latter was involved in a famous mail case, which included collecting for mail routes then operated only once a month instead of daily. Bob Ingersoll was his lawyer at the trial and Dorsey was freed. Then he and Ingersoll established Triangle Dot Ranch in Union and Colfax counties. Post office, 1888—. CLAYTON CREEK (Catron). 18 mi E of Mogollon. CLAYTON MOUNTAIN (Union). CLAYTON WELLS (Eddy). SE part of county on John Lusk Ranch.

CLEAR CREEK (Catron). Rises 20 mi E of Mogollon and flows into Middle Fork of Gila River. CLEAR CREEK (Colfax). Rises near Clear Creek Mtn. and flows N to Cimarron River in Cimarron Canyon. The waters of Clear Creek prompted its naming, as they are fed by snows and run deep through a heavily wooded section. CLEAR CREEK (Socorro). Post office, 1904-06; changed to GLENWOOD. CLEAR CREEK MOUNTAIN (Colfax). In NE part of county.

CLERMONT (Catron). Sprang up in 1878, 5 mi N of Mogollon, and died five years later when everyone moved to Cooney. Small outcroppings of gold continued to be found in the 1890's along Copper Creek. Said to have been the first mining camp in the Mogollon region. Post office, Clairmont, 1881-83.

CLEVELAND (Mora). 2 mi NW of Mora on the Rio de la Casa. Settled in 1835 and originally known as SAN ANTONIO. Named in honor of Grover Cleveland, president of the United States for two terms, 1885-89 and 1893-97. Post office, 1892—.

CLIFF (Grant). 24 mi NW of Silver City on US 260. Settled in 1884 or 1885 and named for the Cliff family, who had recently settled here. Post office, 1894—.

CLIFF DWELLINGS (Grant). In north-central part of county, 2 mi N of Gila River.

CLIFTON, CLIFTON HOUSE (Colfax). 6 mi S of Raton on Canadian Red River. Built in 1867 by Tom Stockton, a rancher, as headquarters for cattle roundups in this section. During the 1870's and 1880's, it was leased for a station of the Barlow-Sanderson Stage Line, which added a blacksmith shop and stables. With the arrival of the AT&SF RR in 1879, the stage was discontinued, and so was Clifton House. Nothing remains at the site but the graveyard with its board markers. Post office, 1869-79.

CLINES CORNERS (Torrance). Tourist stopover and settlement at junction of US 66 and 285, 56 mi E of Albuquerque. Named for Ray Cline who set up a service station here about 1934. Post office, 1964—.

CLINTON (Luna). Siding on SP RR, just E of Akela.

CLOSSON (Cibola). Post office and mountain settlement in Zuñi Mts., 30 mi SE of Gallup. Named for Ed Closson, owner of general store and trading post. Post office, 1916-40.

CLOUDCROFT (Otero). On NM 83 at crest of Sacramento Mts. Established in 1899 when SP RR built a branch line to timber. Primarily a summer resort for El Pasoans. Name was descriptive of location among the clouds at an altitude of 8,640 ft. Post office, 1900—.

CLOVERDALE (Hidalgo). In SW corner of state, near Arizona line and Mexican border. Founded about 1893 by Bob Anderson and John Weams. Named for grass covering the fields. Post office, 1913-43. CLOVERDALE CREEK (Hidalgo). Rises in Coronado National Forest and flows S of Cloverdale.

CLOVIS (Curry). Agricultural, stock, and commercial center on AT&SF RR, at junction of US 60, 70, 84, and NM 18. In 1907, "where Clovis now stands there was already a siding and a few shack buildings and this spot was known as Riley's Switch. Santa Fe Railroad officials then decided upon Riley's Switch as the proper location for the new town that was to be the division point of the Belen cut-off. The story goes that at the time of this decision, the daughter of a Santa Fe Railroad official was reading early French history and she was much attracted to the character of Clovis, King of the Franks, who was converted to Christianity in 496 and thereafter was regarded as the champion of the Catholic Church among the barbarians. When it was suggested that she be given the honor of naming the new town in the Southwest, she immediately formed expression of her admiration of King Clovis by passing the name on to the new town. This was in 1906 . . . thus Riley's Switch became Clovis. . . ." *Clovis Evening News Journal,* June 3, 1935. Post office, 1907—. CLOVIS AIR FORCE BASE. See CANNON AIR FORCE BASE.

CLYDE (Socorro). 3 mi E of San Marcial. Thriving farming community named for the Clyde family, pioneer homesteaders in this region. Settlement was overrun by the Rio Grande flood in 1939, and homes, farms, and equipment were swallowed up in the silt of the river bed. Post office, 1897-1938.

COAL BASIN (McKinley). Mining area near Gallup. Named for large bituminous coal deposits in the area. COAL CANYON (Colfax). The Maxwell Land Grant of 1889 shows two canyons with this name, one extending W from Dillon Canyon near Swastika coal camp, the other extending SW from mouth of Canadian Red River Canyon. COAL CREEK (San Juan). Flows into Chaco River 6 mi S of Chaco. See TIZ NAT ZIN.

COALORA (Hidalgo). On SP RR, 12 mi SW of Lordsburg and 6 mi E of Road Forks. COALORA (Lincoln). 1 mi NW of Capitan. Established in 1899 and named for coal fields when EP&NE RR built the line here. The road was abandoned when the line was built to Dawson. Post office, 1903-05; mail to Capitan.

COATS LAKE (Otero). 15 mi NE of Cienaga.

COCA (San Miguel). Post office, 1889; mail to Sanchez.

COCHITI (Sandoval). Large Indian pueblo 30 mi SW of Santa Fe on the Rio Grande. Cochiti is the northernmost member of the Keresan language group and the name seems to be a Spanish pronunciation of *k-ot yayte,* the meaning of which, according to J. P. Harrington, is obscure. The Tewa Indians, however, give it a folk etymology, *kao,* "stone," *tay-ay,* "estufa, kiva." Cochiti on L'Atlas Curieux (1700). Post office, 1907-08; mail to Thornton. COCHITI CANYON (Sandoval). On NE side of Jemez Mts. COCHITI CREEK (Sandoval). Enters the Rio Grande. COCHITI PUEBLO GRANT (Sandoval). The old Spanish land grant of 1689 was confirmed by the U.S. on Dec. 22, 1858, and surveyed for more than 24,000 acres in 1859. The holdings today are about the same. See PUEBLO LAND GRANTS.

CODY (Luna). See CAMP CODY.

COCKLEBUR LAKE (Chaves). 8 mi N of Melina. COCKLEBUR LAKE (Lincoln). 3 mi W of Lone Tree.

COFFEE POT CANYON (Socorro). In SW corner of county, 11 mi NE of Dusty; NE of Sim Yaten Canyon.

COLD SPRINGS (Valencia). Post office, 1911-12; mail to Sawyer.

COLEMAN (Colfax). Community started in 1885 in Maxwell Land Grant, when many war-weary Southerners were seeking new homes and settling down in NE part of the state. Coleman was the name of people living near

Elkins in the 1870's. COLEMAN CANYON, CREEK (Colfax). At head of Vermejo River Canyon, near ghost town of Elkins.

COLFAX (Colfax). On US 64, 5 mi S of Dawson and on a branch of the AT&SF RR. Enjoyed its peak of prosperity in the 1890's, during the mining boom at Dawson. Post office, 1908-21.

COLFAX COUNTY. Created on Jan. 25, 1869, and named for Schuyler Colfax, Vice-President of the United States, 1869-73. At this time it extended from Taos County to the Texas—Oklahoma line and included the larger part of the Maxwell Land Grant. Present area is 3,771 sq mi.

COLLINS PARK (Catron). Once a settlement in a large meadow on the Continental Divide. Post office, 1908-55. Supplied from Horse Springs.

COLLINSVILLE (Catron). Point 45 mi NE of Reserve and 10 mi SE of Green's Gap. COLLINSVILLE (Quay). First postmaster, Absalom G. Collins. Post office, 1908-12; mail to Ima.

COLMOR (Colfax). On US 85 and AT&SF RR 11 mi S of Springer. The railroad came through on July 4, 1879, and Colmor came into existence ten years later. First settlement was in February 1887. Name came from joining the first three letters each of Colfax and Mora counties, whose edges the town touches. Post office, 1887—.

COLONIAS (Guadalupe). Span., "colonies, plantations." On NM 379, 14 mi NW of Santa Rosa on SP RR. The term could apply to a group of workers on various ranches who needed to build living quarters for their families and thus establish a community. Post office, 1900-47. UPPER and LOWER COLONIAS (San Miguel). Two communities about 7 mi apart on Cow Creek, E of Pecos. Post office, 1895.

COLORADO. A number of small communities have Spanish place names descriptive of red earth or red hills in the neighborhood. COLORADO (Doña Ana). Just S of Hatch. So named before it adopted the newer name of RODEY for Congressman B. S. Rodey. Post office, 1879-86; mail to Rincon. COLORADO CREEK (San Miguel). Enters Sapello River at Las Tusas. COLORADITO (Bernalillo).

COLUMBINE CREEK (Taos). Small tributary of Red River, entering above Questa.

COLUMBUS (Luna). 32 mi SE of Deming on NM 11. Named by first settlers for Columbus, O. Post office, 1891—.

COMANCHE CANYON (Rio Arriba, Taos). Marks county line, NE of Ojo Caliente. Scene of numerous battles in eighteenth century between Spanish garrisons and Indians. COMANCHE CREEK (Colfax). Waters of this creek originate in N end of Moreno Valley, flow into Moreno Creek, and then on into Eagle Nest Lake. It was a marauding spot for Comanche Indians and therefore named for them. COMANCHE CREEK (Taos). Enters the Rio Costillo, 10 mi NE of Red Lake. COMANCHE SPRING (Chaves). 4 mi NE of Oasis. COMANCHE TRAIL (Curry, Quay). An old Indian trail N from Clovis to San Jon, used by Comanches to hunt buffalo. In pioneer days, American emigrants followed it despite Indian raids.

COMMISSARY CREEK (San Miguel). 12 mi SE of Pecos.

COMPAÑERO CREEK (Rio Arriba). Span. "friend, pal." The stream must have some story behind it of friendship or association of friends.

CONANT (Guadalupe). Post office, 1902-10. See NEWKIRK.

CONCEPCION (San Miguel). Community 7 mi SE of Las Vegas. Probably a commemorative name for Our Lady of the Immaculate Conception. This title was given in the seventeenth century to the pueblos of Quarai and Hawikuh. The main church of Santa Fe originally "of the Assumption," assumed this title around 1650; it was destroyed by Indians in 1680. This was the title of the Alameda church in 1776 and of churches established at a later date.

CONCHAS. Span., "shells." References to tribes of Indians known as Conchos and to a Conchos River appear in the *Mercurio Volante*, written by Don Carlos Sigüenza y Gongora in 1693, as an account of the recovery of the Provinces of New Mexico by Don Diego de Vargas. The discovery of shells at the mouth of certain streams on the Gulf of Mexico may have suggested, initially, the name which was later transferred to Indian groups, using the masculine form of *Los Conchos*. CONCHAS (San Miguel). 6 mi NE of Gate City. CONCHAS DAM (San Miguel). Settlement E of the masonry structure. Established in 1936. CONCHAS LAKE STATE PARK AND RECREATION AREA (San Miguel). CONCHAS RIVER (San Miguel). Flows E into Conchas Reservoir. Became the source of a flood-control and reclamation project which started as a public works project in 1935 and was completed in 1939.

CONE (Harding). Former settlement 9 mi W of Hayden; then moved 8 mi NW of Rosebud. Named for William W. Cone. First postmaster, Mystice Cone. Post office, 1908-35.

CONEJOS CREEK (Chaves). Span., "rabbits." So named because of the large numbers of rabbits, both cottontail and jack rabbits, that are found along the creek and in nearby mesquite thickets. Early pioneers who found their rations running low could always depend on a plentiful supply of rabbits along this creek. It is still a game refuge. CONEJOS (Bernalillo). CONEJOS (Chaves). CONEJOS CREEK (De Baca). 13 mi S of Ricardo.

CONKLIN CAVE (Doña Ana). In the side of Bishop Cap, a peak of Organ Mts. Named for Roscoe P. Conklin, who was instrumental in having the cave excavated.

CONRAD (Hidalgo). On SP RR, 12 mi SW of Lordsburg and 16 mi E of Road Forks.

CONTADERO (Socorro). Span., "counting place," from *contar*, perhaps because sheep and cattle were counted in this vicinity. Farming community 4 mi S of San Marcial across the river from old Ft. Craig. There are a number of references to this stopping-place in the Otermin documents of 1682.

CONTINENTAL. Several spots in the state mark the course of the Continental Divide (the "backbone" of the North American continent along the Rocky Mts.), which begins at the N boundary of the state just E of Lumberton and crosses into Mexico on the S between Cloverdale and Antelope Wells. CONTINENTAL (Grant). CONTINENTAL (Luna). 6 mi NE of Hachita. CONTINENTAL DIVIDE (McKinley). On US 66, 5 mi W of Thoreau. Post office, 1949—.

CONTRERAS (Socorro). Settlement 25 mi N of Socorro. Named for Matias Contreras, who raised cattle and sheep in the neighborhood. An ancestor of Matias may have been one of two persons with this name in NM by 1692: Jose de Contreras, a native of San Luis Potosi, who joined the NM exiles at Guadalupe del Paso as early as 1687, and Simon de Contreras, a native of Zacatecas, who settled at Santa Cruz. Post office, 1919-35.

COOKE'S (Luna). 20 mi N of Deming. Named for Capt. Philip St. George Cooke, who was in charge of Mormon Batallion when first wagon train of expedition passed this way in November 1846. Most maps omit the final *e*. Post office, 1889-1914. COOKE'S MOUNTAIN or PEAK (Luna). COOKE'S SPRING (Luna). COOK'S PEAK (Valencia). See SIGNAL PEAK.

COOLIDGE (McKinley). 20 mi SE of Gallup on US 66. Newspaper stories refer to a shooting and a hanging at Coolidge as early as 1882. Thomas Jefferson Coolidge, for whom the town was named, served as a director of the old A&P RR, now a part of the Santa Fe line. Post office, 1888-95; mail to Mitchell; re-established 1926-57.

COOLY LAKE (De Baca). 3 mi E of Pecos River, 18 mi S of Fort Sumner.

COONEY (Catron). In S part of county in Mogollon Mts. Named for James C. Cooney, sergeant of the 8th U.S. Cavalry, who came to Ft. Bayard in 1870. While on duty as a scout, he discovered silver-bearing rock, but said nothing about it. After his discharge, he came here in 1876 with two companions to work the claim. He was killed by Victorio's Apaches on Apr. 29, 1880. His brother, Capt. Mike Cooney, and friends carved a sepulcher out of a rock in the canyon where he was killed and buried him there, sealing the tomb with the silver-bearing ore taken from the mine he discovered. Post office, 1884-1915. COONEY PRAIRIE (Catron). Area 30 mi E of Cooney settlement.

COOPER (Lea). Abandoned settlement and cemetery 6 mi N, 2 mi W of Jal. Post office, 1915-38. COOPER CANYON (San Miguel). Joins Iron Creek where Willow Creek, at Jenks Cabin, leaves it.

COPELAND CANYON (Lincoln). Small stream on N side of Capitan Mts. about 15 mi E of Encinoso. Named for Roy Copeland who ranched in this district before turn of the century.

COPPER (Sandoval). Post office, 1883-90; mail to Cuba. COPPER CITY (Valencia). See COPPERTON. COPPER CREEK (Catron). 2 mi N of Cooney. COPPERAS CREEK (Grant). Word means "green vitriol," a sulphate of various metals in its crystallized form especially of copper, iron, and zinc. COPPER MOUNTAIN (Grant). ¾ mi N of Leopard. COPPERTON (Valencia). Abandoned mining location W of Grants and S of US 66, where Valencia Mining Corp. had a copper mine and post office 1901-11.

CORAZON. Span., "heart." In view of the numerous names derived from such religious terms as *Ave María, Belén, Florida, Las Cruces, La Luz, Nacimiento, Sacramento, Santa Fe*, etc., this one may be commemorative of "the Sacred Heart of Jesus," *El Sagrado Corazón de Jesus*. CORAZON (San Miguel). Community

40 mi SE of Las Vegas. Post office, 1903-09.
CORAZON CREEK (San Miguel). SE of Corazon. CORAZON PEAK (San Miguel). 4 mi E of Corazon.

CORDILLERAS (Taos). Span., "mountain ranges." Community near Ranchos de Taos.

CORDOVA (Rio Arriba), also CORDOBA. 14 mi E of Española. Once named EL PUEBLO QUEMADO, as confirmed by Span. Arch. NM, I, 1046, dated June 22, 1751, in which Juan de Rios sells a plot of land to Francisco Monte Vigil, situated in the Pueblo of Quemado. The name was changed to Cordova when post office was established here in 1900. It honored Don Miguel Peralta de Cordova. Fray Angelico Chavez lists Antonio de Cordoba, a native of Mexico City, as a settler in the new town of Santa Cruz after the Reconquest of New Mexico in 1692. From there his children moved up the valley to Chimayo and doubtless to Cordova. Post office, 1900—. CORDOVA (Torrance). 5 mi W of NM 10 at Tajique.

CORDUROY CANYON (Catron). Long canyon in upper SE corner of county. Enters Beaver Creek 1 mi S of Beaverhead.

CORN MOUNTAIN (McKinley). See TAAIYALONE MOUNTAIN.

CORNUCOPIA CANYON (Otero). Two canyons seem to have this name: one W of Orogrande, where mining operations were carried on at Brice, and the other in southern Sacramentos W of Piñon.

CORNUDAS MOUNTAINS (Otero). Span., "big horns." In S part of county. These mountains rise abruptly from a mesa to an elevation of approximately 7,000 ft. The rock formations are said to have suggested the name. CORNUDO HILLS (Mora). 6 mi E of Wagon Mound.

CORONA (Lincoln). Span., "crown, summit." On US 54, 35 mi SW of Vaughn, at Torrance County line. Established when EP&NE RR (now Southern Pacific), built the line to Dawson coal fields. The railroad company chose the name. Two residents of Corona say the name was selected because this station was the highest point on the line (altitude 6,657 ft). Another antiquarian believes the authorities chose the name because of a small peak nearby which appears to have a crown. Once called GREATHOUSE'S TAVERN. Post office, 1902—.

CORONADO. Francisco Vasques de Coronado was the first of the Conquistadores to explore NM. In 1540-41, he traversed the state from Zuñi to the Pecos Valley, spending one winter at an Indian pueblo near present Bernalillo. Parties of the expedition pushed as far west as the Grand Canyon in Arizona and as far east as the plains of Kansas. CORONADO NATIONAL FOREST (Hidalgo). In SW corner of state, extending over into Arizona. Originally created on Nov. 5, 1906, and called PELONCILLO FOREST. On July 1, 1910, designated as CHIRICAHUA FOREST. On June 6, 1916, officially named Coronado National Forest. It has a gross area of 128,323 acres in NM. CORONADO STATE MONUMENT (Sandoval). 2 mi NW of Bernalillo. Created on Mar. 7, 1935; consists of a museum on the site of two prehistoric Tiguex Pueblo ruins, Kuaua and Puaray. Here Coronado made his headquarters in 1540-42. The 400th anniversary of the entrada of Coronado was celebrated in 1940 with the Coronado Cuarto-Centennial, which included dedication ceremonies at the monument.

CORRAL. Historically, a "corral" was any enclosure, being used in medieval days to name an innyard where the horses of guests as well as other livestock in transport were kept. In western America the corral was usually a circular pen built of posts and rails used to hold horses and cattle. It became the center of men's activities, both horse work and horseplay. CORRAL (Eddy). On AT&SF RR, 31 mi SE of Carlsbad, and 1½ miles N of the Texas line. CORRAL CANYON (San Miguel). 5 mi SW of San Miguel. CORRAL DE PIEDRA (Rio Arriba). CORRALES (Sandoval). Farming community 10 mi NE of Albuquerque. Listed in Escudero's Noticias (1849). Post office, 1885-99; changed to SANDOVAL. CORRAL DE LOS SOLDADOS (Rio Arriba). Named for some American soldiers who had their barracks here at some undetermined time. CORRALES CREEK (San Miguel). Joins Commissary Creek 5 mi N of San Jose and flows into El Rito. CORRALES RIVERSIDE DRAIN (Sandoval). Drainage canal on W side of the Rio Grande above the Alameda Bridge.

CORREO (Cibola). Span., "mail." Post office, general store, and gas station on US 66, 30 mi W of Albuquerque, next door to the AT&SF station at Suwanee. So named because it was the only place for many square miles where mail could be received and dispatched. Post office, 1914-59.

CORRUMPA (Union). An Indian word meaning "wild or isolated." Former settlement on headwaters of Corrumpa Creek where FDW

Ranch was founded by Frederick D. W. Wright. Now headquarters for Ferol Smith Ranch. Post office, 1905-19. CORRUMPA CREEK (Union). 10 mi E of Des Moines, at headwaters of North Canadian. First named Mc-Nees Creek by the traders on the Santa Fe Trail, in memory of a young man who was murdered here by Comanche Indians in 1828. Later the name was changed to Corrumpa. Capt. William Becknell crossed the creek in 1822. Also called CURRUMPAW CREEK.

COSTILLA. Span., "rib." Used in the eighteenth-century Southwest for a long slope along a mountain range, i.e., a diminutive of *costa*, "coast, side." COSTILLA (Taos). On NM 3, in Latir Mts. 2 mi S of Colorado line. Said to take its name from Costilla Creek. Post office, 1872—. COSTILLA CREEK (Taos). Also called RIO DE COSTILLA. Heads at Colorado line and flows S into Costilla Lake, and then via Colorado into the Rio Grande. So named because of a rib-shaped curve. COSTILLA LAKE (Taos). Also called COSTILLA RESERVOIR. In NE corner of county in Vermejo Park. COSTILLA PARK (Colfax). 6 mi W of Van Bremmer Park.

COTTON CITY (Hidalgo). 20 mi SW of Lordsburg on NM 338.

COTTONWOOD. More than a dozen names identify the giant trees which grow in river bottoms and marshy spots of NM. Called "cottonwood" in English and *álamo* in Spanish. COTTONWOOD (Chaves). COTTONWOOD (Colfax). Former small town 10 mi N of Dawson, on Cottonwood Creek. COTTONWOOD (Doña Ana). See BERINO. COTTONWOOD (Eddy). Named for a line of trees near a spring on land obtained by Wallace Holt with government script in 1900. COTTONWOOD CANYON (Colfax). 4 mi S of Raton and S of mouth of Canadian Red River Canyon. There is also a second COTTONWOOD CANYON (Colfax). 15 mi N of Dawson and E of Vermejo River Canyon. COTTONWOOD CREEK (Colfax). Former settlement in Maxwell Land Grant; now deserted. COTTONWOOD CREEK (Eddy). Flows E near Chaves County line, into Pecos River. COTTONWOOD CREEK (Hidalgo). On E slope of the Continental Divide, 17 mi S of Playas. COTTONWOOD CREEK (Valencia, McKinley). Rises SE of Closson, Valencia, crosses into McKinley, and enters Azul Creek 5 mi SW of Thoreau. COTTONWOOD PASS (San Juan). See WASHINGTON PASS. COTTONWOOD SPRINGS (Catron). 6 mi S of US 60 near Arizona line.

COTTONWOOD SPRINGS (Doña Ana). 4 mi NE of Las Cruces on W side of San Andres Mts.

COUNCIL ROCK (Socorro). NW of Magdalena on an unnumbered road just W of junction of NM 52 and US 60. Post office, 1881-83.

COUGAR MOUNTAIN (Lincoln). 7 mi W of Corona.

COUNSELOR'S (Sandoval). Store—station named for the owner, Jim Counselor, who began to trade with the Indians in 1916, and established several trading posts, including this one in 1930. His name is also given to the mission school here and to the community grazing area, within grazing district No. 7.

COUSINS (McKinley). See ROUND HOUSE.

Cow. When the word "cow" appears in an old place name, the term may refer to buffalo rather than beef or dairy cattle. Cow CREEK (Catron). Heads at Elk Mts. Cow CREEK (Colfax). Cow CREEK (Mora). See ELK CREEK. Cow CREEK (Sandoval). Cow CREEK (San Juan). Cow CREEK (San Miguel). Heads in Santa Fe National Forest and joins Bull Creek 6 mi SE of Pecos; flows into Pecos River. Cow CREEK, LOWER, UPPER (Rio Arriba). Rises near Vallecitos. Cow OSHA CREEK (San Miguel). Flows SW into Chaparito Creek, 3 mi E of Macho. Cow SPRING (Santa Fe). See OJO DE LA VACA. Post office, 1899-1906; mail to Lamy. Cow SPRING (Socorro). 8 mi S of Riley. Cow SPRINGS (Grant). Cow SPRINGS (Luna). In N part of county, near Grant County line. Originally called OJO VACA, because a herd of buffalo cows was always here.

COWAN (Quay). Post office, 1908-12.

COWBOY CREEK, COWBOY SPRING (Hidalgo). 15 mi NE of Cloverdale. A stop on the route of the Butterfield Overland Mail. Creek flows NE from spring.

COWLES (San Miguel). On Pecos side of Sangre de Cristo Mts. at terminus of NM 63. Established in 1900 as a hunting and fishing resort by a man of this name. Post office, 1905—.

Cox CANYON (Otero). Settlement, 20 mi E of Alamogordo on NM 24. Named for the canyon where Tom Cox homesteaded about 1872. Cox CANYON (Otero). A canyon, the upper section of which lies within a block of SW edge of Cloudcroft. Cox LAKE (Catron). 12 mi E of Mangas. Named for John W. Cox, whose ranch house stood at S end of lake. Cox PEAK (Catron). 14 mi E of Mangas. Named for three brothers, John, Tom, and Joe Cox, who had ranches in the area.

COYOTE. At least four settlements, three creeks, two canyons, an arroyo, a draw, and a valley are called Coyote, the Spanish-Nahuatl term for an animal part fox, part wolf, inhabiting the desert wastes from central Mexico to Canada. The place which the coyote holds in American experience, among three peoples—Indian, Spanish, Anglo—is emphasized by the frequency of the place name. COYOTE (Lincoln). Pumping station on SP RR, 12 mi N of Carrizozo. About 1900, named HURLBURT, for first agent of EP&NE RR, who had his office in a box car. Name changed to BOGLE, for Roy Bogle, a pumper here. At a later time, the station became Coyote, because it was at the mouth of Coyote Canyon. COYOTE (Mora). See RAINESVILLE. COYOTE (Rio Arriba) 25 mi W of Abiquiu. Named for Coyote Valley and settled in 1862. The settlers had to dispossess the coyotes before they took possession themselves. Post office, 1885, intermittently, to present. COYOTE (Sandoval). COYOTE ARROYO (Santa Fe). COYOTE CANYON (Lincoln). COYOTE CANYON (McKinley). COYOTE CREEK (Colfax). COYOTE CREEK (Mora). Flows SW into Mora County. COYOTE CREEK (Rio Arriba). Rises near Sandoval County line; flows to the Rio Puerco. COYOTE DRAW (Torrance). COYOTE LAKE (Chaves). In E part of county, 18 mi W of Caprock. COYOTE SPRINGS (Bernalillo). Spring producing carbonated water; now in limits of Sandia Base. COYOTE SPRINGS (Valencia). 25 mi W of Belen. COYOTE VALLEY (Rio Arriba).

CRAIG (Socorro). Post office, 1880-85; mail to San Marcial.

CRAMER CREEK (Union). 1½ mi S of Centerville.

CRANES (Cibola). Post office, 1881-88; changed to COOLIDGE, 1896-98; mail to Ft. Wingate.

CRATER (Doña Ana). Former trading point on US 80, W of Las Cruces near Luna County line. Named for the extinct volcano nearby. Post office, 1933-35. CRATER OF ADEN (Doña Ana). Large lava-lined hole in S of county, near Hunt's Hole and Kilbourne Hole. Named for the Rock of Aden, the volcanic mountain fortress on the sea route from Suez to India. Like NM's Crater of Aden, the Rock of Aden is an extinct volcanic cone.

CRAZY PEAK (Quay). 12 mi S of Tucumcari and about 8 mi W of NM 18. Named for an incident that happened here in the early days. A pioneer and his wife came from the East and settled in the valley near the peak. The woman, unaccustomed to the vast country, with its overpowering silences and its harsh extremes in weather, became demented. One day her husband missed her from their home, and after long searching finally found her body lying at the base of a high bluff on the N side of the peaked hill from which she had jumped. From that time the peak has been known as Crazy Peak.

CRESCO (Rio Arriba). Train switch and station on D&RGW RR, 9 mi N of Chama.

CRIBBENVILLE (Rio Arriba). Post office, 1884-96; mail to Vallecitos.

CRISTOBAL DE LA SERNA GRANT (Taos). In 1748 Cristobal de la Serna applied for a land grant in the Talpa—Rio Chiquito area S of Ranchos de Taos. Extends from Picuris Pueblo Grant to San Fernando de Taos Grant.

CROCKER (Sierra). On AT&SF RR 28 mi NE of Truth or Consequences.

CROCKETT DRAW, SPRING (Chaves). 14 mi W of Olive.

CROMER (Roosevelt). 10 mi W of Causey. First postmaster, Richard A. Cromer. Post office, 1907-18; mail to Richmond.

CROOKED CREEK (Eddy). 3 mi N of Carlsbad Caverns.

CROSBY CREEK (Catron). Flows E 8 mi W of Datil. Named for homesteaders. CROSBY SPRINGS (Catron). Source at Crosby Mtn. CROSBY MOUNTAIN (Catron). 8 mi W of Datil.

CROSSROADS (Lea). Oil field and ranching community on NM 18, 18 mi N of Tatum. Named because there was an intersection here when the post office was established in 1923.

CROW CREEK (Colfax). Flows from mountains past Koehler into Canadian Red River, W of Eagle Tail Mtn. Named in an early day for the vast quantity of crows that flew over the country. They built nests in the cottonwoods on the streams, and the early American settlers used poison to cut down their numbers. Creek flows across CROW CREEK FLATS. See RATON CREEK. CROW FLAT (Otero). 15 mi NW of Queen. Post office, 1898-1900. CROW'S NEST WASH (McKinley).

CROWNPOINT (McKinley). On NM 56, 20 mi N of Thoreau at edge of a plain surrounded by low-lying hills; a crown-shaped butte.

CROZIER (San Juan). Appears on nineteenth-century maps after 1858 when soldiers led by Capt. Tom Crozier marched up the arroyo here and across the Chuska Mts. Post office, 1903-19. See TWO GREY HILLS.

CRYSTAL (San Juan). Trading post and settlement on the Navajo Reservation 16 mi SW of Sheep Springs. The Navaho name is *tqunlts'ili,* "crystal water flows out." Post office, 1903-14.

CUATES (Union). Trading point 20 mi N of Clayton. Borrows the Mexicanism *cuate,* "twin," as a place name. The term has generalized to mean "close friend and companion." Post office, 1903-38.

CUB CREEK (Catron). Rises 1 mi N of Mogollon Peak; flows NE to West Fork of Gila River.

CUBA (Sandoval). Span., "trough, or tank." 55 mi NW of Bernalillo on NM 44. Late eighteenth-century Spanish community which was resettled in 1879 by families named McCoy and Atencio, who came from the Jemez region. First named NACIMIENTO, along with the Sierra Nacimiento to the E. Name changed to Cuba when the post office was established, 1887—. A small locality across the Rio Puerco was once called CUBETA, "little trough or tank." On Jan. 6, 1964, Cuba was incorporated as a village.

CUBERO (Cibola). Just off US 66, 8 mi NW of Laguna. Name may honor Gov. Pedro Rodriguez Cubero (1697-1703), who succeeded Don Diego de Vargas and received the doubtful allegiance of the Indians in this area following the Pueblo Revolt at "the place called Cubero, near the pueblo of Laguna" in Span. Arch. NM, I, 910, dated Aug. 27, 1835. However, there was once a settlement W of the Rio Grande between the pueblos of San Felipe and Santo Domingo that might have been named for Governor Cubero, and the present Cubero, which was founded in the nineteenth century, may have been named for a family of Cuberos who lived for a brief period in the Cebolleta region. Post office, 1879—. CUBERO GRANT (Cibola). Bisected by US 66 at village of Cubero. This was a colony grant to Juan Chaves and sixty-one others made in 1833 by the Republic of Mexico through the Governor of New Mexico, Francisco Sarracino.

CUCHILLA, CUCHILLO. The traditional meaning is some variety of cutting blade, but the word extended its meaning in NM to describe a geological outcropping or sharp ridge. CUCHILLA, LA CUCHILLA (Rio Arriba). CUCHILLO (Sierra), 8 mi W of US 85, 9 mi NW of Truth or Consequences. Post office, 1883-1902; 1906—. CUCHILLO NEGRO (Sierra). Settlement 12 mi N of Winston. Named for Cuchillo Negro, famous Apache chieftain, who was a contemporary of Geronimo. CUCHILLO NEGRO CREEK, RIVER (Sierra). Empties into the Rio Grande N of Truth or Consequences. CUCHILLO NEGRO MOUNTAINS (Sierra). Long, narrow range between Cuchillo Negro and Ojo Caliente. CUCHILLO NEGRO PEAK (Sierra). Also called BLACK PEAK. 8 mi NE of Winston.

CUERVO (Guadalupe). Span., "crow." 18 mi NE of Santa Rosa on US 66. The SP RR was built through here in 1901 or 1902. Name is probably descriptive of an infestation of crows in countryside. Post office, 1902—. CUERVO CANYON (Guadalupe). CUERVO CREEK (Guadalupe, San Miguel). Rises in Guadalupe and flows N into Conchas Reservoir, entering it 5 mi W of Gate City.

CUBESTA (Sandoval). See CUBA.

CUESTA DEL OSHA PEAK (Colfax). Span., "hill or peak of the osha plant." On Colfax, Taos border, 5 mi SE of Tienditas. Named for the osha plant which grows abundantly here. Osha has a stem which tastes like celery, and the root is used for medicine.

CUEVA (Sandoval). See LA CUEVA. CUEVA LAKE (Mora). See LA CUEVA.

CULEBRA (Torrance). Span., "snake." Named for a section on AT&SF RR between Lucy and Encino, where it bends out or "snakes" SE, east of Lucy.

CULP CANYON (Otero). Heads SW from the peak at S extremity of Sacramento Mts. Named for an early settler, John Culp, who came here about 1893. CULP PEAK (Otero).

CUMBERLAND (Chaves). 9 mi SE of Roswell on AT&SF RR and US 285. Named by the first settler, the Rev. Charles W. Lewis for Cumberland Presbyterian Church. The town was organized in 1907 by Cumberland Development Co. of which Reverend Lewis was president. A church was built in 1908. Cumberland College was located in church building for three years. World War I put an end to the college, and a building in process of construction was not completed. Post office, 1907-33.

CUMBRES (Rio Arriba). 8 mi NE of Chama. Post office, 1882; mail to Antonito, Colo.

CUMMINGS (Luna). See FLORIDA.

CUNDIYO (Santa Fe). 20 mi N of Santa Fe on NM 4. Name is a corruption of Tewa word *kudijo;* the Nambe Indians, a Tewa group, described it as "round hill of the little bells." Ruins of an ancient pueblo are here, but the community now is chiefly Spanish. Post office, 1922-63. CUNDIYO GRANT (Santa Fe). Small tract 3 by 3½ mi SE of Santa Cruz surrounding settlement of Cundiyo. Granted on Sept. 12, 1743, by Governor Mendoza to Joseph Isidro de Medina, Manuel de Quintana, Marcial Martinez, and Miguel Martinez.

CUNICO (Colfax). On NM 193, 30 mi SE of Raton. Post office, 1927-42. See KIOWA.

CUNNINGHAM (Colfax). Settlement 15 mi SE of Raton on the old Maxwell Land Grant. Named for Dr. J. M. Cunningham of Las Vegas, who was one of the New Mexicans who left the state just to ride in on the first train of AT&SF RR in 1879. In 1901, he was involved in litigation centering around land grant suits with Charles Springer as defendant. CUNNINGHAM BUTTE (Colfax). 9 mi SE of Raton.

CURETON (Grant). Community 8 mi below Cliff. Named for the Cureton family, who came to NM from Bosque County, Tex., in 1903, and owned the Walking X Ranch for thirty-seven years.

CURRUMPAW CREEK. See CORRUMPA CREEK.

CURRY COUNTY. Created by the Territorial Legislature in 1909 from a sector of Roosevelt County. Named for George Curry, who came to New Mexico from Dodge City, Kans., in 1877, served as sheriff of Lincoln County in 1892, and as territorial governor, 1907-1910. Area covers 1,404 sq mi. CURRY (Quay). Post office, 1907-21; mail to Lucille.

CURTIS CREEK (Colfax). Flows across Crow Creek Flats from mountains to Canadian Red River, almost paralleling Crow Creek 2 or 3 mi to the S. Named for old "Dad" Curtis, pioneer, who started Curtis Ranch.

CUTTER (Sierra). Community 14 mi SE of Truth or Consequences. Named for a railroad construction official who worked on this section of AT&SF line. Post office, 1907-56.

CUYAMUNGUE. Name is a Tewa Indian word, ḳooya mooghay-ong-wee, "place where the Spanish live near." The Spanish are described as the "bringers of ḳwaḳoongya," "iron": ḳwa, "oak," plus ḳos, "stone." In reoccupying New Mexico, General de Vargas was at Cuyamungue on Sept. 30, 1692. Span. Arch., NM, I, 506, Public Survey Office, dated Aug. 23, 1719/20, spells the name Cullamunque. F. W. Hodge and J. P. Harrington give as meaning of the name: "place where they hurled stones down." CUYAMUNGUE (Santa Fe). 12 mi N of Santa Fe on US 64. CUYAMUNGUE GRANT (Santa Fe). In 1731, Fernando de la Sena, Thomas de Sena, and Luis Lopez petitioned Gov. Juan Domingo de Bustamente for a grant of land in the abandoned pueblo of Cuyamungue; grant was made on Jan. 2, 1731.

CYBAR (Doña Ana, Luna). Post office, 1900-04; mail to Deming.

DAHLIA (Guadalupe). Post office, farming, and ranching community 12 mi N of US 66, 35 mi NW of Santa Rosa, on Canyon Blanco. Not to be confused with Dilia, which is 12 mi NE.

DAILY CANYON (Mora). South Fork of Manuelitas Creek above Hilton Lodge near Rociada.

DALE (Harding). 1 mi W of Union County line and 6 mi S of Cejita de los Comancheros. Post office, 1908-15; mail to Ione.

DALIES (Valencia). Railroad section and water tank on Belen cut-off of AT&SF RR, 7 mi W of Belen. Named for Paul B. Dalies, a member of the Becker-Dalies Co., of Belen.

DALTON CREEK (Santa Fe, San Miguel). Rises in Sangre de Cristo Mts., E of Santa Fe; enters Pecos River 2 mi S of Macho in San Miguel County.

DALY (Doña Ana). Post office, 1881-82; changed to LAKE VALLEY.

DANDAS CREEK (Taos). Flows into the Rio de Costilla; has many small tributaries which join it at Amalia. Among them are Datil, Carnero, and Del Medio creeks.

DANGEROUS PARK (Catron). 13 mi S of Luna.

DARK CANYON (Eddy). Long canyon which empties just S of Carlsbad into Pecos River. It has some narrow, dark ravines in Guadalupe Mts. where it originates. DARK CANYON (Lincoln). In Mescalero Apache Indian Reservation, on US 70, between Ruidoso and Mescalero. DARK CANYON (Socorro). 9 mi E of Aragon. DARK THUNDER CANYON (Grant). Runs S just E of Yellow Jacket Peak.

DARLING CREEK (Hidalgo). 15 mi S of Playas.

DATIL (Catron). Span., "date." On US 60, 34 mi W of Magdalena. Settled in 1884. Post office, 1886—. Town is named for Datil Mts. Two versions account for the name. One is that the seedpods of the broad-leafed yucca sufficiently resembled dates to bestow the name. The other is that the Spanish applied the name to the fruit of the prickly pear cactus. DATIL FOREST (Catron). See APACHE NATIONAL FOREST. DATIL MOUNTAINS (Catron). In Cibola National Forest, in NE corner of county.

DAVID (Harding). 10 mi E of Mosquero at foot of DAVID HILL. Center of a sheep-raising district. Post office, 1915-22. DAVID LAKE (San Miguel). See LAKE DAVID.

DAWN LAKE (Taos). See BLUE LAKE.

DAWSON (Colfax). 14 mi NE of Cimarron in the Maxwell Land Grant. Named for two brothers, J. B. and L. S. Dawson, who settled on Vermejo River in 1867. John Barliley Dawson started to develop the coal mine which after 1901 was made productive by the Phelps-Dodge Corp. and the SP RR. After railroads started converting to diesel power, the community gradually disappeared. The mine closed on Apr. 30, 1950. Post office, 1900-54. DAWSON CANYON (Colfax).

DAYTON (Eddy). Former community 8 mi S of Artesia and 1 mi E of US 285. Named for J. C. Day, founder of the town in 1902. First located NE of Peñasco River. A townsite was laid out on W side of railroad during winter of 1904-05, and everything but the post office and a store which belonged to a Captain Chase, moved to that location. Post office, 1903-44.

DEAD HORSE CANYON (Colfax). 11 mi N of Dawson, up Vermejo Canyon.

DEAD MAN (Union). Post office, 1909-12; changed to CAPULIN. DEAD MAN'S ARROYO (Union). A few miles E of Sierra Grande Mts. where Seneca Creek heads. Received its name from the last Indian raid in Union County (then a part of Colfax County) on July 4, 1874. Ute Indians came through the country on the warpath, killing several Spanish Americans and two Anglos. The Anglos were killed in Corrumpa Creek and the Spanish in this arroyo. DEADMAN CANYON (Otero). Runs NW into Alamo Canyon, 3 mi SE of Alamogordo. DEADMAN'S CANYON (Grant). In Big Burro Mts. W of Tyrone; drains into Mangas Creek. Named after the body of an unknown murdered man was found here in the early days of Grant County. DEAD MAN'S CURVE (Bernalillo). On NM 85, 2 mi S of Albuquerque; scene of a number of automobile fatalities. DEAD MAN'S CURVE (Socorro). A curve between Socorro and Luis Lopez. So named because several have died here: some murdered, some victims of automobile accidents, and one reported dead from a heart attack. DEAD MAN DRAW (Eddy). Runs E through Seven Rivers Hills into Rocky Arroyo. DEAD MAN GULCH (Grant). Runs N 1 mi W of Leopard. DEAD MAN LAKE (Otero). DEAD

MAN'S PEAK (Rio Arriba). 10 mi NE of Llaves. Said to be named because a gambler was slain here after he ran away with another man's wife. DEAD MAN'S WASH (Hidalgo). DEADMAN WATER HOLE (Otero). On Dog Canyon, E of Broke Off Mtn.

DEAD NEGRO DRAW (Roosevelt). Valley W of Elida named for a Negro according to the following circumstances. When Dr. Caleb Winfrey came to the Pecos River country in the early 1880's, he brought a Negro servant with him. After a few years' residence on the Pecos, the doctor bought the H Bar Ranch near the present site of Portales. One cold winter a blizzard had drifted his cattle many miles to the south. The Negro was riding with the cowboys. Late in the afternoon, he complained of being cold, although the weather was not freezing. He got off his horse, but was put back on by the cowboys, who tried to laugh him out of his chill, but failed. In a little while the Negro died and was taken to the home ranch on a pack horse. Another version of the story says that the storm occurred in July or August, and that the cowboys with the "Winfrey Negro" made him get off the horse and walk to keep his blood in circulation. Finally, they helped him back on the horse and rode on each side to hold him. When they reached the ranch, he was already dead. Dr. Winfrey had a fence built around his grave and planted a willow tree to shade the spot. For many years this lonely spot was the only marked grave in the county.

DEAD NEGRO HILL (Roosevelt). Hill rising some 100 ft above the surrounding terrain and covering some 150 acres of land. History is not clear about how it came to be named. One version is that a detachment of Negro soldiers was being transferred from old Ft. Sumner to Colorado City, Tex. They traveled afoot by the old military road that ran by way of Portales Springs. One of the sudden blizzards common to the plains country struck them and they wandered many miles south of the road, drifting with the wind. Weary, hungry, and cold, they wandered to the south side of this hill. There they stayed, in spite of their commanding officers' efforts to keep them moving. Many of them froze to death by the side of the hill, but the white officers and a few more survived and made their way to civilization with the story of the tragedy.

DEAN (Colfax). On NM 234, 20 mi NW of Maxwell. Probably named for the canyon.

DEAN CANYON (Colfax). With its little stream, the canyon begins at a point on the Ponil, 4 mi N of Cimarron and extends westward. Named for an early settler who had a cabin here.

DE BACA COUNTY. Created from Roosevelt County, Feb. 28, 1917, and named for Ezequiel Cabeza de Baca, the second state governor. He died in 1917, while in office. Area of county is 2,366 sq mi. The family name originated in the thirteenth century during the Moorish wars in Spain. See BACA.

DEDMAN (Union). Post office, 1909-23. See CAPULIN.

DEEP CREEK (Catron). 2 mi N of Cooney. DEEP LAKE (Lincoln). 5 mi W of Lonetree.

DEER CREEK. Incident names for the discovery of deer in these places. DEER CREEK (Hidalgo). 15 mi E of Cloverdale. DEER CREEK (Sandoval). 7 mi NW of Upper Cañon. DEER CREEK (Santa Fe). 2 mi W of Glorieta. DEER CREEK (Taos). 7 mi SE of Questa. DEER SPRING (Socorro). 10 mi S of Riley. DEER TRAIL CREEK (Rio Arriba). Rises 2 mi SE of Hopewell; flows NE to the Rio Tusas.

DEFIANCE (McKinley). Small trading point located on US 66, 12 mi SW of Gallup. Post office, 1881-87. DEFIANCE VALLEY (McKinley). NW of Ft. Defiance. Mentioned in an 1885 report.

DEHAVEN (Harding). Sometimes written DE HAVEN. 3 mi from Union County line, in north-central part of county. First postmaster, George W. De Haven. Post office, 1895-1920.

DEL BADO GRANT (San Miguel). 18 mi SW of Las Vegas. Town of San Miguel is about the center of this location.

DE LO MORA (Mora). See MORA COUNTY.

DEL MEDIO (Guadalupe). 5 mi SE of Anton Chico on US 84. DEL MEDIO CANYON (Taos, Rio Arriba). See JICARITA PEAK.

DEL MUERTO CREEK (Harding). See ARROYO DEL MUERTO.

DELPHOS (Roosevelt). Community on US 70, and AT&SF RR, 12 mi SW of Portales. Name is said to be a transfer from Delphos, in Allen County, O., named for the classical Delphos in Greece. Post office, 1905-40.

DEL VALLE CANYON (Taos, Rio Arriba). See JICARITA PEAK.

DEMING (Luna). County seat, on US 260 and US 80-70, in irrigated vegetable and fruit country. Mining activities in valleys to the N and S. Settled about 1880 and once known as "the city of windmills." Named for Mary Ann Deming, daughter of John Jay Deming, a sawmill owner in Indiana. She married Charles Crocker, who was one of four men who built the early lines of SP RR in this territory, including the line through Deming. The AT&SF RR also has a terminal here. Post office, 1881—. See LUNA COUNTY.

DERENO (De Baca). 17 mi SE of Ft. Sumner, and 12 mi S of Tolar. Probably called *Ciudad de Reno* (city of reindeer) because of its location in the mountains, and later through popular speech the word *ciudad* was dropped. Post office, 1907-34.

DERRAMADERO (Torrance). Span., "drain, sink." Trading point 15 mi NE of Encino.

DERRY (Sierra). On US 85, 26 mi S of Truth or Consequences. Post office, 1893-94; 1911—.

DESEO (Lincoln). Span., "desire." SE of White Oaks on the edge of Lincoln National Forest. Post office, 1917-19.

DESERT (Otero). On SP RR, 1 mi E of US 54 and 38 mi S of Alamogordo.

DES MOINES (Union). On US 87 and C&S RR, 38 mi SE of Raton. Transfer name from Des Moines, Ia. Post office, 1906—.

DETROIT (Doña Ana). Post office, 1889-92; mail to Rincon.

DE VARGAS (Cibola). Homesteading community in W end of county, E of Cerro Alto Mts. May be a commemorative name for Don Diego de Vargas Zapata Lujan Ponce de Leon, Governor and Captain General of New Mexico, 1691-1697, but more likely commemorates another person.

DEVIL'S CREEK (Catron). DEVIL'S LAKE (De Baca). 10 mi W of Dunlap. A large cave-in of the surface covering about 10 acres and from 150 to 200 ft deep. Descent into this hole is very hazardous and the bottom is covered with rocks. DEVIL'S RACE TRACK (Chaves). 4 mi N and 25 mi E of Roswell, 3 mi N of US 380. It is a 2-ft-high igneous dike that extends easterly, probably subsurface to caprock. So named because of its resemblance to a low, jagged racetrack, slightly elevated.

DEVOY PEAK (Union). 2½ mi from Colorado line, 10 mi NE of Folsom. Named for Michael Devoy, early pioneer.

DEWEY (Bernalillo-McKinley). Post office, 1899-1902. See GUAM.

DEXTER (Chaves). 16 mi SE of Roswell, on AT&SF RR and on US 285. Named by Albert E. Macey, a farmer and pioneer in the community who chose the name of his home town in Iowa. Articles of incorporation were filed in January 1903, showing Theodore Burr, a native of Denmark, Milton H. Elford, a native of Canada, who came to NM from North Dakota, and Macey, as members of the Dexter Townsite Co. Post office, 1902—.

DIABLO RANGE (Grant). In north-central part of county, N of Gila River.

DIAMANTE (Rio Arriba). Post office, 1909-12; changed to OJO SARCO (ZARCO).

DIAMOND CAVE (De Baca). 12 mi W and 6 mi S of Dunlap. A large cave of gypsum rock with passages leading back 500 ft. The crystals reflect the light and shine like diamonds. An early pioneer discovered the cave and went East to interest investors. When they sent trained men to investigate, they discovered nothing but gypsum crystals. To commemorate his folly, the cave was named Diamond Cave. DIAMOND CREEK (Sierra, Catron). Tributary of East Fork of Gila River crossed by Beaver Head—Black Canyon Road. SE of Winston on W side of Black Range and about 50 mi from Truth or Consequences. DIAMOND PEAK (Sierra). 8 mi NW of Hermosa.

DIENER (Cibola). 16 mi S of Thoreau. Post office, 1916-31.

DILIA (Guadalupe). On US 84, 28 mi NW of Santa Rosa. Founded in 1898 and named for the daughter of a first settler. Post office, 1911—.

DILLMAN CREEK (Catron). Runs S into San Francisco River, 1 mi E of Luna.

DILLON (Colfax). On AT&SF RR, 3 mi S of Raton. Named for Richard C. Dillon, governor of NM from 1928 to 1932 (eighth governor since statehood in 1912). Town established by the railroad company shortly after the railroad was built through county in 1880. At this point, the railroad branches, and these lines extend up Dillon Canyon to former coal camps of Gardiner, Swastika, Brilliant, and Blossburg. DILLON CANYON (Colfax). Starts about 3 mi SW of Raton and winds in a N direction about to Colorado line. DILLON MOUNTAIN (Catron). In Apache National Forest, 1 mi N of San Francisco River and 10 mi from Arizona.

DIMAS (San Miguel). 16 mi S of Las Vegas, on US 84 between Chapelle and Los Montoyas. Spanish surname derived from St. Dismas, The Good Thief. Some descendants of Dimas Jiron de Tejeda (d. 1736) began

using his first name instead of Jiron or Tejeda.

DIMMIT LAKE (Chaves). 1 mi SE of Bottomless Lakes State Park. Named for one of the Dimmit family of the Roswell area.

DISMUKE (Socorro). On a secondary road about 21 mi SW of Magdalena. Named for a miner who located one of the original claims here.

DIXON (Rio Arriba). On NM 75, 20 mi NE of Española. The general area was settled by the Spanish in the seventeenth century and was called EMBUDO because the valley resembles an overturned *embudo* or funnel. When a post office was established, the name Dixon was selected to honor the first schoolteacher in the area, Collin Dixon. Post office, 1900—.

DOCTOR CREEK (San Miguel). Flows E into Holy Ghost Creek, 4 mi SW of Cowles.

DODSON (Quay). 12 mi SW of Tucumcari. Post office, 1901-16.

DOG CANYON (Otero). On W slope of Sacramento Mts. SW of Alamogordo in White Sands National Monument. About 1850, a band of settlers from the Rio Grande Valley entered this canyon in pursuit of marauding Indians. They found only a dog which the Indians had left behind. The canyon has been the scene of several encounters with Apache Indians, who stole cattle from settlers on the Rio Grande, and from United States troops. Col. Christopher (Kit) Carson with five companies of his regiment, the 1st New Mexico Cavalry, reoccupied Ft. Stanton, and completely subdued the Mescalero Apaches taking four hundred of them prisoner. A railroad station here was called DOG CANYON. See VALMONT. DOG CANYON TRAIL (Otero). An "eyebrow" trail that leads up and out of Dog Canyon. DOG CREEK (Mora). Small creek which flows S into Mora River on S edge of county. DOG LAKE (McKinley). Near Valencia County line, 3½ mi S of Ramon. DOG MOUNTAIN (Hidalgo), DOG TOWN (Otero). See VALMONT. DOG TOWN CANYON (Otero). See VALMONT. DOG TOWN DRAW (Eddy). 7 mi SE of Loving. Named for colonies of the rodents called prairie dogs. See SEVEN RIVERS.

DOLORES. Many communities using this name commemorate *Nuestra Señora de los Dolores,* one of the titles of the Blessed Virgin Mary. DOLORES (Santa Fe). Former gold mining community, 4 mi SE of Madrid. Named for the *Placer de Dolores* which precipitated a gold rush in 1828. Post office, 1887-90; 1894-

1901. DOLORES (Union). On Ute Creek at Harding County line. Post office, 1913-14.

DOMINGO (Sandoval). Trading point for Santo Domingo Indian Pueblo, near US 85, 39 mi NE of Albuquerque. Named for the pueblo. Post office, 1909-42. See SANTO DOMINGO.

DOMINGUEZ (Sandoval). Just N of Cabezon Peak. Probably in the category called possessive names, identifying one of the landowners or a family who lived here. DOMINGUEZ (San Miguel). 12 mi SW of Las Vegas.

DOÑA (Doña Ana). On SP RR near Luna County. See DOÑA ANA.

DOÑA ANA (Doña Ana). Farming settlement 5 mi N of Las Cruces on NM 28, 15 mi W of Organ Mts. Mentioned in reports of Governor Otermin, as he left NM after trying to recapture Santa Fe in 1682. On Feb. 4, members of his party wrote, "We marched on the 4th to another place which they call Doña Ana, where the señor governor and captain-general prepared to go in person to a sierra which is in sight about six leagues away, called Los Organos." A legendary woman, Doña Ana Robledo, was reported to have lived here in the seventeenth century and to have been outstanding for her charity and good deeds. There are also legends of the daughter of a Spanish or Mexican army officer who was captured by the Apaches and never seen again. A letter from a Spanish officer to the Viceroy states that the Apaches in the region of Los Organos (the Organ Mts.) had killed three Spaniards and raided the sheep ranch of Doña Ana Maria Niña de Cordova. In 1839, the Governor of Chihuahua issued a grant known as EL ANCON DE DOÑA ANA (The Doña Ana Bend Colony) to Don Jose Maria Costales and a hundred and sixteen colonists. American military forces came in contact with the community in 1846. In 1853 there was an additional grant of land from the Governor of Chihuahua. In 1854 Mexico sold this added territory to the U.S. in the Gadsden Purchase. Post office, 1854, intermittently, to present. DOÑA ANA COUNTY. Created from S part of Socorro County, Jan. 9, 1852. The village of Doña Ana was the original county seat. In 1853, the county offices were moved to Las Cruces. County area is 3,804 sq mi. DOÑA ANA MOUNTAINS, PEAK (Doña Ana). 5 mi N of Doña Ana.

DON CANUTO (Bernalillo). Cluster of homes and school district S of US 66 between Carnuel and Tijeras. Named for Don Canuto Sanchez, who gave the ground for the school about 1920.

DON CARLOS CREEK (Union). Rises along Colfax County line and flows S to join Holkeo Creek. Name probably is associated with a landowner in the area. DON CARLOS HILLS (Union). In SE corner of county, 6 mi NE of Gladstone.

DON FERNANDO DE TAOS. See TAOS.

DORA (Roosevelt). On NM 18, 16 mi S of Portales. Founded in 1905 and first located 1 mi W and ¾ mi S of present site. According to one account, this was the homestead of two elderly sisters named Lee, one of whom had the first name Dora. The first postmaster was Frederick Humphrey, and the postmistress in 1940 testified that he submitted the name Dora because it was the name of his daughter. When NM 18 went through the area, the settlement grew at its present site. The Dora post office moved from Sec. 33 of the same township to the present location in 1915 when Dora and Lingo school districts consolidated. Post office, 1906—.

DORETTA (San Miguel). Point on AT&SF RR 18 mi SW of Las Vegas. Post office, 1916-39; mail to Serafina.

DORIS (Quay). Post office, 1908-13.

DORSEY (Colfax). 1 mi W of Canadian Red River near Eagle Rock Mtn. Named for Dorsey Lake. Post office, 1879, intermittently, to 1912. DORSEY LAKE (Colfax). Small lake 2 mi S of Koehler Junction, on Crow Creek Flats. Named for Stephen W. Dorsey, U.S. Senator from Arkansas, co-owner of the Ingersol-Dorsey-Alley Ranch. When Ingersoll successfully defended Dorsey in a suit over government mail contracts, Dorsey paid him with 5,000 acres of land and some cattle. Dorsey lived at one time at Chico.

DOUGLAS (Guadalupe). Post office, 1901-02; changed to TUCUMCARI.

DOVER (Colfax). See GATO.

DOWLIN'S MILL (Lincoln). See RUIDOSO.

DRIPPING SPRINGS (De Baca). 3 mi E and 1 mi N of La Lande; flows into Red Lake. At one time called WILCOX SPRINGS after a cattleman made it his headquarters. Dripping Springs and the lake which feeds it (Red Lake) used to be one of the stops for travelers and cattle drivers across this section of the country. Here Billy the Kid and Charley Bowdre spent the night after Tom O'Folliard was shot near old Ft. Sumner. DRIPPING SPRINGS (Doña Ana). In Organ Mts., 15 mi E of Las Cruces.

Named for springs that trickle from the rocks. There are ruins of a hotel, built in the 1880's when the place flourished as a resort. Also called VAN PATTEN's. DRIPPING SPRINGS (Socorro). Post office, 1892-93; mail to Lava. DRIPPING SPRINGS (Torrance). At entrance of Abo Pass on the way to Scholle. DRIPPING SPRINGS (Union). Located in a cave in Peacock Canyon. Gets its name from the way water drips from stalactites. DRIPPING SPRINGS (Cibola). On a ranch 25 mi W of Belen. Also known as LA GOTERA.

DROLET (San Juan). Oldest trading point on US 666, 41 mi N of Gallup. Named for owner, J. M. Drolet.

DRY CIMARRON RIVER (Colfax, Union). The Cimarron River, known by the name "Dry" in NM only, is believed to have been a "disappearing river" because of the notable feature of sinking and rising again farther on. Flows from foot of Johnson Mesa, cuts a deep canyon across N part of Union County, crosses a corner of Oklahoma, and finally empties into Arkansas River near Dodge City, Kans. DRY CREEK (Catron). Flows S and W to join San Francisco River, 4½ mi S of Pleasant. DRY GULCH (Lincoln). See NOGAL. DRY GULCH (San Miguel). 3 mi SW of Macho; enters Pecos River. DRY ICE FIELDS (Harding, Torrance). DRY LAKE (Luna). DRY SALT LAKE (Mora). Just N of Wagon Mound. DRY SANDY ARROYO (San Juan).

DUCK CANYON (Catron). Rises E of Wahoo Peak and runs E into Socorro County. DUCK CREEK (Grant). Flows SE into Gila River entering near Cliff.

DULCE (Rio Arriba). Span., "sweet." Ranching community on NM 17, and D&RGW RR, 23 mi W of Chama. Named for a sweet water spring which is still here. Founded in 1882. Post office, 1892—. DULCE LAKE (Rio Arriba). 4 mi S of Dulce.

DUNES (Otero). On US 54 and the SP RR, 17 mi S of Alamogordo.

DUNKEN (Chaves). On NM 24, 45 mi E of Alamogordo. Named for Oscar J. Dunken, first settler and postmaster. Post office, 1908-20.

DUNLAP (De Baca). Community on NM 20, 34 mi SW of Ft. Sumner. Named for W. O. Dunlap, founder and locater for early settlers. After the early boom of land filing, Dunlap soon was left behind when the settlers failed to make a living on their claims. Town is now an inland supply point for ranchers,

on the highway between Roswell and Ft. Sumner. Post office, 1907-61.

DUNMOOR (Torrance). On AT&SF RR, 23 mi E of Willard. Named for chief engineer James Dunn and his wife, née Moore.

DUORO (Guadalupe). Sheep-raising community on AT&SF RR, 18 mi SE of Vaughn.

DURAN, DURANES. Family name first listed in NM with the Oñate colonists. Several descendants escaped in the Pueblo Rebellion of 1680 and returned in 1693 after the Reconquest. Estevan Duran, a native of San Buenaventura, near present Chihuahua, settled in the Rio Abajo area after the Reconquest and may be associated with Los Duranes in Bernalillo County. However, a Juan Bautista Duran, listed as a European, that is, as a Spaniard or possibly a Frenchman, was living in the Albuquerque area in 1740 and later. He was a merchant and the descendants of his two marriages would constitute a community. DURAN (Torrance). Ranching community on US 54, 15 mi SW of Vaughn. Founded about 1900 by Spanish families named Duran who were employed by AT&SF RR. Post office, 1902—. DURAN CREEK (Taos). Joins the Rio La Junta to empty into the Rio Pueblo 8 mi E of Llano Largo. DURAN LAKE (Lincoln). 6 mi NE of Tecolote. DURAN SPRINGS (Valencia).

DURAZNO (Rio Arriba). Post office, 1887-89; changed to RINCONADO.

DUSTY (Socorro). Name in descriptive category for a ranching and mining community on NM 52 in SW corner of county. In the 1870's the Apaches under Victorio, Geronimo, and Cochise were held at the Ojo Caliente Indian Reservation. The agency and the cavalry post were located just S of Dusty on Alamosa Creek. Later the Indians were moved to the San Carlos Reservation in Arizona. Site of a U.S. cavalry post and headquarters on Alamoso Creek.

DUTCHMAN's CANYON (Colfax). Extends W from Dillon Canyon where Blossburg was at one time a busy coal camp. Named because of an old Dutchman who lived in the canyon when mining operations first started at Blossburg.

DUTCH SPRING (Chaves). See SOUTH SPRING RIVER.

DWYER (Grant). On NM 61, 16 mi SE of Santa Rita. Named for one of early settlers on Mimbres River, G. W. Dwyer, who homesteaded the site in 1883. Post office, 1895-1917.

DYKE SPUR (Santa Fe). Formerly a station on NMC RR, 30 mi S of Santa Fe and 8 mi S of Kennedy. The line ran from Kennedy S to Willard prior to 1907; then was taken over by AT&SF RR and later abandoned.

EAGLE CREEK (Lincoln). Source is at head of EAGLE CREEK CANYON in Sierra Blanca Mts. Named for Eagle Mining and Milling Co., that bought the Parson holdings. Creek flows SE through Alto into Devil's Canyon, where it unites with Little Creek about 3 mi NW of Glencoe and empties into Ruidoso River at Bonnell Ranch. EAGLE HILL (Roosevelt). 8 mi NW of Milnesand. There was a high chalk hill on the DZ Ranch, ½ mi S of the location, where many eagles roosted. Post office, 1914-18. EAGLE NEST (Colfax). Settlement on US 64, 20 mi NE of Taos. Established in 1920 and called THERMA, Greek, "hot". Name Eagle Nest advocated in 1935 because golden eagles live in the mountainous regions. Their feathers are used by Taos Indians for ceremonial worship. EAGLE NEST LAKE (Colfax). Created by a dam finished in 1919 by Charles Springer at head of Cimarron Canyon. 5 mi long and 2 mi wide, midway between Taos and Cimarron. EAGLE NEST MOUNTAIN (Luna). EAGLE PARK (Colfax). Referred to by Lewis H. Garrard in 1846. Probably an early name for Ute Park. EAGLE PEAK (Catron). In Tularosa Mts. EAGLE ROCK MOUNTAIN (Colfax). 5 mi W of Eagle Tail Mtn. on W bank of Canadian Red River, in Maxwell Land Grant. EAGLE TAIL CREEK (Colfax). N of Eagle Tail Mtn., about 15 mi S of Raton, flowing into Uña de Gato Creek. Name comes from the mountain, whose shape resembles the long, sweeping tail of a resting eagle. See BLOSSER CREEK, GAP. EAGLE TAIL MESA (Colfax). At E edge of Maxwell Land Grant, near Eagle Tail Mtn. Named for the mountain. EAGLE TAIL MOUNTAIN (Colfax). About 25 mi NE of Springer. See TINAJA MOUNTAIN.

EARLHAM (Doña Ana). On Rio Grande 10 mi NW of Anthony. Post office, 1888-1911; mail to La Mesa. See VADO.

EASLY (Luna). Siding on AT&SF RR, 28 mi NE of Deming. Named for a railroad employee.

EASTERN NEW MEXICO STATE PARK (Roosevelt). On US 70, 9 mi S of Clovis. Created by the state legislature in 1934. It covers 380 acres.

EAST LAS VEGAS (San Miguel). Post office, 1885-1903; 1906-28.

EAST POTRILLO MOUNTAINS (Doña Ana). See POTRILLO.

EAST RED CANYON (Socorro). See RED CANYON.

EAST VAUGHN (Guadalupe). 1 mi E of Vaughn. Post office, 1911—. See VAUGHN.

EAST VIEW (Torrance). 10 mi NW of Mountainair. Post office, 1890-1919.

EDEN (San Miguel, Guadalupe). A town in Maine has this place name; so does a town in Concho County, Tex. Both are named for individuals, not for the Biblical garden. (Henry Gannett). Post office, 1885-94; mail to Santa Rosa.

EDDY (Eddy). Post office, 1888-99. See CARLSBAD.

EDDY COUNTY. Organized from Lincoln County on Feb. 25, 1889. Named for Charles B. Eddy, promoter of Carlsbad Irrigation Project, who owned ranches in southeastern NM during the 1880's and 1890's. He was instrumental in building the railroad from Pecos, Tex., to Carlsbad and on to Roswell. In 1917, the E part of Eddy County was cut off to help form Lea County. Present area is 4,180 sq mi.

EDGEWOOD (Santa Fe). Bean- and wheat-farming community on US 66, 30 mi E of Albuquerque.

EICHEL (Lincoln). Post office, 1906-13; mail to Ancho.

EIGHT MILE DRAW (Chaves). 12 mi W of Roswell, emptying into South Berrendo Creek. EIGHTMILE WELLS (Hidalgo). 8 mi SW of Hachita. See NUMBER.

EIGHTY MOUNTAIN (Grant). 2 mi NW of Silver City. Eighty Ranch is just S of the peak, and used the number as a brand.

EILAND (Roosevelt). 5 mi SW of Arch. Named for Thomas C. Eiland. Post office, 1909-18.

EL ALTO (Mora). Suburb of Mora.

EL ANCON DE DOÑA ANA (Doña Ana). Span., "the bend of Doña Ana." See DOÑA ANA.

EL BARRO PEAKS (San Miguel). Span., "clay." 5 mi SW of San Geronimo.

EL BURRO (San Miguel). 10 mi SW of Las Vegas and 3 mi W of US 85 and La Manga. See BURRO.

EL CAMINO DEL DIABLO (Chaves). Route S of Mesa Diablo and W of Poe.

EL CAMINO REAL. Span., "The Royal Road." Travel and transportation in the Southwest followed natural routes between settlements even in prehistoric times. With the coming of the Spanish, one of these pathways became known as El Camino Real, which at its N end extended from Chihuahua, Mexico, via El Paso del Norte to Santa Fe, the capital of NM. South of Chihuahua, the road went to Durango, Mexico City, and Vera Cruz. Horses mules, burros, and oxen accompanied and transported both human cargo and freight over this famous highway until such antique methods were superseded by power-driven engines. Part of it was called CHIHUAHUA TRAIL.

EL CERRITO (San Miguel). Span., "little hill, peak." Post office, 1910-16; mail to Villanueva.

EL CERRO (Doña Ana). "Hill, peak." Visited by the Tortugas Indians on a pilgrimage on December 12, in celebration of Guadalupe Day. Also known as EL CERRO DE LOS MULEROS. "Mule drivers." See SIERRA DEL CRISTO REY. EL CERRITO DEL TU-RU-RU-TU (Valencia). On E side of the Rio Grande between Los Lunas and Belen.

EL CUERVO (San Miguel). Span., "raven or crow." Post office, 1888-92; mail to Bell Ranch. EL CUERVO BUTTE (Santa Fe). Possessive name for a high elevation in SE corner of county.

ELDA (Lincoln). On SP RR, 17 mi S of Varney in N part of county. Could be a transfer name from a county in Valencia, Spain. Blind siding named by EP&NE RR Co. when they built their line in 1902, through El Paso, Tex., to Tucumcari. Also called RATTLESNAKE SIDING, because there were so many rattlesnakes here.

ELENA GALLEGOS GRANT (Bernalillo). Large grant N of Albuquerque and E of Rio Grande to Sandia Mts. Brothers named Gallegos were among the seventeenth-century settlers. Their children returned after 1692, and one lived at Bernalillo in 1699. In that year, a sister named Elena was married to Santiago Gurule. The U.S. Court of Private Claims ruled that the Elena Gallegos or Ranchos de Albuquerque Grant was made to Diego Montoya by the crown of Spain in 1694, and that Diego Montoya conveyed to Elena Gallegos in 1716 through the Governor and Captain General, Felix Martinez.

ELEPHANT BUTTE (Sierra). Small settlement and fishing resort on Elephant Butte Lake, 5 mi E of US 85 and Truth or Consequences. Named for hill in center of reservoir, which resembles an elephant. Post office, 1910—.

ELEPHANT BUTTE LAKE STATE PARK AND RECREATION AREA (Sierra). Rubble-construction dam, 1,162 ft long and 321 ft high. The reservoir is 40 mi in length, covering 40,000 acres. Built by the U.S. Reclamation Service, and completed in 1916 at a cost of $5,000,000. At that time it was the largest structure to impound water ever constructed in the U.S. ELEPHANT MOUNTAIN (Socorro). 3 mi S of Magdalena.

EL GALLO SPRING (Cibola). See FORT WINGATE.

EL GOBERNADOR KNOB (Rio Arriba). Span., "governor, ruler." NE from El Huerfanito Peak. Probably describes the elevation as chief or outstanding feature in the landscape.

EL HUERFANO (San Juan). Span., "orphan." 10 mi E and S of Simpson. One of the sacred mountains of the Navajos, which they called dzil naodili. Name is derived from appearance of isolated peak as it rises from a flat landscape. EL HUERFANO MESA (San Juan). EL HUERFANITO PEAK (San Juan). "Little orphan." 14 mi E and N of Simpson and 8 mi N and E of El Huerfano.

ELIDA (Roosevelt). Ranching and farming town on US 70 at AT&SF RR, 25 mi SW of Portales. There are three accounts of the name. One is that J. H. Gee, who platted and sold the first lots in the town in 1902, named it for two of his daughters, Ella and Ida. However, Mrs. J. D. Marlow, whose family were settlers in Elida in 1906, reported that Mr. Gee always told old-timers that when he laid out the town he found a stake in the ground where the old Thompson Letton lumberyard was later built, with the word "Elida" on it. Mrs. Marlow said that Mr. Gee was never able to explain why the name was on the stake, but he adopted the name. T. N. Pendergrass is authority for the report that a construction engineer named the place for his home town in Ohio. Early-day settlers of the town deny that there were ever two residents named Ella and Ida. Post office, 1902—.

ELIZABETH PEAK (Colfax). A short distance NE of Elizabethtown E of Moreno River; elevation 12,491 ft. Named for the daughter of a first settler in Elizabethtown, possibly Elizabeth Moore. See ELIZABETHTOWN. Also called BALDY MOUNTAIN. ELIZABETHTOWN (Colfax). Former copper- and gold-mining camp on NM 38, 5 mi NE of Eagle Nest, in N end of Moreno Valley. First house was built in

1865, when the place was called VIRGINIA CITY. In 1866 a group of prospectors found gold near Willow Creek. As the first semblance of a city appeared, it was named Elizabethtown in honor of Elizabeth Moore, daughter of John W. Moore. A ditch was excavated from Red River for a placer dredge called "The Eleanor." Prospecting continued in Old Baldy Mountain as late as 1930. Town was first county seat of Colfax Co. Now deserted. Post office, 1868-1931.

ELK (Chaves). Farming and ranching community in foothills of Sacramento Mts., on US 83, 37 mi E of Alamogordo. Name derived from Elk Canyon, which runs through ranch lands. Established in 1885 and 1887 when large herds of elk were found here. Elk was formerly called YORK or YORKTOWN, from the York Ranch in the canyon. Post office, 1894-1958. ELK CREEK (Mora). Uppermost tributary to Cow Creek entering 3 mi above Martin's Ranch. ELK HORN PARK (Catron). 3 mi NW of the settlement of Apache Creek. ELK MOUNTAINS (Catron). 9 mi NE of Negrito on the Continental Divide.

ELKINS (Chaves). Former community on US 70 and AT&SF RR, 37 mi NE of Roswell. Post office, 1907—. ELKINS (Colfax). 5 mi S of Vermejo Peak, down Vermejo River, which is about 5 mi from Colorado line. Center for stockmen of the valley. May be commemorative of Stephen B. Elkins, territorial delegate to Congress, 1873-77, and later chairman of the Republican National Committee and holder of other political posts. Post office, 1876-1900.

ELLIS CREEK (Bernalillo). Small swift stream flowing out of N end of Sandia Mts. Named for Ellis Ranch in the vicinity. Also called LAS HUERTAS CREEK since it flows through Las Huertas Canyon.

EL LLANITO (Sandoval). Trading point on US 85, 3 mi N of Bernalillo.

EL MACHO (San Miguel). Span., "mule, male animal"; also "spur, buttress." On NM 63, 8 mi N of Pecos. EL MACHO CREEK (San Miguel). Small tributary of Pecos River between Dalton and Indian creeks.

ELMENDORF (Socorro). 1 mi E of US 85, and on AT&SF RR, 20 mi S of Socorro. Site of a large general store run by the Elmendorf brothers, serving ranchers of this area. First postmaster, Charles H. Elmendorf. Post office, 1906-18.

EL MONTON DE LOS ALAMOS (San Miguel). 9 mi N of Las Vegas, active in days of Santa Fe Trail as a supply center of corn and other produce for Ft. Union. Also a stopping place for the Barlow-Sanderson Stage Line. In the 1870's Charles Ilfeld rented a store here from a prominent freighter and merchant, F. O. Kihlberg.

EL MORRO (Cibola). Span., "headland, bluff, fortress." Farming and ranching community on NM 53, 37 mi SW of Grants. Named for El Morro National Monument. Post office, 1927-63. EL MORRO NATIONAL MONUMENT (Valencia). Just S of town of El Morro. Established in 1906 by President Theodore Roosevelt to preserve Inscription Rock. Since 1933 monument has been under National Park Service. The great triangular rock at this spot is made of light-colored sandstone, soft enough to be cut with a knife or sword point. For centuries, the Spaniards carved names, dates, and short messages on this great "autograph album." More than five hundred separate carvings have been preserved. The earliest dated inscription is by Juan de Oñate, a mine owner of Zacatecas, who became New Mexico's colonizer and first governor in 1598. In translation it reads: "Passed by here the Adelantado Don Juan de Oñate from the discovery of the Sea of the South, the 16th of April of 1605." Oñate was returning from a journey to the Pacific Coast, and the "Sea of the South" was the Gulf of California. EL MORRO MESA (De Baca). 10 mi SE of Buchanan.

EL OJITO (Doña Ana). Span., "little spring." Near Anthony.

ELOTA (Sandoval). On AT&SF RR, 14 mi NE of Bernalillo. Mexican, elote, "ear of green corn," from Nahuatl elotl. In NM the word was extended to the dry or mature ear of maize as well.

EL PASO CANYON (Otero). Span., "pass." EL PASO CANYON (Eddy). Runs S from Sacramento Mts., 18 mi E of Escondida. EL PASO GAP (Eddy). Trading point in SW corner of county on NM 137, 44 mi SW of Carlsbad and 6 mi N of Texas.

EL PERILLO (Doña Ana). See OJO DEL PERILLO.

EL PINO (San Miguel). Cluster of adobe houses between Los Montoyas and Anton Chico, near US 84.

EL PORVENIR (San Miguel). Span., "future." Tourist resort on NM 65, 17 mi NW of Las Vegas, built by Margarito Baca in 1905.

Named for a giant stone monolith, a mountain of rock, to which the name El Porvenir has long been attached. Post office since 1896, with interruptions, as PORVENIR. EL PORVENIR CREEK (San Miguel). See GALLINAS, NORTH FORK.

EL POSO CREEK (Rio Arriba). Span., "sediment, calm." Fork of Cañones Creek. EL POSO LAKE (Sandoval). Small lake near head of Cañones Creek.

EL PRADO (Taos). Span., "meadow." Small farming and ranching community on NM 3, 2 mi NW of Taos. A number of artists and writers live here.

EL PUEBLO (San Miguel). Span., "town." 22 mi SW of Las Vegas. Settlement in the 1880's on the old trail to Ft. Sumner, between San Miguel and Sena. Now called LA FRAGUA. Post office, 1876-98.

EL RANCHITO (Bernalillo). Span., "little ranch." Also called LOS RANCHITOS. Farming area N of Los Griegos, just outside present Albuquerque city limits.

EL RANCHO DE JOSE MIGUEL DE LA PEÑA (Sandoval) See PEÑA BLANCA.

EL RANCHO DE LA PEÑA BLANCA (Sandoval). See PEÑA BLANCA.

EL RIO DE SAN LAZARO (San Juan). See MANCOS RIVER.

EL RITO (Rio Arriba). Ranching community on NM 96 and 110, 26 mi N of Española. Town gets its name from El Rito River. Northern New Mexico State School is here. Post office, 1870—. EL RITO (Sandoval). Site of Bandelier National Monument established in 1916. See BANDELIER NATIONAL MONUMENT. EL RITO (Valencia). EL RITO DE LOS FRIJOLES CREEK (Sandoval). Archeologists favor Span., "rite, ceremony of the beans." Rito also means "little river." Heads in Jemez Mts. and flows SE through Bandelier National Monument into the Rio Grande. EL RITO MOUNTAINS (Rio Arriba). In Carson National Forest. Tewa word for these mountains is pee-speeing ya, "pinkish mountains." EL RITO RIVER (Rio Arriba). Rises in Carson National Forest and flows S to the Chama River.

EL SABINO (Bernalillo). Span., "juniper tree." 4 mi S of US 66 at Tijeras and 1 mi E of NM 10, near Juan Tomas.

EL TABLAZON (Bernalillo). Settlement in Manzano Mts., 20 mi SE of Albuquerque.

EL TAJO GRANT (Bernalillo). Land on E side of the Rio Grande between town of Las Barelas and grant of Isleta Indians. Given to

Diego Padilla on May 14, 1718, by Governor Cassio.

EL TERROMOTE (San Miguel). New Mexican Span., "whirlwind, sandstorm." 18 mi N of Las Vegas, about 6 mi W of Sapello. The word can be confused with terremoto, "earthquake."

ELVA (Chaves). Post office, 1910-16; mail to Acme.

EL VADO (Rio Arriba). Span., "ford of a river." Trading and resort community on NM 112, 15 mi SW of Tierra Amarilla. Post office, 1904-08. EL VADO LAKE STATE PARK AND RECREATION AREA. (Rio Arriba). Dam built in 1935 on Chama River 15 mi SW of Tierra Amarilla to impound and control waters tributary to the Rio Grande.

EL VALLE (Taos). Span., "valley." Near Dixon, 5 mi E of Ojo Zarco.

ELVIRA (De Baca). Former settlement on De Baca County line S of Santa Rosa. Post office, 1908-24.

ELWOOD (Otero). On SP RR, 6 mi SW of Orogrande.

EMBERSON (Union). Post office, 1908-09; mail to Centerville.

EMBOM LAKE (Rio Arriba). Small lake on Jicarilla Apache Reservation.

EMBUDO (Rio Arriba). Span., "funnel." Settlement on US 64 and D&RGW RR, 20 mi NE of Española. Given this name in the seventeenth century by Spanish settlers because Embudo Creek flows through a narrow pass resembling a funnel. In the will of Juan Francisco Martin, Embudo is given as SAN ANTONIO DEL EMBUDO. Former Indian pueblo and then a Spanish farming community. Post office, 1881-1902; 1905—. EMBUDO ARROYO (Bernalillo). Flows W from Sandia Mts. through Albuquerque to the Rio Grande. EMBUDO CREEK (Rio Arriba). Formed by the Rio Pueblo and Santa Barbara Creek and extends from their junction near Peñasco to the Rio Grande above Embudo.

EMERY (Bernalillo). Post office, 1891-92; mail to Bernalillo. EMERY GAP (Union). First known as CIMARRON PASS, it led from Colorado through the mountains to the Dry Cimarron country; 7 mi E of Colfax County line. Post office, 1906-08; 1909-25; mail to Branson, Colo. EMERY PEAK (Union). On S bank of Dry Cimarron River, 8 mi from Colorado line in NW corner of county.

EMZY (Roosevelt). Small community on NM 92, 25 mi SE of Portales, and 3 mi W of Texas border. Named for Emzy Roberts who opened a store and established a post office here in 1918. Post office, 1918-25; mail to Causey.

ENCHANTED MESA (Cibola). Beetling rock 431 ft high, 3 mi N of Acoma; covers 40 to 50 acres. The Indians of Acoma call the great mesa *katzimo*, "enchanted," because of a belief that the Nature Gods have their dwelling on its summit. There is also a tradition that a millenium ago the Acomans dwelt on the flat top, but a fall of rocks caused the stairway to be closed and those who were caught on the height perished of starvation. Another version says that a war party of Acomans were defeated by their enemies and, climbing to the mesa top, starved rather than surrender. Adventurous souls who have scaled the rock find no evidence of buildings, although some pottery fragments remain here. Also called MESA ENCANTADA.

ENCIERRE (Mora). Span., "enclose." Post office, 1887-90; mail to Wagon Mound.

ENCINADA (Rio Arriba). 3 mi NE of Tierra Amarilla.

ENCINO. A popular Mexicanism for *encina* "evergreen oak." ENCINAL (Valencia). "Oak grove." Trading point 5 mi N of US 66, 27 mi E of Grants, and 17 mi W of Laguna. One of six Indian villages inhabited by the Laguna Pueblo Indians and once the site of a government school. ENCINO (Torrance). Ranching town on US 60, 285, and AT&SF RR, 16 mi W of Vaughn. Post office, 1904—. ENCINO CREEK (Taos). Flows E into Mora River, 3 mi N of Mora. ENCINOSO (Lincoln). On NM 48, 22 mi E of Carrizozo. Named because of a stand of oak trees in vicinity, and settled in 1915 by R. A. Durn and Sam Farmer, who put in a general merchandise store and became postmaster. Post office, 1915-20; mail to Capitan. ENCINOSO CANYON, CREEK (San Miguel). Rises just NE of Maes; flows N to Mora River.

ENDEE (Quay). Ranching and farming community on US 66, served by CRI&P RR, 37 mi E of Tucumcari. Name is said to have been adopted from the brand of the ND Ranch established by the Day brothers, John E. and George, in 1882. The two letters in the brand were joined so that the straight line forming the right side of the N also became the straight line forming the front end of the D. Post office, 1886-1955.

ENGLAND (Colfax). Post office, Apr. to Dec. 1881.

ENGLE (Sierra). On NM 52 and AT&SF RR, 9 mi E of Elephant Butte Reservoir. Named for R. L. Engle, one of the engineers who supervised construction of the railroad through the town. The postmaster sent the name through as ANGLE and it stayed that way for six months. Became a siding on the railroad in 1879 and a cattle shipping point. In 1923 and 1924 an effort was made to change the name of the town to Engel, honoring Edward J. Engel, the vice-president of the railroad. The Postmaster General was about ready to give his consent to the change when the novelist Eugene Manlove Rhodes got Sen. Bronson Cutting to intercede. Post office, 1881-1955.

ENSENADA (Rio Arriba). Span., English equivalent is "mountain cave or little valley." Ranching and lumbering community on NM 162, 3 mi NE of Tierra Amarilla. Post office, 1906-58.

EPRIS (Guadalupe). On US 54, and SP RR, 5 mi SW of Vaughn. Post office, 1905-07.

ESCABOSA (Bernalillo). Corruption of Span., *escobosa*, "broom grass." Farming community on NM 10, 23 mi SE of Albuquerque in Manzano Mts. Name signifies brushy country, because it was covered with thick growth of broom grass or other like grasses. Post office, 1900-04; mail to Chilili; 1922-34; 1937-43; mail to Zamora.

ESCALANTE LAKE (Lincoln). 7 mi SE of Corona.

ESCARVADA WASH. Also called ESCARABADA and ESCARRADA WASH. This describes a long, usually dry stream bed running E to W into Chaco River. May be a corruption of Span., *excavada*, derived from *excavar*, "to dig, excavate." One of the pottery types at Chaco ruins is called Escavada B/W and named after this wash.

ESCOBAS (Santa Fe). Span., "brooms." ESCOBAS PEAK (San Miguel). 3 mi SW of Pecos near Santa Fe County line.

ESCONDIDA (Otero). Span., "hidden." On US 54 and SP RR, 20 mi S of Alamogordo. ESCONDIDO (Lincoln). On NM 368, 9 mi N of Tinnie, on SE side of Capitan Mts. Settled about 1887 by Long Moore, who ran sheep in this part of the country. ESCONDIDO (Socorro). Small settlement on US 85, 3 mi N of Socorro. Post office, Feb.-Aug., 1931. ESCONDIDO MOUNTAINS (Catron). ESCONDIDO SPRING (Otero). At foot of Capitan Mts.

ESMERALDA (Valencia). Span., "emerald." Post office, 1894-96; mail to Belen.

ESPAÑOLA (Rio Arriba). Variation of Hispaniola, "New Spain"; Also means "Spanish lady." This ranching and farming community on US 84 and 285, 25 mi NW of Santa Fe, is not named in the list of settlements given by Escudero's *Noticias* (1849). The locality, then, seems to have been settled chiefly after the middle of the nineteenth century. Early settlers listed in the files of the Writers' Project were Juan de Jesus Naranjo and his wife Maria Juan Duran, and the families of Nicolas Vigil and Gregorio Garcia. Post office, 1881—.

ESPINOSA CANYON (Torrance). Span., "thorny"; also "thicket." 7 mi E of Mountainair. ESPINOSA LAKE (Torrance). 12 mi SE of Mountainair. Nicolas de Espinosa was an original settler of Santa Cruz. His marriage is recorded in 1697. Pedro de Espinosa is listed in Santa Fe and Albuquerque after the Reconquest.

ESPIRITU SANTO (Sandoval). Spanish land grant. See OJO DEL ESPIRITU SANTO GRANT.

ESPUELA (Eddy). Span., "spur." Community on US 285 and AT&SF RR, 5 mi N of Artesia. Name means "railroad spur or siding," but it is reported that Hyland G. Southworth at one time changed the spelling to ESPUELLA for his wife, Della Southworth.

ESQUIBEL (San Miguel). 12 mi W of Las Vegas, E of Barillos Peak. ESQUIBEL CANYON (Rio Arriba, Taos). 3 mi N of Tres Piedras. Named for a family whose earliest sojourner, Juan Antonio de Esquivel, is mentioned among the De Vargas colonists of 1693.

ESTACA SETTLEMENT (Rio ' Arriba). Span., "stake." On W side of the Rio Grande 1½ miles N of Alcalde.

ESTALINE CANYON (Socorro). May be a corruption of Span., *estalino*, "stopping place." 13 mi SW of Magdalena.

ESTANCIA (Torrance). Span., "large estate, cattle ranch, resting place." County seat, ranching and farming community on NM 41, and AT&SF RR, 40 mi SE of Albuquerque. Natives say there was a lake here where the cattle came for water. Present settlement began with the coming of the railroad between 1901 and 1904, but sheepmen and cattlemen lived here for many years before. In early days the place was called a plain, but it is believed that John W. Corbett, one of the leading settlers, proposed the name "Valley," that is, ESTANCIA VALLEY, which is now in regular usage. Post office, 1903—. ESTANCIA PARK LAKE (Torrance). Small lake in town of Estancia, covering one acre. ESTANCIA SPRING (Torrance). Held by Don Fernando Otero for years. Settlement here became Estancia. In early days the spring was a resting place for travelers, as it was on one of the trails from Chihuahua to Santa Fe.

ESTERO LARGO (Doña Ana). Span., "long estuary or pond." Campground about 65 mi N of El Paso mentioned in accounts of the Spanish explorers. Named for shape of the waterhole. ESTERO REDONDO (Doña Ana). Span., "round." N of El Paso. ESTEROS CREEK (Guadalupe). "Inlet; (pl.) bottomlands along a river which are sometimes flooded by the river waters." Tributary of Pecos River, entering it 8 mi N of Santa Rosa.

ESTEY (Lincoln). Post office, 1901-03; mail to Oscuro; 1904-31.

ESTRADA (San Miguel). Post office, 1920-21.

ESTRANIA ARROYO (Union). Possible corruption of Span., *extrañar*, "strange." In extreme SE tip of county, flowing E into Monia Creek.

ESTRELLA (McKinley). Span., "star." Trading point and mission 32 mi SW of Cuba on Chacra Mesa. Also known as STAR LAKE TRADING POST. Post office, 1922-25; mail to Cabezon.

E-TOWN (Colfax). See ELIZABETHTOWN.

EUNICE (Lea). Ranching and oil community on NM 8, and TNM RR. Named in 1909 for Eunice Carson, whose father, J. N. Carson, was a homesteader at the site on which the town stands. His son, E. O. Carson, was first postmaster. Post office, 1909—.

EVANOLA (De Baca). On AT&SF RR, 20 mi W of Ft. Sumner.

EVANS (Mora). Small station house on AT&SF RR, 2 mi E of edge of Ocate Mesa. See LEVY.

EXTER (Union). Post office, 1890-1903; changed to VALLEY.

FAHADA BUTTE (San Juan). Span., "belted," or "cinch for a saddle"; possibly a stripe resembling a belt, marked on the formation. *Fajado* is a Spanish surname which could appear in colloquial speech as *fahada.* Equally possible that name is a corruption of *fachada,* "facade." 4 mi SE of Pueblo Bonito.

FAIR. Names of this type have sometimes been considered in the euphemistic or idealistic category, expressing both the imagination and hopes of the original settlers. FAIRACRES (Doña Ana). Farming community on US 80, 4 mi W of Las Cruces. Post office, 1926—. FAIRBANKS (Chaves). On AT&SF RR, 32 mi N of Artesia. FAIRFIELD (Curry). FAIRPOINT (San Juan). Post office, 1894-98; mail to Largo. FAIRVIEW (Bernalillo). FAIRVIEW (Rio Arriba). Shopping center on US 64, about 2 mi NE of Española. A Mormon community in the 1890's, but after 1900 the Mormons moved to Carson, between Taos and the old D&RGW RR. Post office, 1952—. FAIRVIEW (Sierra). Post office, 1881-1930. See WINSTON. FAIRWEATHER (Lea).

FALLS CREEK (San Miguel). Tributary of Tecolote Creek W of San Geronimo.

FARLEY (Colfax). Ranching and farming community on NM 193, 13 mi NE of Abbott. A branch of AT&SF RR formerly ran here from Mt. Dora. Established in 1929, taking the name of its first postmaster. Post office, 1929-32.

FARMINGTON (San Juan). In north-central part of county, 23 mi from Colorado line. Named by Milt Virdin, one of the first settlers, who was helping Judge S. D. Webster, L. C. Coe, and a man named Boran lay out the townsite in 1879. Stockmen came to this place to buy green vegetables and forage for their animals. They called it the "farming town." Virdin suggested dropping the w and combining the two words into Farmington. All agreed, and so the town and new post office took the name. The Navajo Indians had a special name for this spot, calling it *tqo,* "water," *tah,* "three," which could be translated "three waters, blending waters," since the San Juan, Animas, and La Plata rivers join here. Post office, 1879—.

FAULKNER (Sierra). Post office, 1893-98; mail to Hillsboro.

FAYWOOD (Grant). Small community 3 mi W of US 260, and 6 mi NE of Faywood Hot Springs. Settled in 1850 by a Dutch family. Name was a blend of the names of two lumbermen, J. C. Fay and William Lockwood, who were partners of T. C. McDermott in rebuilding the old hotel at the springs after it burned in 1890. Post office, 1901—. FAYWOOD HOT SPRINGS (Grant). 22 mi NW of Deming. Originally named HUDSON HOT SPRINGS for the owner, Col. Richard Hudson, who came to NM with the California column in 1862, later settling in Grant County. The springs were once famed for their curative

qualities. FAYWOOD STATION (Luna). On AT&SF RR, 24 mi NW of Deming.

FELIPE (Valencia). Span., "Philip." On AT&SF RR, 6 mi NW of Belen. Possessive or commemorative name from Spanish settlers.

FELIPE TAFOYA GRANT (McKinley). 13 mi NW of San Mateo along San Miguel Creek. A Felipe Tafoya became *alcalde mayor* of Santa Fe and Lieutenant General of the Kingdom in the mid-eighteenth century. He died in 1771. The grant was made by Gov. Pedro Fermin de Mendinueta to Felipe Tafoya, Diego Antonio Chaves, and Pedro Chaves on June 20, 1767. They took possession fourteen days later.

FELIX (Chaves). Spanish masculine name. Ranch community 40 mi E of Alamogordo. Post office, 1903-18. Also FELIZ (Chaves). Span., "happy." Post office, 1894-95; changed to HAGERMAN.

FENCE LAKE (Cibola). Farming and ranching community on NM 32, 25 mi NW of Quemado. Named for a large reservoir enclosed by stockmen. Most of the settlers came in 1930 and 1931, from the dust bowl. Post office, 1936—.

FENTON LAKE (Rio Arriba, Sandoval). An artificial, 30-acre lake in Jemez Mts., 21 mi N of Jemez Springs. Constructed as an integral part of the Fenton feeding and nesting area for waterfowl. Named for an early surveyor who homesteaded here.

FERNANDEZ CREEK (Taos). See RIO FERNANDEZ DE TAOS. FERNANDEZ DE TAOS (Taos). Post office, 1852-85. See TAOS.

FERRY (Valencia). Post office, 1881.

FEVERAS (Mora). 3 mi NW of Ocate and 2 mi W of NM 120. In 1849 or 1850 a carpenter named Manuel La Favre worked for Lucien B. Maxwell and lived at Rayado, 12 mi NE of this community.

FIELD (Curry). Former trading point 18 mi NE of Melrose on NM 89. Post office, 1907-24. FIELD (Socorro). On NM 52, 35 mi NW of Magdalena. Named for Nelson Field, a cattleman and former land commissioner of New Mexico, in whose home the post office was located. Post office, 1930-43.

FIERRO (Grant). Span., "iron." 6 mi NE of Bayard and 2 mi N of Hanover. Name comes from iron ore located here. Post office, 1899—.

FIFTEEN SPRINGS (Rio Arriba). 8 mi S of Hopewell. See NUMBER.

FIGUEREDO (McKinley). FIGUEREDO WASH (Mc-Kinley). NW corner of county, E of Mexican Springs. Spanish family surname.

FILLMORE (Doña Ana). Trading point on US 80 and 85, 6 mi S of Las Cruces. Named for Ft. Fillmore which occupied the site from 1851 to 1862.

FIVE DOLLAR CANYON (Colfax). 7 mi N of Dawson, extending E from near mouth of Caliente Canyon, and just NE of upper Vermejo River Canyon. Said to be named for a pioneer settler who always wanted to bet five dollars, but never had it. FIVE DOLLAR CREEK (Colfax). Flows through canyon of the same name. FIVE MILE ARROYO (Chaves). Begins N of Chaves and crosses US 285 to enter Pecos River. FIVE POINTS (Bernalillo). Suburb of Albuquerque, where five local highways converge.

FLAG MOUNTAIN (Taos). In Carson National Forest, 5 mi S of Questa.

FLAT LAKE (Eddy). 14 mi E of Espuela.

FLEMING (Grant). 9 mi NW of Silver City. Named for M. W. Fleming, early mining engineer. Post office, 1883-87.

FLORA ARROYO (Eddy). Flows E and enters Pecos River 24 mi below Carlsbad. This place name appears in at least two counties and must be descriptive of wild flowers produced by the intermittent floods in the arroyo beds. FLORA VISTA (San Juan). Ranching and farming community on US 550, 6 mi S of Aztec. Post office, 1878-80; 1884—.

FLORENCE (Eddy). Post office, 1894-1908. See LOVING.

FLORIDA (Luna). Span., "flowery." Trading point on NM 26, 14 mi NE of Deming. Established 1881 when AT&SF RR was built. Named for nearby FLORIDA MOUNTAINS. So called for the many flowers that grow on the slopes, which are watered from Cooke's Peak. First called PORTER STATION; then CUMMINGS; finally Florida. Post office, 1928-40. FLORIDA (Socorro). Small town N of Socorro. In some Spanish communities the name is associated with Pascua Florida, the customary term for Easter. Post office, 1947-55. FLORIDA LAKE (Luna). N of US 70, 7 mi E of Deming.

FLOYD (Roosevelt). On NM 88, 16 mi W of Portales. Named by its first postmaster, Simon W. Lane, who selected the name after three others had been rejected. He gave no reason for the choice and denied selecting the name for a friend. Post office, 1903—.

FLUORINE (Catron). A mineral element (calcium fluoride) found in the springs and wells has contributed this name. Post office, 1910-18; mail to Chloride.

FLYING HIGH (Chaves). Ranching community on NM 13, 42 mi NW of Artesia. Named for Flying H Ranch on Felix River. Post office, 1938—. FLYING W MOUNTAIN (Luna). Named for brand of Flying W Ranch in Cedar Mts.

FOLSOM (Union). Cattle-shipping and ranching community at junction of NM 72 and NM 325, 6 mi E of Colfax County line. Named for President Cleveland's wife Frances Folsom. Post office, 1888—. Name has become associated with a culture period in the history of human life in the Southwest. Chipped stone darts of unique shape, dating from the time when men hunted the giant ground sloth and the mammoth, have been found in the Capulin-Folsom region. These spearheads indicate the existence of a human race here some 15,000 years ago. FOLSOM CAVES (Colfax). On Robinson Peak, SW of Folsom. Contain stalactites of smooth red lava.

FORD (Quay). Post office, 1907-10; mail to House.

FORREST (Quay). Farming and ranching community on NM 18, 36 mi S of Tucumcari. Named for Forrest Farr, son of first postmaster and storekeeper, Watt Farr, who moved here from Missouri with his family in 1907. When a new school building was constructed in 1928, Forrest was moved 1 mi N of its first location. Neighboring communities, including Plain, Stockton, Kirk, and Frio were started in the early days, but only Forrest survived. Post office, 1908-19; 1932—.

FORT BARCLAY (Mora). 2 mi N of Watrous. Not a government fort, but a forage camp, often referred to as a fort. The large, square enclosure, with high adobe walls and a heavy gate that could be locked, was used as a camping place for pioneers and wagon trains. The stockade furnished protection from Indian raids. Post office, 1851-54, under name of BARCLAY'S FORT.

FORT BASCOM (Quay). In a horseshoe bend on S side of Canadian River, 12 mi N of Tucumcari. Established in 1863 under the direction of Brig. Gen. James H. Carleton, then acting commander of the Military Department of New Mexico. Built on land leased from the owners of old Pablo Montoya

Grant. Named to perpetuate the memory of gallant Capt. George N. Bascom, 16th U.S. Infantry, who fell at the Battle of Valverde on Feb. 27, 1862. Ft. Bascom was abandoned by the military in 1870, the land reverting to the owner, John S. Watts, from whom the government had leased the site. The soldiers were moved to Ft. Union. Post office, 1874-92; changed to JOHNSON.

FORT BASSETT (San Miguel). U.S. Army Cavalry Post, established at Mesa Rica, 51 mi NW of Tucumcari, as protection against Indian raids.

FORT BAYARD (Grant). 10 mi E of Silver City. Began when a troop of cavalry, operating in southern NM, camped at a spring among the foothills in this area in 1863. A regular garrison did not arrive until August 1866, and later in that year the post was established. Named in honor of Gen. G. D. Bayard, who served on the frontier with 1st Cavalry and was badly wounded in engagement with Kiowa Indians. General Bayard died in the battle at Fredericksburg, Va. Ft. Bayard was active as a post until 1899. Then it became an Army hospital for tuberculars. After 1920, the facilities were used by U.S. Public Health Service and the Veterans' Administration. In 1965, hospital came to New Mexico Department of Public Welfare to care for chronic-disease patients. Post office, 1867—. See BAYARD.

FORT CONRAD. See FORT CRAIG.

FORT CRAIG (Socorro). On W side of the Rio Grande, 35 mi S of Socorro and E of US 85. Originally called FORT CONRAD, when the post was first built by Col. E. V. Sumner in 1851 to protect the lower Rio Grande Valley. In 1854, the troops moved S to Ft. Craig on W side of the river. In August 1861, after conventions had been held in the previous two years at Mesilla and Tucson, southern NM and southern Arizona were proclaimed the Territory of Arizona under the Confederate States of America. An army of Texans under Gen. H. H. Sibley moved N toward Santa Fe in February 1862. At Valverde, they met General Canby with 3,800 men from the fort. After an all-day battle, the Confederates triumphed and the Union soldiers retreated to Ft. Craig. This was the first battle of the Civil War in NM. Sibley captured Albuquerque and Santa Fe without a fight at either place. He then moved on to take Ft. Union. The fall of Ft. Union would have carried the Southern armies into

Colorado and would have forced the North to send forces westward which were needed east of the Mississippi. This was not to be. Col. E. R. S. Canby, head of the Military Department of New Mexico, had asked for help, and on March 27 and 28 the Colorado Volunteers re-enforced the troops from Ft. Union for a decisive battle in Apache Canyon near Glorieta, 18 mi SE of Santa Fe. Although the Confederate soldiers drove the Union forces back, a detachment of soldiers guided by Col. Manuel Chaves of the New Mexico Volunteers crossed a difficult mountain trail and fell on the supply camp of Sibley's men, destroying wagons, mules, and cannon. General Sibley retreated down the Rio Grande and, after a few more skirmishes, pulled back into Texas. Ft. Craig, like Ft. Fillmore and Ft. Union, had seen the rise and fall of the Confederacy in New Mexico. Post office, 1855-79.

FORT CUMMINGS (Luna). Near the entrance of Cooke's Canyon at Cooke's Spring, 6 mi NW of Florida. Designed by Gen. George B. McClellan with a high wall of adobe entirely enclosing the barracks and headquarters, it was built near a stagecoach station of the Butterfield Overland Mail in 1863 to protect mail carriers, emigrant trains, and freighters from the bands of Apaches. Named for Maj. Joseph Cummings; permanently abandoned in 1891. Post office, 1866-87; 1890-91.

FORT FAUNTLEROY (McKinley). See FORT WINGATE.

FORT FILLMORE (Doña Ana). 6 mi S of Las Cruces on US 85 and 1 mi E of Brazito. Established Sept. 23, 1851, by Col. E. V. Sumner, commander of the Military Department of the Territory. Named for President Millard Fillmore. The fort was built for the protection of early-day travelers. It was abandoned in 1862. Now a trading point and farm community. Post office, 1852-63. See BRAZITO.

FORT FLOYD (Grant). See FORT WEBSTER.

FORT LYON (McKinley). See FORT WINGATE.

FORT MARCY (Santa Fe). First U.S. Army Post in NM. Building started on Aug. 23, 1846, soon after General Kearny occupied Santa Fe. Fort was abandoned in 1897. Named for Capt. R. B. Marcy, discoverer of the headwaters of the Canadian River, and author of *The Prairie Traveller* (1861).

FORT McLANE (Grant). See FORT WEBSTER.

FORT SELDEN (Doña Ana). Ruins of fort are 15 mi N of Las Cruces near US 85, and 9 mi N of Doña Ana, on E bank of the Rio Grande. There were garrisons here from 1865 until April 1879. Name honors Col. Henry R. Selden, 1st New Mexico Infantry and one time captain of the 5th U.S. Infantry. Post office, 1866, intermittently, to 1923; changed to LEASBURG. FORT SELDEN SPRINGS (Doña Ana). See RADIUM SPRINGS.

FORT STANTON (Lincoln). 4 mi SE of Capitan. Formerly a military reservation established in 1855 (although a treaty for use of the land was made with the Mescalero Apaches in 1852). Named for Capt. Henry W. Stanton, who lost his life in a battle with Indians in the Sacramento Mts. on Jan. 19, 1855. After 1896 the Army turned the buildings and site over to the U.S. Public Health Service, which established the Fort Stanton Marine Hospital for the treatment of members of the U.S. merchant marine who were suffering from tuberculosis. While it was still a military post in the 1880's General Pershing (then a lieutenant) was stationed here. In 1953, the federal government turned the area around the fort back to the state for use as a hospital, and a year or so later the federal government reclaimed the land for the Department of the Interior, permitting the state health department to continue the use of the buildings as a hospital. Post office, 1857-63. FORT STANTON CAVE (Lincoln). 1 mi SE of Ft. Stanton and about 5 mi SE of Capitan.

FORT SUMNER (De Baca). On US 60, NM 20, and AT&SF RR. Center of an irrigation district and headquarters for construction of Alamogordo Dam. Named for the fort which was established in 1862 by General Carleton, and which honored Gen. Edmond Vose Sumner, commander of the 9th Military District. Post office, 1866, intermittently, to present.

FORT THORNE (Doña Ana). At upper end of Mesilla Valley on W bank of the Rio Grande; N of present community of Hatch and W of Salem. Established in 1853 by Col. E. V. Sumner and abandoned in 1859. Named by W. H. Emory in honor of Capt. Herman Thorne. Post office, 1855-59.

FORT TULAROSA (Catron). See ARAGON.

FORT UNION (Mora). Ruins of an abandoned, dismantled U.S. fort, on NM 477, 8 mi N of Watrous. The mile-square, open post without stockade was built in 1851 by Col. Edmond Vose Sumner and was used by soldiers, officers, and their families throughout the Indian wars and the Civil War. The fort was an important commercial center as well as a strategic military post. Finally abandoned in 1890. In 1956 Fort Union became a national monument. Post office, 1851-91. FORT UNION MILITARY RESERVE (Mora). Includes the W two-thirds of Turkey Mt., a tract of about 7 by 9 mi, and also flats SW of the mountains and around old Ft. Union, a tract about 3 by 6 mi.

FORT WEBSTER (Grant). Built 15 mi S of Santa Rita copper mines in 1851 to control the southwestern Apaches and offer protection to the Boundary Commission. According to Army records, the fort was renamed FORT FLOYD in the same year and FORT McLANE in the next, and abandoned in 1861. The site was later named UPPER MIMBRES, then TEEL, and finally returned to an earlier name in the area, SAN LORENZO.

FORT WEST (Grant). Reported in 1862 at intersection of Gila and Mangas rivers.

FORT WINGATE (McKinley). Mining, ranching community, and site of the fort, S of US 66, 12 mi SE of Gallup, and 3 mi S of Wingate Station. In 1850 the U.S. War Department established a fort at Cebolleta, N of Laguna, naming it for Capt. Benjamin Wingate. In 1862 Captain Wingate was killed at the Battle of Valverde. In this same year the fort was moved to EL GALLO SPRING (OJO DEL GALLO) 3 mi S of Grants, where Kit Carson made it his headquarters when he rounded up the Navajos. In 1868 the fort moved again, this time to its present site, which was then called BIG BEAR SPRING (OJO DEL OSO). Here there was already a military establishment called FORT FAUNTLEROY, founded in 1860 by Col. Thomas T. Fauntleroy and named for himself. In 1866 the name had been changed to FORT LYON, after Colonel Fauntleroy had resigned his command and joined the Confederacy some years before. In 1868 the two forts were consolidated. Today the FORT WINGATE MILITARY RESERVATION still has storage plants for explosives, but most of the area (64,000 acres) is used as Indian grazing land. Near the highway is a school for Navajos, established after 1925, with dormitories and recreation areas. Post office, 1874—.

FORTY-NINER RIDGE (Eddy). 32 mi E of Carlsbad.

FOSSIL BEDS (San Juan). In San Juan Basin at Four Corners area, locality of well-known Paleocene formations, the Puerco and the Torrejon, with their unique fossil mammals.

FOSTER (Hidalgo). On SP RR, 23 mi NW of Lordsburg.

FOUR CORNERS (San Juan). Here is the only place in the U.S. where citizens from four states, each standing in his own state, can shake hands. In 1949 the governors of Utah, Colorado, Arizona, and NM held a luncheon each sitting in his own state, passing food to his neighbor, using the western theory that once you have broken bread together, the bonds of friendly understanding are strengthened for the working out of mutual problems.

FOUR MILE DRAW (Eddy). Enters Lake McMillan 12 mi S of Artesia, 4 mi N of Lakewood. FOURMILE WELLS (Grant). 4 mi SW of Hachita. See NUMBERS.

FOURTH OF JULY CANYON (Taos). On Colfax border, 5 mi SE of settlement of Red River. FOURTH OF JULY SPRINGS (Torrance). 6 mi NW of Tajique, recreation area known for a rare stand of maple trees.

Fox (San Miguel). On AT&SF RR, 10 mi NE of Lamy. Named for F. C. Fox, general manager of the railroad. Fox MOUNTAIN (Catron). 12 mi NE of Spur Lake.

FRA, also FRAY, CRISTOBAL (Sierra). Mountain range along E bank of the Rio Grande, parallel with the Jornada del Muerto. Named for one of the pioneer Franciscans, Fray Cristobal de Salazar, Oñate's cousin and *sargento mayor,* who died in 1599 on his way back to Mexico, where he went to seek re-enforcements. It is said that a peak at the end of the range resembles the hand and face of an old friar. In the seventeenth century, a military post and stopover about 40 mi S of Socorro was known by this name. The proper Spanish form is *Fray* though *Fra* seems to be chosen by many cartographers.

FRALEY (Socorro). Post office, 1893-96; mail to San Antonio.

FRAMPTON (Colfax). Post office, 1892; mail to Clapham.

FRANCES CREEK (Rio Arriba). Estuary of San Juan River between Archuleta and Rosa, 30 mi W of Bloomfield.

FRANKLIN (Colfax). 9 mi SE of Springer. Post office, 1876-79. FRANKLIN MOUNTAINS (Doña Ana). Small range extending N and S 4 mi E of Berino.

FRAY CRISTOBAL (Sierra). See FRA CRISTOBAL; also PARAJE DE FRAY CRISTOBAL.

FRAZER MOUTAIN (Taos). 1 mi SE of Twining. Named for William Frazer, who organized the Frazer Mountain Copper Co. in 1895. See TWINING.

FRAZIER (Chaves). On US 70 and AT&SF RR, 20 mi NE of Roswell. Post office, 1937-54.

FRENCH (Colfax). Trading point on US 85, 9 mi N of Springer. Named for Capt. William French, who came to America in 1883 from French Park, Ireland. He owned the W-S (William Slaughter) Ranch, first in Grant County; when it moved to Cimarron, he organized the French Tract, a group of farms with French as a center. Because of litigation over water rights, the plan failed and little remains today of the farms and town. French was the author of *Recollections of a Western Ranchman, 1883-1889* (1927). Post office, 1908-45. FRENCH LAKE (Colfax). 7 mi E of Cimarron. See FRENCH.

FRESNAL (Otero). Span., "ash tree." Community in Doña Ana County until the creation of Otero County in 1899. Post office, 1894-1901; changed to HIGHROLLS. FRESNAL CANYON (Otero). In W side of Sacramento Mts., between High Rolls and Cloudcroft. First settlers came in the 1870's and established an agricultural center with orchards and truck gardens. FRESNAL CREEK (Otero). Runs W through Fresnal Canyon and, with La Luz Creek, drains 75 sq mi. First gristmill in county was built on this creek about 1887 by a French-Canadian named William Ostic. Location was near present site of High Rolls and made use of creek water for power.

FRIJOLES (Sandoval). Span., "beans." Trading point 15 mi NE of Peña Blanca. Named for chief crop in area. FRIJOLES CANYON, LOWER (Sandoval). Its small stream flows through the canyon into Bandelier National Monument and empties over high falls into the Rio Grande. FRIJOLES CANYON, UPPER (Los Alamos). Source for headwaters of the stream entering Bandelier National Monument. FRIJOLES CREEK (Mora, Taos). Rises on border of the two counties and flows NW into the Rito de la Olla.

FRIO (Quay). Community shown on 1936 map 3 mi NW of Forrest. Post office, 1919-22. See FORREST.

FRISCO. Popular shortening of San Francisco, "St. Francis." FRISCO (Catron). Small farming and cattle-ranching community 4 mi S of Reserve; on Tularosa River, which is used for irrigation. Scene of the famous fight when Elfego Baca stood off a crowd of Texas cowboys, variously estimated at from thirty to eighty in number. Imprisoned in an adobe hut, he shot it out with his attackers for 33 hours, killing one of his foes and wounding several others. He emerged unscathed. Post office, 1885-1914. FRISCO UPPER PLAZA (Catron). See RESERVE.

FROST (Quay). Post office, 1909-10; mail to Porter. FROST (Bernalillo). Farming community 1 mi E of San Antonito; named for early settler. FROST ARROYO (Bernalillo). Flows E from slopes of Sandia Mts. past San Antonito into Santa Fe County.

FRUITLAND (San Juan). On US 550, 10 mi W of Farmington. Once called OLIO. *Olio* may come from Spanish *olla podrida,* "pot, stew, hotchpotch," or from English for a musical medley. For many years the post office of Olio, with John Moss as postmaster, served the valley. In 1881 a small Mormon colony came to this section to join the few other settlers already located here. The place was called BURNHAM by many, in honor of the Mormon bishop, Luther C. Burnham. Bishop Burnham and John R. Young, first postmaster, became interested in growing fruit. Post office, 1891—.

FRYING PAN CANYON (Catron). Rises in Kelly Mts., flows S and W into San Francisco River.

FULLERTON (Catron). An old ranching settlement on S side of St. Augustine Plains, 61 mi SW of Magdalena. FULLERTON (Grant). Post office, 1882-83; mail to Gage.

FULTON (San Miguel). Post office, 1888-94; 1895-1911; mail to Ribera.

G ABALDON (San Miguel). Named for Juan Miguel Gabaldon, an early settler, who came from Puebla, Mexico, before 1737 and first settled in Santa Fe. Some of his children moved into the Rio Abajo area. Post office, 1941—. A village in Valencia County is called Los GABALDONES. Span., "the Gabaldon folks." GABALDON GRANT (Santa Fe). NE of Santa Fe and W of Tesuque, bisected by Tesuque Creek. Granted to Juan de Gabaldon on June 7, 1752, by Governor Cachupin.

GABILAN. (Rio Arriba). See GAVILAN.

GAGE (Luna). On US 70, 80, and SP RR, 20 mi W of Deming. Settled in 1880 and named for a construction engineer on SP RR. Post office, 1882-89; 1894—.

GALENA (Lincoln). 10 mi SE of Carrizozo on NM 37. Named for lead ore in vicinity. First called DRY GULCH. Post office, 1880-82; changed to NOGAL.

GALESTENA CANYON (McKinley). On Zuñi Indian Reservation 5 mi SE of Zuñi Pueblo. Name may be a Spanish family surname.

GALISTEO (Santa Fe). Originally an Indian Pueblo 22 mi S of Santa Fe. First mentioned by the Fray Rodriguez exploration party in 1581. Governor Oñate reports that he changed the name to SANTA ANA, which has not survived. Name is an old term for a native of Galicia, but it may have been transferred from a town in Estremadura in Spain. Galisteo became the seat of a Franciscan mission established between 1617 and 1629. In the Pueblo Revolt, the Indians killed the resident priest, the father custodian, and other missionaries. The name appears as "Galisto" on L'Atlas Curieux (1700). In 1706 the community was re-established at Galisteo by Gov. Cuervo y Valdez. Between 1782 and 1794 the inhabitants moved to Santo Domingo to escape the Comanche raids. Post office, 1876-1959. GALISTEO CREEK (Sandoval). Flows into the Rio Grande 2 mi N of Santo Domingo Pueblo. GALISTEO CREEK (Santa Fe). Rises near Lamy and flows W into the Rio Grande near Santo Domingo Pueblo. GALISTEO GRANT (Santa Fe). Present maps show a tract about 1 mi square, just S of Galisteo. A land grant is recorded in 1814 and then confirmed in 1861 to Ignacio Chavez and others. GALISTEO LAKE (Santa Fe). 1½ mi S of Galisteo. GALISTEO RIVER (Santa Fe). See GALISTEO CREEK.

GALLEGO. Span., "Galician." In the plural form, Gallegos is a proper name dating back to the earliest Spanish colonists in NM. GALLEGO CREEK (Valencia, Socorro). Rises in Valencia and flows S entering the Rio Salado 10 mi W of Puertecito. GALLEGOS (Harding). Farming and stock-raising community, 2 mi E of Ute Creek in S part of county, on NM 39. Established in 1840 by Don Jesus Maria Gallegos. Post office, 1884, intermittently, to 1955. GALLEGOS (Rio Arriba). 8 mi S of Coyote, near the Rito Seco. GALLEGOS SPRING (Rio Arriba). 5 mi SE of Costilla. GALLEGOS (San Miguel). 18 mi SW of Las Vegas. GALLEGOS (Torrance). In NW part of county, 9 mi W of Moriarty. GALLEGOS CANYON (San Juan). Flows N into San Juan River, 3 mi SE of Farmington. GALLEGOS CANYON (Torrance). Called CAÑON GALLEGOS. Runs NE and SW near settlement of Gallegos. GALLEGOS

LAKE (Mora). 5 mi SW of Wagon Mound just E of AT&SF RR.

GALLINA. Span., "hen." Although *gallina* means "hen or chicken," the wild turkey that is called *pavo* in Spain and *guajalote* in Mexico, goes by the name of *gallina de la tierra* in NM, "chicken of the region." The name appears in a number of places in the state since prairie chickens, pheasants, and other wildfowl may be described. GALLINA (Rio Arriba). 12 mi SE of Lindrith, on NM 96. Settled in 1818 by Antonio Ortiz. Post office, 1890—. GALLINA MESA (Valencia). GALLINA PEAK (Rio Arriba). 7 mi S of El Vado in Santa Fe National Forest. GALLINA PLAZA (Rio Arriba). 2 mi W of Capulin. GALLINAS (Lincoln). Ranger station in Lincoln National Forest, on US 54, 8 mi SW of Corona. Established in 1901 as a water stop for EP&NE RR; later used by SP RR. Named for Gallinas Mts. GALLINAS (Mora). 3 mi NW of Ocate near Colfax County line. GALLINAS (San Miguel). On Gallinas River, 10 mi NW of Las Vegas. GALLINAS MOUNTAINS (Socorro). In Cibola National Forest, 20 mi NW of Magdalena. Named for the waterfowl here. Tewa word for the mountain was *ndee peeng ya,* "turkey mountain." GALLINAS PEAK (Lincoln). In Lincoln National Forest, 1 mi from Torrance County line. GALLINAS RIVER (Rio Arriba). See RIO GALLINAS. GALLINAS RIVER (San Miguel). Formed by various streams NW of Las Vegas, including Beaver and Hollinger creeks; flows SE to join Pecos River in Guadalupe County, 6 mi NW of Colonias. Folklore tells how the stream originated as a teardrop from the "eye" in the rock face of "Big Mike," a peak in San Miguel Mts. GALLINAS SPRING (San Miguel). Post office, 1874-1906; mail to Chaperito. GALLINEROS (Santa Fe). Span., "chicken houses." Named for a nearby mesa of that shape. GALLINEROS MESA (Santa Fe).

GALLO ARROYO (Lincoln). Span., "rooster, cock." GALLO LAKE (Catron). 10 mi NW of Aragon. GALLO MOUNTAINS (Catron). Part of Apache National Forest, in west-central part of county. GALLO PEAK (Catron). 12 mi NW of Aragon. GALLO SPRING (Catron). 11 mi NW of Aragon.

GALLUP (McKinley). In west-central part of county on US 66 and AT&SF RR. Railroad, commercial, and mining center. Founded in 1881 and incorporated in 1891. Old-timers say that the railroad workers would announce that they were "going to Gallup's," meaning it was pay day and they were going to collect from David L. Gallup. He was auditor and paymaster for A&P RR, and then became comptroller in the New York office. The A&P RR was later purchased by the AT&SF RR. Gallup is famed for its Inter-Tribal Indian Ceremonial held annually in late summer. Post office, 1882—. GALLUP TWO WELLS AREA (McKinley). See TWO GREY HILLS.

GAMERCO (McKinley). Coal-mining settlement on US 66, 2 mi N of Gallup. Established in 1920 and named by combining syllables from Gallup American Coal Co. Post office, 1923—.

GARCIA. Alvaro Garcia Holgado, the earliest Garcia of record in NM, came in the Oñate period, and between 1598 and 1692 other Garcias came from Zacatecas, Mexico City, and Puebla. A cluster of these families NW of Belen gave the name Los Garcias, "the Garcia folks," to the settlement in Valencia County; now NORTH and SOUTH GARCIA. GARCIA (Mora). First postmaster, Placida R. de Garcia, Post office, 1892-98; mail to Beenham. GARCIA (Union). First postmaster, Lino Garcia. Post office, 1904-09; mail to Barney. GARCIA FALLS CANYON (Socorro). GARCIAS LATERAL (Valencia). Large irrigation ditch S of Belen.

GARDINER (Colfax). Coal-mining camp 3 mi W of Raton in Dillon Canyon. Owned in 1897 by the St. Louis, Rocky Mountain and Pacific Coal Co. The Gardiner-Swastika branch of the AT&SF RR extended from Dillon to the camp to take out coal. Post office, 1897-1940. GARDINER CANYON (Colfax). Runs W from mouth of Dillon Canyon, starting about 3 mi SW of Raton.

GARFIELD (Doña Ana). On US 85, 10 mi NW of Hatch. Post office, 1896—. GARFIELD MONUMENT (Rio Arriba).

GARITA (San Miguel). 48 mi SE of Las Vegas, 16 mi W of Gate City. Established in 1885 and named by cattlemen who used the town as a trading post. Post office, 1918—. The Spanish word may mean everything from "watchtower" to "jail." If it were *garito,* it could mean "gambling house." The *garito* at Nogales, Ariz., is the passenger gate at the U.S. Customs Office. As *garrita,* it means a "small rag" or perhaps remnant of land left over from a larger whole. In medieval literature *Garita* was an allusive name for a mythical city at the western edge of the world where the sun goes down, usually identified with Cadiz, Spain.

GARRAPATA CANYON, CREEK (Taos). Span., "sheep and cattle tick." 3 mi N of San Cristobal; near NM 3 on the way to Questa.

GARRISON (Roosevelt). 29 mi S of Portales and about 5 mi SW of Causey. Post office called LEACH, 1909-11; changed to Garrison for the postmaster, Joel J. Garrison, who served from 1911 to 1919.

GARY (Hidalgo). Siding on SP RR, 7 mi SW of Lordsburg.

GASCON (Mora). In sheep-raising district, 10 mi SW of Mora. Name means native of Gascony, France. Post office, 1898-1901; 1905, intermittently, to 1930. GASCON CREEK (Mora). Flows past Gascon above Rociada.

GATE CITY (San Miguel). Trading point on NM 129, 17 mi N of Newkirk and 4 mi S of Conchas Reservoir.

GATLIN LAKE (Catron). In W part of county, 6 mi NW of Fox Mtn. Named for a prominent ranching family.

GATO (Colfax). Span., "cat," perhaps, "wildcat, mountain lion." On AT&SF RR, 3 mi S of French. Formerly called DOVER.

GAVILAN. Span., "sparrow hawk." The term in NM is applied to all sorts of hawks or falcons except eagles; the NM spelling is often *gabilán*. GAVILAN (Rio Arriba). On NM 95, 6 mi N of Lindrith. Post office, 1929-46. GAVILAN CREEK (Rio Arriba). Tributary to the Rio Brazos, 6 mi W of Hopewell. GAVILAN LAKE (Rio Arriba). 3 mi SW of Gavilan.

GEM COMMUNITY (Union). Between Bible Top Mtn. on E and Mt. Dora on W, and US 87 and Seneca Creek on N and S. Named for George E. Merrilatt, one of the first homesteaders, whose initials spell "Gem." Settled about 1914 and 1915, it was once a thickly settled dry-farming community, but now is owned by a few cattlemen.

GENOVA (Union, Harding). Shown on 1895 map 10 mi SE of Gallegos, in present Harding County. Post office, 1884-98; mail to Gallegos; 1904-05; mail to Logan.

GEORGETOWN (Grant). 18 mi NE of Silver City, 3 mi W of Mimbres. Silver-mining town which flourished from 1876 to 1886. Two disasters destroyed its prosperity: smallpox drove out many of the families and the price of silver fell. Named for George Magruder, one of the first residents, who came from Georgetown, D.C., which was his birthplace. Magruder and his brother, John R., moved

from Georgetown, D.C., to Grant County in 1872. Post office, 1875-1903.

GERONIMO (San Miguel). Span., "Jerome." Post office, 1896-1902. See MINERAL HILL. GERONIMO PEAK (Sierra). Anglicized Spanish. In Caballo Mts. where ruins of an old fort mark the U.S. Army campaign against the Apaches. Named for the famous Apache chief, Geronimo, 1829(?)—1904, who led the Chiricahua Apaches from their reservation in Arizona between 1881 and 1886, raiding ranches and settlements in NM and Arizona. He surrendered in Mexico to U.S. troops who had pursued him there under three different commanders. GERONIMO LOOKOUT (Sierra). N and W of Kingston and Santa Rita.

GIBSON (McKinley). In 1890 a mining community 3 mi N of Gallup. Named for a coal mine official. Post office, 1890-1947.

GIGANTES. Span., "giants." Name given by the Spanish to two mesas associated by the Indians with supernatural powers. GIGANTES (Santa Fe). On top of Buckman Mesa, near San Ildefonso where the most famous of the giants was *Tsahveeyo*, associated with Black Mesa at San Ildefonso and elsewhere. MESA GIGANTE (Valencia). N of the AT&SF RR and US 66 at Laguna.

GILA (Grant). Mining community on NM 211, 22 mi NW of Silver City. Named for tribe of NM Indians; possibly the Spanish spelling of Apache word for mountain, *tsihl* or *dzihl:* analogous to Nahuatl and Mexican-Spanish interchanges of *tz, x, s,* and *j.* Benavides in 1634 refers to the "Apaches de Xila." Post office, 1875, intermittently, to present. GILA CLIFF DWELLINGS NATIONAL MONUMENT (Catron). Created Nov. 16, 1907. Three groups of small prehistoric dwellings in this primitive area 30 mi N of Silver City, are accessible by auto. GILA HOT SPRINGS (Grant). Just S of Catron County line, on Middle Fork of Gila River. GILA NATIONAL FOREST (Grant, Hidalgo). Composed of areas originally established as Datil and Gila Forests on Mar. 2, 1899, and the Big Burros Forest on Feb. 6, 1907. These areas were combined on Dec. 4, 1931, and now extend over 2,458,505 acres. GILA RIVER (Grant). Rises in Black Mts. in SW part of state; flows SW, crosses Arizona and joins the Colorado at Yuma. Named for the old Gila Indian Pueblo. GILA RIVER, LOWER (Grant). N of Cliff and extends from about 3 mi below the box canyon to junction of middle and west fork. GILA RIVER, MID-

DLE FORK (Grant). GILA RIVER, WEST FORK (Grant). GILITA CREEK (Catron). 5 mi S of Negrito. GILITA CREEK (Grant). At head of Middle Fork of the Gila.

GILLESPIE (Colfax). GILLESPIE (De Baca). Siding, switch, and section house for AT&SF RR. Named for Powers Gillespie, a resident of Yeso Creek at time of construction of the railroad through De Baca County. GILLESPIE CREEK (Hidalgo). Flows E from the Continental Divide 20 mi NE of Cloverdale. GILLESPIE PEAK (Hidalgo). At N edge of Coronado National Forest, 22 mi S of Antelope.

GISE (San Miguel). On AT&SF RR, 25 mi E of Lamy. Named for C. C. Gise, who was connected with Brown Manzanares Wholesale Co.

GIVENS (Roosevelt). Community 3 mi NE of Inez. First postmaster, Joel E. Givens, 1908-13; mail to Arch.

GLADIOLA (Lea). Ranching and farming community on US 380, 24 mi NE of Lovington, 8 mi E of Tatum. Originally called WARREN. Post office, 1929-57.

GLADSTONE (Union). Farming and ranching community on NM 58, 36 mi E of Springer, near Colfax County line. Founded about 1880 by William Harris, and said to have been named for the English statesman, W. E. Gladstone, whom Harris knew. The original inhabitants were from Texas, Oklahoma, and Kansas. Post office, 1888—.

GLASSCOCK (Eddy). In Guadalupe Mts., 20 mi S of Hope. Named for Lee Glasscock, owner of a sheep ranch here.

GLEASON CANYON (Union). On Cross Ell Ranch, about 24 mi NE of Raton. A prong of Cimarron Canyon, the mouth of which is not far from US 64. Named for Fritz Gleason, who came here in the later 1860's bringing a herd of cattle. GLEASON SPRINGS (Union). On the Cross Ell Ranch.

GLEN (Chaves). Post office, 1899-1908; mail to Sunnyside.

GLENCOE (Lincoln). Farming, ranching, and fruit-growing community in Ruidoso Valley, on US 70, 30 mi SE of Carrizozo. Named for Mrs. Frank B. Coe when the family settled here in 1880. First postmaster, Jasper N. Coe. Post office, 1901—.

GLENRIO (Quay). English "glen," plus Spanish rio, "river." One of the rare combinations of English and Spanish to create a place name blend. On US 66, 41 mi E of Tucumcari on Texas line. Founded in 1903, when CRI&P RR was built here. Post office, 1916—.

GLENWOOD (Catron). Mining and ranching community on US 260, 3 mi N of Pleasanton. Fauster and Diming built the first house in 1878. When Allen Bush settled here, the name was BUSH RANCH; then later the place was called WHITE WATER. At one time it was known as GLENWOOD SPRINGS, a former stage stop during the days of the Apache raids in the Mogollon area. Mrs. Sarah Kitt chose the name Glenwood in 1901. Post office, 1906—.

GLOBE (Eddy). Former community 12 mi NW of Carlsbad on AT&SF RR between Avalon and McMillan dams. Named for the Globe Mills and Mining Co., which mined gypsum and made it into plasterboard, operating here from 1915 to 1923. Globe had a post office during this period.

GLORIETA. Span., "bower, arbor." A common term in Mexico for a small square or gathering place surrounded by trees and other vegetation. It is also used for an intersection of a street or road. GLORIETA (Santa Fe). 18 mi SE of Santa Fe, on US 84 and 85. Founded in 1879 when the old A&P RR was under construction. Post office, 1880—. GLORIETA PASS (Santa Fe). A gateway through the Sangre de Cristo Mts. to Santa Fe. Here on Mar. 8, 1862, a Union force under the command of Maj. John M. Chivington defeated Confederate troops in an action which was decisive to the Southern cause in NM.

GOAT SPRING (Lincoln). Near the foot of Tucson Mts. GOAT SPRINGS (Catron). 8 mi E of Arizona line and 15 mi N of US 60.

GOBERNADOR. Span., "governor," also the name of a plant native to the dry sections of northern Mexico, la gobernadora (Zygophillum tridentatum). This shrub, rather than a Spanish governor, may be responsible for the place name. GOBERNADOR (Rio Arriba). Farming and ranching community on NM 17, 36 mi E of Aztec. Established as a mining camp in 1875. Post office, 1916-42. GOBERNADOR CREEK (Rio Arriba, San Juan). Rises in Carson National Forest; flows NW across county line into San Juan River.

GODFREY HILLS (Lincoln). Grazing land in SW part of county, SE of Oscura. Named for a government Indian agent of the 1870's.

GOEBELS (Socorro). General store established by Barney Goebels in 1902 to serve nearby cattle ranchers.

GOLD CANYON (Valencia). In Zuñi Mts., NW of Grants. GOLD DUST (Sierra). A one-time thriving gold-mining center; now a ghost town on NM 180, 29 mi SW of Truth or Consequences. GOLD GRADE (Torrance). Post office, 1907; mail to Willard. GOLD GULCH (Grant). 24 mi SW of Silver City in Big Burro Mts., running SE to NW. Noted for placer mining from early days to the present. GOLD HILL (Hidalgo). 41 mi SW of Silver City in Gila Forest. Named for a very rich deposit of gold in the mountains. Post office, 1886-1906; mail to Lordsburg. GOLD HILL (Taos). 10 mi SE of Questa in Carson National Forest. GOLD CANYON (Valencia). In Zuñi Mts., NW of Grants.

GOLDEN (Santa Fe). Trading point on NM 10, 33 mi NE of Albuquerque and 16 mi SW of Cerrillos. Founded in 1879 and so named because it was in the center of a gold-mining district. Placer gold was discovered in 1839 on Tuerto Creek, named for a spur of San Pedro Mts. A town named TUERTO was N of present Golden, and a settlement named REAL DE SAN FRANCISCO previously occupied the same site as Golden. Post office, 1880-1928.

GOLDENBURG CANYON (Doña Ana). In San Andres Mts. near a military road that crossed the mountains. Named for two brothers who built a trading post and saloon here about 1880.

GOLONDRINA CREEK (Otero). Span., "swallow." See THREE RIVERS. GOLONDRINAS (Mora). 18 mi N of Las Vegas. GOLONDRINAS (San Miguel).

GOMEZ PEAK (Grant). A Francisco Gomez came to New Mexico in 1598, but his male descendants left in 1680 and seem not to have returned. Early in the eighteenth century, a family named Gomez del Castillo held a homestead near San Ildefonso. The name is widely known in later periods.

GONZALES. A well-known Spanish surname which appears among the settlers with De Vargas in 1692 and in early records after that time. GONZALES (McKinley). Former trading point on US 66, 20 mi SE of Gallup. GONZALES (San Miguel). Post office, 1904-13; name changed to MAES. GONZALES CANYON (Colfax). In extreme NW corner of county; extends N and S from Vermejo Canyon to Colorado line. GONZALES LAKE (McKinley). 3 mi W of Thoreau. GONZALES MESA (Colfax). 12 mi W of Springer in Maxwell Land Grant. GONZALES RANCH (San Miguel). Settlement 4 mi S of Rowe, 6 mi W of Ilfeld. Post office, 1953—. GONZALES SPRING (Lincoln). On top of Tucson Mts. GONZALITOS (Sandoval).

GOOD HOPE (Rio Arriba). Post office, 1884-87; mail to Tres Piedras.

GOODSIGHT MOUNTAINS (Luna). 24 mi NE of Deming.

GOOSE CREEK (Taos). Small tributary to Red River 3 mi SW of town of Red River. GOOSE LAKE (Taos). At head of Goose Creek. Both creek and lake are named for wildfowl abundant in area.

GOOSEBERRY SPRING (Cibola). In San Mateo Mts.

GOTERA (Quay). Span., "leakage, drip, gutter." GOTERA DE GUIDOI GRANT (Santa Fe). Tract consisting of about 1,800 acres, which was N of Ortiz Mine Grant and crossed by Galisteo Arroyo. Granted to seven persons by Territorial Deputation of New Mexico in name of the Mexican nation in 1830.

GOULD (Union). Post office, 1906-08; mail to Mosquero.

GRADE (Hidalgo). On NM 9, and SP RR, 15 mi E of Animas.

GRADY (Curry). On NM 18 and 39, 29 mi N of Clovis. Founded on Dec. 13, 1906. A dugout served as a shelter for the first people who came here to file on land. Named for Mrs. Pearl B. Grady, former postmaster, who owned much of the land where the community was established. Post office, 1907—.

GRAFTON (Sierra). Mining camp in the 1880's and 1890's, 7 mi NW of Chloride. Post office, 1881-1904; mail to Phillipsburg.

GRAHAM (Socorro). A man named Graham was superintendent of the Confidence mine at Mogollon. Post office, 1895-1904; changed to CLEAR CREEK.

GRAMA (Doña Ana). On AT&SF RR, 11 mi NE of Hatch. Named for a pasture grass, called by the Spanish grama (genus Boutelona). GRAMA FLAT (De Baca). See WHITE FLAT.

GRANADA (Doña Ana). Post office, 1896-98; mail to Mesilla.

GRANDE (Union). Span., "large or great." Small community on US 87, and C&S RR, 11 mi NW of Grenville. Named for Sierra Grande Mtn., directly E of settlement. Post office, 1908, intermittently, to 1913.

GRANNY MOUNTAIN (Grant). 9 mi S of Gila Cliff Dwellings National Monument.

GRAN QUIVIRA. This name at one time was associated with all the unknown land W of the Mississippi and E or N of the Gulf of California. Michael Lok's 1582 map shows Quivira at the tip of the western continent with Culiacan, Galicia, and Florida covering the rest of the area between Canada and Mexico. Twitchell, *Leading Facts of NM History, I,* 231-33, note 250, quotes Adolph Bandelier: "At foot of the Mesa de los Jumanos there was Tabira now famous under the misleading name of 'La Gran Quivira.'" However, on L'Atlas Curieux (1700) both *Tavira* and *Gran Quivira* are shown: *Tavira* E of Socorro and S of Santa Fe; *Gran Quivira* in large letters at the N edge of the *Mar de las Californias o Carolinas* (Gulf of California or Carolinas). Francisco Vasquez de Coronado sought Quivira in 1540-42, as the country was reported to him by the Indian called The Turk. Benavides, in 1634, refers to "the kingdom of Quivira" in the west and to another of the same name in the east. The references are too numerous to cite. It has been suggested that the word comes from French, *cuivre,* "copper," and that Indians got the term from Jacques Cartier, who was on the St. Lawrence before Coronado was on the Rio Grande. Professor Lansing Bloom proposed that *Quivira* may have been derived from the Arabic word *quivir,* "big," illustrated in Spanish place names as *Guadalquivir.* A third etymology is a Spanish corruption of Wichita *Kirikurus,* named for that tribe. The great Spanish mission in Torrance County is completely disintegrated, but the earliest church was built in 1629 and the massive walls of the second church and its attached monastery and convent, on which work began about 1649, are still standing. In the latter part of the nineteenth century these ruins became identified with the Quivira of Coronado and other Spanish explorers. In 1909, the ruins and an area of 160 acres surrounding them, were dedicated as the GRAN QUIVIRA NATIONAL MONUMENT. GRAN QUIVIRA (Torrance). On NM 41, 19 mi SE of Mountainair. Anglo-American settlement of the area began in the 1880's. Post office, Socorro County, 1904-09; Torrance County, 1909-12; mail to Willard; reinstated later to present.

GRANT (Hidalgo). See SHAKESPEARE. GRANT COUNTY. Formed Jan. 30, 1868. Named in honor of Gen. Ulysses S. Grant by Territorial Legislature, Jan. 30, 1868. In the following November, Grant was elected the eighteenth President of the United States. Area is 3,981 sq mi.

GRANTS (San Miguel). 21 mi SW of Las Vegas.

GRANTS (Cibola). Mining, ranching, and lumbering town on US 66 and NM 53, and AT&SF RR. Originally a coaling station for the railroad, and for years called GRANTS STATION. Named for the Grant brothers, Angus A., Lewis A., and John R., contractors in the construction of the railroad, who maintained a camp for workers called "Grants' Camp." Post office, 1882-1935 under name GRANT; GRANTS, 1936—.

GRAPEVINE CANYON (Otero). In Lincoln National Forest on W slope of Sacramento Mts., about 35 mi SE of Alamogordo. Named for the many wild grapevines growing near the springs and streams. Once used as a range by the Circle Cross Cattle Co. In early days, Indian tribes left pictographs of sotol at the entrance of a cave in the canyon. Sotol is a desert plant used in making a drink called mescal.

GRASS MOUNTAIN (San Miguel). A low mountain used as grazing land, 2 mi NE of Cowles and SE of Pecos Baldy.

GRATTAN (Catron). SE of Datil, across Plains of St. Augustine.

GRAVEL PIT (Quay). Named in 1906 when CRI&P RR started mining gravel for its own use.

GRAVEYARD IN THE SKY (Harding). Stone formation near Bueyeros. So called because of graves of the pioneers on top.

GRAY (Lincoln). First postmaster, Seaborn T. Gray. Post office, 1894-1900; changed to CAPITAN.

GREATHOUSE'S TAVERN (Lincoln). See CORONA.

GREENFIELD (Chaves). Cotton-loading point on AT&SF RR, 4 mi NW of Hagerman on US 285. Named for the Green Ranch 1 mi S which was developed by J. J. Hagerman and named by him for a friend. Post office, 1911-12.

GREEN MOUNTAIN (Colfax). 15 mi SE of Raton.

GREENS GAP (Catron). 18 mi SW of Datil, on NM 12. Named for the M. M. and the G. C. Green families, pioneer homesteaders in this region. Post office, 1920-42.

GREEN TREE (Lincoln). Farming and resort town on US 70, 35 mi NE of Tularosa. Originally named PALO VERDE, but changed by Post Office Department because another town had the same name. Post office, 1946-58. *Palo verde* means "green wood" and names a desert tree. On Oct. 1, 1958, this community by popular approval became RUIDOSO DOWNS. The area adjoins the Ruidoso Downs racetrack.

GREENWOOD CREEK (Colfax). Stream NW of Cimarron, tributary to the Ponil.

GRENVILLE (Union). Dairying and ranching town on US 87, NM 120, and C&S RR, 27 mi NW of Clayton. At this point NM 120 begins. Named for a Mr. Grenville, a prominent man in pioneer days. Post office, 1888—. GRENVILLE CAVES (Union). 8 mi W of Grenville and 4 mi S of US 87. The entrance is on top of a little knoll.

GRIEGOS (Bernalillo). Spanish family surname which originally meant "Greeks." Suburb in NW Albuquerque. Post office, 1903-13.

GRIER (Curry). Farming community on US 60, 84, and the AT&SF RR, 11 mi W of Clovis. Organized in 1910 and named for the wife of an official (maiden name). Post office, 1921-56. Originally called HAVENER.

GROVE CREEK (Grant). Flows into San Vincente Arroyo 3 mi NW of Whitewater. The correct Spanish is *Vicente;* the *n* is intrusive from English.

GRUMBLE GULCH (Socorro). N of Bingham and 13 mi W of Claunch near NM 41.

GUACHEPANGUE (Rio Arriba). Almost certainly a corruption of words in Tewa, although the "guache" element is puzzling. The Tewa (Santa Clara) name is *pot see pa-angay.* The "guache" element may be an approximation of *potsee.* The nearest thing to *ts* in Spanish is *ch.* GUACHE SETTLEMENT (Rio Arriba). The term sounds like a loan word from Tewa. On W bank of Rio Grande 3 mi S of San Juan Pueblo.

GUADALUPE (De Baca). Trading point 12 mi NW of Ft. Sumner. Named for the Virgin of Guadalupe by the Casaus family when they settled here in the 1860's. GUADALUPE (Guadalupe). On SP RR, 15 mi W of Santa Rosa. Post office, 1900-41. GUADALUPE (Sandoval). Small farming and ranching community on the Rio Puerco, 25 mi W of San Ysidro. Also called OJO DEL PADRE because of a little spring now housed in a small stone structure. GUADALUPE COUNTY. Created by the Territorial Legislature on Feb. 26, 1891. Named for Our Lady of Guadalupe, the patron saint of Mexico. Area is 2,999 sq mi. GUADALUPE MIRANDA GRANT (Doña Ana). See MIRANDA GRANT. GUADALUPE

MOUNTAIN (Taos). 3 mi W of Questa. GUADALUPE MOUNTAINS (Eddy, Chaves, Otero). Adjacent to S end of Sacramento Mts. They rise in the S part of Chaves County, extend through the corner of Otero County, along the W border of Eddy County. Perhaps named for the seventeenth-century mission at El Paso del Norte, the southernmost headquarters of the NM Franciscan Missions. Shown on Mapa de los EUM (1828). A spur of these mountains extends E and was named by the Spaniards Sierra de Cenizas, "Ashes Mountain," because of volcanic evidence. GUADALUPE RIVER (Sandoval). Tributary of the Jemez; extends from its junction 7 mi below Jemez Springs for 12 mi to junction of the Rio Las Vacas and Cebolla Creek. GUADALUPITA (Mora). Span., "Little Guadalupe." Farming, lumbering, and sheep-raising community on NM 38, in Rincon Range 16 mi N of Mora. Post office, 1879—.

GUAJE CANYON (Santa Fe). American Span., "gourd." Called by the Tewa at San Ildefonso *tseeso-o,* "great canyon." GUAJE CREEK (Santa Fe). Flows E into Rio Grande, 7 mi S of Santa Clara Creek at Otowi; heads against the Baca Location in Jemez Mts. GUAJE MOUNTAIN (Sandoval). 1 mi from Santa Fe County line, 4 mi SW of Puye.

GUAJOLOTES (San Miguel). New Mexican Span., "water dog or salamander," a corruption of Aztec *axolotl,* "salamander," by confusing it with Aztec *huexolotl,* "turkey."

GUAM (McKinley). On US 66, 20 mi SE of Gallup. Post office, DEWEY, 1899-1902, changed to GUAM, 1902-13; changed to PEREA.

GUILLOU (San Miguel). First postmaster, H. C. Guillou. Post office, 1899-1904; mail to Las Vegas.

GUIQUE (Rio Arriba). On W bank of the Rio Grande opposite Alcalde. Post office, 1906-12; mail to Chamita. See QUIQUI.

GUNSIGHT CANYON (Eddy). Heads in Guadalupe Ridge about 36 mi SW of Carlsbad. From head of canyon, looking out, there is a small hill between the mountains, which gives the viewer the impression of looking over a gunsight.

GURULE (Bernalillo). Spanish family surname. Listed as early as 1699, when Santiago Grole or Gurule married Elena Gallegos in Bernalillo. First postmaster, Felipe J. Gurule, 1892; mail to Albuquerque.

GUSDORF (Taos). Small settlement on US 64 W of Agua Fria. Named for Alexander Gusdorf, pioneer Taos trader and banker, whom the natives called Don Alejandro.

GUT-ACHE MESA (Grant). See BELLY-ACHE MESA.

GUY (Union). Former settlement on NM 370, 37 mi NW of Clayton. Once headquarters for Colorado—Arizona Sheep Co., founded by Edmund D. Hunig. Post office, 1910-45.

GUZMAN's LOOKOUT MOUNTAIN (Doña Ana). 42 mi SW of Las Cruces and 3 mi N of the Mexican border. Probably named for lake in northern Mexico which commemorates a sixteenth-century governor of New Spain, Niño de Guzman.

H AAG (Curry). First postmaster, George F. Haag. Post office, 1909-13.

HACHITA. Span., *hacheta,* "little hatchet," or possibly "little torch," that is, "signal hill." The diminutive form resulted in the English "hatchet" as applied to the Little Hatchet and Big Hatchet Mts., W and S of Hachita Valley. HACHITA (Grant). Small community on NM 9, 81, and the SP RR, 37 mi SE of Lordsburg. The trading point for the HACHITA VALLEY, which lies to the S, crossing the border of Grant and Hidalgo counties. Post office, 1882-98; 1902—.

HACIENDA DE SAN JUAN BAUTISTO DEL OJITO DEL RIO DE LAS GALLINAS GRANT (Guadalupe, San Miguel). See PRESTON BECK GRANT.

HACKBERRY DRAW (Eddy). 2 mi W of Carlsbad. Named for the Western hackberry tree (genus *Celtis reticulata*) which finds its way into some NM canyons. A small tree with veiny, thick leaves that seems very much a stranger in the arid NM environment. HACKBERRY LAKE (Eddy). 25 mi E of Lakewood.

HADLEY (Grant). Post office, 1890-95; mail to Cooks. HADLEY (San Miguel). Post office, 1904-05; mail to Rociada.

HAGAN (Sandoval). Former coal-mining camp 20 mi E of Bernalillo. Post office, 1902, intermittently, to 1931; mail to Placitas; HAGAN JUNCTION (Sandoval). Railroad spur built in mid-1920's as a promotional enterprise by Dr. J. J. DePraslin.

HAGERMAN (Chaves). Ranching and farming town on US 285, and AT&SF RR, 22 mi SE of Roswell. Named in 1906 for J. J. Hagerman, president of PV&NE RR, which was later acquired by AT&SF RR from whom the Hagerman Canal was bought. Post office, 1895—.

HAHN (Bernalillo). On US 85, 4 mi N of Albuquerque. Established about 1910, and named for W. H. Hahn, an early Albuquerque merchant.

HAILE (Guadalupe). First postmaster, James W. Haile. Post office, 1907-18.

HALE LAKE (Lincoln). 6 mi E of Hollywood.

HALFMOON PARK (Catron). 2 mi E of Mogollon Baldy Peak.

HALF WAY HOUSE (Doña Ana). See ANTHONY.

HALL's PEAK (Mora). Community on Ocate Creek near Colfax County line in Mora Grant. Named for the nearby peak. Post office, 1887-1912. HALL's PEAK (Mora). Rises to an elevation of 9,800 ft, in NW corner of county.

HALONA (McKinley). See ZUÑI INDIAN PUEBLO.

HAMILTON (San Miguel). Post office, 1883; mail to Glorieta. HAMILTON MESA (Mora). In W part of county, W of the Rio Valdez.

HANLEY (Quay). Post office, 1907-18.

HANOVER (Grant). Mining community on AT&SF RR and NM 180, 5 mi NE of Bayard. Post office, 1892—. Also called HANOVER JUNCTION.

HANSBURG (Grant). First postmaster, Emma J. Hansburg. Post office, 1892-94.

HANSONBURG (Socorro). Post office, 1906-10; mail to San Antonio.

HAPPY VALLEY (Eddy). Suburban settlement W of Carlsbad.

HARDCASTLE CANYON (Catron). Runs SE into Apache Creek. Capt. E. L. Hardcastle served on Boundary Commission in 1849. HARDCASTLE GAP (Catron). 5 mi SW of Fox Mtn.

HARENCE (Sandoval). Post office, 1911; mail to Señorita.

HARDING COUNTY. Created by state legislature on Mar. 4, 1921. Named for Warren G. Harding, twenty-ninth President of the United States, 1921-23. Area comprises 2,138 sq mi.

HARGIS (Quay). On SP RR, 6 mi W of Tucumcari, just W of Tucumcari Metropolitan Park. Named for settlers.

HARLAN (Colfax). Named for T. B. Harlan, of St. Louis, chief counsel of the Maxwell Land Grant Co.

HARMON (Cibola). 7 mi NE of Grants and 7 mi W of Mt. Taylor. Named for a Mr. Harmon, who farmed extensively in carrots. He came to the valley in the 1940's.

HAROLD LAKE (Chaves). At Roosevelt County line, 7 mi S of Kenna.

HARRINGTON (Union). Post office, 1910-18.

HARRIS (Quay). First postmaster, Otto W. Harris. Post office, 1908-18.

HARRISON LAKE (Lincoln). Just N of Spindle.

HARTFORD (Quay). Post office, 1907-10; mail to Looney.

HASSELL (Quay). Ranching community in SW corner of county, 20 mi NE of Ft. Sumner. First postmaster, John W. Hassell. Post office, 1907-48.

HATCH (Doña Ana). Farming and ranching community on US 85 and AT&SF RR, 33 mi NW of Las Cruces. Named for Gen. Edward Hatch, who was in charge of Ft. Santa Barbara on E bank of the Rio Grande, N of Hatch. He was commander of the district from 1880 to 1895. Once called HATCH'S STATION. HATCH'S RANCH (San Miguel). Post office, 1878-79; changed to CHAPMAN. HATCH'S STATION (Doña Ana). See HATCH.

HATCHET MOUNTAINS (Grant, Hidalgo). See HACHITA (Grant). Big and Little Hatchet ranges are in SW corner of NM where the San Luis and Animas mts. form the NW terminus of the Sierra Madre of Mexico. See HACHITA.

HAVENER (Curry). Post office, 1910-21. See GRIER.

HAWIKUH RUINS (Cibola). A few miles SW of Zuñi Pueblo. Referred to by Castañeda as the place where the Indians opposed Coronado on July 6, 1540.

HAWKINS (Grant). On SP RR, 16 mi SE of Lordsburg. Said to be named for a Mr. Hawkins, at one time an attorney for AT&SF RR, and later general attorney for the old EP&SW RR.

HAWKS (Guadalupe). 5 mi NE of Santa Rosa, on SP RR.

HAYDEN (Union). Trading point in ranching area 29 mi N of Nara Visa. Originally platted as CENTRAL CITY on line of survey for the Denver and New Orleans Railroad never constructed. Renamed Hayden by George L. Cook. Site of annual Hayden Rodeo. Post office, 1908—.

HAYNES (San Juan). On NM 56, 50 mi SE of Farmington. First postmaster, Samuel H. Haynes. Post office, 1908-29. HAYNES (Doña Ana).

HAYSTACK MOUNTAIN (Catron). 1 mi N of Grant County line and 12 mi SE of Pleasanton. HAYSTACK MOUNTAIN (Valencia). W of Grants; site where Paddy Martinez made his discovery of uranium ore in 1950.

HAYTON (Cibola). Ranching community in Zuñi Mts. at head of Bluewater Creek, W of Sawyer and 15 mi S of Thoreau. Named for the parents of Vern and Stan Hayton of Grants, who first settled in that area.

HEADQUARTERS (Otero). On US 70, 13 mi SW of Alamogordo. White Sands National Monument is nearby.

HEART LAKE (Taos). 1 mi W of Baldy.

HEATHDEN (Doña Ana). 22 mi N of Las Cruces, on AT&SF RR, near Radium Springs.

HEATON (McKinley). Post office, 1909-22.

HEBRON (Colfax). On AT&SF RR, 11 mi S of Raton, at Hebron Dam. Post office, 1902-10. HEBRON DAM (Colfax). An artificial reservoir for irrigation purposes. According to Henry Gannett, twenty-five cities, towns, and villages bear the name of the ancient city in Palestine. See BLOSSER CREEK, GAP.

HECK CANYON (Colfax). On NM 199, 18 mi W of Springer, on Sweet Water Creek, in the center of a lumber district. Named for the Matthew Heck family, who owned property in the canyon. Post office, 1927-43. HECK SPRINGS (Colfax). On NM 21, 25 mi W of Springer.

HELENA (Torrance). On SP RR, 21 mi SW of Vaughn. Said to commemorate the broken romance of a railroader whose sweetheart bore that name.

HELL. As a place name, this ancient Anglo-Saxon word is only moderately active. However, in the famous story, "The Devil in Texas," his Satanic Majesty on a trip to that corner of the Southwest meets a sandstorm which takes all the skin off his face and blows his clothes inside out. He explodes on Texas chile, falls into a cactus patch, and is kicked by a longhorn steer. Perhaps these circumstances of climate and environment explain the significance of the following place names, in a contiguous territory. HELL CANYON (Bernalillo). On W side of Manzano Mts., 14 mi E of Isleta Pueblo. HELL CANYON (Sierra). 10 mi N of Kingston, E of Mud Lake. HELL CANYON (Socorro). 5 mi E of Magdalena. HELL ROARING MESA (Catron). 3 mi N of Luna. HELL'S CANYON (Grant). 17 mi N of Silver City. HELL'S HALF ACRE (Grant). 10 mi NW of Silver City, W of Windmill Canyon. Almost entirely rock, with unexplored caves and canyons. HELL'S MESA (Socorro). 5 mi SW of Riley.

HELWEG (Bernalillo). 3 mi from Santa Fe County line, 21 mi NE of Albuquerque. Named for Benjamin N. Helweg, who filed a claim on government land about 1913 and started a store here. Post office, 1922-34.

HEMATITE (Colfax). Post office, 1897-99; mail to Elizabethtown.

HENDRIX (San Juan). See RIVERSIDE. 2 mi E of US 550 and 2 mi S of Riverside.

HENPECK (Eddy). See SEVEN RIVERS.

HENRY (Lea). 6 mi S of Eunice. First postmaster, Henry B. May. Post office, 1909-12.

HEREFORD (Otero). On SP RR at Texas border. Post office, 1904-06; changed to NEWMAN.

HERMANAS (Luna). Span., "sisters." On NM 9 and SP RR, 32 mi S of Deming. Founded in 1879, and named for Tres Hermanas Mts. to the E. Post office, 1903-25.

HERMIT'S PEAK (San Miguel). A great granite hump near Las Vegas, where an Italian hermit, named Juan Maria Agostini, made his home in the 1860's. Through his piety and example, he gave new spirit to the depressed and ill in the Sangre de Cristo area. He was reputed to have been an Italian nobleman who gave up title and riches. After he left the peak he went to Las Cruces, where he lived in a cave. He was killed there in 1869.

HERMOSA (Grant). Span., "beautiful." HERMOSA (Sierra). Former mining settlement on S Fork of Palomas River, 28 mi W of Hot Springs. Post office, 1884-1929.

HERNANDEZ (Rio Arriba). Farming community on US 84 and 285, 6 mi N of Española. First name proposed for the post office was ALABAM, suggested by a local saloon of that name. Congressman B. C. Hernandez disapproved. The people then sent back a request for HERNANDEZ, a name known in NM records from the sixteenth century.

HERRERA (Bernalillo). First postmaster, Nicholas Herrera. Post office, 1900; mail to Albuquerque.

HERRON (Doña Ana). First postmaster, C. M. Herron, Post office, 1886-88; changed to EARLHAM. See VADO.

HERSHFIELD (San Miguel). Oil-drilling camp 10 mi SW of Garita, at foot of Pino Mesa. Named for Harry A. Hershfield, whose company carried on operations here from 1928 to 1938.

HEWITT CREEK (Colfax). In S Moreno Valley; flows into the Cienaguilla, thence into Eagle Nest Lake.

HICKMAN (Catron). Abandoned settlement, 14 mi N of US 60, 10 mi E of NM 36. Post office, 1937-55.

HIDALGO COUNTY. Created by the state legislature on Feb. 25, 1919. Doubtless commemorative of the Treaty of Guadalupe Hidalgo, which ended the Mexican War and ceded NM and Upper California to the U.S. Since the treaty was signed on Feb. 2, 1848, at the Mexican city of Guadalupe Hidalgo, the name also commemorates the patriot Miguel Hidalgo y Costilla, leader of the Mexican Revolution in 1810. Area is 3,447 sq mi.

HIDDEN LAKE AND CAVE (Guadalupe). On NM 91, 2 mi SE of Santa Rosa. Surrounded on all sides by low rocky hills and completely hidden from view; hence its name. About 150 ft in diameter and less than 80 ft deep; fed by springs which rise from the bottom. HIDDEN PASTURE CANYON (Catron or Grant).

HIGH LONESOME (Chaves). HIGH LONESOME (Lincoln). Abandoned settlement on US 70 SE of Lincoln. HIGH LONESOME (Hidalgo). This intriguing name seems to have been sufficiently appropriate and popular to be used in three separate counties. The Lincoln County location was in a resort area and usually less lonesome than the name implied.

HIGH ROLLS—MOUNTAIN PARK (Otero). Community on NM 83, 8 mi NE of Alamogordo. Originally called FRESNAL. The postmaster at High Rolls says that if you ever lie down and start rolling, you won't stop until you reach the next county—forty miles away. Between Cloudcroft and La Luz, the road descends nearly 4,000 ft, twisting and turning, offering fine views of the Sacramento Mts., and across to the White Sands National Monument. However, "rolls" in local usage is applied to the rapids of a mountain stream, and Fresnal Creek tumbles down the slopes here at a rapid rate, making "high rolls." Post office, High Rolls, 1901, intermittently, to 1936; High Rolls—Mountain Park, 1936—. See MOUNTAIN PARK.

HIGHWAY (Roosevelt). Trading point on NM 18, 9 mi S of Dora, and 26 mi S of Portales. Name is descriptive of its location on a state highway.

HILARIO (San Miguel). Post office, 1910-33. See SAN HILARIO.

HILL (Doña Ana). Former trading point on NM 28, 10 mi NW of Las Cruces. Named for the Hill family, a member of which, a Las Cruces dentist, was at one time a candidate for governor. Post office, 1914-37. HILLCREST (Rio Arriba). Trading point 16 mi SE of Dulce.

HILLSBORO (Sierra). On NM 180, 33 mi SW of Truth or Consequences. Once the county seat and center of a rich mining district. There is still prospecting in the hills which once produced six million dollars in gold and silver. When first settled in August 1877, the settlers selected names, put them in a hat, and the one picked was "Hillsborough," which was later reduced to Hillsboro. Post office, 1879—. HILLSBORO PEAK (Sierra). In Mimbres Mts. on Grant County line, 5 mi NW of Kingston.

HILO PEAK (Hidalgo). Span., "thread," but also in mining, a "seam" or "fault, break." In S end of Animas Mts.

HILTON (Doña Ana). Post office, 1887-94, mail to Weed. HILTON LODGE (San Miguel). 2 mi W of NM 105, and 8 mi from Rociada. Named for Ivan J. Hilton, mayor of East Las Vegas, 1950-54. Post office, 1935-46.

HINKSON (Cibola). N of Zuñi Plateau in SW corner of county, 1 mi from Arizona line.

HIQUE (Rio Arriba). See QUIQUI.

HI-WAY (Lea). A location for a rural school, 12 mi E of Tatum. So named because three country schools were consolidated and moved to US 380.

HOBART (Santa Fe, Rio Arriba). On Rio Grande, 5 mi SW of Española. Post office, 1894-1912.

HOBBS (Lea). Ranching, farming, and oil-producing town on US 62, 180, NM 18, and TNM RR. Informants have reported J. B. Hobbs, James Isaac Hobbs, and "Grandma" Hobbs as the initial homesteaders in 1907. Berry Hobbs was the first postmaster in 1911. In November 1928, the Midwest Oil Co.'s discovery well, No. 1 State, established Hobbs as an oil town. Post office, 1910—.

HOCKETT (Doña Ana). Water stop 1 mi S of NM 26, on AT&SF RR, 9 mi W of Hatch.

HODGES (Taos). Post office, 1909-13.

HOGBACK (San Juan). Oil field in San Juan Basin where oil was first produced in that area. See HOGBACK MOUNTAIN. HOGBACK MOUNTAIN (San Juan). A few miles SE of Stanolind. Named for the geological formation.

HOGADERO (San Miguel). Span., ahogar, "drown, choke." Post office, 1884-85; mail to Ft. Bascom.

HOLDEN PRONG (Sierra). Stream flowing N into Arunas Creek, 9 mi NW of Kingston.

HOLKEO CREEK (Colfax-Union). Rises near Peck's Mesa in SW corner of county and flows into Ute Creek after crossing Union County line. Holkeo is reported to be an Indian name, but further data is lacking.

HOLLAND (Union). Post office, 1905-17.

HOLLENE (Curry). Farming community on NM 40, 27 mi N of Clovis, and E of NM 18, near Texas line. Named for Hollene Thompson, small daughter of a Texico man who was active in selling lots in the townsite in 1906 and 1907. Post office, 1907-53.

HOLLINGER CANYON, CREEK (San Miguel). Empties into Beaver Creek 5 mi N of Gallinas town.

HOLLOMAN AIR FORCE BASE (Otero). Early in the history of the base, the post office was listed under the name MONISTA; then HOLLOMAN, 1947-56; HOLLOMAN AIR FORCE BASE, 1956—. See AIR FORCE MISSILE DEVELOPMENT CENTER.

HOLLOWAY (Lincoln). First postmaster, James M. Holloway. Post office, 1908-15.

HOLLYWOOD (Lincoln). Farming community on US 70, just E of Ruidoso. Post office established May 22, 1926, and named for Hollywood, Fla., by first postmaster, George A. Freidenbloom.

HOLMAN (Mora). Farming and sheep-raising community in W part of county, 5 mi NW of Mora. First postmaster, Charles W. Holman. Post office, 1894—.

HOLY CROSS (Luna). Post office, 1935-36. See CAMP CODY.

HOLY GHOST CREEK (San Miguel). Empties from Spirit Lake into Pecos River, 20 mi NW of Glorieta. Said to have been named by a priest who was concealed from Pecos Indians by the mist that collects here.

HONDALE (Luna). Post office, 1908-34.

HONDO (Lincoln). Span., "deep." In modern Spanish the "h" is silent; centuries ago this name was spelled jondo, with the "j" pronounced as "h." Ranching and farming community on US 70 and 380, 48 mi W of Roswell. Named for the Rio Hondo, which is formed at this point by the junction of the Bonito and Ruidoso rivers. Post office, 1900—. Formerly known as LA JUNTA, Span., "junction." HONDO (Santa Fe). HONDO (Taos). 9 mi NW of Taos. HONDO CANYON (Taos). HONDO RESERVOIR (Chaves). 9 mi SW of Roswell. HONDO RIVER, LOWER (Taos). 12 mi N of Taos where it breaks out of the mountains to the Rio Grande. HONDO RIVER, SOUTH FORK (Taos). Fork just N of Taos. HONDO RIVER, UPPER (Taos). Has its source at timber line above Twining.

HOOD (San Juan). On US 550, 3 mi NE of Farmington. First postmaster, George S. Hood, 1898-1906; mail to Farmington.

HOPE (Eddy). Ranching and farming community on NM 83, 21 mi W of Artesia. First settlers called the place BADGERVILLE, from 1884 to 1888, because they had to live in dugouts like badgers. Permanent settlers came in 1888-89, and named the community Hope when the first post office was established. Two of the settlers, Elder Miller and Joe Richards, threw a dime in the air and shot at it in order to decide who was to name the town. "I hope you lose," exclaimed Richards. His opponent did and the winner chose the name Hope. An irrigation district was formed on Peñasco River in 1887 and lasted until 1922. About 1906 a railroad bed was laid to Hope from Artesia and was to be carried to El Paso. The money to complete the project, coming from English capitalists, was on board the ill-fated *Titanic.* Portions of the unfinished roadbed can still be seen. Post office, 1890—. HOPE (Colfax). Post office, 1888-89; mail to Grenville.

HOPEWELL (Rio Arriba). 20 mi SE of Chama. Post office, 1894-1906. HOPEWELL LAKE (Rio Arriba). 2 mi N of Hopewell. These two names may be associated with W. S. Hopewell, a promoter engaged in cattle and mining enterprises, 1878 and later, in Socorro, Sierra, Grant, Torrance, and Rio Arriba counties.

HORACE (Cibola). Flag stop and section track on AT&SF RR, 6 mi E of Grants. At this point US 66 overpasses the tracks and a feeder road (secondary) from the S joins US 66. Named for the contractor who erected and supervised the overpass. HORACE MESA (Cibola). SW of Mt. Taylor.

HORNOS (Santa Fe). Siding on AT&SF RR, between Cañoncito and Lamy. It was named for charcoal ovens which in the 1880's and as late as 1915-20 turned piñon wood into charcoal. The wood was unloaded and the charcoal loaded here, and at night the place was a delightful sight with the glowing fires.

HORSE. The horse was introduced into the Americas by the Spanish, and into NM from the Spanish settlements to the south. Castañeda reports that "the most essential thing in new lands is horses. They instill the greatest fear in the enemy and make the Indians respect the leaders of the army." *Narratives,* 1540-42 (Albuquerque, 1940), p. 282. Place names using the Spanish word for horse may be found listed under *Caballo.* HORSE CAMP (Hidalgo). HORSE CREEK (Chaves). Tributary

of Pecos River, flowing in from NW. HORSE-HEAD CANYON (McKinley). HORSE LAKE (Grant), 10 mi NW of Cliff. HORSE LAKE (Rio Arriba). Also called NORTHERN LAKE, 1½ mi long, fed by underground springs. A sizeable lake of 600 or more acres, half on the Jicarilla Apache Indian Reservation, 20 mi W of Parkview. Many horses have been drowned in it during the winter months when snow is deep. They wander onto the lake to feed on the tall tules and fall through the ice. HORSE LAKE CREEK (Rio Arriba). Flows SE from Horse Lake, to join Willow Creek, 3 mi NE of El Vado Reservoir. HORSE PEAK (Catron). HORSESHOE LAKE (Colfax). A 10-acre lake just below timber line at head of main East Fork of Red River. HORSE SPRINGS (Catron). Ranching community on NM 12, 26 mi SW of Datil. ½ mi E of the original Horse Springs, a very large spring. Named because some soldiers on the way to Ft. Tularosa from Socorro lost a horse and on the way back found it here. Post office, 1879-82. HORSE THIEF CREEK (San Miguel). Tributary of Panchuela Creek.

HOSPAH (McKinley). Trading point 35 mi NE of Thoreau.

HOSTA BUTTE (McKinley). 4½ mi SW of NM 56, SW of Chaco Canyon. Reported to have been named for a favorite Indian guide of Lt. W. H. Simpson. Hosta was lieutenant governor of the Jemez tribe. The Jemez form was *wash e hoste,* and was translated "the lightning."

HOT SPRINGS (San Miguel). On US 65, 1 mi W of Montezuma. Post office, 1902-04; 1905-07. HOT SPRINGS (Sierra). Two neighboring settlements on US 85 took this name at one time or another. The older one became Truth or Consequences in 1950. See TRUTH OR CONSEQUENCES. One week after the original Hot Springs had changed its name, a community called WILLIAMSBURG, just S of Truth or Consequences, adopted the name Hot Springs. On Feb. 3, 1959, its citizens voted to return to the designation Williamsburg, which originally had been selected in honor of Dr. Thomas B. Williams. For place names in Spanish meaning "hot springs," see OJO CALIENTE.

HOUSE (Quay). An agricultural and ranching community on NM 86, 33 mi NW of Melrose. Named for either Lucie J. House, who in December 1902 settled on the 160 acres where House is now located, or for John L.

House who built the first grocery store here in 1904. First postmaster, Lucie J. House. Post office, 1906—.

HOXIE (Colfax). 20 mi S of Raton where US 85 and 64 separate, the former leading to Santa Fe by way of Las Vegas, and the latter by way of Cimarron and Taos. SANTA FE FORKS is the original name, dating from the 1820's when the Santa Fe Trail forked at about this spot. However, of late years the little crossroads filling station has been known as Hoxie because William Hoxie owned and operated the place in 1925.

HOYT CREEK (Catron, Sierra). 19 mi NW of Hermosa.

HUB, THE (Catron). Mountain 9 mi NW of Mangas.

HUBBELL (Catron). 12 mi W of NM 117, and 3 mi S of Valencia County line.

HUDSON (Quay). On SP RR and US 54, 11 mi SW of Logan. Started when CRI&P RR built a line between Dalhart, Tex., and Santa Rosa in 1901. First called REVUELTO and known as a railroad switch; then named Hudson, for a civil war veteran who lived here. Post office, 1908-26. HUDSON (Grant). Post office, 1881-1901; changed to FAYWOOD. HUDSON HOT SPRINGS (Grant). Post office, 1879-81. See FAYWOOD HOT SPRINGS.

HUECO (Otero). Span., "hollow, gap"; Southwestern Span., "water hole, spongy place." On US 54 and SP RR, 24 mi S of Orogrande and 6 mi N of Texas border. Named for features in terrain of the sandy Tularosa Valley. Hueco has been Anglicized in Texas as Waco. HUECO MOUNTAINS (Otero). Just N of Texas border, 18 mi E of Newman.

HUERTO DE LOS BRACITOS (Doña Ana). See BRAZITO.

HUGGINS CREEK (Chaves). 20 mi W of Olive.

HULBURT (Lincoln). See COYOTE.

HULSEY CIENEGA (Catron). Marsh 4 mi NE of Luna.

HUMBLE CITY (Lea). Oil community 9 mi NW of Hobbs, on NM 18 and TNM RR, a branch of the T&P running from Monahans, Tex., to Lovington. Named for the Humble Oil Co., because of drilling interests in the vicinity. Post office, 1930—.

HUMBUG CREEK (Colfax). In NE end of Moreno Valley. Flows into Moreno River and thence into Eagle Nest Lake.

HUNTER (Rio Arriba). Post office, 1893-94; mail to Abiquiu.

HUNT'S HOLE (Doña Ana). In S part of county, 22 mi W of Anthony; one of the large cavities or holes made by erosion and volcanic disturbances, Kilbourne Hole and Philip's Hole being its neighbors.

HURLBURT (Lincoln). First postmaster, F. Hurlburt. Post office, 1908-15. See COYOTE.

HURLEY (Grant). On US 260, 10 mi SE of Silver City. A company village owned by the Chino mine of the Nevada Consolidated Copper Co. and named for J. E. Hurley, once general manager, AT&SF RR. Hurley is directly connected by railroad with Santa Rita and was called HURLEY SIDING until 1910. Then the town was started as the result of the purchase of the Santa Rita Mining Co. by the Chino Copper Co. Post office, 1910—.

HURSCHBURGER PEAK (Otero). See ALAMO PEAK.

HYCE CREEK (San Miguel). Joins Cabo Lucero Creek, 3 mi N or San Geronimo.

HYDE PARK (Santa Fe). State park, a memorial to B. T. B. Hyde, prominent Santa Fean. 8 mi NE of Santa Fe.

HYER (Santa Fe). 12 mi S of Madrid. First postmaster was Charles O. Hyer. Post office, 1908-26.

ICE CAVES (Cibola). A short distance from El Morro on NM 53, in lava beds about 25 mi S of Grants. A perpetual wall of ice 100 ft underground, 12 to 20 ft thick, flat on top and sheer in front, extending back about 100 ft beyond a pool of clear, cold water. It looks like a huge section of NM onyx because of the bluish strata, formed by the winter snow that settles and hardens, with yellow horizontal bands of dust and volcanic ashes that blow into the cave. The sun never enters beyond a point 10 ft back from the perpendicular top of the cliff, thus forming a crescent-shaped face.

IDEN (Guadalupe). 5 mi SE of Vaughn, on the AT&SF RR. Named for Earl Iden, a partner of W. C. Reid, attorney for many years for AT&SF RR.

IDLEWILD (Colfax). Settlement 3 mi W of Eagle Nest.

IGNACIO CHAVEZ GRANT (McKinley, Sandoval). Long, narrow grant spanning two counties 22 mi N of Cebolleta. Made by Governor Mendinueta to Ignacio Chaves and three other Chaves men on Jan. 20, 1768.

ILDEFONZO (Santa Fe). Post office, 1901-15. See SAN ILDEFONSO.

ILFELD (San Miguel). Farming and ranching community on US 84 and 85, 23 mi SW of Las Vegas. Formerly called JUNE. The late Charles Ilfeld was a pioneer merchant of NM in Las Vegas. His son, Louis C. Ilfeld, an attorney, was a member of the first New Mexico senate. Post office, 1928—.

ILLINOIS CAMP (Eddy). 17 mi SE of Artesia. Named for the Illinois Oil Co., which was operating here in 1924-25. This was the original oil discovery E of Pecos River.

IMA (Quay). Farming and ranching community on NM 156, 12 mi S of Montoya and 26 mi SW of Tucumcari. In 1902, I. W. Moncus, with his wife, daughter, and brother-in-law, settled in the canyon used by the notorious outlaw, Black Jack Ketchum, for a hideout. In 1908, farmers came into the community, filing on each 110 acres of land. In 1909, Moncus established a store. He named the post office for his oldest daughter. Post office, 1908-55.

INCA (San Juan). On D&RGW RR, 7 mi NE of Aztec.

INDIAN. Without any particular reference as to which Indians, this general designation appears both for settlements and field names (geographical features). INDIAN (Rio Arriba). On Mills Lake, 10 mi S of Dulce. INDIAN CAMPS (Colfax). At entrance of Cimarron Canyon. Once a camp of traveling Indian bands, where many arrowheads can be found. INDIAN CREEK (Catron). Flows E to Gilita Creek, 6 mi SW of Negrito. INDIAN CREEK (Chaves, Otero). Rises in Mescalero Apache Indian Reservation and flows E across county line to Felix Canyon. INDIAN CREEK (Eddy). Small tributary of the Pecos, entering from W opposite Brush's resort. INDIAN CREEK (Otero). See THREE RIVERS. INDIAN CREEK (San Miguel). INDIAN CREEK (Socorro). Flows SE into Nogal Canyon. INDIAN CREEK (Taos). Rises 2 mi S of US Hill; flows SW to the Rio Pueblo. INDIAN DIVIDE (Lincoln). On SP RR, 12 mi SE of Carrizozo, in Tucson Mts. Highest point between Capitan and Carrizozo. INDIAN HEAD (Colfax). 5 mi N of Cimarron, W of highway. Name comes from likeness of a head and face showing in sandstone rimrock. INDIAN PEAKS (Catron). A group of five or six peaks, 7 to 10 mi SE of Pelona Mtn. INDIAN TRAIL (Chaves, Otero).

INDIOLE (Torrance). ON SP RR, in SE part of county, 1 mi from Guadalupe County line.

INEZ. Given names appear less frequently as place names than do surnames or family names. The list of first names used as NM place names includes both Spanish and Anglo, e.g., Inez, Lucy, Ramon, Thomas. Mrs. Devine Cook is authority for the statement that INEZ (Roosevelt) was "named for Inez Mullins, daughter of an early settler. She was a very pretty girl." Inez is a trading point on NM 92, 20 mi SE of Portales and 5 mi from the Texas border. Post office, 1908-30.

INGLEVILLE (De Baca). 5 mi N of Dunlap. First postmaster, James L. Ingle. Post office, 1908-23.

INSCRIPTION ROCK (Cibola). See EL MORRO.

INGRAM (Roosevelt). Community 12 mi NW of Elida. Post office, 1907-16; mail to Benson.

IOLA (Luna). 16 mi SW of Deming. Post office, 1911-17.

IONE (Union). In SW corner of county, 3 mi S of NM 65, and 9 mi SE of Rosebud. Settled in 1908 by Iowa farmers. E. F. Snyder was the first postmaster. He is reported to have named the place for a girl he left behind in Iowa. Post office, 1908-62.

IRON CREEK (Catron). Small tributary of Middle Fork of Gila River SE of Reserve. IRON CREEK (Grant). 4 mi W of Tyrone; joins Willow Creek, W of Sugarloaf Mtn.

ISIDORE. An Anglicized Spanish given name, honoring San Ysidro (St. Isidore) Labrador, the patron of farmers. ISIDORE (Guadalupe). On Gallegos Ranch at San Miguel—Guadalupe line. Post office, 1906-09; mail to Montoya. The post office later was re-established 8 mi NE of Newkirk, just W of NM 129, and from 1919 to 1928 about 3 mi E of present highway. ISIDORE (Sandoval). See SAN YSIDRO.

ISLETA (Bernalillo). Span., "little island." 13 mi S of Albuquerque on US 85. Named for the fact that when the Spanish arrived, the pueblo was literally on an island, with the river curving on each side. Today the Rio Grande is to the E and the pueblo is on high ground around which the river bends. The Tiwa name was tsugwevaga, meaning "kick flint," for the Indians played a kicking race using a piece of obsidian or flint. Isleta at one time belonged to the old Tiguex Indian province. During the Pueblo Rebellion of 1680, the Isleta Indians gave shelter to the Spanish people who came here, and finally joined them in their flight to the south. Shown on L'Atlas Curieux (1700). In 1733, known as

SAN AGUSTIN DE LA ISLETA. ISLETA PUEBLO LAND GRANT. Established by the Spanish government in 1689; confirmed by the U.S. government in 1858. 18 mi long on each side of the Rio Grande and 5 mi wide. A grant to the Pueblo of San Antonio de Isleta is recorded on Aug. 13, 1828, by the Governor of Chihuahua. Post office, 1882-83; 1887—. See PUEBLO LAND GRANTS.

IVANHOE (Grant). Site of a mill near the San Jose mine and the present town of Vanadium.

J ABALINA BASIN (Lea). Span., *javelina*, "sow of a wild boar"; in Southwestern Span., a wild pig; the peccary. 7 mi SW of Jal and 4 mi above the Texas line.

JACK'S CREEK (San Miguel). Enters Pecos River 1 mi above Cowles in NW corner of county. Source is near Pecos Baldy, S of Truchas Peak. JACK'S LAKE (McKinley). 11 mi NW of Terrero. JACK'S PEAK (Lincoln). In Jicarilla Mts. Named for an old prospector, whose last name has not been recorded.

JACKSON (Grant). Former trading point at junction of US 260 and NM 78, 50 mi NW of Silver City, 8 mi from Catron County line. Now ranch country. Post office, 1913-16; mail to Buckhorn.

JACONA (Santa Fe). Small community on S side of Pojoaque Creek, about 1 mi from Pojoaque, W of US 64 and 84. A Tewa Indian pueblo here was abandoned in 1696. The name is the Spanish approximation of *Sakona*, "at tobacco barranca," Tewa name for the pueblo. A location S of Santa Fe is shown as Hacona on L'Atlas Curieux (1700), and a settlement with this name is reported in Escudero's *Noticias* (1849). JACONA GRANT (Santa Fe). Small triangular tract about 3 mi W of Tesuque. The abandoned pueblo grant became the property of Ignacio de Roybal and Francesca Gomez, his wife, Oct. 2, 1702, by act of Governor Cubero.

JAL (Lea). On NM 18, a farming community also producing oil and natural gas, in SE corner of county, 8 mi N of Texas border. Named for the old JAL Ranch in Monument Draw, 6 mi E of present site. The cattle brand was brought to NM on a herd of cattle purchased by the Cowden Land and Cattle Co. from John A. Lynch of east Texas, whose initials formed the name. "Uncle" Alonzo Edwards sold his ranch to the Cowden brothers.

The settlement moved to its present location in 1916. Post office, 1910—.

JALAROSO (Cibola). Probably a corruption of Span., *jaralosa;* see JARA. Post office, 1898-99; mail to Zuñi.

JAMES DAM (Union). Large earth-rock dam on Corrumpa Creek 8 mi E of Des Moines; used for irrigation. At former headquarters of Thomas P. James Ranch. Now called WEATHERLY LAKE for present owner, A. D. Weatherly.

JAQUEZ (Rio Arriba). Settlement named for Spanish colonial family. Post office, 1888-90; changed to GALLINA. See CAÑADA JAQUEZ.

JARA. Span., "thicket, small oak;" but NM Span., "reed, willow, osier." JARA CREEK (Valencia). 4 mi N of Paxton. JARALES (Valencia). "Osier thickets." Community 3 mi S of Belen, 2 mi E of US 85. Post office, 1895-98; 1900—. Also called JARALOSA. JARALOSA CANYON, CREEK (Valencia). JARALOSA CREEK (Rio Arriba). N of Pound's Mill; flows W through JARA CANYON to become La Jara Creek, before it enters San Juan River. JARALOSA CREEK (Socorro). Flows N to join the Rio Salado 1 mi W of Puertocito. JARA PEAK (Socorro). See LA JARA PEAK. JARILLA (Otero). "Small bushes." Post office, 1899-1904; changed to BRICE. JARILLA JUNCTION (Otero). Post office, 1905-06; changed to OROGRANDE. JARILLA MOUNTAINS (Otero). Narrow range about 12 mi long, in S part of Tularosa Basin, 38 mi SW of Alamogordo. Separated from Sacramento and Organ mts. by low flats covered with desert growth. The Nannie Baird mines here were once known as the "Two-Barrel Mine," because S. M. Perkins, the discoverer and first white prospector, traded his entire right to it for two barrels of water. He was captured, at one time, by the Apache Indians who stripped him of his clothes and prepared to murder him but discovering his hunchback and owing to their superstition about deformity he was released unharmed. He found several rich lodes. JARITA CREEK (Colfax). Correct name for JACETAS CREEK. Flows into Canadian Red River at S Colfax boundary. Named for the many willows on its banks. JAROSA (Mora). 6 mi W of Wagon Mound on slopes of Turkey Mtn. in Mora Grant. So named because of the location near a grove of willow trees. JAROSA (San Miguel). JAROSA CANYON (Mora). Runs S, just N of Hamilton Mesa. JAROSA CANYON (Rio Arriba). Flows N to join the Rio Puerco, 2 mi N of Cañones.

JAROSA CREEK (San Miguel). Small fork of the main Pecos, just above Pecos Falls in high country. JAROSA CREEK (Taos).

JARAMILLO. Spanish family name. The earliest Jaramillo of NM record was Pedro Varela Jaramillo, who is named in the 1680-81 lists and who died at Guadalupe del Paso (modern Ciudad Juarez). His sons Cristobal and Juan returned to NM with the Reconquest of 1692 to resettle in the Rio Abajo region. They are later reported as living in Bernalillo. JARAMILLO (Rio Arriba). 6 mi S of Hopewell. JARAMILLO (Sandoval). 10 mi W of Los Alamos. JARAMILLO (San Miguel). First postmaster, Benigno Jaramillo. Post office, 1892-93; mail to Las Vegas. JARAMILLO CREEK (Sandoval). West Fork of Valle Grande Creek on Baca Location No. 1, in Jemez Mts.

JARDIN (San Miguel). Post office, 1902-04; mail to Rociada.

JAWBONE MOUNTAIN (Rio Arriba). 3 mi NW of Hopewell.

JEMEZ. The name is from the Tanoan Indian dialect in which it has the form *hay mish,* "people." In 1583, the Spanish explorer Espejo visited Jemez, and a few years later the colonizer Oñate visited the pueblo and received promises of friendship. The great mission church here was destroyed in the Pueblo Rebellion of 1680. It was known as San Jose de Giusewa, for the large pueblo nearby. The location is shown as *Los Emes* on L'Atlas Curieux (1700). JEMEZ MOUNTAINS (Sandoval, Los Alamos). In SE quarter of Sandoval and in Los Alamos. Named for the pueblo. JEMEZ PUEBLO (Sandoval). On NM 4, 26 mi NW of Bernalillo. Post office, Jemes, 1879-1907; changed to PUTNEY, 1907-08; Jemes, 1908-50; Jemez Pueblo, 1950—. JEMEZ PUEBLO GRANT (Sandoval). Area 5 mi square surrounding the pueblo: the standard "N one league, E one league, W one league, S one league, to be measured from the four corners of the Church in the center of the Pueblo." The grant was legalized by Governor Cruzate at Guadalupe del Paso, Sept. 20, 1689, after the Jemez Indians had agreed not to rebel again through the testimony of their representative that "they were very much intimidated by their recent defeats at the hands of the Spanish soldiers." See PUEBLO LAND GRANTS. JEMEZ RESERVOIR (Sandoval). Dam on Jemez River, 8 mi N of Bernalillo. JEMEZ RIVER (Sandoval). Rises in Jemez Mts.; flows S and E to join the Rio Grande 6 mi N of Bernalillo.

JEMEZ SPRINGS (Sandoval). Settlement 12 mi N of the pueblo. Post office, 1907—.

JENKINS (Lea). One-time store, post office, and school in Baker Flat, 5 mi W of Crossroads. Named for founder, a Methodist preacher. First postmaster, William L. Jenkins. Post office, 1910-27. JENKINS CREEK (Catron). 9 mi N of Luna.

JERKY MOUNTAINS (Catron). 22 mi E of Pleasanton, N of W fork of Gila River.

JEWETT (Catron). N of Apache Mtn. and 10 mi N of NM 12 at Apache Creek. JEWETT (San Juan). Post office, 1884-1907; mail to Fruitland. See LIBERTY.

JICARILLA. Span., "little cup"; NM Span., "little basket cup." The Apaches in this neighborhood were named in Spanish, "Basket Maker Apaches." JICARILLA (Lincoln). Mining and stock-raising community 27 mi NE of Carrizozo. Post office, 1892-1942. JICARILLA APACHE INDIAN RESERVATION. (Rio Arriba, Sandoval). In W part of county. JICARILLA MINING DISTRICT (Otero). Formerly called SILVER HILL DISTRICT. JICARILLA MOUNTAINS (Lincoln). The S half of this range is in the N end of Lincoln National Forest and extends NE for 15 or 20 mi. Some old Spanish mines have been found in this vicinity near White Oaks. JICARILLA PEAK (Rio Arriba). JICARITA MOUNTAIN (Mora). Rounded like an inverted basket. It is sacred to the Picuris and has a shrine on its summit. JICARITA PEAK (Taos, Rio Arriba). Between Taos and Rio Arriba. Named because on its W slope there is a cup-shaped hole or extinct crater from which a strong current of air continually flows. Three canyons have their source here: the Santa Barbara, Del Medio, and Del Valle.

J. J. LOBATO GRANT (Rio Arriba). Large grant on each side of Chama River with Abiquiu at the center. The marriage of Juan Jose Lobato is recorded at San Juan on Nov. 27, 1733. On Aug. 24, 1740, this grant was made to Lobato by Governor Mendoza, and he took possession on September 11 of that year.

JOFFRE (Guadalupe). On AT&SF RR, 12 mi SE of Vaughn.

JOHN MILLS LAKE (Rio Arriba). 11 mi S of Navajo.

JOHN SCOLLY LAND GRANT (Mora, San Miguel). An area 6 mi square surrounding town of Watrous. Granted by Governor Armijo about 1844, within Mora Grant. Litigation continued between heirs of the two grants for half a century.

John's Creek (San Miguel). Small stream at head of the Sapello.

Johnson (San Miguel). Post office serving Ft. Bascom, 1892-95; mail to Liberty. Johnson (Union). First postmaster, David C. Johnson. Post office, 1906-11; mail to Kenton, Okla. Johnson Canyon (Catron). Little fork of White Creek, in Mogollon Mts. on trail from Jenks Cabin to Cliff. Johnson Lake (Santa Fe). Little timber-line lake 2 mi N of Santa Fe Baldy Mtn., near Mora County line. Johnson Mesa, Park, (Colfax). 16 mi E of Raton and N of US 64 and 87. Named for Lige Johnson, first settler in the park, which is S of the mesa.

Jones (McKinley). Jones Camp (Socorro). E of Chupadera Mesa, S of Gran Quivira near Claunch; shown on a territorial map in 1908. Jones Canyon (Colfax). Extends from Colorado line to Canadian Red River, 10 mi W of Raton. Jonesville (Quay, Curry). First postmaster, Joseph C. Jones. Post office, 1908-11; mail to Pleano.

Joneta (Lincoln). Post office, 1923-26. See Lon.

Jordan (Quay). SW part of county, on US 156, 28 mi S of Tucumcari. Named for Jim Jordan, who established the post office, 1907-55. From 1902 to 1909, the locality was the scene of constant fights between cattlemen and sheepmen. Homesteaders came later.

Jornada (Sierra). On AT&SF RR, 37 mi N of Hatch. Post office, 1903-04; mail to San Marcial. Jornada del Muerto (Socorro, Sierra, Doña Ana). Span., "journey of death." This celebrated topographic feature lay on the caravan routes from Chihuahua to Santa Fe, and was chosen for travel because it shortened the route by at least a day. It was a waterless stretch of nearly 90 mi from Rincon to San Marcial between San Andres Mts. on E and Fray Cristobal Range on W. In addition, many miles were sandy, and sometimes the Indians made their attacks from hiding places in the mountains or the arroyos. Oñate in 1598 named one of the arroyos *Los Muertos*, "The Dead," and the phrase *jornada del muerto* in Spanish is "journey of the dead man." However, since hundreds perished in this crossing, women and children as well as men, "journey of death" seems a much more fitting translation. Jornada Experimental Reserve (Doña Ana). W of San Andres Mts., 10 mi N of Doña Ana Peak.

Jose (Luna). Post office, 1902-05; mail to Cooks.

Jose Antonio Lucero Grant (Santa Fe). Original grant by Gov. Gervasio Cruzat y Gongora, Sept. 20, 1732, to Jose Antonio Lucero, one fanega of planting land on Santa Fe River above and near the city of Santa Fe.

Jose Garcia Grant (Sandoval). Granted in 1742 to Capt. Jose Garcia near the M. and S. Montoya Grant at the place called Guadalupe.

Joseph (Rio Arriba). Post office, 1884; changed to Abiquiu. Joseph (Socorro). Post office, 1887-98; mail to Frisco; 1901-06; changed to Aragon.

Jose Trujillo Grant (Santa Fe). Also called Pueblo Quemado Grant. Descendants of the original settlers reported a decree prior to the year 1743, citing references in contiguous grants to the Town of Quemado. However, their claim was dismissed for lack of documents and evidence as to the boundaries of the allotted area.

Juana Lopez (Santa Fe). Post office, 1866-70. See Sitio de Juana Lopez Grant.

Juan Bautista Vigil et al. Grant (Doña Ana, Sierra, Socorro). A grant of 2½ million acres by Gov. Manuel Armijo, Jan. 10, 1846, to three petitioners who agreed to dig wells in the center of the Jornada and defend them against Indians, in order to aid travellers through the "journey of death." Since the planned improvements were not made, the grant was later cancelled by the U.S.

Juan de Dios Peña Grant (Santa Fe). On Galisteo River near Ortiz Mine Grant. Petitioners claimed the grant was made by legislative assembly on May 22, 1830, to Juan de Dios Peña and others.

Juan de Mestas Grant (Santa Fe). Extends below the Pueblo of Pojoaque to the Pueblo of Jacona. On Dec. 10, 1699, Lieut. Gen. Roque Madrid, chief alcalde and war captain for Pedro Rodriguez Cubero, Governor and Captain General, placed Juan de Mestas in possession of the said land with the formalities prescribed by law.

Juan la Cruz Canyon (Colfax). At head of Vermejo River, near the former site of Elkins post office. Named for Juan La Cruz who first had a home in the canyon in 1875.

Juan's Lake (San Juan). 7 mi W of Chaco Canyon National Monument.

Juan Tabo Canyon (Bernalillo). Boulder-strewn canyon on W slope of Sandia Mts., 10 mi NE of Albuquerque. Established by the U.S. Forest Service in 1936 as a public recreation area. On April 5, 1748, a petition designated La Cañada de Juan Taboso as W

of Sandia Mtns. Twitchell, *Span. Arch.*, I, 235.
Taboso Indians were akin to Apaches of Texas.
Tabo is a Spanish word in the Philippines
meaning "cup made from coconut shell." The
name is listed by Elsie Clews Parsons as one
used by members of a ceremonial society at
Jemez, some 30 mi NW of this area. (*The
Pueblo of Jemez*, 1925, p. 38.)

JUAN TAFOYA (Cibola). Post office, 1895-99;
mail to Seboyeta.

JUAN TOMAS (Bernalillo). Former bean-growing
community 20 mi SE of Albuquerque, and 1
mi E of NM 10. Named for John Thomas, a
ranch owner about 1870.

JUDSON (Roosevelt). Community 4 mi SW of
Elida. First postmaster Judson Hunter. Post
office, 1907-18; mail to Elida.

JUNCTION (San Juan). Post office, 1895-96; mail
to Farmington. JUNCTION CITY (San Juan).
Post office, 1891-95; changed to Junction.

JUNE (San Miguel). Post office, 1918-28. See
ILFELD.

K AISER LAKE (Eddy). Artificial lake 8 mi
SE of Artesia; formed after 1917 when the
U.S. Reclamation Service planted tamarisks
to prevent silt from being washed into Lake
McMillan. The lake at that time covered 12
acres and from 1926 to 1940 was used for
fishing and as a game preserve. Named for
three Kaiser brothers who homesteaded here
from 1906 to 1910. A. A. Kaiser was county
school superintendent about 1910. The red,
yellow, orange, and white cliffs rising on its
E side are encrusted with "Pecos diamonds,"
valueless but of sparkling stone. After 1940,
the area was drained by the Carlsbad Irrigation Project and at present the river flows in
a big ditch entirely through the old lake bed.

KAPPAS ARROYO (Colfax). Side stream from Canadian Red River.

KAPPUS (Quay). First postmaster, Anthony Kappus. Post office, 1910-13.

KARR CANYON (Otero). Narrow, scenic canyon
about 5 mi long in high altitude, where orchards and flowers grow abundantly. Named
for an early settler, Will Karr, who homesteaded here in 1886.

KARRUTH CREEK (Catron). 9 mi N of Luna.

KATHERINE LAKE (Santa Fe). At timber line
1 mi NE of Santa Fe Baldy Mtn.; 8 mi by
trail up Windsor Creek from Cowles. Named
for Katherine Chavez Page Kavanagh, owner
of Los Pinos Guest Ranch on Pecos River.

KEARNEY (Otero). On SP RR, 2 mi W of US
54, 5 mi NW of Alamogordo. Named for
Perry Kearney, a rancher who ran cattle on
shares for T. B. Catron at this location.

KEARNY'S GAP (San Miguel). A cut through
a range of hills about 5 mi NW of Las Vegas
through which US 85 passes. According to
the *New Mexico*, American Guide Series
(1940), this gap was named for Gen. Stephen
W. Kearny, commander of the Army of the
West, who passed through here on Aug. 17,
1846, to encounter the Mexican governor,
Armijo. For a number of reasons, Armijo dismissed his men and fled south. Kearny occupied both Las Vegas and Santa Fe without
firing a shot.

KELLAR LAKE (Eddy). 4 mi NW of Carlsbad
Caverns National Park.

KELLY (Socorro). 27 mi W of Socorro, and 2
mi SE of Magdalena. A townsite was laid out
here in 1870 and named for Andy Kelly, a
sawmill operator who also operated a lead-
zinc mine. In the 1880's silver was also mined
here and zinc recoveries supported the community until 1931. As many as 3,000 people
once lived here. Kelly is now a ghost town.
Post office, 1883-1945. KELLY MOUNTAINS
(Catron). 13 mi S and W of Reserve.

KEMP (Bernalillo). First postmaster, Dina
Kemp. Post office, 1907-08; mail to Albuquerque.

KENNA (Roosevelt). On US 70, 35 mi SW of
Portales. Originally named URTON for two
brothers who came to the region from Missouri in 1884. One of them became a foreman
on the old Bar V Ranch that extended W to
Pecos River. There are two reports as to the
changing of the name. One is that a contractor
named Kenna camped here during the construction of the roadbed for AT&SF RR. The
stages from Amarillo, Tex., and from the
west stopped here to exchange mail and pas-
sengers at Kenna's Camp. Then after the
railroad was built, the name Kenna remained.
The vice-president of the railroad was E. D.
Kenna, and this may have contributed to the
choice of a name. Post office, 1902-05; changed
to URTON. Restored to Kenna; 1906—.

KENNEDY (Lincoln). First postmaster, Silas A.
Kennedy. Post office, 1888-90; mail to Lower
Peñasco. KENNEDY (Santa Fe). At junction
of AT&SF RR, and NMC RR; 20 mi due S
of Santa Fe. Post office, 1906-18.

KENT (Doña Ana). F. H. Kent was general
manager of the Doña Dora mines about 1909.

First postmaster, Garard W. Kent. Post office, 1904-11; mail to Organ.

KENTUCKY MESA (San Juan). Mesa N of San Juan River W of Fruitland. So named because a group of Kentuckians homesteaded here in 1910.

KENZIN (Doña Ana). On SP RR, 20 mi SW of Las Cruces and 5 mi NW of Afton.

KEOTA (Colfax). Station tunnel on AT&SF RR, 3 mi N of Raton.

KEPHART (Union). Former store and post office on farm of Tom Kephart, 20 mi SE of Abbott. Dwelling became headquarters of Jay Lemon Ranch.

KERMIT (Roosevelt). On AT&SF RR, 15 mi SW of Portales. One version of the naming reports it as commemorative of President Theodore Roosevelt's son, who was killed in World War I. Another account traces it to D. Kermit Fitzhugh, one of two brothers from Clovis who laid out a townsite here. Post office, 1910-18. Previously called PLATEAU.

KETTNER (Cibola). Former logging camp 32 mi W of Grants in Zuñi Mts. Once operated by the Kettner Co. Post office, 1904-09; changed to SAWYER.

KIDNEY WATER SPRING (Sandoval). See SULPHUR SPRINGS.

KILBOURNE HOLE (Doña Ana). Large subsidence crater, more than 1 mi across and 600 ft deep, in lava beds of Crater of Aden area, 22 mi W of Anthony.

KIMBALL (Colfax). Post office, 1890; changed to SPRINGHILL. KIMBALL (Hidalgo). Mining camp near Stein's Peak.

KIMBROUGH (Lea). On TNM RR, 7 mi NW of Hobbs.

KING (Lea). Former homesteading village, 10 mi SE of Tatum; E of McDonald. Now abandoned. Named for family who had early-day post office here. Post office, 1909-18.

KINAHOLI (San Juan). Navajo trading post and settlement. In Navajo kin bi neo'li means "a drafty house."

KINGSTON (Sierra). Community on NM 180 9 mi W of Hillsboro. Now partially deserted town and tourist attraction of the old mining days; just inside Gila National Forest. Silver was discovered here in 1880. The townsite was laid out by the Kingston Townsite Co., and derives its name from the Iron King Mine. Post office, 1882-1957.

KINIBITO (San Juan). Navajo trading post and settlement, 10 mi S of Haynes. To the Navajos, gini bit' o means "hawk's nest."

KINNEY (Bernalillo). Railroad switch 4 mi S of Albuquerque. Named about 1929 or 1930 for a clay pit and manufacturing plant of the Kinney Brick Co., founded by B. H. Kinney of Albuquerque.

KIOWA (Colfax). 15 mi SW of Capulin. Known as the Kiowa District, which was first known as the KIOWA CAMP. Although the Kiowa Indians never lived here, at certain seasons they liked to stop at this place en route to the East, to fish and hunt and give their ponies rest and food. Kiowa district post office, 1877, intermittently, to 1904; mail to Folsom. This post office was also sometimes called CUNICO, a family name often heard in the section. KIOWA MOUNTAIN (Rio Arriba). 3 mi SW of Tusas.

KIRK (Quay). Post office, 1908-21. See FORREST.

KIRTLAND (San Juan). Fruit-farming community on US 550, 9 mi W of Farmington. Post office at Olio before 1903. KIRTLAND AIR FORCE BASE (Bernalillo). At SE edge of Albuquerque city limits. Air Corps Advanced Flying School was established in 1941 to train bomber pilots, copilots, bombardiers, and mechanics. Named for Col. Roy S. Kirtland, pioneer Air Corps pilot. Atomic testing and engineering activities began in 1946. Major Air Force organizations at Kirtland are the Special Weapons Center, the Weapons Laboratory, the Directorate of Nuclear Safety, and the New Mexico Air National Guard. Primary mission of Kirtland is nuclear research, development, and testing.

KIT CARSON'S CAVE (McKinley). 6 mi NE of Zuñi. Named for Kit Carson who was said to have taken shelter here during his campaign against the Navajos in 1864. KIT CARSON PEAK (Colfax). Small peak at mouth of Little Red River about 3 mi S of Raton. Some people call it SQUAW PEAK, and others Kit Carson Peak because a small group stood off an Indian attack from its top, while one of their party rode to the settlement for help which routed the Indians two days later.

KLONDIKE HILLS (Luna). Between Hermanas and Gage, NE of Hachita. CEDAR GROVE is part of these hills.

KNOB CREEK (Taos). 1 mi S of Tres Ritos.

KNOWLES (Lea). Former ranching community on NM 132, 13 mi SE of Lovington and 9 mi N of Hobbs. Once the largest settlement in the county, but now abandoned. Named for Rube Knowles who furnished mail service on horseback as early as 1903, at first without pay. Called OASIS for a short time. With the discovery of oil at Hobbs, people tore down buildings and moved them S to the new oil settlement. Post office, 1903-44.

KOEHLER (Colfax). 16 mi SW of Raton on NM 375. Named for Henry Koehler, one-time chairman of the Maxwell Land Grant Board. The land was owned for sixty years by the St. Louis, Rocky Mountain and Pacific Coal Co., but in 1955 the Kaiser Steel Corp. purchased the coal-mining properties, and in 1957 the mining operations were reactivated. Post office, 1907-57. KOEHLER JUNCTION (Colfax). On Ute Division of AT&SF RR where the tracks for Koehler coal camp begin; the junction is 2 mi E of Koehler.

KOOGLER (San Miguel). Post office, 1921-31. See TECOLOTEÑOS.

KORNEGAY (Lea). Siding and stock pen on TNM RR 7 mi S of Hobbs. Named for the Kornegay Ranch which the railroad crossed when it was constructed in 1930.

KRIDER (Roosevelt). On AT&SF RR, 33 mi NW of Portales.

KROENIGS (San Miguel). On AT&SF RR, 5 mi SW of Watrous.

KUTZ CANYON (San Juan). Empties into San Juan River 3 mi W of Bloomfield.

LA BAJADA (Santa Fe). Span., "descent." Trading point on NM 22, 15 mi NE of Domingo, and 7 mi E of Peña Blanca. Named for the mesa and road, formerly a steep series of hairpin curves on the old Santa Fe Trail between Santa Fe and Albuquerque. Post office, 1870-72. LA BAJADA MESA (Santa Fe). One of the most famous landmarks on the Chihuahua Trail was the descent (and ascent) of the mesa shelf between Santa Fe and Albuquerque. Some 19 mi S of Santa Fe, the freighters wound down the cliff of black basalt for more than a mile, bracing their wagons with boulders when they stopped, and, after the days of automobile traffic, pouring water into boiling radiators. In 1932, the highway was moved 5 mi S and E, on a longer but less precipitous grade. La Bajada has always been the dividing line between the section of the state called Rio Arriba "upper river," and Rio Abajo, "lower or down river," symbols of divisions in both economy and politics. The original name of this area was LA MAJADA, "a sheltered place where shepherds put up for the night with their flocks." Later, the road

from Santa Fe to the Rio Abajo district descended from the higher plateau near this point, and so the transition from Majada to Bajada was easy and natural.

LABELLE (Taos). Post office, 1895-1901; mail to Elizabethtown.

LABORCITA. In Spanish, the Latin word for work, labor, came to mean the plowing and tilling of land. Hence, a labrador is not a laborer, but a farmer. In NM, labor was extended to mean the very land that was tilled, and so laborcita means a small patch of tilled land. Also spelled LAVORCITA. LABORCITA (Socorro). Little town between Socorro and San Antonio. Named because it was originally a group of small farms. Also called RIVER VIEW because of its clear view of the Rio Grande. LABORCITA CANYON (Otero). Small farm or ranch in Lincoln National Forest on W slope of Sacramento Mts. The stream is a tributary of La Luz Creek and is about 6 mi long. Settled in 1885 by Frank and Jesus Borunda because of its numerous springs for irrigation.

LA CAÑADA (Rio Arriba). In 1680, there was a settlement of Spaniards here near the old Tewa pueblo of Santa Cruz de la Cañada, in the neighborhood of San Juan and Santa Clara. Post office, 1852-57. See SANTA CRUZ.

LA CASA LAKES (Mora). Span., "house." Several small lakes W of Cleveland.

LA CIENAGA (Santa Fe). Post office, 1906-07; mail to Santa Fe. See CIENAGA.

LA CINTA (San Miguel). Span., "ribbon, band, strip." Post office, 1877-88; mail to Bell Ranch. LA CINTA CREEK (Harding, San Miguel). Flows 1 mi S of Roy into San Miguel County, through Pablo Montoya Grant, to join Canadian River.

LA COLONIA (Doña Ana). See LAS COLONIAS.

LA CONCEPCION (San Miguel). Post office, 1882-85; mail to Las Vegas. See CONCEPCION.

LA CRUZ DE ANAYA (Sierra). Span., "cross of Anaya." Seventeenth-century Spanish campground on the Jornada del Muerto. Named because of a cross over a grave.

LA CUARA (Torrance). 5 mi N of Mountainair, S of Punta.

LA CUESTA (San Miguel). Post office, 1873.

LA CUESTA DE DON FRANCISCO (Doña Ana). Slope of Mt. Frank, just N of Las Cruces.

LA CUEVA (Mora). Span., "cave." Ranching community on the Rio de la Casa, at junction of NM 3 and NM 21, 5 mi SE of Mora. Post office, 1868—. LA CUEVA (Rio Arriba). Also known as LA CUEVA REGION. Caves here extend 30 yd into the cliffs. According to Tewa legend, this is where the Keres people entered into this world. LA CUEVA (Sandoval). Sawmill site on NM 4 just W of Porter. LA CUEVA (San Miguel). LA CUEVA (Santa Fe). 3 mi E of Glorieta. LA CUEVA LAKE (Mora). 1 mi E of La Cueva, and 5 mi SE of Mora. LACY (Roosevelt). 4 mi NW of Floyd. Named for Lacy Crabtree, who, with his father, had a store here. Post office, 1907-17.

LADD (Colfax). First postmaster, Charles B. Ladd. Post office, 1886-89; mail to Springer.

LADIM (Grant). On SP RR, 18 mi SE of Lordsburg.

LADRON MOUNTAINS (Socorro). 25 mi NW of Socorro. Also called Los LADRONES. These mountains became a hideout for Navajo and Apache horse thieves and later for American rustlers. They are very rocky and trails are passable only on foot or single file on horseback. One of the American bandits had a ranch in the area which lent cover to his marauding activities. He is said to have had a spy in Socorro who was thought to be a simpleton, but nevertheless reported to his master information which aided in the robberies.

LA FRAGUA (San Miguel). Span., "forge, blacksmith's shop." On NM 3 about 4 mi S of Ribera. Formerly called EL PUEBLO. LA FRAGUA CANYON (Rio Arriba). In Carson National Forest; flows W into La Jara Creek, 8 mi N of Gobernador.

LAGARTIJA CREEK (San Miguel). Span., "wall lizard, rock lizard." Sometimes misspelled LAGARTIGA. Rises 5 mi NE of Trujillo; flows NE near Sanchez.

LA GLORIETA (San Miguel). Post office, 1875-80. See GLORIETA.

LA GOTERA (Cibola). See DRIPPING SPRINGS.

LAGUNA (Cibola). Span., "lake." Name of an Indian pueblo on US 66, 46 mi W of Albuquerque. The Laguna Indians are a Keresan group who were given a land grant by the King of Spain in 1689. They had named their locality pokwindiwe onwi, "pueblo by the lake." There were other Keres forms meaning "lake, water dammed up, much water," but the Spanish word laguna seems to cover them all. Nothing remains of the lake, the original bed of which is now a meadow. The present village was built toward the close of the eighteenth century, and a number of other Indian groups seem to have joined the Lagunas in building it. Post office, 1879—. LAGUNA AMBROSIA (McKinley). See AMBROSIA

LAKE. 12 mi NE of Prewitt. LAGUNA DEL MUERTO (Sierra). "Dead man." E of Fray Cristobal Range. In G. F. Ruxton, Adventures in Mexico (1848), p. 175, there is a reference to Laguna del Muerto, in the Jornada del Muerto. LAGUNA DEL PERRO (Torrance). "Dog." 7 mi W of Lucy. In Tewa, known as the "accursed lakes." LAGUNA GATUNA (Lea). N of US 180, 10 mi W of Lea. LAGUNA LARGA (Rio Arriba). Large lake, covering 25 acres, 6 mi SE of San Miguel. LAGUNA LINDA (Mora). On the flat ridge between the Rio La Casa and Cebolla Creek, near Cleveland. LAGUNA PLATA (Lea). N of US 180, 12 mi W of Lea. LAGUNA PUEBLO (Cibola). See LAGUNA. LAGUNA PUEBLO GRANT (Cibola). On Sept. 27, 1870, the U.S. Surveyor General confirmed the Laguna Land Grant of 1689, measuring 5 mi square and including the lake. Today the lake has disappeared, but the Rio San Jose still furnishes water for the irrigation of crops. LAGUNA SALADA (Catron). See ZUÑI SALT LAKE. LAGUNA SECA (San Miguel). "Dry." LAGUNA TONTO (Lea). N of US 180, 11 mi NW of Lea. LAGUNA TOSTON (Lea). N of US 180, 14 mi W of Lea. LAGUNITA (San Miguel). "Little lake." Settlement 3 mi W of US 84, 15 mi S of Las Vegas on Bernal Creek, which must have provided the water to inspire this descriptive name. LAGUNITAS (Sandoval). 3 mi SW of Cuba. LAGUNITAS LAKES (Taos). Several small lakes at head of San Antonio Creek, N and S of Tres Piedras.

LA HUERTA (Eddy). Span., "garden." On AT&SF RR, 2 mi N of Carlsbad. The water supply from Lake Avalon seems to have made possible this place name.

LA JARA. In Spain this is the name for the European labdanum tree, but in NM the term was applied to the scrub willow. The place name use is widespread. Its English equivalent would be Willow Place, The Willows, Willow Creek, etc. LA JARA (Mora). Settlement, 3 mi N of Rainsville. LA JARA (Sandoval). Farming community on NM 126, 15 mi W of Los Alamos. Post office, 1911—. LA JARA CANYON (Rio Arriba). Runs N and W past Pounds. LA JARA CANYON (Taos). 1 mi from Colfax County line, entering the Rio Fernando de Taos to the W. LA JARA CREEK (Mora). Flows E and S near Rainsville to enter Coyote Creek 2 mi from Mora River. LA JARA CREEK (Rio Arriba). Rises E of Gobernador in Carson National Forest; flows NW into San Juan River. LA JARA CREEK

(Sandoval). In the Valle Grande on Baca Location No 1, in Jemez Mts. LA JARA LAKE (Rio Arriba). On Jicarilla Apache Indian Reservation. LA JARA PEAK (Sandoval). 7 mi NW of Riley.

LA JENCIA (Socorro). 10 mi NE of Magdalena.

LA JENCIA CREEK (Socorro). Joins the Rio Salado 8 mi SE of Riley.

LA JOLLA (Rio Arriba). See VELARDE.

LA JOYA (Socorro). Span., "ornament, jewel." Farming community on NM 47 and AT&SF RR, 20 mi N of Socorro, on the Rio Grande. Formerly called LA JOYA DE SEVILLETA, and later RANCHOS DE LA JOYA. Another possible identification is with *hoya,* "valley, river basin." A stopover settlement for caravans and pioneer travel along the Rio Grande. It is in the Sevilleta Grant and near the Indian pueblo named Sevilleta by Oñate. Post office, 1871—.

LA JOYITA (Socorro).

LA JUNTA (Guadalupe). Span., "union, junction." LA JUNTA (Lincoln). See HONDO. LA JUNTA (Mora). Post office, 1868-79; changed to WATROUS. LA JUNTA CREEK (Taos). Main fork of the Rio Pueblo or Tres Ritos Creek, joining the main stream at Tres Ritos.

LAKE ALICE (Colfax). In Sugarite Canyon about 2 mi S of Lake Maloya. The lake is Raton's supplementary water supply. Named for Alice Jelfs, the daughter of John Jelfs, a prominent banker in Raton at time lake was constructed by AT&SF RR. LAKE ALICE (Rio Arriba). One of three small lakes at head of Las Trampas River. The other ones are Lake Hazel and Lake Ruth.

LAKE ARROYO (Colfax). Side stream from Canadian Red River. Named for the character of its location.

LAKE ARTHUR (Chaves). Ranching and farming community on US 285, 8 mi S of Hagerman. Named for the lake, which served as a memorial to Arthur Russell, who in 1893 settled on a ranch 3 mi N of the town. Post office, 1904—. LAKE ARTHUR (Chaves). 3 mi NE of the town.

LAKE BALDES (Torrance). Probably a variant of Spanish Valdez, a family name. 3½ mi N of Socorro County line, 15 mi SW of Progreso.

LAKE BURFORD (Rio Arriba). On NM 95, 8 mi W of El Vado Lake; drains into Chama River. Also known as STINKING LAKE, and its Tewa name bears out the description, *pokwee,* "lake" and *soo,* to "smell."

LAKE DAVID (San Miguel). Near Mora County line 5 mi E of Sapello.

LAKE EIGHT, ELEVEN (Colfax). Part of a group of numbered lakes in an area 5 by 7 mi NW of Maxwell. See NUMBERS.

LAKE ERIN (Catron). 12 mi NW of Luna.

LAKE FORK (Taos). The small upper reaches of the Rio Hondo N and E of Taos.

LAKE FOURTEEN (Colfax). See LAKE EIGHT.

LAKE HAZEL (Rio Arriba). One of three small lakes at head of Las Trampas Creek.

LAKE ISABEL (San Miguel). 8 mi W of Watrous.

LAKE JOHNSON (Santa Fe). See JOHNSON LAKE.

LAKE KATHERINE (Santa Fe). See KATHERINE LAKE.

LAKE LA TULE (Curry). Southwestern Span., "cattail, reed." 5 mi S of Melrose.

LAKE LUCERO (Doña Ana). An alternately dry and filled alkali lake at SW end of White Sands National Monument, at Otero County line. Special permission is necessary to visit the area. See LUCERO.

LAKE MALOYA (Colfax). 6 mi NE of Raton; near head of Sugarite Canyon. It impounds water from springs, rain, and melting snow for Raton's municipal water supply; also used for fishing and recreation.

LAKE McMILLAN (Eddy). Large storage dam on Pecos River, about 10 mi long and 4 mi wide. Named for W. H. McMillan, a wealthy early-day resident of Carlsbad, who was prominent in the organization of the Pecos Valley Land and Ditch Co. in 1887. This company later became the Pecos Irrigation and Investment Co. It was taken over by the U.S. Reclamation Service as the Carlsbad Irrigation Project.

LAKE PEAK (Santa Fe). Just S of Santa Fe Baldy Mtn. Considered by the Tewa Indians as the "sacred mountain of the East." They held summer ceremonials at the lake on top of the peak.

LAKE RUTH (Rio Arriba). One of three small lakes at head of Las Trampas River.

LAKE TWO, SEVEN, TWELVE, THIRTEEN, TWENTY (Colfax). See LAKE EIGHT.

LAKE VALLEY (Doña Ana, Sierra). 2 mi W of Monument Peak, 18 mi S of Hillsboro on NM 27. Once a prosperous mining town in center of Lake Valley mining district, one of the heaviest silver-producing districts in NM. Productive ore was discovered by George W. Lufkin in August, 1878, and a mining rush followed. He chose the name DALY, but the site was renamed Lake Valley for a small lake near the settlement. Production between 1882 and 1888 exceeded four million dollars. Then mining activity declined. Even the lake dried up. Post office, 1882-1955. Also called SIERRA CITY. LAKE VALLEY (Socorro). Post office, 1880-81.

LAKEVAN (Chaves). Post office, 1897-98; mail to Hagerman.

LAKEWOOD (Eddy). Former farming and ranching community 14 mi S of Artesia and 2 mi E of US 285. So called because of its proximity to Lake McMillan. Post office, 1904—; formerly called McMILLAN.

LA LAGUNA DEL DIFUNTO AMBROSIO (McKinley). See AMBROSIA LAKE.

LA LANDE (De Baca). Ranching community on US 60, 7 mi E of Ft. Sumner. Different versions are given about the name. A merchant of Kaskaskia sent a Frenchman, La Lande, in 1804 over the Santa Fe Trail. Zebulon Pike refers to Baptiste La Lande in his *Expedition* (1810), but there is nothing to confirm this early visitor in association with a later settlement. There is an unconfirmed report that the town was named for a long-time employee of the SF RR who died during its construction, around 1905. All trains on the system were stopped on the day of his burial. The early homesteaders here were unable to make a living on the barren land and soon left when the county seat was established at nearby Ft. Sumner. Post office, 1906-55.

LA LIENDRE (San Miguel). Span., "string of nits." Ghost town 21 mi SE of Las Vegas on NM 67. So called because the houses were strung along the roadside. It was settled about 1845 and 1850 by people named Duran and by Juan de Dios Maes. Post office, 1878, intermittently, to 1942.

LA LOMA (Guadalupe). Span., "small hill." Farming and ranching community on NM 119, 34 mi SE of Las Vegas. Named because of its location on the slope of the neighboring mountain range. LA LOMA DE PEDRO BARBON (Sandoval). Also called LOMA BARBON. 5 mi S of Santa Ana Pueblo.

LA LUZ (Otero). Span., "light." Near US 54 and NM 83, 7 mi N of Alamogordo. Oldest settlement in Tularosa Basin. Once the site of a nationally known pottery works. The first chapel was built here in 1719. Two missionaries on their way to northern NM stopped, baptized a number of Indians, and built a chapel which they named "Our Lady of Light." Post office, 1886—. LA LUZ CANYON (Otero). On W slope of Sacramento Mts. Settlement made in 1864 just a few miles

above the present village of La Luz. The canyon is 10 mi long, while its width varies from a narrow gorge to broad meadows, not exceeding ½ mi. LA LUZ CREEK (Otero). Has a high source on W slope of Sacramento Mts.; flows SW into Fresnal Creek. LA LUZ DITCH (Otero). A man-made channel which conveys water to Alamogordo for irrigation purposes.

LAMA (Taos). Span., "mud, ooze." Settlement 3 mi N of San Cristobal near Lama Canyon.

LA MADERA (Rio Arriba). Span., "wood, lumber." Mining, ranching, and farming community on NM 111, 32 mi N of Española. Settlement dates from 1820 and a founder Juan de Dios Chacon, but the name may be a later selection based on sawmill operations in the ponderosa pine forest of the Halleck and Howard Lumber Co. of Denver. Post office, 1906-08; mail to Ojo Caliente; 1911—. LA MADERA (Sandoval). Winter sports area in Sandia Mts., 17 mi NE of Albuquerque city limits.

LA MAJADA (Santa Fe). See LA BAJADA. LA MAJADA GRANT (Sandoval, Santa Fe). Tract begins 3 mi N of Pena Blañca and extends NE 8 mi, crossing Santa Fe County line. Given to Capt. Jacinto Pelaez on Feb. 10, 1695, and revalidated by Governor Cubero on Dec. 13, 1698.

LAMANCE (Cibola). Stock-farming settlement on W edge of lava flow about 40 mi SW of Grants near Fence Lake. Among its settlers is a colony of Seventh-Day Adventists, the place being named for one of them in 1930.

LA MANGA (San Miguel). Span., "sleeve, fringe of land." Settlement 5 mi S of Las Vegas on NM 3.

LA MESA (Bernalillo). Span., "tableland." LA MESA (Doña Ana). Farming community on NM 28, 6 mi S of Las Cruces. Named for nearby lava flow called Black Mesa. Founded 1854-57 by Spanish Americans, and a few Anglo-American pioneers. In the nine years, 1845 to 1854, this part of the Rio Grande Valley remained in Mexico until the Gadsden Purchase became effective on Nov. 16, 1854. Settlement was desirable here because it was a higher tract of land and free from overflow by frequent floods that submerged nearly all other parts of the valley. First post office, named VICTORIA, but locally called La Mesa. Post office, 1908—. LA MESA DE SAN MARCIAL (Socorro). See SAN MARCIAL. LA MESA ENCANTADA (Cibola). See ENCHANTED MESA. LA MESILLA (Doña Ana). See MESILLA.

LA MOSCA CANYON (Valencia). Span., "fly." Runs NW from La Mosca Peak. LA MOSCA PEAK (Valencia). 1 mi N of Mt. Taylor.

LAMY (Santa Fe). Community on US 285, 17 mi SE of Santa Fe. When the AT&SF RR was extended into Santa Fe (1880), the junction of the main line and the spur into Santa Fe was named Lamy, honoring Archbishop John B. Lamy who entered the newly created American diocese in 1851, five years after Territory was occupied by U.S. troops. Bishop Lamy carried on a notable educational and missionary work in the Southwest. He is the central figure in Willa Cather's memorable novel *Death Comes for the Archbishop* (1926). Settled by people who used to live in Cañoncito or Hornos, about 4 mi away. Post office, 1881—. LAMY GRANT (Santa Fe). Tract of irregular shape, about 4 mi at widest part, surrounding the village of Lamy. Archbishop Lamy took the land claim in trust for the Roman Catholic Church on Sept. 29, 1857. Area is 16,546.85 acres.

LANARK (Doña Ana). On SP RR, 25 mi NW of El Paso, Tex. Post office, 1905-21.

LANCY CREEK (Grant). 12 mi N of Pinos Altos.

LANE SALT LAKE (Lea). 4 mi SE of Roberts.

LANGSTROTH CANYON (Catron). Small tributary of White Creek in Mogollon Mts. W of Gila Cliff Dwellings National Monument.

LANGTON (Roosevelt). Named for Joe Lang, who operated a ranch in the vicinity and was an early sheriff in the county. Post office, 1904-30.

LA PLACITA (Taos). Span., "little place or plaza." On NM 3, about 2 mi N of Taos Plaza; in existence since 1778. LA PLACITA DE LOS GARCIAS (Bernalillo). Area on Guadalupe Trail 1 mi S of Alameda.

LA PLATA (San Juan). Farming and ranching community on NM 17, 14 mi N of Farmington. Named for the river. Founded in 1877 and settled by Edward Williams. Originally, the area was in the Jicarilla Apache Reservation. The government tried to settle the Ute Indians on it, but they refused. It was then thrown open for settlement for a little while, with claims on 160 acres per person. Post office, 1881, intermittently, to present. LA PLATA RIVER (San Juan). Rises in Colorado Mts. and empties into San Juan River below Farmington. May have been named by Juan Rivera, who led a party of Spaniards to La Plata Mts. in Colorado in 1765, by way of San Juan River. The purpose of the trip was to investigate rumors of gold and silver. Rivera crossed Dolores River to San Miguel, thence to Uncompahgre River. In 1776, Escalante and Dominguez, two friars, came into Colorado from Santa Fe, blazing a route known as the Old Spanish Trail.

LA POSTA (Sandoval). Span., "post stage." See CABEZON.

LA PUENTE (Rio Arriba). Span., "bridge." Farming and ranching community 14 mi S of Chama. Named for small settlement near Abiquiu with the same name. Post office, 1920-44.

LA QUESTA (San Miguel). LA QUESTA (Socorro). In SW corner of county at Sierra line. See QUESTA.

LARGO (De Baca). Span., "long, extended." On AT&SF RR, 28 mi W of Ft. Sumner. LARGO (Lincoln). Small community on US 54 and SP RR, 19 mi N of Carrizozo. LARGO (San Juan). Said to be descriptive of extent of San Juan River. Navajo, *tqahot tquel,* "where the water spreads." Post office, 1883-1927. LARGO CANYON, CREEK (Catron). Fed by several tributaries which head in Gallo Mts. and Mangas Mts.; flows NW. LARGO CANYON (Lincoln). Rises in Lincoln National Forest; flows S, then W into Socorro County. LARGO CREEK (Rio Arriba, San Juan). Rises in Sandoval County and flows N to the San Juan, entering it near Blanco.

LA RINCONADA (Bernalillo). Span., "corner." In the Southwest, the word means "small, secluded place." Settlement in foothills 1 mi N of Alameda.

LARKSPUR PEAK (Taos). Mountain 12,000 ft high N of Taos Pueblo.

LA SALINA GRANT (Torrance). Tract about 1 mi square containing salt deposits; 6 mi SW of Lucy. Simon Prada owned it on Jan. 5, 1846, and transferred it to George W. Paschal for whom a survey was made by the deputy surveyor for Bexar County, Tex., on July 22, 1859. Sometime after this it belonged to Henry Voelker.

LAS ANIMAS CREEK (Sierra). See ANIMAS CREEK.

LAS COLONIAS (Guadalupe, San Miguel). Post office, 1873-75; 1878-99. See COLONIAS.

LAS CORNUDAS MOUNTAINS (Otero). See CORNUDAS.

LAS CRUCES (Doña Ana). Span., "crosses." County seat on US 70, 80, 85, and AT&SF RR; heart of the Mesilla Valley on the Rio Grande and the site of New Mexico State University. Authorities differ as to why the town received this name. There is one report that a Spanish caravan was attacked by Apaches in 1848, and massacred near the southern border. Searching parties, discovering the mutilated bodies of the victims, gave them decent burial, erected wooden crosses to their memory, and from these crosses Las Cruces got its name. Another account is that a caravan of oxcarts at an earlier date, en route from Chihuahua, was attacked by Indians, and a few days later a second party of freighters found the bodies and erected crosses over their graves. The only certainty seems to be that a collection of crosses marked a burial ground here in the 1840's and suggested the name. Post office, 1854—.

LAS CUEVAS (Doña Ana). Span., "caves." Rock formation on W side of Organ Mts. So called because the formation contains several caves.

LAS DISPENSAS (San Miguel). NM Span., "store rooms for food." Community 8 mi NW of Las Vegas, on NM 65.

LAS FABRES (Mora). See FEVERAS.

LAS GALLINAS (Mora). See GALLINAS.

LAS HUERTAS (Sandoval). Settled by the original grantees of San Antonio de las Huertas Grant, made by the Spanish on Dec. 31, 1767. See SAN ANTONIO DE LAS HUERTAS GRANT. LAS HUERTAS CANYON, CREEK (Sandoval). Runs N through San Antonio de las Huertas Grant W of Placitas. LAS HUERTAS OJO LAKE (Valencia). 10 mi E of Tome.

LAS MANUELAS (Mora). Small community in a cluster of Spanish settlements N of Ocate.

LA SMELTA (Socorro). Hispanicized form of English "smelter." Name given to SW part of Socorro when the Billings smelter was here. Also called PARK or PARK CITY. Original survey made in 1882. Post office, 1892-94; mail to Socorro.

LAS NUTRIAS (McKinley). Span., "beavers." Zuñi Indian farming village of Taiakwin. LAS NUTRIAS (Socorro). Settlement on NM 47, 14 mi S of Belen. Governor Otermin reports that he and his Spanish forces were at this place in January 1582 on their second withdrawal from NM.

LAS PALOMAS (Sierra). 7 mi S of Truth or Consequences, and just E of US 85. Settled by the Garcia and Tafoya families, both bringing in numerous peons who were released from obligation by law soon afterwards. At one time a place to which the natives and Indians made pilgrimages in order to be benefited by the remedial natural springs here. Post office, 1881—.

LAS PEÑUELAS (Doña Ana). Span., "big rocks." Seventeenth-century Spanish campground now known as POINT OF ROCKS, because of the distinctive rock formations.

LAS PLACITAS DEL RIO (Rio Arriba). Span., "little plazas of the river." LAS PLACITAS (Sierra).

LAS TABLAS (Rio Arriba). Span., "boards, planks." Mining, lumbering, and ranching community 8 mi S of Tres Piedras. Name refers to lumber. Post office, 1911—. LAS TABLAS (Lincoln). See ARABELLA. LAS TABLAS CANYON (Lincoln). Tiny stream in Capitan Mts., 9 mi N of Lincoln.

LAST CHANCE CANYON (Eddy). In Guadalupe Mts., 35 mi NE of Carlsbad; flows E to Dark Canyon. Named in 1881, when a party following a band of marauding Indians was about to turn back for lack of water, and discovered, as a "last chance," the running stream here.

LAS TORRES (San Miguel). 19 mi SE of Las Vegas.

LAS TRAMPAS (Taos). See TRAMPAS. LAS TRAMPAS CREEK (Taos). Heads N of Truchas Peak, flowing NW near Trampas. LAS TRAMPAS GRANT (Taos). W of Las Trampas and Embudo River. Granted by Governor Cachupin on July 15, 1751, to Juan Arguello and others, heads of twelve families, to supplement a concession one month earlier from the land of Sebastian Martin.

LAS TRUCHAS CREEK (De Baca). Heads in Quay County and flows into Pecos River near Ft. Sumner. LAS TRUCHAS GRANT (Rio Arriba). Given to Francisco Montes Vigil in 1754.

LAS TUSAS (San Miguel). NM Span., "prairie dogs." Trading point, 4 mi W of Sapello and 15 mi NW of Las Vegas.

LAS UVAS MOUNTAINS (Doña Ana). See SIERRA DE LAS UVAS.

LAS VEGAS (San Miguel). Span., "meadows." County seat, agricultural and livestock center on US 85 and AT&SF RR. Home of New Mexico Highlands University, founded in 1893. Greater Las Vegas is composed of two communities, the city on the E side of Gallinas River and Old Town or West Las Vegas on the W side. Community originally known as NUESTRA SEÑORA DE LOS DOLORES DE LAS VEGAS, "Our Lady of Sorrows of the Meadows." During Mexican War, on Aug. 15, 1846, Gen. Stephen Watts Kearny with his Army of the West arrived in Las Vegas, and from a housetop in the old plaza read his proclamation. The city was a resting place for caravans before venturing into the dangerous canyons on the way to Santa Fe. Escudero in *Noticias* (1849) shows the locality as Vegas on his caravan map, and calls it VEGAS DE LAS GALLINAS in his list of settlements. Post office, 1850—. LAS VEGAS GRANT (San Miguel). 35 mi E to W and 20 mi N to S. In 1821 Luis Maria Cabeza de Baca petitioned the Mexican governor for a grant of land bordering on the Rio Gallinas, then called the VEGAS GRANDES, for himself and his seventeen sons. Though the grant was made in 1823, it was never completely occupied because of encroachment by the Indians. First settlement of any size was made in 1833, when a group of men from San Miguel del Bado, on Pecos River, petitioned for a grant. It was given under condition that a plaza be erected for protection against the Indians. This grant was confirmed by action of the U.S. Congress on June 21, 1860. See BACA LOCATION No. 2. LAS VEGAS HOT SPRINGS (San Miguel). 5 mi NW of Las Vegas where AT&SF RR operated a series of luxury hotels between 1880 and 1903. Post office, 1882-1902. See MONTEZUMA.

LAS VIEJAS MESA (Rio Arriba). Span., "old women." S of Alire and the Rio Cebolla and W of US 84. Indian name was *kwee yo-o-ah*, which meant "old woman, steep slope." There would seem to be a relationship to the Spanish, *las viejas*. It appears as MESA DE LOS VIEJOS on the Geological Survey Map. Provisional Edition (1955).

LA TETILLA PEAK (Santa Fe). See TETILLA PEAK.

LATIR LAKES (Taos). Group of seven lakes at head of LATIR CREEK, a tributary of Costilla Creek. Name has been reported to be a French surname. There is however, a Spanish verb, *latir*, "to howl, bark," which could have associations with coyote or wolf calls. LATIR PEAK (Taos). E of Questa and N of Baldy.

LA TULE LAKE (Curry). See LAKE LA TULE.

LA TUNA (Doña Ana). See ANTHONY.

LAUGHLIN (Colfax). LAUGHLIN PEAK (Colfax). In E end of county near Union County line.

LA UNION (Doña Ana). On NM 28, 29 mi S of Las Cruces. Post office, 1909-57.

LAVA (Socorro). Community on AT&SF RR, 16 mi S of San Marcial and 22 mi N of Engle. Post office, 1886-1903. LAVA (Rio Arriba). LAVA BEDS (Lincoln). 3 mi W of Carrizozo. They are about 60 miles long and 4 mi wide where US 380 crosses them. The

crater from which the molten lava flowed is 15 mi NW of Carrizozo, and is called LITTLE BLACK PEAK. Within the confines of the malpais are enormous blow holes, 30 to 40 ft wide and nearly as deep, where often the original ground level may be seen as a lighter patch of grass-covered soil at the bottom. LAVA BEDS (Socorro). So named because of location near edge of lava flow just E of upper end of Elephant Butte Reservoir and just N of Sierra County line. The area is reached by a county road from San Marcial. LAVA BEDS (Valencia). Scattered over NE and NW parts of the county are scores of extinct volcano craters, which in eruption, almost covered the area from a point W of McCarty's to Grants, and 25 mi S. Near the Ice Caves is one of these craters whose molten lava flowed like a river over the area E of the Continental Divide. US 66 has been cut through this deposit, some of which is 20 ft thick. The flow between Grants and McCarty's is of comparatively recent origin, possibly only a few thousand years old. "The year of the fire," of which the Laguna Indians speak, may refer to a lava flow. Crossing the lava is almost impossible, except by paths, as it is broken with upheavals and fissures. The largest crater, in San Mateo Mts., is almost 80 ft deep.

LA VEGA DE SAN JOSE (Cibola). See SAN FIDEL.

LA VENTANA (Sandoval). Span., "window." Coal-mining and ranching community on NM 44, 45 mi NW of Bernalillo; in Nacimiento Mts.; it provides a windowlike view. Post office, 1925-32.

LA VILLITA (Taos). Span., "little village." 2 mi N of Alcalde, 7 mi N of Española.

LAVORCITA (Socorro). See LABORCITA.

LAWYER CANYON (Eddy, Otero). Heads on E slope of Guadalupe Mts. 18 mi NE of Cienaga; flows E into Rawhide Canyon.

LEA (Lea). Formerly oil camp and electric generating plant on NM 176, 15 mi W of Oil Center, and 26 mi SW of Hobbs. Named for the county. Post office, 1929-31. LEA COUNTY. Created on Mar. 17, 1917. Named for Capt. Joseph C. Lea of Roswell, who came to NM from Cleveland in 1876. He lived for a time in Elizabethtown, and came to Roswell in 1877. He is known as "the father of Roswell" and the founder of New Mexico Military Institute. He died in 1904. Lea County was formed from parts of Chaves and Eddy counties and has a present area of 4,394 sq mi.

LEACH (Roosevelt). Post office, 1909-11; changed to GARRISON.

LEASBURG (Doña Ana). Trading point on US 85, 14 mi N of Las Cruces. First postmaster, Adolphe Lea. Post office, 1866, intermittently, to 1898. LEASBURG DAM (Doña Ana). 3½ mi NW of Leasburg.

LECHUGUILLA CANYON (Eddy). Southwestern Span., "agave." In Guadalupe Mts., SE of Queen.

LEDOUX (Mora). Village 4 mi S of NM 3; named for early fur trapper. Post office, 1902—.

LEE LAKE (Cibola). 6 mi NE of Mt. Taylor lookout. Named for the Lee family, owners of a large sheep ranch with headquarters at San Mateo.

LEE'S PEAK (Hidalgo). In Pyramid Mts. 3 mi SW of Lordsburg, and about ½ mi from the ghost town of Shakespeare. Known by old-timers as the location of the "Great Diamond Fiasco." See SHAKESPEARE.

LEGANSVILLE (Curry). First postmaster, John W. Legan. Post office, 1907-14. See BELLVIEW.

LEGGETT (Catron). See WET LEGGETT SPRING.

LEIGHTON (Union). First postmaster, Hampton W. Leighton. Post office, 1890-1904; mail to Folsom.

LEMITAR (Socorro). Farming community on US 85, 7 mi N of Socorro. There is some question as to the origin of the name. Consensus seems to be that it was originally named for a Mexican family called something like Lemitar, the present name being a corruption. There is, however, a plant called *lemita*, "buckbrush, skunk brush, *rhus trilobata*," which produces berries found here. They have a lime taste. Children used to make a sort of lemonade from these berries crushed in sugar and water. Post office, 1866, intermittently, to present.

LEON (Harding). Span., "lion." Now deserted; was on E bank of Ute Creek, 20 mi NE of Mosquero. Post office, 1898-1911. LEON (Mora). Post office, 1892-1912; mail to Baca. LEON CREEK (Harding, Union). Small creek that flows SW into Pinabete Arroyo. LEONCITO (Guadalupe). Span., "little lion." On SP RR 5 mi NE of Vaughn. Named for a rock formation that resembles a small lion.

LEOPOLD (Grant). 11 mi SW of Silver City, in Little Burro Mts.; sister town of Tyrone in the canyon just above it. In 1908 the commercial center of Burro Mtn. mining region. Nothing is left of the town but its jail, which remains because it was an old mine tunnel, with a grilled iron door at the entrance. Post office, 1904-14.

LEROUX GRANT (Taos). 10 mi N of Taos and W of Wheeler Peak. Named for the family to whom the grant was made. Joaquin Le Roux is mentioned in chronicles of the 1840's in the company of Uncle Dick Wooten, Kit Carson, and Pedro Miranda of the Beaubien-Miranda Grant family.

LE RUE (Rio Arriba). Cluster of homes W of NM 95, 12 mi N of Lindrith. Possibly a transfer name from settlers on Antoine Leroux Grant.

LESBIA (Quay). On CRI&P RR, 9 mi E of Tucumcari. Named when the railroad started through Amarillo, Tex., to Tucumcari in 1901-02, and known as a railroad switch. Transfer name from an Aegean island famed as the home of the Greek poetess, Sappho. Formerly called RUDOLPH. From 1910 to 1913, as CASTLEBERRY, for the first postmaster. Post office, 1914-18.

LESLIE SPRING (Chaves). 4 mi N of Acme.

LESPERANCE (San Miguel). First postmaster, Pedro Lesperance. Post office, 1890-96; changed to GERONIMO.

LEVY (Mora). Ranching and farming community on US 85 and AT&SF RR, 5 mi N of Wagon Mound. Named on July 12, 1883, to honor the manager of the railroad commissary. Formerly called EVANS. Post office, 1908—. LEVY (San Miguel). See PECOS.

LEWIS (Curry). N of Grady on the caprock. Named for the old Jack Lewis Ranch. First postmaster, John H. Lewis. Post office, 1907-10. LEWIS LAKE (Chaves). 3 mi E of Pecos River in N part of county, 50 mi N of Roswell.

LEWISTON (Roosevelt). W of Elida. First postmaster, Nettie Lewis, 1907-11; mail to Elida. LEWISTON LAKE (Roosevelt). 11 mi SE of Floyd.

LEW WALLACE PEAK (Taos). 7 mi W of Eagle Nest Lake. Named for Gen. Lew Wallace, who was territorial governor of New Mexico from 1878 to 1881.

LEYBA (San Miguel). Farming and ranching community 13 mi E of US 285, 28 mi SW of Las Vegas. The family name first appears in the person of Pedro de Leyva, who is named in Spanish archives of the colony as early as 1661. He was a captain and lieutenant governor for the Salinas Pueblo district. First postmaster, Francisco S. Leyba. Post office, 1908—.

LIBERTY (Doña Ana). LIBERTY (Quay). A roaring cowtown in the 1870's on Pajarito Creek. It was the mecca for cowpunchers a hundred miles around. Now not even a ghost town, as it has vanished completely from its location 3 mi from the present city of Tucumcari. The settlement died when the railroad came to Tucumcari in 1901. LIBERTY (San Juan). 17 mi W of Farmington. Post office, 1907-20; formerly JEWETT. LIBERTY (San Miguel). Post office, 1880-1902. LIBERTY (Valencia). Site of one-room school built in 1936 for children of homesteading families, 50 mi SW of Grants. Name selected by community as representative of the freedom of homesteaders.

LIGHTNING LAKE (Otero). 5 mi S of Marcia.

LILLY MOUNTAIN (Catron). 12 mi NW of Gila Cliff Dwellings National Monument. LILLY PARK (Catron). On W Fork of Gila River, 1 mi S of Lilly Mtn. Called park because it was a clearing in timber country and a natural preserve for game. Named for a rancher-prospector who was killed here by the Apaches in 1885. His name was spelled both Lilly and Lilley, resulting in confusion with Ben Lilley, who hunted lions in the same territory later.

LIMESTONE CANYON (Socorro). Begins 8 mi S of Dismuke and runs to the head of Alamosa Creek.

LINCOLN (Lincoln). Ranching community on US 380, 32 mi SE of Carrizozo, on Bonito River in El Capitan Mts. Settled in 1849 and first named LAS PLACITAS, "little plazas or settlements"; then called BONITO for river of the same name. After the county was created in 1869, the name of the town was changed to honor Abraham Lincoln, sixteenth President of the United States, 1861-65. It became the county seat, but in 1909 the county offices were moved to Carrizozo. A rock formation to the right of US 380, 1 mi E of Capitan, strongly resembles the profile of the Civil War President. The town became famous between 1878 and 1881 as the center of the Lincoln County War featuring William (McCarty) Bonney, "Billy the Kid." His escape from the Lincoln County jail on Apr. 28, 1881, fifteen days before the date set for his hanging, is re-enacted annually with a local cast and the original setting. Post office, 1873—. LINCOLN CANYON (Lincoln). Runs from Capitan Mts. SW into Rio Hondo near Lincoln. LINCOLN COUNTY. When established, Jan. 16, 1869, it embraced all the territory between 34th parallel on the N, Texas boundary on

the S, Pecos River on the E, and San Andres Mts. on the W. In 1889, Chaves and Eddy counties were cut off the E side and ten years later Otero County was taken from the SW corner. At present, the area is 4,859 sq mi LINCOLN NATIONAL FOREST (Lincoln). Composed of areas originally created as Sacramento Forest on July 26, 1902, Gallinas Forest on Nov. 5, 1905, Guadalupe Forest on Apr. 19, 1907. On July 2, 1908, these areas were combined and designated as ALAMO FOREST. On July 1, 1918, the name was changed to its present form. Gross area is 1,444,311 acres.

LINDRITH (Rio Arriba). Farming and ranching community on NM 95, 20 mi NW of Cuba. Named for Lindrith Cordell, the son and stepson of Mr. and Mrs. C. C. Hill, when they established a post office and store on their homestead. Post office, 1915—.

LINGO (Roosevelt). On NM 92, 30 mi SE of Portales. Originally named NEED, July 26, 1916, but the Post Office Department said it was too much like WEED, in Otero County. Name changed to LINGO, Mar. 6, 1918, and site moved 3 mi N of old location. Despite reports that the name had something to do with the way people talked on the E slope next to Texas, the town probably commemorates a family name. Post office, 1918—.

LISBOA SPRINGS (San Miguel). LISBOA SPRINGS HATCHERY (San Miguel). Built in 1921 on Pecos River, 28 mi E of Santa Fe.

LISBON (Hidalgo). Siding 11 mi SE of Lordsburg, on SP RR. Site on Culberson Ranch, known in days of the Butterfield Overland Mail.

LISTON (Chaves). First postmaster, Henry G. Liston. Post office, 1907-14.

LITTLE BEAR LAKE (McKinley). 6 mi SW of Ft. Wingate.

LITTLE BLACK PEAK (Lincoln). Extinct volcano, 15 mi NW of Carrizozo. Source of the lava beds. See LAVA.

LITTLE BLUE LAKE (Taos). 5 mi NE of Latir Lakes, N of Baldy.

LITTLE BURRO PEAK (Socorro). In San Andres Mts. in SE corner of county.

LITTLE BURRO MOUNTAINS (Grant). Run NW beyond Tyrone, E of Big Burro Mts.

LITTLE CHAMA RIVER (Rio Arriba). Main fork of Chama River, emptying into it just below Chama. See CHAMA.

LITTLE CREEK (Grant). Small tributary of West Fork of Gila River, emptying into it 2 mi above XSX Ranch.

LITTLE CREEK (Lincoln). Flows S through Alto.

LITTLE CROW CREEK (San Miguel). Flows into Canadian Red River directly W of Eagle Tail Mtn. Drains a portion of Crow Creek flats.

LITTLE CUERVO CREEK (San Miguel). Rises at San Miguel and flows NE to Cuervo Creek.

LITTLE DEEP CREEK (Catron). Flows W from Bearwallow Mtn., 7 mi W and S of Negrito.

LITTLE DOG CANYON (Catron). Flows S from above Cantrell Lake; in Guadalupe Mts.

LITTLE FLORIDA MOUNTAINS (Luna). See FLORIDA.

LITTLE HATCHET MOUNTAINS (Hidalgo). See HATCHET.

LITTLE PINE CREEK (Catron). Rises on W slope of Brushy Mtn. and flows NW.

LITTLE RED RIVER CANYON (Colfax). Named for Little Red River which flows through it. See CANADIAN RIVER.

LITTLE RIO GRANDE, LOWER (Taos). Consists of the Little Rio Grande from its junction with Taos Creek up to the mouth of Pot Creek. Flows through Ranchos de Taos. LITTLE RIO GRANDE, UPPER (Taos). Consists of the Little Rio Grande from Pot Creek to its head; flows through canyon N of U.S. Hill on road from Taos to Mora.

LITTLE SALT LAKE (Roosevelt). 11 mi SE of Portales.

LITTLE SAN PASCUAL MOUNTAINS (Socorro). See SAN PASCUAL.

LITTLE TURKEY CREEK (Grant). The S fork of Little Creek.

LITTLE WALNUT CREEK (Grant). Flows NW between Juniper Hill and Stewart Peak, 3 mi NE of Bear Mtn.

LIZARD (Doña Ana). On SP RR, 12 mi NW of El Paso, Tex., and 4 mi N of Texas border.

LLANO (Guadalupe). Span., "plain." Near San Miguel County line, just S of Anton Chico. LLANO (Taos). Lumbering and farming community on NM 75, 20 mi S of Taos. Post office, 1898—. LLANO DE SAN JUAN (Taos). LLANO ESTACADO (Quay). "Staked plains." There has been considerable debate both as to the origin and meaning of this colorful term for a great plateau stretching from Canadian River in NM and Oklahoma S for 400 mi. The Pecos River is, roughly the W edge of the Staked Plains, and the Palo Duro Canyon, 200 mi away, is the E border line. Curving along the N and W rim is the caprock, like a stockade or *estacada* in Spanish, "palisade, fence." This rough barrier made the canyons and grassed areas a refuge for game and wild horses, and famous as pasture land for cattle. Other explanations for the name have ranged from the yuccas as "stakes" in the area to the belief that caravan trains from Chihuahua to Arkansas in the nineteenth century, or from Texas W, marked their trail with stakes. The name does not appear, however, on the caravan map in Escudero's *Noticias* (1849). LLANO LARGO (Taos). Village on the Rio Santa Barbara, 6 mi E of Trampas. LLANO QUEMADO (Taos). "Burnt." Settlement on NM 3, ½ mile S of Ranchos de Taos. Name was first applied to Indian ruins excavated here by the Smithsonian Institution in 1920. LLANO VIEJO (Guadalupe). On NM 119, W of Dilia.

LLAVES (Rio Arriba). Span., "keys." Trading point on NM 112, 10 mi N of Gallina. Post office, 1940—.

LLOYD (Colfax). On NM 85, 6 mi SW of Maxwell.

LOBATO (Rio Arriba). On D&RGW RR, 4 mi N of Chama. The first man of this name in NM, Bartolome Lobato, arrived in 1695 and settled in Santa Cruz; from there the family spread throughout the N part of the province. J. J. LOBATO GRANT (Rio Arriba). Abiquiu is in the center of this large land grant in SE section of county.

LOBO (Taos). Span., "wolf." Formerly AQUA DE LOBO, corruption of AGUA DEL LOBO. Post office, 1905-11; mail to Arroyo Seco. LOBO CREEK (Taos). Flows down Lobo Peak into Arroyo Hondo. LOBO CREEK (Valencia). Flows into Lobo Canyon 6 mi W of Mt. Taylor. LOBO PEAK (Taos). A broad-based mountain of Sangre de Cristo Range, 4 mi E of San Cristobal. Here D. H. Lawrence came to Del Monte (also called Kiowa) Ranch in September 1922 and stayed until spring. He returned in 1924 and 1925 after trips to Mexico and England. He was joined by several other writers and artists during these years and a small colony existed on the slopes of Mt. Lobo. Lawrence died in France on Mar. 2, 1930. His ashes were brought to the ranch on Lobo Peak in 1936 and interred in a small white chapel. Both ranch and chapel were deeded by Mrs. Lawrence to the University of New Mexico in 1956. On August 11 of the same year Frieda Lawrence died in Taos and was buried two days later in front of the chapel.

LOCKNEY (Quay). Former settlement 15 mi W of Nara Visa, near Harding County line. Post office, 1909-35.

Loco Arroyo (Colfax). Span., "insane." Flows into Canadian Red River. The so-called "crazy" creek was named because of its intermittent risings. Loco Hills (Eddy). Settlement on US 83, 14 mi W of Maljamar. Loco Hills (Eddy). Run N and S just E of the town.

Lo de Mora (Mora). See Mora County.

Lo de Padilla Grant (Bernalillo, Valencia). Situated in two counties E of the Rio Grande below Isleta Pueblo. Granted to Diego de Padilla by Governor and Captain General Cosio on May 14, 1718.

Logan (Quay). Ranching community 24 mi NE of Tucumcari, on NM 39 and US 54. Named in honor of a Captain Logan of the Texas Rangers. Post office, 1901—.

Logville (Socorro). Deserted place on US 60, 30 mi W of Magdalena, on San Augustin plains and surrounded by cattle country.

Lola Creek (Rio Arriba). Flows N into the Rio de los Pinos at San Miguel near Colorado line.

Loma (Taos). Span., "hill." Loma Alta (De Baca). "High." Adjoins highway between Yeso and Vaughn. Named because it rises 200 to 300 ft above the surrounding plains. Loma Grande (Lincoln). On NM 37, 10 mi SE of Carrizozo. Loma Parda (Mora). "Gray." In modern Spanish, pardo, a, denotes a "brownish shade," resulting from a mixture of black, white, yellow, and red. In old Spanish and in NM usage, only black and white are considered; thus "gray" is the result. Ghost town on N bank of Mora River, 6 mi NW of Watrous. During the heyday of Ft. Union 6 mi NE, Loma Parda entertained the soldiers with saloons, dance halls, and gambling houses. Post office, 1872-1900; mail to Watrous. Loma Vista (Luna). Lomito Ojo Lake (Valencia).

Lon (Lincoln). Trading point on NM 42, 30 mi SE of Corona. In 1924, it was first called Joneta for Mrs. Joneta Bagley, but in 1931 Ben Moseley established a general store and was appointed postmaster. He named the place for his son, Lonnie. Post office, 1934-42.

Lone Mountain (Grant). In central part of county, about 2 mi NW of Hurley. So named because it is the only mountain in the immediate vicinity, and is surrounded by level plateaus. In the 1870's a gold-mining camp was here. See Newton. Lone Mountain Peak (Lincoln). A lone peak at S end of Jicarilla Mts., containing deposits of iron ore

and extensive beds of white, black, and mottled marble. Lone Pine (Socorro). Post office, 1882-83; mail to Gila. Lone Star (Quay). Lone Tree Lake (Lincoln). 28 mi E of White Oaks. Lone Tree Lake (San Miguel). See Truchas Peak Lake.

Long Canyon (Otero). Tributary of Sacramento River. Long Canyon (Taos). Tributary of Upper Hondo, N of Taos. Long Canyon Mountains (Catron). E of Tularosa Mts. 9 mi SE of Aragon. Longs (Roosevelt). Post office 8 mi NW of Causey from 1907 to 1920, during which there were two postmasters, Thomas H. and Robert F. Long.

Lookout (Eddy). Post office, 1883-92; changed to Malaga. Lookout Canyon (Catron). Steep, rough fork of Mogollon Creek, heading against Mogollon Peak. Lookout Mountain (Valencia). Ranger station on a peak in Zuñi Mts., between McGaffey and Paxton Lumber camps in Cibola National Forest. Name applied because this peak makes an admirable lookout and observatory station for the U.S. Forest Service.

Looney (Quay). First postmaster, Henry J. Looney. Post office, 1908-13; changed to Woodrow.

Lopez. The name is found in both seventeenth- and eighteenth-century NM archives. A Nicolas Lopez was killed at Santo Domingo in the Pueblo Rebellion of 1680. The widow and three sons returned to NM in 1693 after the Reconquest. Pedro Lopez del Castillo also returned at the time of the Reconquest, with his wife Maria de Ortega, and was living at Bernalillo in 1699. His family, and that of his sister, Juana Lopez del Castillo, are thought to have come from Bernalillo with the original families to found Albuquerque in 1706. Lopez (San Miguel). 5 mi SW of San Miguel. Lopezville (San Miguel). Post office, 1881-86; mail to Cabra Spring.

Lordsburg (Hidalgo). County seat, mining and ranching town on US 70 and 80, on SP RR. 20 mi N is the Solar Radiation Observatory maintained by the Smithsonian Institution. Founded Oct. 18, 1880, when SP RR reached here from the W. The community at Grant, or Shakespeare, moved to the new location at the tracks. Lordsburg was named for an engineer in charge of the construction crew. Post office, 1881—. See Shakespeare.

Loretta (Colfax). Community in coal mining area 2 mi N of Dawson. Named for the Loretta coal mine.

Los ABEYTAS (Socorro). See ABEYTAS.

Los AGUATES (San Miguel). Span., "puddles, small pools of water." So named because this condition prevails in a deep arroyo in the neighborhood.

Los ALAMOS (Los Alamos). Span., "poplars, cottonwoods"; *álamo temblón*, "aspen." 24 mi NW of Santa Fe. There was a settlement here as early as 1880, but it was named by Ashley Pond when he established the Los Alamos Ranch School for boys here in 1917. Taken over by the Manhattan District of the U.S. Army in 1943 to build a laboratory for research in nuclear physics. From its beginning, the Los Alamos Scientific Laboratory has been managed and operated by the University of California as a contractor, first for the Army and since Feburary 1947 for the U.S. Atomic Energy Commission. The University of New Mexico has a graduate center here. Los Alamos became county seat in 1949. Post office, 1941, intermittently, to present. Los ALAMOS (San Miguel). Trading point 13 mi NE of Las Vegas. Post office, 1878-1919. Los ALAMOS CANYON, RINCON (Los Alamos). 5 mi NW of Los Alamos. Los ALAMOS COUNTY. In north-central portion of state, W of the Rio Grande, about 16 mi NW of Santa Fe in Jemez Mts. Created on June 10, 1949, from portions of Sandoval and Santa Fe counties by action of the state legislature. Area comprises only 111 sq mi. Los ALAMOS CREEK (San Miguel). Los ALAMOS RESERVOIR (Los Alamos). Water-supply lake for Los Alamos project.

Los AMOLES (Doña Ana). See AMOLES.

Los ARENALES (Bernalillo). See ARENAL.

Los BRAZOS (Rio Arriba). Post office, 1922-26. See BRAZOS.

Los CAVOS (San Miguel). Community 7 mi N of US 66 at Clines Corners.

Los CERRILLOS (Santa Fe). See CERRILLOS. Los CERRILLOS GRANT (Santa Fe). Original grantee was Alfonso Rael de Aguilar, who received this land NW of Galisteo on Sept. 18, 1692, from Gov. Diego de Vargas.

Los CHAVEZ (Valencia). Trading point on NM 47, 10 mi N of Belen. Named for descendants of Don Fernando de Chaves. Post office, 1929-34. See CHAVEZ.

Los CHUPADEROS (Mora). 6 mi NE of Mora on old wagon road to Guadalupita and Ocate.

Los CORRALES (Sandoval). See CORRALES.

Los DIEGOS (San Miguel). Span., "the James folks." 28 mi SW of Las Vegas; 8 mi S of San Miguel.

Los DURANES (Bernalillo). See DURAN.

Los ESPINOSAS (Rio Arriba). Settlement 5 mi S of El Rito. See ESPINOSA.

Los GABALDONES (Valencia). See GABALDON.

Los GALLEGOS (Rio Arriba). See GALLEGOS.

Los GARCIAS (Valencia). See GARCIA.

Los GRIEGOS (Bernalillo). Suburb in NW Albuquerque. Family name which originally meant "people of Greek origin."

Los GUAJALOTES (Bernalillo). See PADILLAS TABLELAND.

Los HORNILLOS (Doña Ana). Span., "little ovens, fireplaces." See ROUGH AND READY.

Los HUEROS (Mora). Mexican Span., "fair, blond." Settlement in hills N of Ocate.

Los JARALES (Valencia). See JARALES.

Los LADRONES (Socorro). See LADRON MOUNTAINS.

Los LENTES (Valencia). Farming area W of the Rio Grande between Isleta Indian Reservation and Los Lunas. Named for three Indian families who settled S of Isleta about 1850. The original name, as listed in 1730, was ENTE and in 1736, EL ENTE, colloquial Span., "guy"; *los lentes*, "those guys."

Los LUCEROS (Rio Arriba). Span., "the Lucero folks." 3 mi N of Alcalde. Shown on 1862 map. Post office, 1855-77; changed to PLAZA DEL ALCALDE. See LUCERO.

Los LUNAS (Valencia). Span., "the Luna folks"; the masculine article is used here because of the family name. Farming community and county seat on US 85 and AT&SF RR, 21 mi S of Albuquerque. Named for descendants of Diego de Luna, who was born in 1635. Post office, 1855-57; 1865—. See LUNA.

Los MARTINEZ. (Bernalillo). Part of Albuquerque, between Broadway and Edith, NE. Settled by Trinidad Martinez about 1900. Also called MARTINEZ TOWN. See MARTINEZ.

Los MONTOYAS. (San Miguel). On U.S. 84, 12 mi S of Las Vegas. See MONTOYA.

Los NARANJOS, "the Naranjo folks." This family name came to New Mexico in 1600, but there is no connection between the first pioneer and the few individuals of this name who were here in 1680 and returned in 1693. Los NARANJOS (Mora). "Orange trees." On NM 120, 20 mi NW of Wagon Mound.

Los NUTRIAS (Rio Arriba). See TIERRA AMARILLA.

Los OJITOS (De Baca). Span., "little springs." Los OJITOS (Guadalupe). See BESS. Los

OJITOS (Rio Arriba). 5 mi E of Laguna Peak.
Los OJITOS (San Miguel). Post office, 1878-81.
Los OJOS (Rio Arriba). Span., "springs." The
Tewa name for this place is *ohoo*, from the
Spanish *ojos* plus *boo-oo*, "town." Los OJOS DE
SANTA CLARA (Rio Arriba). Not far from San
Miguel. See OJO.
Los ORGANOS (Doña Ana). See ORGAN MOUN-
TAINS.
Los PACHECOS. Span., "the Pacheco folks." A
Geronimo Pacheco was listed as a soldier in
1628 and accused of participating in pagan
games at San Juan Pueblo. A soldier named
Luis Pacheco was in Santa Fe in 1632; and
perhaps the same Luis was companion to
Vicente Pacheco in the escort of soldiers listed
in 1636. Other Pachecos are named in seven-
teenth-century archives both before and after
the Pueblo Rebellion of 1680. Los PACHECOS
(Rio Arriba).
Los PADILLAS (Bernalillo). See PADILLAS.
Los PINOS (Rio Arriba). Span., "pine trees."
Trading point 68 mi NW of Taos, 3 mi W
of US 285, and 1 mi from Colorado border.
Juan Bautista Pino was a traveling merchant
from Mexico City who lived in the area of
Isleta and Belen as early as 1747. His sons
were also merchants, living in Tome. Among
his descendants was Don Pedro Bautista Pino,
who in 1810 became the first and only Deputy
from New Mexico to the Spanish Cortes,
where he presented a report about the province which was published in Cadiz, Spain,
in 1812. The Rito de Pino, in Valencia County, was first claimed from the Indians by original members of the Pino family. Los PINOS
(Valencia). Post office, 1865-66. See PERALTA.
Los PINOS RIVER (Rio Arriba). See RIO DE LOS
PINOS. Los PINOS RIVER (San Juan). Enters
NM at Colorado line to join the San Juan
35 mi E of Farmington. Also called PINE
RIVER.
Los PUERTOS DE ABO (Valencia). Span., "gaps
of Abo." Maj. J. H. Carleton in 1853 reported
that there were two passes through the mountains to the E of the Rio Grande and W of
the ruined mission named Abo. The summit
of the right-hand pass was 19 mi from Casa
Colorado in Valencia. This may be pertinent
to the meaning of Puerto de Luna.
Los QUELITES GRANT (Valencia). In NM, *los
quelites* describes an herb, "lamb's quarter."
Also called SAN FRANCISCO DEL VALLE GRANT.
Possession of this grant, bordering the settle-

ment of Tome, was given on May 4, 1761.
Governor del Valle ordered that the village
be built in "one or two squares, and that they
shall be joined, the walls of the houses of the
settlers serving for each other, and the plazas
they may establish must each be garrisoned by
the round towers opposite each other for defense from enemies."
Los RANCHITOS (Bernalillo). See EL RANCHITO.
Los RANCHOS DE ALBUQUERQUE (Bernalillo). Village in the valley 2 mi N of Albuquerque
city limits. Incorporated Dec. 29, 1958. Name
comes from the Elena Gallegos or Los Ranchos
de Albuquerque Grant. See ELENA GALLEGOS
GRANT.
Los SISNEROS (Mora). 14 mi N of Mora and E of
NM 38.
Los TANOS (Guadalupe). 11 mi NE of Santa
Rosa, on SP RR. Name is Indian from the
Towa group of Tanoans whose villages spread
over the great plain S of the Tewa country. It
was E of the Rio Grande and included communities of the Galisteo Basin. According to
J. P. Harrington, the name means "live down
country people." Post office, 1907-25.
LOST BEAR LAKE (Mora). 2 mi above Pecos
Falls, and 11 mi W of Mora; source of one
of tributaries of Pecos River.
Los TEMASCALITOS (Doña Ana). Span., "the
little steam baths." A group of hills about 12
mi S of Las Cruces. According to Conkling
in *Butterfield Overland Mail,* the hills were
probably named because of their resemblance
to the tentlike steam baths used by Mexican
Indians.
LOST LAKE (McKinley). 7 mi S of Fort Wingate. LOST LAKE (San Miguel). 4 mi W of
Rociada; a source of Maestas Creek. LOST LAKE
(Taos). Head of West Fork of Red River in
high country.
Los TOMASES (Bernalillo). Old settlement now
included in NW Albuquerque, N of Sawmill Road and E and W of Los Tomases
Drive. Name follows the family pattern of
Los Duranes, Los Candelarias, Los Griegos,
and others.
Los TORREONES (Socorro). See LUIS LOPEZ.
Los TORRES (San Miguel). Span., "the Tórres
folks." Settlement in Antonio Ortiz Grant, 20
mi SE of Las Vegas on Gallinas River. Named
by families of this name. The earliest member,
Juan de Torres, appears in the Oñate lists of
1597. A Francisco Gomez de Torres is listed
as captain of the wagon-train escorts in 1619

and 1621. Other members of this family are named in reports after the Pueblo Rebellion of 1680.

Los TRIGOS GRANT (San Miguel). Span., "wheat fields." Small tract spanning US 85, S of Rowe and 24 mi SW of Las Vegas. The title papers for this grant were made under the government of Spain in 1815.

Los TRUJILLOS (Valencia). 1 mi E of Tinaja, N of NM 53; presently abandoned. Named for Spanish families.

Los VALLES DE SAN AGUSTIN (San Miguel). See SAN AUGUSTIN, AGUSTIN.

Los VALLES DE SAN JERONIMO (San Miguel). See MINERAL HILL.

Los VIGILES (San Miguel). Just E of Montezuma. Named for members of the Vigil family. Post office, 1918-24.

LOUIS (Mora, Union). Formerly TRAMPERAS. First postmaster, Louis R. Garcia. Post office, 1892-96; mail to Clapham. See MIERA.

LOURDES (San Miguel). On Gallinas River, 10 mi SE of Las Vegas. Post office, 1919—. See SAN AUGUSTIN, AGUSTIN.

LOVING (Eddy). Farming and ranching community on US 285 and AT&SF RR, 10 mi SE of Carlsbad. First named VAUD, in 1893, for Swiss settlers, who imported Italian laborers to work on their farms. Post office named FLORENCE, 1894-1908; changed to Loving in honor of John Loving, who was one of the first men to drive cattle up the Pecos Valley from Texas about 1889. The Goodnight-Loving Trail from Texas to Cheyenne by way of Ft. Sumner, Las Vegas, Raton, Trinidad, and Denver, was named for John Loving and Charles Goodnight. Post office, 1908—.

LOVINGTON (Lea). At junction of NM 83 and 18, 22 mi NW of Hobbs. Community was established near the turn of the century by two traders, E. M. and J. W. Caudle from Seminole, Tex. The Caudles built the first store here. Named for R. F. (Florence) Love, who in 1903 settled upon a section where the town of Lovington is located. He was state representative from Eddy County before Lea County was formed. His brother, James B. Love, became the first postmaster in 1908, and had the post office in a store on his homestead. Post office, 1908—.

LOWER CAÑONES (Rio Arriba). Settlement on Cañones Creek 1 mi N of Cañones.

LOWER COLONIAS (San Miguel). 5½ mi E of NM 63, and 7 mi NE of Rowe.

LOWER GALLINAS (San Miguel). 5 mi E of Gallinas.

LOWER PEÑASCO (Chaves). Ranching and farming area in SW corner of county on NM 83, 54 mi SW of Roswell. Named for the Rio Peñasco, on which it is situated. The river was dry in many places; yet there were sinkholes with water in them. So the settlers dug out ditches around the sinkholes, and packed the river bed by driving cattle over it. In this way they created a man-made river which lengthened the Peñasco some 25 mi. Post office, 1884-1920.

LOWER ROCIADA (San Miguel). 3 mi from the Mora County line, on NM 105.

LOWER SAN FRANCISCO PLAZA (Catron). Trading point 5 mi S of Reserve.

LOWER VALLECITOS (Sandoval). See VALLECITO.

LOWERY CANYON (Colfax). 15 mi N of Baldy Mtn. on North Fork of Ponil Creek.

LOYD (Quay). Post office, 1906-14.

LUCAS (Mora). First postmaster, Anna Lucas. Post office, 1908-11; mail to Roy.

LUCERO. Pedro Lucero de Godoy, a native of Mexico City, came to NM early in the seventeenth Century. His sons and grandsons figured prominently during the Reconquest. Their descendants heavily populated both Rio Arriba and Rio Abajo districts in Spanish times. LUCERO (Mora). On NM 38, 7 mi NE of Mora. Post office, 1885-1936. LUCERO (Torrance). 10 mi W of Moriarty. LUCERO CREEK (Taos). Heads at Lucero Lake. LUCERO DE GODOI GRANT (Taos). See MARTINEZ or GODOI GRANT. LUCERO LAKE (Doña Ana). See LAKE LUCERO. LUCERO LAKE (Taos). Timber-line lake at head of Lucero Creek in Taos Mts. LUCERO LAKES (Rio Arriba). 7 mi NE of Hopewell. LUCERO MESA (Valencia). LUCEROMONTOYA (Quay). See MONTOYA.

LUCIA (Torrance). First postmaster, Lucy A. Pierce. Post office, 1908-14; changed to LUCY.

LUCIANA, LOUISIANA MESA (Quay). Large mesa connected by a narrow strip of land to the Llano Estacado, 20 mi SW of Tucumcari. The people at Bell Ranch say Luciano is the old name corrupted in recent times to Louisiana, and that it was owned by a pioneer Spanish settler named Luisiano or Luciano.

LUCILLE (Quay). Post office, 1911-34; previously ORTON.

LUCY (Torrance). On AT&SF RR, US 60, 12 mi NE of Willard. Settled by homesteaders about 1905. Three versions of the naming are given:

first for the wife of James Dunn, chief engineer of AT&SF RR; second, for an AT&SF RR attorney's mother from Las Vegas; third, for Lucy Myers, daughter of Frank Myers, a construction engineer for the railroad when the Santa Fe cutoff was being built. Formerly, LUCIA; in 1914 the name was changed to Lucy. The railroad station no longer exists, but the point is still marked on the line and the highway as Lucy. Post office, 1915-42.

LUERA MOUNTAINS (Catron). S of San Augustin Plains and N of NM 78.

LUIS LOPEZ (Socorro). Community 5 mi N of San Antonio. Named for the man who once owned the land. By the middle of the seventeenth century there was an estancia or hacienda of Luis Lopez in the vicinity. Once called LUIS LOPEZ RANCH. Bosquecito, Span., "little bosque," is across the Rio Grande and here stand Los Torreones, "the towers, fortresses," exceedingly thick walls built in circle formation. This may have been a fortress planned for the battle of Valverde. LUIS LOPEZ CREEK (Socorro). 5 mi N of San Antonio. LUIS LOPEZ DRAIN (Socorro). Near Luis Lopez, along the Rio Grande.

LUJAN CREEK (Mora). East Fork of Mora River above Chacon; rises in Rincon Range in extreme NW corner of county.

LUMBERTON (Rio Arriba). Ranching and oil-producing community 18 mi W of Chama, on NM 17. A Mr. Biggs bought 40 acres from a ranch owned by Francisco Lobato; then he surveyed streets and lots. Named about 1894 for the many sawmills in the vicinity. Post office, 1894—; formerly AMARGO.

LUMBRE (Rio Arriba). Span., "fire, light." Post office, 1907-10; mail to Abiquiu.

LUNA. Named for the Luna family, descendants of Diego de Luna, who returned to NM after the Reconquest. His seventeenth-century ancestor was, to all appearances, Juan Gomez de Luna, who came from Zacatecas sometime after 1621. LUNA (Catron). 14 mi NW of Reserve on San Francisco River. Named for Don Salomon Luna, who for more than a quarter of a century was leader of the Republican party in the territory and state. Post office, 1886—. LUNA (Lincoln). Abandoned pump station, on SP RR. LUNA COUNTY. Created on Mar. 16, 1901, when Salomon Luna was a dominant political figure. Present area is 2,957 sq mi. LUNA CREEK (Mora). W fork of Mora River above Chacon; heads in Rincon Range. See Los LUNAS.

LUXOR (Luna). Siding on SP RR 5 mi E of Deming. No longer in use.

LYBROOK (Rio Arriba). Trading point 30 mi SW of Lindrith, on NM 44, between Farmington and Cuba. Will Lybrook came here from North Carolina to homestead in 1918 and was joined by his brother Sam and other members of the family who also homesteaded and set up sheep and cattle ranches.

LYDEN (Rio Arriba). Farming community 30 mi N of Santa Fe. Post office, 1902, intermittently, to 1957.

LYKINS (Roosevelt). Near Benson, W of Floyd. First postmaster, Richard N. Lykins. Post office, 1909-13.

LYNCH (Lea). Former community and oil-pipeline station near Lea. Named for early ranch in area.

LYNN (Colfax). On AT&SF RR, 6 mi N of Raton. Railroad settlement at S entrance to famous Raton Pass Tunnel, highest point on the line. Post office, 1891-1910; mail to Wooten, Colo.

MACHO CREEK (Sierra). Span., "mule, strong." 4 mi W of Lake Valley.

MACY (Roosevelt). 12 mi W of Portales. The name has been reported as an English corruption of Span., mesa, "tableland," but this is an English surname and also in use by an Indian agency post office in Nebraska, where it was coined from the "ma" in Omaha the "cy" in agency. Post office, 1907-13.

MADISON (Union). 8 mi NE of Folsom, in Dry Cimarron Canyon. First town in what is now Union County. All that is left are ruins of the old gristmill. Named for Madison Emery, who settled in NM in 1865. Post office, 1874-88.

MADRE MOUNTAIN (Catron). Span., "mother." In Datil Mts., 9 mi from Socorro County line.

MADRID (Santa Fe). 24 mi SW of Santa Fe, on NM 10. Former coal-mining community. Francisco de Madrid, in NM shortly after the Oñate Conquest, is the ancestor of the Madrid family which returned with the De Vargas Reconquest in 1692. One of the latter's captains, Roque Madrid, was interested in lead mines throughout the general area of the present coal mines where Madrid is located. The settlement dates from 1869, and may commemorate both the Madrid family and the capital city of Spain. Post office, 1896—.

MADRONE (Valencia). Perhaps Span., *madroño,* New Mexican "evergreen oak." On AT&SF RR, 5 mi SW of Belen. Name created when railroad cutoff was built into Belen.

MAES (San Miguel). Ranching community 36 mi E of Las Vegas. The earliest recorded member of the Maese family was Juan Maese, who was in NM as early as 1631. Settlers with this name left when the Pueblo Indians rebelled in 1680, and members of the family returned in 1693, after the Reconquest. They spread E from the Santa Fe area to settle in Mora and San Miguel counties. Post office, 1914-57; formerly GONZALES.

MAESTAS. During the nineteenth century the name Mestas came to be spelled "Maestas," probably influenced by the family name of Maese. MAESTAS CANYON, CREEK (San Miguel). Fork of Manuelitas Creek W of Rociada. A settler with the name Juan de Mestas Peralta returned with his wife to Santa Fe in 1693. In 1710 he was living at Pojoaque. MAESTAS CREEK (Mora). 3 mi W of Rociada. MAESTAS LAKE (San Miguel). At head of Maestas Canyon.

MAGDALENA (Socorro). On US 60, 20 mi W of Socorro. About 1884, when it was settled, one of the largest cattle-shipping centers in the Southwest. One tradition says that an early Spanish priest named the mountains in honor of Mary Magdalene. A more familiar story relates that the name is taken from the face and bust formed by a combination of rocks and shrubbery, seen on N end of the mountain range, which is thought to resemble the head of Mary Magdalene. This stone image is said to have been a sanctuary to which the hunted fugitive could flee in safety. A well-known story in early days tells that a band of Apaches surrounded a party of Mexicans here and were about to overpower them when the face of Mary Magdalene appeared on the mountainside, frightening the Apaches away. Post office, 1880—. MAGDALENA MOUNTAINS (Socorro). In Cibola National Forest, S of Magdalena. MAGDALENA PEAK (Doña Ana). 12 mi S of Hatch. Named because of its supposed resemblance to the head of Mary Magdalene. MAGDALENA MINES (Socorro). Post office, 1878.

MAHILL (Otero). See MAYHILL.

MAIZE (Curry). See PORTAIR.

MAJOR LONG'S CREEK (Union). Flows SE across S tip of county into Texas. Possibly commemorative of Stephen H. Long (1784-1864), American explorer and engineer, who led a U.S. Army expedition in 1819-20 to the Rocky Mts. returning by the Arkansas and Canadian rivers. Long's Peak in Colorado was named for him.

MALAGA (Eddy). Farming community on US 285 and AT&SF RR, 15 mi SE of Carlsbad. Founded in 1892 and named for a sweet Spanish wine made from a variety of grape which grew well here sixty years ago. Settled by Swiss who located on 5-acre tracts and imported Italian labor. Due to impoverishment of the land and plant diseases, most of the grapevines have been plowed under and the land is now the Carlsbad Irrigation Project. Post office, 1892—; formerly LOOKOUT.

MALAGRO HILL (Lincoln). See MILAGRO HILL.

MALDONADO (Mora). Post office, 1896-97; mail to Wagon Mound.

MALJAMAR (Lea). Ranching and oil-producing community on NM 83, 26 mi SW of Lovington. Named for three children of William Mitchell: MALcolm, JAnet, and MARgaret. He was a member of the New York Stock Exchange and started the Maljamar Oil and Gas Co., just south of the present town. He was president of the corporation when it began in 1926, and later became chairman of the board. Post office, 1943—.

MALLETTE CREEK (Taos). Flows SW to Red River, joining it just above the town of Red River.

MALONE (Hidalgo). 15 mi N of Lordsburg. Site of the old Caesar Brook home. Post office, 1884-88; mail to Gold Hill.

MALPAIS. Span., "badlands." See LAVA BEDS. Name appears in three counties of state and describes the lava beds in areas which were once volcanic. MALPAIS (Doña Ana). 2 mi N of Mexican border on SP RR, 22 mi E of Columbus. MALPAIS (Lincoln). Here, the lava beds have been whitened by the drifting dust from the White Sands National Monument farther south. MALPAIS HILL (Harding). 1 mi W of Ute Creek and S of Sierra Negra Mts. MALPAIS HILL (Union). 3 mi SW of Dora and near Farley—Mt. Dora branch of AT&SF RR right of way. MALPIE (Union). Formerly called MALPAIS. This spelling is a clue to the widespread pronunciation in the West: "mal pi." Former trading point 12 mi S of Capulin and NE of Chico near Union County line. Named for the great quantity of volcanic rock found in the hills and area near the settlement. Post office, Malpais, 1909-11; mail to Des Moines; Malpie, 1916-39.

MANBY HOT SPRINGS (Taos). Also called HOT SPRINGS. Medical springs long known by the Indians; 12 mi NW of Taos. Purchased by A. R. Manby, an English mining engineer who came to Taos in 1894-95 and whose decapitated body was found in his Taos house on the evening of July 3, 1929. The murder was never solved.

MANCHESTER (Lincoln). Post office, 1881.

MANCO BURRO, MANCO DE BURRO PASS (Colfax). Span., "crippled." See CHICARICA MESA. Between Chicarica Mesa and Raton Mesa, SE of Raton. "Manco de Burro Pass got its name first from a burro getting crippled, and the stream; also I understand, from the old settlers, that there was a pack train going through to trade with the Indians. Up on the mountains the burro put his knee out of place and limped and when anything limps they say it is 'manco.'" Testimony of Calvin Jones in litigation over Maxwell Land Grant, Sept. 13, 1883. (W. A. Keleher, *Maxwell Land Grant*, p. 90.) MANCOS RIVER (San Juan). In extreme NW corner of state. Originally called EL RIO DE SAN LAZARO.

M. AND S. MONTOYA GRANT (Sandoval). Small area along the Rio Puerco 2 mi N of Cabezon. Granted by Governor Cachupin on Feb. 14, 1767, to Miguel and Santiago Montoya, cousins, whose grandfather had previously owned a house and land at Abiquiu.

MANGAS. Span., "sleeve, fringe of land"; also could be a transfer from Mangas, Colo. Fray Angelico Chavez points out that *mangas* is also used in a figurative sense for "shreds" or "sleeves" of rain pouring from clouds in a sky that is clear in other parts of the heavens. MANGAS (Catron). Community 28 mi W of Datil and 16 mi SE of Quemado. This region is in the heart of the old country of the Apaches, one of whose chieftains was called Mangas Coloradas, "Red Sleeves," but it is doubtful that the place names are Apache commemoratives. Post office, 1909-43; formerly PINOVILLE. MANGAS CREEK (Catron). Rises in Mangas Mts. and flows N to Largo Creek. MANGAS CREEK (Grant). Rises at Tyrone on the Continental Divide and flows NW into Gila River. MANGAS MOUNTAINS (Catron). Short range in center of county, N of San Augustine Plains, and 8 mi S of Mangas. MANGAS VALLEY (Catron). MANGAS (Grant). Post office, 1896-98; mail to Cliff.

MANN (Roosevelt). 10 mi S of Portales. First postmaster, Jasper N. Mann. Post office, 1907-17.

MANSFIELD (Hidalgo). Flag station on SP RR, when it was first built; 20 mi W of Lordsburg. Located on the 712 Ranch owned by J. P. Mansfield.

MANSKER (Union). Site of former consolidated school, 9 mi S of Clayton on NM 18. Named for Robert W. Mansker, old-time peace officer.

MANUELITAS (San Miguel). Span., "little Manuelas." 15 mi N of Las Vegas near Sapello. The masculine name, Manuel, is the Hebrew form of Emmanuel meaning "God with us." Name was often given in baptism to women by simply adding a feminine ending. It is said that a farmer in this area had three daughters, each named Manuela. MANUELITAS CREEK (San Miguel). Above Sapello and flows through Rociada. MANUELITO (McKinley). Settlement on US 66, 16 mi SW of Gallup on AT&SF RR. Named for a famous Navajo leader called Manuelito. It is the center of an area populated by several hundred Navajo Indians. Post office, 1881—.

MANZANA (Torrance). Post office, 1871-72. See MANZANO.

MANZANARES CREEK (San Miguel). Flows through Upper Colonias 2 mi E of Pecos and empties into Cow Creek. Name is an old one in NM, members of this family appearing in records before and after the Pueblo Rebellion in 1680.

MANZANITO CREEK (Grant). Span., "little apple." MANZANO (Torrance). "Apple tree." Near this town on NM 10, 15 mi NW of Mountainair, are two old apple orchards, which tradition claims were planted during the mission period before 1676. But Dr. Florence Hawley Ellis, University of New Mexico, dates the trees, from ring growth, as no earlier than 1800. They are said to be the oldest apple orchards in America. Tradition held that they were planted when Manzano was still one of the pueblos in the Salinas region. However, the Spanish village dates from 1829. Houses of present-day settlement are around a lake. E of the lake is a *torreón* or defense tower, which was constructed as protection against Indian attacks. Post office, 1876, intermittently, to 1919. MANZANO GRANT (Torrance). An area 5 mi square largely SE of Manzano. Settlement dates from Nov. 28, 1829, when the Territorial Deputation passed a decree ordering the Justice of the Jurisdiction to place the petitioners in possession of lands for which they had asked, "giving each one the tillable land he may be able to cultivate, leaving the remainder for such other individuals who in future may establish themselves therein." MANZANO MOUNTAINS (Torrance, Bernalillo). Extend SE of Albuquerque and S of Sandia Mts. Name derived from the town and old apple orchards. MANZANO PEAK (Torrance). High elevation 6 mi SW of village of Manzano for which it is named.

MAQUINA CREEK (Colfax). Span., "machine." 14 mi S of Cimarron. Named for a sawmill here in the early 1870's.

MARBLE CANYON (Otero). On W slope of Sacramento Mts., at base of Alamo Peak within Lincoln National Forest. Named for vast deposits of marble found here. Operations in the quarry were begun by Frank Falcony with the founding of Alamogordo in 1898.

MARCIA (Otero). Lumbering community 12 mi SE of Alamogordo in Sacramento Mts. Named for Marcia Logging Co. Post office, 1923-42.

MARGUERITA (San Miguel). Post office, 1891-92; mail to Genova.

MARIANA (Rio Arriba). Post office, 1891-1906; mail to Abiquiu. MARIANO LAKE (McKinley). Trading post and Indian school operated by U.S. Bureau of Indian Affairs, 8 mi E of Pine Dale and NE of Ft. Wingate. Named for Navajo chief Mariano whose decendants live in this area.

MARINO (Cibola). MARINO LAKE (McKinley). Trading point 35 mi E of Gallup. Name is a Spanish surname. The marriage of Luis Marino appears in Roman Catholic Church records on May 21, 1778. He may have been a brother of Fray Jose Marino, priest of Acoma in 1776.

MARION (Sierra). Post office, 1907-10; mail to Cutter.

MARMON (Cibola). On AT&SF RR, 10 mi SW of Laguna. Two brothers with this name were traders and settlers at Laguna in the latter part of the nineteenth century. One was a civil engineer with AT&SF RR when it came into NM. In 1880-81, he laid out the streets of Albuquerque. He married into the Laguna tribe.

MARQUEZ (Sandoval). Farming and ranching community 20 mi NE of Laguna on NM 279. Named for the Marquez family. Post office, 1901—.

MARTINEZ. Family name traceable to Herman Martin Serrano, a settler who arrived with Oñate in 1598. The Martin Serrano family returned to NM after the Reconquest in 1692. By the nineteenth century the many descendants had dropped the Serrano and had given a z ending to the plural form, resulting in Martinez. MARTINEZ (Bernalillo). First postmaster, Daniel Martinez. Post office, 1902-09; mail to Alameda. MARTINEZ (Colfax). First postmaster, Marcelina V. Martinez. Post office, 1889-1902; mail to Aurora. MARTINEZ (San Juan). MARTINEZ (Taos). Near county line in SE corner, W of Chacon. MARTINEZ CANYON (Rio Arriba, Taos). 9 mi E of Hopewell.

MARTINEZ OR GODOI GRANT (Taos). Also called LUCERO DE GODOI, ANTONIO MARTINEZ GRANT. Area W of Taos Pueblo Grant between Arroyo Hondo and Ranchito. The various grants in the neighborhood were in litigation from 1869 to 1911. At a trial before the U.S. Surveyor General for New Mexico, in Santa Fe on Jan. 6, 1908, the Taos Valley Land Co. sued to settle claims between the Antonio Martinez Grant (whose title purported to have been legalized Oct. 26, 1716, by Gov. Felipe Martinez) and the Antoine Leroux Grant (said to have been conferred upon Pedro Vigil, Juan Bautista Vigil, and Cristobal Vigil on Aug. 9, 1742). The U.S. Court decreed that the Lucero de Godoi Grant was made to Antonio Martinez on Oct. 26, 1716, as a royal grant and the title belonged to heirs of the original grantee.

MARTINS (Rio Arriba). LOS MARTINITOS (San Miguel).

MASSACRE GAP (Doña Ana). Pass in Sierra de Las Uvas, NW of Las Cruces. Named because a whole Mexican family was massacred here in 1870. MASSACRE PEAK (Luna). In Cook's Range, 3 mi S of Ft. Cummings.

MASSEY (Curry). Post office, 1909-10; mail to Ard.

MASTODON (Doña Ana). Point on SP RR, 2 mi N of Texas border, 12 mi W of El Paso.

MATER (Quay). 17 mi NE of Tucumcari on US 54, between Logan and Hudson. Started when CRI&P RR put in the line between Dalhart, Tex., and Santa Rosa in 1901. The name is a family name.

MAVERICK CANYON (Grant). 4 mi W of Tyrone, S and W of Sugarloaf Mtn. Name is the term for a motherless calf and is derived from Samuel A. Maverick of Decro's Point, Tex., who took over a bunch of cattle for debt before the Civil War and placed them in charge of a Negro who failed to brand them. Subsequently, unbranded range cattle in the area were called mavericks, and this term spread throughout the entire cattle kingdom of the west. MAVERICK MOUNTAIN (Grant). 7 mi SW of Kingston.

MAXWELL (Colfax). Farming and ranching town on US 85, 13 mi N of Springer. Established in the late 1880's by Maxwell Land and Irrigation Co. on Canadian Red River. Named for owner of Maxwell Land Grant. Post office, 1879, with suspensions and name changes, to present. Maxwell Land Grant (Colfax). Once covered not only the extent of western Colfax County, but parts of southern Colorado, eastern Taos County, all of Union County, and embraced a total of 1,714,764.93 acres of land, largest single land holding in the Western Hemisphere. Named for Lucien B. Maxwell, a hunter and trapper who came to NM from Kaskaskia, Ill., about 1849. He settled on land granted by Governor Armijo in 1841 to Carlos Beaubien, a French trapper, and to Guadalupe Miranda of Taos. Maxwell married Beaubien's daughter, Luz, and, after Beaubien's death in 1864, bought out the remaining heirs for $3,000. Grant was not approved finally by the U.S. Congress until June 21, 1860.

MAYHILL (Otero). Farming and ranching community on NM 83, 28 mi E of Alamogordo. In Lincoln National Forest and Sacramento Mts., on an elevated mesa above the depression where James and Peñasco canyons meet. Named for John F. Mahill, one of the pioneer settlers, who came here in 1881 from Missouri. An early postmaster spelled the name Mayhill instead of Mahill. Post office, 1902—; formerly UPPER PEÑASCO.

MAYPENS (Lea). TNM RR siding and stock pen, 5 mi S of Eunice.

MAZON's (Cibola). A series of ranches in W part of county. Formerly constituted very large holdings of cattle and sheep by Mazon family in latter part of the nineteenth century. The pastures extend W and S from Tinaja to county line. Only a few remain in the hands of the Mazon family.

McALISTER (Quay). Farming community on NM 86, 36 mi S of Tucumcari and 19 mi NE of Tolar. Named for A. I. McAlister, who built the first store here and whose wife was the first postmaster. Post office, 1907—. Mc-

ALLISTER LAKE (San Miguel). Natural lake about 10 mi S of Las Vegas.

McCARTY'S (Cibola). Trading community on Acoma Indian Reservation on US 66, 13 mi SE of Grants. Named for the contractor whose camp was here when AT&SF RR was built through this section. Just above the settlement, is a beautiful church recently built by the Indians, which is an exact replica, half size, of the ancient mission church of old Acoma. Its wood carvings are notable works of art. Called SANTA MARIA DE ACOMA by some residents. Post office, intermittently, 1887-1911, as both McCarty's and McCarty.

McCAULY (Grant). Settlement 8 mi S of Cliff, just E of Black Mtn.

McCHRISTOBAL CREEK (Colfax). Small tributary to Ponil Creek on CS Cattle Co. ranch, NW of Cimarron.

McCUNE (McKinley). On AT&SF RR, 10 mi E of Gallup.

McDONALD (Lea). Farming and ranching community on NM 18, 14 mi N of Lovington; originally 1 mi E of present site. Named for William C. McDonald, the first state governor, 1912-17. McDONALD LAKE (Otero). 10 mi E of Sacramento.

McEWAN LAKE (Otero). 1 mi NW of Weed.

McGAFFEY (McKinley). Farming and ranching community 16 mi SE of Gallup, and 10 mi S of Wingate Station. In 1906 Horabin-McGaffey started a sawmill in Zuñi Mts. Post office, 1919-44. McGAFFEY LAKE (McKinley). Artificial lake about 6 mi S of Wingate Station.

McGREGOR (Taos). Post office, 1882-83; mail to Ranches of Taos.

McGREGOR RANGE (Otero). Missile firing range under control of the Commanding General, U.S. Army Air Defense Center, Fort Bliss, Tex. Extends from the Texas line at Newman eastward from US 54. Named for Malcolm McGregor, who owned the property when the U.S. leased it on July 1, 1954. On June 26, 1956, the area became U.S. property in fee simple.

McINTOSH (Torrance). Farming and ranching community on NM 41 and AT&SF RR, 38 mi SE of Albuquerque. Post office, 1906—.

McKINLEY (Torrance). Former settlement 32 mi SE of Albuquerque, near Arroyo de Tajique. McKINLEY COUNTY. Created on Feb. 23, 1899, and named for William McKinley, twenty-fifth President of the United States, 1899-1901. Area is 5,461 sq mi.

McKittrick Creek (Eddy). 11 mi SW of Carlsbad Caverns National Park.

McKnight Gap (Catron). Between Spur Lake and Luna in San Francicso Mts.

McLean (Curry). Former community named for George McLean, one of the original homesteaders N of Pleasant Hill, who had a little store and post office here. First postmaster, Ollie McLean. Post office, 1907—.

McMillan (Eddy). Post office, 1894-1904; changed to Lakewood. McMillan Lake (Eddy). 10 mi S of Artesia.

McNees Creek (Union). See Corrumpa Creek.

McPherson (Mora). See Sands.

McWilliams Canyon (Colfax). Extends from Colorado line to Canadian Red River, 15 mi W of Raton. Named for a Baptist minister who made his home here during the 1870's.

Meadow Creek (Grant). Flows N from Pinos Altos Mts. into Sapello Creek, 15 mi above Silver City.

Medanales (Rio Arriba). Span., "sandhills." On US 84, 8 mi SE of Abiquiu. Spanish family name. Post office, 1947—.

Medio (San Miguel). Span., "halfway, middle." On SP RR, 10 mi S of Mosquero. Medio Creek (Santa Fe). See Rio en Medio. Medio Dia Canyon, Creek (Sandoval). On S side of Jemez Mts. across ridge, 1 mi E of Bland. Medio Dia Canyon (Sandoval). 5 mi NW from Cochiti Pueblo.

Medler (Doña Ana). Also known as Medler Radium Springs. Flagstop about 1912 on AT&SF RR, 18 mi N of Las Cruces. Named for Judge Edward L. Medler who, at that time, was interested in Radium Springs nearby. A hotel for health seekers operated here.

Meek (Lincoln). On Salt Creek, 15 mi NE of Lincoln. First postmaster Thomas B. Meek. Post office, 1904-22.

Meloche (Colfax). 10 mi S of Raton and 4 mi W of Thompson. Named for the first owner of TO Ranch, Tony Meloche, who is listed as postmaster at Vermejo from 1874 to 1883.

Melrose (Curry). On US 60, NM 88, and AT&SF RR, 25 mi W of Clovis. Settled in 1882 and called Brownhorn for Walter "Wildhorse" Brown, and a Mr. Horn, owner of Pigpen Ranch. AT&SF RR was responsible for renaming the town. Railway officials in 1906 selected Brownhorn as the site of repair shops and laid out a townsite here. They, however, called their part of the townsite Melrose, reported to have been a transfer name from Melrose, O. Post office, 1906—.

Melvin (Mora). Post office, 1895-99; mail to Wagon Mound.

Mentmore (McKinley). Former coal-mining community ½ mi N of US 66, on AT&SF RR, 5 mi W of Gallup. Now a Baptist mission and day school for Indians. Post office, 1917—.

Me Own Hills (Sierra). ½ mi S of Diamond Creek and 7 mi from Catron County line, in Gila National Forest. Described as singular in one version. Named by an old man in the neighborhood who said, "Me own it."

Mesa. Span., "table, tableland." In the Southwest, the name of a unique landscape feature usually volcanic; any high, flat, plateau. However, it has been customary to call any relatively high, flat country a mesa. The term is so widespread in its use that it is both localized and general in its application, i.e., "out on the mesa" and "the mesa pasture." At least nine counties in NM make use of this place name. Mesa (De Baca). On US 285, at Chaves County line. Mesa Chaves (Chaves). See Chaves. Mesa del Oro (Valencia). "Gold." In SE part of county, 12 mi N of Puertecito. Mesa de los Padillos (Bernalillo). See Padillas Tableland. Mesa de los Viejos (Rio Arriba). "Old people." See Las Viejas Mesa. Mesa del Rito Gaviel (Chaves). "Little Gaviel River." Mesa del Yeso (Rio Arriba). "Gypsum," 2 mi SW of Yeso settlement. Mesa Diablo (Chaves). 11 mi SE of Melena. Mesa Encantado (Valencia). See Enchanted Mesa. Mesa Gigante (Valencia). North of US 66 at Correo. See Gigante. Mesa Jumanes (Torrance). "Jumanes Indians." Mesa Largo (Colfax). "Long." 7 mi W of Capulin. Mesa Lauriano (San Miguel). 11 mi E of Lourdes; a given name. Mesa Montosa (San Miguel). Corruption of montuoso, "hilly." 8 mi E of Chaperito. Mesa Pinca (Quay). Also called Pinco Mesa. "Orphan sheep." An expression similar to dogie, "an orphan calf." 3 mi W of Quay. An interesting trace of the language in the sheep-raising country. Mesa Pinebestosa (Rio Arriba). W of Coyote Creek, 6 mi N of county line. Mesa Prieta (Rio Arriba). "Dark." 4 mi N of Coyote. Mesa Prieta (Sandoval). In SW corner of county, E of Puerco River. Mesa Redondo (Quay). "Round." A high, flat-topped mountain towering above the surrounding valley, 6 mi W of

Norton. Covers ten or twelve sections of land that are excellent cattle range. It was the hangout of the Spikes gang of outlaws and cattle thieves, which was broken up by cattlemen and posses in the early 1890's. MESA RENTADA (Valencia). "Income yielding." 12 mi NW of Field. MESA RICA (San Miguel). "Rich." Trading point on NM 129, 51 mi NW of Tucumcari. Received its name from a legend that Indians attacked a burro train of gold. During this fight, a few white men slipped away with the gold and hid it on the mesa. No one ever found it. Post office, 1938-41. MESA VERDE (San Juan). "Green." At Colorado line, 15 mi N of Shiprock.

MESCALERO. Span., Mexican *mezcal,* stalk and leaf base of agave plant, from which an intoxicating drink is made, and the buttonlike tops are chewed as a stimulant. MESCALERO (Otero). 19 mi NE of Tularosa. Headquarters for the Apache Indian tribe whom the Spanish called Mescaleros because they were "mescal eaters." Post office, 1887—. MESCALERO APACHE INDIAN RESERVATION (Otero). On US 70, 18 mi NE of Tularosa, where Sacramento and White mts. join. The reservation was set up in 1872, but the present boundaries were not established until 1883. Previously, the Mescaleros had been quartered at Ft. Stanton with the Navajos. When disputes and quarreling developed between the two groups, the Mescaleros broke away and pillaged through eastern and southern NM. The Army captured the larger number of them and brought them back to Ft. Stanton. Then the reservation was established at Mescalero, 39 mi to the S. Post office, 1887—. MESCALERO RIDGE (Chaves, Lea, De Baca). Runs N and S along county lines. Named for the Apaches who came here to hunt. MESCALERO VALLEY (Chaves). W of Mescalero Ridge.

MESILLA (Doña Ana). Span., "little table." Farming community on NM 28, 2 mi S of Las Cruces. So named because it is built on a little piece of tableland that rises above the Rio Grande. Settled in 1850. The historic plaza was made a state monument during the 103rd Pan-American Fiesta in September 1957. Post office, 1858—. Also known as LA MESILLA. MESILLA (Rio Arriba). MESILLA PARK (Doña Ana). Unincorporated village adjoining University Park at Las Cruces on US 80. Named for nearby La Mesilla. With the routing of AT&SF RR through Las Cruces in 1881, the town of La Mesilla lost prestige and all pub-lic offices were removed to Las Cruces 3 mi away, which then became the county seat. Six years later, a group of citizens formed two land companies; the second was called the Mesilla Park Tract, taking its name from Mesilla Valley. When the New Mexico College of Agricultural and Mechanic Arts (now New Mexico State University) came into existence in 1889, the small village grew considerably. Post office, 1892—. MESILLA CIVIL COLONY GRANT TRACT (Doña Ana). Grant obtained after the Mexican War by Spanish Americans who petitioned the Mexican government for land then in the province of Chihuahua. Grant was approved in 1853, but when the Gadsden Purchase was signed in the same year, the territory became part of the U.S.

MESITA (Cibola). Span., "small tableland." In NE part of county. The diminutive ending suggests a small, low mesa with sides sharply defined. On it is a modern Indian village which is an outgrowth of Laguna Pueblo. MESITA DE GUADALUPE (Guadalupe). Small mesa 16 mi NW of Santa Rosa. MESITA DE JUANA LOPEZ GRANT (Santa Fe). 8 mi E of Santo Domingo Pueblo and bisected by Galisteo Creek. Granted to Domingo Romero, Miguel Ortiz, and Manuel Ortiz, in January 1782.

MESQUITE (Doña Ana). English spelling of Mexican-Span., *mezquite,* "desert shrub," and from Nahuatl *mizquitl.* Farming and ranching community on US 80, 12 mi S of Las Cruces on AT&SF RR. Established in 1881 and named by railroad executives for the many mesquite bushes here. Post office, 1913—. MESQUITE LAKE (Luna). 12 mi N of Arena.

MESTEÑO (Harding). American Span., "wild, untamed," usually applied to an animal, as "wild horse." American English "mustang" is derived from this Spanish adjective. On SP RR near Mills.

METCALF CANYON (Colfax). N of North Ponil Creek, about 6 mi N of former Stern post office.

MEXICAN CREEK (Colfax). In N part of Moreno Valley; flows into Moreno Creek, which in turn, flows into Eagle Nest Lake. Named by the Mexican gold miners of Elizabethtown who congregated along this creek to make their adobes. MEXICAN SPRINGS (Hidalgo). See SHAKESPEARE. MEXICAN SPRINGS (McKinley). An agricultural experiment station 24 mi N of Gallup. Post office, 1939—.

MEYERS (San Miguel). Settlement 10 mi S of Las Vegas, on US 84.

MIAMI (Colfax). Farming and ranching community on NM 199, 12 mi W of Springer. Settled in 1908. The first colonists were from Miami County, O., which got its name originally from a tribe of Indians who made their home in SW Ohio and SW Indiana. Post office, 1908—. MIAMI LAKE (Colfax). Artificial reservoir, 8 mi W of Miami.

MICE LAKE (Colfax). 5 mi NE of Raton.

MICHALLAS CANYON (Lincoln). Short stream in Capitan Mts.

MICHO (Lea). 3 mi SE of Tatum. Post office, 1921-22; mail to Tatum. MICHO CREEK (Lea). Empties into Pecos River from Capitan Mts.

MIDDLE FORK LAKE (Taos). At head of Middle Fork of Red River, 2 mi E of Twining.

MIDDLETON LAKE (Lincoln). 23 mi E of White Oaks.

MIDNIGHT (Colfax). A gold-mining and boom town that was on Bitter Creek in NW corner of Moreno Valley. Finally abandoned when the factions fought over the belle of the dance hall. Midnight was the liveliest time of the day; so the name was chosen by the miners. Post office, 1895-98; mail to Cerro.

MIDWAY (Luna). Townsite mapped in 1909, midway between Deming and Hermanas on EP&SW RR. Small community that disappeared when the track from Deming was taken up. Post office, 1909-18.

MIDWEST CITY (McKinley). MID-WEST (San Juan). Drilling locations in oil fields of San Juan Basin. Named for Mid-West Refining Co.

MIERA. The earliest record of this name is that of a soldier, Bernardo y Miera y Pacheco, who appeared in Santa Fe as early as 1756, at which time he was *alcalde mayor* of Galisteo and Pecos. His son, Anacleto (also Cleto), although born in Chihuahua, is said to have been the founder of the family which settled at MIERA (Mora, Union). 9 mi S of Barney, at Harding County line. At one time called TRAMPERAS, also LOUIS. First postmaster, Francisco Miera. Post office, 1889, intermittently, to 1927. MIERA (Bernalillo). Post office, Feb. to Aug. 1935; mail to Chilili. MIERA (Roosevelt).

MIESSE (Luna). Siding on SP RR 4 mi W of Carne. A tract of land by this name was opened during the land boom of 1910-14 for sale to farmers. The name is no longer used except on railroad maps. Post office, 1915-19.

MIGUEL CREEK (McKinley). Runs through Felipe Tafoya Grant, 22 mi S of Estrella.

MIKE MOUNTAIN (Taos). See SAN MIGUEL MOUNTAIN and PUEBLO CREEK.

MILAGRO (Guadalupe). Span., "miracle." 1 mi S of US 66, 35 mi W of Santa Rosa. Once a filling station and bus stop between Amarillo, Tex., and Albuquerque. Post office, 1916, intermittently, to 1935. MILAGRO HILL (Lincoln). In SW part of the county about 1 mi E of Oscura. It is well adapted for grazing. MILAGRO SPRING (Lincoln). At Milagro Hill. MILAGROS (Bernalillo). Post office, 1902-06; mail to Chilili.

MILAN (Cibola). Incorporated in 1957, 2 mi W of Grants on US 66. Named for Salvador Milan, owner of the land through his wife, Veneranda Mirabal, whose father had large holdings here.

MILESEVENTEEN (Sandoval). 17 mi N of San Ysidro where a depot and watering stop were arranged for the SFNW RR. The project failed after 1927 and the installations were abandoned. See TILDEN.

MILK HOUSE DRAW (Grant). Named for such a structure in or near the draw.

MILL (Grant). MILL (Socorro). MILL CREEK (Grant). 2½ mi N of Pinos Altos.

MILLER (Eddy). See ARTESIA. MILLER (Sandoval). On the Rio Puerco 7 mi SW of Cabezon. Post office, 1898-1905. MILLER (Valencia). 12 mi S of Acoma. Post office, 1911-12. MILLER-STEGMAN (Eddy). See ARTESIA.

MILLIGAN (Socorro, Catron). Post office, 1907-13; a post office name for Upper Frisco Plaza. Also called MILLIGAN PLAZA. See RESERVE.

MILL-IN-THE-SAND (Roosevelt). See MILNESAND.

MILLS (Harding). Farming and ranching settlement along NM 39, 11 mi N of Roy on SP RR. Name honors Melvin W. Mills, early-day attorney and rancher of Springer and Elizabethtown. Post office, 1898—. MILLS BUTTE (Mora). 3 mi W of Canadian Red River in E part of county, and halfway between N and S boundaries. MILLS CREEK (Colfax). Small creek in N end of Moreno Valley; flows into Moreno River which goes on to Eagle Nest Lake. Named for Judge M. W. Mills. MILLS LAKE (Rio Arriba). 6 mi N of Pounds. MILLS PASS (Colfax). 3 mi NW of Baldy Mtn., in Maxwell Land Grant. See MILLS CREEK.

MILLSITE CREEK (Hidalgo). 18 mi S of Playas.

MILNESAND (Roosevelt). Ranching community on NM 18, 38 mi S of Portales. A popular tradition remains that the name was MILL-IN-THE-SAND, because there was a windmill so designated on the old DZ Ranch. Later it was spelled as one word. Mrs. Lillian Curl established the first store in 1910 and was made postmaster. Post office, 1915—.

MIMBRES (Grant). Span., "willow trees." mining and ranching community on NM 61, 6 mi NE of Santa Rita. Named for Mimbres River. An early Indian tribe who built pit houses lived near here and were named by the Spanish, *Mimbreños*. Post office, 1886, intermittently, to present. MIMBRES (Luna). Point 1 mi N of Mexican border on SP RR, 7 mi W of Columbus. MIMBRES HOT SPRINGS (Grant). Post office, 1878-79. MIMBRES LAKE (Grant). Just W of the Sierra County line, 12 mi NW of town of Kingston. MIMBRES MOUNTAINS (Grant). Named because they are near Mimbres River. MIMBRES PEAK (Grant). MIMBRES RIVER (Grant, Luna). Heads in the Black Range N of Mimbres and flows toward Deming in Luna County. Ranches extend length of the river for 40 mi.

MINCO (Roosevelt). 6 mi NW of Causey. Post office, 1909-14.

MINEOSA (Quay). Possibly a misspelling of *miniosa*, Span., "containing *minio*, red lead." Near Union County border, 9 mi NW of Nara Visa. Post office, 1908-13.

MINERAL CITY (San Miguel). Post office, 1881-83; mail to Las Vegas. MINERAL CREEK (Catron). Beyond the ridge N of Mogollon, emptying into San Francisco River near Alma. MINERAL CREEK (Sierra). Runs through Chloride into South Fork Creek. MINERAL HILL (San Miguel). Trading point 17 mi W of Las Vegas. Post office, 1902, intermittently, to 1935. In the 1890's the name was Los VALLES DE SAN JERONIMO. Post office, GERONIMO, 1896-1902. MINERAL SPRINGS (Valencia). Post office, 1877-78.

MINERO (Grant). Span., "miner, mine operator." On SP RR, 3 mi E of Hachita.

MINNIE BUTTE (Harding). In NE corner of county about 3 mi W of Union County line.

MIRAGE (Luna). On AT&SF RR, 7 mi NE of Deming.

MIRANDA GRANT (Doña Ana). Also known as GUADALUPE MIRANDA GRANT. Guadalupe Miranda certified in a notarized document dated Jan. 18, 1888, that he had conveyed one *sitio* and three *caballerías* of land to J. F. Crosby, which Miranda was put in possession of by Judge Jose Maese on Dec. 3, 1851.

MIRIAN (Luna). Point 2 mi N of Texas border, 7 mi E of Columbus.

MISHAWAKA (San Miguel). Settlement 18 mi SE of Las Vegas, founded about 1908 by six families from Mishawaka, Ind. It ended during the 1930's with the failure of their dryland farms. Post office, 1910-11.

MITCHELL (Bernalillo-McKinley). Post office, 1892-96; mail to Bluewater; re-established 1898-99; changed to THOREAU.

MOCKINGBIRD GAP (Sierra, Lincoln). At NE corner of Sierra County, in San Andres Mts., crossing from Sierra into Lincoln. Named by U.S. soldiers who were in this neighborhood pursuing Indians. Mockingbirds have been reported here as early as 1883, according to an old man who prospected for copper in the area at that time. The Western mockingbird is common in NM, breeding N as far as Taos and Farmington, and most abundant along the Rio Grande from Albuquerque south. The birds nest at the lower altitudes from 3,800 to 7,000 ft, but outside of the breeding season, they live as high as 9,000 to 10,000 ft. This is why they are frequently heard only in June in the cities of the Rio Grande Valley. Travelers have said that the Western mockingbird surpasses even the English nightingale in the beauty and variety of its song.

MODOC (Doña Ana). Post office, 1901-03; mail to Las Cruces.

MOGOLLON. The name commemorates that of Don Juan Ignacio Flores Mogollon, governor of the Province of New Mexico from 1712 to 1715, who may have discovered mineral deposits in what is now Catron County and encouraged their development. MOGOLLON (Catron). Former mining village, now a ghost town on NM 78, 22 mi S of Reserve, and 7 mi E of NM 12. Mines have produced over $15,000,000 in gold, silver, and copper since 1889. Named for the mountains. Post office, 1890—. The Mogollon Apaches were named for Mogollon Mesa and mountains in NM and Arizona, because that was their country. MOGOLLON CREEK (Grant). Rises in Catron County and flows out of the Mogollon Mts. S to Gila River. MOGOLLON MOUNTAINS (Grant). In S part of county E of Mogollon. A majestic monument to the memory of Governor Mogollon. MOGOLLON PEAK (Catron). In Mogollon Mts. 16 mi E of Pleasanton. MOGOLLON, WEST FORK (Catron). The West Fork of Mogollon Creek.

MOGOTE (Mora). Span., "hummock"; New Mexican Span., "horns of young animals." MOGOTE PEAK (Rio Arriba). W of El Rito River, 7 mi E of Canjilon. MOGOTE RIDGE (Rio Arriba).

MOLYBDENUM (Taos). On NM 38, between Questa and Red River, in Carson National Forest. Named for deposits of this metallic element.

MOLLOY LAKE (Colfax). See LAKE MALLOY.

MONDEL (Hidalgo). Siding on SP RR, 16 mi SW of Lordsburg, E of Steins and near Road Forks.

MONERO (Rio Arriba). Coal-mining community on NM 17, and D&RGW RR, 18 mi W of Chama. In Italian, *monero* means "money." A number of Italians lived here when it was settled in 1884. Post office, 1884-1963.

MONGOLA (Luna). On SP RR, 15 mi W of Deming.

MONIA CREEK (Union). Doubtless a misspelling of Span., *monilla,* a shrublike plant producing a hard, black seed, found in NM. Area first called MONIA ARROYO. Creek flows E across S tip of county into Texas.

MONICA CANYON (Socorro). SW of Magdalena on NM 52. In the 1880's there was a settlement called MONICA and a MONICA SPRING here. Post office, 1881-83; mail to Socorro.

MONISTA (Otero). Post office, 1944-47. See AIR FORCE MISSILE DEVELOPMENT CENTER.

MONJEAU MOUNTAIN (Lincoln). 15 mi W of Glencoe. Elevation 10,000 ft, a U.S. Forest Service lookout station here affords a spectacular view of the south-central part of the state.

MONTAÑO. Members of the Montaño family lived in the Salinas district in the middle of the seventeenth century. A different individual, Antonio Montaño de Sotomayor, came some years before the Pueblo Rebellion of 1680. Descendants of both families returned with the Reconquest of 1692. MONTAÑOS (Sandoval).

MONTECITO (Rio Arriba). MONTE PRIETO (Socorro). 10 mi S of Gran Quivira National Monument, near Blue Creek. MONTE VERDE (Colfax). On NM 38, 7 mi S of Eagle Nest.

MONTERREY (Otero). Post office, 1909-11; changed to WEST TULAROSA.

MONTEZUMA (Bernalillo). Post office, 1879-80. MONTEZUMA (San Miguel). Farming community on NM 65, 6 mi NW of Las Vegas. Site of Montezuma Seminary, which occupies the building formerly known as the Montezuma

Hotel. Named by AT&SF RR people for Montezuma (Moctezuma) pre-Spanish Aztec ruler of Mexico, who was conquered by Cortez. Post office, 1924—. MONTEZUMA (Socorro). Post office, 1896-1900; mail to Eastview.

MONTICELLO (Sierra). Ranching and farming community on NM 142, 21 mi NW of Truth or Consequences. Settled in 1856 and reportedly named by a prospector who came from Virginia and who chose to commemorate the Monticello Estate of Thomas Jefferson in the Old Dominion. However, an old settler, when interviewed, testified that it was originally named CAÑADA ALAMOSA and that the place was headquarters for the Southern Apache Agency before the establishment of the Ojo Caliente Apache Reservation in 1874. He said that in the 1880's a man named John Sullivan (who had been a freighter and who came from Monticello, N.Y.) became postmaster and named the town Monticello. Post office, 1881—. MONTICELLO CANYON (Sierra). Arroyo crossing US 85, 12 mi N of Truth or Consequences. MONTICELLO CREEK (Sierra). Flows SE through Monticello.

MONTOSO MESA (San Miguel). See MESA MONTOSA.

MONTOYA. Bartolome de Montoya, a native Spaniard who had married Maria de Zamora in Mexico City, came with his family to Santa Fe in 1600. The marriages of his five children and their descendants are recorded in the growing Spanish colony in the seventeenth century. See LOS MONTOYAS (San Miguel). MONTOYA (Quay). Also LUCERO-MONTOYA. Farming and ranching community on US 54 and 66, 21 mi W of Tucumcari. Established in 1902 when CRI&P RR built a siding here. Formerly called ROUNTREE. Post office, 1902—. M. AND S. MONTOYA GRANT (Sandoval). See M. AND S. MONTOYA GRANT.

MONUMENT (Doña Ana). 1 mi N of Texas border on NM 8 and SP RR, 25 mi E of Columbus. MONUMENT (Lea). Oil-field community on NM 8, 9 mi SW of Hobbs. Established in 1885 and named for an old Indian monument built before 1870 at Monument Spring to mark the location of water. Jim (Lane) Cook built a general store here in 1900 and became the first postmaster. There is now a cement statue of an Indian along the highway in town. Post office, 1900—. See MONUMENT SPRING. MONUMENT CANYON (Otero). On SE slope of Sacramento Mts. within Lincoln National Forest. Named for the monument marking the water hole. Stream in canyon flows SW into Sacramento River. MONUMENT CREEK (Sierra). Enters South Fork Creek, 1 mi W of Chise. MONUMENT DRAW (Lea). 6 mi W of Jal, near Texas line. Extends over 36 mi within the county, running N and S from above Oil Center. MONUMENT PEAK (Sierra). 2 mi E of Lake Valley. Named for the large, black, rock formation which rises from the steeper end of the mountains. On the more sloping end, a rock formation resembles a giant lizard. This mountain was one of several in southern NM from which mirror heliograph messages were sent from Ft. Bliss at El Paso to former Ft. McRae, a total distance of 150 mi. MONUMENT ROCK (San Miguel). MONUMENT SPRING (Lea). Named for a 45-ft-high caliche rock marker built by Indians to show the spring here. The monument was visible for 35 mi. In the mid-1870's, it was torn down by buffalo hunters and used to construct a fort and corrals which are still standing. The spring was sold in 1885 for $400 to a man named Kennedy; it changed hands several times, finally becoming a part of the HAT Ranch. MONUMENT SPRING (Sierra). 5 mi S of Chloride.

MOONHULL CANYON (Grant). Runs E to Gila River at McCauley, 9 mi S of Cliff.

MOORE (Quay). Postmaster, John A. Moore. Post office, 1903-12. MOORE (Rio Arriba). Small community 20 mi SW of Tierra Amarilla, near El Vado.

MOQUINO (Cibola). Community N of Laguna and S of Cebolleta. Thought to have been named for Moqui (Hopi) Indians but probably named for Miguel Moquino, one of four individuals who claimed ownership of the area around Paguate and Moquino prior to the Paguate Purchase. MOQUINA ARROYO (Cibola).

MORA (Mora). On NM 3 and Mora River, in W part of county. County seat and shopping center for many small rural communities. Post office, 1864—. See MORA GRANT. MORA COUNTY. Formed Feb. 1, 1860, with the town of Mora as county seat. Present area is 1,944 sq mi. MORA FLATS (San Miguel). Flat area 6 mi NE of Cowles at Mora County line. MORA GRANT. The entire district was designated as LO DE MORA and DE LO MORA in early documents. This peculiar designation led to stories. One was that the name was a con-

traction of Span., el ojo, "the spring," and la mora, "the mulberry." Another relates how the first Spanish settlers lived on game in the region and supplemented their diet with moras or mulberries growing on the mountainsides. A third legend tells how Cerain St. Vrain, a French trapper from Taos, found a dead man in 1823 on the banks of the Rio de la Casa and called the place L'Eau de Mort, "the water of the dead." The facts are that the Spanish neuter article lo, in this place name, is the equivalent of "thing, that which belongs to" and is used not only here but in other place names: Lo de Padilla, "the possession of Padilla." The Mora surname comes from one or more individuals, such as Mora Pineda, and Garcia de la Mora, who came to NM after the Reconquest of 1692. People of this name were living on the frontier of Mora County at the end of the eighteenth century. In 1835 a decree dated September 28 by Col. Albino Perez, then governor, gave each of seventy-six settlers a strip of land on which they settled, subsequently founding the towns of San Antonio de lo de Mora (now Cleveland) at the upper end of the valley, and Santa Gertrudis de lo de Mora (now Mora proper) at the lower and wider end. The grant is a large one, extending from Mora to Wagon Mound and covers most of the central part of the state. MORA RIVER (Mora, San Miguel). Rises in Rincon Range, E of Sangre de Cristo Mts.; flows through W and S sections of county into San Miguel County where it joins Canadian River N of Sabinoso. Shown as RIO MORA on Mapa de los EUM (1828). MORA RIVER (San Miguel); also called MORA PECOS. See RIO MORA.

MORAGO CANYON (Catron). Span., "sheaf, bundle." S of Long Canyon Mts. and 3 mi E of the Continental Divide. There were members of the Moraga family in NM both before and after 1680.

MORENO CREEK, NORTH, SOUTH (Colfax). Span., "dark, swarthy." These two creeks rise in extreme N and W end of Moreno Valley and join to form Moreno River. Named for Moreno Valley. MORENO RIVER (Colfax). Flows S to Eagle Nest. These waters were used at one time for placer-mining operations, when gold was washed off the ground in the Elizabethtown district. MORENO VALLEY (Colfax). In mountains on watershed between Colfax and Taos counties.

Morgan (Sierra). 2 mi NE of Monticello. Morgan Creek (Sierra). 17 mi NW of Hillsboro, and W of Hermosa.

Moriarty (Torrance). On NM 41, 2 mi S of junction with US 66. Michael Timothy Moriarty left Indianapolis in the early 1880's to seek a cure for his rheumatism. He settled in the Estancia Valley intending to return N when his condition cleared. He died in 1932 on the sheep ranch he operated here. Post office, 1902—.

Morley (Catron). Named for William R. Morley, civil engineer who built AT&SF RR line through Raton Pass. He was the father of Ray Morley of Magdalena and of Agnes Morley Cleaveland, author of *No Life for a Lady* (1941).

Mosca Peak (Torrance). Span., "fly." One of the highest elevations in Manzano Mts.

Moses (Union). There are two communities with this name, an "old" and a "new" Moses. "Old" Moses was located near Corrumpa Creek, 18 mi NE of Clayton. This settlement was known in the days of the Santa Fe Trail. Upon the sale of the Espinosa ranch (Delfin Espinosa was the last owner of the old Moses store), a new store and post office was started at a curve in NM 18. The first postmaster was Frank Moses. Post office, 1909-55.

Mosquero. Span., "flytrap or flypaper," but never used in this sense in NM. The meaning here is a "swarm of flies, fleas, or mosquitoes." Mosquero (Harding). County seat on SP RR and NM 39, 19 mi SE of Roy. Stock-raising and farming community and the site of dry-ice plants. Post office, 1908—. Mosquero (San Miguel). Mosquero Creek (Harding). Rises E of Mosquero, and flows SE to join Ute Creek in south-central part of county.

Mott Well (Otero). 7 mi NE of Desert and 5½ mi SE of Elwood.

Mountainair (Torrance). Ranching and farming community on US 60, at AT&SF RR, 32 mi E of Belen. At top of Abo Pass, it is surrounded by ancient Indian ruins, Abo, Quarai, and Gran Quivira. Incorporated in 1901; settled by a Mr. Corbett, George Hanlon, and C. C. Maning. Named because of its situation. Post office, 1903—.

Mountain Park (Lincoln). Mountain Park (Otero). Post office, 1904-55. See High Rolls —Mountain Park. Mountain View (Luna). Post office, 1911-14.

Mount Capulin (Union). See Capulin Mountain. Mount Clayton (Union) 8 mi W of Mt. Dora and 3 mi S of C&S RR right of way. Named Round Mountain by traders on the the Santa Fe Trail, who crossed here in 1822 under the leadership of Colonel Becknell. In 1887, name changed to Mount Clayton by U.S. Senator Stephen W. Dorsey of Arkansas, in honor of his son Clayton. Mount Dora (Union). 15 mi NW of Clayton. Named for Senator Dorsey's sister-in-law. Mount Dora (Union). Ranching community on US 87, 18 mi NW of Clayton; 3 mi from Mt. Dora, for which it was named. Established in 1887. Shipping point for cattle, sheep, and grain on the C&S RR. Post office, 1908—. Mount Franklin (Doña Ana). In Organ Mts. Mount Pelado (Sandoval). See Mount Redondo. Mount Picacho (Santa Fe). 2 mi E of Santa Fe. On its summit, in August 1937, the ashes of Mary Austin, folklorist, poet, and novelist were buried in a cairn of rocks. Mount Powell (McKinley). 17 mi E of Ft. Wingate and 4 mi N of Thoreau. Mount Redondo (Sandoval). A high, conspicuous mountain with a Jemez pueblo ruin at its base. Named for its round shape. Also called Mount Pelado. Mount Riley (Doña Ana). Community 2 mi N of Texas border on SP RR, 22 mi E of Columbus. Mount Sedgewick (Valencia). 50 mi W of Grants in Cibola National Forest. Mount Taylor (Valencia). The old Spanish name was Cebolleta Mountain, "little onion." The Navajo name is *tso dzil*, "big, tall mountain." The ceremonial name is *dzil dotlizi*, "turquoise mountain." Anglo-Americans named the peak for Zachary Taylor, twelfth President of the United States. Highest of the San Mateo Mts., it marks the S border of the Navajo universe. Mount Taylor Lake (Valencia). On Mt. Taylor. Mount Vernon (Roosevelt). Small community 11 mi NE of Causey. Post office, 1910-13. Mountview (Colfax). Post office, 1895-1900; changed to Dawson. Mount Washington (Socorro). 6 mi NW of Rosedale.

Mowry City (Luna). On Bell Ranch, 25 mi N of Deming. Formerly called Rio Mimbres when it was a stage stop on the route of the Butterfield Overland Mail, and then named for Maj. Sylvester Mowry, who in 1859 sent out literature trying to promote a land boom. Some of his advertisements showed steamboats navigating what were actually dry stream beds. When his efforts failed, along with the Butterfield Overland Mail, Rio Mimbres returned to the range land from which it had been briefly removed. Major Mowry had been stationed with the 3rd Artillery at Ft. Webster in 1853.

Mud Lake (Sierra). 10 mi N of Kingston. Mud Spring (Rio Arriba). 7 mi N of Costilla. Mud Springs Mountains (Sierra). 6 mi NW of Truth or Consequences. Muddy Creek (Colfax). Small stream in N end of Moreno Valley, which at one time supplied water to placer miners of Elizabethtown district. Flows into Moreno River; waters are always riled and muddy, giving the stream its name.

Muir (Grant). Flagstop on AT&SF RR, when it was first built. On Muir Ranch 11 mi S of Robert. Named for John T. Muir, a pioneer in this area. Once called Muir Service.

Mule Creek (Grant). Farming and ranching community on NM 78, 46 mi NW of Silver City. First settled by Dan McMillen in 1877, on the place now owned by A. O. Steyskan. So named because John McMillen had found a mule track here. Post office, 1916—. Mule Creek (Grant). Runs N into San Francisco River. Mule Mountains (Catron). W of Mule Creek. Mule Peak, Mule Canyon (Otero). In Sacramento Mts. Some time prior to the Civil War, a band of marauding Indians who had raided settlers along the Rio Grande and stolen mules, were trailed to this canyon. Here the settlers found one of the mules. From that event, both the peak and canyon derived their names. Mule Shoe (Socorro). 9 mi S of Magdalena near Bear Canyon. Mule Spring (Grant). 2 mi S of town of Mule Creek.

Mulligan Gulch (Socorro). Rises on Cat Mts. and flows SE into Elephant Butte Reservoir, 6 mi SW of San Marcial.

Mundo (Rio Arriba). Span., "world." 9 mi S of Colorado line; 4 mi SE of Lumberton.

Muñoz Canyon (San Juan). Runs N and empties into San Juan River between Largo Canyon and Armenta Canyon SE of Bloomfield. Muñoz Creek (Rio Arriba). Rises in Rio Arriba and flows W to junction of Compañero Creek. The Muñiz, or Muñoz, name appears several times in eighteenth century NM documents, but the names may not be related to the Rio Arriba or San Juan settlers indicated here.

Murdock (Quay). 12 mi NW of Melrose. Post office, 1907-17.

Murray (Socorro). First postmaster, John P. Murray. Post office, 1909-13.

Mush Mountain (Valencia). 9 mi SE of Acoma Pueblo, near Arroyo Colorado.

Mustang Creek (San Miguel). Anglicized Spanish, mesteño, "small, half-wild horse." Joins Arroyo de la Cinta Creek, 5 mi below Bell Ranch.

Myndus (Luna). Siding on SP RR, 18 mi E of Deming and 4 mi W of Akela. Post office, 1913-22.

Nacimiento. Span., "birth, scene representing the Nativity"; also "source of a river or spring." One of the most popular days of commemoration in the calendar year of the Roman Catholic Church is El Nacimiento de Nuestra Señora, "the Birthday of Our Lady," celebrated on September 8. Nacimiento (Sandoval). See Cuba. Nacimiento Mountains (Sandoval, Rio Arriba). See Sierra Nacimiento Peak (Rio Arriba). In SE corner of county, in Santa Fe National Forest.

Nadine (Lea). On NM 18, 5 mi S of Hobbs. Once called Roberts, but later named for Nadine Hughes, daughter of James H. Hughes, the first postmaster. Post office, 1910-34. Nadine (Hidalgo).

Nageesi (San Juan). Probably Navajo, nayi'ze, "squash." On NM 44, 26 mi S of Bloomfield, near Cuba. Post office, 1941—.

Nakaibito (McKinley). Trading point near US 666, 24 mi N of Gallup. Navajo nakai means "a Mexican," plus tqo, "water," i.e., "Mexican Springs."

Nambe (Santa Fe). Rural settlement near a pre-Spanish Tewa-speaking Indian pueblo on NM 4, 16 mi N of Santa Fe, and 4 mi E of Pojoaque. Namba on L'Atlas Curieux (1700). The word is Tewa, nambay-ongwee "people of the roundish earth," and was applied to the pueblo of their ancestors, the ruins of which are 5 or 10 mi NE on Panchuelo Creek. Site is said to be on a kind of mound. Post office, 1901-22. Nambe Creek (Santa Fe). N of Nambe Pueblo. Nambe Falls (Santa Fe). On Nambe Creek, 5 mi above pueblo. Named for pueblo. Three portions of the falls all have individual Indian names. Nambe Lake (Santa Fe). 1½ mi S of Santa Fe Baldy Peak. Nambe Pueblo Grant (Santa Fe). About 4 mi by 5 mi in dimension, with Nambe in NW part. The Indians from Nambe testified on Sept. 29, 1856, before the U.S. Surveyor General for New Mexico, that they had a land grant from the Spanish king, but many years earlier a dispute arose between the Indians and Mexican citizens who wished to trespass on their land. The case was taken before the acting governor of the Territory to whom the governor of Nambe delivered the grant. It has not been heard of since. They claimed one league from each corner of the church in the pueblo. NAMBE RIVER, LOWER (Santa Fe). Portion of the river below falls. NAMBE RIVER, UPPER (Santa Fe). Above falls to source at Santa Fe Baldy Peak.

NARANJO. Span., "orange tree." Family name which came to NM in 1600, but there is no connection between the pioneer of this line and other individuals of the name who were in NM at the time of the Pueblo Rebellion of 1680 and returned in 1693 after the Reconquest. NARANJO (Doña Ana). NARANJOS (Mora). "The Naranjo folks." Settlement on NM 120, 20 mi NW of Wagon Mound. Post office, 1886-88; 1913-17.

NARA VISA. "Narvis" may be a corruption of the Spanish surname Narvaez, which residents of the area pronounced, in informal conversation, "Nara Visa." NARA VISA (Quay). On US 54 and NM 18, and also CRI&P RR. Established in 1902 with the building of CRI&P RR through that county to Tucumcari. Named for the creek. Post office, 1902—. NARA VISA CREEK (Quay). Tributary of Canadian River. Named for Spanish sheepherder, "Narvis," who lived on the creek in the late 1800's.

NASCHITI (McKinley). Navajo "badger water"; may mean "scratching for water." Trading post started in 1886; mission and day school also established here.

NAVA (San Juan). See NEWCOMB.

NAVAHO, NAVAJO. The Spanish called the Indian tribe Navajos de Apache. It has been suggested by Dr. Edgar Lee Hewett (see Bibilography) that a Tewa word na-ba-hu-u, "arroyo of cultivated fields," may be the language source. Another etymology may be Span., navaja, "clasped knife," because the Navajo men carried great stone knives, but Fray Alonso de Benavides writes in Revised Memorial of 1634 (1945), pp. 307-08, that the Navajos were great farmers and the name signified "great planted fields." NAVAJO (McKinley). Settlement on Arizona line, 11 mi NE of Window Rock, Ariz. Site of large sawmill owned by Navajo tribe. NAVAJO (Rio Arriba). On

D&RGW RR, 8 mi NW of Lumberton. NAVAJO (Taos). Post office, 1880-81. NAVAJO DAM (McKinley). Post office, 1963—. See NAVAJO LAKE STATE PARK AND RECREATION AREA. NAVAJO INDIAN RESERVATION (San Juan, McKinley). Created originally by the treaty of June 1, 1868. Since that time a number of additions have been made by Executive Orders. The largest addition was by Executive Order of Jan. 15, 1917. NAVAJO LAKE STATE PARK AND RECREATION AREA (San Juan). Scenic area on San Juan River 25 mi E of Aztec via NM 511 from NM 117. The Bureau of Reclamation Dam is second largest earth-filled dam in the United States. Started in 1958 and dedicated in September 1962, the lake when full will extend 35 mi and will provide fishing, recreational, and wildlife conservation facilities. In addition, the storage will regulate flow of the San Juan and provide water to irrigate 110,000 acres on Navajo Reservation. Post office, Navajo Dam, 1963—. NAVAJO MINE (McKinley). NAVAJO RIVER (Rio Arriba). Heads in Colorado and returns N of Dulce. NAVAJO SPRING (Rio Arriba). On W side of Canjilon Creek. The Tewa name sah bay po, "athabaskan water," is probably related to the Spanish Ojo Navajo. NAVATA (McKinley). Trading point on US 666, 4 mi N of Gallup.

NEED (Roosevelt). Post office, 1917-19. See LINGO.

NEGRA (Torrance). Span., "black." On US 60, 5 mi W of Encino. This town was started when AT&SF RR built the Belen cutoff about 1905 and 1906. Name selected on account of the black soil. Post office, 1909—. NEGRITO "Little black"; colloquial, "darling." 20 mi SE of Reserve. NEGRITO CREEK (Catron). Two forks, North and South, are in central part of county, and join to empty into Tularosa River, which flows to San Francisco River S of Reserve.

NESTER DRAW (Catron). A long dry wash 6 mi SE of Mangas. "Nester" was a term of contempt among cattlemen, for it described the farmers who frequently homesteaded on range land. The term seems to be a metaphor, both descriptive (as it applied to a house and trees that looked like a nest in a wide-open space) and psychological (as it identified a lonesome, wandering cowboy who decided to settle down and farm).

NEW ABBOTT (Colfax). See ABBOTT.

NEW ALBUQUERQUE (Bernalillo). Post office, 1881-82; changed to ALBUQUERQUE.

NEWCOMB (San Juan). On US 666 and Captain Tom's Wash, 52 mi N of Gallup. Originally called NAVA, from first syllables of Navajo. In 1914, Arthur J. Newcomb and his wife, Frances L. Newcomb, established a trading post here. In 1920, the post office at Crozier was located at Newcomb Trading Post. A day school and houses for the teachers and other employees were built by the U.S. Bureau of Indian Affairs. Today the locality bears the name Newcomb. The trading post is otherwise designated. Post office, 1929-44.

NEW DOMINGO (Sandoval). Trading point on US 85, and AT&SF RR, 36 mi N of Albuquerque. Transfer name from neighboring Santo Domingo Pueblo.

NEW HOBBS (Lea). 1 mi S of Hobbs, but really a part of the town. Post office, 1930-32. See HOBBS.

NEWHOPE (Roosevelt). Small community 1 mi W of NM 18, 29 mi S of Portales. Named about 1902 when a homesteader finally found water after digging several wells. Post office, 1910-20; mail to Elida.

NEWKIRK (Guadalupe). Trading point on US 54, 66, and SP RR, 27 mi E of Santa Rosa. Settled in 1901 when CRI&P RR came through. Named for James P. Conant, early rancher, and called CONANT. Changed to Newkirk by a settler from Newkirk, Okla. Post office, 1910—.

NEW LAGUNA (Cibola). Farming and ranching community on US 66, and AT&SF RR, 26 mi SE of Grants. Named for "old" Laguna, the Indian pueblo 2 mi W. Post office, 1920—.

NEWMAN (Otero). Trading point on US 54 and SP RR, 20 mi NE of El Paso, Tex., on Mexican border. Named for L. E. Newman, early real-estate man of El Paso, who sold building sites to home seekers. Archaeologists say there was once a Pueblo Indian city here of prehistoric date. First postmaster, Henry L. Newman. Post office, 1906-14.

NEW MEXICO. Territory of the United States since 1846, when it was occupied by military forces during the Mexican War, although more or less peaceful penetration had occurred after the opening of the Santa Fe Trail in 1821. Officially annexed by the Treaty of Guadalupe Hidalgo, May 30, 1848. First petitioned for statehood in 1850, but not admitted until Jan. 6, 1912, when New Mexico became the forty-seventh state in the Union.

Since the admission of Alaska, New Mexico is the fifth largest in size, embracing 121,666 sq mi. The name of the state is of Nahuatl derivation, being a transfer from Mexitli, a name for Tenochtitlan, the capital city of the Aztec nation. The Nahuatl Indians were called Azteca from Aztlán, their traditional place of origin, or Méxicas from Mexi, their traditional leader when they migrated to the Valley of Mexico. The Aztec tongue also has the forms metztli, "moon," and xihtli, "center or central place." Thus, Mexico means "place of the moon," or "in the center of the moon." Cabeza de Vaca, Friar Marcos de Niza, and Coronado were early sixteenth-century travellers into the area known as Cibola and Quivira, but not until 1562 did an explorer refer to the region as un otro, or Nuevo, Méjico, "another," or "New" Mexico. This comparison was made by Don Francisco de Ibarra after his appointment as governor of the Mexican province of Nueva Vizcaya. Ibarra thus seems to have the distinction of having named the American state that is oldest in point of organized government. Francisco del Cano was sent to explore the country west of Monterrey and found a large lake which he called Laguna del Nuevo Mexico. When Antonio de Espejo, a wealthy Spaniard living at Santa Barbara, below Chihuahua, returned from an exploration in 1582-83, he referred to "visiting and exploring the provinces of New Mexico, to which I gave the name of Nueva Andalucia, as I was born in the district of Cordoba." Luxan, the chronicler of the Espejo expedition, used the name Nuevo Mejico on the title page of his journal dated 1583, and when Don Juan de Oñate took possession of the land in 1598, he called himself "governor, captain general, and adelantado of New Mexico, and of its kingdoms and provinces, as well as those in its vicinity—and contiguous thereto." In 1771, New Mexico was reduced from a "kingdom" to a "province." Four years after occupation by American troops in 1846, it became the Territory of New Mexico. Then after seventy-two years and more than fifty bills and memorials to Congress, New Mexico was admitted to the Union. The name is a remarkable and distinguished one, with its American Indian roots, Spanish modification, and present American-English form.

NEWTON (Grant). Post office, 1883; mail to Silver City. Formerly called LONE MOUNTAIN.

NICOLAS DURAN DE CHAVES GRANT (Valencia).

Small grant between the Rio Grande and the Rio Puerco W of Tome. Nicolas Duran de Chaves was twenty-four years old and a resident of Atrisco in 1714. Early in 1739, he petitioned Governor Mendoza for a tract of land on the Rio Grande and on June 1 the Governor approved the grant, directing the alcalde of Albuquerque to put Duran de Chaves in possession. On Aug. 26, 1739, the alcalde did so.

NIESLEY CANYON (Catron, Socorro). 5 mi SW of Dusty.

NIGGER CREEK (Colfax). A young Negro, whose name is unknown, came to Elizabethtown some time during the boom years of 1865-90. He made his home apart from the whites on a little creek in the N end of Moreno Valley, which leads into the Moreno River. NIGGER DIGGER (Socorro). 13 mi SE of Dusty. Negroes worked in the ranch camps both as cooks and as cowhands. Howard N. (Jack) Thorp in his book *Pardner of the Wind* (1945) pays tribute to the part they played in range balladry. NIGGER HEAD (Socorro). In W part of county, N of Gallinas Mts. NIGGER HILL (Roosevelt). Said to be named for a group of Negro soldiers from Company A, 10th U.S. Cavalry, who died of thirst here while hunting a band of hostile Indians. The story is that when Indians were sighted, many of the Negro cavalry took to saddle without filling their canteens. They trailed the Indians through an insufferably hot day. At nightfall the men dismounted, and the next day pursued the Indians until mid-afternoon; then they turned back to hunt for water. At a mound in Roosevelt County, some buffalo hunters who had joined the Negro cavalry, left for a lake to the NE. Some of the hunters succeeded in reaching the lake, and took water to their brethren along the trail. Most of the soldiers finally reached a small lagoon, but before they reached it, they killed and drank the blood from twenty-two of their horses. Five of the soldiers perished. The legend around Roosevelt County always has been that a group of the Negro soldiers were left on Nigger Hill, and that they either died of thirst or were slaughtered by the Comanches. NIGGER MESA (Union). On Colorado line between Branson and Folsom. Named by the cowboys after a fight between a Negro and a cowboy which was staged at the foot of the mesa in the early 1880's.

NIMENIM RIDGE (Eddy). Extends N and S for 15 mi NE of Carlsbad.

NINE MILE CREEK (Colfax). In S end of Moreno Valley. Flows into Cieneguilla Creek, which then flows into Eagle Nest Lake. Named because it was 9 mi S of Elizabethtown, which, in the early days, was the center not only of Moreno Valley, but the NE part of the state during the hectic mining years between 1865 and 1890. NINE MILE HILL (Bernalillo). From Albuquerque city limits W on US 66. See NUMBERS.

NO AGUA (Taos). Span., "no water." Trading point on NM 74, 34 mi NW of Taos. Site of extensive perlite production. NO AGUA MOUNTAIN (Taos). 2 mi SE of Skarda, near Rio Arriba County line.

NOBE (Roosevelt). 16 mi W of Causey. Post office, 1907-16.

NOGAL (Lincoln). Span., "walnut tree." 10 mi SE of Carrizozo on NM 37, at mouth of Nogal Canyon, between Sierra Blanca and Tucson mts. There is a big walnut tree growing in town and others grow in the canyon along the Hondo River and in the Sierra Blanca Mts. About 1879, free gold was discovered here. Original name was DRY GULCH, probably given by early prospectors. Post office, 1882—; formerly GALENA. NOGAL CANYON (Lincoln). The stream here rises N of Nogal Peak and flows NE near Nogal entering Nogal Arroyo. NOGAL CANYON (Otero). Heads 6 mi N of Cloudcroft; flows NW, entering the Rio Tularosa W of Bent. NOGAL CANYON, CREEK (Socorro). Rises in county and flows E to Elephant Butte reservoir. NOGAL LAKE (Lincoln). 10 mi SE of Carrizozo. Once belonged to SP RR, but the water has now been sold to neighboring cities of Ruidoso and Carrizozo. NOGAL PEAK (Lincoln). 3 mi N of Parsons in SW part of county. Named for the town of Nogal, 6 mi NE. NOGAL PEAK MINE (Lincoln). Brought in $500,000 in gold ore in twenty-four years. The Helen Rae and American gold mines here were also great producers in the early 1880's.

NOLAN (Mora). Community on US 85 and AT&SF RR, 11 mi N of Wagon Mound. The majority of the inhabitants were rail-railroad employees. Post office, 1908-44.

NOMBRE DE DIOS. Span., "name of God." 21 mi S of Las Cruces. Destroyed by a flood in 1884.

NOONDAY CANYON (Grant). In NE part of county in the Black Range. In the early days when

Kingston was an important point in the Southwest and Pinos Altos was a booming mining town, the settlers in both places traveled back and forth. They always expected to make the trip on horseback in one day. As there was always water at Noonday Canyon, it became the rule to try to get here at noon. This accounted for the name.

NORIA (Doña Ana). Span., "water well." 1 mi N of Texas border, on SP RR, 25 mi W of El Paso, Tex. The word comes from the Arabic and denotes a kind of water wheel used in N Africa and S Spain to raise the flow of water from a ditch or well for irrigation. In NM the word was applied to a dug well as early as the mid-seventeenth century.

NORTH (Lincoln). Blind siding an SP RR, 6 mi SW of Oscuro on US 54. Established and named by EP&NE RR in 1899, when it built the line through Capitan.

NORTH BAR LAKE (Catron). 13 mi NE of Mogollon.

NORTH CANADIAN (Union). See CORRUMPAW.

NORTH CANADIAN RIVER. See CANADIAN RIVER.

NORTH CHAVES (McKinley). On AT&SF RR, 4 mi E of Thoreau.

NORTH DES MOINES (Union). Post office, 1909-16. NORTHERN LAKE (Rio Arriba). See HORSE LAKE.

NORTH FORK, LARGO CREEK (Rio Arriba). Span., "long." North Fork rises in N part of county SW of Regina and flows W to Largo Creek.

NORTH GARCIA (Valencia). On AT&SF RR, 25 mi NW of Belen. See GARCIA.

NORTH GUAM (McKinley). On AT&SF RR, 25 mi E of Gallup.

NORTH LUCY (Torrance). 12 mi SE of Clines Corners; 2 mi from US 285. Named for Lucy, a railroad point, 25 mi SW of it. See LUCY.

NORTH MANZANARES (San Miguel). On Manzanares Creek, 6 mi N of Pecos.

NORTH PONIL (Colfax). Creek near Baldy Mtn. See PONIL.

NORTH SAN YSIDRO (San Miguel). 6 mi E of Rowe, 1 mi N of Pecos River. NORTH SEVEN RIVERS (Eddy). See BRANCH SEVEN RIVERS.

NORTH SPRING RIVER (Chaves). Had its origin in a small lake, fed by springs, 1 mi W of Roswell; then flowed E through city to junction with Hondo River, the total length being 5 or 6 mi. Before the coming of Van Smith to the place where Roswell now stands, the river which he and Wilburn named North Spring was known as OLD MAN SPRING, the old man being Robert Casey, father of Mrs.

Lillie Casey Klassner. Twenty-five years ago, the river was a good-sized stream, but now the upper half is completely dry because of the lowering of the water table through the drilling of artesian wells.

NORTH STAR MESA (Grant). 35 mi NE of Silver City on W side of Mimbres River. Named for the North Star Mine, off Pine Canyon N of Grafton. The mesa is 10 or 12 mi long, perfectly level, and has a dense forest over the entire area.

NORTH STAR ROAD (Grant, Catron). Runs N from Mimbres (Grant) to Beaverhead (Catron), at foot of W slope of the Black Range, known as early as 1885 and named for the North Star mine. The U.S. Forest Service rebuilt the road between 1933 and 1938.

NORTON (Quay). Former ranching and farming community on NM 88, 20 mi SE of Tucumcari. Named for Michael J. Norton, who established a store here in 1907 and became the first postmaster. Post office, 1907-41.

NUESTRA SEÑORA DE BELEN GRANT (Valencia). See BELEN GRANT. NUESTRA SEÑORA DE GUADALUPE (Doña Ana). See TORTUGAS. NUESTRA SEÑORA DE LA LUZ (Otero). See LA LUZ. NUESTRA SEÑORA DE LA LUZ DE LAS LAGUNITAS GRANT (Sandoval). Between the Rio Puerco and Cebolleta Mts. in SW corner of county. Granted by Gov. Francisco Marin to Antonio Baca and others before 1761, but they were dispossessed within a year and the land given to Joaquin Mestas and others. Baca commenced proceedings before acting governor Manuel Portillo Yrrisola, and in 1762 the new governor, Tomas Velez Cachupin, regranted the land to Antonio Baca, awarding Mestas payment for improvements. NUESTRA SEÑORA DE LOS DOLORES DE LAS VEGAS (San Miguel). See LAS VEGAS. NUESTRA SEÑORA DE SOCORRO DE PILABO (Socorro). See SOCORRO.

NUEVE (Sandoval). Span., "nine." On AT&SF RR, 9 mi NE of Bernalillo.

NUMBERS. The use of numbers as both descriptive and locating devices occurs in the place-name procedures of this state. Numbers as descriptive designations are illustrated by names such as THREE RIVERS and FIFTEEN SPRINGS. A type of description appears in the numbering of a group of artificial lakes created by the Maxwell Irrigation District in the 1920's to hold water from the Vermejo River. These lakes appear as LAKE TWO, LAKE FIVE, LAKE THIRTEEN, and so on. Canyons and arroyos bear names that tell their distance from a fixed point, as SIX MILE CANYON or THIRTEEN MILE DRAW. Stream beds follow the same pattern, as NINE MILE CREEK. Even hills are so named, as SIX MILE HILL. SEVENTY-FOUR DRAW and SEVENTY-FOUR MOUNTAIN are associated with ranch names in the area and their cattle brands. Into what category SIX SHOOTER SIDING falls may be left to the imagination. For further information on the names mentioned here, see their specific listings.

NUTRIA. Span., "otter"; NM, "beaver." The nutria is an otterlike mammal, the fur of which was made into felt by the Spanish colonists. When they saw the North American beaver, they called it *nutria*. NUTRIA (McKinley). Small Indian village 20 mi S of Ft. Wingate, on Rio Creek. NUTRIA CREEK (McKinley). Rises below Pinehaven and flows S to join the Rio Pescado. NUTRIAS (Rio Arriba). Farming community on US 84, 9 mi S of Tierra Amarilla, on Nutrias Creek. NUTRIAS CREEK (Rio Arriba). "Beaver Creek." Also called NUTRITAS CREEK. Rises SE of Tierra Amarilla and flows W and N to Chama River. NUTRIAS LAKE (Rio Arriba). At bend of Nutrias Creek, SE of Tierra Amarilla.

NUTT (Luna). Former station and trading point on NM 27, and AT&SF RR, 19 mi SW of Hatch. Named for a Colonel Nutt, an original stockholder and director of AT&SF RR, which was organized by Boston people in the late 1860's. When the line was being built from Rincon to Deming, many mines opened up at Lake Valley and Hillsboro, and there were prospects in the Black Range for producers of silver ores. Nutt was the logical point of shipment to refineries. When the road was extended to Lake Valley in 1884, nearly all the people moved there. Post office, 1881, intermittently, to 1939. NUTT MOUNTAIN (Sierra). 3 mi N of Nutt. See SUNDAY CONE.

O AK. Oak trees do not flourish in the dry climate of NM, except the scrub oak, known as Span., *chaparral,* a dwarf evergreen or thicket of these trees. The place names refer to this dwarf oak. OAK CAÑON, CREEK (Union). 4 mi S of Emery Gap. OAK GROVE (Grant). OAK SPRINGS (Catron).

OAKWOOD SPRINGS (San Miguel). Post office, 1891-93; mail to Lesperance.

OASIS (Chaves). On NM 255, 8 mi SE of Roswell, E of Bottomless Lakes State Park, commonly known as the OASIS RANCH, where the largest artesian well in the world was drilled in 1931; original flow 9,225, still about 5,000 gallons per minute and remains the world's largest. OASIS (Lea). See KNOWLES. OASIS STATE PARK (Roosevelt). Recreation area of 200 acres, 5 mi NW of Portales. Opened July 22, 1962. In 1934 the discovery of a flint spear point in the leg bone of an ice-age mammoth proved that man lived here with prehistoric animals 12,000 to 13,000 years ago.

OBAR (Quay). Settlement on NM 54, 8 mi SW of Nara Visa. Formerly called PERRY; then Obar, for the Circle Bar Ranch, whose brand is a circle with a bar under it. The owner of the ranch was named Howrey. Settlement started in 1906-07. Prior to that, the spot was a switch on CRI&P RR. Post office, 1908-53. O BAR O CANYON (Catron). In south-central part of county. Named for a ranch brand. O BAR O MOUNTAIN (Catron). On the Continental Divide, 12 mi NW of Black Springs.

OCATE (Mora). Perhaps Mexican *ocate,* "white pine." Ranching, lumbering, and dry-farming community on NM 120, 24 mi NW of Wagon Mound, on Ocate Creek and 5 mi S of Colfax County line. Name is reported to be Apache for "windy gap," but linguistic support for this is lacking. Post office, 1866—. OCATE CRATER (Mora). 18 mi NE of Mora, at W end of Ocate Mtn. OCATE CREEK (Mora, Colfax). Rises in Colfax County then flows SE through Ocate, below which it is diverted into Upper Charette Lake and then into Canadian River. OCATE CREEK, SOUTH FORK (Mora). Small stream at the Schiele Ranch above Ocate. OCATE GRANT (Mora). On Oct. 15, 1837, Manuel Alvarez petitioned Governor Armijo for land to introduce Merino sheep, and on October 16 the governor approved the grant, confirming it on Dec. 5, 1845. OCATE MESA (Mora). Large mesa extending 10 or 12 mi; starts 3 mi NW of Wagon Mound. OCATE MOUNTAIN (Mora). 18 mi NE of Mora.

OCHO (Luna). Span., "eight." Siding on AT&SF RR, 8 mi NW of Deming.

OCHOA (Lea). Trading point on NM 256, 14 mi W of Jal. Said to be named for Ochoa, Tex. Name is more likely to be for a Spanish family who settled here in relatively modern times. Today only an old school and an abandoned oil plant remain. Post office, 1917-40.

ODEN (Grant). Post office, 1913-18; mail to Sherman.

OGLE (Quay). Settlers by this name operated a grocery store when there was a post office here, 15 mi SW of Tucumcari. Post office, 1906-13.

OHAYSE (Otero). On SP RR near Orogrande. Post office, 1917-21.

OIL. As a place name, this word has chiefly been significant in NM since the discovery of oil at Hobbs in 1927. OIL (Grant). OIL CENTER (Lea). Community 16 mi SW of Hobbs on NM 8. Post office, 1937—. OIL CITY (Eddy). 14 mi SE of Artesia. OIL SIDING (Hidalgo). In Lordsburg on a spur of SP RR. Named because it is a point where oil cars are unloaded. OIL SPUR (Quay).

OJITA (San Miguel). Spa.... "little spring." OJITA (Mora). OJITA (Rio Arriba). In a gasfield drilling basin, 11 mi N of Lindrith and 4 mi W of NM 95. Post office, 1941. OJITOS CANYON (Rio Arriba). Heads just W of the Continental Divide and flows SW into Cañada Larga, 15 mi W of Lindrith. OJITOS CANYON (Rio Arriba). A second canyon of the same name in the same county; heads NE of Gallina and flows NE into the Chama River. OJITA DE LAS CONCHAS (San Miguel). "Shells." OJITOS FRIOS (San Miguel). "Cold." Trading point 12 mi W of Las Vegas.

OJO. Span., "eye, keyhole, spring." The ordinary Spanish word for spring is fuente, a full-flowing burst of water from the ground, a type which is rare in NM. Ojo is an archaism in Spanish for a small, slow flow of water, and the term was widely adopted in this state as a place name. The springs are described by their size, color, temperature, location, and a dozen other characteristics. OJO ALAMO (San Juan). "Cottonwood." OJO AMARILLO CANYON (San Juan). "Yellow." OJO ANALLA (Otero). Spanish family name, Anaya. A large family by this name was wiped out in the Pueblo Rebellion of 1680. The only male survivor, Francesco de Anaya Almazan, remarried in 1682, and returned with his wife upon the Reconquest of 1692. His name is recorded on Inscription Rock at El Morro National Monument. OJO CALIENTE (Rio Arriba, Taos). "Hot." Unincorporated community in two counties along banks of Vallecitos River. Health resort on US 285, 26 mi N of Española. Place names in both Tewa and Spanish have described the hot springs here: Tewa, posee po pee, "green springs." It has been conjec-

tured that posee was originally compounded of po, "water" and see, "stink," and that posee referred to stinking water which usually had a green moss color. The Tewa called it "green spring" since the high temperature causes the growth of blue-green algae, covering the rocks with an emerald-green color. The Tewa regarded the place as the dwelling of tribal gods. The springs themselves were the openings between this world and the "down below world," whence their first people came. The grandmother of Poseyemo, a Tewa hero, is said still to live in one of the springs. The Spaniards had a settlement here that might have existed before the Pueblo Rebellion. Listed as a settlement by Gov. Manuel Armijo in Santa Fe on July 7, 1840. Post office, 1871—. OJO CALIENTE (Socorro). In SW area of county 3 mi SE of Dusty. Site of an old fort and the Hot Springs Apache Reservation in 1874. OJO CALIENTE (Valencia). Small place in NW edge of county just within the Zuñi Reservation. In the neighborhood may be found as many as thirty-one ancient Indian ruins of various sizes. OJO CALIENTE GRANT (Rio Arriba). Small grant lying S of Ojo Caliente. Settlers may have been there before the Pueblo Rebellion, and were certainly living at the place by 1689. This date is carved on a beam in an old church in the settlement. The grant dates from Sept. 11, 1793, when Governor Concha approved the petition of Sgt. Luis Duran, District Lt. Jose Antonio Espinosa, and forty-nine others for this tract in the valley between the Cañada de los Comanches and a "monument of stone and mud with a holy cross of cedar placed in the heart." OJO CHAMISO (Sandoval). 5 mi E of Jemez Springs. OJO CHERISCO (San Miguel). Perhaps churresco, "thick, oozy, dirty." OJO CHICO (Otero). "Small." OJO CHIQUITO (Valencia). "Very small." OJO DE ALBERTO (San Miguel). OJO DE BERNAL (San Miguel). 7 mi from San Miguel. OJO DE CASA (Sandoval). Settled in 1661 when the mines near here were opened by the Spaniards. OJO DE CHAPELLE (San Miguel). OJO DE LOS INDIOS (Torrance). NE of fire-lookout station on Capilla Peak. OJO DE LA CASA (Santa Fe). OJO DE LA GOTERA (Bernalillo). "Dripping." Near Chilili. OJO DE LA LOMITA (Otero). "Little hill." OJO DE LA MOSCA (Valencia). "Fly." In San Mateo Mts. OJO DE LA PARIDA (Socorro). "Woman lately delivered of a child." OJO DE LAS GALLINAS

(Harding). "Chickens or wild fowl." Ojo de la Turrieta (Bernalillo). "Spring of the Turrieta family." Ojo de la Vaca (Santa Fe). "Cow." Trading point 20 mi SE of Santa Fe. Ojo del Borrego Grant (Sandoval). Area measuring 5 by 6 mi, about 6 mi E of Jemez Pueblo. Made to Nerio Antonio Montoya, Mar. 4, 1768. Ojo del Carnero (Quay). "Sheep." In the Plaza Larga area E of Tucumcari. Named because of the wild sheep that came to water here. Ojo del Espiritu Santo Grant (Sandoval). "Holy Spirit." Large Spanish land grant W of Jemez Pueblo. Made to Luis Maria Cabeza de Vaca on May 24, 1815, by Gov. Alberto Maynez. Said to have been named by a peon who stood guard one night and saw two wraithlike spirals rising from the ground. He rushed toward the camp crying, "El Espiritu Santo!" Others followed him and discovered the spring. Ojo del Gallo (Cibola). See Fort Wingate. Ojo de los Ajuelos (Bernalillo). Perhaps "wild garlic," from ajo, "garlic." Near Chilili. Ojo de la Casa (Bernalillo). "House spring." S and E of Placitas. Ojo de los Montoyas (San Miguel). Ojo del Oso (Torrance). "Bear." Ojo del Padre (Sandoval). "The father," possibly "priest." Post office, 1940-58. See Guadalupe. Ojo del Perrillo (Doña Ana). "Little dog." The chronicler of the Oñate expedition in 1598 writes that while crossing the Jornada del Muerto, the colonists had traveled a day and a night without water. On May 23 a dog appeared with muddy paws and hind feet. Two of the men searched and found water holes. The spot became named for this incident. Indians in the area were called Apaches del Perrillo. The place is called El Perillo in the Otermin documents, 1680-82 (C. W. Hackett, editor). Ojo del Perro (Hidalgo). Ojo de San Jose Grant (Sandoval). Small area 3 mi NE of Jemez Pueblo. Granted to Paublin Montoya and six associates on Sept. 16, 1768. Ojo Escondida (Rio Arriba). Near Sandoval County line, 17 mi E of Cuba. Ojo Feliz (Mora). "Happy." Ranching and lumbering community 1 mi E of NM 21, 57 mi W of Wagon Mound. Post office, 1922—. Ojo Hediondo (San Miguel). "Stinking." Ojo la Casa Lake (Torrance). 4 mi S of Vallecitos. Ojo la Jara (Los Alamos). 2 mi N of Los Alamos. Ojo Lomito Trigo (Valencia). 13 mi E of Belen. Ojo Perrito (Torrance). 4 mi NE of Tajique. Ojo Perro (Torrance). 4 mi E of Riley. Ojo Redondo (Cibola).

"Round." In Zuñi Mts. NW of Grants. Ojo Salas Lake (Valencia). 9 mi W of Manzano. Ojo Terrero (Torrance). 4 mi NW of Tajique. Ojo Vaca (Luna). See Cow Springs. Ojo Zarco (Mora). "Clear, blue." Ojo Zarco (Rio Arriba). Farming community W of NM 76, 6 mi N of Truchas. Post office formerly called Diamante. Also spelled Ojo Sarco. Post office, 1913—. Ojo Zarco or Sarco Creek (Rio Arriba). Enters Embudo River N of Ojo Sarco.

O.K. Creek (San Miguel). Flows NE through O.K. Ranch into Mora River, 13 mi E of Watrous.

Old Albuquerque (Bernalillo). Post office, 1886—. See Albuquerque.

Old Baldy (Otero). See Sierra Blanca Mountain.

Old Man Hill (Chaves). See Six Mile Hill.

Old Man Spring (Chaves). See North Spring River.

Old Mesilla (Doña Ana). See Mesilla.

Old San Jose (Cibola). Settlement on edge of Cubero Grant, 5 mi NE of McCarty's. The name San Jose in this area is in honor of San Jose de Acoma, the patron of the great mission church whose holy image on a painting is reported to have been brought to Acoma Pueblo either by Fray Ramirez in 1629 or by a later priest between 1665 and 1710 as a gift of the Spanish king, Charles II.

Olguin (San Miguel). Post office, Olquin, misspelling of Spanish name Olguin. First postmaster, Juan B. Olquin. Post office, 1905-11; mail to Anton Chico.

Olio (Rio Arriba, San Juan). Post office, 1884-1903; changed to Kirtland. See Fruitland.

Olive (Chaves). Former ranching community 16 mi NW of Kenna. Founded about 1906 in the San Juan Mesa area. Abandoned by 1938. Post office, 1909—.

Omega (Catron). Post office, 1938—. See Sweazeville.

Omlee (Otero). Community on US 54, and SP RR, 5 mi S of Alamogordo. Name is a blend of initials letters and the surname of Oliver M. Lee, the owner of large ranch holdings near S end of Sacramento Mts. and in the valley at Wildey Wells.

Onava (San Miguel). Cattle pens on US 85, 10 mi NE of Las Vegas. Post office, 1902, intermittently, to 1924.

One Butte (Otero). See Tres Montosos.

Opal (Otero). Post office, 1904; mail to Cloudcroft.

OPTIMO (Mora). Span., "best, very good." Farming and ranching community 1 mi E of US 85 and 9 mi SW of Wagon Mound. Formerly called TIPTON. The railroad imported settlers from Pennsylvania who were called Dunkards, a sect of the German-American Baptists. They settled on land E of the railroad right of way and attempted farming. Post office, 1909-47. ORAN (Otero). Post office, 1904-07; mail to Avis. ORANGE (Otero). Former trading point in SE part of county, 5 mi SW of Cienaga and 3 mi N of Texas border. Post office, 1904-25. ORCHARD PARK (Chaves). On US 285, and AT&SF RR, 13 mi SE of Roswell. Named by early settlers who planted orchards in 1893, which soon failed. Post office, 1907-25. Formerly ALELLEN.
OREJAS MOUNTAIN (Taos). See TRES OREJAS PEAKS.
ORGAN (Doña Ana). Mining community on US 70, 14 mi NE of Las Cruces, in foothills of Organ Mts., for which it was named. In 1908, famed sheriff Pat Garrett was shot to death on the road leading from this old mining camp to Las Cruces. Millions in lead, copper, and silver have been earned here, but very little in gold. The mines are now half-filled with water, but U.S. Bureau of Reclamation officials say it would be too massive a job to lower the water table throughout the mountain range, in order to drain or pump out all the water. Post office, 1881, intermittently, to present. ORGAN MOUNTAINS (Doña Ana). At S end of Rocky Mts. in central part of the state; 10 mi E of Las Cruces. Oñate refers to them as Sierra del Olvido, "Sierra of Oblivion," but the Otermin documents of 1682 (C. W. Hackett, editor) use the name Los Organos, "pipe organs." On De Lafora's map (1771), the peaks are shown as Los Organos and in De Lafora's text, written from 1766 to 1768, the author refers to the sierra of Los Mansos which "are commonly called Los Organos because of irregular peaks in this chain which resemble pipes of an organ."
ORIENTAL (Eddy). Post office, 1910-16.
ORNAS (Santa Fe). See HORNOS.
OROGRANDE (Otero). Span., "big gold." On SP RR and US 54, 26 mi from Texas line. Named because of numerous gold-mining operations in vicinity. Post office, 1906—. See JARILLA JUNCTION.
ORO QUAY PEAK (Santa Fe). In San Pedro Mts., 12 mi SW of Ortiz, and same distance N of

Edgewood. Contains extensive deposits of silicon.
ORTEGA MOUNTAINS (Rio Arriba). 3 mi W of Ancones.
ORTIZ (Santa Fe). 5 mi W of Galisteo. Two men named Ortiz, and their families, are known to have lived in this area. Nicolas Ortiz, a native of Mexico City, came in 1693, settled in the Santa Cruz region, and acquired lands and mines in the Galisteo basin S of Santa Fe. The second man was a Señor Ortiz who discovered gold in 1828 in this region. ORTIZ MINE GRANT (Santa Fe). Area approximately 10 by 11 mi lying between Golden and Madrid. The original grantees were Jose Francisco Ortiz and Ygnacio Cano, whose petition to register a vein of ore was approved Dec. 18, 1833. ORTIZ MOUNTAINS (Santa Fe). Formerly called SIERRA DE SAN LAZARO. Span., "mountain of St. Lazarus." E of NM 10 and S of Madrid.
ORTON (Quay). Post office, 1908-11; changed to LUCILLE.
OSCURA (Socorro). Span., "dark, heavily shaded." Post office, 1881-82. OSCURA (Lincoln). Ranching community on US 54, and SP RR, 17 mi SW of Carrizozo. Established by EP&NE RR in 1899 when the road was built through to Capitan. Named for Oscura Mts. just W of it. In 1906 E. G. Rafferty of Chicago purchased the land and laid out a townsite. He also drilled for oil, but was unsuccessful in finding any. Post office, OSCURO, 1901-47; Oscura, 1947-51. OSCURA MOUNTAINS (Socorro). See SIERRA OSCURA. OSCURA PEAK (Socorro). In Sierra Oscura Mts. on Lincoln County border, 21 mi NW of Oscura.
OSHA. The name of an herb, wild angelica root, found in various parts of the state and used for medicinal purposes. OSHA (Colfax). Post office, 1894-1903; changed to BLACK LAKE. OSHA CANYON (Mora). OSHA CANYON (Taos). 2 mi E of Llano Largo. OSHA CREEK (San Miguel). Small tributary to Cow Creek, 10 mi W of Gallinas. OSHA MOUNTAIN (Taos, Colfax). See CUESTA DEL OSHA PEAK. OSHA PASS (Colfax). Near Taos County line, 3 mi N of Osha Mtn. OSHA PEAK (Torrance). 6 mi W of Manzano.
OSO CREEK (Lincoln). Span., "bear." Empties into Salado Creek, 3 mi NW of Capitan. OSO RIDGE (Valencia). Spur of Zuñi Mts, 20 mi W of Grants.

OTERO. The family name first appears in 1659, when Pedro Otero is listed in marriage records at Santa Fe. The names of other members of this family are found in eighteenth-century records at Albuquerque and Tome. The family acquired lands and achieved prominence in this and the following century. OTERO (Colfax). A lively spot near the foot of Raton Pass when AT&SF RR reached here in 1878. After the division point was removed 5 mi N to Raton in the following year, most of the settlement moved with it. OTERO (Valencia). Post office, 1905-06; mail to Los Lunas. OTERO COUNTY. Created from S part of Lincoln County and E part of Doña Ana. Second largest county in state, containing an area of 6,638 sq mi. Named for Miguel A. Otero, territorial governor at time the county was created, Jan. 30, 1899. Governor Otero was appointed by President William McKinley in 1897 and served until 1906. OTERO CANYON (Bernalillo). Runs N into Cedro Canyon, 2 mi W of Sabino.

OTIS (Eddy). Farming community on US 285 and AT&SF RR, 6 mi S of Carlsbad. Named for T. E. Otis, director of AT&SF RR. Post office, 1893-1901; mail to Carlsbad. OTIS (San Juan). Trading post started in 1919. Named for its founder.

OTOWI (Santa Fe). Tewa, p'otsuivi, "gap where water sinks." Trading point on NM 4, 35 mi NW of Santa Fe and 7 mi W of San Ildefonso. Official gaging station for water on the upper Rio Grande. Nearby is one of the important pueblo ruins in the Pajarito region. During 1923, a post office was requested for Los Alamos Ranch, using the ranch name, but since a place near Las Vegas already had that name, three others were submitted and the department chose Otowi. How Otowi brought the Indian world to the edge of this Los Alamos nuclear physics laboratory is told by Peggy Pond Church in her book The House at Otowi Bridge (1960). Post office, 1921-41.

OTTO (Luna). OTTO (Santa Fe). A map in Twitchell, Leading Facts NM History, II, shows two towns with this name: one between Moriarty and Stanley, almost due S of Santa Fe; another S of Golden. First postmaster, Otto H. E. Goetz. Post office, 1907-23.

OVERTON (De Baca). 10 mi SW of Yeso.

OZANNE (Socorro). Known in the 1880's as a stopping place between Carrizozo to San Antonio. Named for Urbane Ozanne, who had the stage line between Carthage and White Oaks. Post office, 1906-09; mail to San Antonio.

OWL CANYON (Hidalgo). Runs NW to a point 2 mi S of Rodeo.

PAAKO RUINS (Bernalillo). The ruined houses of an ancient Tiwa settlement in Paako State Monument. They were constructed of stone rubble and were two stories in height. Adolphe Bandelier writes that they were inhabited as late as 1626, but abandoned before 1670. PAAKO STATE MONUMENT (Bernalillo). In San Pedro Valley, E of Sandia Mts. and 8 mi N of Tijeras. Created July 16, 1933.

PABLO MONTOYA GRANT (San Miguel). Very large area including portions of two counties, the greater area being in E San Miguel and a small corner in NE Guadalupe. Grant was made Nov. 19, 1824, and boundaries were described as lying on Red Canadian River from bend of Cinta Creek to La Trinchera and from Arroyo del Cuervo to Mule Spring. "Trinchera" here refers to a stone boundary marker set in the center of a natural earthen fortification within the Trinchera hills.

PACHECO CREEK (Santa Fe). Flows NW, 3 mi above Tesuque. PACHECO GRANT (Santa Fe). Small tract 7 mi SW of Santa Fe and 2 mi W of US 85. Granted by the King of Spain through Governor Mendinueta in 1769 to Jose Pacheco and Salvador Pacheco.

PACKSADDLE CANYON (Catron). Heads N of Mogollon Peak; runs E into West Fork of Gila River. PACKSADDLE CANYON (Grant). Heads in Pinos Mts. and runs into Gila River.

PADDY'S HOLE (Catron). See PATTIE'S HOLE.

PADILLAS, Los PADILLAS Bernalillo). Span., "the Padilla folks." On US 85, 9 mi S of Albuquerque. Ruins of Tiwa Indian villages are nearby. The first Padilla in NM was Jose de Padilla, who came from Queretaro before the Pueblo Rebellion of 1680. His children settled in the Rio Abajo after the Reconquest of 1692, several families giving the name later to this settlement. Post office, 1903-17. PADILLAS TABLELAND (Bernalillo). Also called MESA DE LOS PADILLAS. Lava-capped butte SW of Padillas. On the mesa are some old ruins which may be the Tiwa Indian pueblo of Los GUAJOLOTES mentioned by Espejo in 1582-83. Charles Fletcher Lummis heard of a tradition that this pueblo was abandoned because of the great number of venomous snakes here. Isleta claimed it as an ancient site of her people. PADILLA CREEK (Lincoln and Chaves). Rises in Lincoln and flows E to Pecos River. PADILLA CREEK (De Baca). Joins Fifteen-Mile Arroyo 10 mi NW of Chaves. PAGE (McKinley). Former logging and farming settlement in Zuñi Mts. 25 mi SE of Gallup. Named for Gregory Page, Gallup businessman in the early 1900's. Post office, 1913-16. PAGUATE (Cibola). Trading point 8 mi N of Laguna. Both Paraje and Paguate grew out of summer Indian settlements of the Laguna Indians, which were temporary locations prior to 1870, but which have now become permanent settlements. Named for Antonio Paguat, one of the four Mexicans from whom the Lagunas purchased the land subsequently known as Paguate Grant. The name Paguat or Paguate appears in late eighteenth-century records of local parishes. Post office, 1905, intermittently, to present; PACQUATE, 1922-27. PAGUATE CREEK (Cibola). Flows S to join the Rio San Jose, 3 mi E of Laguna. PAGUATE GRANT (Cibola). Extends approximately 24 mi E to W, 6 mi N to S, with Paguate at the center. PAGUATE MESA (Cibola). Site of Cebolleta village. Post office, 1905-08; mail to Laguna. PAINTED CAVE (Sandoval). In Bandelier National Monument. PAINTER (Roosevelt). In the neighborhood of Floyd. First postmaster, William A. Painter. Post office, 1908-12. PAJARA (Lincoln). Span., "bird." PAJARITA (San Miguel). "Little bird." On US 85, 3 mi SE of Rowe. PAJARITO (Bernalillo). 6 mi S of Albuquerque on W bank of the Rio Grande in Pajarito Grant. First mentioned in middle of the seventeenth century. Name may be descriptive of many birds in the cottonwood groves along the river. Pajarito is also a surname found among Indian families, and is mentioned in the Cebolleta Grant area 40 mi W and settled at a later period. Post office, 1868-1929. PAJARITO CANYON (Sandoval, Santa Fe). PAJARITO CREEK (Quay). Rises in Guadalupe County and flows NE to Canadian River. PAJARITO GRANT (Bernalillo). Long narrow grant, S of Albuquerque, running from Pajarito settlement to the Rio Puerco. It was also called SITIO DE SAN YSIDRO DE PAJARITO GRANT. The title passed not from a

known grant but from documents proving possession by Doña Josefa Baca in 1746, and passed on to her heir Antonio Baca and those who claimed ownership from him. PAJARITO PEAK (Otero). The only high, isolated peak in E area of Mescalero Indian Reservation. PAJARITO PEAK (Sandoval). 10 mi NW of Jemez Pueblo. PAJARITO PLATEAU (Sandoval, Santa Fe). Tewa name tchirage, "place of the Bird People," is applied to a large Puye ruin on top of N rim of Pajarito Canyon. PALIZA or POLICA CREEK (Sandoval). Little creek on S side of Jemez Mts., heading at Cerro Pelado and emptying into Jemez River at Jemez Pueblo. PALMA (Torrance). Span., "palm, palmetto"; in this case, "yucca." Small settlement on US 66, 32 mi NW of Vaughn. Post office, 1903-55. PALMILLA (Taos). "Little palm." On NM 285, 8 mi S of Antonita, Colo. Named for the abundance of yucca plants in the vicinity. PALO BLANCO (Colfax). Span., "white tree, pole." PALO BLANCO CREEK (Colfax). Flows S to Holkeo Creek, 15 mi N of Gladstone. Named for Blanco Mtn. to the N. PALO BLANCO MOUNTAIN (Colfax). 4 mi NW of Malpie. PALO BLANCO PEAK (Colfax). 15 mi SW of Capulin in E end of county. PALO CIENTE CREEK (Taos). Enters the Rito de la Olla, 10 mi SE of Talpa. PALODURA (Socorro). "Hardwood." PALO FLECHADO (Colfax, Santa Fe). "Tree pierced with darts." Mountain pass near Agua Fria. Named because many arrows were found sticking in the trees after an Indian fight. However, another explanation is that it comes from an old Taos Indian custom of shooting the remaining arrows into a large tree after buffalo hunts. At the summit of the mountain near the pass is the tree containing the arrows. PALO FLECHADO CREEK (Colfax). Rises in Taos Mts. and flows E to Agua Fria where it joins Agua Fria Creek. PALO VERDE (Lincoln). See GREEN TREE. PALOMAS (Quay). Span., "doves, pigeons." 15 mi W of Tucumcari. Railroad switch for passing trains when CRI&P RR built its line in 1901-02 between Dalhart, Tex., and Santa Rosa. PALOMAS ARROYO (Luna). Runs from the NW to Midway. PALOMAS CREEK (Sierra). Empties into Palomas River 10 mi SW of Cuchillo. PALOMAS HILLS (Quay). 1 mi S of Palomas. PALOMAS RIVER (Sierra). Flows S from Cuchillo and empties into Caballo Reservoir. See LAS PALOMAS. PALOMAS SPRINGS (Sierra). Post office, 1911-14; mail to Hot

Springs; changed to TRUTH OR CONSEQUENCES.

PANCHUELA CREEK (San Miguel). Span., feminine given name, "little Frances." One of the streams which join Pecos River 4 mi above Cowles. PANCHUELA CREEK (Santa Fe). Flows N from Nambe Pueblo into Cundiyo Creek. At least three pueblo ruins are along this creek, which flows through deep canyons in places. PANCHUELA CREEK, WEST (Mora). Heads across the divide from Panchuela Creek, and constitutes the headwaters of Frijoles Creek, which flows past Cundiyo to Santa Cruz Lake.

PANKEY CANYON (Socorro). 43 mi N of Truth or Consequences. Named for Ruben Pankey of the family which owned a 43-section ranch here. Also called SAN JOSE CANYON.

PAQUITA (Valencia). Span., diminutive of Francisquita, "little Frances, Fanny." Other forms are Quica and Quiquita, or Pancha, Panchita, and Panchuela. On AT&SF RR, 5 mi N of Los Lunas.

PARADISE PLAINS (Guadalupe). Post office, 1909-10; mail to Potrillo.

PARAJE. Span., "place, residence." Historically, the word has a slightly different meaning here as a place name. Many an old settlement started with a name like *Paraje de Belén*, *Paraje de Bernalillo* because it served as a "stopping point" for people traveling. PARAJE (Socorro). Post office, 1867-1910; mail to Milligan. PARAJE (Cibola). Laguna Indian village, 3 mi W of New Laguna; land irrigated from San Jose Creek. PARAJE DE FRAY CRISTOBAL (Sierra). Locality or camping place on the Rio Grande near the present San Marcial. This was the last stopping place for water at N end of Jornada del Muerto. Name is that of Fray Cristobal Salazar, a Franciscan who came with Oñate and was later notary at the trial of Villagra, the poet and chronicler of Oñate's expedition. Townsite submerged by water of Elephant Butte Lake.

PARK. In certain areas of NM, chiefly N and W, "park" is used, as it is in Colorado, to describe a valley shut in by high hills or mountains. This is an old English usage but it also was common to the early French trappers who came to the Rocky Mts. for beaver and other furbearing animals. They spelled the word *parc*, applying it to a cleared, grassy basin that served as a kind of enormous pen or corral for deer, buffalo, and other wild animals. PARK, PARK CITY (Socorro). Post office, 1892-94; mail to Milligan. See LA SMELTA.

PARKS (Grant). First postmaster, W. J. Parks. Post office, 1882-83; mail to Lordsburg. PARK SPRINGS (San Miguel). 5 mi E of US 84, 30 mi SE of Las Vegas. Post office, 1914-19.

PARK VIEW (Rio Arriba). Farming and ranching community on US 84, 15 mi S of Chama, and 5 mi N of Tierra Amarilla. Settled in 1878. Before descending the hill, there is a view of timber and clearings that look like a park. Post office, 1877—.

PARKER ARROYO (Colfax). 1 mi W of Hebron; connects with Canadian Red River in north-central part of county. PARKERS (Otero).

PARMA (Luna). Siding and tracks on SP RR, 5 mi W of Deming. Used as a loading station for Camp Cody in World War I.

PARSONS (Lincoln). Camp for miners on South Fork of Bonito River, 5 mi above Bonito Dam. Started in 1892 and named for R. C. Parsons, who made a gold strike here in 1886. Post office, 1888-1926. PARSON'S MINE. In Sierra Blanca Mts., at 10,000 ft.

PARTON (Colfax). Formerly TROYBURGH. Post office, 1884-86; mail to Raton.

PASAMONTE (Union). Span., "pass or opening between mountains." On NM 58, 33 mi W of Clayton. Lies between rolling hills, which is doubtless the explanation of the name. Established in 1899 by Carl Gilg, its first postmaster. Post office, 1899-1947. PASAMONTE LAKE (Union). N and W of Pasamonte.

PASCHAL (Grant). Post office, 1882-83; mail to Silver City.

PASTURA (Guadalupe). Span., "pasture, feed." Pasture, in the Western sense of the word, means grazing land and applies to any area where there is good grass or wild hay. Trading point on US 54 and SP RR, 19 mi SW of Santa Rosa. Founded in 1901 by employees of the railroad, and of the Pastura Trading Co., owned by the Charles Ilfeld Co. Post office, 1903—.

PATO (Torrance). Span., "duck." PATO MESA (Valencia). Span., "duck tableland." PATOS CREEK (Lincoln). Heads in Patos Mts.; flows N and E into Cienega del Macho. PATOS LAKE (Lincoln). In the early days the lake had lots of water and many wild ducks; hence the name. Now it is dry most of the year. Freighters between Socorro and Lincoln used to camp here overnight. PATOS MOUNTAINS (Lincoln). 5 mi E of White Oaks. Named for the lake. A good quality of coal was discovered here in the early days, and was used for light and power plants.

PATTERSON (Catron). 6 mi W of Horse Springs. Named for George Patterson, a soldier who retired as a rancher at Patterson Spring. Post office operated from 1884 to 1906, with R. C. Patterson as postmaster, but was transferred in that period from Patterson to Joseph to Whitfield and back to Patterson. PATTERSON (Union). First postmaster, Gertie Patterson. Post office, 1910-18.

PATTIE'S HOLE (Catron). 6 mi from Socorro County line, SE of Luera Mts. Also called PADDY'S HOLE. Name may have come from James O. Pattie, author of *The Personal Narrative of James O. Pattie of Kentucky* (1831), who hunted and trapped for six years through Arizona and NM. This water hole was the only watering place between Magdalena and the large ranches to the west. Here cattlemen and sheepmen often met and several disputes led to murders.

PATTON CREEK (Colfax). Small stream which flows into Canadian Red River at its source near Colorado line in NW part of county. PATTON CREEK (Sierra). 8 mi S of Kingston.

PAXTON (Otero). Community on US 54 and SP RR, 5 mi S of Escondida and 25 mi S of Alamogordo. PAXTON SPRINGS (Valencia). Also called PAXTON. Former logging camp on NM 56, 15 mi SW of Grants and once the terminus of the Breece Co. RR, 4 mi from the Ice Caves. Named for the Paxton family who were early settlers. Post office, 1929-30.

PEACOCK CANYON (Union). Prong of Cimarron Canyon 35 mi NE of Folsom. A family of this name located here in the early 1870's. See DRIPPING SPRINGS.

PEARL (Lea). Former trading point 20 mi W of Hobbs. Named for Mrs. Pearl Roberts, postmaster. Post office, 1908-29.

PEARSON (Roosevelt). Post office, 1907-11; changed to BENSON.

PECK'S MESA (Colfax). N of Holkeo Creek in extreme SE corner of county. Named for an early family in the neighborhood.

PECOS. The name is pre-Spanish, but may be a Spanish approximation of the Keresan Indian form *payokona*, possibly from the Towa *pa*, "water," *kyoo*, unexplained, *la*, locative, i.e., "place where there is water." Name on L'Atlas Curieux (1700) locates the Indian pueblo now in ruins. PECOS (San Miguel). Settlement on US 63, 3 mi from the old Indian pueblo and 6 mi N of Rowe. Before July 12, 1883, known as LEVY. Post office, 1883, intermittently, to present. PECOS BALDY (Mora). Peak

located in SW tip of county in Sangre de Cristo Mts. PECOS BALDY LAKE (Mora). At E base of Pecos Baldy Mtn., 7 mi N of Cowles. PECOS GRANT (San Miguel). Tract 5 mi square surrounding Pecos Pueblo. Made by Governor Cruzate on Sept. 25, 1689, and confirmed by U.S. Congress on Dec. 22, 1858. PECOS MINES (San Miguel). PECOS PUEBLO (San Miguel). Ruins 23 mi SE of Santa Fe on US 84, 85. F. W. Hodge fixed the date for the abandonment of Pecos Pueblo as August 1838. Driven forth by Comanche Indian raids and sickness, the inhabitants first went to Sandia, and then later joined the Jemez, to whom the Pecos people were related linguistically. PECOS RIVER (San Miguel, Guadalupe, De Baca, Chaves, Eddy). Flows through these counties into Texas to join the Rio Grande N of Del Rio. PECOS STATE MONUMENT (San Miguel). 1 mi E of Pecos. Created Feb. 20, 1935, at site of Pecos Pueblo. PECOS STATION (San Miguel). See SAN MIGUEL DEL BADO.

PEDERNAL. Span., "flint or quartz, extreme hardness." Probably descriptive of the mountain 10 mi SE of Clines Corners. Tewa, *tsee peeng ya* "flaking stone mountain." PEDERNAL (Torrance). Small settlement 3 mi S of US 60, 9 mi SW of Encino. Post office, 1917-55. PEDERNAL CREEK (Rio Arriba). SW corner of county in Polvadera Grant; 15 mi NW of Los Alamos. Flows N into Polvadera Creek. PEDERNAL HILLS (Torrance). Low mountains in north-central part of county. So called by the Indians and Spanish in the early days because of its flint rock. Indian signs show that they used it as a stopping place because of the springs as well. PEDERNAL MOUNTAINS (Rio Arriba). 3 mi SE of Youngsville. PEDERNAL PEAK (Torrance). 14 mi N of Pedernal.

PEDRO ARMENDARIZ No. 33, No. 34 GRANTS (Sierra, Socorro). Two grants which extend from Engle in Sierra nearly to San Antonio in Socorro. The owner of these grants was a lieutenant in the Santa Fe garrison in 1808 and received the land grant in 1820. He was forced to abandon it because of Indian attacks and left NM for Chihuahua after 1822.

PEDROSO CREEK (San Miguel). 6 mi NW of Cherryvale.

PELADO MOUNTAIN (Rio Arriba). Span., "bald, hairless." The Tewa called it "mountain of the west," and performed sacred ceremonies on its summit. It may also be the Navajo sacred mountain of the East. Highest of the Jemez range, elevation 11,260 ft.

PELEA (Doña Ana). On US 85, N of El Paso at Texas line.

PELONA MOUNTAIN (Catron). Span., "bald." In SE part of county on the Continental Divide. The English would be "Baldy Mtn."

PELONCILLO FOREST (Hidalgo). See CORONADO NATIONAL FOREST. PELONCILLO MOUNTAINS (Hidalgo). Possibly a misspelling of *piloncillo,* meaning "sugarloaf," NM derivation from *pilon de azúcar.* However, the name could mean "little baldy" mountains. In SW corner of county, running N and S 1 mi from Arizona border.

PEÑA BLANCA (Sandoval). Span., "white rock." Farming and ranching community 8 mi N of US 85, 23 mi SW of Santa Fe. This early nineteenth-century town might have been named for the alkali-saturated knoll halfway between it and Santo Domingo Pueblo, or else from the whitish cliffs of Peralta Canyon which stand out prominently against the dark Jemez Mts. in the distance. It must be noted, however, that the first, or at least one of the first, to establish himself in this territory was a Jose Miguel de la Peña, and the settlement was known as EL RANCHO DE JOSE MIGUEL DE LA PEÑA up to the time it was first referred to as EL RANCHO DE LA PEÑA BLANCA. Post office, 1867, intermittently, to present. PEÑA BLANCA ARROYO CREEK (San Juan). Heads SE of Beautiful Mtn. and flows E into Chaco River. PEÑA FLOR POST OFFICE (Colfax). Shown on Department of Interior map, 1936, as 4 mi S of Colorado line on upper Vermejo River. May be a corruption of *pina flora,* "pine flower." Post office, 1888-1901; mail to Catskill. PEÑAS NEGRAS (Sandoval). "Black rocks." Largest fork of the Rio de las Vacas in heart of Jemez Mts. PEÑASCO (Taos). "Rocky." 3 mi E of Chamisal on the Rio Chiquito. Named because it is in a valley denuded of its primeval forest, with all its rocks exposed. Post office, 1874, intermittently, to present. PEÑASCO BLANCO (San Miguel). "White crag." Settlement on NM 94, 4 mi E of Rociada, 1 mi from Mora County line. PEÑASCO CREEK (Taos). Joins Picuris Creek E of the pueblo, to form Embudo Creek. PEÑASCO PEAK (Sierra). 9 mi W of Elephant Butte reservoir, 1 mi from Socorro County line. PEÑASCO RIVER (Eddy, Otero, Chaves). See RIO PEÑASCO. PEÑASCO SPRING (Sierra). 1 mi SE of Peñasco Peak.

PENDARIES (San Miguel). On NM 94, 10 mi NW of Sapello. Jean Pendaries was a Frenchman who settled on a ranch near here in the early days. He founded the community of Rociada and later moved up to Gascon, in Mora County on the Rito de Gascon, naming the stream and settlement for his native province. He was the great-grandfather of Consuelo Baca La Farge, wife of the novelist Oliver La Farge, who has described the life in these communities in a number of story-sketches. Post office, 1918-26.

PENDLETON (San Juan). Post office, 1903-22. PENDLETON CANYON (Otero). Runs S of Weed and W toward Sacramento Mts.

PEÑASTAJA (Sandoval). Span., *peña,* "boulder." NW part of county on NM 197, 6 mi from the Continental Divide and 18 mi W of Cuba. Named for rocky formations. Post office, 1931-43.

PENITENTE PEAK (Santa Fe). 10 mi NE of Santa Fe and 2 mi S of Santa Fe Baldy Peak. Named for a religious confraternity of the Roman Catholic Church, called *Los Hermanos de la Luz,* "The Brothers of Light," and popularly known as *Los Hermanos Penitentes* or simply Penitentes. The most notable religious services of the group are held during Holy Week when processions of men carrying crosses and being whipped commemorate the Road of the Cross traveled by Christ. Another name of the group is *Los Hermanos de Sangre de Cristo* or "The Brothers of the Blood of Christ." This title may have named the mountain range NE of Santa Fe where Penitente Peak is located.

PENNINGTON (Union). 17 mi SW of Mt. Dora. Post office, 1914-21.

PENRITH (Union). On C&S RR, 3 mi SE of Mt. Dora. Once a blind siding and shipping point for cattle. Now grazing land.

PEP (Roosevelt). On NM 18, S of Dora and 24 mi S of Portales. Said to have been named by Harold Radcliff in the depression days, for the breakfast cereal of the same name. Post office, 1936—.

PERALTA (Valencia—). Village on NM 47, 4 mi NE of Los Lunas. Derives its name, not from the second Spanish governor, Don Pedro de Peralta, but from the families that lived here, descendants of Andres and Manuel de Peralta who came to NM before 1680, and of Pedro de Peralta, a native of Valladolid, in New Spain, who came after 1693. Site of the first Methodist missions established in this section of the Southwest in October 1871, although a Protestant group had been organized here in 1855. Post office, 1861-65; changed to Los

PINOS, 1865-66; Peralta, 1866—. PERALTA CANYON (Sandoval). PERALTA CREEK (Sandoval). Heads NW of Bland on S side of Jemez Mts., and empties into the Rio Grande at Cochiti. PERALTA, LOWER RIVERSIDE DRAIN (Valencia). Heads E of the Rio Grande 7 mi S of Isleta and empties into river at Belen. PERALTA, UPPERSIDE DRAIN (Valencia). Begins below the Isleta Diversion and empties into the Rio Grande near Los Lunas on E side of river.

PERCHA (Sierra). Span., "chicken perch, snare for birds." On NM 180, 2 mi W of Hillsboro. Post office, 1882-83; mail to Kingston. PERCHA CITY (Sierra). Originally a mining camp near Robinson's Cave. PERCHA CREEK (Sierra). Flows through Hillsboro, to the Rio Grande above Caballo Dam. Sections of the creek are called NORTH, MIDDLE, and SOUTH PERCHA.

PEREA (Bernalillo, Sandoval). First postmaster, Francisco Perea. Post office, 1894-1907; mail to Jemez Springs. Formerly ARCHULETA. PEREA (McKinley). Trading post on US 66, 15 mi SE of Gallup. The ancestors of the Perea family in NM first appear at Guadalupe del Paso (Ciudad Juarez) in 1681. They joined the exiles in their return to NM in 1693 and settled in the Rio Abajo district. Post office, 1915-20.

PERICO (Union). Post office, 1886-88; changed to CLAYTON. PERICO CANYON (Union). Span., "parakeet," but also a family name. Rises near Tripod Mtn., flows E, passes 6 mi S of Mt. Dora and 5 mi S of Clayton into Texas.

PERRY (Quay). Post office, 1907-08. See OBAR. PERRY (Roosevelt). PERRY (San Juan). PERRYVILLE (Colfax). Locality in Cimarron Canyon. Post office, 1894-95; mail to Elizabethtown.

PETACA. Span., "trunk for clothes." An old word denoting a hamper made of hide; now used also for modern American trunks and lockers. Some Mexican lexicographers think the word comes from Nahuatl, petlacalli. PETACA (Rio Arriba). Settlement 11 mi SW of Tres Piedras and 36 mi N of Española. Mica has been mined here for a number of years. Post office, 1900—. PETACA GRANT (Rio Arriba). 11 mi S of Tres Piedras. Petition on Feb. 25, 1836, by Julian Martinez, his father Antonio, and Francisco Antonio Atencia and his sons to gain land granted twelve years before to other grantees who had failed to improve or occupy it. They said they intended to engage in agriculture on a tract of land called Petaca. They received and accepted possession, in virtue of which "they plucked up herbs,

leaped, cast stones, and shouted for joy, saying 'God be praised, long live the Nation, long live the Sovereign Congress, and the law that governs and protects us.' "

PETRIFIED FOREST (Quay). 6 mi SW of Tucumcari, and 1 mi S of US 66. Logs and fragments of petrified wood lie on the ground although they have been greatly depleted by souvenir hunters.

PHANTOM BANKS (Eddy). In SE corner of county near Texas line.

PHILLIPSBURG (Sierra). On NM 52 about 6 mi NW of Chloride. Post office, 1904-06; mail to Fairview. PHILLIPS HILLS (Lincoln). In SW part of county about 2 mi W of Oscuro. In the early days, these hills showed a good vein of coal, but it was never developed. Named for a family who homesteaded at this place. There is also a PHILLIPS SPRING on this old homestead. PHILLIPS' HOLE (Doña Ana). Volcanic crater 17 mi W of E county line and 10 miles N of Mexican border.

PHILMONT ROCKY MOUNTAIN SCOUT CAMP (Colfax). A Boy Scout camp and game refuge covering 55 sq mi. Established in 1938, as a gift of Waite Phillips, owner of the nearby Philmont Ranch. Covers 128,000 acres and stretches N and S of Cimarron about 25 mi. First named PHILTURN, combining Phillips and "turn in."

PHILTURN (Colfax). See PHILMONT ROCKY MOUNTAIN SCOUT CAMP.

PICACHO (Doña Ana). Span., "top, peak, summit." Village 6 mi NW of Las Cruces. Named for the mountains. Once a stopping place for the Butterfield Overland Mail. PICACHO (Lincoln). On US 380 and 70, 46 mi SE of Carrizozo and 40 mi W of Roswell on the Rio Hondo. Settled about 1868 by a Frenchman named Leopoldo Scheney. Named for the peak a mile from town. Post office, 1891, intermittently, to present. PICACHO MOUNTAINS (Doña Ana). A few miles NW of Las Cruces. PICACHO MOUNTAIN (Santa Fe). See MOUNT PICACHO NEGRO DE ENCINAL (Valencia). Volcanic plug or peak 3 mi N of Cubero, which served as the SW corner of Baltazar Baca Grant. PICACHO PEAK (Lincoln). 1 mi from town of the same name.

PICURIS (Taos). Indian settlement and ancient pueblo ruins 12 mi E of Embudo and US 64, on the Rio Pueblo. Governor Oñate visited "the great pueblo of Picuries" on July 13, 1598. Though Picuris is in the Tewa subgroup of Tanoan, the name may be the Spanish corruption of Jemez (Towa) *pay kwee lay ta,* "at mountain gap," or possibly the Jemez name for Picuris people, *pay kwee layish;* also Keresan, *pee-koo-ree-a,* "those who paint." Called SAN LORENZO DE PICURIS in 1732; it appears on Mapa de los EUM (1828). PICURIS CREEK (Taos). Rises in mountains E of the town. PICURIS PEAK (Taos). 7 mi E of Cieneguilla. PICURIS PUEBLO GRANT (Taos). Small area surrounding the parish of San Lorenzo de Picuris Pueblo. One of the Governor-General Cruzate grants, dated Sept. 25, 1689. See PUEBLO LAND GRANTS.

PIEDRA ABURUJACA (Rio Arriba). Span., "lumpy rock." Peak in Carson National Forest, 8 mi SW of Dulce. PIEDRA LUMBRE. Either *piedra de alumbre,* "alum rock," or *piedra de lumbre,* "rock of fire," because of the abundance of flint. PIEDRA LUMBRE ARROYO, CREEK (Mora). Flows E into Canadian River at Harding County line. PIEDRA LUMBRE GRANT (Rio Arriba). Spans Chama River 10 mi W of Abiquiu; crossed by US 84 and NM 96. Gov. Velez Cachupin approved this grant to Pedro Martin Serrano, lieutenant of the Militia Company of Chama, on Feb. 12, 1766, and Martin took possession on February 17 of that same year.

PIE LAKE (Cibola). 14 mi N of Atarque.

PIERCE CANYON (Eddy). 28 mi SE of Carlsbad. Named for M. L. Pierce, who was wounded here in 1880, when the shot fired by Bob Ollinger killed John Jones and passed through Jones's body to hit Pierce. It is the oldest cow camp in the area and was used as early as 1874. PIERCE PEAK (Hidalgo). High point in Alamo Hueco Mts.; in SE corner of county, 8 mi from Mexican border.

PIE TOWN (Catron). On US 60 and NM 117, 21 mi NW of Datil. The grandson of a baker still lives in this community and he reports that his grandfather specialized in pie-making and advertised his profession with a big sign on the highway at this point. His fame spread among road workers and travelers, resulting in the name which now marks the settlement on all maps.

PIGGLY WIGGLY CANYON (Colfax). NE of Johnson Mesa.

PIGPEN CREEK, NORTH and SOUTH (Hidalgo). Flows N to enter Animas Creek 15 mi S of Animas.

PILAR (Taos). Span., "pillar." Trading point on US 64, 17 mi SW of Taos. Granted to settlers in 1795 by Fernando Chacon, military governor of NM, 1794-1805. Possibly named for a woman called Pilar, a feminine name derived from Nuestra Señora del Pilar, whose shrine in Zaragoza is one of the chief sanctuaries in Spain. However, it is also reported that the name comes from a male Indian called Pilar Vigil. Post office, 1918-21.

PIÑA (Colfax). Span., "pine cone." PIÑA (Taos). 5 mi SE of Costilla. Post office, 1900, intermittently, to 1920. PINABETAL MESA (Rio Arriba). 3 mi NE of San Antonio. PINABETE ARROYO (San Juan). "Fir tree." Rises in center of county and flows W into Chaco River. PINABETE ARROYO (Union). Lear Creek flows into it. PINABETITOS CREEK (Union). "Little fir trees." Rises SW of Pasamonte and joins Major Long's Creek below Stead. PINATASO CANYON (Lincoln). Perhaps *pinatasa,* "stand of measured pine."

PINCO. Span., *ir de pingo,* "wander about." The term, in NM Spanish, describes an orphan lamb, and is used in areas where sheep-grazing is common. It is also written *penco,* perhaps from *hacerse de pencas,* "to be coaxed." PINCO (Quay).

PINE (San Miguel). Trading point 28 mi SW of Las Vegas. Post office, 1943—. PINE CIENEGA CREEK (Grant). 2 mi E of community of Mule Creek. PINE CREEK (Colfax). Flows out of the pine-covered mountainside in N Moreno Valley and joins Moreno River which flows into Eagle Nest Lake. PINE CREEK (Grant). Flows S into Duck Creek 15 mi N of Cliff. PINE DALE (McKinley). Trading post and school operated by U.S. Bureau of Indian Affairs, 18 mi NE of Gallup. PINE FOREST (Doña Ana). Post office, 1860-61. PINE GROVE (Torrance). PINEHAVEN (McKinley). Farming and ranching community E of NM 32, 14 mi S of Gallup. Post office, 1939-43. PINE LAKE (Rio Arriba). 9 mi SW of Pounds. PINE LAWN (Catron). See PINE PARK. PINE LODGE (Lincoln). On N side of Capitan Mts., 2 mi S of NM 48. In 1909 the site was leased from the government by a group of Roswell businessmen for the purpose of establishing a summer resort. PINE LODGE CREEK (Lincoln). On N side of Capitan Mts. at the village of Pine Lodge. PINE PARK (Catron). Trading point on US 60, 10 mi W of Reserve. Also called PINE LAWN. PINE RIVER (San Juan). See LOS PINOS RIVER. PINES (Sandoval). 2 mi W of Bandelier National Monument. Post office, 1907-13. PINE SPRING, also PINESPRING (Otero). An abandoned settlement 9 mi down James Canyon from Cloudcroft. Post office, 1890-92; mail to Cloudcroft. PINITOS (Valencia). Span., "little pine trees." Ranching settlement near El Morro on highway between Zuñi and Atarque, 35 mi S of Gallup. Named for the pine groves in this area. PIÑON (Otero). Span., "nutpine, pine kernel." Village on NM 24 near Piñon Draw, 44 mi SE of Cloudcroft. When the post office was established, John W. Nations, a schoolteacher, selected the name because of the piñon variety of pine trees growing here. These trees produce edible nuts. Post office, 1907—. PIÑON CREEK (Chaves). Flows E of Piñon in SW corner of county, in Lincoln National Forest. PIÑON CREEK (Otero). Rises in county and flows S. PIÑON DRAW (Otero). On E slope of Sacramento Mts. PIÑON HILLS (Colfax). 10 mi W of Springer in Maxwell Land Grant. PINOS ALTOS (Grant). "High pines." 7 mi NE of Silver City on NM 25 in the Black Range. The discovery of gold in 1860 led to this settlement, which was first called BIRCHVILLE for a Mr. Birch, one of the three men who made the discovery. Changed to PINO ALTO and PINOS ALTOS. Post office, 1867—. The Apache Indians were so destructive to life and property that the settlers entered into a compact with them. It was agreed that a large cross should be placed on the summit of the hill just N of the town, and that as long as it was left there no killing would be done. This was strictly adhered to, and no resident was killed thereafter by an Indian. PINOS WELLS (Torrance). Point 29 mi SW of Vaughn. Post office, 1884-1919. PINOVILLE (Catron). Post office, 1905-09; mail to Mangas. Mangas.

PINKERTON (Mora). Post office, 1881-82; changed to WAGON MOUND.

PINTADA (Guadalupe). Span., "painted." Ranching community 8 mi S of US 66, 24 mi W of Santa Rosa. Named for color in arroyo nearby. Post office, 1909-47. PINTADA ARROYO (Guadalupe). 8 mi S of Santa Rosa. PINTADA CANYON (Torrance). In NE part of county; runs E into Pintada Creek. PINTADA CREEK (Guadalupe). Flows E through Sombria and Pintada. PINTADA MESA (Guadalupe). Named for varied colors of earth. PINTADO (McKinley). See PUEBLO PINTADO. PINTADO SPRINGS (McKinley).

PINTO (Otero). Span., "mottled." Community on NM 83 and the old EP&SW RR, 11 mi E of Alamogordo. The name is most familiarly used for a piebald or spotted horse. However, there is also a bean by this name.

PIONEER (Chaves). Post office, 1910-11; mail to Bronco, Tex. PIONEER CREEK (Taos). Comes into Red River from the S just below the town of Red River. Commemorates first settlers who lived here. PIONEER LAKE at head of Pioneer Creek.

PIPELINE CANYON (Otero). 22 mi S of Alamogordo. Named for a water line laid to Orogrande; station of SP RR for mining operations in vicinity.

PITCHFORK (Lea). 25 mi NE of Tatum and 15 mi E of Crossroads; originally 6 mi W of its present site. Named for the Pitchfork brand, used on a ranch where the school is now located. Once changed to SLATON; then later back to Pitchfork. PITCHFORK CANYON (Catron). Heads in Elk Mtn. and runs S, paralleling Hay Canyon.

PITT (Sierra). In San Andres Mts., 30 mi E of Engle.

PITTSBURG (Colfax). Once a community 25 mi E of Springer in center of a farming district. Post office, 1924-32.

PLACER. A Spanish word for washing gold from sandy soil. There is not enough water in most parts of NM where gold deposits are located to make use of placer mining on a large scale, but some place names do remain. PLACER CREEK (Rio Arriba). Small stream N and W of Tusas; a tributary to the Rio Vallecitos. PLACER CREEK (Taos). Flows N into East Fork of Red River. PLACER FORK (Taos). Flows W into Columbine Creek.

PLACITA, PLACITAS. Span., "little plaza." These place names are found under PLAZA.

PLAIN (Curry). PLAIN (Lea). See PLAINVIEW. PLAIN (Quay). 3 mi NE of Forrest. Post office, 1907-32. See FORREST. PLAINS OF SAN AUGUSTINE (Catron). See SAN AUGUSTIN. PLAINVIEW (Lea). Formerly called RAT, for the Rat Mill, an old watering place. An early settlement of homesteading days, 15 mi NE of Lovington. RAT was the brand on cattle once run here by Bud Ratcliff. Post office, 1907-30.

PLATEAU (Roosevelt). On AT&SF RR, 19 mi SW of Portales. Post office, 1906-10; changed to KERMIT.

PLATERO (Bernalillo). Span., "silversmith." Community in the Cañoncito Navajo Reservation, 6 mi N of US 66 and 4 mi W of the Rio Puerco, on the road to Cañoncito Day School. Once a post office, 1916-19, operated by the

Platero family for whom the locality is named. PLATERO (Sandoval).

PLAYAS (Hidalgo). Span., "beaches." Community on NM 9, and SP RR, 12 mi E of Animas. Name given to depressed, sandy areas that are dry except when rainfall is collected. A *playa* is usually a closed drainage basin, a saline lake. Post office, 1913-18. PLAYAS LAKE (Hidalgo). 14 mi long, but only a mile or less wide, W of Little Hatchet Mts. and S of Playas. PLAYAS VALLEY (Hidalgo). Runs N and S, from the border of Mexico, E of Animas Mts.

PLAZA. Span., "square, marked place." All the original settlements of NM were built around a plaza, as New England towns were built around a commons. The plazas were not only a traditional custom in village planning but they were an assembly place for protection against marauding Indians, the outer walls of buildings constituting a kind of rampart. Gradually the word "plaza" came to signify any village, whether built around a square or not, and finally it supplemented the terms *villa, pueblo,* and *aldea,* even *ciudad* to some extent. *Placitas,* a diminutive plural of *plaza,* came to describe a small cluster of houses. PLACITAS (Doña Ana). "Little plazas, little towns." See SANTA TERESA. PLACITAS (Sandoval). Farming community on NM 44, 7 mi E of Bernalillo in center of San Antonio de las Huertas Grant. Built on site of an ancient Indian pueblo; many Indian artifacts have been unearthed here. Post office, 1901, intermittently, to present. PLACITAS (Sierra). Small settlement 2 mi S of Monticello. PLAZA (Doña Ana). See SALEM. PLAZA (Quay). Post office, 1908-11; mail to Tucumcari. PLAZA BLANCA GRANT (Rio Arriba). Narrow grant crossing Rio Arriba line into Taos County; made to Manuel Bustos on July 18, 1739, by Gov. Gaspar Domingo de Mendoza. PLAZA COLORADO (Rio Arriba). "Red." Small village below Abiquiu, now mostly in ruins. PLAZA COLORADO GRANT (Rio Arriba). A narrow tract within the J. J. Lobato Grant 1 mi N of Abiquiu; W of Plaza Blanca Grant. On June 25, 1739, Governor Mendoza granted this land to Rosalia, Ignacio, and Juan Lorenzo de Valdez, brothers and sister, residents of the Villa Nueva de Santa Cruz. PLAZA DE ARRIBA (Guadalupe). PLAZA DEL ALCALDE (Rio Arriba). Post office, 1877-82; formerly PLAZA DE LOS LUCEROS. PLAZA DE LOS ABEYTAS (Socorro). See ABEYTAS. PLAZA DE LOS LUCEROS (Rio

Arriba). Post office, 1855-77. PLAZA DE MEDIO (Rio Arriba). PLAZA LARGO (Quay). "Long." 14 mi E of Tucumcari. PLAZA LARGO (Rio Arriba). PLAZA LARGO CREEK (Quay). Runs N from center of county to join Revuelto River at US 66, between Tucumcari and San Jon. Named for its appearance of a dry flat. However, in rainy seasons it becomes a raging stream.

PLEANO (Quay). Post office, 1907-14.

PLEASANT (Union). Former settlement and school district in farming region 10 mi E of Des Moines. Also called PLEASANT VALLEY. Post office, 1914-15. PLEASANT HILL (Curry). Trading point on NM 108, 15 mi NE of Clovis. Organized in 1910. Originally part of Brown Ranch and Shenault Ranch. Lee Barnes is credited with naming the town. He suggested the name at a meeting of "nesters" who came to decide where a school should be placed and what to call the thriving community. Mrs. Lucy Barnes, widow of Lee Barnes, says her husband got his idea from Pleasant Hill, Tex., a favorite town of his. PLEASANTON (Catron). A Mormon settlement 4 mi S of Glenwood and 10 mi SW of Mogollon, on US 260. Founded in the 1870's and named for an Army officer. Small tributary of San Francisco River here irrigates the orchards. Post office, 1882-86; mail to Alma. PLEASANT VALLEY (Doña Ana). PLEASANT VALLEY (Harding). 6 mi SE of Buena Vista. PLEASANT VALLEY (Quay). 17 mi E of Atarque. PLEASANT VALLEY (Roosevelt). PLEASANT VALLEY (Union). See PLEASANT.

PLOMO (Doña Ana). Span., "lead." 46 mi NE of Las Cruces. A big mill and smelter were built here and abandoned immediately when the lead mine played out. Post office, 1902; mail to Las Cruces.

POE (Chaves). On AT&SF RR, 5 mi NE of Roswell. Named for the Poe family, pioneer settlers in the region..

POINT OF ROCKS (Colfax). A mound of syenite rocks, rising from the prairies, from which runs a clear, crystal spring. At E county line near Ute Creek. A noted battleground and landmark of the Santa Fe Trail. POINT OF ROCKS (Doña Ana). See LAS PEÑUELAS. Point OF ROCKS (Sierra). In SE corner of county, 6 mi S of Upham.

POISON SPRING (Cibola). 45 mi S of Ft. Wingate. Named because a man and several horses and mules died here after drinking the water.

POJOAQUE (Santa Fe). Village on US 64, 18 mi

NW of Santa Fe. J. P. Harrington says that the Spanish name is an approximation of the Tewa words *posoong wa ghay,* "drink water place." A Nambe Indian volunteered the information that the name is a corruption of a Santa Clara word, *povi age,* meaning "place where the flowers grow along the stream." Abandoned after the Pueblo Rebellion in 1680 and resettled in 1706 by the Spanish. Since 1900, it has not been used as an Indian pueblo. Post office, 1870-1919. POJOAQUE PUEBLO GRANT (Santa Fe). Tract 4 by 5 mi in area surrounding present settlement of Pojoaque. The governor, the war chief, and the preserver of the peace for the pueblo appeared before the Surveyor General for New Mexico and testified that the pueblo had received a grant from the King of Spain, and that forty years earlier a lawsuit had occurred between the pueblo and a Mexican and the title deed of the pueblo was presented to the alcalde of Chimayo as evidence in the case. Since that time the grant has not been heard of. Asked how long the pueblo had been in existence, the Indians said the bell of the church bore the date 1710 and was cast for the church. They said their title was for one league from each corner of the church and that they raised wheat, corn, fruits, and stock, and subsisted entirely by agricultural pursuits. POJOAQUE RIVER (Santa Fe). Named for the town through which it flows. Above Pojoaque, however, it is called NAMBE CREEK. Flows W to the Rio Grande.

POKER LAKE (Lincoln). 24 mi E of White Oaks.

POLLY (Lincoln). Blind siding on AT&SF RR, 7 mi SW of Carrizozo on US 54. Established and named by EP&NE RR in 1899 when the road was built to Capitan.

POLVADERA (Socorro). 10 mi N of Socorro, on US 85. Corruption of Spanish *polvareda,* which means "dusty." The story is that the Lord told the people that if it did not rain by August 10 the place would be a desert. It did not rain; therefore the name was given. August 10, fiesta day, in honor of the patron saint, San Lorenzo, is said always to bring rain. Post office, 1895, intermittently, to present. POLVADERA CREEK (Rio Arriba). Rises S of Abiquiu Peak and joins Cañones Creek to flow into Chama River. POLVADERA GRANT (Rio Arriba). Semitriangular area N of Abiquiu Peak, extending to town of Cañones. The U.S. Surveyor General's office on Dec. 14, 1886, approved a claim made by the heirs of Juan Pablo Martin to this grant made Feb. 12, 1766, in Rio Arriba County. POLVADERA MOUNTAIN (Socorro). 4 mi W of Lemitar.

PONCE DE LEON HOT SPRINGS (Taos). 7 mi SE of Taos. Mineral springs long known to the early Indians and first Spanish for the cure of rheumatism.

POND CREEK (Colfax). Rises in county and flows S to junction of Carisso Creek. POND MILL (Rio Arriba). See POUNDS MILL.

PONDEROSA (Sandoval). Farming, ranching, and lumbering community on NM 290, 31 mi N of Bernalillo. Named for a stand of Ponderosa pine. Post office, 1932, intermittently, to present.

PONIL (Colfax). Post office, 1879-1913. PONIL CREEK (Colfax). An Indian word, naming an important creek with three branches at the source called the NORTH, MIDDLE, and SOUTH branches. They all rise N of Cimarron in adjacent canyons, join and flow to Cimarron River, 2 mi E of the town, from Vermejo Park area. PONIL PARK (Colfax). In Sangre de Cristo Mts. at head of Ponil Creek; about 3 by 6 mi in size.

POOL OF SILOAM (Otero). Low spot E of White Sands, which US 70 skirts 20 mi S of Tularosa. An oil well was dug here which produced sulphur water instead, forming a pool covering many acres.

POPE (Socorro). On AT&SF RR, 7 mi S of San Marcial. May have been named for William Hayes Pope, first district judge in 1917.

PORTAIR (Curry). On US 60, 7 mi W of Clovis, on AT&SF RR. As its name signifies, it is the airfield, and was once on the TAT airline. Now used only for local planes. Once named BLACKTOWER by AT&SF RR because of the large, black, water tank visible for miles around. Name later changed to MAIZE, for the grain sorghum produced in the area. Subsequently, changed to Portair.

PORTALES (Roosevelt). Span., "porches, gates." County seat and center of agricultural area on US 70 and NM 18. Named for Portales Springs. Founded in 1898 when PV&NE RR was being built. The locality was part of the H Bar Ranch, and a construction camp for railroad builders. Eastern New Mexico University was established here in 1934. Post office, 1899—. PORTALES SPRINGS (Roosevelt). 6 mi SW of Portales. One of the regular watering places on the Ft. Sumner trail. The earliest settler here was Doak Good, who moved to the springs in 1881. When he first arrived, he lived in the caves from which the springs flow. The caves resemble the porches of Mexican adobe houses, hence the name. PORTER (Quay). On NM 392, 8 mi N of San Jon. Named for a family that began settlement here. First postmaster, Mary Porter. Post office, 1908-15. PORTER (Rio Arriba). Post office, 1881-82; formerly BLOOMFIELD and returned to Bloomfield. PORTER (Sandoval). 3 mi W of NM 4, 23 mi SE of Cuba. Post office, 1933-37. PORTER STATION (Luna). See FLORIDA. PORVENIR (Mora). Post office, 1896, intermittently, to 1922. See EL PORVENIR. POTATO CANYON (Colfax). Begins about 4 mi up Canadian Red River and extends SW 7 mi. An Eastern farmer settled here and raised potatoes, selling them to the miners in Blossburg; hence the name. POTATO MOUNTAIN (Colfax). 5 mi E of Raton. POT CREEK (Mora). North Fork of the Little Rio Grande into which it empties, a short distance below U.S. Hill. POT HOOK (Grant). On SP RR, at Hidalgo County line. POTRILLO (Doña Ana). Span., "colt." Community 3 mi N of Texas border on SP RR, 36 mi W of El Paso, Tex. Named for two mountain ranges in SW part of county. Post office, 1908-14. EAST POTRILLO and WEST POTRILLO, separated by Mt. Riley. POTRILLO CANYON (Santa Fe). POTRILLO CREEK (Guadalupe). Runs S into Alamogordo Creek. POUNDS (Rio Arriba). 21 mi NW of El Vado on Jicarilla Apache Indian Reservation. POUNDS MILL (Rio Arriba). Former trading point 40 mi W of Tierra Amarilla; now range land. POVERTY CREEK (Sierra). In Winston area, 11 mi S of Dusty and just S of Socorro County line. POWDER HORN CANYON (Grant). Heads 2 mi W of Mimbres Lake; runs W and S into Mimbres Canyon, 2 mi from its entrance to Mimbres River. POWELL MOUNTAIN (McKinley). See MOUNT POWELL. PRAIRIE. "Prairie," wide tract of level or rolling grassland, is not too common in NM and the word is not Spanish but French. In early days, the grass on grazing land was higher and the top soil deeper. The Spanish word might be *pradera* or *llanura*. In the Southwest, *llano* is heard for a treeless plain. PRAIRIE CROW CANYON (Colfax). Just W of Koehler, 18 mi SW of Raton. PRAIRIE DOG CANYON (Colfax). Small canyon extends N from mouth of Cali-

ente Canyon, which is off Vermejo River Canyon, 8 mi N of Dawson. PRAIRIE VALLEY (Curry). PRAIRIE VIEW (Lea). PRAIRIE VIEW (Quay). Post office, 1908-15. PRATT (Hidalgo). SP RR siding on NM 9, 28 mi SW of Lordsburg. Post office, 1905-13. PREACHER'S HEAD (Grant). Large rock 16 mi NE of Silver City. Resembles the head of a man in serious study. Also called PREACHER'S POINT. PRESTON (Colfax). On Ute division of AT&SF RR, 10 mi SW of Raton, where the track branches for Van Houten. Established in 1900. PRESTON (Curry). Shown on 1921 map 30 mi N of Clovis. Post office, 1907-10; mail to Legansville. See BELLVIEW. PRESTON BECK GRANT (Guadalupe, San Miguel). Large grant spanning the present San Miguel and Guadalupe county lines, E of Antonio Ortiz and Anton Chico grants. Gov. Bartolome Baca made the grant to Juan Estevan Pino, Dec. 23, 1823. The full title was HACIENDA DE SAN JUAN BAUTISTO DEL OJITO DEL RIO DE LAS GALLINAS. Pino held the land until 1838 or 1839 and was succeeded by his sons until 1844 or 1845. They abandoned the land because of Indian troubles. Title passed to Preston Beck, Jr., in 1853 and 1854. PREWITT (McKinley). Ranching community on US 66, and AT&SF RR, 18 mi NW of Grants. Trading post here was started by Robert C. Prewitt, Sr. Post office, 1928—. PRIMA AGUA (Bernalillo). Span., "first water." Settlement 16 mi E of Albuquerque, on old US 66. Named for a spring that has never gone dry. PRIOR CREEK (Catron). 8 mi NW of Gila Cliff Dwellings National Monument. A man named Pryer was killed here by Apaches who were stragglers from Geronimo's band when he returned to Mexico. PRITCHARD (Roosevelt). Post office, 1907-08; mail to Texico. PROGRESSO (Torrance). Formerly spelled PROGRESO, Span., "progress, civilization." 14 mi SE of Willard on NM 42 and 20 mi E of Mountainair. Change in the spelling of the name has not been explained. Post office, Progreso, 1894-1901; 1904; Progresso, 1909-30. PRONTO (Doña Ana). Span., "prompt." On SP RR, 25 mi SW of Las Cruces, and 8 mi NW of Afton. PUARAI (Sandoval). Also PUARAY. On W bank of the Rio Grande, 2 mi S of Coronado Monument. Historic Indian pueblo ruin in the Tiguex province visited by Coronado and later Spanish explorers. The site is shown on L'Atlas Curieux (1700) S of Santa Fe. PUEBLITO (Rio Arriba). Suburb of San Juan, just across the river. PUEBLITO (Socorro). 4 mi N of Socorro, on E bank of the Rio Grande. PUEBLITOS (Valencia). Post office, 1902-06; mail to Jarales. PUEBLO. Span., "village, people." Castañeda, chronicler of the Coronado expedition of 1540-42, calls the Indian villages *pueblos,* "towns" in traditional Spanish usage, and refers to them as a pueblo-dwelling group. The name, therefore, was given to various sites and settlements, and in later times to the Indians themselves and to geographical features. PUEBLO ALTO (San Juan). See CHACO CANYON (McKinley, San Juan). PUEBLO ARROYO (Valencia). 6 mi N of Laguna Pueblo. PUEBLO BLANCO (Torrance, at Socorro County line). Abandoned town near Gran Quivira. PUEBLO BONITO (San Juan). The largest of eighteen major ruins in Chaco Canyon National Monument, a cluster of prehistoric villages, dating from A.D. 919 until 1127 or later. This tremendous apartment house contained over eight hundred rooms and sheltered perhaps fifteen hundred people at one time. See CHACO CANYON (McKinley, San Juan). PUEBLO COLORADO (Torrance). An abandoned town near Gran Quivira, at Socorro County line. PUEBLO CREEK (Catron). Flows into San Francisco River, 6 mi N of Alma. PUEBLO CREEK (Taos). Heads at Blue Lake against Old Mike Peak in Taos Mts., and flows on through Taos Pueblo and into Taos Creek W of Taos. PUEBLO LAND GRANTS. A good many of the pueblo grants go back to a series of declarations by Don Domingo Jironza Petriz de Cruzate, who succeeded Governor Otermin in 1682, two years after the Pueblo Rebellion had driven the New Mexican Spanish down to Guadalupe del Paso. Cruzate, an experienced officer, carried on a series of campaigns against the border Indians. Then in 1688, when he returned for a second term as Governor, he warred against the Indians in the north. On Sept. 20 and 25, 1689, he dictated a series of documents in which he granted land to various pueblos, telling how he waged his military campaigns against these hostile and apostate groups in the "kingdom of New Mexico"; how he took captive a prisoner from Zia who was "one of the most conspicuous in battle, lending his aid

everywhere," but, being wounded, he surrendered. This captive, a twenty-one-year-old warrior named Bartolome Ojeda, upon being interrogated, claimed to be familiar with many of the warring groups, and testified that each of them had been "very much intimidated" by the Spanish troops, and that he judged it would be unprofitable for them to fail in giving their allegiance to the Spanish crown. Upon this promise of co-operation and obedience to Spanish rule, Governor Cruzate issued grants to some sixteen Pueblo groups in NM and to the Pueblo of Moquino in what was to become Arizona. The NM groups listed were Acoma, Cochiti, Galisteo, Jemez, Laguna, Pecos, Picuris, San Cristobal, San Dia [sic], San Felipe, San Juan, San Lazaro, Santa Ana, Santo Domingo, Zia, and Zuñi. These grants were later confirmed by various acts of Congress and decrees of the Surveyor General. However, some doubt has been cast upon the authenticity of the Cruzate documents. On June 21, 1856, Donaciano Vigil, who was Secretary of the Territory under the Republic of Mexico, swore before the U.S. Surveyor General for New Mexico, that from the year 1840, when he took charge of the public archives, until that present day, there were no title deeds of grants made to the Indian pueblos in the archives under his charge. Whatever the legality of the archives in question, no one could challenge the claim of the Pueblo groups to possession and use of the land around their central church for subsistence and maintenance of their communities. The exact definition of boundaries in relation to neighboring land grants has resulted in litigation lasting until this day. PUEBLO PARDO (Torrance). An abandoned site near Gran Quivira, at Socorro County line. PUEBLO PEAK (Taos). NE of Taos Pueblo. A sacred mountain to the Taos Indians. PUEBLO PINTADO (McKinley). "Painted." Trading point in Chaco Canyon on NM 56, 60 mi NE of Thoreau, and 12 mi NW of Estrella. PUEBLO QUEMADO GRANT (Santa Fe). See JOSE TRUJILLO GRANT. PUEBLO SABINAL (Socorro). "Cedar." PUERCO RIVER (McKinley). See RIO PUERCO OF THE WEST. PUERCO (Valencia). See RIO PUERCO.

PUERTECITO (Colfax). Span., "small pass through mountains." PUERTECITO (Sandoval). 8 mi E of Placitas. PUERTECITO (Socorro). On NM 52, 21 mi NW of Magdalena, at end of Puertecito Canyon. Said to be so narrow that from a distance the space seems too small to pass through. Post office, 1903-30; changed to FIELD. PUERTO (Quay). 18 mi SE of Tucumcari. Post office, 1901-18. PUERTO DE LUNA (Guadalupe). Farming and ranching town on NM 91, 11 mi SE of Santa Rosa. Settled in 1863 by the following people and their families: Don Melquitades Ramires, Sixto Ramirez, Mercedes Carvajal, Fabian Brito, Pablo Pacheco, and Miguel Chaves. Present-day inhabitants believe that the name means "gateway of the moon," because of a narrow gap in the tall mountains near the village, where at certain times in the month, the moon shines through into the river valley. They affirm that the explorer Coronado so named it as he slept on the spot. Perhaps he said *"puerto de la luna."* Documentary confirmation is lacking. The name probably means "Luna's Gap," and reports the fact that members of the Luna family settled here about 1862-64. Members of this family are still living in the area. Just beyond and on the road to Borica (old Ft. Sumner road), the settlement was called simply PUERTO, "pass or gap." Post office, 1873—.

PUNTA (Torrance). Span., "point." On NM 10, 6 mi NW of Mountainair, at edge of Cibola National Forest. One of the Quarai Mission ruins. Post office, 1894-1913. PUNTA DE AGUA (Torrance). "Water." Village and spring in a grove of cottonwood trees 5 mi N of Mountainair. Post office, 1890-93.

PUP CANYON (Otero). 2 mi W of Little Dog Canyon and S of Cantrell Lake, in Guadalupe Mts.

PUTNAM (San Juan). Trading point at Pueblo Bonito, 22 mi N of Bloomfield, for visitors to the main cluster of Indian pueblo ruins in Chaco Canyon National Monument. Named for Dr. Frederick Ward Putnam, of Harvard University, who prepared the first plans for the study of the archeology here. Post office, 1901-11.

PUTNEY (Sandoval). Formerly JEMES. Post office, 1907-08; changed to JEMEZ PUEBLO. PUTNEY MESA (Valencia). 10 mi NW of Acoma. The Putney family were nineteenth-century traders and wholesalers with headquarters in Albuquerque.

PUYE (Rio Arriba). Also called RIVERSIDE. Settlement on US 285 and 64 near Española. Named for Puye Ruins. PUYE RUINS (Rio Arriba). On NM 5, 11 mi SW of Española. A Tewa Indian name: *pu*, "cottontail rabbits,"

and *ye*, "to assemble," probably a place for hunting rabbits. The site of one of the most extensive and interesting of the ancient cliff villages. Supervised by the U.S. Bureau of Indian Affairs and the Santa Clara Indians who own the land. These Indians claim the ruins are the homes of their ancestors, from which they were driven by the drought.

PYRA (Hidalgo). Siding on SP RR, 4 mi W of Lordsburg.

PYRAMID (Hidalgo). Post office, 1882-97; mail to Lordsburg. PYRAMID MOUNTAINS (Hidalgo). S of Lordsburg. So named because one of the peaks looks like a pyramid. PYRAMID ROCK (McKinley). A formation resembling a pyramid, in the Red Rock area about 8 mi E of Gallup.

QUAHADA RIDGE (Eddy). Corruption of Span., *quijada*, "jaw." 14 mi NE of Carlsbad, S of US 62 and 180. So named because its outline resembles a jaw.

QUAKING ASP CANYON (Grant). Heads at Sierra County line; runs NW into Yates Canyon. QUAKING ASP CREEK (Catron). 15 mi E of Mogollon, N of Gilita Creek.

QUALACU (Socorro). The most southerly pueblo of the Piro Indians, on E bank of the Rio Grande, 24 mi S of present Socorro. Mentioned by Oñate in 1598.

QUARAI (Torrance). Tigua Indian, *kwa-ri'*. Site of a Spanish mission 10 mi NW of Mountainair. Founded in 1629; now in ruins. The remains of the old church are the most imposing left standing of the "Cities that Died of Fear." The stone walls were over 60 ft high and 5 or 6 ft thick, but have crumbled to 20 ft in height. This was a Tiwa pueblo which was abandoned between 1671 and 1680 when the road to Salinas was blocked by Apache Indians. Created a state monument on Feb. 20, 1935. Post office, 1917-19.

QUARTZITE PEAK (Rio Arriba). 6 mi W of Tusas.

QUARTELEZ (Rio Arriba). Also spelled *cuartelez*. This could mean "district, barracks for the quartering or housing of soldiers." Farming community on NM 76, 4 mi E of Española, on the Rio Arriba—Santa Fe border.

QUAY (Quay). Ranching community on NM 18, 17 mi S of Tucumcari. Established in 1902 by a Mr. Adams. It is not known whether the place was named for the county or for QUAY FLAT on which it is located. The town was moved 1 mi SE of its first location in 1917.

Post office, 1904—. Quay County. Jan. 28, 1903. The name of Matthew S. Quay, U.S. Senator from Pennsylvania, 1887-1904, seems to have played a part in all these names. Present area is 2,905 sq mi.

Queen (Eddy). Former settlement on NM 137, 40 mi SW of Carlsbad, in Guadalupe Mts. Started by J. W. Tulk, who built a store and post office here in 1905. The nearest water was on the ranch of two brothers, J. C. and M. J. Queen, and Mr. Tulk agreed to name the place Queen for the use of the water. Now known as the Dr. Womack Ranch. Post office, 1905-20. Queens Head (Catron). Peak in Apache National Forest, 10 mi NW of Aragon.

Quemado (Catron). Span., "burned." Ranching and vegetable-producing community on US 60, 81 mi W of Magdalena in north-central part of county. About 1880, Jose Antonio Padilla and his family moved from Belen to a place they called Rito Quemado, because both sides of the creek had the sage and rabbitbush burned off by the Indians. He brought sheep and started the stock industry in this part of the state. A few years later the name was shortened to Quemado. A second explanation has been that the town is located on an extinct volcanic area and appears to have been scorched. Post office, 1886—. An early Spanish settlement in the canyon 5 mi NE of Quemado was called Rito.

Querecho Plains (Eddy, Lea). A broad stretch of high, flat plain, rising to Mescalero Ridge, midway between Carlsbad and Lovington. Name is used by the chronicler Castañeda for the Indians who met Coronado after he left the Rio Grande Valley on his search for Quivira in 1541. They were probably Apaches.

Questa (Taos). Seems to be a corruption of Span., cuesta, "slope or grade." Farming and mining community on NM 3 and 38, 22 mi N of Taos. Originally called San Antonio del Rio Colorado. Changed to Questa when the community acquired a post office. Post office, 1883—. Questa del Puerta de Capote (San Miguel).

Quien Sabe Creek (Taos). Span., "who knows?" E of US 64, between Taos and Ranchos de Taos.

Quigui (Sandoval). See Quiqui.

Quijosa Grant (Taos). Area S of Taos River between Hondo Canyon and Ranchito. Grant made on June 16, 1715, to Francisco Antonio de Quijosa.

Quincy (Luna). On SP RR, 25 mi W of Deming and 16 mi E of Separ.

Quini (McKinley). See Zuñi.

Quintana Mesa (Rio Arriba). 21 mi W of Dulce, 4 mi S of Colorado line.

Quiqui (Rio Arriba). Known as San Rafael del Quiqui. 2 mi N of San Juan Pueblo and W of the Rio Grande. In 1765, Antonio Abeytia made his will certifying that he lived at San Antonio del Bequiu del Guyqui, jurisdiction of Santa Cruz. See Guique.

Quigui (Sandoval). According to Bandelier, the Santo Domingo Indians once lived at two pueblos, each of which was called Quigui. The earlier Quigui stood on the banks of the Arroyo de Galisteo, more than a mile E of the present Santo Domingo; the later Quigui was built farther westward.

Quirk (Cibola). Loading point on AT&SF RR for Laguna Indians' livestock, 30 mi E of Grants. A spur was built in 1955-56 from Quirk to the Jackpile mine, the world's largest open pit uranium mine.

Quivira (Socorro, Torrance). See Gran Quivira.

Rabbit Ear Creek (Union). First called Rabbit Ears Creek, later renamed Cienaga Creek, Span., "marsh," and still later, Big Spring. Name for the mountain ridge to the E, Las Orejas de Conejo, "Ears of the Rabbit." Freighters on the Santa Fe Trail called it Cienega del Burro, or "jackass swamp." Known today as Seneca Creek. It flows E between Rabbit Ear Mtn. and Clayton, continuing into Texas. Rabbit Ear Mountain (Union). 6 mi N of Clayton, near US 87. Named for a Comanche chief, called Rabbit Ears, Orejas de Conejo, because his ears had been frozen. He was killed in battle and buried on the mountainside. In 1717 at this place, a volunteer army of five hundred Spaniards killed several hundred Comanches and took seven hundred of them prisoner, after which a long truce followed. Rabbit Mountain (Sandoval). In Jemez Mts. 10 mi SW of Otowi.

Rabenton (Lincoln). 20 mi NE of Carrizozo. Once a small community that flourished during the heyday of nearby White Oaks. Post office, 1910-28. Formerly Raventon.

Radium Springs (Doña Ana). Formerly known as Fort Selden Springs; also Randall Station. Community centered around a health resort, 1 mi NE of US 85, on AT&SF RR,

18 mi N of Las Cruces. Named for the radium reported in the springs, which are said to have been known by the Indians in pre-Spanish times, and were used by the soldiers at Ft. Selden. Post office, 1926—.

RAEL (Colfax). Post office, 1901-02; mail to Springer.

RAFAEL CREEK (Union). Rises SE of Sierra Grande Mtn. and empties into Corrumpaw Creek (now the North Canadian). Said to have been named by U.S. Senator Stephen W. Dorsey of Arkansas, who sojourned in NM in the 1880's.

RAGLAND (Quay). Formerly CAPROCK. Trading point on NM 18, 25 mi S of Tucumcari. Named in 1906 for a Mr. Ragland, who filed a claim on which a small store and post office were erected. First postmaster, Maud Ragland. Post office, 1908-17.

RAILROAD CANYON (Colfax). Extends from Raton to the Raton Tunnel on AT&SF RR, about 8½ mi, running N and S. The tracks follow this canyon to the highest point on the system, 7,622 ft. RAILROAD MOUNTAIN (Chaves). An igneous dike, 25 to 30 ft high; 50 mi NE of Roswell and crossed by US 70. The bank extends E from Capitan Mts. for 50 mi, probably beyond subsurface. So named because the unique formation runs straight and smooth like a railroad.

RAIN CREEK (Catron). Tributary of Mogollon Creek joining that stream below the falls and heading between Black Mts. and Center Baldy.

RAINY MESA (Catron). 12 mi SE of Reserve.

RAINY MESA DIVIDE (Catron). Runs N and S below South Fork of Negrito Creek, 6 mi NW of Negrito.

RAINSVILLE (Mora). Farming community 2 mi E of NM 21, 8 mi E of Mora. Formerly called COYOTE. Post office, 1921—.

RALSTON (Hidalgo). Post office, 1870-71. See SHAKESPEARE. RALSTON (San Juan).

RAMAH (McKinley). Farming and lumbering community on NM 53, 31 mi SE of Gallup. Settled in 1874 by Mormons, and named for a figure in the Book of Mormon. Post office, 1884—. RAMAH LAKE (McKinley). 1 mi N of Ramah settlement.

RAMAN (McKinley). Settlement 2 mi from Valencia County line, 23 mi S of Ft. Wingate.

RAMON (Lincoln). One Spanish form of the name "Raymond." Ranching community on US 285, 32 mi SE of Vaughn, in NE corner of county. Name chosen in Washington from a list of names submitted for a post office

founded in 1924 and continuing until 1945. RAMON (Union). Post office, 1911-14; changed to DAVID.

RAMON VIGIL GRANT (Sandoval). Semimountainous region traversed by NM 4 in the Bandelier National Monument area. The names of Ramon Vigil and Pedro Sanchez both appear with this grant which dates from Mar. 28, 1742.

RANA (Quay). Span., "frog." Settlement 28 mi NE of Tucumcari, and 12 mi NW of Glenrio. Said to be one name of the ranch upon which the post office was established, 1908-25. RANA CANYON (Quay). Heads N of Bard; runs NE into Canadian River.

RANCH. The Anglicized form of Span., *rancho* occurs more than a hundred times, but unless the name has come to be associated with a public settlement or commercial center, it has not been listed in this dictionary. This may be unfortunate, for all of these ranches are centers of human activity and they stamp names upon large geographical areas. In some cases, ranch names are perpetuated in present-day town names. See BELL, ENDEE, JAL, OBAR, OMLEE. RANCHVALE (Curry). 8 mi NW of Clovis on NM 277. Named by Vernon Tate, one of the first settlers, and its first postmaster. The Ranchvale School, completed in 1919, was the first consolidated school in NM. Post office, 1913-17.

RANCHES OF TAOS (Taos). See RANCHOS DE TAOS.

RANCHOS. Span., "hamlet, cluster of dwellings"; American Span., "cattle range and buildings." In American use, the word originally was applied to the dwellings of workers, herdsmen, or farmers, but eventually it was used for a landed estate, called *hacienda* in other Spanish-American countries, and in NM it became synonymous with *aldea*, "village." *Ranchito*, of course, is a smaller settlement than *rancho*, and *ranchería* is still another term describing a cluster of buildings in cattle country. *Ranchería* was used, for many years to designate Apache brush camps. *Ranchos de* may be considered a synonym for English "suburb."

RANCHITO (Taos). Settlement along Taos Canyon, 2 mi W of Taos. RANCHITOS (Bernalillo). Farming area N of Albuquerque, between Los Ranchos de Albuquerque and Alameda. RANCHITOS (Rio Arriba). Trading point on US 64, 10 mi N of Española. Post office, 1905-07. Also called RANCHITOS DE SAN JUAN.

RANCHO (Roosevelt). 14 mi NW of Melrose, in extreme NE corner of county. Post office,

1913-25. RANCHO DE LA POSTA (Sandoval). Former community on W side of the Rio Puerco 15 mi S of present site of Cabezon. Settled about 1780 and abandoned in the 1880's when land was purchased for sheep grazing. RANCHOS DE ALBUQERQUE (Bernalillo). Old area of settlement between Albuquerque and Alameda. See LOS RANCHOS DE ALBUQUERQUE. RANCHOS DE ATRISCO (Bernalillo). Suburban area S of city limits of Albuquerque. See ATRISCO. RANCHOS DE LA JOYA (Socorro). See LA JOYA. RANCHO DEL RIO GRANDE GRANT (Taos). Large area between Picuris and Fernando Mts., S of Talpa. The original grant was by Gov. Fernando Chacon and was dated Feb. 4, 1795. Names are given of ten people who asked to be put in possession of the land. They took possession on Apr. 9, 1795. RANCHOS DE TAOS (Taos). 5 mi S of Taos on US 64. In 1837, called SAN FRANCISCO DEL RANCHO DE TAOS. The famous St. Francis of Assisi Church was built in 1772 by Franciscan missionaries. This was a pre-Spanish settlement of Taos Indians, and later settled by Spanish in 1716. Post office, Ranches of Taos, 1875—.

RANDALL STATION (Doña Ana). See RADIUM SPRINGS.

RANGEL (McKinley). 13 mi SW of Estrella, near the Continental Divide.

RANGER LAKE (Lea). Abandoned settlement 12 mi N of Tatum. Named for a lake usually dry, 2 mi SW, which received its name from the legend that Texas Rangers had trouble with Indians here. Post office, 1908-20.

RAT (Lea). See PLAINVIEW.

RATON. Span., "mouse." *Ratona*, "female mouse or rat." New Mexicans applied the term *raton* not only to ordinary house and field mice but also to the rock-squirrel and probably to the kangaroo rat, which flourishes in arid regions of the western United States. The bat was not known by Spanish *murciélago*, but as *ratón volador*, "flying mouse." RATON (Colfax). On US 85 and 87 and NM 72, 8½ mi S of Raton Pass. Started in 1879, Raton grew with the arrival of AT&SF RR to become the county seat and principal town in NE corner of the county. Once called WILLOW SPRINGS: then named for the mountains. Post office, 1880—. RATON CREEK (Colfax). First called WILLOW ARROYO, then WILLOW CREEK. Flows S of Railroad Canyon, N of Raton across Crow Creek flats to join Uña del Gato River, 7 mi S of Raton, and then into Canadian Red River. RATON MOUNTAINS (Colfax). Form part of the long range which divides northeastern NM from Colorado. Named for numerous rodents which feed here on the piñon nuts. RATON PASS (Colfax). Famed from days of covered wagon caravans on Santa Fe Trail. Highest point on AT&SF RR; altitude 7,622 ft. RATON PEAK (Colfax). Central and tallest peak of the range, directly N of Raton, almost at Colorado line. RATON SPRINGS (McKinley).

RATTLESNAKE (San Juan). Trading point and oil-drilling landmark 32 mi W of Farmington, in San Juan Basin oil fields. RATTLESNAKE CREEK (Sandoval). Flows into Canadian River 6 mi NW of Bascom. RATTLESNAKE HILL (Torrance). RATTLESNAKE PEAK (Doña Ana). Rocky peak which rises abruptly from the desert S of Cambray. Site of a large prehistoric Indian campground. Name may have been conferred because of snakes found among the rocks, or because of petroglyphs of snakes discovered in several places on the peak. RATTLESNAKE SIDING (Lincoln). See ELDA. RATTLESNAKE SPRING (Eddy). The water supply of Carlsbad Caverns National Park comes by pipeline from this spring.

RAVENTON (Lincoln). Post office, 1896-1900; mail to White Oaks. See RABENTON.

RAWHIDE CANYON, DRAW (Otero, Eddy). The draw heads in the Guadalupe Mts. 2 mi N of Coats Lake; enters the canyon and then Rocky Arroyo, flowing NE.

RAW MEAT CREEK (Catron). Flows into West Fork of Gila River, N of Diablo Range. Said to have been named by the famous old hunter, Bear Moore, after he discovered a man here eating his meat raw because he did not have matches to make a fire.

RAYADO. Span., "streaked," as with lines drawn straight across a surface. Lines were often drawn on the ground with a stick to mark the outlines of a lot or of a house to be built on it. Geographical features could be marked, as cliffs with fault lines. Certain tribes of Plains Indians were called *Rayados* by early Spaniards because they tattooed, scarred, or painted their faces with vertical or horizontal lines. RAYADO (Colfax). Trading point on NM 21, 23 mi W of Springer. Post office, RYADO, 1873-81; RAYADO, 1881, intermittently, to 1919. RAYADO CREEK or RIVER (Colfax). Passes through Rayado and joins Urreca Creek 11 mi W of Springer. RAYADO MESA (Colfax). 14 mi W of Springer in Maxwell Land Grant. RAYADO PEAK (Colfax). On Rayado River near Rayado Pass. RAYADO STATION (Colfax). 5 mi S of Springer.

RAYO (Socorro). Span., "ray of light, thunderbolt." Former settlement 32 mi NE of Socorro and 12 mi S of Scholle, on W side of Chupadera Mesa. Post office, 1917-40.

RAY RODGERS (Catron). Named for H. R. (Ray) Rodgers, land commissioner (1947-50), in appreciation for his interest in this sawmill settlement, one of the most remote from a railroad in the state.

READING CANYON (Grant). Runs NW of Reading into Steamboat Canyon and then to Bear Creek. READING MOUNTAIN (Grant). In Pinos Altos Mts. 16 mi SE of Gila. These two names may be associated with Pierson B. Reading, a mining engineer who explored the Trinity River country in California about 1848 and thereafter.

REAL DE DOLORES (Santa Fe). Post office, 1869-70.

REAL DE SAN FRANCISCO (Santa Fe). See GOLDEN.

RECHUELOS (Rio Arriba). Settlement on the Rio del Oso, 15 mi NW of Española.

RECONA (San Miguel). See RENCONA.

REDAMADERA (Torrance). See DERRAMADERO.

RED BLUFF (Eddy). Community 1 mi E of US 285 on AT&SF RR, 28 mi S of Carlsbad. RED CAÑON (Socorro). Post office, 1886-88; mail to White Oaks. RED CANYON, WEST (Socorro). E of NM 52, 1 mi S of Dusty. RED CLOUD (Torrance). 20 mi E of Gran Quivira. Post office, in Lincoln county, 1882-90; in Valencia and Torrance counties, 1904-06; mail to Mountainair. RED HAIR CANYON (Catron, Grant). Parallels White Rock Canyon ½ mi SE; runs into Little Creek 4 mi S of Sheridan Mtn. and 18 mi E of Arizona. RED HILL (Catron). Ranching and lumbering community on US 60, 23 mi SW of Quemado, and 8 mi from Arizona line. Post office, 1935-57. RED LAKE (De Baca). Formerly known as WILCOX LAKE. See DRIPPING SPRINGS, which it feeds. 3 mi E of La Lande and 1 mi N of US 60. Has a reddish color from clay soil in the region. Watering hole for early travelers and cattle drivers across the plains to Ft. Sumner and other places. RED LAKE (Eddy). 3 mi NW of Carlsbad Caverns National Park. RED LAKE (McKinley). 5 mi S of San Juan County line, 16 mi W and N of Tohatchi. RED LAKE (Roosevelt). 12 mi W of Rogers. Named for nearby lake. Post office, 1907-29. RED LAKES (Colfax). Former community 10 mi SW of Black Lakes on NM 38. REDLAND (Roosevelt).

Community 4 mi E of Causey. Name is descriptive of color of soil. Post office 1907-17; changed to EMZY. RED MOUNTAIN (Luna). RED MOUNTAIN (McKinley). 20 mi W of Estrella. RED MOUNTAIN (San Miguel). Post office, 1917-18. RED RIVER (Taos). Mining and mountain resort on NM 38, 11 mi E of Questa, on N bank of Red River. First prospected by miners from Elizabethtown about 1869-70. Named for the river, which was called by the Taos Indians *pee ho ghay po*, "red river creek," for the pigment which colors it. Townsite was laid out by the Mallette brothers in 1894. Post office, 1895—. RED RIVER (Taos). Flows W into the Rio Grande. Also called RIO COLORADO, because of its color. Rises in eastern chain of Rocky Mts., 100 mi N of Santa Fe. RED RIVER CANYON (Colfax). Begins at Red River Peak, 4 mi S of Raton and flows into Canadian Red River at NW corner of county. RED RIVER PASS (Colfax). At Taos County line at N end of Moreno Valley where NM 38 crosses the mountains into Red River country. RED RIVER PEAK (Colfax). Small pointed peak at mouth of Little Red River Canyon. Named before the stage coaches came across Raton Mts. RED RIVER SPRINGS (San Miguel). Post office, 1878-84; mail to Hogadero. REDROCK (Grant). Farming and ranching community 24 mi N of Lordsburg. Post office, 1896—. RED ROCK (McKinley). 9 mi SE of Ft. Wingate. RED TIP (Chaves). RED WASH (San Juan). Also called STANDING ROCK WASH.

REDONDO CREEK (Sandoval). East Fork of Sulphur Creek, a fork of San Antonio Creek in the Baca Location in Jemez Mts. REDONDO PEAK (Sandoval). 5 mi E of Cueva.

REED CANYON (Colfax). Ghost town near site of Elkins at head of Vermejo River. Named for "Cump" Reed from Missouri, an early settler here in 1875.

REED'S RANCH (Doña Ana). Post office, 1879.

REESE HILL (Union). On NM 18, 5 mi S of US 64 at Clayton. Named for a family who lived near the foot of the hill. NM 18, leading from Cimarron River Canyon S to Clayton, emerges from the canyon at this point.

REFUGIO COLONY GRANT (Doña Ana). Granted in 1852 by the Republic of Mexico, for an area along the Rio Grande between Chamberino and La Union.

REGINA (Sandoval). Farming community on NM 112, 11 mi N of Cuba. Founded in 1911 by J. H. Haleri, W. F. Fish, and a Mr. Collier. Name is transferred from Regina, Sask., Canada. Post office, 1911—.

REHOBOTH (McKinley). Community on US 66, 8 mi E of Gallup. Location of Rehoboth mission, boarding school, and hospital. Founded in 1903 by the Christian Reformed Church. Post office, 1910—.

RENCONA (San Miguel). Farming community on NM 34, 32 mi SW of Las Vegas, and 13 mi S of Rowe. Post office, 1917, intermittently, to present.

RENDEZVOUS (Sierra). Up Mineral Creek, NW of Chloride. A native claims it is RENDEZVILLE. According to G. Adlai Feather, Rendezvous and Rendezville are both approximations. The only town (camp) up Mineral Creek is ROUNDVILLE at the Dreadnought mine.

RESERVE (Catron). Farming and ranching community on NM 12, 22 mi N of Mogollon; settled in the late 1870's. Known as UPPER FRISCO PLAZA in the 1880's, and locally as MILLIGAN'S PLAZA for a prominent merchant and saloonkeeper here. In 1882, a deputy sheriff named Elfego Baca held off a mob of Texas cowboys here in a gun battle that lasted thirty-three hours. Called Reserve after John Kerr established U.S. Forest Ranger headquarters here later. The name, therefore, indicates U.S. forest reserves. Post office, 1901—.

RESOLANA (McKinley). Span., "sunny place." In Chaco Canyon area where a small rise protects it from the wind but not from the sun.

REVUELTO (Quay). Span., "turn." Post office, 1897-1916. See HUDSON. REVUELTO CREEK (Quay). "Muddy, turbid." Flows N into Revuelto River 6 mi E of Lesbia. REVUELTO RIVER (Quay). Flows NE into Canadian River near Logan.

REYES (Harding). Span., "kings." In NE part of county on NM 171, and 57, 35 mi NE of Mosquero. A Christian name formerly common to both men and women in honor of the Three Kings of Epiphany. Perhaps named for the Magi themselves or for an individual bearing the name. Post office, 1910-18.

RHODES CANYON (Sierra). On NM 52 in San Andres Mts. between Engle and Tularosa. See ENGLE. RHODES PASS (Socorro). Between Tularosa and Hot Springs; NM 52 once crossed San Andres Mts. through Rhodes Pass. Named for Eugene Manlove Rhodes, cowboy-novelist, whose ranch was here. The area today is within the White Sands Missile Range, but in June the range is opened each year for a pilgrimage to the grave of the author, which is marked by a stone tablet bearing the dates 1869-1934 and the inscription *Pasó Por Aquí* ("He passed by here"), the title of one of his memorable works.

RIBERA (San Miguel). Span., "shore or bank of a river." Farming and ranching community on NM 3, 23 mi SW of Las Vegas. Named for a Ribera family of Santa Fe, who were among the pioneer settlers of San Miguel del Vado. The ancestor was Salvador Matias de Ribera, a native of Puerto de Santa Maria in Spain, who came to NM in 1693. The surname is often alternately spelled Rivera. Post office, 1894—.

RICARDO (De Baca). Ranching community 5 mi S of US 60, on AT&SF RR, 10 mi SW of Ft. Sumner. Said to have been named for a railroad official with this given name. Post office, 1908-54.

RICE (Quay). First postmaster, Clara S. Rice. Post office, 1907-08; changed to HUDSON.

RICHARDSON (Lincoln). Stock-raising community on NM 48, on N side of Capitan Mts. First postmaster, Andy Richardson. Post office, 1895-1912.

RICHEY (Guadalupe). Former post office and store 10 mi E of Riddle on rural mail route from Tucumcari to Santa Rosa, about 1912-20.

RICHLAND (Roosevelt). Trading point 5 mi E of NM 18, 30 mi S of Portales. Post office, 1908-33.

RICHMOND (Hidalgo). Post office, 1875-84; mail to Lordsburg. See VIRDEN.

RICOLITE (Grant). Named for a peculiar type of marble or serpentine found only at this location. Post office, 1890-91; mail to Lordsburg.

RIDDLE (Guadalupe). Former trading point 10 mi SE of Puerto de Luna. Named for owner of store here. Post office, 1909-20.

RIDGE CREEK (Harding). See ARROYO DEL CESITA.

RILEY (Socorro). Trading point 20 mi N of Magdalena, on the Rio Salado. Early Spanish settlement here is confirmed by one of the older small mission churches in the state. The Anglo name was contributed by the owner of a sheep ranch. Post office, 1890, intermittently, to 1931; mail to Magdalena. RILEY (Torrance). 3 mi N of NM 10 at Tajique. RILEY, RILEY'S SWITCH (Curry). Former name of AT&SF RR station at Clovis. Post office, 1906-07.

RINCON (Bernalillo). Span., "corner, box canyon." Former settlement on old US 66, 17 mi E of Albuquerque. RINCON (Doña Ana). On NM 40 and AT&SF RR, 5 mi E of Hatch. Named because it is built in a corner formed by two nearby mountains. Marks the S end of the dreaded Jornada del Muerto. Early-day travelers, immigrants and animals, died of thirst while trying to cross the desert. Its S end is also the beginning of the old Chihuahua Trail. Post office, 1883—. RINCON (San Miguel). Post office, 1875-83; changed to ROCIADA. RINCONADA (Rio Arriba). "Little box canyon." See DURAZNO. RINCONADA (Taos). RINCONADA CANYON (Otero). Heads in White Mts.; runs S and W. RINCONADO (Rio Arriba). Settlement 4 mi E of Embudo, where three creeks meet. Post office, 1880-81; 1889-1918. RINCON BONITO (San Miguel). RINCON DE LA PARIDA (Socorro). RINCON RANGE (Mora). Extends N and S in W Mora County, from Lucero to Colfax County line, W of Coyote Creek.

RING (Colfax). At one time in Ponil Park on North Ponil Creek in Maxwell Land Grant. So called because the Ring Road ended in a circle where an engine could be turned. RING CANYON (Catron). Runs NE into West Fork of Gila River, NW of Gila Cliff Dwellings National Monument.

RIO ABAJO. Span., "lower river." Albert Pike in *Prose Sketches and Poems* (1834), p. 174, describes the Rio Abajo district as "halfway between Santa Fe and the Paso del Norte." The name is still applied to the area in the central and southern reaches of the Rio Grande Valley in NM, as distinguished from that of the northern territory, or Rio Arriba. La Bajada Mesa, 19 mi S of Santa Fe, is the dividing line between Rio Arriba and Rio Abajo, since the drop from the Santa Fe Plateau at this place is about 1,500 ft. RIO ARRIBA. "Upper river." G. F. Ruxton, an English soldier of fortune, reported in the mid-nineteenth century that "the settled portion of the province of New Mexico is divided into two sections which from their being situated on the Rio del Norte, are designated Rio Arriba and Rio Abajo, or up the river and down the river." (*Adventures in Mexico*, p. 186.) RIO ARRIBA COUNTY. Formed Jan. 9, 1852, when the boundaries included a strip of country from the Sangre de Cristo Mts. to a line S of Taos County. On Feb. 10, 1880, this county was enlarged, giving it all the country W of the present Taos—Rio Arriba county line. When

San Juan County, which adjoins on the W was formed on Feb. 24, 1897, Rio Arriba was given the present boundaries, with the exception of a part of the SW section, which was added to Sandoval County. Its area is 5,871 sq mi, the fifth largest county in the state. RIO BONITO (Lincoln). "Pretty river." Rises in the Sierra Blanca, near Parsons in Lincoln National Forest, flowing SE to the Ruidoso to form the Hondo at the town of Hondo. The Rio Bonito was robbed of its beauty through the diversion of practically all the water to the SP RR across the mountain range to the W. RIO BRAVO DEL NORTE. See RIO GRANDE. RIO CANADIAN. See CANADIAN RIVER. RIO CAPULIN (Santa Fe). "Chokecherry river." North Fork of Nambe Creek, 3 mi N of Santa Fe Baldy. RIO CHAMA (Rio Arriba). See CHAMA RIVER. RIO CHIQUITO (Santa Fe, Rio Arriba). "Very small river," but it seems to be a translation of the Tewa name *po ay po hoo oo,* "little water creek." Fork of the Little Rio Grande coming out of mountains NE of Ranchos de Taos, and a tributary of Santa Cruz Creek. RIO CHIQUITO (Sandoval). 5 mi E of Jemez Pueblo. RIO CHIQUITO (Taos). 5 mi E of Las Trampas. RIO CHUELOS (Rio Arriba). See RIO EN RECHUELOS. RIO COLORADO (Taos). Post office, 1871-72; 1877-78. RIO COLORADO (Valencia). See ARROYO COLORADO. RIO CUBERO (Valencia). See RIO SAN JOSE. RIO DE. In the place names using *de,* academic Spanish would require the article with names of topographical features, of families, and of animals and wildlife, e.g., El Rio de la Arena, El Rio de los Luceros, El Rio de las Vacas. In NM, however, where place names have undergone changes from one language to another, and in some cases a change to even a third language, the standard academic forms have frequently been lost. Names may appear in several different ways, as Rio de las Perchas, Rio las Perchas, Perchas River. These factors may explain some of the irregularities in the place names employing *río,* "river," and *rito* "little river." RIO DE ARENAS (Grant). "Sandy places." Flows S from Ft. Bayard, 5 mi E of Silver City. RIO DE ARENAS (Luna). RIO DE CHAMOS (Rio Arriba). See CHAMA RIVER. RIO DE COSTILLA (Taos). See COSTILLA CREEK. RIO DE LA CASA (Mora). "River of the house." Also known as RIO LA CASA, LOWER and UPPER. Rises in west-central part of county and flows SE to join Mora River. Named for the many beaver houses or dams, along the stream.

RIO DE LA LAMA (Taos). Flows through Lama Canyon into Red River. See LAMA. RIO DEL PLANO (Colfax). "River of the flat or plain." NE of Springer and flows into Canadian Red River. May be an Anglicism in Spanish. *Rio del Llano* would be standard Spanish. RIO DE LAS VACAS (Sandoval). "River of the cows." Flows S from San Pedro Mts. at S border of Rio Arriba County to join Jemez River below Jemez Springs. RIO DE LAS ANIMAS (San Juan). See ANIMAS RIVER. RIO DEL NORTE Y DEL NUEVO MEXICO. See RIO GRANDE. RIO DEL OSO (Rio Arriba). "Bear river." In SE corner of county, 9 mi N of Española; flows into Chama River from the SW. Indian name means "shove stick creek," taken from a pueblo ruins named for a game played by the Puebleños. RIO DE LOS PINOS (Rio Arriba). Rises in Colorado and flows E at San Miguel, returning to Colorado, 1 mi N of Los Pinos. RIO DEL PUEBLO PLAZA (Mora). "River of the town plaza." RIO EN RECHUELOS (Rio Arriba). "Small streams." Flows N to enter Polvadera Creek 4 mi NW of Tschicoma Peak. RIO EN MEDIO, "Middle river." Perhaps a parallel to this Spanish descriptive name would be the English place name "Midway." RIO EN MEDIO (Mora, Santa Fe). Also called RIO DEL MEDIO and MEDIO CREEK. Mountain stream heading on NW side of Pecos Baldy and flowing W for 18 mi to Santa Cruz River. RIO EN MEDIO (Santa Fe). Community 10 mi N of Santa Fe on NM 22. Usually called RIO MEDIO. RIO FELIX (Otero, Chaves). "Happy river." Rises in Mescalero Indian Reservation near its E boundary; flows E through Chaves County and empties into Pecos River above Hagerman. RIO FERNANDO DE TAOS (Taos). Also called RIO TAOS and TAOS CREEK. Flows into the Rio Grande W of Taos and parallels NM 64 to E of Taos for 12 mi up to Tienditas. RIO FRIJOLES (Taos, Mora). "Bean river." Refers to bean-growing patches irrigated by the stream's flow. RIO FRIJOLES (Santa Fe). Heads N of Baldy Peak and flows NW; a tributary of Santa Cruz River. RIO GRANDE. Span., "great river." Rises on E slope of the Continental Divide, near Silverton, Colo., entering New Mexico northwest of Ute Peak. Flows south through the western half of the state crossing into Texas at Anthony. When Don Juan de Oñate took possession of New Mexico in 1598, he announced, "I take possession, once, twice, and thrice, and all the times I can and must, of the actual jurisdic-

tion, civil as well as criminal, of the lands of the said Rio del Norte, without exception whatsoever, with all its meadows and pasture grounds and passes." This was the Rio Grande of today. The great river valley had been visited by earlier explorers, Chamuscado and Espejo in 1581 and 1583; but Oñate and his successors, by colonizing along its banks, brought the name into New World prominence. In 1519 Alonso Alvarez de Pineda had seen the river as it entered the Gulf of Mexico and named it El Rio de las Palmas, "the River of Palms," but this name never extended farther north than the palm-growing belt. RIO DEL NORTE Y DEL NUEVO MEXICO appears on L'Atlas Curieux (1700), and Escudero in *Noticias* (1849) calls it the RIO BRAVO DEL NORTE. Translated, this last title is "Bold River of the North," and such it has been, though in seasons of drought the flow scarcely seems to merit either "grand" or "bold." In the story of Western America, however, history, politics, and the life cycle of races and individuals have been told and written along the banks of this stream. RIO GRANDE (Doña Ana). Community 1 mi N of Texas border on SP RR, 5 mi NW of El Paso. RIO GRANDE DE LOS RANCHOS (Taos). "Big river of the ranches." Flows W and N to Cordova, where it joins Rio Pueblo de Taos, which enters the Rio Grande. RIO GUADALUPE (Sandoval). Flows S to join the Jemez at Cañon. RIO HONDO (Chaves, Lincoln, Taos). See HONDO. RIO HONDO (Taos). Settlement 4 or 5 mi from San Fernandez de Taos. RIO LA CASA (Mora). See RIO DE LA CASA. RIO LA JUNTA (Taos). "Junction river." Enters the Rio Pueblo at Tres Ritos in a recreation area crossed by NM 3. RIO LA JUNTA (Mora). See WATROUS. RIO LAS PERCHAS (Rio Arriba). "Snares." Tributary entering the Rio de las Vacas about 7 mi E of Cuba and 14 mi N of NM 126. See PERCHA CREEK. RIO LUCERO (Taos). Flows S from Arroyo Seco, E of Taos to join Taos River. Name should be El Rio de los Luceros, "the river of the Lucero folks." RIO LUCIA (Mora). Close to Peñasco on W side of mountains; at entrance to Picuris Pueblo. Post office, 1921-23. RIO MEDIO (Santa Fe). See RIO EN MEDIO. RIO MIMBRES (Grant). Post office, 1866-75. RIO MIMBRES (Grant, Luna). See MIMBRES RIVER. RIO MIMBRES (Luna). See MOWRY CITY. RIO MOQUINO (Valencia). Rises in Cebolleta Grant and flows S into the Rio Paguate, N of Laguna. Spanish surname. See

Moquino. Rio Mora (Mora, San Miguel). See MORA RIVER. Rio Mora (San Miguel). Rises in NW corner of county and flows S into the Pecos. Also called MORA PECOS. Rio NUTRIA (McKinley). See NUTRIA CREEK. Rio NUTRIAS (Rio Arriba). See NUTRIAS CREEK. Rio Ojo CALIENTE (Rio Arriba). "Warm spring river." Flows S from La Madera through Ojo Caliente; parallels NM 285 to join Chama River near Hernandez. Rio PAGUATE (Valencia). See PAGUATE CREEK. Rio PEÑASCO (Eddy, Otero, Chaves). "Cliff river." Tributary of Pecos River; heads in Sacramento Mts. in Lincoln National Forest, then flows SE; joins Eagle Creek 1 mi before entering Lake McMillan. Rio PESCADO (McKinley). "Fish river." Rises in Zuñi Mts. and flows W to Zuñi River. Rio PLANO (Colfax). "Level, even, smooth." Flows W from Chico to enter Canadian River N of Springer; course is over high, relatively smooth terrain, explaining the descriptive name. Rio PUEBLO (Taos). "River town." Trading point on NM 3, 20 mi S of Taos. Post office, 1910-14. Rio PUEBLO DE TAOS (Taos). Rises near Colfax County line and flows W to the Rio Grande. Rio PUERCO (Bernalillo, Sandoval, Socorro, Valencia). Rises in Sandoval County, at SE corner of Apache Reservation, looking like an ordinary gully; runs S to empty into the Rio Grande S of Bernardo. Rio PUERCO (McKinley). "Muddy river." Rises S of Crownpoint and flows SW through Gallup to cross into Arizona where it becomes the Rio Puerco of the West. Rio PUERCO (Rio Arriba). Rises in Santa Fe National Forest and flows N to Chama River. Rio QUEMADO (Rio Arriba). Flows through Rosario Grant S of Truchas. Rio QUEMADO (Taos). "Burnt, scorched." Heads on NW side of Truchas Peak and flows W to Cordova and Santa Cruz River. RIO RANCHO (Sandoval). Suburb about 10 mi N of Albuquerque. RIO RUIDOSO (Lincoln). "Noisy." Rises in Otero County and flows E through Lincoln County to the Rio Hondo. RIO SALADO (Sandoval). "Salty." Flows SE to Jemez Creek near San Ysidro; has its source in Salado Canyon. Contains calcite and has warm currents caused by springs. RIO SALADO (Socorro). Rises in Catron County and flows E to the Rio Grande, crossing US 85 about 8 mi N of Polvadera. RIO SAN ANTONIO (Rio Arriba). Flows N through San Antonio to Los Pinos. RIO SAN JOSE (Cibola). Drains E part of county, where it begins as an outlet of Bluewater Reservoir and empties into the Rio Puerco in

SW corner of Isleta Indian Reservation. En route, it touches Grants, crosses the Acoma and Laguna reservations. In dry weather, a tiny stream with quicksand, but in wet weather, a torrent. In early times, called Rio CUBERO, in honor of the old Spanish governor (1697-99). Rio TANQUE DEL MEDIO CANYON (Rio Arriba). See CAÑADA TANQUES. Rio TAOS (Taos). See Rio FERNANDO DE TAOS. Rio TULAROSA (Catron). Has its source in a small mountain meadow NE of Aragon, joins San Francisco River near Reserve. Rio TULAROSA (Otero). Rises in Mescalero Indian Reservation on W slope of the Sierra Blanca and flows W through Tularosa. Rio TUSAS (Rio Arriba). New Mexican Span., "prairie dogs." Flows SE near Taos County line through Tusas and Servilleta Plaza to enter the Rio Vallecitos at La Madera. Rio VALDEZ (Mora, San Miguel). North Fork of the Mora Pecos in SW corner of county, joining that stream at upper end of Mora Flats and crossing into San Miguel County. Rio VALLECITOS, LOWER (Rio Arriba). Joins the Rio Tusas at La Madera and flows into the Rio Ojo Caliente N of settlement of Ojo Caliente. Rio VALLECITOS, UPPER (Rio Arriba). Refers to the river from Ancones up to the source W of Hopewell high in the mountain meadows. Rio WILLOW (Rio Arriba). Rises in county and flows S to Chama River.

RIP LAKE (Lincoln). 29 mi E of White Oaks.

RITCHY (De Baca). Trading point shown on 1921 map, N of Ft. Sumner and 10 mi E of Riddle, about 1 mi from Guadalupe County line. Said to have been named for owners of store here. Post office, 1914-19.

RITO. Span., "little river." Diminutive form of a Spanish generic term, widely used in NM, where the commingling of Spanish and English terms for streams has left the distinction between *río, rito, river, creek* rather vague, both as to dimensions and the quantity of water. RITO (Catron). See QUEMADO, SWEAZEVILLE. RITO (Valencia). On AT&SF RR, 9 mi E of Laguna. RITO AZUL (Mora). "Little blue river." Fork of the Rito de los Chimayoses, S of Truchas Peak. RITO BERNAL (Colfax). In NW corner of county, flows into Vermejo River. RITO COLORADO (San Miguel). "Little red river." Flows W into Sapello Creek at San Ignacio. RITO CREEK (Catron). Former settlement on Rito Quemado Creek, mentioned as early as 1740; 8 mi E of present Quemado and N of Rito Hill on the old route of US 60. Rito de la Olla (Taos). "Jar." Flows W into the Rio Grande del Ranchos, 5 mi below Talpa. Rito de las Sillas (Rio Arriba). "Seats, saddles." Settlement and creek 2 mi S of Coyote. Rito de los Chimayoses (Mora). "The Chimayo folks." The biggest fork of the Rito del Padre or Beatty's Fork of Pecos River; heads against E side of Truchas Peak. Rito de los Esteros (Mora). "Estuary"; Mexican Span., "flooded, marsh." Small fork of the Mora Pecos entering from E at lower end of Mora Flats, 5 mi NE of Cowles. Rito de los Indios (Sandoval). "Indians." North fork of San Antonio Creek on Baca Location in Jemez Mts. Rito del Oso (Mora). "Bear." Fork of the Mora Pecos, along Rociada Trail. Rito de los Pinos (Sandoval). "Pines," or "the Pino folks." Little stream heading in W side of Jemez Mts. E of La Jara and NE of Cuba. Rito del Padre (Mora). "Father or priest." Also known as Beatty's Fork of the Pecos. Extends from Beatty up to source at Truchas Peak. Rito de Oro (Colfax). "Gold." In NW corner of county; flows into Vermejo River. Rito de Pino (Valencia). See Los Pinos. Rito la Cueva (Sandoval). Flows E from Nacimiento Mts. into Rio de las Vacas at Porter. Rito Lake (Catron). At Omega; overflow makes the stream at Rito Quemado. Rito las Palomas (Sandoval). "Doves." Fork of the Rio de las Vacas joining this stream near where the Cuba—Jemez Springs road crosses it. Rito Leandro (Colfax). In NW corner of county; flows into Vermejo River. Rito los Steros (Mora). See Rito de los Esteros. Rito Maestas (Mora). "The Maestas folks." East Fork of the Rito del Padre in upper Pecos country, 15 mi W of Mora. Rito Medio (Taos). "Little middle river." Swift-flowing stream emptying into Latir Creek near Sunshine Valley in N Taos County. Rito Molina (Santa Fe). 7 mi E of Cundiyo. Rito Moquino (Valencia). W of Baltazar Grant and S of Cebolleta. See Moquino. Rito Pacheco (Santa Fe). "The Pacheco folks." Little stream E of Tesuque and S of Aspen Hill. Rito Perro (Mora). "Dog, prairie dog." East Fork of Panchuela Creek; just below Pecos Baldy Peak. Rito Presa (Colfax). "Dam, trench, ditch." Small tributary of Cimarron River. Perhaps named for a dam in the stream for fish or irrigation. Rito Quemado (Catron). "Burned, scorched." See Quemado. Rito Quemado (Santa Fe). Joins the Rio Medio 4 mi

S of Truchas. Rito Quemazon (Taos). "Conflagration, burned." Name probably describes a burned area, perhaps caused by a grass or forest fire, through which the stream passes. Rito Sabadiosis (Mora). Enters the Rito del Padre just above Beatty, 7 mi N of Cowles. Rito Seco (Rio Arriba). Flows NW into Coyote Creek below Mesa Pinebestosa. Riverside (Rio Arriba). A modern commercial district along US 64 and 285, 1 mi E of Española. Formerly known as Puye. Riverside (Lincoln). Trading point on US 380, 31 mi W of Roswell. Named because of its location on Hondo River. First called "Big Hill Filling Station" by W. O. Norman in 1925 because it is at the foot of the big hill here. When he sold the place in 1930, the name was changed to Riverside Camp. Riverside (San Juan). Also known as Hendrix. Trading point on US 550, 13 mi NE of Aztec and the D&RGW RR. Post office, 1905-33. Riveryard (Sandoval). River View (Socorro). See Lavorcita.

Road Canyon (Colfax). Extends between Canadian Red River Canyon and Vermejo River Canyon in N part of county near Colorado line. One of the trails into the Vermejo country came down through this canyon; thus the name Road Canyon. Road Canyon (Union). S of Reese Hill. So named because the first road leading through Cimarron Canyon to Clayton went through it. Road Forks (Hidalgo). 17 mi SW of Lordsburg, at junction of US 80 and NM 14. Settled about 1925 and named by Mr. and Mrs. G. H. Porter. Post office, 1925-55.

Roanoke (Chaves). On AT&SF RR and W bank of Pecos River, near Elkins, 25 mi SE of Dunlap. Post office, 1908-11.

Robert (Hidalgo). Flag stop and watering place on A&NM RR which used to operate from Clifton, Ariz., to Hachita; 6 mi SE of Lordsburg. Named for a partner in the Roberts and Banner Cattle Co.

Roberts (Eddy, Lea). Near Chaves County line, 18 mi W of Crossroads. Named for Gene Roberts, who established first store. First postmaster, James D. Roberts. Post office, 1908-10; mail to Elkins; changed to Nadine.

Robinson (Colfax). See Rayado. Robinson Mountain (Colfax). NW of Capulin, just inside county line. Named for the Robinson-Hoover Commission Co. of Kansas City, Mo., which served the livestock men of Colfax and

Union counties in the early days. Post office, 1882-83; mail to Fairview.

ROBLEDO (Doña Ana). Settlement on W bank of the Rio Grande, between Doña Ana and Radium Springs. Pedro Robledo, a native of Toledo, and the first person in the Oñate colony to die in NM, was buried here on May 21, 1598, and the site, including a promontory nearby, may commemorate him. The name, however, may also be known through Doña Ana Robledo, the legendary (perhaps mythical) seventeenth-century lady for whom Doña Ana settlement seems to have been named. The site *Robledillo* is shown on Mapa de los EUM (1828). ROBLEDO EL CHICO (Doña Ana). Span., "little oak grove." Spanish campground a short distance S of Robledo. ROBLEDO MOUNTAIN (Doña Ana). 10 mi S of Radium Springs. Named for Pedro Robledo.

ROBSART (Lincoln). On SP RR, 7 mi N of Carrizozo. There is a folk tale which says that an old Indian fighter used to drive his mule down to watch the railroad construction. The man had a speech deficiency and when he called to his mule, Rob, he would cuss and raise sand because he couldn't get Rob to "sart" (start).

ROCIADA (Mora). Span., "dew-sprinkled." ROCIADA (San Miguel). Farming and ranching community on NM 105, 22 mi NW of Las Vegas. Post office, 1883—. See PENDARIES; SANTO NIÑO.

ROCK CREEK (Sandoval). Enters the Rio de las Vacas, 9 mi SE of Cuba. ROCK CREEK (Socorro). Empties into East Canyon 7 mi SE of Rosedale. ROCK ISLAND (Quay). Post office, 1909-15; changed to GLENRIO. ROCK LAKE (Torrance). 9 mi SW of Progresso. ROCK SPRINGS (McKinley). 2 mi S of NM 68 and 7 mi NW of Gallup. ROCK SPUR (Eddy). Point on AT&SF RR, 7 mi S of Malaga. ROCKY WATER HOLE CANYON (Otero). Runs into Bug Scuffle Canyon NE of Escondida; on SW slope of Sacramento Mts.

RODARTE (Taos). Farming and ranching community near Peñasco, 3 mi S of NM 75 and 19 mi SW of Taos. Cristobal de Rodarte was among the first settlers of Santa Cruz in 1696, one of the colonists sent by the Viceroy. The family name was confined mostly to the mountain region E and N of Santa Cruz. Post office, 1917—.

RODEO (Hidalgo). Settlement established in 1902 on US 80 and SP RR, 48 mi S of Lordsburg at Arizona line. Bears the name of the Spanish word that means "roundup, enclosure for cattle" because cowmen came here to separate, brand, and ship their cattle each year. Post office, 1903—.

RODEY (Doña Ana). See COLORADO. Trading point on US 85, 3 mi SE of Hatch. Post office, 1904-27.

ROEBUCK (Roosevelt). 3 mi E and 2 mi N of Causey. Named for a settler who homesteaded here. The schoolhouse was moved years ago, but the cemetery is still called Roebuck Cemetery.

ROGERS (Roosevelt). Farming and dairying community on NM 235, 25 mi SE of Portales. Named for Rogers, Ark., by Rev. Andrew J. Maxwell, who laid out the townsite in 1908. Post office, 1908—.

ROMERO. The many Romeros in NM are descended from Bartolome Romero, a native of Toledo who came in 1598, and from other colonists of the same name who came with the Reconquest of 1692 and later. ROMERO (Catron). ROMERO (Santa Fe). First postmaster, Carlos Romero. Post office, 1895-1900; mail to Santa Fe. ROMERO (San Miguel). Post office, 1904-08; mail to East Las Vegas. ROMERO LAKE (Taos). 2 mi W of Chacon, on Mora County line. ROMEROVILLE (San Miguel). A combination of the family name Romero and the English-used French word *ville*. Trading point on US 84 and 85, 5 mi S of Las Vegas. Settled in 1880, and named for Don Trinidad Romero, a rancher and member of the U.S. Congress. He entertained President and Mrs. Hayes and General Sherman in his $100,000 mansion here. The building was destroyed by fire in 1932. Post office, 1877-80; 1927-53. ROMEROVILLE CANYON (San Miguel). A gorge cut 800 ft in the mesa S of Romeroville. Named for the town.

ROOSEVELT (Quay). 4 mi SW of McAlister, near Roosevelt County line. Post office, 1906-19. ROOSEVELT COUNTY. Organized from Chaves and Guadalupe counties on Feb. 28, 1903. Named for Theodore Roosevelt, twenty-sixth President of the United States, 1901-09. Present area is 2,487 sq mi.

ROPES SPRING (Doña Ana). In San Andres Mts. about 40 mi from Las Cruces. Named for Horace Ropes of Massachusetts, who settled here in 1885.

ROSA (Rio Arriba). Span., "rose." Community on San Juan River 1 mi S of Colorado line. Post office, 1888-1921.

ROSARIO (Santa Fe). Span., "rosary." Early station on AT&SF RR, 5 mi E of Santo Domingo. Abandoned after closing of coal mine in the Cerrillos district, but reactivated when mining of gypsum deposits began in 1960.

ROSARIO GRANT (Rio Arriba). In SE corner of county. Truchas is the chief settlement in this area. Grant made to families named Romero, Espinosa, Bernal, and Martin, on Mar. 18, 1754, by Governor Cachupin.

ROSEBUD (Harding). On NM 65, 29 mi E of Mosquero. Settled in 1908 by three young sisters. A new barn was being painted a bright red; upon finishing the job, the painters painted three green rosebuds at the end of the barn to represent the sisters. M. T. Nix, upon applying for a post office several months later, sent in the name Rosebud. Post office, 1909-50.

ROSEDALE (Socorro). Former trading point 6 mi W of NM 107, 24 mi S of Magdalena. Site of an historic mining town where Jack Richardson discovered gold in the 1880's. He is reported to have honored a lady friend in the naming. The property was developed by the Martin brothers and sold to Rosedale Mining and Milling Co. After the plant burned in 1910, the holdings were leased by T. B. Everhart, who operated them for some time. Now in ruins. Post office, 1899-1928.

ROSING (San Juan). On D&RGW RR, 6 mi NE of Aztec. Post office, 1909-19.

ROSWELL (Chaves). Principal town on US 70, 380, and 285, 7 mi W of junction of Pecos and Hondo rivers. Once a favorite Indian camping place. Today, a commercial and cultural center, site of the New Mexico Military Institute, and of Walker Air Force Base, one of the leading Air Force installations in the U.S. Named by Van C. Smith for his father, Roswell Smith, of Omaha, Neb. Smith was a professional gambler, who came from Omaha in 1869 with his partner, Aaron O. Wilburn. They built two adobe buildings for a general store, post office, and overnight stopping place for paying guests. When Smith filed the first land claim on Mar. 4, 1871, he chose the name Roswell. Capt. Joseph C. Lea bought Smith's holdings in 1877, and during the next decade he and his family owned the entire town. Roswell is in the nation's most important artesian basin; it became the county seat on Feb. 25, 1889. Gov. Miguel A. Otero proclaimed the town a city on Sept. 5, 1903. Post office, 1873—. ROSWELL AIR FIELD, ROSWELL ARMY AIR FIELD, ROSWELL ARMY FLYING SCHOOL (Chaves). See WALKER AIR FORCE BASE.

ROUGH AND READY (Doña Ana). The name for hills about 20 mi N and S of Las Cruces, and a station for the Butterfield Overland Mail. Also known as LOS HORNILLOS, Span., "the little fireplaces or ovens," because the building had two fireplaces. ROUGH CREEK (Hidalgo). Flows E from the Continental Divide, 14 mi SE of Antelope. ROUGH MOUNTAIN (Lincoln). 6 mi SW of Corona.

ROUND HOUSE (McKinley). Former trading point, known also as COUSINS, on NM 32, 18 mi S of Gallup. Post office, 1930-31. ROUND MESA and ROUND MOUNTAIN (Santa Fe). See BLACK MESA. ROUND MOUNTAIN (Mora). In SW tip of county N of Cowles. Named for its circular formation. ROUND MOUNTAIN (Otero). A conical-shaped knoll which, because of its location overlooking the Tularosa Basin, was used as a lookout by the Indians. Scene of a battle won by a Sergeant Glass on Apr. 17, 1868, against a band of Apache Indians who were trailing a supply wagon under his guard. Glass was leading Company H, U.S. Cavalry, with additional re-enforcements from settlers of Tularosa. ROUND MOUNTAIN (Socorro). Post office, 1878-79. ROUND MOUNTAIN (Union). See MOUNT CLAYTON.

ROUNTREE (Guadalupe). First postmaster, Henry K. Rountree. Post office, 1901-02; changed to MONTOYA.

ROWE (San Miguel). Farming community on US 84, 85, and on AT&SF RR, 32 mi SE of Santa Fe. Established in 1876. Named for a railroad contractor. Post office, 1884—. ROWE MESA (Santa Fe). NW of Rowe.

ROUNDYVILLE (Sierra). See RENDEZVOUS.

ROY (Harding). On NM 39, 120, and SP RR, 9 mi E of Canadian River. Center of a ranching and farming area that also produces carbon dioxide. Established by Frank and William Roy in 1901, and named for Frank, the first postmaster. Original town was 2 mi W of present site. New town was started when the railroad was built, and incorporated in 1916. Post office, 1901—.

ROYCE (Union). Community 8 mi W of Clayton on C&S RR, US 64 and 87. Ranchers received their mail here, and brought cattle for shipment.

RUDOLPH (Lincoln). First postmaster, Milnor Rudolph. Post office, 1878; changed to SUNNYSIDE in San Miguel County.

RUDULPH (Quay). First postmaster, Carolina Rudulph. Post office, 1908-10; changed to CASTLEBERRY.

RUDY TOWN (San Miguel). Once a settlement of the American Metals Co. mine at Terrero, 18 mi N of Pecos.

RUIDOSO (Lincoln). Span., "noisy." Ranching and tourist town on NM 37, 24 mi SE of Carrizozo. Picturesque setting on Ruidoso River, at foot of Old Baldy Peak. Name describes the fast-flowing, noisy creek that runs through the town. Formerly known as DOWLIN'S MILL. Post office, 1882—. RUIDOSO DOWNS (Lincoln). See GREEN TREE. RUIDOSO RIVER, LOWER, MIDDLE, and UPPER, also NORTH FORK and SOUTH FORK (Lincoln). In Lincoln National Forest. See RIO RUIDOSO.

RUIZ. Spanish family name, the first bearer of which, Pedro Ruiz, was in the soldier-escorts to NM in 1608 and 1609. Other men with the name appear in seventeenth-century records, and a Juan Ruiz de Caceres is listed as a property owner in Santa Cruz in 1698. RUIZ (Bernalillo). RUIZ (Sandoval).

RUSSELL (Chaves). Spur on AT&SF RR 3 mi NW of Hagerman, built about 1912. Named for Howard Russell, who, along with his neighbors, used it for loading hay.

RUSSIA (Otero). Station on old EP&SW RR, 25 mi E of Alamogordo. A lumber camp, terminus of the Cloudcroft branch of the railroad; abandoned before World War II. Post office, 1904-06.

RUSTLER CANYON (Grant). In Big Burro Mts., W of the Continental Divide, 6 mi SW of Tyrone.

RUTH (Guadalupe). Locality 6 mi W of Ima, where there were early-day buffalo hunts. Named for Ruth Darnell of Tucumcari. Post office, 1905-17.

RUTHERON (Rio Arriba). Ranching community on NM 95, 13 mi S of Chama. Named by a rancher, Heron, for his daughter Ruth; hence Ruth-eron. Post office, 1927—.

RUTTER (Doña Ana). On SP RR, 20 mi SW of Las Cruces, and 5 mi SE of Afton.

RYADO (Colfax). Post office, 1873-81; changed to RAYADO.

SABADO CREEK (Sandoval). Span., "Saturday." 7 mi N of Cuba.

SABINA. Span., "savin, juniper"; in NM, "dwarf juniper." *Sabina* is the correct Spanish term for certain species of fragrant juniper. The early colonists applied the name to the common scrub cedar or juniper that covers most of the hills. In time, the word took on a masculine ending. SABINAL (Socorro). "Place of junipers." On AT&SF RR, 11 mi N of Bernardo, on US 60 and 85. Post office, 1866-1907. SABINAL RIVERSIDE DRAIN (Socorro). Heads W of the Rio Grande at Belen and empties into the river 10 mi below, near San Juan. SABINO (Bernalillo). 4 mi SE of US 66, at Tijeras. SABINO (Harding). Trading point 21 mi E of Roy. SABINOSO (San Miguel). "Place overgrown with junipers." Ranching community 5 mi N of US 65, 21 mi SW of Roy. Post office, 1914, intermittently, to present.

SACATON CREEK (Grant). *Sacatón* is a misspelling of *zacatón*, an American-Spanish term for a kind of fodder grass that grows in bunches along river bottoms or other lowlands where there is moisture. This creek is in Mogollon Mts.; heads on S slope of West Baldy in Catron County and flows S into Grant to Duck Creek 1 mi above Buckhorn. SACATON (McKinley).

SACRAMENTO. Span., "sacrament." A contraction of El Santísimo Sacramento, "the Most Blessed Sacrament," alluding to the Holy Eucharist. When thus used for place names in Spanish countries, it refers to this particular sacrament, and not to any of the other six sacraments of the Catholic Church. SACRAMENTO (Otero). 15 mi SE of Cloudcroft. Post office, 1935—. SACRAMENTO MOUNTAINS (Otero). Lie E of S part of the Tularosa Basin and form about 50 mi of its mountain wall. This plateau descends gently E toward the Pecos Valley for about 75 mi. Name appears as SIERRA DEL SACRAMENTO on Mapa de los EUM (1828). SACRAMENTO RIVER (Otero). Has its source near summit of Sacramento Mts. Drains the areas of the Pecos Valley and the Tularosa Basin; heads S of Marcia and flows to the Circle Cross Ranch.

SACRED FIRE MOUNTAIN (Santa Fe). See BLACK MESA.

SADDLEBACK MESA (Quay). 15 mi S of Tucumcari and 7 mi W of NM 18. Named for its peculiar shape, which resembles that of a saddle. The headwaters of Plaza Largo Creek are here.

SAIL ROCK (Colfax). Peculiar rock formation in Cimarron Canyon, resembling the sail of a boat moving in the shallow waters.

SAINT ANN'S MISSION (Lincoln). Directly across US 70 from Bonnell's Ranch, where Eagle

Creek enters Ruidoso River. Services of the Protestant Episcopal Church have been held for over fifty years at this site, first in the old schoolhouse formerly located here. The present chapel was erected in 1934, the only non-Roman Catholic place of worship on the highway between Roswell and Alamogordo. SAINT PATRICK (San Miguel). Post office, 1892-94; mail to Las Vegas.

SAINT VRAIN (Curry). Farming community on US 60, 84, and AT&SF RR, 8 mi E of Melrose. Named for Ceran St. Vrain, who came from St. Louis in 1830 to Taos, where he became a colonel of the First New Mexico Volunteer Infantry. Ill health caused him to resign and his lieutenant colonel, Kit Carson, assumed command. When St. Vrain first arrived, he was accompanied by as many as a hundred trappers to catch beaver on the upper Rio Grande and the Colorado and Gila rivers. At one time, he was a partner of Charles Bent, the governor of NM, 1846-47, who was murdered in a revolt against American rule at Taos. Post office, 1907—.

SAIS (Valencia). Small town on AT&SF RR, 20 mi SE of Belen. The progenitor of this family was Ambrosio Saiz, a native of San Bartolome in New Spain, who came to NM shortly after 1665. His son and family returned with the Reconquest of 1692.

SALADITO CREEK (Quay). Span., "little salty." Rises S of Tipton, and flows NE into San Jon Creek. SALADO (Guadalupe). Post office, 1892-99; mail to Ft. Sumner; resumed, 1899-1913. SALADO (Harding). SALADO (Sandoval). At San Ysidro. SALADO ARROYO (Harding). Comes out of Union County and flows SE to Ute Creek in central part of county. SALADO CREEK (De Baca). Rises in county and flows into Pecos River. SALADO CREEK (Harding). Heads in Union County; flows S into Del Muerto Creek above Bueyeros. SALADO CREEK (Rio Arriba). SALADO CREEK (McKinley, Sandoval). Heads in Cebolleta Mts. in McKinley, crosses the county line and flows E into Rio Puerco. SALADO PEAK (Sierra). 18 mi W of Truth or Consequences.

SALAZAR. Francisco de Salazar is mentioned as a soldier in 1625. For complicity in the murder of Governor Rosas, this Salazar was executed in 1643, but a Bartolome de Salazar was *alcalde mayor* of the Zuñi area in 1663, and Salazars are listed in 1693 and later. SALAZAR (Sandoval). See CASA SALAZAR. SALAZAR (San

Miguel). SALAZAR LAKE (Rio Arriba). 4 mi E of Lindrith.

SALEM (Doña Ana). Farming community on US 85, 5 mi NW of Hatch. Named in 1908 when a group of New Englanders from Salem, Mass., settled here. Previously called PLAZA. Post office, 1908—.

SALINA (Catron). Span., "salt mines." SALINA LAKE (Torrance). "Salty." 6 mi SE of Willard. Contains natural salt deposits. SALINAS (Otero). 1 mi E of US 54, on SP RR, 11 mi N of Tularosa. Post office, 1902-12; changed to THREE RIVERS. SALINAS PEAK (Socorro). Near Zuñi Salt Lake. SALINE LAKE (Torrance). 2 mi SW of Silio.

SALIZ CANYON (Catron). Heads E of Aspen Mtn. and runs into San Francisco River NW of Kelly Mts. May be a family name, perhaps a corruption of Salaices. SALIZ MOUNTAINS (Catron). Begin 6 mi SW of Reserve.

SALT CREEK (Chaves). Rises in Lincoln County and flows E to Pecos River. SALT CREEK (Otero). Has its source at Malpais Spring near W side of the lava bed. In its last few miles, it has a flat bottom ¼ mile or more wide and precipitous walls up to 40 ft high, of gypsum and clay of pure white and a delicate shade of red. In the vicinity of Salt Creek, the slope of the underground water table is such that the creek has cut down to and tapped these waters to become a permanent stream. SALT CREEK (Socorro). Rises in Lincoln County and flows S. SALT LAKE (Catron). Trading point on NM 32, 25 mi NW of Quemado. Curtis Salt Co. is here. Commonly called ZUÑI SALT LAKE. It is mentioned by Captain Farfan of Oñate's army in 1598. Tons of salt are taken from here, where one volcanic cone lies within another and salt is found in the water around the outer cone. Indians make a pilgrimage here each year. Post office, 1902-40. SALT LAKE (Eddy). 6 mi NE of Loving. SALT LAKE (Mora). Near Wagon Mound. SALT LAKE (Otero). 15 mi SW of Tularosa. SALT LAKE (Roosevelt). 4 mi SE of Arch. SALT LAKE BEDS (Torrance). Chain of salt deposits in old lake beds N of Progresso, referred to as early as 1668 in a Spanish document that tells how burros were loaded here with salt and driven seven hundred miles to Chihuahua where the salt was used in the smelting of silver. SALTPETER CREEK (Colfax). Begins 5 mi below Dawson where it empties into Vermejo River, and flows S through a

canyon of the same name. SALTPETER MOUN-
TAIN (Colfax). 5 mi SE of Dawson, on banks
of Saltpeter Creek. SALT WELLS (Lea).
SALVATION CANYON (Catron). Heads N of O
Bar O Mts., and runs N for 6 mi.
SALYERS CANYON (Colfax). Begins in NW part of
county; runs SE to Vermejo near former Elkins post office. An early settler had this name.
SAN ACACIA (Socorro). Farming and ranching
community on US 85 and AT&SF RR, 14 mi
N of Socorro. Named for the San Acacio who
was represented by the *santeros* (image mak-
ers) as crucified and dressed in a Spanish
military uniform. He was said to have been a
Roman soldier slain for his faith in early
Christian times. The change from *o* to *a* in the
last syllable of the name may be from confusion with the word *acacia,* a kind of tree.
Post office, 1881—.
SAN AGUSTIN (Bernalillo, Catron, *et al*). See SAN
AUGUSTIN.
SAN ANDRES (Socorro, Bernalillo). Span., "St.
Andrew the Apostle." Mountain range N of
Organ Mts. and the old settlement of Los
Padillas. There are St. Andrews for the months
of May, July, August, and November. No
doubt the date the town was founded deter-
mined which saint it should be. SAN ANDRES
CANYON (Otero). Tiny stream in a deep box
canyon SE of Alamogordo, on W side of
Sacramento Mts. SAN ANDRES CREEK (Doña
Ana). On E slope of San Andres Mts. 20 mi
N of Organ. SAN ANDRES MOUNTAINS (Doña
Ana, Socorro, Sierra). Run N and S between
San Agustin Mts. and the Sierra Oscura.
SAN ANDRES PEAK (Doña Ana). In San
Andres Mts. 6 mi W of Lake Lucero.
SAN ANTONE LAKES (Rio Arriba). Anglicized
Span., "St. Anthony." In Carson National
Forest. SAN ANTONIO (Bernalillo). Settlement
at Cedar Crest, on US 10, 18 mi E of Albu-
querque, in foothills of Sandia Mts. Named
for its patron saint. Very old village, a trad-
ing point when ox *carretas* (carts) creaked all
the way to Santa Fe. Although there are sev-
eral St. Anthonys, it was St. Anthony of
Padua, disciple of St. Francis, that the people
of NM favored as patron for several places.
SAN ANTONIO (Mora). Old town 3 mi SW of
Mora in sheep-raising section of county in
Mora Grant. SAN ANTONIO (Rio Arriba). 11
mi NE of Hopewell. SAN ANTONIO (Socorro).
Farming community on US 60 and 85, 11 mi
S of Socorro. Named for the mission founded

in 1629 by Fray Antonio de Arteaga and Fray
Garcia de Francisco de Zuñiga. Post office,
1870—. SAN ANTONIO (Taos). Post office, 1867-
68. See VALDEZ. SAN ANTONIO CREEK (San-
doval, Rio Arriba). 3 mi W of San Antonio
Mts.; rises in Sandoval County and flows S to
Jemez Mts. SAN ANTONIO DE LAS HUERTAS
GRANT (Sandoval). Area of about 7 sq mi
surrounding community of Placitas. Granted
to twenty-one petitioners by Governor Mendi-
nueta on Dec. 31, 1767, and the families took
possession on Jan. 13, 1768. SAN ANTONIO DEL
BEQUIU DEL GUYQUI (Rio Arriba). See
QUIQUI. SAN ANTONIO DEL EMBUDO (Rio
Arriba). See EMBUDO. SAN ANTONIO DE LO DE
MORA. See CLEVELAND. SAN ANTONIO DEL RIO
COLORADO (Taos). See QUESTA. SAN ANTONIO
DE PADUA (Socorro). The parish of Socorro.
Named for the favorite Anthony. SAN AN-
TONIO DE SENECU (Socorro). A Piro pueblo,
prior to the Pueblo Rebellion of 1680; 13
mi below Socorro on the Rio Grande. SAN
ANTONIO MOUNTAIN (Rio Arriba). W of 285,
10 mi S of Colorado line, NE of San Antonio.
Marks N boundary of the Tewa-speaking In-
dian world according to their mythology. SAN
ANTONIO MOUNTAIN (Sandoval). 6 mi NW
of Redondo Peak. SAN ANTONIO RIVER (Rio
Arriba). Rises in county and flows N to Colorado; a tributary of Los Pinos River in Carson
National Forest, heading at Lagunitas Lakes
and flowing past San Antone Ranger Station.
SAN ANTONIO SPRINGS (McKinley). Mission
church on NM 58, 5 mi NE of Thoreau. SAN
ANTONITO (Bernalillo). Span., "little St. Anthony." Trading point on NM 10, 10 mi NE
of Tijeras and 23 mi E of Albuquerque. 2 mi
to the N is the ancient pueblo of Paako, which
is owned by the University of New Mexico
and used for field work in archeology.
SAN AUGUSTIN. Also spelled AGUSTIN and
AUGUSTINE. St. Augustine of Hippo was a
Father and Doctor of the Roman Catholic
Church, fourth century. *Agustín* is the Spanish form but "Augustin" seems to be prevail-
ing. SAN AUGUSTIN (San Miguel). Small community on Gallinas River, 9 mi SE of Las
Vegas; known today as LOURDES, commemo-
rating the French shrine. SAN AUGUSTINE
(Doña Ana). Post office, 1876-88; mail to
Organ. SAN AUGUSTIN PASS (Doña Ana).
Separates Organ Mts. from San Andres Mts.
SAN AUGUSTIN PEAK (Doña Ana). Pointed
mountain on S tip of San Andres Mts. SAN

AUGUSTIN PLAINS (Catron). SW of Datil between Mangas Mts. and the Continental Divide.

SAN BLAS (Valencia). St. Blase, or Blaise, of Sebaste, was a fourth-century Christian hero. Throats are blessed on his feast day throughout the Roman Catholic Church. He was a patron of the now extinct eighteenth-century settlement of Nustra Señora de la Luz.

SAN BUENAVENTURA (Sandoval). Name of the Roman Catholic parish at Cochiti Pueblo. St. Bonaventure, Cardinal Bishop, Doctor of the Church, pioneer and reorganizer of the Franciscan Order, has been patron of Cochiti Pueblo since the beginning of the seventeenth century, and was patron also of Humanas Pueblo, believed to be the same as Gran Quivira. Spanish folk who received his name in baptism usually shortened it to Ventura. SAN BUENAVENTURA DE CHIMAYO (Santa Fe). See CHIMAYO.

SAN CARLOS (Bernalillo). Name of the Roman Catholic parish at Alameda. Commemorates St. Charles Borromeo, Cardinal Archbishop of Milan in the sixteenth century. He was patron of the church in Alameda at the end of the eighteenth century. SAN CARLOS (Socorro). Post Office, 1875-78.

SANCHEZ (San Miguel). Trading point on NM 65, 50 mi S of Sabinoso. Settled about 1832. One of the families with Oñate in 1597-98 bore this name. First postmaster, Manuel A. Sanchez. Post office, 1898-1927. SANCHEZ (Socorro). On Alamocito Creek, 26 mi N of Augustine. SANCHEZ (Torrance). 10 mi W of Mountainair. SANCHEZ CANYON (Sandoval). Small stream E of Cañada. SANCHEZ SPRINGS (Catron). S of Datil on San Augustin Plains.

SAN CLEMENTE (Valencia). Former settlement near Los Lunas. Name honors St. Clement I, Bishop of Rome and Pope in the years A.D. 92-101. His name was given to the eighteenth-century Rancho de San Clemente. SAN CLEMENTE GRANT (Valencia). The land extended W of Los Lunas from the Rio Puerco to a few miles E of the Rio Grande. Granted to Don Felix Candelaria in 1716. Subsequently owned by the Luna family and granted to their heirs by the U.S. in 1899.

SAN CRISTOBAL, also CRISTOVAL. Span., "St. Christopher." This title was first given to one of the early seventeenth-century Tanos Missions in the Galisteo Basin. Name is usually spelled Cristóbal in NM. SAN CRISTOBAL (Taos). Farming community on NM 3, 14 mi N of Taos. The earliest Anglo settlers came in 1860. SAN CRISTOBAL ARROYO, CREEK (Santa Fe). Flows W from San Miguel County to enter Galisteo Creek, 1 mi S of Galisteo. SAN CRISTOBAL CREEK (Taos). Little stream on W side of Mt. Lobo, E of San Cristobal. SAN CRISTOBAL GRANT (Santa Fe). Large area crossed by San Cristobal Arroyo, extending 2 mi N of Galisteo and 12 mi S. SAN CRISTOBAL GRANT (Taos). Granted to Severino Martinez on Aug. 4, 1815.

SANCTUARIO (Santa Fe). Span., santuario, "sanctuary." Settlement on Santa Cruz River, 1 mi S of Chimayo.

SAND CREEK (Catron). 7 mi N of Luna.

SANDIA (Sandoval). Span., "watermelon." Fray Alonso de Benavides in his Revised Memorial of 1634 (1945) refers to a Franciscan convent called San Francisco de Sandia, which he says is located in the principal pueblo of the Tiwa Indians. His reference is to an Indian settlement 13 mi N of Albuquerque and today just E of US 85. The population then was more than three thousand. Tradition has it that watermelons grew abundantly in the canyons of the mountains near the pueblo or in the pueblo itself. However, the Tiwas called their pueblo na-fi-at, "dusty place," which casts doubt upon the theory that "watermelons" were the chief feature of the locality. "Dust," no doubt, describes the sandy stretches of the Rio Grande Valley, and melons could refer to squash or pumpkin vines in irrigated patches. Watermelons, Citrullus vulgaris, having a hard green rind and a pink or red pulp, are not native to the Southwest, but Spanish priests could have brought seeds and planted them. Popular belief holds that the striped appearance of the rocks or the pinkish reflections of the surfaces at sunset led to the name "watermelon mountains" in Spanish. According to the testimony of one paisano in Granada, Spain, there is a block of hills in the contrafuertes of the Sierra Nevada Mountains which is known locally as El Corazón de la Sandía because the shape of the mountain mass is like that of the heart of a melon, the pulpy center. (Letter from Professor Nicholas Baum, Granada, Spain, Apr. 7, 1959.) Thus a transfer name could have been suggested by topographical similarities in Spain and NM. Sandia Pueblo post office, 1892-95. SANDIA (Valencia). Settlement near NM 6, 6 mi W of Los Lunas. SANDIA BASE (Bernalillo). On the SE outskirts of the city of Albuquerque is the Field Command of the Defense Atomic Support Agency, which was activated as the Armed Forces Special Weapons Project in 1947 concurrently with the dissolution of the Manhattan Engineering District which developed the first atomic weapons during World War II. The Defense Atomic Support Agency is a joint service command and is staffed by personnel from the Army, Navy, Air Force, and Marine Corps. Also on Sandia Base is the Albuquerque Operations Office of the Atomic Energy Commission and Sandia Corporation, one of AEC's prime contractors and the state's largest non-government employers. SANDIA CANYON (Santa Fe). The tradition that watermelons grew in the upper canyon has been referred to above. The Indian name, *posoo gay hoo-oo,* means "where water slides down arroyo." SANDIA MOUNTAINS (Bernalillo, Sandoval). Lofty range E of Albuquerque, which may be entered from US 66 from the S, or from US 85 from the NW. They are, with the Manzanos directly S, the most prominent geological feature in central NM. In pueblo mythology, the Sandias are one of the four sacred mountains, marking the S boundary of the Tiwa-speaking Indian world; the N boundary was San Antonio Peak in Rio Arriba County; the E boundary was Lake Peak in Santa Fe County; the W boundary was the Pelado Mts. in Sandoval County. The Tiwas called the range *o-ku-piu,* "turtle mountain." An aerial tramway lifts visitors from valley to crest and E side ski run. SANDIA PARK (Bernalillo). Small community on the Loop Road, NM 44, 23 mi NE of Albuquerque. Post office, 1926—. SANDIA PEAK (Santa Fe). SANDIA PUEBLO (Sandoval). Near US 85, 3 mi S of Bernalillo. Discussed at the beginning of this name cluster. SANDIA PUEBLO GRANT (Bernalillo, Sandoval). The pueblo is spelled *San Día* in the Cruzate grant of 1689, leading to the conjecture that the name may be associated with *El Día Santo,* "Holy Day." After the Spanish troops reconquered NM in 1692, these Indians fled to the Hopis in Arizona. They did not return until 1742, and then six years later their grant was renewed by Governor Codallas y Rabal. In 1858, the U.S. Congress confirmed this grant, which conveys to the pueblo about 24,000 acres of land.

SAN DIEGO (Doña Ana). Span., "St. James." Mountain about 10 mi SE of Hatch. Campground site of the early Spanish explorers, at

the beginning of the Jornada del Muerto. Formerly called TONUCO. A settlement by this name appears on the Mapa de los EUM (1828). SAN DIEGO CANYON (Sandoval). Picturesque red sandstone formations on NM 4, N from San Ysidro.

SANDOVAL (Sandoval). Trading point and residential community on NM 46, 10 mi N of Albuquerque. Named for Francisco D. Sandoval, a leading stockman of this vicinity. Post office for Corrales area, 1899—. SANDOVAL COUNTY. Created by the Territorial Legislature on Mar. 10, 1903. Named for the Sandoval family which settled in this region. The first appearance of this name comes from Juan de Dios Sandoval Martinez, a native of Mexico City, who came with the Reconquest of 1692. His immediate descendants dropped the "Martinez." Area is 3,871 sq mi.

SANDS (San Miguel). On AT&SF RR, 6 mi from Rowe. Before July 12, 1883, known as McPHERSON. SAND SPRINGS (Quay). 32 mi NE of Tucumcari, on CRI&P RR. SAND SPUR (Hidalgo). On SP RR, 13 mi W of Lordsburg.

SAN ESTEVAN (Valencia). Settlement named for the original patron of Acoma Pueblo, St. Stephen the Protomartyr, mentioned in the New Testament.

SAN FELIPE (Sandoval). Span., "St. Philip." A pre-Spanish Keresan-speaking pueblo, 10 mi N of Bernalillo and 27 mi N of Albuquerque. Thought to have been named by De Sosa when he visited NM in 1591. St. Philip the Apostle has been patron of the pueblo of San Felipe since the mission's founding. The pueblo is named on L'Atlas Curieux (1700). Post office, 1929-36. SAN FELIPE DE NERI (Bernalillo). The title used for the Villa of Albuquerque in 1777 and for some time later, since it had been so named by the Viceroy in 1706. See ALBUQUERQUE. St. Philip Neri was a sixteenth-century priest of the city of Rome and founder of a religious cogregation. He is the patron saint of the Roman Catholic Church in Old Albuquerque to this day. SAN FELIPE PUEBLO GRANT (Sandoval). Small grant extending 2 mi N and 6 mi S of San Felipe Pueblo. Awarded by Governor Cruzate on Sept. 20, 1689, upon promise that the Indians would not revolt against the Spanish. The boundaries are one league E and W, with a grove on the N called the Bosque Grande, and a grove on the S in front of a hill called Culebra.

SAN FERNANDES (Valencia). Settlement between Tome and Valencia, 3 mi SE of Los Lunas.

SAN FERNANDO (Valencia). Former settlement named for the parochial saint, St. Ferdinand III, thirteenth-century King of Castile and member of the Third Order of St. Francis. With San Blas he was patron of the now extinct settlement on the Rio Puerco. SAN FERNANDO DE TAOS GRANT (Taos). Small triangular-shaped area at SW line of Taos Pueblo Grant. In 1796, the *alcalde mayor* and war captain of Taos Pueblo and its districts, following the order of Governor Chacon, gave possession of a place known as Don Fernando de Taos, to sixty-three families; later in 1797, 1798, and 1799, he gave further possession to other families in the same area.

SAN FIDEL (Cibola). Small village on US 66, 18 mi E of Grants. Named for one of three saints: St. Faith, St. Fidelis, or St. Fidharleus. Originally called LA VEGA DE SAN JOSE. Post office, 1919—. BALLEJOS, for the family name "Vallejos"; changed to San Fidel. Name suggested by the pastor, Fr. Robert Kalth, O.F.M. The first settler was Baltazar Jaramillo and his family, about 1868.

SAN FRANCISCO. Franciscan pioneers of NM named many places for the founder of their order, St. Francis of Assisi, who lived from 1182 to 1226. The first was the extinct pueblo of Puaray, which was originally selected as headquarters for the missions; from it the patronage was transferred to its successor, the seventeenth-century pueblo of Sandia. St. Francis was also patron of Nambe Pueblo, the town and parish of Santa Fe, Los Ranchos de San Francisco, now called Ranchos de Taos, and Frisco, near the county seat of Catron County. SAN FRANCISCO (Rio Arriba). SAN FRANCISCO (Socorro). Post office, 1879-82; mail to Horse Springs. SAN FRANCISCO DE ALBUQUERQUE. (Bernalillo). See ALBUQUERQUE. SAN FRANCISCO DEL RANCHO DE TAOS (Taos). See RANCHOS DE TAOS. SAN FRANCISCO DEL VALLE GRANT (Valencia). See Los QUELITOS GRANT. SAN FRANCISCO MESA (Colfax). Formerly called AHOGADERA, "place of the drowned," because a sheepherder had lost eight hundred sheep in the stream. Named by Judge Bransford in the early 1880's. SAN FRANCISCO MOUNTAINS (Catron). On W border of county. SAN FRANCISCO PASS (Colfax). Connects NW part of county with Colorado, 5 mi E of Taos County line. SAN FRANCISCO PLAZA (Catron). See FRISCO. SAN FRANCISCO RIVER (Catron). Heads in San Francisco Mts., in SW part of state along the Continental Divide. The river follows the valley between San Francisco and Mogollon ranges in a southerly direction, and turns W into Arizona where it empties into Gila River. SAN FRANCISCO XAVIER (Bernalillo). See ALBUQUERQUE.

SAN GABRIEL (Rio Arriba). This was an old Tewa pueblo at confluence of Chama River and the Rio Grande. The original inhabitants abandoned the pueblo so that Oñate and his colonists could have a home in their new territory. Arriving here on July 11, 1598, Oñate christened the pueblo SAN JUAN, adding DE LOS CABALLEROS as a tribute to the Spanish gentlemen who had accomplished this mission. The Indian name for the pueblo was *yoong ghay*, "down at the mockingbird place." After three years, the Indians moved across to the E bank of the river, taking the name San Juan to their new quarters. The site which the Spanish occupied became San Gabriel del Yunque. Thus, San Gabriel can lay claim to the site of the first capital of New Mexico. In 1610, the Spanish moved from San Gabriel to the present location of Santa Fe. San Gabriel today is in ruins, which have recently been excavated, confirming occupancy by Oñate's group.

SAN GERONIMO DE TAOS (Taos). Name given to the mission church established at Taos Pueblo by Fray Pedro Miranda in 1617, but destroyed in 1680 during the Pueblo Rebellion. Also used for the pueblo known today simply as Taos Pueblo. San Geronimo is the St. Jerome, fourth-century Father and Doctor of the Roman Catholic Church, famed as the collector and editor of manuscripts which went into the Latin Bible called the Vulgate. Two mission churches have been built since the first one was destroyed. SAN GERONIMO (San Miguel). 9 mi W of Las Vegas on Tecolote Creek. Once a prosperous community, it is almost depopulated today.

SANGRE DE CRISTO MOUNTAINS (Santa Fe, Colfax, Taos). This range runs N and S, in the southernmost section of the Rockies, extending from S Colorado to Santa Fe and Pecos. It forms the W boundary of Mora County. Some of the peaks are Latir, Lobo, Wheeler (13,160 ft, the highest in the state) and Pueblo. As late as 1790, called SIERRA MADRE

MOUNTAINS. Present name started at the beginning of the nineteenth century and seems to be associated with the birth of the Penitente religious confraternity and its accentuated devotion to the Passion and Death of the Savior. Penitente Peak is one of the lofty eminences in this range, 10 mi NE of Santa Fe. SANGRE DE CRISTO GRANT (Taos). Very large tract bounded by the Rio Grande on NW, by Latir Creek, Latir Lakes, and Ortiz Peak on W and S, and by Cimarron Mts. on E. Grant made by Governor Armijo to Luis Lee and Narciso Beaubien, Dec. 27, 1843. Narciso Beaubien died in the Taos Massacre of 1847 and his father, Charles Beaubien, inherited his son's share. Subsequently, Charles Beaubien purchased the remainder from the other grantees.

SAN GREGORIO LAKE (Rio Arriba). Cee CIENAGA GREGORIO.

SANGSTEE (San Juan). See SANOSTEE.

SANGUILUELA CREEK (San Miguel). Enters the Gallinas, SE of Las Vegas. May be a corruption of Span., sanguijuela, "leech, cheat."

SAN HILARIO (San Miguel). Commemorative name for St. Hilary, a fourth-century Doctor of the Roman Catholic Church. Post office, 1878-86; mail to La Cinta. SAN HILARIO (Bernalillo).

SAN IGNACIO (Guadalupe). Farming and ranching community S of US 66, 18 mi W of Santa Rosa. Name commemorates St. Ignatius of Loyola, founder of the Jesuits and a Spaniard, who was the only St. Ignatius known to the people of NM. Post office, 1908, intermittently, to 1946. SAN IGNACIO (San Miguel). 5 mi W of Sapello. Post office, 1886-1901; mail to Sapello. See TECOLOTEÑOS.

SAN ILDEFONSO (Santa Fe). Pre-Spanish Tewa-speaking Indian pueblo, on NM 4, 10 mi S of Española. The Tewa name is pok-wo ghay ongwee, "pueblo where the water cuts down through." This was the place Oñate calls BOVE and which he changed to San Ildefonso. The Navajo name is tsay-tu kiune, "houses between the rocks," and refers to the space between Round Mtn. and Buckman Mesa. Spanish name commemorates St. Ildephonse, Archbishop of Toledo in the seventh century. The mission was built here in 1617, and St. Ildephonse has been its patron since that year. Named on L'Atlas Curieux (1700). SAN ILDEFONSO MESA (Santa Fe). See BLACK MESA. SAN ILDEFONSO PUEBLO GRANT (Santa Fe). On June 16, 1856, the governor and two chiefs of San Ildefonso testified that the pueblo received a grant from the King of Spain but, as it was torn and scarcely legible, the priest of the pueblo took it to Santa Fe to have it copied. That was a long time ago and they had not seen it since. The grant was confirmed by Act of Congress, Dec. 22, 1858, for 17,292 acres.

SAN ISIDRO (Doña Ana). Span., "St. Isidore." Small village 2 mi N of Las Cruces. SAN ISIDRO (Sandoval). At junction of NM 4 and 44, 5 mi SW of Jemez Pueblo. Post office, 1910-12. SAN ISIDRO, NORTH and SOUTH (San Miguel). 23 mi SW of Las Vegas on Pecos River. See SAN YSIDRO.

SAN JON (Quay). The word, as it now stands, is meaningless. It is probably a corruption of Spanish zanjón, "deep gully"—with sandy banks. Ranching and farming town on US 66, 23 mi E of Tucumcari on CRI&P RR. Tom Jones built the first building here in 1902. Construction of the railroad in 1904 caused the town to boom. Named in October 1906 by W. D. Bennett, the first postmaster. Post office, 1906-. SAN JON CREEK (Quay). Flows NE from San Jon to cross the Texas line N of Glenrio. Appears as San Jon on U.S. Geological Survey map (1955), but as San Juan on General Land Office map (1936).

SAN JOSE. Span., "St. Joseph." The name of the foster-father of Jesus is commemorated in a number of NM place names. He was the patron of the first mission established among the Jemez Indians in 1617, but destroyed by the Navajos five years later. After the Spanish returned in 1692, St. Joseph was named patron of the new church at Laguna Pueblo. Often settlements were known by the name of the parish church, as SAN JOSE DEL CERRO CABEZON, a village mentioned at start of the nineteenth century. SAN JOSE (Bernalillo). Small village now incorporated into Albuquerque. SAN JOSE (Eddy). SAN JOSE (Grant). SAN JOSE (San Miguel). Farming community on US 85, 22 mi SW of Las Vegas. On Pecos River; camp site for General Kearny on march to Santa Fe in 1846. Post office, 1858, intermittently, to present. SAN JOSE (Sierra). Once on San Jose Arroyo and US 85; now buried under Elephant Butte Lake. SAN JOSE (Socorro). Post office, 1892-96; mail to Sabinal. SAN JOSE (Valencia). See SUWANEE and CORREO. SAN JOSE CANYON (Socorro). See PANKEY CANYON. SAN JOSE RIVER (Valencia). Begins in Cibola National Forest, along E slope of Zuñi Mts.; drains SW along AT&SF RR and US 66. Finally connects with the Rio Colorado and then with the Rio Puerco. These rivers are dry most of the time.

SAN JUAN. Span., "St. John the Baptist." Don Juan de Oñate conferred this title upon the Indian pueblo he occupied on July 11, 1598, adding DE LOS CABALLEROS in tribute to the rank and knightly virtues of the Spanish founders. This formula was not unique in that Jerez de los Caballeros is a place name in the old province of Estremadura, Spain, from which a number of Oñate's colonists came. SAN JUAN (Rio Arriba). Post office, 1870-81; mail to Chamita. SAN JUAN PUEBLO (Rio Arriba). On US 64, 4 mi NE of Española. Still bears this name, though it is across the river from its original site. The old San Juan which Oñate rechristened SAN GABRIEL in 1601, is the site of the pueblo ruins today on W bank of the river. Oñate remained at San Juan Bautista and San Gabriel until he left in 1610. His successor, Don Cristobal de Peralta, arrived in the fall of 1609 and ordered a new capital built. This was Santa Fe, located some 30 mi to the S at the foot of the great mountain range which was later called Sangre de Cristo. Name appears on L'Atlas Curieux (1700). Post office, 1944—. SAN JUAN (Grant). On Mimbres River and NM 61, 9 mi SE of Santa Rita. SAN JUAN AREA. Navajo name for this area is dine ḳehat eh sah, "ancient land of the Navajos." SAN JUAN CANYON (Sandoval). Runs S into Vallecitos Creek at the settlement of Lower Vallecitos. SAN JUAN CANYON, CREEK (Quay). Flows NE into San Jon River at San Jon. SAN JUAN COUNTY. Created by the Territorial Legislature on Feb. 4, 1887, and named for the river. Area is 5,476 sq mi. SAN JUAN PUEBLO GRANT (Rio Arriba). Made by Governor Cruzate, Sept. 25, 1689. See PUEBLO LAND GRANTS. SAN JUAN RIVER (Rio Arriba, San Juan). Flows down from Colorado into Rio Arriba County, and returns to Colorado in San Juan County.

SAN LAZARO (Santa Fe). Span., "St. Lazarus," whom Christ raised from the dead. Title first given to one of the early seventeenth-century Tanos Missions in the Galisteo Basin. The Otermin documents relate that these Indians in 1680 took part in the Pueblo Rebellion.

SAN LEONARDO LAKE (Rio Arriba). Small lake of the Las Trampas watershed. SAN LEONARDO RIVER (Rio Arriba). 7 mi W of Truchas.

SAN LORENZO (Grant). Span., "St. Lawrence." Ranching community on NM 180, 10 mi E of Santa Rita. Founded in 1714 by Gov. Juan Ignacio Flores Mogollon, in honor of St. Lawrence, third-century deacon, killed for his Christian faith at Rome. He was Spanish born; hence his feast has always been a major one among Spanish peoples. Post office, 1886—. See FORT WEBSTER. SAN LORENZO (San Miguel). Named by Lorenzo Lopez to commemorate his patronal saint and his own name. A military outpost during the American occupation. Post office, 1876-77. SAN LORENZO (Valencia). SAN LORENZO ARROYO (Socorro). Runs E into the Rio Grande near Polvadera. Also called ARROYO DE SAN LORENZO. SAN LORENZO DE PICURIS (Taos). An Indian pueblo N of NM 75, 16 mi SW of Taos. The Tewa name peeng wee ongwee means "mountain gap pueblo." Why this description was used is not known since no gap exists anywhere near the pueblo. See PICURIS.

SAN LUIS (Sandoval). Small settlement on NM 279, 20 mi W of Jemez. Name commemorates St. Louis IX, King of France in the thirteenth century, the son of Louis VIII and Blanche of Castile. SAN LUIS OBISPO (Socorro). St. Louis, Franciscan bishop of Toulouse in the thirteenth century, and a grandnephew of King St. Louis. He was reared in Spain and chosen patron of the seventeenth-century pueblo of Sevilleta. SAN LUIS PASS (Hidalgo). SAN LUIS REY (Valencia). "St. Louis, King."

SAN MARCIAL (Socorro). Trading point 2 mi E of US 85, 30 mi S of Socorro. Named for St. Martial of Limoges, France, third century. This nineteenth-century town was the successor of the older town of Paraje on the opposite side of the Rio Grande. Founded after the American Occupation as LA MESA DE SAN MARCIAL, on E bank of the Rio Grande. Perhaps named by one of the French clergy, although the name itself was given in baptism among New Mexicans in the early eighteenth century. Wiped out by a flood in 1866, the inhabitants moved over to the higher W bank to found another San Marcial, which was completely destroyed by a flood in 1929. New San Marcial was established with the coming of the railroad in 1880. Post office, 1869-1944.

SAN MARCOS (Santa Fe). Span., "St. Mark." This title was first given to one of the early seventeenth-century Tanos Missions in the Galisteo Basin. SAN MARCOS PUEBLO GRANT (Santa Fe). Area 2 mi square, 2 mi NE of Los

Cerrillos. Made to Antonio Urban Montaño by Governor Cachupin. Montaño was placed in possession on July 26, 1754.

San Mateo (Cibola). Span., "St. Matthew." On the McKinley—Cibola line, at foot of Mt. Taylor, 18 mi NE of Grants. One report dates the founding as in 1835 by Col. Manuel Chaves who, while crossing the place on his way to Seboyeta from fighting the Indians, rested under an oak tree and decided to build a home and chapel here, naming the place for St. Matthew. Another version tells that Roman A. Baca, a half-brother of Chaves, led a group of colonists to the site after the Navajo campaign of 1855. The Navajo name means "the meadow." Post office, 1876—. San Mateo Canyon (Socorro). Runs to the Sierra County line, W of San Mateo Peak. San Mateo Creek (McKinley, Valencia). Joins Bluewater Creek 4 mi NW of Grants to form San Jose River. San Mateo Mesa (McKinley). San Mateo Mountains (Socorro). In SW part of county in Cibola National Forest. San Mateo Mountains (Valencia). Also called Sierra de San Mateo. S of the village of San Mateo, and SW of Jemez Mts. San Mateo Peak (Socorro). In SW part of county 12 mi E of Dusty. San Mateo Springs Grant (McKinley). Small area extending S of San Mateo and crossed by San Mateo Creek. Grant made by Governor Mendinueta to Santiago Duran y Chaves, Feb. 5, 1768, but litigation occurred in the 1880's between the Duran y Chaves heirs and the heirs of Roman A. Baca, who filed a counterclaim.

San Miguel (Doña Ana). Span., "St. Michael." Trading point on NM 28, 5 mi S of Las Cruces. Post office. 1952—. Formerly called Telles. San Miguel (Rio Arriba). On the Rio de los Pinos in NE corner of county, 2 mi from Colorado line. San Miguel (Sandoval). Farming community beginning 1 mi E of NM 44 and 9 mi S of Cuba. San Miguel (San Miguel). On US 85, 22 mi SE of Las Vegas. Post office, 1851, intermittently, to 1910. See San Miguel del Bado. San Miguel County. Created by the Republic of Mexico in 1844, and re-established by the U.S. Territorial Legislature on Jan. 9, 1852. Named for the town San Miguel del Bado. Area is 4,894 sq mi. San Miguel Creek (McKinley). Rises in county and flows N to Chico Creek. San Miguel del Bado (San Miguel). "River crossing." (Pecos River). 5 mi S of Ribera. One of the oldest towns in NM. Originally settled by a group of Indians who were cast out because of their conversion to Catholicism. An important way-stop on the Santa Fe Trail, between Santa Fe and Las Vegas. Here many Texans were imprisoned when they invaded NM in 1847. San Miguel del Bado became the town of San Miguel. San Miguel del Bado Grant (San Miguel). Small grant N of Pecos River, 20 mi SW of Las Vegas. On Nov. 25, 1794, Governor Chacon granted to Lorenzo Marquez and fifty-one men with him a tract known as San Miguel del Bado. Marquez and the others said they had twenty-five firearms and promised to enclose themselves with bulwarks and towers as defense against the Indians. After granting the request, the governor ordered the alcalde of Santa Fe to put them in possession, which he did on Nov. 6, 1794. San Miguel del Socorro (Socorro). San Miguel Mountain (San Miguel). Called Big Mike; 10 mi NW of Las Vegas. Has the profile of a human face, as viewed from US 85. Mythology surrounding this stone giant makes a pygmy of Paul Bunyan. He was reputed to be twenty-seven miles tall and his walk-around money was said to be the gold received in ransom by Cortez, the Conquistador, for the release of Montezuma. The Pueblo Indians said, "The face of God is in all mountains. Only here has time replaced parts of the mountain with space in the proper places so that all can see the human likeness of the Great Spirit."

Sanostee (San Juan). Trading point 7 mi W of US 666, 30 mi SW of Shiprock. The name is Navajo and may be *tse-nas-tse*, "rocks around it."

San Pablo (Guadalupe). Span., "St. Paul the Apostle." San Pablo (San Miguel). Trading point 15 mi SW of Las Vegas. San Pablo (Sandoval). San Pablo Canyon (Sandoval). Heads on Blue Bird Mesa, flows W into the Rio Puerco, 5 mi S of Lagunitas.

San Pasqual (Socorro). Ruined Indian pueblo described in the Otermin documents, 1680-82, C. W. Hackett, editor. Within sight of Senecu, 10 mi S of Socorro.

San Patricio (Lincoln). Span., "St. Patrick," patron of Ireland. Fruit-raising and ranching community on US 70, 36 mi SE of Carrizozo. In the area originally called Ruidoso from the river on which it is located. About 1875, when the Roman Catholic church was built and named San Patricio, the name of this community was changed to correspond with it.

El Chivato (Billy the Kid) is supposed to have attended dances here. Among the early settlers were Feliz Trujillo, Ramon Olguin, Jose M. Sedillo, and their families. Post office, 1904—.

SAN PEDRO (Rio Arriba). Span., "St. Peter." SAN PEDRO (Santa Fe). 32 mi NE of Albuquerque on NM 10; former mining town in San Pedro Mts. Post office, 1881-1918. SAN PEDRO (Socorro). Old Spanish settlement on the Rio Grande and US 360, 1 mi E of San Antonio. SAN PEDRO CREEK (Sandoval). Flows N and W into Coyote Arroyo, 3 mi NW of Hagan. SAN PEDRO GRANT (Bernalillo, Sandoval, Santa Fe). Lies between San Antonio and Golden, and cuts the corners of three counties. Named for the parish of San Pedro del Cuchillo, at the Tewa mission of Paako. Abandoned before 1670. The later grant measures about 50 sq mi and was made on Aug. 23, 1839, to Antonio Sandoval, who in turn passed title to Serafin Ramirez. The latter deeded to Jesus Miera, Ramon Gurule, and others, who took possession on Nov. 27, 1844. SAN PEDRO MOUNTAINS (Rio Arriba). In SW corner of county, S of Capulin. SAN PEDRO MOUNTAINS (Santa Fe). Small range E of the Sandias and S of Golden. SAN PEDRO PARK (Rio Arriba). On NE slope of San Pedro Mts.

SAN RAFAEL (San Miguel). Span., "St. Raphael." 4 mi W of NM 65, 2 mi W of Trementina. SAN RAFAEL (Valencia). On NM 174 and 53, 4 mi SW of Grants. Post office, 1881, intermittently, to present. SAN RAPHAEL DEL GUIQUE or Quique (Rio Arriba). See QUIQUI.

SAN RAMON (San Miguel). On NM 65, 5 mi N of Trementina.

SAN SIMON CIENAGA (Hidalgo). Span., "marsh of St. Simon." SAN SIMON SINK (Lea). South-central part of county below Lea, between NM 176 and 256. SAN SIMON SWALE (Lea). A 30-mi depression with occasional rank water holes.

SANTA ANA (Sandoval). Span., "St. Anne." Pre-Spanish Keresan pueblo N of NM 44, 10 mi NW of Bernalillo. Destroyed by Gov. Pedro Reneros de Posada in 1687 as an aftermath of the Pueblo Rebellion. The Indians returned and the church was rebuilt by De Vargas. St. Anne, traditional name of the Mother of the Virgin Mary, has been honored by the name of this Queres pueblo on Jemez River from the beginning of the mission. Shown on L'Atlas Curieux (1700). SANTA ANA (San Miguel). SANTA ANA (Santa Fe). See GA-

LISTEO. SANTA ANA PUEBLO GRANT (Sandoval). Tract 5 mi square with the pueblo at the center. Representatives of Santa Ana produced a Cruzate document dated Sept. 25, 1689, and the grant was confirmed by special act of Congress, Feb. 9, 1869, because Santa Ana had been omitted in the annual report of the Surveyor General, Sept. 30, 1855, when he recommended approval of the Spanish land grants to Zia, San Juan, Jemez, and Pecos. See PUEBLO LAND GRANTS.

SANTA BARBARA CANYON, CREEK (Rio Arriba). Tributary to the Rio Pueblo consisting of three forks all heading against the high divide between Truchas Peak and Jicarita Peak. SANTA BARBARA GRANT (Taos). In Carson National Forest between Tres Ritos and El Valle. Made to Valentin Martin and forty-one petitioners who took possession on Apr. 3, 1796.

SANTA CLARA (Grant). See CENTRAL. SANTA CLARA (Mora). Post office, 1876-77. SANTA CLARA (Rio Arriba). On NM 5, 4 mi S of Española. Pre-Spanish pueblo named ka po by the Tewa Indians. The Navajo name for these people means "tribe like bears." Spanish name honors St. Clare of Assisi, with whose assistance St. Francis founded his Second Order, composed of strictly cloistered nuns. Santa Clara was also the original name of WAGON MOUND in Mora County. Shown on L'Atlas Curieux (1700). SANTA CLARA (Santa Fe). Trading point 5 mi W of US 64 and 84, 20 mi NW of Santa Fe. SANTA CLARA CREEK (Rio Arriba). In Santa Clara Indian Reservation on E side of Jemez Mts. SANTA CLARA INDIAN RESERVATION (Rio Arriba). Established in 1689 by the Spanish government. SANTA CLARA PUEBLO GRANT (Rio Arriba). Tract about 5 mi square with the pueblo at the center. On June 14, 1856, the young men of Santa Clara Pueblo testified that the older men said they had a grant from the King of Spain, but it had been lost. One Indian testified that the authorities of the Mexican government took the Indian deeds in order to have them copied and revalidated. The Indians claimed one league from the church to the four points of the compass.

SANTA CRUZ (Santa Fe). Span., "Holy Cross." Farming and ranching community on NM 76, 2 mi E of Española. Seventeenth-century settlement important in religious and political history of the state. Second villa decreed in NM by the Spanish government and founded by De Vargas in 1695. "La Villa Nueva de

Santa Cruz de los Españoles Mejicanos del Rey Nuestro Señor Carlos Segundo" is the impressive title, but old Spanish records usually refer to it as "La Villa Nueva de Santa Cruz de la Cañada." Santa Fe was the first official villa in 1610; Santa Cruz, the second in 1695; Albuquerque, the third in 1706. Post office, 1878, intermittently, to present. SANTA CRUZ GRANT (Rio Arriba). Approved by Governor de Vargas, Dec. 1, 1703. SANTA CRUZ LAKE (Los Alamos). See FRIJOLES CANYON. SANTA CRUZ RESERVOIR (Santa Fe). Irrigation reservoir, impounding waters of the Rio Medio and Frijoles Creek in a deep canyon, 10 mi E of Española. SANTA CRUZ RIVER (Santa Fe). Flows S of Santa Cruz to empty into the Rio Grande below Española.

SANTA FE (Santa Fe). Span., "Holy Faith." On US 85, 20 mi E of the Rio Grande, in north-central part of county. Capital city of NM and the oldest European community W of the Mississippi. Cultural center with museums, research institutions, historical monuments of Indian, Spanish, and pioneer American interest. Founded as a villa by Don Pedro de Peralta in 1610, after the first Spanish governor and colonizer, Oñate, moved his headquarters to Santa Fe. Peralta was instructed to establish a capital for "The Kingdom of New Mexico," which he did at the edge of a great chain of mountains where a Tano Indian village had been abandoned. Although Twitchell, in *Old Santa Fe* (1925), p. 17, refers to the founding of La Villa Real de Santa Fe de San Francisco, Fray Angelico Chavez can find no early document that refers to the city by this title. He believes the capital was named in accord with the Conquistador tradition of naming towns in the New World for Santa Fe, Spain, near Granada, which Ferdinand and Isabella had founded and named in honor of the Holy Faith during their final conquest of the Moors in 1492. Fray Alonso de Benavides refers simply to the "villa de Santa Fe." Until 1680, Santa Fe was the only Spanish incorporated town north of the settlements in Mexico. The capital was evacuated on Aug. 21, 1680, when an Indian named Pope, from San Juan Pueblo, led a revolt which drove Governor Otermin, the military garrison, and the civilians down the river valley to Guadalupe del Paso, present Ciudad Juarez. In 1692 and 1693, a good many of them returned with the new Governor and Captain General Don Diego de Vargas, who was able to enter

the city without warfare. Strife followed in some of the pueblos, as it also continued through the next two hundred years with hostile bands of nomadic Indians, but Santa Fe met only one other military occupation. That was the entry of American forces under Gen. Stephen W. Kearny on Aug. 18, 1846, who, like De Vargas, occupied the city without firing a single shot. Twenty-five years earlier the first Anglo-Americans had entered Santa Fe to begin the Santa Fe trade. Post office, 1849—. SANTA FE COUNTY. Named for the city which became the county seat when the county was designated by the Territorial Legislature on Jan. 9, 1852. Created by the Republic of Mexico in 1844. Present area is 1,973 sq mi. SANTA FE BALDY (Santa Fe). Peak 12,628 ft high; 14 mi NE of city. SANTA FE CREEK or RIVER (Santa Fe). Flows SW into the Rio Grande from Santa Fe Lake in Sangre de Cristo Mts., NE of city. SANTA FE FORKS (Colfax). See HOXIE. SANTA FE GRANT (Santa Fe). Area 5 mi square surrounding the original Villa Real de Santa Fe. The City of Santa Fe was represented before the Court of Private Land Claims, Jan. 31, 1893, stating that the land grant had been issued by the King of Spain before the Pueblo Rebellion of 1680. SANTA FE LAKE (Santa Fe); also called SANTA FE BALDY LAKE. 7 mi NE of Santa Fe. SANTA FE NATIONAL FOREST (Santa Fe, San Miguel, Mora). Lies E and NE of Santa Fe in the corners of three counties.

SANTA GERTRUDIS (Mora). Town in the Mora Valley named for St. Gertrude, a German abbess of the thirteenth century who was a favorite in Spanish countries. Originally called SANTA GERTRUDIS DE LO DE MORA.

SANTA MARIA DE ACOMA (Cibola). See MC-CARTY'S.

SANTA RITA (Grant). Span., "St. Rita." Copper-mining community on NM 180, 6 mi NE of Bayard, on AT&SF RR. Settled in 1803 by Francisco Elguea, a Chihuahua businessman, and originally named SANTA RITA DEL COBRE. Span., "copper." The mine was known in early Spanish times, and continued digging has made it one of the greatest open-pit excavations in the world. Post office, 1881—. SANTA RITA (San Juan). SANTA RITA (Socorro).

SANTA ROSA (Guadalupe). County seat on Pecos River, on US 84, 54, and 66, and SP RR. Settled in 1865, and named about 1890 for a chapel built by Don Celso Baca, in honor of his mother, and dedicated to St. Rose of Lima, a maiden who became the first canonized saint of the New World. She was also the patroness of the eighteenth-century pueblo church of Abiquiu, as well as of the chapel of the Spanish settlers living close by. Post office, 1873—. SANTA ROSA CREEK (Guadalupe). Flows from Blue Hole Spring at Santa Rosa into Municipal Lake. SANTA ROSA CREEK (Sandoval). Small tributary of Upper San Antonio Creek at the Baca Location W of Los Alamos. SANTA ROSA DE CUBERO GRANT (Sandoval). Small tract just N of San Felipe Pueblo. Granted to Bartolome Fernandez and Joseph Quintana prior to 1805. The heirs again applied for possession of the land in 1815 and were duly possessed. SANTA ROSA VALLEY (Sandoval). Grassy meadows on W side of Jemez Mts. Called by the Tewa *pim paenge,* "beyond the mountains."

SANTA ROSALIA (Sandoval). Span., "St. Rosalie." A Sicilian girl-hermit of the twelfth century mentioned as patroness of Corrales in 1799. There are many paintings of her in NM. Also name of parish.

SANTA TERESA (Doña Ana). Span., "St. Therese." Spanish-American village adjoining Hatch. Also called PLACITAS.

SANTIAGO. Contraction of Santo Iago, the ancient Spanish rendering of St. James the Greater, who is believed to have established Christianity in Spain. "Santiago!" is the traditional battle cry of Spain, and because St. James is said to have appeared on horseback aiding the Spanish armies, he has been so represented in Spanish art. Although no major church was dedicated in his honor, many a small chapel was, and his image could be found everywhere. The feast of Santiago used to be celebrated in every village as a sort of traditional national holiday. Races and games on horseback were the chief nonreligious features. SANTIAGO (Mora).

SANTILLANOS. Probably from Span., family name Santillanes. The earliest members, Juan Simon de Santillan and his wife, were living in the Isleta district as early as 1744. SANTILLANOS (San Miguel). 3 mi W of San Geronimo. SANTILLANOS CREEK (San Miguel). Joins Falls Creek N of Santillanos.

SANTO DOMINGO (Sandoval). Span., "St. Dominic." Pre-Spanish Indian pueblo 4 mi N of US 85, near AT&SF RR, 29 mi SW of Santa Fe. Formerly called QUIQUI or QUIGUI. Tradition has it that Oñate contributed the name

because he arrived here on Sunday, Span., *domingo.* Whatever the circumstance, it is certain that the name of the mission church commemorates St. Dominic, thirteenth-century Spanish preacher and founder of the order of Friars Preacher, known as Dominicans. The old pueblo of Cundiyo also had him for a patron. Post office, 1960—. SANTO DOMINGO PUEBLO GRANT (Sandoval). Running from NW to SE, the grant extends about 10 mi on each side of the Rio Grande. Santo Domingo presented a Cruzate document granting lands to the pueblo on Sept. 20, 1689; but the pueblo also has a document signed by Governor Mendinueta on Sept. 10, 1770, presenting contiguous grants to Santo Domingo and to San Felipe pueblos. See PUEBLO LAND GRANTS.

SANTO NIÑO. Span., "Holy Child." Devotion to Christ in His infancy was common in the first century of NM history, and increased in later periods. The term Santo Niño has not survived as a place name where it was formerly used in Mora and San Miguel counties, although one of the twin villages of Rociada in San Miguel is still called by this name. El Santo Niño de Atocha, "the Holy Child of Atocha," is represented in medieval pilgrim attire, wearing a cape and wide-brimmed hat with cockleshell, and carrying a staff and a basket said to have supplied food to prisoners at Atocha in Spain. Chapels in Mora and San Miguel especially honored this religious figure. SANTO NIÑO (Santa Fe). Village between Riverside and Santa Cruz.

SANTO TOMAS. St. Thomas the Apostle was selected in 1754 as patron of the new settlement of Trampas, but the church built some years later was dedicated to St. Joseph. When Governor Tomas Velez Cachupin refounded the pueblo of Abiquiu, he designated his namesake as patron. SANTO TOMAS (Doña Ana). Settlement 10 mi S of Las Cruces. SANTO TOMAS (Rio Arriba). SANTO TOMAS DE ITURBIDE (Doña Ana). Span., "St. Thomas of Iturbide." Originally a Spanish-American village 8 mi S of Las Cruces. Named for a Mexican grant, Aug. 19, 1848. Now the headquarters for the Stahmann Farms. Possession of this grant seems to have been taken on Aug. 3, 1853, as authorized by Guadalupe Miranda, land grant official for the Republic of Mexico.

SANTO TORIBIO (Sandoval). St. Turibius was Archbishop of Lima in the sixteenth century.

The full name of the old village of VALLECITO, near Jemez, was SANTO TORIBIO DEL VALLECITO. See VALLECITOS.

SAN VINCENTE. Span., "St. Vincent." Name is probably a misspelling of San Vicente. There are well-known saints of this name: St. Vincent Martyr, killed by the Romans at Valencia in A.D. 303; St. Vincent Ferrer, a Dominican preacher, famous in Spain in the fourteenth century; and St. Vincent de Paul, a Frenchman known for his charitable works. The first two would be choices of the early Spanish clergy; the French priests in the second half of the nineteenth century would have chosen the third. SAN VINCENTE ARROYO (Grant, Luna). Heads just W of Silver City; runs SE into Mimbres River 1 mi below Spalding. SAN VINCENTE DE LA CIENAGA (Grant). See SILVER CITY.

SAN YSIDRO (Sandoval). Farming community on NM 44, 23 mi NW of Bernalillo. Settled in 1699 by Juan Trujillo and others. Named for St. Isidore the Farmer, who lived at Madrid in the eleventh century and who is represented with a plow and ox team, sometimes also with an angel who does the plowing while the saint is at prayer. San Ysidro is widely honored in NM during May, when his image is carried through the fields as a blessing for crops. Post office, 1874, intermittently, to present. SAN YSIDRO GRANT (Sandoval). Narrow area 2 mi wide running 6 mi E and 6 mi W of San Ysidro. Given by Governor de Anza to Antonio Armenta and Salvador Sandoval on May 4, 1786. In 1936 much of this grant was acquired by the Rural Resettlement Administration for the use of the Zia Indians.

SAPELLO. One of the most puzzling names in NM place history. There are several Spanish words which are said to account for the name, sapillo, "toad," sepelio, "burial, interment," among them. Ina Sizer Cassidy quotes a cleaning woman as calling a scrubbing brush el sapello, standard Span., cipello. Western Folklore, XII (October 1953), 286-89. But the accent in these words does not stress the final syllable. Fray Angelico Chavez, writing in New Mexico, 34 (October 1956), 5, says there was a French priest, Pierre l'Esperance, who in 1839 applied for land at a place and river called Shapellote. He quotes the historian Twitchell as believing the place was Sapello. This seems to be confirmed by a reference on Jan. 16, 1821, in the Las Vegas Grant to a N boundary on Chapellote River; 14 years later a conflicting grant in the same area refers to a N river boundary as the Sapello. Fr. Chavez suggests the word is of Plains Indian origin, since this was long their stamping ground. It resembles chapalote, the name of a Kiowa or French-Kiowa, who married in Taos. The word lasted as a surname for a couple of generations. A French priest at Las Vegas, in 1853, unmistakably referring to Sapello, wrote Chapellon. SAPELLO (San Miguel). Farming settlement 13 mi N of Las Vegas. Post office, 1874—. SAPELLO CREEK (Grant). Also spelled SAPILLO. 15 mi N of Silver City. SAPELLO CREEK (San Miguel). Tributary of the Mora from Las Tusas to Tecoloteños. SAPELLO RIVER (San Miguel). Rises in NW corner of county and flows E into Mora River.

SAPILLO CREEK (Grant). See SAPELLO.

SARDINE MOUNTAIN (Chaves). 13 mi S of Elkins

SATAN PASS (McKinley). S of Chaco Canyon National Monument on NM 56 between Crown Point and Thoreau.

SATEKON (San Juan). Corruption of Span., zacatón, a tall grass growing in clumps where the ground is moist. Post office, 1900-01; mail to Jewett.

SAUA CREEK (Colfax). Perhaps a corruption of Span., savia, "sap." Flows into Canadian Red River at Harding County line. Named for maple trees along its bank.

SAUZ (Mora). Span., "willow." Post office, 1904-05; changed to ABBOTT.

SAUZAL (Valencia). Span., "place of willows." Former Spanish settlement between Belen and Las Nutrias.

SAVOIA (McKinley). Shown in Valencia County (1884 map) at edge of Zuñi Reservation, 28 mi S of Ft. Wingate. Post office, 1882-87.

SAVOYA (Luna). In SE corner of county, 13 mi above Mexican border.

SAWMILL CANYON (Colfax). Heads in Gallo Mts.; runs NE into Largo Creek, 13 mi E of Agua Fria Mtn. SAWMILL CREEK (Colfax). There are two Sawmill Creeks in Colfax County. One in N end of Moreno Valley empties into Moreno River, which flows into Eagle Nest Lake. The other flows into Canadian Red River above town of Red River. Along both creeks there were early sawmills. SAWMILL CREEK (Grant). Joins Cienaga Creek, 3 mi E of Mule Creek settlement. SAWMILL PEAK (Sierra). In Black Range, 3 mi SW of Fluorine.

SAWTOOTH MOUNTAINS (Catron). 6 mi E of Tres Lagunas.

SAWYER (Cibola). Abandoned sawmill site of the American Lumber Co. N of Oso Ridge near the headwaters of Bluewater Creek, a little E of the Notches in Oso Ridge. SAWYER CREEK (San Miguel). Flows SE into Pecos River 1 mi N of Macho. Post office, 1909-16.

SCHIELE LAKE No. 1, 2, and 3 (Mora). Small lakes on mesa above Schiele Ranch headquarters N of Ocate.

SCHOLLE (Socorro, Torrance). Ranching community on US 60 and AT&SF RR, 32 mi SE of Belen. Founded in 1904 and named for Fred Scholle, one of the pioneer merchants of Belen. Post office, 1908, intermittently, to present.

SCHOMBERG (Colfax). On AT&SF RR, 5 mi N of Maxwell. Named for one of the managers of the Maxwell Land Grant.

SCHOOLHOUSE CANYON (Grant). Heads at Schoolhouse Mtn. and runs NW into Gila River 7 mi S of Cliff. SCHOOLHOUSE MOUNTAIN (Grant). 12 mi SE of Cliff.

SCHROEDER (Chaves). First postmaster, August Schroeder. Post office, 1908-13.

SCHUREE CREEK (Colfax). Tributary to the Ponil, NW of Cimarron.

SCOTT (Lea). 6 mi SE of Tatum. Named for C. C. Scott, early district attorney. Nothing remains of this settlement which consisted of stores, a post office, and a school. Post office, 1909-21.

SEAMA (Cibola). Laguna Indian village, 1 mi S of US 66 from Cubero. Site of a government Indian school and medical center. An early Spanish name for the area was CAÑADA DE LA CRUZ. The valley met the Rio San Jose, forming a cross, and the Spaniards noted this and designated the village, in translation, "ravine of the cross." Present name is Keres-Laguna word meaning "door," i.e., "gateway, passageway." Because of the contour of the land enclosing a wide valley, the site of Seama offers a natural gateway. Post office, 1905-32.

SEBADILLA CREEK (San Miguel). 11 mi E of Pecos.

SEBASTIAN DE VARGAS GRANT (Santa Fe). Begins 1 mi S of Santa Fe and runs for 7 mi on each side of US 285. Made as early as 1728 by authority of the King of Spain.

SEBASTIAN MARTIN GRANT (Rio Arriba). Lies E of the Rio Grande between Alcalde and Velarde. Owner of this large estate was Sebastian Martin Serrano, who was 22 years old in

1696. He became a captain in 1708 and earned fame as an Indian fighter. In 1714, he was alcalde of Santa Cruz. A number of land transfers are recorded to him in the Santa Fe region between 1710 and 1751. This particular grant was made by the Spanish crown on May 23, 1712.

SEBOLLA (Rio Arriba). Post office, 1907-10; changed to CEBOLLA.

SEBOYETA (Cibola). The name is believed to be a corruption of Span., cebolleta, "a place prolific with onions," and transferred to the village from the name of the mountains directly N. Today a trading point on NM 279, 12 mi N of Laguna, the community was established as a military outpost about 1804-08 by the heads of thirty families from the Rio Grande Valley. From its founding, this town was preyed upon by the Navajos, and a 10-ft wall was built around it for protection, having a narrow gate for entrance, closed by 2-ft-thick planks. At one time more than five thousand Indians besieged the place, and there are many stories about the bravery of these early pioneer men and women. Post office, 1885—.

SECO CREEK (Sierra). Span., "dry." Rises in county and flows E to the Rio Grande. SECO RIVER (Rio Arriba). Rises in county and flows S to Chama River.

SEDAN (Union). Farming community on NM 102, 24 mi S of Clayton, 5 mi W of Texas line. Named by Ames B. Christerson, who located on a homestead here and was its first postmaster, in memory of Sedan, Kans., his home town. Post office, 1910—.

SEDILLO (Bernalillo). Trading point on US 66, 23 mi E of Albuquerque. Pedro de Cedillo is the earliest member of the family for whom the locality is named, and he is described as a native of Queretaro who arrived in NM before the Pueblo Rebellion of 1680. At that time he was a captain living in the Rio Abajo district. His descendants are known after the Reconquest of 1692, when the Spanish returned from northern Mexico. SEDILLO HILL (Bernalillo). E of Albuquerque, in Tijeras Canyon.

SEELY CANYON (Colfax). Begins near Gardiner in Dillon Canyon and extends W.

SEGAL CREEK (Colfax). 10 mi SE of Maxwell.

SELDEN (Doña Ana). Post office, 1911-13; changed to FT. SELDEN.

SENA (San Miguel). Farming community W of NM 3, 23 mi SW of Las Vegas. Named for the Sena family, the earliest member of whom was Bernardino de Sena. He came to NM in 1693 with his foster parents. He was then only nine years of age. In 1708 he was living at Pojoaque, and from the time of his marriage until his death he lived in Santa Fe, where Sena Plaza still records his memory. Post office, 1895—.

SENECA (Union). May be Anglicized form of Span., *cienaga,* "swamp." Once a heavily populated farming community on NM 18, 14 mi NE of Clayton. After the "dust bowl" of the 1930's, much of the land was retired or leased by the U.S. Forest Service to ranchers. Post office, 1908—. SENECA CREEK (Union). Known to the early freighters over the Santa Fe Trail by the Spanish name CIENAGUILLA DEL BURRO, "jackass swamp." Heads E of Sierra Grande Mts., crossing county from W to E. As Union County was settled by homesteaders from the East, the name was shortened to Seneca. It is possible, of course, that identification occurred with the names of other places, such as the Senecas in Kansas, New York, and other states. See RABBIT EAR CREEK.

SENECU (Socorro). Abandoned Piro pueblo and Franciscan mission on W bank of the Rio Grande 10 mi S of Socorro, at site of present village of San Antonio. Named in 1629 by Fray Antonio de Arteaga and Fray Garcia de San Francisco, its founders.

SENODAN CREEK (Colfax). In S end of Moreno Valley, flowing into Cienaguilla Creek, which flows into Eagle Nest Lake. Senodan was a family name in the district.

SEÑORITO (Sandoval). Span., "young gentleman, little master of the house." Former trading point on NM 126, 4 mi SE of Cuba. Established as a mining camp in 1893. Post office, 1901-24. SEÑORITO CANYON (Rio Arriba).

SENTINEL BUTTE (Hidalgo). W of Alamo Hueco Mts., 9 mi N of Mexico border.

SEPAR (Grant). The story has grown that there was a construction camp here called CAMP SEPARATION on US 70 and 80. Now a station on SP RR, about 20 mi SE of Lordsburg in S extension of county. One story of the name is in Owen Wister's *Red Men and White* (1895), where the author writes that the name was chosen because the construction camp was the point where railroad-building crews from the East met those from the West. The facts are that the station here was called SEPAS not SEPAR, possibly from Span., *cepas,* "tree

stump, shoots from base of tree." Post office, 1882—.

SERAFINA (San Miguel). Farming community 17 mi SW of Las Vegas. The word is a feminine given name, taken from Span., *serafín,* the highest order of angels. Post office, 1923—.

SERNA (San Miguel). SERNA's (Valencia). Location of a one-room schoolhouse, originally for the children of Rancher Serna and his neighbors, in Zuñi Mts. near Atarque.

SERPENT LAKE (Taos). 8 mi W of Holman.

SERVILLETA (Taos). Span., "napkin, flat plain." Farming and ranching community on US 285 and old D&RGW RR, 21 mi NW of Taos. Name first applied to SERVILLETA PLAZA in Rio Arriba, an old Spanish settlement on the Rio Tusas, 2 mi from Taos County line. When the railroad was built, 1880-85, the name was transferred to the railroad siding, where the village grew. One of the commemorative titles of the Virgin Mary is La Madona de la Servilleta suggested by the painting of Murillo. Post office, 1913-49.

SETON VILLAGE (Santa Fe). Small settlement off US 84 and 85, 10 mi SE of Santa Fe. Named for Ernest Thompson Seton, author of stories dealing with nature and animal life, who made his permanent home here from 1930 until his death in 1946. He established his Woodcraft League of America and his School of Indian Wisdom here. His library and collections remain in the care of his wife.

SEVEN BROTHERS MOUNTAIN (Sierra). 4 mi SW of Kingston. SEVEN CITIES OF CIBOLA. See ZUÑI INDIAN PUEBLO. SEVEN LAKES (McKinley). Small settlement on NM 56, 43 mi NE of Gallup. There used to be seven lakes, named by the old-timers SIETE LAGUNAS. At present, there is only one small lake, which is usually dry. SEVEN RIVERS, NORTH (Chaves, Eddy). Rises in Chaves County and flows E to Lake McMillan. SEVEN RIVERS, MIDDLE (Eddy). Rises in Chaves County and flows E to North Seven Rivers. SEVEN RIVERS, SOUTH (Eddy). Rises in Eddy County and flows E to Middle Seven Rivers. SEVEN RIVERS (Eddy). Former town named for the seven branches of the stream which flows into Lake McMillan on the Pecos River at this point. The first settlers came in 1867, drove out the Indians, and called the place DOGTOWN, because of the great number of prairie dogs here. Dick Reed set up a trading post in the fall of this year. In 1878 the site was named Seven Rivers. In the 1880's the town was moved farther N and called HENPECK; later, still farther N and called WHITE CITY. The move was caused by water shortage on account of the drilling of artesian wells. Post office, 1877-95; mail to McMillan. SEVEN RIVERS HILLS (Eddy). 10 mi NW of Carlsbad. SEVEN SPRINGS (Sandoval). In Jemez Mts. 17 mi SE of Lagunitas, and 4 mi W of San Antonio Mts. SEVEN SPRINGS ICE POND (Sandoval). Small pond formed by a dam at Seven Springs fish hatchery in Jemez Mts. SEVEN TROUGHS SPRING (Catron). 16 mi NE of Luna, and 7 mi SW of Fox Mtn.

SEVENTY-FOUR DRAW (Sierra). Joins Turkey Run to flow W into Hoyt Creek and Gila River. Named for a brand in use before brands were registered. Not derived from Seventy-Four Mtn. SEVENTY-FOUR MOUNTAIN (Grant). In Diablo Range. 2 mi S of Catron County line, 15 mi N of Cliff. According to the U.S. Forest Service, the name is derived from a brand used by a rancher in the area.

SEVILLETA GRANT (Socorro). Very large grant spanning the Rio Grande from San Acacia to Sabinal, and from Los Pinos Mts. to the Ladrones. Made by Governor Melgares to sixty-seven petitioners, May 29, 1819. A Piro pueblo, about 20 mi N of Socorro, was named SEVILLETA by Oñate in June 1598 because of the resemblance of the location to that of Seville, Spain.

SHADYBROOK (Taos). Trading point on US 64, 10 mi E of Taos, on the Rio Don Fernando in Taos Canyon. Named for the large cottonwoods growing here.

SHAGGY PEAK (Santa Fe). 6 mi SE of Santa Fe near Glorieta.

SHAKESPEARE (Hidalgo). Ghost town at N tip of Pyramid Mts., 2 mi S of Lordsburg. In the 1850's a watering spot here was known as MEXICAN SPRINGS. A station was established in 1858 on the alternate route of the original Butterfield Overland Mail. In 1867, the National Mail and Transportation Co. placed a stage stop here naming the locality GRANT, in honor of General U. S. Grant. After a prospector in 1870 interested William C. Ralston, a San Francisco banker, in ore he found in the Pyramid Mts., the name was changed to RALSTON. In 1872, two miners, Philip Arnold and John Slack, reported that they had found diamonds at Lee's Peak. They produced specimens which were exploited into the great diamond hoax, like that in Wyoming at the same period. When the diamonds were discovered to have been salted, the community was ready for another name change, and encouraged by Col. John Boyle, who established the Shakespeare Mining Co., they changed the name of the town to Shakespeare. Col. Boyle built the Stratford Hotel. When the ore deposits failed and SP RR bypassed the town, trade and people shifted to Lordsburg on the railroad line. Post office, 1879-85.

SHAKESPEARE (Socorro). 6 mi SE of Magdalena, 11 mi NW of Socorro.

SHALAM (Doña Ana). Religious colony founded in 1885 by Dr. John B. Newbrough of New York City, 8 mi N of Las Cruces. Name taken from the cult's religious book "Oahspe." Some nine hundred acres were purchased by the Faithists, but after the death of their leader in 1891 the property was abandoned or otherwise disposed of. The locality is still known by that name.

SHAMROCK (Otero). Post office, 1910-16. See VALMONT.

SHANDON (Sierra). Post office, 1904-06; mail to Garfield.

SHEEP CANYON (Catron). Runs E from the Continental Divide, 1 mi N of Sierra County line. SHEEP SPRING CREEK (Colfax). In Raton Mts.; flows into Canadian Red River. SHEEP SPRINGS (McKinley). SHEEP SPRINGS (San Juan). Trading point on US 666, 40 mi S of Shiprock.

SHELLY PEAK (Grant). In Diablo Range, N part of county.

SHEPHERD's CANYON (Grant). See CITY OF ROCKS.

SHERIDAN OJITA (San Miguel). Near NM 3, 2 mi S of Romeroville.

SHERMAN (Grant). Farming, ranching, and mining community on NM 61, 12 mi SE of Bayard, and 16 mi SE of Santa Rita. Post office, 1894-98; 1902—. SHERMAN (San Juan).

SHIELD LAKE (Lincoln). 28 mi E of White Oaks.

SHILLINGSBURG (McKinley). 7 mi NW of Crownpoint, W of NM 56.

SHILOH DRAW (Otero). In southern Otero Mts., 14 mi from Texas line.

SHIPROCK (San Juan). Ranching and farming community on US 84 and 666, 30 mi W of Farmington. Called NEEDLES before 1848, and established in 1903 by the U.S. as a northern Navajo Indian agency. The name comes from a majestic rock called by the Navajos *tse bida' hi*, "rock with wings." Three folk myths are associated with this natural phenomenon: one that the Navajos crossed a narrow sea beyond the setting sun and landed among an unfriendly people which caused the Great Spirit to send a stone ship to carry them to this spot; another is that they were brought by a great bird which was turned into stone when the mission was finished; the third is that the Navajos were cast up from the earth at this spot and the ship is a symbol of their voyage. All these stories may be modern, since there is no mention of any of them in *An Ethnologic Dictionary of the Navajo Language* (1910) or in Mary Wheelwright's *Navajo Creation Myth* (1942). Post office, 1904—. SHIPROCK HILL (Union). On S side of US 64, 13 mi W of Oklahoma line. The hill is of dark red sandstone formation, having a strong resemblance, when seen from the W side, to the prow of a ship. It rises to about 350 ft.

SHOEMAKER (Mora). Ranching and farming community 3 mi S of US 85, 19 mi SW of Wagon Mound. Named for Capt. W. R. Shoemaker, Civil War ordnance officer at Ft. Union near Las Vegas. He was esteemed and respected by the civilian population as well as by the military. Post office, 1882-1957. SHOEMAKER CANYON, E of Ft. Union Military Reserve, also bears his name.

SIA (Sandoval). Post office, 1906-08; mail to Jemes. See ZIA.

SIBLEY (San Miguel). Post office, 1903-09; mail to Las Vegas.

SIDE PRONG (Sierra). Small stream entering Holden Prong, 8 mi NW of Kingston. In southern Appalachians and farther S and W, "prong" means a branch of a stream or inlet.

SIEGA (Curry). On AT&SF RR, 4 mi E of Clovis.

SIENEGA. See CIENEGA.

SIERRA. Span., "saw." Presumably named for the Sierra de los Caballos Range. In Spain the word applies to high, sawtooth mountains and it was appropriately transferred to the Southwestern ranges by the Spanish colonists. The term has been adopted into the English language. It is also a family name. Nicolas de la Sierra, a native of Spain, lived at Guadalupe del Paso in the middle of the eighteenth century, and moved to Santa Fe around 1766. Members of his family could be found in the N region of El Paso. SIERRA BLANCA MOUNTAIN (Otero). Span., "white ridge." 7 mi NW of Ruidoso and 1 mi S of Lincoln County line. So named because it is snow-capped for a large part of the year. Elevation 12,003 ft; southernmost point in U.S. on which Arctic life zone con-

ditions exist. Also known as OLD BALDY. SIERRA BLANCA RIDGE (Rio Arriba). Snow-covered most of the year. SIERRA CITY (Sierra). See LAKE VALLEY. SIERRA COLORADO (Valencia). "Red." SIERRA COUNTY. Created by Territorial Legislature on Apr. 3, 1884. Presumably named for the mountain range within its limits. Area is 3,118 sq mi. SIERRA DE CENIZAS (Otero-Eddy). "Ashes." See GUADALUPE MOUNTAINS. SIERRA DE LAS UVAS (Doña Ana). "Grapes." S of Hatch. Probably named for wild grapes that grow in the canyons. SIERRA DE LA VENTANA (Socorro). "Window." Near Los Ladrones Mts. Named for the shape of a window seen in one of its walls. SIERRA DEL CRISTO REY (Doña Ana). "Christ the King." Formerly known as EL CERRO DE LOS MULEROS. In southernmost tip of NM just outside El Paso, Tex. On it stands a 45-ft statue of Christ. SIERRA DEL ORO (Santa Fe). "Gold." Peak in Ortiz Mts. Named because of a gold strike in 1833. SIERRA DE LOS CABALLOS (Sierra). See CABALLO MOUNTAINS. SIERRA DEL SACRAMENTO (Otero). See SACRAMENTO MOUNTAINS. SIERRA DE SAN LAZARO (Santa Fe). See ORTIZ MOUNTAINS. SIERRA DE SAN MATEO (Valencia). See SAN MATEO MOUNTAINS. SIERRA DIABLO (Sierra). "Devil." SIERRA GRANDE MOUNTAIN (Union). On US 85, in NW part of county. A symmetrical basaltic cone more than 40 mi around the base and said to be the largest individual mountain in North America. SIERRA LA ESCOBA (Valencia). See BROOM MOUNTAIN. SIERRA MONTOSA (Socorro). "Rugged." SIERRA MOSCA (Santa Fe). "Fly." SIERRA MUJER (Valencia). "Woman." Near SIERRA MUJER PEAK. Site of a school built by the WPA for children of scattered homesteads nearby. SIERRA NACIMIENTO (Rio Arriba, Sandoval). "Birth of Christ." In north-central part of county, extending N into Rio Arriba. See NACIMIENTO. SIERRA NEGRA (Harding). "Black." On W bank of Ute Creek in central part of county. SIERRA OSCURA (Socorro). "Dark." So named because the undergrowth and lava make them look dark. A part of this range is in SW corner of Lincoln County, and the rest, in Socorro County, has some copper mines. SIERRA RICA (Hidalgo). "Rich." Name of a settlement and a mountain. SIERRA SOMBRERO (Sierra). "Mexican hat." Isolated peak near Lake Valley. Named because of its conical shape. SIERRITA (San Miguel). "Little mountain."

Siete Lagunas (McKinley). See Seven Lakes.

Signal Peak (Luna). 18 mi N of Deming. Also called Cooke's Peak. Used in Indian days as a signal hill by Lt. Col. Philip St. George Cooke, leader of the Mormon Battalion in 1846-47. Captain Cooke established a second signal station at Soldier's Farewell Hill. For another mountain used as a signal peak see Tucumcari.

Sile (Sandoval). Settlement on W bank of the Rio Grande, 4 mi S of Cochiti.

Silio (Torrance). Span., "silo." On AT&SF RR, 6 mi E of Willard. Although the round, towerlike silo is uncommon on the big range pastures, a trench silo, dug with or without board side walls, serves the same purpose and probably is the type of silo referred to in this place name.

Silman Lake (Chaves). 16 mi S of Elkins.

Silver City (Grant). On US 260 and AT&SF RR. The Spanish name was San Vicente de la Cienaga when settlement was founded about 1870. A few years later, Anglos changed the name to Silver City because of the mine boom. In 1874, it became the seat of Grant County, formerly a part of Doña Ana County. The settlement was incorporated in 1876. Before the railroad was built in 1881, twelve- and fourteen-horse teams hauled ore and bullion into the city, and bricks of gold and silver were stacked on sidewalks outside shipping offices. Silver City is a major center of the ranching industry and the site of New Mexico State Teachers College. Post office, 1871—.

Silver Creek (Catron, Socorro). Flows E to join Alamosa River S of Ojo Caliente. Silver Hill District (Otero). See Jarilla Mountains. Silver Ledge (Grant). Midway between Mimbres and Santa Rita rivers E of Santa Rita. So called because the Indians claimed they made bullets out of the metal found on this hill, where there was pure silver. Silver Spring Canyon (Otero). Small stream NE of Cloudcroft.

Simmons (Guadalupe). On SP RR, 30 mi NE of Santa Rosa.

Simpson (San Juan). 6 mi W of NM 44; 17 mi S of Bloomfield. Simpson Creek (San Juan). Settlement 12 mi S of Farmington near Gallegos Canyon. Named in honor of J. H. Simpson. The Navajo name is *besh lichee begez*, "streams coming together."

Sim Yaten Canyon (Socorro). In S corner of county E of NM 52 and N of now abandoned Warm Springs Apache Indian Reservation.

Sim Yaten Hills (Socorro). 8 mi NE of Dusty.

Sink Holes (Guadalupe, De Baca, Lincoln, Chaves). Thousands of water holes, some of which are as deep as 80 ft, lie within the Vaughn, Santa Rosa, Roswell area. They are formed by moisture erosion of rock layers called the Permian "Red Beds."

Sipapu Winter Sports Area (Taos). Skiing, skating, and toboggan slopes 27 mi S of Taos. The word has been used from ancient times by Pueblo Indians to identify a hole in the firepit of their council chambers. The sipapu is associated with the Creation Myth of the emergence from the earth wombs or Underworld.

Site of Coronado's Bridge (Guadalupe). On Pecos River NE of Anton Chico. Coronado is supposed to have crossed the river here in 1541.

Sitio de Juana Lopez Grant (Santa Fe). Tract beginning about 16 mi SW of Santa Fe and extending into Ortiz Mine Grant below Madrid. No record is known to exist of the original grant, but on Dec. 30, 1762, Don Bartolome Fernandez, a resident of Santa Fe, sold and conveyed said land to Joseph de Alire, as appears by his deed made before the *alcalde mayor* of Santa Fe.

Sitio de los Cerrillos Grant (Santa Fe). Small tract on NM 85, 11 mi SW of Santa Fe, 7 mi N of Cerrillos. Original grantees were Cleto de Miera and Pedro Bautista Pino, who took possession on Feb. 11, 1788.

Sitio de San Ysidro de Pajarito Grant (Bernalillo). See Pajarito Grant.

Sitting Bull Falls (Eddy). 25 mi SW of Carlsbad, in arid country. One bright, moonlit night in 1881, a small group of Indians led by old Chief Sitting Bull stole about thirty-five head of cattle and nine horses from Seven Rivers. The next morning Jim, John, and Bill Jones, Pete Corn, Marion Turner, Mart Fanning, Joe Woods, and Charlie Slaughter pursued them. They overtook the Indians at the ridge where the Bill Jones ranch is now and found them eating one of the saddle horses. The cowboys attacked the Indians and recovered some of the horses. For two days they trailed the Indians. They followed a stream, and when they came to the falls they named them after the chief of the Indians who had been the cause of their discovery. See Last Chance Canyon. Sitting Bull Falls Canyon (Eddy). Heads N of

Queen, runs NE into Wilson Canyon. Named for the falls in the canyon.

SIXELA (Union). Switch point on C&S RR, 9 mi SE of Clayton at US 87 near Texas line. At this point tracks become Denver and Fort Worth Railway. Named in 1886.

SIX MILE CANYON (Socorro). About this distance SW of Socorro. SIX MILE CREEK (Colfax). Flows E from the Taos Peak region into Eagle Nest Lake, in Moreno Valley. SIX MILE HILL (Chaves). 6 mi W of Roswell; this ridge is crossed by US 380 and 70. Called OLD MAN HILL in the 1860's by Robert Casey. The original road to Picacho and W passed just S of this knob. SIX MILE SPRING (Chaves). W of Olive. SIX SHOOTER SIDING (Quay). See TUCUMCARI. Also see NUMBERS.

SKARDA (Taos). 37 mi NW of Taos, on Rio Arriba County line. Named for a rancher. Post office, 1922-42.

SKATES CANYON (Grant). Heads on the Continental Divide; runs N into Sapillo Creek, 7 mi NW of Mimbres.

SKELETON CANYON (Hidalgo). At Arizona line, 10 mi NW of Cloverdale.

SKINNED ASS CANYON (Catron). Narrow canyon near Reserve. Named by the cowboys because it was such a tight fit for burro pack trains passing through.

SKULL CANYON (Hidalgo). On Arizona line 20 mi NW of Cloverdale.

SLAGLE (Colfax). First postmaster, Florence B. Slagle. Post office, 1901-02; mail to Chico. SLAGLE CANYON (Colfax). 5 mi W of Chico post office.

SLATTON (Lea). See PITCHFORK.

SLAUGHTER CREEK (Eddy). Near Texas line; flows SE into Grapevine Creek, then into Black River, and finally into Pecos River. SLAUGHTER MESA (Catron). N of Twin Springs and SE of Tule Lake.

SLEEPING UTE MOUNTAIN (San Juan). Shrine of Ute Indians, NW of Farmington, and a part of the Ute Range. It somewhat resembles a huge giant who has lain down to rest for eternity.

SMITH. The Smith place names do not quite equal the Baca or Chavez names on the topography of NM, because the Smiths came later and names, generally speaking, have age in the locality on their side. SMITH (Eddy). Post office, 1928-41; changed to LOCO HILLS. SMITH (San Juan). E of Amarilla Canyon, 8 mi S of Farmington. SMITHS (McKinley). SMITH (Union). Post office, 1914-18. SMITH'S LAKE

(McKinley). On NM 56, 15 mi NE of Thoreau, and 40 mi E of Gallup. Also called SMITH LAKE.

SMOOTHING IRON MESA (Catron). 8 mi SW of Alma.

SNOW CREEK (Grant). Small tributary to Middle Fork of Gila River, SE of the Negrito ranger station.

SOCORRO (Socorro). Span., "help, aid." County seat and trading center 72 mi S of Albuquerque, on US 60, 85, and AT&SF RR. Name was given by Juan de Oñate on June 14, 1598, to the Piro Indian pueblo of Teypana, N of present city of Socorro, because, as he said, the Indians "gave us much corn." A mission church was built before 1628 by Fray Garcia de Zuñiga at another Indian settlement nearby and called NUESTRA SEÑORA DE SOCORRO DE PILABO, commemorating the help given to Oñate. At the time of the Pueblo Rebellion of 1680, most of the six hundred inhabitants of the pueblo followed Governor Otermín to Guadalupe del Paso, building a new village designated as SOCORRO DEL SUR, "Socorro of the South." De Vargas in 1692 reports stopping at the ruins of the NM mission, Nuestra Señora de Socorro. Appears on L'Atlas Curieux (1700) as Socora. It was not until 1815 or 1816 that the ancestors of the present families affirmed their claim to a grant from the Spanish crown and settled in Socorro. Between 1867 and 1890, Socorro was the center of one of the richest mining areas in the country. Post office, 1851—. SOCORRO COUNTY. Created by the Republic of Mexico in 1844, but designated by the Territorial Legislature in July 1850; name taken from the original place name. Area is 6,634.4 sq mi, making it third largest county in the state. SOCORRO GRANT (Socorro). Tract about 6 mi square surrounding the city. The town was entitled under the laws of Spain and Mexico to four square leagues of land in a square body measuring one square league from the corners of the Roman Catholic Church. On or about 1815-16, a grant was made by the Governor and Captain General of New Mexico to settlers of the colony of San Miguel del Socorro for a body of land embraced on N by bank of San Lorenzo Arroyo, on E by the summit of Oscuro Mts., on S by Bosque del Apache meadow, and on W by the summit of Magdalena Mts. SOCORRO MINES (Socorro). Post office, 1875-78; changed to MAGDALENA MINES.

SODA DAM (Sandoval). On NM 4, 20 mi N of San Ysidro. A natural dam which extends from the canyon floor and leaves a huge curtain of sodium deposit hanging over the edge of the rock.

SOFIA (Union). Former trading point on NM 120, 36 W of Clayton and 10 mi E of Colfax County line. Once a large bean-growing district, homesteaded by immigrants chiefly from Bulgaria and Hungary. Now all ranching country. Post office, 1914-26.

SOHAM (San Miguel). Farming community on US 84 and 85, 24 mi SW of Las Vegas, and 1 mi N of Sands. Post office, 1917—.

SOLANO (Harding). Community on NM 39 and SP RR, 10 mi SE of Roy. May have been named for St. Francis Solano, a Spanish Franciscan, who evangelized Peru and other parts of South America. Also a surname for the family of Antonio Solano y Castro, who was married in Santa Fe on May 20, 1763. Another man named Solano is named in Santa Fe records in 1790. Post office, 1907—.

SOLDIER CREEK (Grant). Very small W tributary of Cow Creek coming in above the Martin Ranch and heading at SOLDIER CREEK PARK.

SOLDIER HILL (Lea). 5 mi S of Caprock.

SOLDIER'S FAREWELL HILL (Grant). In south-central part of county W of Deming. One of three signal stations used in the early days. Flares were used by night and mirrors by day. Water was carried to this station from a spring at the foot of the hill. A group of seven soldiers signaled that they were ambushed by Indians and, when no aid came, their farewell message to Cook's Peak was that they were going down the hill to combat the Indians because of their intense suffering from thirst. All were killed; that is one story about how it got its name. Another explanation is that an Eastern soldier in the detachment, who was engaged to a girl at home, became despondent because he could not see her more often, and therefore shot himself. A third account is that soldier escorts from Ft. Cummings left the west-going caravans, and returned to the fort, but Ft. Cummings may have been established later than the naming of the peak.

SOLEDAD CANYON (Doña Ana). Span., "solitude." Runs E from Organ Mts., 12 mi E of Las Cruces. Name may be descriptive of loneliness or it may commemorate Nuestra Señora de la Soledad, "Our Lady of Solitude," a title for the Virgin Mary which resulted after a widowed duchess in Spain dressed a statue of Mary in her own widow's weeds. An early name seems to have been SOLDADO CANYON, "soldier," but this may have resulted from a confusion with *soledad*.

SOLITARIO PEAK (San Miguel). Span., "solitary." In Santa Fe National Forest, 3 mi N of El Porvenir.

SOMBRILLO (Santa Fe). Span., "shady." Trading point on US 64 and 285, 3 mi SE of Española.

SOMBRIO (Guadalupe). 28 mi W of Santa Rosa, 6 mi from Pintada. Post office, June-Aug., 1936; mail to Pintada.

SOUTH BERRENDA CREEK (Chaves). 2 mi N of Roswell.

SOUTH CHAVES (McKinley). On AT&SF RR, 5 mi E of Thoreau.

SOUTH CHISUM CAMP (Eddy). See ARTESIA.

SOUTHERN UTE CREEK (San Juan). Flows into La Plata River which empties into the San Juan. Named for Southern Ute Indian Reservation across Colorado line.

SOUTH FORK (Lincoln). Post office, 1875-87; changed to MESCALERO.

SOUTH GARCIA (Valencia). See GARCIA.

SOUTH LATIR LAKE (Taos). Mountain lake at head of South Latir Creek on SW side of Latir Peaks. See LATIR LAKES.

SOUTH MOUNTAIN (Santa Fe). 2 mi S of San Pedro, at Bernalillo County line.

SOUTH PONIL (Colfax). Little stream SW of Cimarron. See PONIL CREEK.

SOUTH PYRAMID PEAK (Hidalgo). In S end of Pyramid Mts.

SOUTH SAN YSIDRO (San Miguel). On Pecos River, 1½ mi NW of Ilfeld.

SOUTHSIDE (Colfax). Post office, 1878-79.

SOUTH SPRING (Chaves). On AT&SF RR, 5 mi SE of Roswell. Post office, 1899-1900.

SOUTH SPRING RIVER (Chaves). Head of this river was a pond fed by springs ½ mi W of AT&SF RR at South Spring Siding. In late 1860's river known as DUTCH SPRING, because a German named Eisenstein lived here. Now only a shallow trickle of water which reaches Hondo River a few yards above the point where it empties into the Pecos at Pecos bridge on US 380. Loss of water has been caused by drilling of artesian wells, lowering the water table.

SOUTH SPRING SIDING (Chaves). Formerly called SOUTH SPRING STATION; a few miles SE of Roswell on AT&SF RR.

SPARKS CANYON (San Miguel). Extreme N fork of Maestas Canyon W of Rociada. SPARKS CREEK (Mora, San Miguel). Joins Manuelitas Creek at Lower Rociada.

SPAULDING (Luna). Siding and section of track 20 mi NW of Deming on AT&SF RR. Named for Spaulding, the sport promoter, who had holdings near here. Name is misspelled, SPALDING, on most maps.

SPIESS (Santa Fe). On AT&SF RR, 2 mi SW of Lamy. Named for Charles A. Spiess of Las Vegas, an attorney for the railroad who also was a member of the New Mexico Constitutional Convention.

SPINDLE (Lincoln). Farming and stock-raising community on NM 48, 22 mi NE of Capitan, on N side of Capitan Mts. Several families named Spindle lived here. Post office, 1917-20.

SPIRIT LAKE (Santa Fe). Shallow lake at head of Holy Ghost Creek, 3 mi W of Cowles.

SPRING ARROYO (Colfax). Small stream that flows into Canadian Red River. SPRING CANYON (Colfax). Extends NW from Vermejo Peak. SPRING CREEK (Colfax). Flows through Spring Canyon, 3 mi E of Dawson and empties into Vermejo River. SPRING CREEK (Rio Arriba). Flows into the Rio Nutrias 3 mi W of Nutrias. SPRING CREEK (Rio Arriba). Flows into the Rio Tusas, 2 mi S of Tusas. SPRING HILL (Union). Post office, 1890-99; mail to Folsom.

SPRINGER (Colfax). Town on US 85, NM 58 and 199, 41 mi S of Raton on Cimarron River. Settled in 1879 and became the third county seat in 1882, before the voters approved Raton in 1897. Two brothers named Springer gave their name to the town: Charles, a rancher near Cimarron, and Frank, a lawyer and official of the Maxwell Land Grant Co. Post office, 1879—. SPRINGER LAKE (Colfax). 3 mi NW of Springer.

SPUR LAKE (Catron). Ranching community 20 mi S of US 60 and 18 mi N of Luna, in a remote region in the foothills of Gallo Mts. Named for Spur Ranch and the lake nearby. SPUR LAKE (Catron). Artificial lake 9 mi NE of Luna. Named for its shape, which resembles a spur on a riding boot. Later destroyed when cattle bogged down in the mud. Post office, 1922-58. SPUR LAKE BASIN (Catron).

SQUARE LAKE (Eddy). 9 mi W of Maljamar.

SQUAW CREEK (Grant). Enters Black Creek 5 mi E of Gila Hot Springs. SQUAW CREEK (Sierra, Catron). Flows from NW corner of Sierra County into Corduroy Canyon. SQUAW PEAK (Colfax). See KIT CARSON PEAK.

STAGE CANYON (Colfax). Begins 5 mi N of Dawson and runs W from Vermejo River Canyon.

STANDING ROCK (McKinley). Settlement 36 mi NE of Gallup and 16 mi NW of Crownpoint. Named for Standing Rock Wash. STANDING ROCK WASH (McKinley, San Juan). Runs N and S just W of Crownpoint. Named for a large, red rock formation.

STANLEY (Santa Fe). Farming and ranching community on NM 41, 42 mi S of Santa Fe, and 12 mi N of Moriarty. Named for an early-day cattleman. Settlement began in 1902.

STANOLIND (San Juan). Formerly an oil community 10 mi SE of Shiprock and 20 mi W of Farmington, on a spur from a secondary road. Named for the Stanolind Co., a wholly owned subsidiary of the Standard Oil Co. of Indiana; name is a blend of first syllables of parent company.

STAR (Guadalupe). Post office, 1909-10; mail to Taft. STAR LAKE (Taos). Small lake high in Taos Mts., 5 mi SE of Twining. STAR LAKE TRADING POST (McKinley). See ESTRELLA. STAR WELLS (Lea).

STARKWEATHER CANYON (Catron). Heads in San Francisco Mts.; runs SE into San Francisco River to Reserve.

STARVATION PEAK (San Miguel). Near Bernal, 15 mi SW of Las Vegas, on old Santa Fe Trail. Said to have been named for a party of a hundred and twenty Spanish colonists who took refuge here from an Indian attack. Men, women, and children were held until they all starved to death. A large Penitente cross now surmounts its summit, accompanied by a beacon light.

STATE COLLEGE (Doña Ana). Post office, Agricultural College, 1912-59. See UNIVERSITY PARK.

STAUNTON (Union). Passing track on US 87 and C&S RR, 4 mi NW of Grenville. Post office, 1914-18.

STEAD (Union). Trading point, farming, and ranching community on NM 18 and Major Long's Creek; 25 mi S of Clayton. Named for father of L. R. (Rock) Stead of Clayton. Post office, 1916—.

STEAMBOAT CANYON (Grant). Near Silver City. Named for a rock formation which resembles a steamboat. STEAMBOAT MOUNTAIN (Union). S of NM 325, E of Folsom. Layers of sandstone resemble a gigantic ship left stranded and immobile endless years ago.

STEEPLEROCK (Grant). Community 5 mi N of Hidalgo County line, and 3 mi E of Arizona line. STEEPLE ROCK PEAK (Grant). In W part of county, 4 mi S of Steeple Rock. Named because it resembles a large steeple.

STEGMAN (Eddy). First postmaster, Sallie L. Stegman. Post office, 1899-1903; changed to Artesia. See ARTESIA.

STEINS (Hidalgo). Former trading point on NM 14 and SP RR, 19 mi SW of Lordsburg. Named for Steins Pass. Founded in 1880 with the building of the railroad. New highway bypasses Steins. Post office, 1905-44. STEINS MOUNTAIN (Hidalgo). Peak 2 mi NW of Steins. STEINS PASS (Hidalgo). One of three mountain gaps which formed portions of the route of the old Butterfield Overland Mail and of early emigrant trails to southern California. Named for Captain Steins, who lost his life defending DOUBTFUL CANYON. Post office, 1888-1905; changed to STEINS. STEINS PEAK RANGE (Hidalgo). Along west-central border of county.

STERN POST OFFICE (Colfax). 10 mi NW of Cimarron on Ponil Creek in Maxwell Land Grant. Named for an early settler.

STEVENS (Catron). Former trading point on US 260, 8 mi SW of Reserve. STEVENS CREEK (Otero). 13 mi S of Sacramento. STEVENS LAKE (Otero). 14 mi S of Sacramento. STEVENS SAWMILL PLAZA (Catron). These places are named for a distinguished Englishman, Montague Stevens of Cambridge, who came to NM in 1881. He was a direct descendant of Mary, Queen of Scots. Another ancestor, Sheffield, Duke of Buckingham, owned the home purchased by the English king, George III, as the original fabric of Buckingham Palace. Mr. Stevens died in Albuquerque on Dec. 16, 1953, aged 94.

STEWART LAKE (San Miguel). Small lake about 6 mi from Cowles.

STINKING LAKE (Rio Arriba). See BURFORD LAKE. STINKING SPRINGS (De Baca). 3 mi S and 1 mi W of Tolar. Named by the early travelers because of the peculiar smell given off by the black ooze and reeds. In the early days, there was a rock house built nearby. In this house, on Dec. 23, 1880, Sheriff Pat Garrett killed Charley Bowdre and captured Billy the Kid after an all-day battle.

STOCKTON'S (Colfax). The Stockton family owned ranches in several NM counties. Post-master, William H. Stockton. Post office, 1878. STOCKTON (Grant). STOCKTON (Quay). See FORREST. STOCKTON (Roosevelt). First postmaster, John J. Stockton. Post office, 1904-05; mail to Langton.

STONE CABIN GULCH (Hidalgo). Runs SW from Little Hatchet Mts. STONE LAKE (Rio Arriba). See BOULDER LAKE.

STONEHAVEN (Union). Post office, 1910-13.

STONG (Taos). Former trading point on US 285, 12 mi NE of Ojo Caliente, and 30 mi W of Taos; on the abandoned Alamosa and Santa Fe narrow-gauge branch of D&RGW RR. Name of station agent of old "Chile Line" when railroad was built here about 1885. Later known as TAOS JUNCTION. Post office, 1920-42.

STORRIE RESERVOIR (San Miguel). Lake 5 mi N of Las Vegas; covers 1,200 acres when full.

STOUT CANYON (Colfax). Begins 7 mi N of Dawson and extends E from Vermejo River canyon. Named for a Pennsylvania pioneer who made his home here.

STRAUSS (Doña Ana). On SP RR, 16 mi NW of El Paso, and 8 mi W of US 80. Post office, 1894-97; mail to El Paso; 1918-43.

STRAWBERRY PEAK (Socorro). 6 mi NW of Socorro.

SUBLETTE (Rio Arriba). On D&RGW RR, 14 mi NE of Chama at Colorado line. SUBLETT MINE (Eddy). Legendary mine, or cache, of gold in Guadalupe Mts. near Carlsbad. Supposed to have been found by William Colum Sublee or Sublette (Old Ben), who came to town with a pouch of reddish-gold nuggets, similar to the kind found in California. Since Old Ben died in 1892, no one has been able to find the "mine."

SUGARITE (Colfax). Post office, 1912-44. See CHICARICA.

SUGARLOAF MOUNTAIN (Sierra). 18 mi SW of Winston.

SULPHUR (Bernalillo, Sandoval). Post office, 1898-1904; 1907-09. See SULPHUR SPRINGS. SULPHUR CANYON (Bernalillo). In Sandia Mts. SULPHUR SPRINGS (Sandoval). Trading point 25 mi NE of Jemez Pueblo and N of Redondo. One of many resorts in Jemez Mts. built around a sulphur spring. Another name was "Kidney Water Spring." The Jemez Towa Indian word is pat-yo-shool-oonu, "place of the boiling water." Post office, 1909-13.

SUMMIT (Hidalgo). 7 mi W of US 70, on SP RR, 19 mi NW of Lordsburg.

SUNDAY CONE (Sierra). Peak on S border of county, 3 mi N of Nutt and 3 mi E of NM 27. Called NUTT MOUNTAIN since the 1880's, at N end of Goodsight Mts.

SUNLAND PARK (Doña Ana). Community 5 mi NW of El Paso, Tex., on SP RR. Formerly ANAPRA. In 1960, the community changed the name to Sunland Park for the race track which operates a winter horse-racing meet here. Post office, 1962—.

SUNNYSIDE (Guadalupe). Post office, 1878-82; 1905-10; changed to FORT SUMNER.

SUNSET (Lincoln). On US 70 and 380, 34 mi W of Roswell.

SUNSHINE VALLEY (Taos). Site of extensive truck farming, 3 mi E of the Rio Grande and 10 mi N of Questa. Formerly called VIRSYLVIA. Post office, 1921-33.

SUNSPOT (Otero). 18 mi S of Cloudcroft. Site of Sacramento Peak Observatory of Air Force Cambridge Research Laboratories. Named because main purpose of observatory is solar research with the object to predict sun-induced disturbances in earth's atmosphere and in outer space. Post office, 1953—.

SUWANEE (Valencia). On NM 6 and AT&SF RR, 30 mi SW of Albuquerque. Formerly called SAN JOSE, having been named for the river near it. Changed to Suwanee in 1902 because there was another station on the line in Oklahoma with the name San Jose. Post office for the locality opened in 1914 and called CORREO.

SWAMP (Eddy). Post office, 1894-95; mail to Eddy.

SWARTZ (Grant). On NM 61, 15 mi SE of Santa Rita, and 21 mi SE of Bayard. First postmaster, Edward J. Swartz. Post office, 1887, intermittently, to 1919.

SWASTIKA (Colfax). Sanskrit, "good fortune." 5 mi W of Raton, in Dillon Canyon. Formerly a coal-mining town owned by the St. Louis, Rocky Mountain and Pacific Co. The Gardiner—Swastika branch of AT&SF RR once extended from Dillon to Swastika for the purpose of shipping coal. Post office, 1919-40; changed to BRILLIANT.

SWEAZEVILLE (Catron). Trading point, 4 mi E of Quemado, on US 60. Formerly known as RITO, but a Mr. Sweaze or Swazea named it for his family when he established a store and filling station here. Later called OMEGA. Post office, 1928-30; mail to Pie Town.

SWEETWATER (Colfax). Post office on Sweetwater Creek, 1878-82; mail to Springer.

SWEETWATER CREEK (Colfax). E of NM 21, 7 mi N of Mora, along S border of county; flows into Ocate Creek, which enters Canadian Red River.

SYCAMORE CREEK (Grant). Flows E to join Gila River 3 mi S of Cliff.

SYLVANITE (Hidalgo). Post office, 1908-13.

TAAIYALONE MOUNTAIN (McKinley). According to F. W. Hodge, Zuñi Indian, "corn mountain," from tâ á, "maize," and yalone, "mountain." Mesa-like mountain 3 mi S of Zuñi Pueblo, where there are altars and shrines to Indian deities, and where ceremonial rites are held at certain seasons of the year. When Coronado reached Hawikuh, a Zuñi village, on July 8, 1540, after a march of four months, the Indians took refuge on Taaiyalone, where the heights and their gods would give them protection. Today an airplane beacon rises near these old-time ruins of refuge. The Navajo name for this mesa is tse hoghan, "rock house." A Zuñi myth associates the mountain with the House of the Gods and the making of rain, lightning, and thunder, which has led to the name used by Anglo-Americans, THUNDER MOUNTAIN.

TABLE MESA (San Juan). 16 mi S of Shiprock. Drilling landmark in San Juan Basin oil field.

TAFOYA (Colfax). Ranching community on county road 8 mi NW of Farley. The first Tafoyas, the three sons of Juan de Tafoya Altamirano, natives of Mexico City, came to NM shortly after the Reconquest of 1692. Post office, 1936-53. TAFOYA (Valencia).

TAFT (De Baca). Former community 14 mi NE of Ft. Sumner. Post office, 1909-27.

TAIAKWIN (Socorro). Site of former Indian village, E of the Rio Grande and N of Lemitar.

TAIBAN (De Baca). Ranching community on US 60, 84, and AT&SF RR, 14 mi E of Ft. Sumner. Taiban is an Indian name, but whether it is Comanche or Navajo is not known. Some say it means "horsetail," because of the tributaries of Taiban Creek, for which it is named. Another meaning given is "three creeks" for the same geographical facts. The townsite was laid out in 1906 by Judge McGill, a Mr. Lindsey, and J. B. Sledge. Post office, 1906—. TAIBAN CREEK (DeBaca). All its tributaries come in from the N throughout the 50-mi course to where it joins Pecos River, 18 mi S of Ft. Sumner. TAIBAN SPRINGS (De

Baca). About ¾ mi SW of Taiban and ¼ mi S of US 60. Known in the early days as BRAZIL SPRINGS, for a Portugese immigrant who settled here in 1871.

TAJIQUE (Torrance). Farming, ranching, and lumbering community on NM 10, 14 mi W of Estancia and 31 mi SE of Albuquerque at foot of Manzano Mts. Post office, 1885, intermittently, to present. Name is probably the Hispanized form of taskike, which designated the Tewa sixteenth-century pueblo nearby. The Tiwa name was tush-vit-yay or tua-yit-yay. The old pueblo stood on the S bank of the stream NW of the present village, and furnished a refuge for the inhabitants of Quarai in 1674. The following year it was abandoned because of Apache raids. TAJIQUE CREEK (Torrance). Little stream heading into Manzano Mts. W of Estancia. TAJIQUE GRANT (Torrance). Area 3 mi square surrounding the old settlement at Tajique. Manuel Sanchez petitioned for himself and nineteen other residents of Valencia County on Mar. 9, 1834, for this tract; approved by the governor on Mar. 17, and on Apr. 9, the justice of the township of Valencia gave possession.

TAJO (Socorro). Span., "cut or opening in a mountain; line or place to which the work of a gang extends."

TAJON (San Miguel). Post office, 1889-92; mail to Bell Ranch.

TALAYA GRANT (Santa Fe). See ATALAYA GRANT.

TALPA (Taos). Span., "knob." On NM 3, 6 mi S of Taos, near the mouth of the Rio Chiquito. Name may be commemorative of Talpa, a town in southern Mexico, which is famous for a shrine of Nuestra Señora del Rosario de Talpa. However, in the mid-nineteenth century there was a Señora Talpa Romero, member of a prominent Taos Valley family whose name may be honored here. Settlement occurred in the early eighteenth century as a part of the general occupation of the Ranchos de Taos area.

TALLONS CREEK (Hidalgo). 20 mi NE of Cloverdale.

TANDY (Roosevelt). First postmaster, Albert M. Tandy. Post office, 1908-09; mail to Melrose.

TANK CANYON (Cibola). Scattered settlement near Cebolleta Mesa, 45 mi SE of Grants. In 1936 the WPA built a small schoolhouse here for the benefit of neighborhood children. Named because of a small reservoir and watering place for cattle in center of this canyon.

TANK MOUNTAIN (Hidalgo). 10 mi E of Rodeo.

TANNER (San Juan). 32 mi S of Farmington.

TANQUE. Indian pueblo listed in Escudero's Noticias (1849) as in the First District, which included present-day Santa Fe and San Miguel counties.

TAOS (Taos). The form is a Spanish approximation of Tewa Indian words, tu-o-ta, "red willow place," or tua-tah, "down at the village." On US 64, 54 mi NE of Santa Fe. Known to explorers and colonizers from the time of Coronado (1540-42). Not settled until 1617 when Fray Pedro de Miranda built a mission as an outpost of Spanish life. A settler named Don Fernando de Chavez was an important landowner here before the Pueblo Rebellion of 1680. His family was slain in the Pueblo Rebellion in that year and he did not return with the Reconquest of 1692. In 1710, Cristobal de la Serna petitioned for a grant of land, referring to its previous owner as Don Fernando. The Spanish settlement thus became known as FERNANDO DE TAOS. A Don Carlos Fernandez in the eighteenth century and a Señor Francisco Fernandez in the early nineteenth century are reported to have mixed names with the original Don Fernando. Early American travelers and later historians confuse the names: Zebulon Pike (1807), "San Fernandez"; H. H. Bancroft (1889), "Taos—known as Fernandez de Taos or Don Fernandez de Taos, a corruption . . . of San Fernando de Taos"; Twitchell, "Don Fernandez or San Fernandez de Taos." The Spanish parish has never been dedicated to a San Fernando or San Fernandez but to Our Lady of Guadalupe. The U.S. Post Office Department in 1852 chose "Fernandez de Taos," but in 1885 settled upon the shorter and less debatable "Taos." French traders came to the Taos fairs in the eighteenth century and Anglo-American trappers and traders appeared here after 1820. About 1890 Taos became known to artists, who were followed by writers, many of whom made Taos their permanent home. Post office, 1852—. TAOS COUNTY. Created by the Republic of Mexico in 1844; designated by the New Mexico Territorial Legislature on Jan. 9, 1852. Area is 2,252 sq mi. TAOS CREEK (Taos). See RIO FERNANDO DE TAOS. TAOS JUNCTION (Taos). Trading point on NM 96, 30 mi W of Taos. Formerly called STONG. TAOS MOUNTAIN (Taos). NW of the pueblo and sacred to the

Indians. Shelters Blue Lake, used for ceremonial purposes. TAOS PASS (Colfax). At S end of Moreno Valley; the pass where US 64 crosses Taos Mts. into Taos County. TAOS PEAK (Colfax). 6 mi W of Eagle Nest Lake almost on Taos County line. TAOS PUEBLO (Taos). 8 mi E of the Rio Grande, 3 mi NE of Taos settlement. Pedro de Castañeda records that this northernmost pueblo, when discovered by Coronado and his soldiers, was known as BRABA, and that the Spanish gave it the name VALLADOLID. The word is used by Juan Velarde, secretary to Don Juan de Oñate who founded the colony in 1598. Oñate says the place was also called TAYBERON at this time. (Don Juan de Oñate, Colonizer of New Mexico, 1595-1628, eds. Hammond and Rey, p. 321.) When a church was dedicated at the Indian pueblo, the community was named SAN GERONIMO DE TAOS. The Taos mission was founded as early as 1629. San Geronimo is still the patron saint of the pueblo, and his feast day on September 30 is celebrated with dancing and sports that make it the most important event of the year. TAOS PUEBLO GRANT (Taos). There is no specific grant paper (as are the Cruzates). See PUEBLO LAND GRANTS. However, an early grant to the pueblo may have been confirmed in measurements ordered by Gov. Fernando de la Concha in 1793 and certified again in 1815 when a dispute occurred between the pueblo and Spanish residents nearby and at Arroyo Hondo and other settlements. The U.S. Surveyor General confirmed documents dealing with the Taos Grant on Dec. 22, 1858.

TAPIA (San Miguel). Span., "adobe wall, fence." Settlement in SW corner of county, 5 mi N of Clines Corners. Name is of Arabic origin signifying fence, or wall, to enclose a garden or part of a patio. Also a family name. Juan de Tapia was already in New Mexico in 1607, and his descendants returned with the Reconquest of 1692. Post office, 1928-39. TAPIA CANYON (San Miguel).

TAPICITOS (Rio Arriba). New Mexican Span., "little ridges," from Span., tapar, "to cover or obstruct the view." Ranching and farming community on NM 95, 40 mi S of Dulce. Post office, 1918-63. TAPICITOS CREEK (Rio Arriba). Starts N of Tapicitos and flows into Cañon Largo.

TATE (Union). Former post office and trading point on Carrizo Creek, 18 mi SW of Clayton. Started by H. H. Tate on old Clayton-

Las Vegas Trail about 1907. Now ranching area. Post office, 1914-23.

TATUM (Lea). Ranching and farming town on US 380 and NM 18, 21 mi N of Lovington. Named for James G. Tatum, owner of first store here in 1909. Built on land formerly part of the LFD Four Lakes Ranch and halfway between two old watering places known as Eight Mile and West Keenum. First postmaster, Mattie G. Tatum. Post office, 1909—.

TAYBERON (Taos). See TAOS PUEBLO.

TAYLOR CREEK (Catron, Sierra). 9 mi S of Beaverhead. TAYLOR SPRINGS (Colfax). 8 mi SE of Springer, on Canadian Red River near NM 58. Sometimes called TAYLOR. Named for Elijah Taylor, who started the Taylor Springs Ranch many years ago. Post office, 1905-09; Taylor Springs, 1909-41.

T BAR CANYON (Catron). S part of county, 16 mi from Grant County line. Named for a ranch brand.

TEAGUE (Lea). 11 mi N of Jal on NM 18; TNM RR siding and stock pen.

TECHADO (Cibola). Span., "roofed over." Post office and small village 35 mi S of El Morro on NM 36, at foot of the lava flow. Named for TECHADO MESA nearby, where an old ruin with a covered well was responsible for the name. See TRECHADO.

TECOLOTE. Mexican Span., "owl," from the Nahuatl tecolotl. This word was used in NM to denote any and all kinds of owls to the total exclusion of Span. buho and lechuza. TECOLOTE (Lincoln). Blind siding on US 54, on SP RR, 30 mi NE of Carrizozo in Jicarilla Mts. Established and named by the railroad. TECOLOTE (Sandoval). Settlement of seven or eight families 1 mi E of Placitas on NM 44. TECOLOTE (San Miguel). Trading point on US 84, 85, and AT&SF RR, 10 mi S of Las Vegas. Settled in 1824 by Salvador Montoya. From 1850 to 1860 it became one of a chain of posts established by the U.S. Army for forage and corn during the campaign against the Indians. The railroad station was named on July 12, 1883. Post office, 1851, intermittently, to 1923. TECOLOTE CREEK (San Miguel, Guadalupe). Tributary of Gallinas River that joins Pecos River in Guadalupe. TECOLOTE GRANT (San Miguel). Triangular-shaped area 6 mi S of Las Vegas and N of Bernal Peak. Granted to Salvador Montoya and five of his neighbors on Nov. 19, 1824. They took possession on Apr. 23, 1825, and lived here three or four years until they were driven off by Indians. TECOLOTE MOUNTAIN (San Miguel). TECOLOTEÑOS (San Miguel). "Natives of Tecolote." Settlement W of NM 3, 18 mi NW of Las Vegas. Name indicates that first settlers were from Tecolote. Also called SAN IGNACIO and KOOGLER. Post office, 1931-47. TECOLOTITO (San Miguel). "Little owl." On Pecos River, 7 mi W of US 84 and 4 mi N of Anton Chico.

TEEL (Grant). On NM 61, 18 mi NE of Bayard. First postmaster, Alma E. Teel. Post office, 1901-26. See FORT WEBSTER.

TEJAR (Guadalupe). Span., "to make tiles; tile works or kiln." 4 mi W of Vaughn near Torrance County line.

TEJON (Sandoval). Span., "badger." 4 mi NE of Placitas, in center of Tejon Grant. TEJON GRANT (Sandoval). Small area 2 mi E of Placitas. The U.S. Surveyor General confirmed the claim of Salvador Barreras and others because they were given possession on Nov. 7, 1840, by the laws of Spain and Mexico.

TEKAPO (McKinley). Former trading point on NM 53, 4 mi SW of Zuñi.

TELEPHONE CANYON (Otero). There are an East and West Telephone Canyon. Named for the telephone wires strung through them. TELEPHONE CANYON (Rio Arriba). Near La Jara Lake 11 mi S of Dulce on the Continental Divide. TELEPHONE CANYON (Taos). Flows S into Osha Canyon and then into Embudo Creek at Vadito.

TELESFORA (Union). Post office, 1901-03; mail to Miera.

TELLES (Doña Ana). Jose Telles Jiron, a native of the suburb of Mexico City called Coyoacan, came to NM sometime before 1660. Members of his family returned with the Reconquest of 1692 and later dropped the second name. Post office, 1894-97; mail to Earlham, 1897-1906; Telles, 1906-17, 1947-52. See SAN MIGUEL.

TELLTALE BLUFF (Eddy). See TRACY.

TEMPLE (Colfax). On the Rio del Plano, 18 mi NE of Springer, near Chico. First started with the Temple Ranch, then became a small community, now abandoned. TEMPLE PEAK (Colfax). In SE corner of county near Chico. Named for the Temple family, owners of the Temple Ranch.

TEMPORAL (Otero). Span., "weather, season." On US 54 and SP RR, 8 mi N of Tularosa. This word has several meanings as does its English equivalent. In New Spain, tierra de temporal came to mean "dry farm," tilled land in an arid region without benefit of

irrigation and entirely dependent on seasonal rains.

TENAJA MOUNTAIN (Colfax). See TINAJA MOUNTAIN

TEN MILE HILL (De Baca). 17 mi S of Ft. Sumner. See NUMBERS.

TENNESSEE CREEK (Grant). Rises near Arizona line; flows into Mule Creek, 1 mi N of Mule Creek settlement.

TEQUESQUITE (Harding). Mexicanism, "alkali." Once a small settlement, now deserted, 10 mi SW of Baca post office, on Tequesquite Arroyo. Post office, 1879-90. TEQUESQUITE ARROYO, CREEK. (Harding). Rises in NW corner of county and runs S from Albert into Ute Creek near San Miguel County line.

TEQUESQUITE CREEK (Hidalgo). TEQUESQUITE SPRINGS (Rio Arriba). The Indians and old inhabitants of this area gather and use the alkali for a purgative medicine; the water can also be used to raise crops and for other purposes. It is pinkish in color and salty in taste.

TERROMONTE (San Miguel). See EL TERROMOTE.

TERRERRO (San Miguel). Span., a corruption or misspelling of terrero, "mound, dump, place for mine and smelter waste." Trading point on NM 63, 40 mi E of Santa Fe, and 20 miles NE of Glorieta. Named for slag dump of American Metals Co. Post office, 1927—.

TERRERO (Valencia). 24 mi SE of Zuñi.

TESUQUE (Santa Fe). Settlement on US 285, 6 mi N of Santa Fe. Named for the pueblo. The Spanish settlers date from 1740. Name is a Spanish form of Tewa Indian tat' unge' onwi, "spotted dry place." The river disappears in the sand and comes through in spots. Post office, 1938—. TESUQUE PUEBLO (Santa Fe). Ruins now called in Tewa tay tsoon ghay, "cottonwood tree place," a corruption of the Spanish way of pronouncing the original Indian name. They have thus made a new folk etymology: tay, "cottonwood tree"; tsooghay, locative. Site of original pueblo when the Spaniards first came was 3 mi E of present village. It is the most southerly of the present Tewa pueblos near Santa Fe. Name is variously spelled, such as Tezuque, Tesuqui, Tesuke, etc. In Spanish and English, the name Tesuque is applied rather vaguely to the whole region about the pueblo. TESUQUE CREEK (Santa Fe). Largest tributary of Pojoaque Creek; flows past the pueblo. The greater part of its drainage was formerly held by the Indians. TESUQUE PUEBLO GRANT (Santa Fe). Original Spanish land grant, confirmed by the Republic of Mexico in 1821; confirmed in the Treaty of Guadalupe Hidalgo, 1848, by the U.S.

TETILLA PEAK (Santa Fe). Span., "small nipple." 4 mi NE of La Bajada settlement and almost due N at top of grade.

TEXICO (Curry). Farming and ranching community on US 60, 70, and 84, 9 mi E of Clovis; on Texas border. Name is a blend of syllables in Texas and New Mexico. The first real settler, Ira W. Taylor, arrived after 1900. He was a section foreman of the old PV&NE RR who took out a 160-acre homestead adjoining railroad property at the depot. The name ESCAVADO was given this XIT Ranch area, adjoining Texas border. Post office, 1902—.

TEYPANA (Socorro). Indian pueblo, formerly of the Piro, which Oñate named SOCORRO because it furnished his company with "much maize." On the W bank of the Rio Grande, 8 mi N of present Socorro. See SOCORRO.

THE MEADOWS (San Juan). Large tract of land about 6 mi N of Fruitland. Named for the thick, tall grass watered by drainage from surrounding higher elevations. In the 1850's and 1860's, this land was unfenced and used for grazing. After homesteading, residences were maintained by cattlemen. Today the area is fenced and used for pasture, but the owners live in nearby settlements.

THE PINES (Grant). 1 mi N of Tyrone.

THERMA (Colfax). Post office, 1821-35. See EAGLE NEST.

THIEVING ROCK (San Juan). 3 mi S of Colorado line, in NW corner of Ute Mountain Indian Reservation.

THIRTEEN MILE DRAW (Chaves). 13 mi S of Roswell on NM 13. See NUMBERS.

THOMAS (Union). Ranching community W of NM 18, 17 mi S of Clayton. First postmaster, Laura F. Thomas. Post office, 1907-44.

THOMPSON (Colfax). 20 mi W of Des Moines. Once a station on the old SLRM&P RR, 4 mi W of Vigil. Named for William Lee Thompson, who moved here from San Lorenzo in Grant County in the 1870's and established a store and a fruit orchard. THOMPSON (Valencia). 16 mi S of Zuñi. THOMPSON CONE (Sierra, Grant). On county line, 13 mi SW of Hillsboro. THOMPSON PEAK (Santa Fe). 8 mi E of Santa Fe, in Santa Fe National Forest; altitude, 10,540 ft.

THOREAU (McKinley). Ranching and lumbering community on US 66, and AT&SF RR,

31 mi E of Gallup. According to M. L. Woodard of Gallup (Letter, Feb. 22, 1940), the settlement was named for the author Henry David Thoreau, probably at the time the railroad established the station. Post office, 1899—. Formerly called MITCHELL.

THORNE (Doña Ana). Post office, 1881-83; changed to RINCON.

THORNHAM (Roosevelt). Post office 18 mi SE of Elida, 1910-15.

THORNTON (Sandoval). Trading point 6 mi S of Peña Blanca. Post office, 1895-1909; changed to DOMINGO.

THREE GUN SPRINGS (Bernalillo). On E slope of Sandia Mts., 2½ mi from Carlito Springs. THREE RIVERS (Otero). Ranching community on US 54 and SP RR, 17 mi N of Tularosa. Named for three mountain streams. In the late 1870's Patrick Coghlan established his headquarters 2 mi from the present station. Later, this became the Tres Ritos Ranch of former Secretary of the Interior, Albert B. Fall. A few years after the Lincoln County War, Mrs. Susan Barber, the widow of Alexander C. McSween of Lincoln, who was killed in the war, acquired extensive holdings and moved her cattle a few miles nearer the mountains than Three Rivers. She was known as "The Cattle Queen of New Mexico." In 1917, she sold out to the Fall interests, and moved to White Oaks. Post office, 1883, intermittently, to present. THREE RIVERS (Otero). Flows W from Sierra Blanca Mts. Receives two affluents, Indian and Golondrina creeks, which join 7 mi E of the village.

THUNDER MOUNTAIN (McKinley). See TAAIYALONE.

TIENDITAS. Span., "little tents, little stores." Trading point on US 64, 13 mi E of Taos. This word was applied to any house of merchandise, no matter what the size or type of building. TIENDITAS CREEK (Taos). Flows E into the Rio Fernando de Taos at Tienditas.

TIERRA AMARILLA. Span., "yellow earth." This is the term applied by New Mexicans to the dark ochre earth with which they paint the lower part of whitewashed walls in rooms and portales. Since Tewa name means the same thing, "earth yellowness," it would seem that the Spanish name was an adaptation of the earlier Indian name. TIERRA AMARILLA (Rio Arriba). County seat and farming community on US 84, 15 mi S of Chama. Townsite first filed in 1832, and originally called Los NUTRIAS. Post office, 1866-

68; 1870—. Tierra Amarilla Creek (Rio Arriba). Small stream flowing W past Tierra Amarilla to the Chama. Tierra Amarilla Grant (Rio Arriba). Large grant measuring about 30 sq mi, with Tierra Amarilla a little S of center. Once owned by Thomas B. Catron. In recent years it has been cut up and bought by different ranchmen. Original grant was approved by Territorial Deputation on July 20, 1832, to Manuel Martinez, his eight children, and those others who volunteered to accompany him to this land. Tierra Azul (Rio Arriba). "Blue earth." On S side of Chama River below Abiquiu. The Indians call it *nantsang waboo-oo*, "blue or green earth flats," which suggested the Spanish place name. Tierra Blanca (Sierra). "White earth." 5 mi SE of Kingston. Name describes a mixture of clay and alkali used for both interior and exterior walls of houses. Post office, 1892-1903; mail to Lake Valley. Tierra Blanca Mountain. Tierra Blanca Creek (Curry). Rises N of Broadview and flows SE into Texas. Tierra Blanca Creek (Luna). Tierra Blanca Creek (Sierra). Flows E 6 mi S of Hillsboro, into the Rio Grande 2 mi N of Derry. Tierra Blanca Mountain (Sierra). 5 mi SE of Kingston.

Tiguex Province (Bernalillo). When Coronado came up the Rio Grande Valley in 1540, he found a group of Indian towns between Isleta and present-day Bernalillo. These made up the province of Tiguex, probably the most densely populated part of the Southwest when first seen by the Spaniards. These villages spoke the Tiwa language, and only two of them survive in this area today, Isleta and Sandia. Coronado made his headquarters at Kuaua (now Coronado State Monument) and Puaray, and went from them on his fruitless tour of the plains in search of Quivira. In 1542, he left Tiguex to return to Mexico. Tijeras (Bernalillo). Span., "scissors." Trading point on US 66, 16 mi E of Albuquerque. Paako State Monument is nearby. A theory has developed that the name is descriptive of the canyons, which form the outline of scissors with the town at the fulcrum. However, the name is a family surname, and a settlement existed in the canyon by 1856. Post office, 1888, intermittently, to present. Tijeras Canyon (Bernalillo). Runs E and W between Sandia and Manzano mts. Seems to have been named for the settlement. An earlier name was Carnue or Carnuel Canyon.

Tilden (Sandoval). 3 mi N of La Ventana and at terminus of SFNW RR when it was completed from Bernalillo. A celebration was held on July 7, 1927, but the project failed and the depot and townsite were abandoned. Post office, 1931-32; mail to Cuba. Tinaja misspelled Tenaja (Colfax). Span., "large earthern jar for holding water or other liquids." Small settlement 16 mi S of Raton. Tinaja (Valencia). 3 mi N of NM 53 and and NE of El Morro. Named because it is close to an Indian ruin in a circular depression or sink in the lava, giving the appearance of a pot or bowl. A walk-in well here is similar to the one made by the Indians at Techado. It formed the source of their drinking water. Tinaja Arroyo, Creek (Colfax). S of Eagle Tail Mtn.; flows into Canadian Red River. Named for Tinaja Mtn., directly E. Tinaja and Eagle Tail Mountains (Colfax). These two peaks lie 12 to 16 mi S of Raton. Descriptive names chosen by early stage drivers on the Santa Fe Trail, for Tinaja is flat on top and has a short, narrow neck like a jar. Eagle Tail reminds one of the sloping, swooping back of an eagle.

Tingle (Cibola). Trading point on NM 36, 8 mi SE of Atarque. Said to be named for a pioneer family. Post office, 1932-39; mail to Fence Lake.

Tinnie (Lincoln). Farming and ranching community on US 70 and 380, 42 mi SE of Carrizozo. Could be called the town of many names, having had four to date. In 1876, named Analla for an early settler, Jose Analla; renamed Tinnie thirty-three years later, in 1909, for the oldest daughter of the first postmaster. At one time it was also called Las Cuevas (the caves) from the large caves in which the first-comers lived. Later named Cuba. "Tinnie" survives. Post office, 1909—. Tin Pan Canyon (Colfax). Extends W of Dillon Canyon a few miles beyond Blossburg. Named for a shining tin pan nailed to a post by a miner as a guide to his friends who were to follow him to his camp.

Tio Grande (Rio Arriba). Creek paralleling the Rio Nutrias, about 2 mi SE, entering the Rio San Antonio just below San Antonio settlement.

Tipton (Quay). On Salidita Creek, 6 mi S of San Jon. Post office, 1909-13. Tipton (Mora). At one time a small town with a post office 2 mi N of Watrous, in John Scolly Land Grant. Named for the Tipton family which was one of the first to settle here. Now part of a very large ranch. Mora River runs through the property and US 85 passes a short distance E. Post office, TIPTONVILLE, 1876-98. See OPTIMO. TIPTON CREEK (San Miguel). Flows N between Watrous and Shoemaker.

TIZ NAT ZIN (San Juan). Navajo, *tse*, "rock," *lizhin*, "black." Arroyo rising W of Lybrook and running into Chaco Canyon 35 mi S of Farmington. Also called COAL CREEK.

TOADLENA (San Juan). Navajo, *tqo-ha-leeh*, "water bubbling up." Government Indian boarding school and trading point, 12 mi SW of Newcomb, 49 mi N of Gallup. Named and settled by the Navajo Indians many years ago. There are many springs on the mountain slope here. Post office, 1917-.

TOAYALLONE MOUNTAIN (McKinley). See TAAI-YALONE MOUNTAIN.

TOBOGGAN (Otero). On NM 83, and old EP&SW RR, 15 mi E of Alamogordo. Post office, 1899-1900; mail to Cloudcroft.

TOBOSA FLAT (Hidalgo). Spanish term for a tough grass that grows on rocky ground. 10 mi W of Lordsburg. Descriptive name of the lavalike soil and coarse growth.

TOCITO (San Juan). Navajo, *tqo-seedo*, "hot water." 10 mi NW of Newcomb. TOCITO WASH (San Juan). Runs E above Tocito to enter Chaco River.

TOGEYE LAKE (McKinley). 6 mi W of Inscription Rock, at Valencia County line.

TOHATCHI (McKinley). Trading post and settlement 1 mi W of US 666, 25 mi N of Gallup. Name is a Navajo word with several meanings, *tqohachee*, "scratch for water, water in rock ledge," and *tqo qachi*, "water dug out." Settlement was built around an Indian school established by the government in 1895 on the Navajo Reservation. Post office, 1898-. TO-HATCHI WASH (San Juan). In extreme NW corner of state; runs NE across Colorado line to enter San Juan River.

TOKAY (Socorro). Former trading point 2 mi S of US 380, on old NMM RR, 8 mi E of San Antonio. Coal was once mined here from an extensive deposit developed by B. H. Kinney. Post office, 1919-32.

TOLAR (Roosevelt). Ranching and sand- and gravel-producing community on NM 86, US 60, 84, and AT&SF RR, 18 mi W of Melrose. Named for Tolar, Tex., by J. W. Coleman, the first postmaster, who had a daughter living here. Post office, 1905-46; mail to Taiban.

TOLBY CREEK (Colfax). Tributary of Cimarron River, emptying into it from the S just below Eagle Nest Dam. Name recalls the mysterious death of a preacher named Rev. Thomas J. Tolby, who was found murdered here, during the Land Grant Wars of Colfax County.

TOLEDO CREEK (Sandoval). Tributary of Upper San Antonio Creek on Baca Location No. 1 in Jemez Mts. Name is a Spanish surname found among Indian families in this area as well as among Spanish settlers.

TOLL GATE CANYON (Union). Branch of Dry Cimarron Canyon, 8 mi from Folsom. Named for toll road built by Bill Metcalf through canyon in 1870-71.

TOLTEC (Rio Arriba). 18 mi W of Los Pinos, at Colorado state line. Name of one of the earliest of the Nahuatl Indian tribes to invade central and southern Mexico. Name chosen by D&RGW RR when this was once a stopping point. TOLTEC (Valencia). Siding on AT&SF RR, 5 mi NW of Grants. TOLTEC GORGE (Rio Arriba). Between Colorado line and the Rio de los Pinos, near Toltec.

TOME (Valencia). Farming and ranching community on NM 47, E of the Rio Grande, 5 mi NE of Belen. Name may be traced to Governor Otermin's *maese de campo*, Tome Dominguez de Mendoza, who built a hacienda near the volcanic hill known as CERRO DE TOME in the days before the Pueblo Rebellion of 1680. Dominguez lost everything in the Rebellion and did not return to his ranch after the Reconquest of 1692; but his name persisted as a place name despite his disappearance from the scene. In 1858, a weathered wooden statue was found in the river near Tome and the people of the village believe it to be the one kept by Tome Dominguez in the chapel at his home. Post office, 1881-85; 1888-. TOME GRANT (Valencia). Large tract S of Tome and E of the Rio Grande, extending to Manzano Mts. Grant made to settlers by Governor Mendoza; they took possession on July 30, 1739. TOME RIVERSIDE DRAIN (Valencia). Heads E of river and empties into Lower Peralta Drain 4 mi above Belen.

TONQUE ARROYO (Santa Fe). On W side of the Rio Grande near Peña Blanca. Name may be related to the old TANQUE Indian pueblo in Rio Arriba, or to TUNQUE, a pre-Spanish pueblo at NE edge of Sandia Mts. F. W. Hodge says the word is Tewa for "village of the basket."

TONUCO (Doña Ana). 4 mi E of US 85, on AT&SF RR, 12 mi SE of Hatch. See SAN DIEGO.

TONY (Guadalupe). On SP RR, 2 mi NE of Vaughn.

TOOTH OF TIME MOUNTAIN (Colfax). W of Philmont Ranch and 9 mi SW of Cimarron. An immense wind-cut rock having the appearance of a tooth, on the top edge of a ridge.

TOP HAT MOUNTAIN (Hidalgo). In Alamo Hueco Mts., near SE corner of county, 3 mi from Mexico.

TORIETTE LAKES (Catron). 7 mi NW of village of Apache Creek.

TORIL (Colfax). Span., "pen for bulls before the fight." On AT&SF RR, 6 mi S of French.

TORNERO (Roosevelt). Span., "one who turns a lathe, one who winds about." Switch at stockyards on AT&SF RR, 30 mi SW of Portales. Name may be a metaphor for wind twisters.

TORRANCE (Torrance). Small settlement 29 mi SE of Vaughn, on US 55 and SP RR. Originally the terminal point of old NMC RR and named for Francis J. Torrance, promoter, connected with the building of this road. Post office, 1902-07; mail to Corona; Torrance, 1935-42. TORRANCE COUNTY. Created on Mar. 16, 1903, and also named for Francis J. Torrance. Present area is 3,369 sq mi.

TORREON (Sandoval). Span., "fortified tower." 14 mi SE of Estrella. TORREON (Torrance). Farming community on NM 10, 14 mi W of Estancia, built on site of the "Piros of the Salinas" pueblo ruins. Named for towers still standing at Manzano and built by the Spaniards as a fortification against the Apache-Navajos. Post office, 1895, intermittently, to present. TORREON ARROYO (McKinley, Sandoval). Runs SE into the Rio Puerco. TORREON GRANT (Torrance). Area approximately 6 by 3 mi surrounding the village of Torreon. On Oct. 16, 1841, Nino Antonio Montoya, authorized by twenty-seven individuals, petitioned Antonio Sandoval, Prefect of the Central District of New Mexico, for this tract, and after approval by the Justice of the Peace the Prefect ordered him to give possession, which he did on Mar. 3, 1841.

TORRES (San Miguel). See LOS TORRES. TORRES (Sierra). Juan de Torres, a native of Mexico City, came with the colonizer Oñate in 1598, and other members of the Torres name appear in both seventeenth- and eighteenth-century records.

TORTUGAS (Doña Ana). Span., "turtles." Mexicanized Tiwa Indian Pueblo 4 mi SE of Las Cruces and 1 mi SE of Mesilla Park on US 80 and 85. The village is divided into two parts, San Juan and Guadalupe. Legend places its founding in 1680 or 1682, when Tiwa Indians accompanied Governor Otermin south from the Pueblo of Isleta near Albuquerque. The aged and ill Indians who could go no further, the "slow ones" or "turtles," stopped here and founded the village. A second theory is that the town was named for a mountain which resembles a turtle. The Indians also call their village NUESTRA SEÑORA DE GUADALUPE.

TOTAVI (Santa Fe). Tewa Indian, "quail." Trailer camp village for workers established in 1948 at Los Alamos. Post office, 1949-53; mail to Santa Fe.

TOWANDA (Union). Passing track on C&S RR halfway between Folsom and Alps.

TOWNDROW (Colfax). 6 mi from Colorado, just S of NM 72. TOWNDROW PEAK (Colfax). On Johnson Mesa 10 mi E of Raton. Named for an early family now scattered over northern NM. The mesa is flat on top, with the exception of two small peaks, one of which is Towndrow.

TOWNER (Mora, Colfax). First postmaster, John C. Towner. Post office, 1877-78.

TOWN OF ABIQUIU GRANT (Rio Arriba). See ABIQUIU.

TOWN OF ALAMEDA GRANT (Bernalillo, Sandoval). Post office, 1910-12. See ALAMEDA.

TOWN OF CHAMITA GRANT (Rio Arriba). See CHAMITA GRANT.

TOWN OF EL RITO GRANT (Rio Arriba). See EL RITO GRANT.

TRACHADO (Socorro). Post office, 1918-19; mail to Quemado.

TRACY (Curry). Post office, 1910-12. TRACY BLUFF (Eddy). On Pecos River, 2 mi SE of Carlsbad. Named for the father of Francis G. Tracy of Carlsbad, who homesteaded in this area about 1890. Some maps call it TELLTALE BLUFF.

TRAGUES CREEK (Quay). Rises in Union County near Ione, and flows SE across NE corner of Quay to Texas.

TRAHEY (Santa Fe). An early station on old NMC RR, between Dyke and Stanley.

TRAIL CANYON (Catron). Very small fork of Mogollon Creek on the trail from 916 Ranch to Jenks Cabin. TRAIL'S END (Chaves). NW of Artesia. Post office, 1921-22; mail to Artesia.

TRAMPAS (Taos). Also called LAS TRAMPAS. Span., "traps, snares." Trading point on NM 76, 22 mi S of Taos; known as the "place of the early settlers." This adobe-walled town is a part of seventeenth-century Spain and Mexico, set down in the heart of NM. The mission church dates from 1760 or earlier and is called Santo Tomas del Rio de las Trampas, which indicates that the settlement takes its name from the stream, which was named because of beaver traps placed in its waters. Shown as Tram on Mapa de los EUM (1828). Post office, 1898—. TRAMPAS MOUNTAIN (Rio Arriba). 7 mi SE of Trampas. Another indication that this was fur-trading country. TRAMPAS RIVER (Rio Arriba, Taos). Rises E of Truchas Peak and heads N into Embudo Creek. TRAMPERAS (Mora, Union). Post office, 1879-92; changed to LOUIS. TRAMPEROS CREEK (Union). "Trappers." 25 mi S of Clayton.

TRAP CORRAL CANYON (Catron). In SE corner of county 9 mi NE of Gila Cliff Dwellings National Monument. So named because the canyon could be closed off after wild horses were driven into it and thus trapped.

TRAVESSER CREEK (Union). Also spelled TRAVASIER CREEK; more commonly known as TRAVASIER CANYON. Heads W of Guy and runs NE to Dry Cimarron River.

TRAVESILLA (Union). Post office, 1892-94; mail to Veda.

TREASURE MOUNTAIN (Grant). 6 mi N of Little Burro Mts. Named by early prospectors.

TRECHADO (Cibola). Said to be a corruption of Span., trecheado, "stopping place." Arthur Bibo, member of a prominent ranching family in Cibola County, says the name is an error for techado, "covered, roofed over," the correct designation for TECHADO MESA nearby. This was named for a ruin at its SE base which has a walk-in well in the center, roofed by early Indians before it was abandoned. The well was uncovered by one of the cowboys working for the Nations Ranch in the early 1900's or before. Post office, 1924-47; mail to Fence Lake. See TECHADO.

TREMENTINA (San Miguel). Span., "turpentine." Farming community on NM 65, 46 mi E of Las Vegas. Named because the farmers obtained turpentine and pine oil here. Settled about 1892, near Corazon Peak. Post office, 1901—. TREMENTINA CREEK (San Miguel). Heads 5 mi E of Trujillo; flows E and SE into Conchas Creek.

TRENTON (Quay). Post office, 1907-08; mail to Hollene.

TRES HERMANAS (Luna). Span., "three sisters." Settlement 14 mi SE of the mountains and named for them. TRES HERMANAS (Luna). 25 mi S of Deming and NW of Columbus. These three peaks stand close together.

TRES HERMANOS (Colfax). Span., "three brothers." 13 mi E of Maxwell and 24 mi S of Raton. The three peaks are close together and and are linked near the summits.

TRES LAGUNAS (Catron). Span., "three lakes." Ranching community 7 mi N of US 60, 24 mi E of Quemado. Close to three "cattle tanks" or mountain lakes formed by water from Datil Mts. Sometimes the lakes are just marshy land. Post office, 1957-62.

TRES MONTOSOS (Otero). Span., "three buttes." 15 mi SW of Alamogordo, 4 mi SE of US 17, and 6 mi W of US 54. Known locally as TWIN BUTTES AND ONE BUTTE; the separate butte is 4 mi SE of the other two. They lie N of Jarilla Mts. While drilling for oil was in process, a vein of artesian water was struck at a depth of 1,000 ft. This has flowed continuously since that time, forming a lake covering 320 acres, which is now part of White Sands National Monument. TRES MONTOSOS (Socorro). Three peaks halfway between Augustine and Magdalena.

TRES OREJAS PEAKS (Taos). Span., "three ears." 14 mi W of Taos. The Tewa name is ndayoyay peeng-ya, "coyote ear mountains," because they are said to resemble coyote ears. Also called OREJAS MOUNTAINS.

TRES PIEDRAS (Taos). Span., "three rocks." Lumbering and ranching community on US 285, 35 mi NW of Taos. Built E of three large extrusions of granite that can be seen many miles away. Settled in 1879. Tewa name is "mountain sheep rock place." Post office, 1880, intermittently, to present. TRES PIEDRAS ARROYO (Taos). Flows into the Rio Grande from the N.

TRES RITOS (Taos). Span., "three little rivers." Established as a lumber camp about 1900. Lies in a pocket in Sangre de Cristo Mts. between U.S. Hill and Holman Hill on NM 3, 27 mi S of Taos. Named for the junction of three streams, the Rio La Junta, Agua Piedra Creek, and the Rio Pueblo. Post office, 1916-27; 1937-40; mail to Peñasco.

TRIGO CANYON (Valencia). Span., "wheat." Mountain camping ground and recreational area 20 mi E of Belen, across the mesa in

Manzano Mts; can be reached from NM 6. Named for the wheat that grew at one time, near mouth of the canyon. Area maintained by U.S. Forest Service in Cibola National Forest.

TRINCHERA (Colfax). Span., "trench." Post office, 1882-83; mail to Madison. TRINCHERA CREEK (Colfax). Rises in NE corner of county; flows N into Colorado to Purgatoire River. TRINCHERA PASS (Colfax). In NE corner of county at E end of Johnson Mesa; cuts through mountains into Colorado, which explains the name.

TRINITY (Otero). Site on White Sands Missile Range 26 mi below Carthage in SE Socorro County. Here the first atomic bomb was detonated on July 16, 1945. Prayer services for peace are held annually on July 16 by worshippers of Protestant, Catholic, and Jewish faiths. According to Dr. Robert Oppenheimer, director of Los Alamos laboratory of nuclear physics when the bomb was designed, the name has no technical content, but was inspired by lines of the English poet John Donne: "As East and West in all flat maps— and I am one—Are one, so death shall touch the Resurrection." (From "Hymn to God, My God, in My Sickness.")

TRIPOD MOUNTAIN (Union). 10 mi SW of Mt. Dora on N bank of Carrizo Creek. A set of three low peaks representing points of a triangle (legs of a tripod), W of the famous "round mound" landmark of old Santa Fe Trail.

TROMPERAS CREEK (Union). Probably Span., tramperas, "trappers." 6 mi S of Clapham.

TROTER (Catron). 3 mi SE of Alma, on Whitewater Creek.

TROUT CREEK (Catron). In the San Francisco watershed 15 mi W of Reserve; site of proposed dam for recreational purposes. TROUT CREEK (Grant). Small stream 20 mi N of Silver City. TROUT LAKE (Rio Arriba). 7 mi NE of Nutrias. TROUT SPRINGS (San Miguel). Stream fed by five springs; a tributary to Gallinas River 12 mi W of Las Vegas. TROUT CREEK (Catron). Enters San Francisco River 2 mi E of Luna.

TROY (Colfax). Named for the Troy family, homesteaders here. First postmaster, Daniel Troy. Post office, TROYBURGH, 1878-84; changed to PARTON.

TRUCHAS (Rio Arriba). Span., "trout." Farming community on NM 76, 18 mi NE of Española and 26 mi N of Santa Fe. Fishing stream

nearby doubtless gave the name. The Tewa Indian names, too, are of interest; for the creek, "crooked chin place arroyo"; for the peak, "rock horn mountain." "Rock horn" seems to refer to upward-projecting rocks at the summit. The reason for "crooked chin" is unknown. Post office, 1894—. TRUCHAS CREEK, RIVER, (Rio Arriba). Heads on Truchas Peak; flows NW into the Rio Grande S of Velarde. TRUCHAS PEAK (Rio Arriba, Mora). 12 mi SE of Truchas settlement. On county line in S end of Sangre de Cristo Mts. Altitude 13,102 ft, the second highest peak in NM, exceeded only by Wheeler Peak. TRUCHAS PEAK LAKE (San Miguel). At head of the Rito de los Chimayoses, E of Truchas; also called LONE TREE LAKE. TRUCHAS RANGE (Santa Fe). In NE part of county.

TRUJILLO (San Miguel). Farming and ranching community on NM 65, 31 mi E of Las Vegas. Name found in families from Estremadura Province in Spain; in NM the first Trujillo settler was Diego de Trujillo, who arrived in 1632. He was a native of Mexico City. The San Miguel settlement dates from about 1836. Post office, 1913, intermittently, to present. TRUJILLO ARROYO (Luna). TRUJILLO CREEK (Sierra). Heads at Grant County line S of Kingston; flows E into the Rio Grande N of Arrey.

TRUTH OR CONSEQUENCES (Sierra). This controversial place name was adopted on Mar. 31, 1950, when the city formerly known as HOT SPRINGS voted to accept the offer of Ralph Edwards, master of ceremonies of a well-known radio show, to adopt the name of the show, Truth or Consequences, in return for a yearly fiesta with the program held in the city. Although Fount Sullivan is said to have started the settlement in 1905, there were residents in the neighborhood from the settlement of Las Palomas in the mid-nineteenth century or earlier. In fact, LAS PALOMAS, PALOMAS SPRINGS OF LAS PALOMAS, all seem to have been nineteenth-century names for the locality. Named for the doves that lived in the cottonwoods along the river. Confusion has resulted from the establishment on Apr. 9, 1874, of the Ojo Caliente or Hot Springs Apache Reservation in Socorro County, 40 mi SE on Alamosa River. However, the map of the Territory of New Mexico, printed for the Department of the Interior, General Land Office, in 1876, shows both the reservation and the community of Hot Springs on the Rio Grande. Today there is a post office at Las Palomas as well as at the incorporated city of Truth or Consequences. Williamsburg, a community just S of Truth or Consequences, for a time appropriated the name of Hot Springs. A good many radio newscasters and newspapermen refer to the city by its initials only, as T or C. Truth or Consequences (when it was called Hot Springs) became the county seat of Sierra County in 1937. The hot springs here still remain an important attraction to health seekers, whether advertised by name or not. Post office, as Truth or Consequences, 1951—.

TSAYA (San Juan). Trading point 45 mi S of Farmington. Post office, 1922-26; mail to Crownpoint.

TSCHICOMA PEAK (Rio Arriba). 13 mi S of Cañones, in Jemez Mts. near Sandoval County line. Also spelled CHICOMA PEAK.

TUCSON MOUNTAINS (Lincoln). In SE part of county. This range is not very high and is adapted to raising cattle, sheep, and goats. Will C. Barnes, in *Arizona Place Names* (1935), p. 455, says that both Hodge and Cones agree that the name comes from Piman Indian *sluyk-son,* "a dark or brown spring." Originally probably a Papago word, *styuk,* "black," and *son,* "foot, base" of a hill, doubtless locating the place of water or a spring. TUCSON SPRINGS (Sierra).

TUCUMCARI (Quay). County seat and commercial center on US 54 and 66. Named for Tucumcari Mtn. Although there was a settlement called Liberty 3 mi north on Pajarito Creek, as early as 1882, the city was not founded until 1902 when the CRI&P RR was built. For a brief period during construction camp days in 1901, the name was SIX-SHOOTER SIDING. The building of the SP RR extension road and the irrigation district from Conchas Reservoir have been important to the entire area. About the name, there has been more surmise than factual information. A folk tale credited to Geronimo relates that an Apache Indian maiden named Kari had a sweetheart, Tocom, who was slain by Tonapon, a rival. After the death of Tocom, Kari is said to have killed Tonapon and then taken her own life. Whereupon, Wautonomah, her father, stabbed himself, crying, "Tocom! Kari!" The Tucumcari area, however, is Comanche territory and Comanche phrases have linguistic support: the phrase for "two fires," *cuchtonaro,* "burn, make a fire," and *uah,* "two." The Comanches are reported to have used the peak for smoke

signals across the valley to the plains. Tucumcari Mtn., therefore, could mean "Signal Peak." The most convincing explanation is contributed by Elliott Canonge, Oklahoma linguist, who writes that the name is Comanche *tukamukaru,* "to lie in wait for someone or something to approach." According to Felix Kowena, his Comanche informant, this particular mountain was frequently used as a lookout by Comanche war parties. Post office, 1902—. TUCUMCARI CREEK (Quay). Formed by Plaza Larga, Barranca, and other creeks which join E of Lesbia; flows N into Canadian River. TUCUMCARI METROPOLITAN PARK (Quay). Site purchased in October 1935 and now maintained by the city as a recreation area.

TUERTO (Santa Fe). See GOLDEN. TUERTO MOUNTAINS (Santa Fe). See SAN PEDRO MOUNTAINS.

TULAROSA. Span., "reddish reeds or willows," i.e., "red of the stems." TULAROSA (Otero). Ranching and farming town on US 54 and SP RR 12 mi NW of Alamogordo; on edge of Mescalero Apache Indian Reservation. Post office, 1868-69; 1873—. TULAROSA BASIN (Otero). See LA LUZ. TULAROSA CANYON, CREEK (Catron). Tributary to Tularosa River, entering it from the E, 1½ mi E of Tularosa Mtn., 3 mi N of Aragon. TULAROSA CREEK (Otero). Heads on Mescalero Apache Indian Reservation and flows W to Tularosa. TULAROSA MOUNTAIN (Catron). 2 mi NW of Aragon. TULAROSA PEAK (Otero). TULAROSA RIVER (Catron). Heads in Mangas Mts.; flows SW into San Francisco River.

TULE LAKE (Catron). 13 mi N of Aragon.

TULOSA (San Miguel). Span., "reedy place." *Tule,* a word perhaps of Nahuatl origin, *tollin,* "common reed or cattail." Settlement 28 mi SE of Las Vegas, and 5 mi S of Alta Vista.

TUNICHA RANGE (San Juan). Spanish adaptation of Navajo *tqu'ntsa,* "large water." In Chuska Mts., SW corner of county. Name may possibly have been derived from Tunsta Wash in the general area.

TUNIS (Luna). Siding on SP RR, 6 mi W of Deming.

TUNQUE RUINS (Sandoval). Probably a Spanish adaptation of Tano-Tewa, *tung-ge,* "village of the basket." Ruins, at N end of the Sandias, were abandoned by the time the Spanish arrived. TUNQUE ARROYO (Sandoval). 10 mi NE of Bernalillo. Named for the Indian pueblo.

TUNSTA WASH (San Juan). Runs NE; joins Captain Tom Wash just E of Newcomb, to flow into Chaco River.

TUNSTALL'S CANYON (Lincoln). Reached by a road that leads S from near Tinnie, on US 70 and 380. Named for an Englishman, John H. Tunstall, who was killed here on Feb. 13, 1878, while going from his ranch on Felix River to Lincoln with a party of friends, among whom was Billy the Kid. It was this killing that precipitated the Lincoln County War.

TURKEY CREEK (Grant). Enters Gila River 11 mi NE of Cliff. TURKEY LAKE (Rio Arriba). 2 mi SE of Hopewell. TURKEY MOUNTAINS (Mora). Series of sandstone foothills in NE part of state, about 5 mi E of US 85 and 15 mi W of Wagon Mound. Named because of the number of wild turkeys found in the range. TURKEY SPRINGS (Valencia). In San Mateo Mts. TURKEY TRACK (Lea).

TURKEYFEATHER CREEK (Catron). Flows SE into West Fork of Gila River, entering 3 mi W of Jerky Mts. TURKEYFEATHER MOUNTAIN (Catron). 17 mi NE of Pleasanton. TURKEYFEATHER PASS (Catron). 2 mi NE of Turkeyfeather Mtn.

TURLEY (San Juan). 1 mi N of NM 17, 17 mi SE of Aztec. First postmaster, Urna B. Turley. Post office, 1906-41.

TURN (Valencia). Trading point on NM 47, 9 mi S of Belen, and 1 mi E of Bosque. Named by a Mr. Conant, a rancher, because of the sharp turn in the highway. Post office, 1927-38. See CASA COLORADO.

TURNER (Roosevelt). Locality near Arch, SE of Portales. Named for W. A. Turner, an early settler. Post office, 1908-11. TURNER PEAK (Catron). 7 mi NW of Luna. TURNERVILLE (Grant). Mining comunity on NM 180, 6 mi N of Bayard and 2 mi SE of Hanover. Post office, 1945—. See WIMSATTVILLE.

TURQUESA (Santa Fe). Post office, 1880-99; mail to Cerrillos. See CARBONATEVILLE.

TURQUILLO (Mora). Span., "little turk." 9 mi NE of Mora in the Rincon Range. Post office, 1910-13.

TURQUOISE (Otero). 1 mi E of US 54, on SP RR, 30 mi S of Alamogordo. TURQUOISE MOUNTAIN (Santa Fe). Just N of Cerrillos, where almost a million cubic yards of stone with turquoise are believed to have been excavated by the Indians in pre-Spanish times. TURQUOISE TRAIL. Traversing NM from the S to Santa Fe. Also known as CHIHUAHUA TRAIL

and EL CAMINO REAL (The Royal Road). Named for the path to turquoise mines, as well as to royal villas and settlements.

TUSAS (Rio Arriba). Span., "prairie dogs." Trading point on NM 111, 6 mi W of Tres Piedras and 32 mi NW of Taos. Tusa is the NM name for this particular rodent of the Southwest which the first Anglo-Americans likened to little dogs. It is not known whether the English term was translated from the Spanish or vice versa. The mountains seem to have been named before the town. Post office, 1898-1930. TUSAS CREEK (Rio Arriba). See RIO TUSAS. TUSAS MOUNTAIN (Rio Arriba). 5 mi NW of Tusas.

TUSCOCOCILLO CANYON (Quay). Heads near Porter and runs N into Canadian River.

TWELVEMILE WELLS (Hidalgo). 12 mi SW of Hachita.

TWIN ANGELS PEAK (San Juan). 12 mi SE of Bloomfield. Named by the stockmen because of a formation on top that resembles two figures at an altitude only wings could reach. An important landmark named as early as July 4, 1876, when this portion of the Jicarilla Apache Indian Reservation was thrown open for white settlement. TWIN BUTTES (McKinley). 4 mi SW of Gallup. TWIN DAMS (Chaves). On Rocky Arroyo and Hondo River, near their confluence, 12 mi S of Roswell. TWIN BUTTES (Otero). See TRES MONTOSOS. TWIN LAKES (Guadalupe). Two lakes, joined by a small stream, 2 mi SE of Santa Rosa. The smaller lake is so deep, it is said to be bottomless. TWIN LAKES (McKinley). 11 mi N of Gallup, on US 666. TWIN MOUNTAINS (Colfax). Two small cinder peaks on NM 7, between Des Moines and Folsom. They supplied C&S RR with cinders for ballast. This source also furnishes cinders for building blocks. TWIN SISTERS CANYON (Grant). Runs S into San Vincente Arroyo. TWIN SISTERS PEAKS (Grant). 3 mi NE of Pinos Altos in Pinos Altos Mts.

TWINING (Colfax). TWINING (Taos). Mining district formerly called AMIZETTE, 15 mi NE of Taos, on W slope of Taos Mt., with placer gold and copper, gold and silver lodes. When Amizette declined in 1895, William Frazer found copper and gold farther E in the canyon and he interested Albert C. Twining, a banker from New Jersey. A smelter costing $300,000 was built. When the smelter was fired, the molten ore froze to the sides of the furnace and the enterprise went bankrupt. Post office, 1902-10 mail to Valdez.

Two GREY HILLS (San Juan). Trading post 7 mi NE of Newcomb, first owned by a Mr. and Mrs. Ritz when it was established near a mission begun by the Dutch Reformed Church. Called by the Navajos *bis da cleetso*, "two yellow adobes." These terms may refer to hills in the vicinity. The Indians here make very fine rugs, which are woven without any red color, and are named for the place of weaving. Post office called CROZIER, 1903-19.

Two WELLS (Valencia). A place called the GALLUP Two WELLS area near Zuñi under a U.S. government purchase program in 1930's; now administered by the U.S. Bureau of Indian Affairs.

TYRONE (Grant). Former turquoise- and copper-mining community in the Burro Mts., 13 mi SW of Silver City. Named by a Mr. Honeyky for Tyrone, Ireland. The community is now largely deserted, although several beautiful buildings are still standing. Post office, 1906—. It was the sister town of Leopold (Grant).

TYUONYI (Sandoval). Name given to the chief ruins in El Rito de los Frijoles Canyon. The word is Keresan and its meaning is unexplained. Bandelier said the word has something to do with a treaty or contract by which certain pueblo tribes agreed that land areas, loosely defined, should belong, in the future, to each of them exclusively. The people of Cochiti claim that the inhabitants of Tyuonyi were their ancestors.

ULMORIS (Hidalgo). On SP RR, 5 mi E of Lordsburg.

UÑA DE GATO (Sandoval). Span., "cat's claw." 1 mi S of Hagan and 2½ mi NW of Puertocito. Named for a little bush, the black locust, because of its thorns. Post office, 1880-82.

UÑA DE GATO CREEK (Colfax). Rises in Johnson Park near Colorado line and flows SW to join Eagle Tail Creek N of Eagle Tail Peak; then joins Raton Creek and flows to Canadian Red River.

UNDERWOOD LAKE (Catron). 8 mi N of Luna.

UNION COUNTY. Created by the Territorial Legislature, Feb. 13, 1893. Formed from other counties and named Union because of the united desire of the people to establish a county government. UNION CHAPEL (Quay).

UNIVERSITY PARK (Doña Ana). Village surrounding New Mexico State University, (formerly New Mexico College of Agricultural and Mechanic Arts), 2 mi SE of Las Cruces and 1 mi E of US 80 and 85. Called STATE COLLEGE until Apr. 1, 1959. Post office, 1959—.

UPHAM (Sierra). Siding on AT&SF RR, 20 mi S of Engle, where cattle were shipped.

UPPER CAÑON (Sandoval). Settlement on Jemez River, 4 mi N of Jemez Pueblo. UPPER COLONIAS (San Miguel). 5 mi E of Pecos. UPPER FRISCO PLAZA (Catron). See RESERVE. UPPER LA JARA (Sandoval). Town on NM 96, 5 mi N of Cuba. UPPER MIMBRES (Grant). Post office, 1877-82; mail to Santa Rita. See FORT WEBSTER. UPPER MORA (Mora). Post office, 1868. UPPER PEÑASCO (Otero). Post office, 1884-1902. See MAYHILL.

UPTON (Roosevelt). Trading point 20 mi W of Portales, and 15 mi N of Elida. Named for W. G. Upton, an early settler. Post office, 1907-30.

URRACA (Colfax). Span., "magpie." Settlement on NM 21, 22 mi NW of Springer and 5 mi S of Cimarron. URRACA CREEK (Colfax). Rises near Clear Creek Mtn. and Black Mtn. in SW part of county; flows E, passing 5 mi S of Cimarron to Canadian Red River. URRACA MESA (Colfax). 12 mi SW of Cimarron.

URTON (Roosevelt). Named for W. G. and George Urton, brothers who came from Pleasant Hill, Mo., in 1884. W. G. Urton was with the Bar V Ranch and was president of the Cass Land and Cattle Co. George was with the LFD Ranch. Post office, 1906-07. See KENNA. URTON LAKE (De Baca). 20 mi S of Ft. Sumner. Large lake which is without water during dry spells. Named for W. G. Urton, foreman on the old Bar V Ranch, which covered this district during the early days.

U.S. HILL (Mora). A grade on the winding mountain road leading from Mora to Taos. Explanation commonly given for name is that the alignment of the road is so irregular that if viewed from the air, it would actually spell out the initials "U.S." Engineers of the State Highway Department have expressed doubts of this etymology, and the manager of the Las Vegas Chamber of Commerce suggests that the U.S. Forest Service, which completed the road, may have had something to do with the name. U.S. Hill was also the name of the military road farther W between Embudo and Taos.

UTAHPO (Rio Arriba). Tewa, "Ute trail." Name of a famous Ute trail, leading from the Rio Grande, across Canal Mesa N into the Ute country. UTE CREEK (Colfax). Post office, 1868-95; mail to Baldy. UTE CREEK (Union, Harding, Quay). Rises in SW part of Union County and flows S to join Canadian Red River in Quay County. Named for the Ute Indians. Some old maps call it ALAMO CREEK. UTE LAKE STATE PARK AND RECREATION AREA. (Colfax). Dam is earth-filled structure 5,750 ft long, impounding the Canadian River just W of Logan. Designed for industrial and recreational purposes. UTE MOUNTAIN INDIAN RESERVATION (San Juan). Area of which 168 sq mi lie in NM; begins 10 mi NW of Farmington and goes across Colorado line. UTE PARK (Colfax). Settlement and area in Cimarron Canyon on US 64, and at terminal of Ute Park branch of AT&SF RR. At one time inhabited by the Ute Indians so they could be near the government agency at Cimarron, which supplied and governed them. Other settlers moved in about 1867. Post office, 1908—. UTE PARK (Taos). In Sangre de Cristo Mts., 4 mi S of Colorado line, SW of Costilla. Named for the Ute Indians.

VACANT (Chaves). See VOCANT.
VADO (Doña Ana). Span., "ford." Farming community of many names on US 80, 15 mi SE of Las Cruces. First known as HERRON, for the name of the earliest Anglo settlers, two brothers. Later changed to EARLHAM, for a town in Ohio or Illinois from which that family came. Later yet, called CENTER VALLEY by one of the postmasters. Present name may be for an early ford or river crossing. Post office, 1911, intermittently, to present. VADITO (Taos). Ranching community on NM 75, 23 mi S of Taos.
VALDEZ (Taos). Farming community 6 mi E of NM 3, 12 mi N of Taos. Settled between 1750 and 1800. Jose Luis Valdez, a native of Oviedo, Spain, who married a native of Mexico City, came to NM with the Reconquest of 1692 and settled in Santa Cruz. Probably named for this family. Formerly called SAN ANTONIO, for Catholic chapel in the village. Post office, 1895—.
VALEDON (Hidalgo). 3 mi SW of Lordsburg. Post office, 1917-32.

VALENCIA (Valencia). Trading point on NM 47, 14 mi N of Belen, and 2 mi E of Los Lunas. Named for Juan de Valencia, who settled in this area in the seventeenth century. His descendants returned here after the Spanish reoccupied NM in 1692. One of the oldest Spanish-American settlements in county and at one time the county seat. Post office, 1884-1904; 1923-34; mail to Los Lunas. VALENCIA COUNTY. Created by the Republic of Mexico in 1844 and confirmed by the New Mexico Territorial Legislature, Jan. 9, 1852. Named for the town in the county.
VALENZUELA (Socorro). See BALENZUELA.
VALLADOLID (Taos). See TAOS PUEBLO.
VALLECITO MOUNTAIN (Taos). Span., "little valley." 6 mi E of Valdez. VALLECITOS (Bernalillo). On NM 10, 15 mi SE of Albuquerque. VALLECITOS (Rio Arriba). Farming and ranching community on NM 111, 36 mi N of Española. Founded in 1776, the same time as Canjilon and the surrounding settlements. Post office, 1886—. VALLECITOS (Sandoval). Also known as LOWER VALLECITOS. Community on Vallecitos Creek and NM 290, 3 mi NE of Jemez. VALLECITOS CREEK (Sandoval). Rises in Paliza Canyon W of Bland and flows into Jemez River N of Jemez Pueblo. VALLECITOS DE LOS INDIOS (Sandoval). 13 mi NW of Jemez Pueblo. VALLECITO GRANT (Rio Arriba). Between the mountains of Santa Clara and the ranch of Jose Reano. Grant made to Brevet Lieutenant Jose Garcia de la Mora, in company with twelve persons. VALLECITO DE LOBATO GRANT (Rio Arriba). Also called TOWN OF VALLECITO GRANT. Near the source of Ojo Caliente River. Granted on Feb. 27, 1824, by Gov. Bartolome Baca to Jose Rafael Samora and twenty-five others. VALLECITOS, LOWER and UPPER (Rio Arriba). See RIO VALLECITOS. VALLE GRANDE (Sandoval). On NM 4, SW of Los Alamos. Grassy valley, 176 sq mi in area, in extinct crater surrounded by mountains. VALLE GRANDE CREEK (Sandoval). Head of East Fork of Jemez River on Baca Location No. 1; in high mountain country, flowing through the Valle Grande. VALLE GRANDE PEAK (Rio Arriba). 5 mi SW of Vallecitos. VALLE MEDIO FORK (San Miguel). Extreme North Fork of Bear Creek. VALLEY (Union). Trading point on NM 325, 2 mi from Colorado line, on Dry Cimarron River. Settled in 1879. Post office, 1903-26. VALLEY AUGUSTINE (San Miguel). VALLEY

RANCH (San Miguel). Settlement on Pecos River, 1 mi N of Pecos at S edge of Alexander Valle Grant. Post office, 1908-50. VALLEY SEVEN RIVER (Eddy). Rises in county and flows E to junction of Branch Seven River. VALLEY VIEW (Roosevelt). 14 mi S of Elida. Post office, 1911-18. Formerly called WOOTEN.

VALMONT (Otero). Trading point of many names, on US 54 and SP RR, 10 mi S of Alamogordo. First called DOG TOWN, from Dog Canyon in vicinity. Later changed to CAMP CITY, for a Mr. Camp an early settler; then to CAMP in 1908. In 1910, the name was again changed to SHAMROCK and finally, in 1915, to its present name, which seems to be a combination of "vale" and "mountain." Post office, 1917-22.

VALMORA (Mora). Farming and ranching community 4 mi E of US 85, and 5 mi NE of Watrous, in John Scolly Land Grant. Formerly a sanatorium-village operated by eastern firms for the benefit of their employees. Post office, 1916—.

VALVERDE (Socorro). Span., "green valley." Trading point 29 mi S of Socorro, at S end of Jornada del Muerto, near Ft. Selden. Bears the name of an early governor or his descendants. Capt. Don Antonio Valverde y Cosio was acting governor of NM from 1717 to 1722; he was well traveled for his time. His only mode of journeying was by walking, but during his term of office he visited all the pueblos of the province, marched to Mexico, and went into what are now Colorado and Kansas. He campaigned against the Comanche and Ute Indians in 1719. In 1722, he moved from Santa Fe to Guadalupe del Paso. A famous battle of the Civil War was fought at Valverde in 1862, when the Confederate Army, moving north, met the Union troops from Ft. Craig. The Confederates were the victors.

VANADIUM (Grant). Mining community on NM 180 and AT&SF RR, 2 mi N of Bayard. Named for the mineral deposits here, which are used as an alloy with steel. Post office, 1912—.

VAN BREMMER CREEK (Colfax). Rises in Van Bremmer Park NE of Cimarron near Dawson Canyon, and flows SE for 25 mi to join Vermejo River 10 mi W of Maxwell. VAN BREMMER PARK (Colfax). Area 4 mi square in the midst of tall, rugged mountains. At head of

Van Bremmer Creek and 6 mi E of Costilla Peak.

VANCE (Union). 14 mi S of Clayton, ½ mi W of NM 18, and 3 mi SE of Thomas. First postmaster, William H. Vance. Post office on farm of Willis R. Vance, 1908-20.

VANDERITOS (Mora, Colfax). Post office, 1886-87; mail to Hall's Peak; 1906-07; mail to Aurora.

VANDER WAGEN (McKinley). 18 mi S of Gallup on NM 32. Once called WHITE WATER, but changed when post office was established in 1949. Commemorates Andrew Vander Wagen, who came to NM in 1897, as a missionary of the Christian Reformed Church, first to the Navajos and later to the Zuñi Indians.

VAN HOUTEN (Colfax). Abandoned mining town 6 mi W of US 85, and 18 mi SW of Raton. Named for Jan Van Houten, of Raton, manager of coal mines and American representative of the Dutch syndicate which acquired the Maxwell Land Grant from Lucien B. Maxwell. He became president of the St. Louis, Rocky Mountain and Pacific Co., associated with the grant. Post office, 1902-52; mail to Raton.

VAN PATTENS (Doña Ana). See DRIPPING SPRINGS.

VAQUEROS (Rio Arriba). Span., "cowboys, herdsmen." Post office, 1919-22; mail to Dulce. VAQUEROS CANYON (Rio Arriba). In Carson National Forest; runs SW into La Jara Creek, 4 mi W of Gobernador.

VARGAS (Union). Siding 5 mi from Mt. Dora where AT&SF RR bought a mountain and built a short track in order to use volcanic cinder material for ballast roadbeds.

VARIADERO (San Miguel). A local coinage from the Span., variar, "to vary, to change," therefore naming a place where a stream frequently changes its course. Trading point on NM 65, 25 mi N of Newkirk. Founded by Jesus Angel of Bernal in 1872. Post office, 1907-23.

VARNEY (Torrance). On SP RR, 4 mi NE of Corona. Named about 1910 for the bookkeeper of the Corona Trading Co. Post office, 1914-18.

VAUD (Eddy). Post office, 1893-94; changed to FLORENCE. See LOVING.

VAUGHN (Guadalupe). Community that is a highway junction, US 60, 54, 285; also a railroad shipping point for cattle, sheep, and wool. Named for Maj. G. W. Vaughn, former civil engineer for AT&SF RR. Post office, 1907—. See EAST VAUGHN.

VAUR (Mora). Post office, 1889-92; changed to LEON.

VEDA (Union). Post office, 1890-98; mail to Spring Hill; 1900-07; mail to Corrumpa.

VEGA BLANCA (San Miguel). Span., "white meadow." VEGA BLANCA (Santa Fe). VEGA BLANCA (Sierra). VEGA BONITA CREEK (San Miguel). Fork of Valle Medio Creek, which flows into Bear Creek. Heads in a meadow with marsh and underground stream, 5 mi SW of Rociada. VEGAS DE LAS GALLINAS (San Miguel). See LAS VEGAS GRANT. VEGAS GRANDES (San Miguel). See LAS VEGAS GRANT.

VEGUITA (Socorro). "Little meadow." Farming community on NM 47, 12 mi S of Belen and 33 mi N of Socorro, W of US 85. Post office, 1918—.

VEITCH (Hidalgo). On SP RR, 10 mi NE of Lordsburg.

VELARDE (Rio Arriba). Fruit-raising community on the Rio Grande and on US 64, 14 mi NE of Española. Juan Antonio Perez Velarde arrived from Spain to settle at Guadalupe del Paso by 1725. The Velardes who are known in Santa Fe, Albuquerque, and the Rio Arriba country would seem to be his descendants. Founded by Matias Velarde in 1875. First named LA JOLLA, a misspelling of La Joya. Many of the finest woven blankets in NM were produced here in the early days. First postmaster, David Velarde. Post office, 1855—.

VENCILL (Luna). Siding on AT&SF RR, 10 mi NW of Deming. Named for Jo Vencill, a long time employee of the railroad.

VENTANAS (San Miguel). Span., "windows." Post office, 1919-27. See TRUJILLO.

VENUS (Santa Fe). Trading point 10 mi NW of Moriarty on the NMC RR. Named for the Venus Mercantile Co., a general store. Post office, 1909-28.

VERA CRUZ (Lincoln). Post office, 1881-83; mail to Nogal.

VERMEJO CREEK (Mora). Span., "brown or auburn." Flows into Canadian Red River at county line. VERMEJO PARK (Colfax). Ranching community on NM 234, 30 mi W of Raton on Vermejo River. When AT&SF RR was built over Raton Mts., most of the inhabitants moved to Raton. Vermejo Park is the center of the old Bartlett Estate, a 350,000-acre ranch with palatial homes. A group of Californians now own the estate and have made a club of it for vacationing. Post offices, Vermejo, 1874-83; Cimilorio, 1883-98; Vermejo, 1902-07; Vermejo Park, 1907—. VER-

MEJO RIVER (Colfax). Rises in NW corner of county; fed by many smaller streams. Flows through VERMEJO CANYON, through Dawson, and SE to join Canadian Red River 6 mi S of Maxwell. Along its banks, the earliest settlers of northeastern NM made their homes.

VERNON (Colfax). Ranching community on SP RR, 18 mi SE of French and 10 mi SE of Taylor Springs. Post office, 1911-17.

VEVAY (Doña Ana). On SP RR, 20 mi NE of El Paso, Tex.

V CROSS T LAKE (Catron). 1 mi N of Beaverhead.

VICK'S PEAK (Socorro). In Cibola National Forest, 4 mi S of San Mateo Peak. Said to be named for Chief Victorio, often referred to as "Old Vic" when he and his Apaches camped here in the 1870's.

VICTOR (Socorro). 5 mi SE of Jarales. Post office, 1910-14.

VICTORIA (Doña Ana). Post office, 1880-1908; changed to LA MESA. VICTORIA PARK (Sierra). W of Victoria Park Mtn. VICTORIA PARK MOUNTAIN (Sierra). 6 mi SW of Hermosa.

VICTORIO (Luna). Siding on SP RR, and NM 9, 12 mi E of Hachita. VICTORIO MOUNTAINS (Luna). Small range 12 mi E of Hachita. Named for the Apache chieftain who left the Mescalero reservation in 1879 and led his braves until he was killed in 1883.

VIGIL. Francisco Montes Vigil and his wife came to Santa Fe as early as 1695, and in 1710 he received a grant of land at Alameda. They were the earliest of a considerable number of Vigils who arrived to settle in NM during the eighteenth century. VIGIL (Quay). 18 mi SE of Conchas Reservoir, 14 mi W of Tucumcari. VIGIL (San Miguel). Post office, 1882; mail to Ft. Bascom. VIGIL (Union). Post office, 1894-98; changed to BUEYEROS. VIGIL CANYON (Catron). Heads in Arizona and runs E into San Francisco River at Alma.

VILLANUEVA (San Miguel). Farming community on NM 3, 12 mi S of Bernal and 27 mi SW of Las Vegas. Named by the Post Office Department in 1890, after petition of the people. Founded in 1808 by Mariano Baros and José Felipe Madrid. Post office, 1890-1912.

VILLITA (Rio Arriba). Span., "small town." On US 64, N of Alcalde. Shown on maps of the 1880's about 30 mi SE of Chama.

VIRDEN (Hidalgo). Farming community on NM 82, 31 mi NW of Lordsburg. Formerly known as RICHMOND, but in 1916 name was changed when that area became populated with Mormon refugees from Mexico. Name chosen for the owner of the land where the village now stands. Incorporated as a village in 1925.

VIRGINIA, VIRGINIA CITY (Colfax). Postal records list Taos, Mora, and Colfax counties for this station between Apr. 9, 1868, and Oct. 22, 1869. See ELIZABETHTOWN.

VIRSYLVIA (Taos). Trading point 3 mi W of NM 3, 10 mi N of Questa. Now called SUN-SHINE VALLEY.

VISTA (Grant). Former trading point on NM 9 and SP RR, 8 mi W of Hachita.

VIVAY (Doña Ana). Point on SP RR between Aden and Chappel.

VOCANT (Chaves). Location S of Rio Feliz on the Roswell-Hope road, 16 mi W of Hagerman. Post office, 1908-13.

VOLCANO (Rio Arriba). Post office, 1922-23; mail to Skarda.

VOUGH (Eddy). See LOVING.

WAGNER (Torrance). Post office, 1908; mail to Mountainair.

WAGON MOUND (Mora). Ranching and dryfarming town on NM 120, US 85, and AT&SF RR, in east-central part of county. Named by stockmen about 1859 for a rocky formation to the E, resembling a covered wagon. SANTA CLARA seems to have been the earliest name for the community. It was here that the Cimarron cutoff joined the main branch of the Santa Fe Trail. Post office, 1882—.

WAGON TONGUE MOUNTAIN (Catron). 1½ mi SE of Aragon.

WAHOO CANYON (Catron). 5 mi W of Dusty. WAHOO PEAK (Catron). 7 mi SW of Dusty. Could be a transfer name from a town in Nebraska 35 mi W of Omaha.

WALDO (Santa Fe). On AT&SF RR, 20 mi W of Lamy, 2 mi NW of Cerrillos. Active about 1892 when the mines were producing at Cerrillos. From 1918 to 1924, a zinc oxide plant operated here. Name honors Judge Henry L. Waldo, who came to Santa Fe from Missouri in 1862. He was appointed chief justice of the Supreme Court of the Territory in 1881. Post office, 1920-26.

WALKER AIR FORCE BASE (Chaves). Established at Roswell in 1942, as a permanent installation of the U.S. Air Force. The ROSWELL ARMY FLYING SCHOOL became successively the ROSWELL ARMY AIR FIELD and the ROSWELL AIR FIELD before finally being renamed Walk-

er Air Force Base in 1948. Name honors Brig. Gen. Kenneth N. Walker, who was killed in the air battle for New Guinea.

WALKING X CANYON (Grant). Runs SE from the Continental Divide, 8 mi S of Cliff. See CURETON.

WALL (Valencia). WALL LAKE (Catron). 15 mi S of Beaverhead.

WALLACE (Sandoval). 10 mi NE of Algodones. Post office, 1882-87; mail to Cerrillos; 1888-95; mail to Peña Blanca. Became THORNTON; later DOMINGO. WALLACE (Colfax). 28 mi W of Des Moines. Said to be named for Gen. Lew Wallace, author of The Fair God (1873) and Ben-Hur (1880). While governor of New Mexico Territory (1878-1881), he tried to settle one of the most famous feuds in western history, called the Lincoln County War.

WALNUT (Lincoln). Formerly on SP RR, 9 mi E of Carrizozo and 1 mi from US 380. Established in 1899 and named by EP&N RR for the walnut trees in nearby Water Canyon. Water station when the trains ran to Capitan every day, but long since abandoned. WALNUT CREEK (Chaves, Eddy). 17 mi NW of Hope. WALNUT CREEK (Socorro). WALNUT WELLS (Hidalgo). Way station on Butterfield Overland Mail route in 1858. The Diamond A Cattle Co. owned the well of water here. Post office, 1914-20.

WALTERS LAKE (Eddy). 15 mi E of Illinois Camp.

WAMPIA SPRING (McKinley). 9 mi SE of Zuñi Pueblo, near Valencia County line.

WAMSLEY CROSSING (Taos). Established in 1892 by Sock Wamsley, who built a bridge across the Rio Grande.

WANETTE (Union). Established about 1911, 5 mi SW of Seneca and NW of Clayton. A Dr. Carpenter, owner of a general store, combined the name of his daughter Nette with that of his freighter, Walter Ciser, to designate the place. Wanette disappeared when isolated by travel and highways. Post office, 1910-16.

WARM SPRINGS APACHE INDIAN RESERVATION (Socorro). Established Apr. 9, 1874, at Ojo Caliente or Hot Springs on Alamosa River, 40 mi SW of Truth or Consequences. Later abandoned.

WARREN (Lea). Post office, 1912-19; 1920-23. See GLADIOLA.

WASHINGTON PASS (San Juan). In Chuska Mts., 10 mi W of NM 666 and 16 mi SW of Newcomb. Named in honor of Lt. Col. John M. Washington, civil and military governor of

New Mexico, 1848-49, and commander of the expedition against the Navajos in 1848. Locally called COTTONWOOD PASS. The Navajos believe that the pass is the neck of the mountain range called *yolth dzil*, "bead mountain."

WATER BIRD LAKE (Taos). Small lake at head of Pueblo Creek, NE of Taos. WATER CANYON (Lincoln). Heads on Nogal Peak; runs N and W 6 mi S of Carrizozo. WATER CANYON (Otero). Small stream in Sacramento Mts., 12 mi SE of Alamogordo. WATER CANYON (Santa Fe, Sandoval). Enters the Rio Grande from the W, 4 mi below Buckman bridge. Tewa name meant "fishweir water thread canyon." WATER CANYON (Socorro). Watering station formerly used by trains on AT&SF RR. Post office, 1887-88; Watercanon, Jan.-Sept. 1899; both names, 1899-1927; Water Canyon, 1927-29 mail to Magdalena.

WATERFLOW (San Juan). Farming and mining community on US 550, 13 mi W of Farmington, through which the San Juan, Animas, and La Plata rivers flow. Post office, 1920—.

WATERLOO (Luna). Former settlement 1 mi W of NM 11 and 10 mi N of Columbus. Established about 1910-11, and faded during the economic depression of the 1930's. Name may be a transfer, but there has been a suggestion that it was selected by some of the settlers because of the ill fate which followed drought and hard times. Post office, 1911-22.

WATROUS (Mora). Old Spanish settlement 20 mi NE of Las Vegas, on US 82, and AT&SF RR. At junction of Sapello and Mora rivers, and once called LA JUNTA or RIO LA JUNTA. Shortly before the Civil War, the community took the last name of Samuel B. Watrous, an early Anglo-American settler. Post office, La Junta, 1868-79; changed to Watrous, 1879—.

WEATHERLY LAKE (Union). See WETHERLY LAKE.

WEAVER (McKinley). Abandoned coal-mining town. Named for Wiley Weaver, a mine official.

WEBER (Mora). Post office, 1898-1905; mail to La Cueva. WEBER CITY (Curry). Former trading point on NM 88, 15 mi N of Melrose. Settled in 1932 and named for a Weber family. Now, the only business establishment is a bar.

WEDDING CAKE HILL (Union). On N side of US 64, 12 mi W of Oklahoma line. Named for its peculiar formation, a round mound

rising about 300 ft from the floor of the canyon. The grass-covered slope is topped by red, white, and brown layers of sandy rock, giving it the appearance of a big layer cake.

WEED (Otero). Truck-farming and lumbering community on NM 24, 27 mi SE of Alamogordo, on E slope of Sacramento Mts. Named for W. H. Weed of White Oaks who established a branch store here in the early 1880's. Post office, 1885—.

WELLS (Eddy). Area E of Salt Lake and E of Loving; a triangle formed by Nash Well on N, Indian Well on E, and South Well on SW. Some say that the word "Wells," first referred only to Indian Wells dug here.

WEMPLE (Luna). Siding to Peru Mills on AT&SF RR, 5 mi NW of Deming.

WERSONICK CANYON (Colfax). Above Yankee, where family of this name lived.

WEST (Quay). Surname of first postmaster, James T. West. Post office, 1908-25. WEST EL PASO (Doña Ana). Formerly ANAPRA. Post office, 1915-19; mail to El Paso. WEST LAS VEGAS (San Miguel). Post office, 1928—. See LAS VEGAS. WEST POTRILLO MOUNTAINS (Doña Ana). Extend S to Mexican border in SW part of county, S of Aden. WEST RED CANYON (Socorro). Heads in Cibola National Forest and runs S to Alamosa River below Dusty. WEST TULAROSA (Otero). Post office, 1911-12. WESTWATER (Eddy). Post office, 1902-03; mail to Carlsbad. WESTYARD (McKinley). On AT&SF RR, 5 mi W of Gallup.

WET CANYON (Colfax). In extreme NW corner of county. WET LEGGET SPRING (Catron). 8 mi W of Reserve and W of US 260.

WETHERLY LAKE (Union). 9 mi SE of Des Moines.

WHEATFIELD LAKE (San Juan). In SW corner of county, 4 mi W of Crystal.

WHEATLAND (Quay). Old trading point on NM 39, 25 mi S of San Jon. Settled about 1915. Name selected by ballot among members of three school districts when these were consolidated: North Bend, a school built and started by an early settler, W. R. Brown, in 1915; Blair School, ½ mi from present site; and Forest School, several miles to SW. Now known as CAMERON.

WHEATON CREEK (Rio Arriba). In Black Lake Valley; tributary to Coyote Creek.

WHEELER PEAK (Taos). NE of Taos in Sangre de Cristo Mts. Probably named for Maj. George M. Wheeler, in charge of surveys W of the 100th meridian between 1871 and

1879. Highest peak in NM, elevation 13,160 ft. WHISKEY CANYON (Sierra). For no reason related to the name, a famous fossil locality, in Caballo Mts. S of Truth or Consequences. WHISKEY CREEK (Colfax). Tributary to the Ponil NW of Cimarron. WHISKEY CREEK (Grant). Small creek 5 mi NE of Silver City; flows into Cameron Creek. There is a story that in the early days the settlers had stills along the creek, and became careless in guarding them. When the Indians stole the whiskey and became intoxicated they decided to massacre the surrounding settlers, but were easily defeated because of their condition. WHISKEY LAKE (McKinley). In NW part of county at San Juan County line, 10 mi N of Tohatchi.

WHITE (Lea). Formerly a one-teacher school, 6 mi SW of Eunice. WHITE CREEK (Catron). Rises in Mogollon Mts., and is a tributary of West Fork of Gila River. WHITEFLAT (Chaves). WHITE FLAT (De Baca). First known as GRAMA FLAT, because of the grama grass that grew on this 3-mi-square area. In the early 1900's a man named White was killed here in a range quarrel and the name was changed. WHITE LAKE (Chaves). 7 mi S of Elkins. WHITE LAKE (Socorro). 5 mi SE of Gran Quivira. WHITE LAKES (Santa Fe). Trading point on US 285, 37 mi S of Santa Fe. WHITE MESA (Sandoval). 3 mi SW of San Ysidro. Named for gypsum deposits here. WHITE MOUNTAIN (Otero). Post office, 1913-22; changed to THREE RIVERS. WHITE MOUNTAINS (Otero). See SIERRA BLANCA. WHITE OAKS (Lincoln). Old mining community on NM 349, 11 mi NE of Carrizozo. Named for many white oak trees surrounding two large springs near the settlement. Famed as the setting for Emerson Hough's novel *Heart's Desire* (1903). Founded as a mining camp in 1879; within twenty-five years nearly three million dollars in gold and silver was taken from the mines. When EP&NE RR bypassed the camp, development faded in these and other minerals which had been discovered. Now almost a ghost town. Post office, 1880-1954. WHITE ROCK (Los Alamos). Built entirely of prefabricated material, and planned originally in 1948 as a construction camp for workers on government projects at nearby Los Alamos. WHITE ROCK (San Juan). Trading point 57 mi NE of Gallup. WHITE ROCK CANYON (Catron, Grant). Runs SW across

county line into Little Creek, 6 mi N of Jackson. WHITE ROCK CANYON (Sandoval, Santa Fe). The Rio Grande flows through White Rock Canyon in Bandelier National Monument at E border of county. WHITEROCKS MOUNTAIN (Catron). On Arizona line, 21 mi SE of Reserve. WHITE SANDS MISSILE RANGE (Doña Ana). Headquarters 25 mi NE of Las Cruces; established July 9, 1945, by Department of Defense; operated by Department of Army for use of all branches of service and NASA. Encompasses 4,000 sq mi. Formerly WHITE SANDS PROVING GROUND; changed to White Sands Missile Range on May 1, 1958. Contains the White Sands National Monument. WHITE SANDS NATIONAL MONUMENT (Otero). An area of 176,000 acres covered with white, granulated gypsum crystals that look like sand, 16 mi SW of Alamogordo on US 70. Extends for 24 mi in length and varies from 10 to 15 mi in width. These dunes are unlike any other in the world. Wild creatures on the edge of this area have taken on protective coloration and one finds white mice, white lizards, and light-colored insects. There is practically no animal or vegetable life in the interior. In 1920, Father Augustine, from Santa Barbara, Calif., discovered some warm ponds here, in very cold winter weather. WHITE SANDS PROVING GROUND (Doña Ana). See WHITE SANDS MISSILE RANGE. WHITES CITY (Eddy). Tourist-resort community on US 62 at entrance to Carlsbad Caverns National Park, 18 mi SW of Carlsbad. Named for Jim White, a cowboy who discovered the Caverns in 1901. Post office, 1942—. See the town of SEVEN RIVERS. WHITE SIGNAL (Grant). Trading point on NM 180, 17 mi SW of Silver City. Post office, 1909-34. WHITE SULPHUR SPRINGS (Lincoln). Post office, 1875; changed to SOUTH FORK. WHITE TAIL (Otero). In E part of Mescalero reservation, 37 mi NE of Tularosa; on US 70 and NM 24, near Cloudcroft. Named for WHITE TAIL DRAW, where many whitetail deer are found. This is a settlement of another tribe of Apache Indians. Post office, 1915-26; mail to Mescalero. WHITE WATER (Catron). See GLENWOOD. WHITEWATER (Grant). 3 mi W of US 60; 18 mi SE of Silver City on AT&SF RR. Post office, 1883, intermittently, to 1952. WHITE WATER (McKinley). See VANDER WAGEN. WHITEWATER BALDY (Catron). WHITE WATER CREEK (Catron). Rises on W side of Mogollon Mts., flowing through Glenwood to San Francisco River. WHITEWATER CREEK (Grant). Rises SW of Santa Rita; flows S to Luna County line. WHITEWATER CREEK (Hidalgo). Parallels border 1 mi above Texas; flows E into Deer Creek. WHITEWATER MOUNTAIN (Hidalgo). WHITEWATER, SOUTH FORK (Catron). South fork of White Water Creek. WHITE WATER SPRINGS (Otero). WHITFIELD (Socorro). Post office, 1890-92; changed to PATTERSON. WHITMIRE CANYON (Hidalgo). 10 mi NW of Cloverdale. WHITMIRE CREEK (Hidalgo). Flows into Animas Creek from the S, 11 mi N of Cloverdale. WHITNEY (Colfax). WHITNEY (Luna). Siding on SP RR. WHITSON (Colfax). Post office, 1878. WILCOX SPRINGS (DeBaca). See DRIPPING SPRINGS. WILCOX LAKE (DeBaca). See RED LAKE.

WILD COW CANYON (Grant). Heads 10 mi SW of Gila Cliff Dwellings National Monument; runs S into Gila River. WILD COW MESA (Eddy). In Guadalupe Mts. SW of Rocky Arroyo. Named because in the old days, it was a hiding place for stolen cattle. Some of these became lost, increased, and their offspring became wild. WILD HORSE CANYON (Socorro). 9 mi SW of Dusty, and 2 mi S of San Mateo Peak. WILD HORSE CREEK (Santa Fe). Heads in Sangre de Cristo Mts. and flows NW into Dalton Creek, 10 mi E of Santa Fe. WILD HORSE PEAK (Grant). 2 mi S of Schoolhouse Mtn. and 4 mi W of Gila River.

WILEY CREEK (De Baca). Joins Pecos River at Chaves. Named for "Old Man" Wiley, who first settled here in the early 1900's. 30 mi long, but has no water except in rainy seasons. WILLARD (Torrance). Farming town on US 60, and AT&SF RR, 13 mi NE of Mountainair. Established in 1902 and named for Willard Samuel Hopewell, Jr., son of W. S. Hopewell, promoter and railroad builder, who came to NM from California in 1878. Became a station on SFC RR in 1903. Post office, 1903—. See HOPEWELL.

WILLIAMS (Lea). 12 mi S of Caprock just E of Mescalero Ridge near Chaves County line. WILLIAMS (San Miguel). WILLIAMSBURG (Sierra). Post office, 1949—. See HOT SPRINGS. WILLIAMS LAKE (Taos). At head of a fork of Hondo River N of Taos. WILLIS (Mora). On Pecos River 15 mi N of Pecos. Post office, 1896-1905.

WILLOW (Colfax). Post office, 1902; changed to VAN HOUTEN. WILLOW ARROYO (Colfax). See RATON CREEK. WILLOW CREEK (Catron). Follows old Bursum Road to Mogollon; headwaters of Middle Fork of Gila River. WILLOW CREEK (Colfax). 3 mi S of Elizabethtown. WILLOW CREEK (Mora). WILLOW CREEK (Rio Arriba). Point on D&RGW RR, 5 mi S of Chama. WILLOW CREEK (Rio Arriba). Heads just W of Chama River and flows S into it above El Vado Reservoir. Plans call for a dam on this creek to deliver water via Chama River into the Rio Grande in order to provide supplemental water for irrigation and for municipal and industrial uses in Albuquerque. WILLOW CREEK (San Miguel). Tributary of Pecos River, entering it at Terrero. WILLOW LAKE (Eddy). 2 mi S of Malaga. WILLOW SPRING (Grant). 1 mi NE of Seventy-Four Mtn. WILLOW SPRINGS (Colfax Union). Post office, 1877-79; 1914-17; mail to Corrumpa. See RATON.

WILNA (Grant). Trading point on US 70, 80, and SP RR, 28 mi W of Deming.

WILSON (Colfax). WILSON (Hidalgo). WILSON CANYON (Catron). Heads at Eagle Peak and runs NW and W into Tularosa River 4 mi NE of Reserve. WILSON CREEK (Grant). Flows SW into Cherry Creek 3 mi N of Pinos Altos Mts.

WIMSATTVILE (Grant). 1 mi W of Santa Rita and E of Hanover. Named for a Mr. Wimsatt who filed a claim, but discovered it was not valuable in paying ore. He built a store instead, around which a small village grew. In recent years renamed TURNERVILLE in order to obtain a post office. The store buildings are vacant but still standing.

WINDMILL CANYON (Grant). Runs N into Bear Creek, 9 mi E of Cliff.

WIND MOUNTAIN (Otero). One of Cornudas Mts., 2 mi N of Mexican border.

WINGATE STATION (McKinley). On AT&SF RR, 12 mi E of Gallup. See FORT WINGATE.

WINKLE (Guadalupe). On SP RR, 12 mi NE of Vaughn.

WINSOR CREEK (San Miguel). Tributary of Pecos River at Cowles, heading at Lake Katherine and Stewart Lake.

WINSTON (Sierra). At foothills of Black Range on NM 52, 28 mi NW of Truth or Consequences. Originally a mining community named FAIRVIEW. Changed to Winston in honor of Frank H. Winston, who set up a mercantile business here in 1882. He was once a member of the State Legislature and a pioneer in cattle raising and mining. Post office, 1930—.

WIRE LAKE (De Baca). 15 mi W of Dunlap.

WISSMATH. (Rio Arriba). At Taos County line, 11½ mi N of Tres Piedras. WISSMATH CRATERS (Taos). 2 mi E of Wissmath.

WITT (Torrance). On NM 41, 5 mi N of Estancia. Dry-ice plant on old NMC RR, built here in 1935 by Witt Ice Co.

WOLF CANYON (Sandoval), also WOLF CAÑON. Post office, 1914-15; mail to Señorita. WOLF CREEK (Mora). Flows S to Mora River, joining it at Valmora. WOLF CREEK (Rio Arriba). Tributary to Chama River, heading in Colorado; flows SW and enters the river 4 mi above Chama.

WOODBURY (Sandoval). Near Bland, 6 mi S of Peña Blanca. The *Santa Fe New Mexican,* Nov. 14, 1900, has a reference to a new mill being built at Woodbury, which is described as on the road from Thornton. First postmaster, A. J. Woodbury. Post office, 1899-1903.

WOODROW (Quay). Post office, 1914-16; mail to Tucumcari. See LOONEY.

WOOLEN MILL (Mora). Abandoned town once located 11 mi E of Watrous on Mora River.

WOOTEN (Otero). On NM 83 and old EP&SW RR, 15 mi E of Alamogordo. WOOTEN (Roosevelt). 14 mi S of Elida. First postmaster, Thomas S. Wooten. Post office, 1909-11; changed to VALLEY VIEW.

WORMEN LAKE (Chaves). 20 mi E of Orchard Park.

WRIGHT (Otero). 6 mi SW of Weed, in Pendleton Canyon area. Post office, 1904-09.

WYNN CREEK (San Miguel). 2 mi E of Atarque.

X RAY (Torrance). 12 mi SE of Mountainair. Post office, 1917-20.

Y ANKEE (Colfax). Former coal town and trading point on NM 72, 8 mi NE of Raton. Founded in 1904 by Wall Street brokerage firm of E. D. Sheppard and Co., and named because several Boston men were involved in this coal-mining venture. A. D. Ensign, representing a group of Eastern investors, was the promoter of the building of AT&SF RR from Raton to Yankee. Town was owned by the railroad, but abandoned because of faulty manipulation of the capital involved. Coal

mining was later resumed. Post office, 1906-22. YANKEE CANYON (Colfax). 10 mi E of Raton. NM 72 winds through this beautiful canyon, which goes up onto Johnson Mesa. YANKEE GULCH (Catron). Heads on Apache Mtn. and runs SW into Apache Creek.

YATES (Harding). 4 mi S of Union County line, and 22 mi NE of Roy on NM 120. Named for "Uncle Jim" Yates, who settled here in 1908. Post office, 1922-31. YATES CANYON (Grants). Heads 4 mi SW of Mimbres Lake; runs SW into East Canyon. YATES SPRING (Grant). Flows into Yates Canyon from N.

YELLOW JACKET PEAK (Grant). 3½ mi from Arizona line, and 3 mi SW of Brushy Mtn.

YERBA (Roosevelt). Span., "herb, grass, weed." On AT&SF RR, 2 mi SW of Portales.

YESO (De Baca). Span., "gypsum." Ranching community on US 60, and AT&SF RR, 22 mi W of Ft. Sumner. Named for Yeso Creek. Established in 1906 with building of the railroad. Post office, 1909—; Yesso, 1912-13. YESO (Rio Arriba). Settlement 7 mi S of Canjilon, E of Arroyo del Yeso. YESO CREEK (De Baca). Flows E into Pecos River 20 mi S of Ft. Sumner. The water is unpalatable, although stock will drink it. The mineral, yeso, is sickening to the taste and discourages all growth in the soil.

YORK, YORKTOWN (Chaves). See ELK. YORK CANYON (Colfax). Near site of former Elkins post office, at head of Vermejo River.

YOUNG CANYON (Colfax). Near former site of Elkins, at head of Vermejo River. Named for the Young family, pioneers from Missouri. YOUNG'S CANYON (San Miguel). Small tributary to Gallinas River at Adam's Ranch. YOUNGSVILLE (Rio Arriba). Farming and ranching community on NM 96, 31 mi NW of Española, and 14 mi W of Abiquiu. Post office, 1914—.

YRISARRI (Bernalillo). Former trading point and community 1 mi E of NM 10, 14 mi SE of Tijeras. Don Pablo Yrisarri established this settlement when he, a Spanish loyalist, was driven out of Vera Cruz by Mexican patriots. He later moved into the Rio Grande Valley and married twice into families of the Albuquerque district, in 1811 and 1822. Some of the people who had come north with him remained at Yrisarri but their descendants have since slowly left the area.

YUNQUE YUNQUE (Rio Arriba). Ancient pueblo site near the confluence of Chama River and the Rio Grande where Juan de Oñate in 1598 established his first capital on his *entrada* into New Mexico. On W bank of Rio Grande, opposite San Juan Pueblo. Yunque Yunque was abandoned twelve years later when the capital at Santa Fe was established.

Zacatosa (San Miguel). Span., "grassy place." Houses and corrals W of Las Vegas on old road through Kearny's Gap to San Geronimo.

Zamora (Bernalillo). Settlement on old highway of US 66, 18 mi E of Albuquerque. A Zamora family furnished one of the postmasters about 1940. A number of Zamora men are listed in seventeenth-century records, two of them in the military companies which came to Santa Fe. Post office, 1939-46; mail to Tijeras.

Zia (Sandoval). Indian pueblo on NM 44, 16 mi NW of Bernalillo; name from the native *Tsia;* a pre-Spanish Keresan-speaking pueblo. Their sun symbol is the state insignia. Castañeda in his account of the Coronado expedition writes that in the winter of 1540-41, the Captain General sent a captain to *Chia* (Zia) to accept the submission of the pueblo, and that the captain left four bronze cannon there which were in bad condition. Shown as *Sia* on L'Atlas Curieux (1700). Zia Pueblo Grant (Sandoval). Area 5 mi square with the pueblo at the center. Grant dates from the Cruzate papers, Sept. 20, 1689; confirmed by U.S. through the annual report of the Office of the Surveyor General, Sept. 30, 1855. See Pueblo Land Grants.

Zildigloi Mountain (McKinley). Navajo, *dzil ditloi,* "stubby mountain." 6 mi S of San Juan County line, 2 mi E of Arizona, and 12 mi W of Tohatchi.

Zombarino Lake (Sandoval). 9 mi SW of Lagunitas.

Zorro (Otero). Span., "fox." Zorro Creek (San Miguel). Rises in county and flows S to Canadian Red River.

Zuñi. Spanish adaptation of the Keresan *sunyi'tsi* or *su'nyitsa,* said by F. W. Hodge to be of unknown meaning. Fray Francisco de Escobar in 1605 called the pueblo Quini. An etymology has been proposed in the Tewa Keresan form *soonyee-ongwee* "casting place pueblo" or "rock slide pueblo." Zuñi (McKinley). Shipping point on AT&SF RR, 5 mi E of Gallup. Zuñi Buttes (McKinley). Twin peaks 4 mi NW of Zuñi. Called by the Zuñis *kwili yalone,* "two mountains." Zuñi Canyon (Valencia). Runs NE into the Rio San Jose, 2 mi W of Grants. Zuñi Mountain (McKinley, Valencia). 26 mi NE of Zuñi pueblo, in Cibola National Forest. Zuñi Plateau (Valencia). In SW corner of county. Zuñi Pueblo (McKinley). 32 mi S of Gallup on NM 36 and 53. In 1539 Fray Marcos de Niza, accompanied·by Estevanico, a Negro who had been with Cabeza de Baca three years earlier, saw one of the Zuñi villages which he called Hawikuh. This pueblo and its neighbor Halona were "the middle ant heap of the world" or the center of the Zuñi universe, and two of the Seven Cities of Cibola sought by the Spanish Conquistadores. In 1540, Francisco Vazquez de Coronado occupied the Zuñi site, and in 1580 Chamuscado visited it, using the name *Cami.* Espejo, in 1583, is considered to have first used the exact form *Zuñi* as a name. *Zuñi* appears on Lafora map in 1771. Post office, 1879, intermittently, to present. Zuñi Pueblo Grant (McKinley). Area about 5 mi square E and S of Zuñi Pueblo, established by Governor Cruzate on Sept. 25, 1689. See Pueblo Land Grants. Zuñi River (Valencia). Begins in SW corner of county on Zuñi Mts., and flows across the reservation to enter the Little Colorado in Arizona. Zuñi Reservoir (McKinley). 4 mi NE of Zuñi Pueblo. Zuñi Salt Lake (Catron). 42 mi S of Zuñi Pueblo. Considered sacred by a number of Indian tribes, but belongs to the Zuñi Indians who have always used its salt for themselves and for trade with other Indians. Governor Oñate visited the lake in October 1598, and on the Miera y Pacheco map (1775), it is shown as the Salina de Zuñi. Alarcon gives the name Guatuzaca as that of an old woman who lived in a lake west of Zuñi. The Zuñi have a tradition of an old woman, Salt Mother, a mythical being who lives in the lake.

BIBLIOGRAPHY

Archivo General de la Nación. Mexico, D.F. Historia, 2.

Archivo General de la Nación. Mexico, D.F. Provincia Internas, 37, No. 2.

Barker, S. Omar. "Place Names—Pleasant and Puzzling," New Mexico (Aug. 1956), 30, 46, 48.

Benavides, Fray Alonso de. Revised Memorial of 1634. Albuquerque: University of New Mexico Press, 1945.

Bloom, Lansing. "Albuquerque and Galisteo Certificate of Their Founding, 1706," New Mexico Historical Review, X (Jan. 1935), 48-50.

Brothers, Mary Hudson. "Place Names of the San Juan Basin, New Mexico," Western Folklore, X (Apr. 1951), 165-67.

Brown, Frances Rosser. "The Spanish Had a Name for Them," New Mexico (Aug., Sept., Oct. 1935; Oct. 1942); also in This Is New Mexico, ed. George Fitzpatrick. Santa Fe: The Rydal Press, 1948.

Bryan, Howard. Albuquerque Tribune column, "Off the Beaten Path": "Dusty," Sept. 1954; "Cabezon," Jan. 3, 1955; "Names for Presidents and Prominent Citizens," Jan. 24, 1955; "Organ Mts.," Jan. 31, 1955; "Place Names," June 4, 1956.

Burnham, Lucy S. "New Mexico Place Names: Fruitland, The Meadows, Burning Hill," Western Folklore, X (Jan. 1951), 74-75.

Carlson, Helen. "Truth or Consequences, New Mexico," Western Folklore, XVI (Apr. 1957), 125-28.

Cassidy, Ina Sizer. "The Story of Sapello or 'Scat Joe,'" Western Folklore, XII (Oct. 1953), 286-89.

———. "Taos, New Mexico. Don Fernando de Taos," Western Folklore, VIII (Jan. 1949), 60-62.

Chant, Elsie Ruth. "The Naming of Tucumcari," New Mexico Folklore Record, III (1948-49), 36-37.

Chavez, Fray Angelico. "Don Fernando de Taos," Western Folklore, VIII (Apr. 1949), 160.

———. "Aztec or Nahuatl Words in New Mexico Place Names," El Palacio, 57 (Apr. 1950), 109-12.

———. "New Mexicanisms in New Mexico Place Names," El Palacio, 57 (Mar. 1950), 67-79.

———. "New Mexico Religious Place Names Other than Those of Saints," El Palacio, 57 (Jan. 1950), 23-26.

———. "New Mexico Place Names from Spanish Proper Names," El Palacio, 56 (Dec. 1949), 367-82.

———. Origins of New Mexico Families. Santa Fe: The Historical Society of New Mexico, 1954.

———. "Saints' Names in New Mexico Geography," El Palacio, 56 (Nov. 1949), 323-35.

Dike, Sheldon H. The Territorial Post Offices of New Mexico. Albuquerque: Dikewood Corporation, 1958.

Directory of Post Offices, pp. 159-61. Washington: U.S. Post Office Department, July 1963.

Escobar, Fray Francisco de. "Diary of the Oñate Expedition to California, 1605," reprinted in Oñate, Colonizer of New Mexico, 1595-1628. Part II, ed. Hammond and Rey (1953).

Escudero, Don José Agustín de. Noticias Históricas Estadísticas de la Antigua Provincia del Nuevo-México, 1849; trans. H. Bailey Carroll and J. Villasana Haggard in Three New Mexico Chronicles. Albuquerque: The Quivira Society, 1942.

File, Lucien A. Ghost Town Map of New Mexico. Compiled by Bureau of Mines and Mineral

Resources, 1964. Available through State Department of Development, Tourist Division, Santa Fe.

Finke, Charles G. "New Mexico Postal History, Present Post Offices of New Mexico." (Mimeographed.) Albuquerque, January 1960.

Forrest, Earle Robert. *Missions and Pueblos of the Old Southwest.* Cleveland: Arthur H. Clarke Co., 1929. 2 vols. Spanish mission names in Arizona and New Mexico, with their English equivalents. I:333-35.

Gannett, Henry. *American Names, A Guide to the Origin of Place Names in the United States.* Washington: Public Affairs Press, 1947.

Greenleaf, Richard E. "The Founding of Albuquerque, 1706: An Historical-Legal Problem," *New Mexico Historical Review* XXXIX (Jan. 1964), 1-15.

Gregory, Herbert E. *The Navajo Country.* Water Supply Paper no. 380. Washington: U.S. Geological Survey, 1916.

Hackett, C. W., ed. *Revolt of the Pueblo Indians of New Mexico and Otermin's Attempted Reconquest, 1680-82.* Albuquerque: University of New Mexico Press, 1942.

Hallenbeck, Cleve. *The Journey of Fray Marcos de Niza.* Dallas: University Press, 1949.

———. *Land of the Conquistadores.* Caldwell, Idaho: The Caxton Printers Ltd., 1950.

Hammond, George P., and Agapito Rey, ed. *Don Juan de Oñate, Colonizer of New Mexico, 1595-1628.* Albuquerque: University of New Mexico Press, 1953.

———. *Narratives of the Coronado Expedition, 1540-1542.* Albuquerque: University of New Mexico Press, 1940.

Harrington, John Peabody. *The Ethnogeography of the Tewa Indians.* Bureau of American Ethnology. Annual Report 29:29-636. 1907-08. Bibliography: pp. 585-87. Includes derivation and meaning of geographical terms and place names in the Tewa language.

———. "Haa'ko, original form of the Keresan name of Acoma," *El Palacio,* 56 (May 1949), 141-44.

———. "Name of Zuñi Salt Lake in Alarcon's 1540 account," *El Palacio,* 56 (July 1949), 220-22.

———. "Old Indian Geographical Names Around Santa Fe, New Mexico," *American Anthropologist,* n.s. 22:341-59. Oct.-Dec. 1920. Also reprinted as a separate.

Hewett, Edgar L. "Origin of the Name Navaho," *American Anthropologist,* n.s. 8:193. Jan.-Mar. 1906. The tribal designation is derived from the Tewa Indian pueblo of Navahu, meaning "the place of great planted fields."

———. *Ancient Life in the American Southwest.* Indianapolis: Bobbs-Merrill, 1930.

Hill, Robert T. "Descriptive Topographic Terms of Spanish America," *National Geographic Magazine* 7:291-302. Sept. 1896. Prepared for reports to director of U.S. Geological Survey on geography of Texas and New Mexico region.

Hodge, F. W. *Handbook of American Indians North of Mexico.* Washington: Bureau of American Ethnology, 1907.

———. "Early Spanish Bungling of Indian Names," *Western Folklore,* IX (Apr. 1950), 153-54.

———. "The Name 'Navajo,'" *Masterkey,* 23 (May 1949), 78.

Keleher, W. A. *Maxwell Land Grant.* Santa Fe: The Rydal Press, 1942.

———. *The Fabulous Frontier.* Santa Fe: The Rydal Press, 1945.

Lafora, Nicolas de. *The Frontiers of New Spain.* Berkeley: The Quivira Society, 1958.

Marshall, James. *Santa Fe, the Railroad That Built an Empire.* New York: Random House, 1945.

Mencken, H. L. *The American Language: Supplement II.* New York: Knopf, 1948. Chap. X. Proper Names in America, 3. Place Names, pp. 525-75.

Mirkowich, Nicholas. "A Note on Navajo Place Names," *American Anthropologist,* n.s. 43:313-14. Apr.-June 1941. Lists Navajo names still in use for a few places in Arizona and New Mexico.

Mitchell, L. B. "The Meaning of the Name Albuquerque," *Western Folklore,* VIII (July 1949), 255-56.

New Mexico in 1610, Juan de Montoyas's Relacion of the Discovery of New Mexico. Albuquerque: The Quivira Society, 1938.

New Mexico: A Guide to the Colorful State. (American Guide Series.) New York: Hastings House, 1953.

Ogburn, Vincent H. "Notes on Place Names in Eastern New Mexico," Eastern New Mexico College *Bulletin,* Studies in Arts, Science, and Letters, Nov. 1944.

Payne, L. Keith. "Post Offices of Roosevelt County, New Mexico." Portales, New Mexico, 1955. Typed ms. in photostat, University of New Mexico Library, Albuquerque.

Pearce, T. M. "Albuquerque Reconsidered," *Western Folklore,* XVI (July 1957), 195-97.

————. "The New Mexico Place Name Dictionary, A Polyglot in Six Languages," *Names*, VI (Dec. 1958), 217-25.

————. "Loving and Lovington: Two New Mexico Towns," *Western Folklore*, VIII (Apr. 1949), 159-60.

————. "New Mexico Place Name Dictionary," *Western Folklore*, VIII (July 1949), 257-59. Report of first collection, New Mexico Place Name Dictionary. Comments on role of railroads, postmasters' families in place naming.

————. "Some Indian Place Names of New Mexico," *Western Folklore*, X (July 1951), 245-47. Points out interplay of languages in place naming and also offers comment on racial response to name situations.

————. "Place Name Pronunciation Guides for Western States," *Western Folklore*, X (Jan. 1951), 72-73. Illustrates difficulties in selecting pronunciations and marking them.

————. "Religious Place Names in New Mexico," *Names*, IX (Mar. 1961), 1-7.

————. "Spanish Place Name Patterns in the Southwest," *Names*, III (Dec. 1955), 201-209.

Siguenza y Gongora, Don Carlos de. *Mercurio Volante, 1693*. Los Angeles: The Quivira Society, 1932.

Sleight, Frederick W. "A Problem of Clarification in Ethnographic Nomenclature," *El Palacio*, 56 (Oct. 1949), 295-300. Gives names of peaks in Jemez Mts.

Stanley, F. More than fifty individual studies of New Mexico settlement names have been published by this writer, who has lived in New Mexico for eighteen years. Information on names and histories in pamphlet form: Abiqui, Acoma, Alamogordo, Alma, Albuquerque (book), Anton Chico, Belen, Bernalillo, Bland, Blossburg, Carlsbad, Catskill, Cerrillos, Chloride, etc. P. O. Box 11, Pep, Texas.

Thatcher, Harold F., and Mary Hudson Brothers. "Fabulous La Plata River," *Western Folklore*, X (April 1951), 167-69.

Thomas, Alfred Barnaby. *Forgotten Frontiers, A Study of the Spanish Policy of Don Juan Bautista de Anza, Governor of New Mexico, 1777-1787*. Norman: University of Oklahoma Press, 1932.

Three New Mexico Chronicles, by Pino, Barreiro, and Escudero. Trans. H. Bailey Carroll and J. Villasana Haggard. Albuquerque: The Quivira Society, 1942.

Tibon, Gutierre. *Mexico—The Name*, Onomastica, No. 17 (1959), Winnipeg, Canada.

Twitchell, Ralph Emerson. *Leading Facts of New Mexican History*. 5 vols. Cedar Rapids: Torch Press, 1911-12.

————. *Old Santa Fe*. Santa Fe: New Mexican Publishing Co., 1925.

————. *The Spanish Archives of New Mexico*. (Vol. I in Office of the Surveyor General, Santa Fe; Vol. II in Library of Congress.) Cedar Rapids: Torch Press, 1914.

Villagra, Gaspar Perez de. *History of New Mexico, 1610*. Trans. Gilberto Espinosa. Los Angeles: The Quivira Society, 1933.

White, Marjorie. "Shakespeare: The West's Most Authentic Ghost Town," *New Mexico Magazine*, 40 (Apr. 1962), 5-7, 35.

White, Rose P. "New Mexico Place Names: Roosevelt County," *Western Folklore*, IX (Jan. 1950), 63-65.

————. "The Town of Portales, New Mexico," *Western Folklore*, VIII (Apr. 1949), 158-59.

Young, Robert W., and William Morgan. "Navajo Place Names in Gallup," *El Palacio*, 54 (Dec. 1947), 283-85.

CONTRIBUTORS

Individual workers who contributed to the Writers' Program of the Works Projects Administration in New Mexico were: Victor Bachelor, T. E. Bowen, Christina Brams, J. C. Brock, Lorin W. Brown, J. M. Burns, Alan A. Carter, F. M. Casey, Ina Sizer Cassidy, W. A. Chapman, Elinor Crans, Edith L. Crawford, Katy Day, Charlie Dunlap, Albert Easley, Keith M. Edwards, W. M. Emory, E. J. Ennis, C. W. Evans, Mrs. Ferris, Kenneth Fordyce, Carl Gerhardt, M. E. Goldberg, Blanche C. Grant, Mollie Holder, J. Inness, Mrs. Billy Khuns, Carl Livingstone, Bright Lynn, C. Marckham, Eli Martinez, Reyes Martinez, Mary Mendoza, Mrs. B. Mosely, M. O. Pate, W. L. Patterson, C. B. Redfield, Bill Reed, Lon Reed, L. E. Roderick, Dan Savage, A. B. Searle, D. D. Sharp, Evelyn Shuler, Claude Simson, Vernon Smithson, C. A. Thompson, C. C. Totty, Bryan Trammel, C. G. Warkins, D. M. Woody, T. P. Wooten.

Collectors for three mimeographed pamphlets prepared between 1949 and 1951 and contributors since the publication of these pamphlets are: R. E. Barton Allen, Salomon Alvarez, E. P. Ancona, Clinton P. Anderson, Lillie G. Anderson, Raymundo Angel, Anton Babichca, Mrs. Charles Bartholomew, Dorothy Baylor, Jacob M. Bernal, Marguerite Bernard, Arthur Bibo, Mrs. Ardath B. Biederman, Hazel C. Billings, Cevil Black, Garette E. Blackwell, C. Blair, Mrs. B. Blount, Helen Green Blumenschein, Grace H. Branch, Mary Hudson Brothers, Frances I. Burch, Lucy S. Burnham, Mrs. Joel B. Burr, Gene Calkins, E. G. Campbell, Elliott Canonge, Ina Sizer Cassidy, Elsie Ruth Chant, Fray Angelico Chavez, Sybel Clagett, Marguerite Codding, Henry B. Coddington, Maj. Clarence E.

Cone, Mareth Cooley, Bill Crane, Perla E. Darbyshire, Albert D. Duke, Bruce T. Ellis, Laura Engelbrecht, Octavia Fellin, Erna Fergusson, Ruth Fish, Julius E. Fitzner, Mr. and Mrs. Sidney Fleming, Dan E. Furse, Jim Garitson, John Gavahan, Marian W. Gibbons, Kay Gilmartin, J. W. Gilstrap, Mrs. E. L. Goats, Harriet Harshfield Goodman, Nellie E. Greet, Reyes Gurule, S. S. Griffin, E. R. Harrington, Mrs. Rodney E. Hatch, Mrs. Charles C. Hill, F. W. Hodge, Harry Hoijer, Marvin Hoster, J. T. Hoy, A. C. Jaquez, Myra Ellen Jenkins, Hugh B. Johnson, Spud Johnson, Walter Johnson, W. A. Keleher, Mrs. W. D. Kelley, Robert Kemm, Troy Kemper, F. M. Kercheville, William Koenig, Nettie Gerhardt Koll, Mrs. E. E. Lane, Louis E. Laney, Helga M. Latham, Jose M. Maestas, Jr., Mabel Major, Mrs. F. L. Malhop, A. J. Manzanares, Mrs. W. K. Marmon, Dave Martin, Joseph M. Martin, Wayne Mason, H. M. McClelland, Walter B. McFarland, Helen Melton, Adeline Miller, Mr. and Mrs. R. L. Miller, Clough Moncus, Hermon Moncus, D. D. Monroe, Hazel Moore, Frances L. Newcomb, A. R. Nykl, Don O'Meara, Robert O'Sullivan, Myrie Ogle, Romeo A. Ortiz, Clora Cox Osborne, Anna L. Owen, Mr. and Mrs. P. A. Pankratz, Luis Paraga, William A. Parish, Mr. and Mrs. T. M. Pearce, George M. Peterson, Daisy Madduz Philips, Mrs. M. H. Phillips, Col. Jack Potter, Edith Rainbolt, John C. Rainer, Epigmenio Ramirez, William D. Reams, Bill Reed, Rev. Sabino Rendon, J. Albert Richards, W. J. Richards, Faris Roberts, Duane C. Rosselot, Janet Royle, T. G. Sanders, Ramon Sender, Philip Shamberger, Howard Sheets, Melvin C. Shockey, Ralph A. Shugart, Milton R. Smith, Mrs. Vene W. Smith, J. B.

Spincer, Rock Stead, J. S. Stearns, Charley Sturges, Harold F. Thatcher, Mr. and Mrs. Joe Tondre, Francis C. Tracy, Theron Trumbo, Elizabeth Tucker, F. W. Vale, Mrs. E. A. Vander Wagen, Raymond F. Waters, Mack S. Webster, Charles Weeks, Harry V. Whatley, Louis P. White, Louis M. Whitlock, Mr. and Mrs. C. V. Wicker, Harold G. Widdison, Roy Almon Wiley, W. W. Williams, J. M. Winchester, B. C. Withers, Betty Woods, Miss S. Zabel.

Finally, we gratefully acknowledge the help of J. O. Kilmartin, of the Board of Geographic Names, U.S. Department of the Interior; Walter W. Ristow, Assistant Chief, Map Division of the Reference Department, Library of Congress; and the co-operation of the following New Mexico Chambers of Commerce: Alamagordo, Albuquerque, Anthony, Artesia, Aztec, Belen, Carlsbad, Carrizozo, Clayton, Clovis, Deming, Farmington, Gallup, Grants, Hobbs, Las Cruces, Las Vegas, Lordsburg, Lovington, Mountainair, Portales, Raton, Roswell, Ruidoso, Santa Fe, Silver City, Socorro, Springer, Taos, Truth or Consequences, and Tucumcari.